The
Notre Dame
Football Scrapbook

The Notre Dame Football Scrapbook

BY

Richard M. Cohen,
Jordan A. Deutsch,
and David S. Neft

BOBBS-MERRILL

Indianapolis/New York

Cover photos courtesy of Notre Dame Sports Information Department.

Library of Congress Cataloging in Publication Data

Cohen, Richard M   1938-
    The Notre Dame football scrapbook.

    1. Notre Dame, Ind. University—Football.
I. Deutsch, Jordan A., joint author.   II. Neft,
David S., joint author.   III. Title.
GV958.N6C64   796.33'263'0977289   77-5262
ISBN 0-672-52335-3

ACKNOWLEDGMENTS

The *Notre Dame Football Scrapbook* is one of the first books in a continuing series of major college scrapbooks. The authors are sure you will enjoy this unique and new concept in sports publishing.

The task of assembling all the material and data contained in this book could not have been accomplished by the three authors alone. In order to make this book a reality, the cooperation of many individuals, institutions, libraries, newspapers and news services was needed. The authors, therefore, would like to express their deep appreciation to the following people, who contributed their time and facilities during the preparation of this book:

> Nancy McCormack, *Visual and Technical Coordinator and Photo Reproduction Consultant*
>
> Roland T. Johnson, *Research Assistant and Advisor*

Notre Dame Sports Information Department:
> Roger Valdiserri, *Sports Information Director*
> Robert P. Best, *Assistant Sports Information Director*

Notre Dame International Sports and Games Research Collection:
> Herb Juliano, *Curator/Researcher*
> Chet Grant, *Consultant*

Notre Dame Publications:
> *The Scholastic*
> *The Dome*
> *The Observer*
> *Notre Dame Football Guides*
> *Notre Dame Football Reviews*
> *Notre Dame Football Game Programs*

Pro Football Hall of Fame:
> Jim Campbell, *Historian*

Hartford Public Library, Reference and General Reading Department:
> Josephine Sale, *Head*
> Martha Nolan, *Administrative Assistant*
> Dorothy Brickett, Rosalie Fawcett, Carol Fitting, Bhaskararao Kali, Shirley Kiefer, Fernando Labault, Beverly Loughlin, Betty Mullendore, Ann Santos, *Research Assistants*

Library of Congress, Serial Division:
> The staff of the Reference Section

Danbury Public Library:
> The staff of the Reference Section

New York Public Library Annex:
> The staff of the Newspaper Division

The authors would also like to thank the following news services and newspapers for the use of their material:
> *Associated Press News Service*
> *The Baltimore Sunpapers*
> *The Cleveland Plain Dealer*
> *The Hartford Courant*
> *The New York Times*

Production:
> Sally Lifland

The Authors' Wives:
> A special thanks to Nancy Cohen, Thea Deutsch, and Naomi Neft for their continuous faith, understanding, and cooperation throughout all our projects.

All comments and inquiries on this book should be sent to
> Sports Products Inc.
> 415 Main Street
> Ridgefield, CT 06877

Foreword

There is no university in the world whose name is more synonymous with "spirit" than the University of Notre Dame, yet there is nothing more difficult to define than the Notre Dame spirit. Who or what, precisely, i. responsible for this spirit has inspired a great deal of speculation. Perhaps the definitive answer lies in the words of Notre Dame's President, Father Theodore M. Hesburgh: "a proud Notre Dame tradition of doing everything with style, spirit and excellence." Or, in the words of another observer, perhaps it is "just one more reflection of Notre Dame's commitment to excellence."

One thing is certain—it is easy to misunderstand Notre Dame without visiting the campus, and it is hard to visit the campus without seeing that Catholic education is Notre Dame's reason for being. Its majesty on the football field is merely an extension of the inspiring leadership provided through the years by the University itself. Its remarkable endurance as a symbol of college football merely reflects an unwavering standard of excellence.

The reputation and glory of Notre Dame football is kept alive from year to year not by any one man, but by many men and boys who come from all walks of life to give more of themselves than might be expected, because they are realizing a dream.

Many people equate the beginning of the Notre Dame football tradition with the games, legends and eras of some of its more prominent and contemporary personalities. To be sure, names like Rockne and Gipp are all but synonymous with Notre Dame football, but it is interesting to note that the Fighting Irish played their first game a year before Knute Rockne was born.

Throughout the first twenty-five years of Notre Dame football, 1887–1912, coaches like James L. Morison, Frank Hering, Thomas Barry, and Jack Marks, to mention a few, were building a tradition with a cumulative 113–31–13 record. During this period, Barry led the Irish to their first undefeated season, and Louis "Red" Salmon, later a Notre Dame head coach, was the University's first All-American.

Around the turn of the century, when baseball was the preeminent college sport, Notre Dame fielded quality teams. Over the years, Notre Dame's basketball teams have consistently defeated larger schools which take pride in their basketball prowess. But the name of the game that made the tradition is football.

This feat is the issue of love and egoism. For most of the past twenty-seven years, this beautiful campus with its hallowed halls, lakes and buildings has been my home. When I first set foot and eyes on the Notre Dame campus, I fell in love with the natural beauty, the mood, the tempo, the spirit, the history and the tradition of this place. It is a love affair which has endured without dimming to this day.

Here at Notre Dame the excitement of growth abounds, just as it has since the gold dome, Notre Dame's familiar landmark and the shining symbol of its traditions, first cast its glint across the Indiana plains. As a campus dweller, I am witness to it daily. Living in the Athletic and Convocation Center, the focal point of activity for present-day coaches and athletes, just across the street from the football stadium, I can almost feel the presence of the greats: George Gipp, perhaps the most controversial and multi-talented man ever to play for Notre Dame, whose untimely death brought him a measure of immortality; the Four Horsemen, who won immortality on the typewriter of Grantland Rice: "Outlined against a blue-gray October sky . . ."

At pep rallies, when the band strikes up the most famous fight song in the land, "Cheer, Cheer for Old Notre Dame," even the most intellectual student finds himself as wildly carried away in the uproar as generations of Notre Dame men before him. The festooning streamers, the firecrackers, the band, the signs, the buttons, the hawkers, the upsets, the classic confrontations, the "games of the year," the "games of the century," the battles of the north, south, east and west—all of these things and more at once reflect and contribute to the ever-living, ever-loving Notre Dame spirit. But, first and foremost, Notre Dame is people.

In my capacity as curator of the International Sports and Games Research Collection, established ten years ago at Notre Dame with a basic commitment to providing resources for serious and scholarly sports research, I encounter living links to the Notre Dame tradition almost daily—Edward "Moose" Krause, Notre Dame's human landmark, its athletic director, and a legend in his own time; Donald C. "Chet" Grant, one of Rockne's great quarterbacks, who later coached under Elmer Layden, and who has written brilliantly of his life and times with Rockne; Rev. Edmund P. Joyce, C.S.C., Notre Dame's Executive Vice President and chairman of its Faculty Board in Control of Athletics, an articulate man with an aura of strength about him.

Notre Dame has long been deeply involved with athletics at all levels—recreational, intramural, club and intercollegiate. There are many and mixed reasons for this involvement, not the least being that we believe sports add a dimension to our sense of what it is to be human, including, as they often do on our campus, welcome interludes of festivity. We have pledged ourselves to excellence in both education and athletics. Sports have been a factor that has held the Notre Dame family together over many difficult years. They have been part of the curious mix that makes Notre Dame "a place with a sense of place."

Though Notre Dame, like most other colleges, is feeling the winds of change, the link back to the past is, remarkably, as strong today as ever. Once a year I am reminded of the founding of the University: at Christmas time, Potawatomi Indians from Dowagiac and other Southern Michigan communities, representing forefathers who inhabited an Indian Mission on the land that would later become Notre Dame, make their annual trek to the campus to accept gifts of food in keeping with a tradition started 135 years ago by Father Edward Sorin, C.S.C., Notre Dame's founder.

I have spent countless hours listening to the old priests tell tales of the "superstition tree"; the ghost of Gipp in Washington Hall; the intriguing chain of events surrounding the jeweled crown presented to the University as a gift from Empress Eugenie, wife of Napoleon III, who was himself a generous benefactor; "coffin hall"; and many other legends from the past. Tradition is reflected everywhere.

As all alumni and "subway alumni" well know, the rise of towering academic buildings has not overshadowed Knute Rockne's cherished stadium, where the green grass on the gridiron is tenderly nurtured year round for the five momentous Saturdays in the fall. Unlike the Ivy League schools, which no longer dominate the All-American selections as they did fifty years ago, Notre Dame has managed to gain in academic prestige without losing its football prowess. Its football prestige rates as high today as it did in the days of Rockne and Leahy.

I am fortunate, indeed, that my life has taken me deeply into the realm of wholesome, exciting Notre Dame football, allowing me to meet and mingle with champions—players, coaches, administrators, trainers and cheerleaders. I cherish these friendships, but much to my dismay I never got around to keeping a scrapbook that would preserve and enrich these memories. Now the people at Sports Products Inc. have done it for me, with this book that enriches an already venerable tradition. Notre Dame followers, especially, owe them a debt of gratitude, though it is a book to be enjoyed not only by Fighting Irish football fans, but by all those who appreciate and recognize the ultimate in sports achievement.

Here is a book that will "wake up the echoes" and "shake down the thunder" a little more subtly than an Irish pre-game pep rally, but it will, nonetheless, help you relive the glory and the tears that went into the making of Notre Dame tradition. Here you will capture the flavor of campus life, the emergence of Notre Dame as a football dynasty, and the exuberance of a nation heralding its gridiron heroes. The authors have collected the outstanding accounts and pictures of the panorama that, through the years, has made Notre Dame mean college football to millions of fans—the players, the coaches, the games, the seasons, the tactics, the institution that is Notre Dame football. From on-the-scene sources, you can now read what was written about the action when it happened.

This unique collection includes records and accounts of the very early days of football under the gold dome; highlights from the greatest intersectional rivalry in collegiate football, Notre Dame and Southern California; the legendary games with Army; the "Game of the Century" against Ohio State; the great quarterbacks; the myths and the magic; the national championships; all the winning and all the losing; the history, traditions and spirit as never before presented. What a marvelous idea! Whatever your particular status, oldest grad or youngest fan, it is a *must* for players, parents, fans and admirers of Notre Dame football.

There is only one Notre Dame . . . with a tradition that even the least sentimental players feel. I hope after reading this book you will sense a small part of this tradition.

Herb T. Juliano, *Curator/Researcher*
International Sports and Games Research Collection
University of Notre Dame

Notre Dame's First Football Team

Back row: Hepburn, Houck, Sawkins, Fehr, Nelson, Melady, Springer.
Front row: Jewett, Cusack, Luhn, Prudhomme.

SCORING VALUES

Seasons	Touchdown	Field Goal	Point After	Safety
1887-1897	4 points	5 points	2 points	2 points
1898-1903	5 points	5 points	1 point	2 points
1904-1908	5 points	4 points	1 point	2 points
1909-1911	5 points	3 points	1 point	2 points
1912-1957	6 points	3 points	1 point	2 points
1958 to date	6 points	3 points	1 point for kick / 2 points for run or pass	2 points

1887
Coach: None
Captain: Henry Luhn

N.23 L Michigan 0-8 H
(0-1-0)

KEY TO ABBREVIATIONS
S. O. N. D.—Month—September, October, November, December
W-L-T—Game won, lost or tied
H—Home game
A—Away game, played at opponent's home stadium
N—Game played at a neutral site; see footnote for city
Nt—Night game
YS—Game played at Yankee Stadium, New York
HC—Homecoming game
TH—Game played on Thanksgiving Day
R—Game played in rain
S—Game played in snow
U—Major upset
0:00—Time remaining in games decided in the final minutes; in case of ties, time followed by team scoring last
C—Capacity crowd

—FOOTBALL.—For some days previous to Wednesday great interest had been manifested by our students in the football game which had been arranged between the teams of the Universities of Michigan and Notre Dame. It was not considered a match contest, as the home team had been organized only a few weeks, and the Michigan boys, the champions of the West, came more to instruct them in the points of the Rugby game than to win fresh laurels. The visitors arrived over the Michigan Central RR., Wednesday morning, and were at once taken in charge by a committee of students. After spending a few hours in "taking in" the surroundings, they donned their uniforms of spotless white and appeared upon the Seniors' campus. Owing to the recent thaw, the field was damp and muddy; but nothing daunted, the boys "went in," and soon Harless' new suit appeared as though it had imbibed some of its wearer's affinity for the soil of Notre Dame. At first, to render our players more familiar with the game, the teams were chosen irrespective of college. After some minutes' play, the game was called, and each took his position as follows:

UNIV. OF M.—*Full Back:* J. L. Duffy; *Half Backs:* J. E. Duffy, E. McPheran; *Quarter Back:* R. T. Farrand; *Centre Rush:* W. W. Harless; *Rush Line:* F. Townsend, E. M. Sprague F. H. Knapp, W. Fowler, G. W. De Haven, M. Wade.
UNIV. OF N. D.—*Full Back:* H. Jewett; *Half Backs:* J. Cusack, H. Luhn; *Quarter Back:* G Cartier; *Centre Rush:* G. A. Houck; *Rush Line:* F. Fehr, P. Nelson, B. Sawkins, W. Springer, T. O'Regan, P. P. Maloney.

On account of time, only a part of one inning was played, and resulted in a score of 8 to o in favor of the visitors. The game was interesting, and, notwithstanding the slippery condition of the ground, the Ann Arbor boys gave a fine exhibition of skilful playing. This occasion has started an enthusiastic football boom, and it is hoped that coming years will witness a series of these contests. After a hearty dinner, Rev. President Walsh thanked the Ann Arbor team for their visit, and assured them of the cordial reception that would always await them at Notre Dame. At 1 o'clock carriages were taken for Niles, and amidst rousing cheers the University of Michigan football team departed, leaving behind them a most favorable impression.

1888 ROSTER

E. Prudhomme (C)
E. H. Coady
J. E. Cusack
F. Fehr
J. L. Hepburn
H. M. Jewett
F. X. Mattes
J. B. Meagher
E. Melady
E. A. Sawkins
F. Springer

1888				
	Coach: None			
	Captain: Edward C. Prudhomme			
Apr.20	L	Michigan	6-24	H
Apr.21	L	Michigan	4-10	H
D.6	W	Harvard School (Chi.)	20-0	H
	(1-2-0)		30-34	

H. Jewett
Football.

UNIVERSITY OF MICHIGAN VS. UNIVERSITY OF NOTRE DAME.

PLAYERS.

U. OF M.		U. N. D.
W. W. HARLESS,	*Center Rusher*	F. FEHR,
G. W. DeHAVEN,	*Rusher*	E. SAWKINS,
J. H. DUFFIE,	"	P. J. NELSON,
G. A. WOOD,	"	G. A. HOUCK,
L. MacMILLAN,	"	E. MELADY,
F. TOWNSEND,	"	J. HEPBURN,
E. M. SPRAGUE,	"	F. SPRINGER,
R. T. FARRAND,	*Quarter Back*	J. E. CUSACK,
J. H. DUFFY (Capt.),	*Half Back*	H. LUHN (Capt.),
J. E. DUFFY,	"	H. JEWETT,
E. MacFADDEN,	*Goal*	E. PRUDHOMME.

POINTS IN THE GAME.

Touch-down, 4 points; Goal kicked from touch-down, 2; Field kick over goal, 5; Safety Touch-down by side in its own goal, 2 (for their opponents).

Notre Dame played two games of football with the University of Michigan last week: one at the Green Stocking Ball Park in South Bend on Friday, and one on the University grounds Saturday. The home team lost both games—the first by a score of 26 to 6, and the second by a score of 10 to 4.

About half-past one o'clock, Friday afternoon, the Notre Dame players and their friends took carriages and started for South Bend. They met the Ann Arbor eleven at the Sheridan House, and after a short drive through the streets of the city drew up at the Ball Park where the game was to be played. The first thing on the programme, however, was a 100 yards dash for a gold medal open to any who cared to enter. There were four starters: James Duffy, of Ann Arbor; H. Jewett and J. Hepburn, of Notre Dame, and a South Bend runner. The race was practically between Duffy and Jewett, and the former led from the start to the finish. Notwithstanding Jewett's bad start, by a wonderful spurt he came in so close to Duffy that the latter had no room to spare. The time was 11 seconds. There are many who still believe that Jewett possesses the more speed of the two. Shortly after 3 o'clock, the football game was called by E. M. Sprague, of Ann Arbor, who acted as referee. The players were: University of Michigan—W. W. Harless (centre), G. W. De Haven, J. H. Duffie, G. A. Wood, G. Briggs, R. S. Babcock, E. Rhodes, *Rushers;* W. D. Ball, *Quarter Back;* E. MacFadden, J. L. Duffy, *Half Backs;* J. H. Duffy (captain), *Goal.* University of Notre Dame —F. Fehr (centre), E. Sawkins, P. J. Nelson, G. A. Houck, E. Milady, J. Hepburn, F. Springer, *Rushers;* J. E. Cusack, *Quarter Back;* H. Luhn (captain), H. Jewett, *Half Backs;* E. Prudhomme, *Goal.* From the time the ball was first kicked, until the end of the second inning, the game was exciting. The first inning was interrupted by a number of wranglings over the rules, but the second went through smoothly. Ann Arbor scored first on a touch-down by James Duffy at 3.28. Then Ball made four more by another touch-down, and John Duffy added two to this by kicking the

ball over the goal. Duffie made another touch-down. Then James Duffy raised the score by four points, and a goal kick by John Duffy increased Ann Arbor's lead two points. That was all the scoring done in the first inning, the Notre Dame eleven failing to do any effective work. In the second inning the score of the Michigan boys received an increase of six on a touch-down by Ball, and a goal kick by John Duffy. This made a total of 26, and Ann Arbor made no more during the game. For Notre Dame Springer got the ball and touched it down beating his opponent's goal, and the spectators manifested their delight by enthusiastic applause. But the referee claimed that Springer had interfered with an Ann Arbor player before getting the ball from him, and the ball was brought back into the field, much to the disgust of the audience. After a few minutes' play, however, Jewett secured the ball, and by a magnificent run made a touch-down in Ann Arbor ground, and Prudhomme raised the ball over the goal for two more points, making a total of six for Notre Dame. Jewett's play was an elegant one, and it caught the fancy of the crowd who were evidently pleased to see the Michigan team's record broken. Little fine playing was shown after that, and when time was called the score was still 26 to 6. About four hundred people witnessed the game.

The Ann Arbor boys came out from South Bend to the University Saturday morning. After an inspection of Notre Dame and her surroundings, and after partaking of dinner in the Senior refectory and a short ride on the lake, they got ready for their second game and appeared on the grounds with their opponents at 2 o'clock. Just after taking their positions, Bonney of South Bend photographed the two teams and the field.

There were some changes in the Ann Arbor team rendered necessary by the departure of Mr. James Duffy who was called home Friday evening. E. M. Sprague was put in the eleven, and R. S. Babcock, who had become too lame to play, having been injured in the previous game, was selected to referee the contest. The game was played with ten men on a side. The home team had the kick off, and forced the ball steadily towards the Michigan goal where 2 was soon scored on a safety touch-down by Harless. Another safety touch by Duffy made the score 4. Ann Arbor could do nothing until the last two minutes of the first inning when Sprague took the ball, while the other players were settling some dispute, and made a touch-down for his side, and a goal kick by Duffy gave them two more points. Notre Dame claimed the touch-down was illegal, asserting that Sprague neglected to put the ball in play, and furthermore went out of bounds to the goal. The referee, however, could not see it in this light. In the second inning Harless, by a touch-down, raised the score to 10 points, and the game closed with a score of 10 to 4 in favor of Ann Arbor. Jewett's touch-down was not allowed, although it was apparently legal. By many it is believed that in all justice Notre Dame won the game, but the referee's decision made it otherwise. However, the record of Ann Arbor was badly broken, and they have not had as hard a tussle for some time as they experienced last week. After a lunch the visitors departed on the 5 o'clock train to Niles, where they made connections for home. They made a favorable impression by their manly bearing and courteous conduct, and we hope that next year may bring with it another friendly contest for football honors.

1889
Coach: None
Captain: Edward C. Prudhomme

N.14	W	Northwestern	9-0	A

(1-0-0)

1890-1891 — No team

1892
Coach: None
Captain: Patrick H. Coady

O.19	W	South Bend H.S.	56-0	H
N.24TH	T	Hillsdale	10-10	H

(1-0-1) 66-10

1893
Coach: None
Captain: Frank M. Keough

O.25	W	Kalamazoo	34-0	H
N.11	W	Albion	8-6	H
N.23	W	DeLaSalle (S)	28-0	H
N.30TH	W	Hillsdale (S)	22-10	H
J.1'94	L	Chicago	0-8	A

(4-1-0) 92-24

1889 ROSTER

E. Prudhomme (C)
S. Campbell
D. E. Cartier
E. H. Coady
T. H. Coady
S. Dickerson
F. Fehr
J. Fitzgibbon
S. B. Fleming
C. B. Flynn
J. L. Hepburn
T. J. McKeon

1892 ROSTER

P. H. Coady (C)
E. W. Brown
P. J. Crawley
N. S. Dinkle
E. F. DuBrul
J. Flannigan
J. J. Kearns
F. M. Keough
E. B. Linehan
F. E. Murphy
M. A. Quinlan
C. F. Roby
E. M. Schaak
F. J. Schillo

1893 ROSTER

F. M. Keough (C)
J. P. Barrett
A. Chidester
J. T. Cullen
N. S. Dinkle
E. F. DuBrul
J. Flannigan
F. H. Hesse
M. D. Kirby
C. F. Roby
F. J. Schillo
R. B. Sinnott
C. W. Zeitler

Football.

NORTHWESTERN VS. NOTRE-DAME.

On Thursday last the Notre Dame eleven defeated the Northwestern University, of Evanston, Illinois, by the score of 9 to 0. It was the first game the boys ever played outside of their own grounds, and the result is the more gratifying for that reason. It plainly proves that they can win when deprived of the encouragements and praises of their fellow-students, and even when surrounded by a crowd of spectators who treat them as mortal enemies, as was the case on the 14th.

Evanston had the kick-off, and at 3.07 p. m. Ridgeway opened the game with a long place kick, which was immediately returned by Cartier, and the real playing was begun. Ridgeway again got the ball and tried to take it towards Notre Dame's goal; but a quiet young gentleman from that University brought him to a stop by sitting on him. Then both sides lined up and the ball again was put in play. The Indiana men gradually forced the sphere towards Evanston's goal, notwithstanding the strenuous objections of their opponents. They reached the twenty-five yard line and then began to see-saw back and forth, neither side accomplishing anything. During the scrimmages Notre Dame lost the services of their best player, Hepburn, who was obliged to leave the game. S. Fleming took his place and filled it admirably. After they had spent some time in hard playing near the Northwestern goal, Cartier managed to get the ball and, although surrounded by a number of his opponents, made an excellent field kick, which gave Notre Dame a "starter" of five points. Ridgeway again opened with a place kick and the ball was in play. Here the Evanstonians began to show their strength; they brought the seat of action near their objective goal, and it looked as though they would make a touch-down. If they ever had a chance it was then; but by hard playing the Notre Dames prevented it, and when time was called the score stood 5 to 0.

In the second half, Notre Dame had the kick-off, and Cartier having dribbled the ball the rushline closed in around him, and as a "human wedge" gained nearly 25 yards. Then the playing became harder than ever. They crossed and recrossed the field, and it seemed that neither side could gain any advantage, and the half was nearly closed when Ed. Coady and S. Fleming played the neatest and most successful trick of the game. Ed. got the ball and hid it, and Steve, pretending to have it, set off across the grounds. Three or four of the Northwesterns followed him, and Ed. had a comparatively clear road. He rushed through and made the only touch-down of the game. This was all that was done, and as time was called the boys realized the fact that they had "shut out" their adversaries, and the 'Rah! 'Rah! 'Rah! was heartily and joyfully given.

Of the men taking part in the game too much cannot be said. Captain Prudhomme and his assistant, Frank Fehr, put up a phenomenal game, and the victory was largely due to their earnest, resolute efforts. In the rushline everyone played well; Hepburn, while on the field, played better than any of the others. McKeon, Fitzgibbons, Campbell, Flynn and Tom Coady played as though their lives depended on it, and showed the Northwestern men several points in rushline tactics. Dickerson, as half-back, was here, there, and everywhere and surprised the natives in many ways. The points were made by Cartier and Ed. Coady, assisted by Fleming, and they understand the good-wishes and thanks of their fellow-students. Of the Evanston eleven, Harris, Moulding and Ridgeway put up the best game, the last named being a wonder as a full-back. The teams were as follows:

EVANSTON:—Rushers—Hotrous (centre), Wilson, Kelly, Kennicon, Clark, Hayes, Stewart, Chapin. Harris, Quarter-back; Noyes and Moulding, Half-backs; Ridgeway, (captain), Full-back.

NOTRE DAME:—Rushers—Fehr (centre), Fitzgibbon, McKeon, Flynn, Campbell, Hepburn, Fleming, T. Coady, E. Coady. Quarter-back; Prudhomme (captain), Dickerson, Half-backs; Cartier, Full-back.

—FOOTBALL.— On Wednesday last a 'bus full of hopeful football players entered the grounds and were unloaded on the campus. A short while afterwards they again got into their 'bus, looking rather disconsolate and dilapidated. These youths hailed from the South Bend High School, and engaged in mortal combat with the college 2d eleven, who were under the efficient generalship of Captain Flannigan. And a combat it was, although nobody was hurt. When the teams went out upon the field the difference between the two was immediately seen. Notre Dame's men were bigger and stronger in every way, while those of the High School were much smaller. In spite of their size, they put up a very plucky game, and were admired for their tenacity. The game opened with a rush by Notre Dame. By a little clever scheming McDermott secured the first touch down without any difficulty, others followed quick and fast. At the end of the first half the score was 22-0 to Notre Dame's credit. The second half began, and a larger and larger score was chalked upon Notre Dame's side of the board, while that of the High School was a perfect blank. At the close of the game the score was 56-0. Touch-downs were made as follows: Brown, 5; McDermott, 1; Dinkle, 2; Cullen, 2; Henley, 1. The High School boys play a very fair game for a team of their size and weight, but Notre Dame's eleven was too heavy for them. The score would have been much larger but for the fact that the team was organized on short notice and could not get very much practice. This game shows that there is good football blood here and it should be worked up. There is no exercise more healthful and more manly than good football. The game is one that develops all the manliness there is in a boy, and is therefore popular among college students.

1894
Coach: James L. Morison
Captain: Frank M. Keough

O.13	W	Hillsdale	14-0	H
O.20	T	Albion	6-6	H
N.15	W	Wabash	30-0	H
N.22	W	Rush Medical	18-6	H
N.29TH	L	Albion	12-19	H

(3-1-1) 80-31

1894 LETTERMEN

F. M. Keough (C)
G. M. Anson
E. E. Brennan
D. V. Casey
A. Chidester
S. J. Corby
C. A. Corry
J. J. Dempsey
N. S. Dinkle
J. Rosenthal
C. W. Zeitler

--The Notre Dame football team, while being entertained at the residence of Mrs. Edward Roby, was tendered a dinner and reception by the hostess which was a very brilliant affair, a number of South Chicago guests being present. The table was spread in the large hall and was beautifully decorated with the college colors, blue and gold. The favors were exquisite, and the table groaned beneath the weight of many substantial viands, as well as the delicacies of the season. The evening's festivities were interspersed with music both vocal and instrumental, also recitations from the college boys, assisted by the Misses Beck. The gem of the evening was a recitation from the ever-willing hostess, entitled "Mary, the Household Minstrel," which was enjoyed by all. At a late hour the guests departed, feeling that they had spent a most delightful evening.—S. Chicago Calumet.

Is Football a Help or a Hindrance to a Student?

A SYMPOSIUM BY THE CRITICISM CLASS.

To assert that football is a hindrance to the true collegiate student would be to bring upon oneself the criticism of thousands who admire this popular sport. And yet I feel safe in saying that there are few sincere football players who would claim that they are aided in the slightest degree by their devotion to the game.

Articles on this subject have been published far and wide, and many pages of our popular magazines have been given up to the sole purpose of proving that football has greatly increased the intellectuality of our college men. Such, at least, seems to be the stand taken by most writers on the subject. After making broad assertions that athletics and intellectuality always go hand in hand, they place before us an ideal student whom the unsuspecting public looks up to and admires. *Mens sana in corpore sano* concludes the idealistic theme on our hero; but I have yet to find him, who can, from experience, claim that football has disclosed to him the secret of applying his time well, and has urged him on to pursue his studies with greater attention and zeal. If I should assert that the student and athlete combined is not a man to be admired, assuredly would I deserve the severest criticism. There have been, and are now, men in our own college who take the keenest delight in aiding the cause of football by indulging in the sport; and these men, moreover, have proven themselves to be students in the truest sense of the word; but does this contradict my statement? Not in the least. Such a man is a student in spite of football. He was a student before he ever played football. He must realize that he is making a great sacrifice by playing; and if he does it from purely uninterested motives, he is to be looked upon as the ideal we are all struggling to attain—a manly man. He is unselfish in giving others pleasure; but that he does it to his own detriment, no one can deny.
RICHARD S. SLEVIN.

1895
Coach: H. G. Hadden
Captain: Daniel V. Casey

O.19	W	Northwestern Law	20-0	H
N.7	W	Illinois Cycling Club	18-2	H
N.22	L	Indpls. Artillery (S)	0-18	H
N.28TH	W	Chicago Phys. & Surg.	32-0	H

(3-1-0) 70-20

1895 LETTERMEN

D. V. Casey (C)
R. P. Browne
T. Cavanaugh
J. Gallagher
J. M. Goeke
E. H. Kelly
W. J. McCarty
J. C. Murphy
J. Rosenthal
W. A. Walsh
L. C. Wheeler

Notre Dame, 18; Illinois Cycling Club, 2.

To football enthusiasts at Notre Dame, Thursday's game was full of significance. It revealed the fact that our Varsity this season will be the strongest the University has ever produced. Every man played for all that was in him, and it would be impossible to pick out anyone as excelling the rest. Three features of our Varsity's playing stand out most conspicuously: the interference, tackling and defensive work. The team has made such marked improvement in interference that it is safe to predict the closest kind of a game with Northwestern. Time and time again, the backs were guarded down the field for twenty, twenty-five and thirty yards. The men played with a snap and dash they have never shown previously, and before the visiting players so much as fingered the ball, two touch-downs and goals had been made in rapid succession. Casey, Cavanagh, Kelly, McCarthy, Mullen and Murphy swept around the ends in a way that set the "rooters" wild with delight. Our opponents were simply helpless before that human snow-plow, and if the good work is kept up, Van Doozer and his champion cohorts will experience an unpleasant surprise in trying to pierce our interference.

The tackling was simply superb. Words cannot describe it. In nearly every tackle made, the runner was nailed in his tracks. It seemed as though a pack of demons had been let loose, for that is about the only way to describe it. Every man contributed his share. Murphy, Walsh and Mullen, however, showed up slightly the best, though Wheeler and McCarthy made two phenomenal tackles back of their opponents' line. Goeke, too, saved a touch-down by bringing down Murphy after the latter's great spurt of thirty yards. Twice in succession Murphy of Notre Dame dove through his opponents' interference, and tackled the runner without any gain; and a little later Mullen downed Diener in a way that made the latter wonder where he was.

THE LINE-UP.		
ILL.-CYCLING CLUB		NOTRE DAME
Chisholm	*Right End*	Mullen
Kinsley	*Right Tackle*	Kelly, Galen
Jackson	*Right Guard*	Casey
Richardson	*Centre* {	Rosenthal Gallagher
Waugh	*Left Guard*	Cavanagh
Hager	*Left Tackle*	McCarthy
Wood	*Left End*	Murphy
Smith	*Quarter Back*	Walsh
Gross	*Right Half*	Wheeler
Diener	*Left Half*	Brown
Murphy	*Full Back*	Goeke

Umpire, Brennan. *Referee*, Bennett. *Timers*, Shiveley and Mott. *Reporters*, McDonough, Burns and Slevin.

Back row: Corby, Casey, Mott, Morrison, Dempsey.
Middle row: Dinkle, Anson, Chidester, Rosenthal.
Front row: Brennan, Keough, Corry, Zeitler.

1896

Coach: Frank E. Hering
Captain: Frank E. Hering

O.8	L	Chicago Phys. & Surg.	0-4	H
O.14	L	Chicago	0-18	H
O.27	W	S.B. Commercial A.C.	46-0	H
O.31	W	Albion	24-0	H
N.14	L	Purdue	22-28	H
N.20	W	Highland Views	82-0	H
N.26TH	W	Beloit (R)	8-0	H

(4-3-0)   182-50

PERDUE

The anxiously awaited game with Purdue is now a matter of history, and, though it did not make us champions of the State, it demonstrated beyond a doubt that Purdue has not an undisputed title to that honor, and furthermore, it proved that Notre Dame can justly claim recognition from the Western "Big Six." We may well be proud of our Varsity, but let us not permit our pride to blind us to the defects which certainly lost Saturday's game. It looked as though we had the advantage on the offensive, but on the defensive we were outclassed by Purdue. Why? Just because the Varsity has not a good scrub team to practice with. When the Varsity had the ball, they played football, as it is supposed to be played by the big teams; but when Purdue had the ball, the Varsity did not appear to such great advantage. Our line was invincible. Every man not only held his opponent, but did a good share of tackling. Purdue's strength lay in her backs, and particularly in Jameson. His ability to squeeze through tacklers is certainly wonderful.

On the defensive Fagan outclassed his man. He worried the quarter-back in proper style and tackled when he had nothing else to do. Cavanagh and Rosenthal also had the advantage over their opponents. Although the latter had to buck against the famous Webb, he was punctured but twice and with no particular effort. The former sustained his reputation as a football player; came in for a good share of tackling and surprised all by his agility. His tackle of Marshall, immediately after the first kick-off, was certainly a pretty one. Alward and Wagner were no match for Hanly and Moritz. The latter broke through at will, and always had a hole ready if Brown or Kegler wanted to hit the line.

Murphy and especially Mullen did splendid work at the ends. The latter never took the ball but kept Halstead helpless. He also broke through at will, and once, unassisted, he carried Jameson eight yards before he could get a start. Moritz and Fagan also broke through and captured the ball before Goben could pass it. The weakness in the defence was centred in our backs. They did not seem to understand Purdue's interference; hence the large end gains. They made up for this deficiency, however, when they were on the offensive. Not once did Purdue down us with a loss, and not once did our backs fumble the ball. A little more speed in starting was all that was wanting.

Daly did magnificent work while he was in the game, and it was his ability to slide through the tackles probably that caused his speedy retirement. Brown and Kegler played a hard game and never failed to get through the line. McDonald always got around the end, and Hanly, Moritz and Schillo sustained their reputation as ground gainers. Captain Hering played his usual hard game; his clever management and varied plays undoubtedly making the Varsity's offensive work so striking. The linemen held their opponents and made the gains possible. Kegler's punting was up to the standard he has set for himself, but he has made little progress in goal-kicking, and it was undoubtedly due to this defect that Purdue won the championship.

THE LINE-UP:

VARSITY	POSITION	PURDUE
Murphy	Left End	Halstead
Hanly	Left Tackle	Wagner
Rosenthal	Left Guard	Bates
Fagan	Centre	Breen
Cavanagh	Right Guard	Webb
Moritz	Right Tackle	Alward
Mullen	Right End	Hall
Hering (C.)	Quarter-Back	Goben
R. Brown	Left Half-Back	Moore
Schillo	Right Half-Back	Jameson (C.)
Kegler	Full-Back	Marshall

Touchdowns, Kegler (2), Murphy (2), Brown, Jameson (4); Goal-Kicks, Jameson (4), Mullen (1), Substitutes, Daly for R. Brown, R. E. Brown for Daly, O'Hara for Kegler, McDonald for Schillo, Bates for Hall, Foulks for Bates; Umpire, Dr. Thompson of Princeton; Referee, L. Downs of Greencastle; Timekeepers, Marmon and Muessel; Linesmen, Corby and Rushell; Halves, 35:00.

1896 LETTERMEN

F. E. Hering (C)
R. E. Brown
T. Cavanaugh
M. T. Daly
W. A. Fagan
F. X. Hanley
W. C. Kegler
J. I. Mullen
J. C. Murphy
J. Rosenthal
F. J. Schillo

CAPTAIN F. E. HERING (Q. B.)

Captain Hering has done his work well. By his efforts the old men were made better, and, by building on their experience, reared for themselves a monument of strength and skill. Besides this improvement, our Captain has made a much greater one. When some men roused themselves from their lethargic state of laziness, and put on the moleskins for the first time, they were surprised to hear they played well. Under Captain Hering's coaching and with a few weeks of practice they were more surprised to find themselves on the Varsity, and their friends were even more surprised than themselves.

Thomas T. Cavanagh (R.G.), William A. Fagan (C.), Jacob Rosenthal (L.G.).

1897

Coach: Frank E. Hering
Captain: John I. Mullen

O.13	T	Rush Medical	0-0	H
O.23	W	DePauw	4-0	H
O.28	W	Chicago Dental Surg.	62-0	H
N.6	L	Chicago	5-34	A
N.13	W	St. Viator	60-0	H
N.25TH	W	Michigan State (R)	34-6	H

(4-1-1)   165-40

1897 LETTERMEN

J. I. Mullen (C)
M. T. Daly
J. W. Eggeman
J. F. Farley
W. C. Kegler
C. J. Lins
W. P. Monahan
C. M. Niezer
F. J. Schillo
F. G. Swonk
F. L. Waters

Chicago, 34; Notre Dame, 5.

We have met the enemy and we are theirs. In Chicago last Saturday, Stagg's men defeated the Varsity by a score of 34 to 5; and we are more proud of our representatives than ever. With weak interference and weaker tackling, and with some of the best players out of the game, the Varsity played a hard, courageous game, and, in spite of all obstacles, proved that for downright perseverance and fearlessness, Notre Dame is at the top. We lost fairly and have no excuses to offer. Chicago's interference was wonderful, and her assaults on our weakened line were terrific; but in many cases we held them. They deserve all the credit for their hard-won victory; to Notre Dame belongs the glory of having made a game fight from start to finish. Painfully injured and weak from repeated charges, Schillo stuck to the game until compelled to retire by the coach. In Schillo we have a man of whom any team in the country might well be proud. Kegler's punting, coming, as it always did, at the critical time, saved us many touchdowns. Only one of his punts was blocked—the rest saved us. Besides this, the full-back hit the line hard, and once carried the ball seventy yards through all the opposing tacklers; but his punting was a feature of a game that was full of features.

For the first time on Marshall Field the Princeton kick was successfully accomplished, and Daly is the man who did it. From the thirty-yard line he sent the ball squarely between the posts, and scored against Chicago for the only time in the afternoon. At centre, Eggeman was in the game all the time, and out-played the much-talked-of Cavanagh at every point. The praises which the spectators lavished upon Big John were well earned. Waters played a splendid game. His passing was perfect, and he tackled with a dash that was exhilarating. At full-back he downed Chicago without fail. Monahan did well, and while they were in the game, Farley, Captain Mullen and Littig put up a pretty game. For Chicago, Kennedy, Clarke and Hamill played well, and Gardner kicked five out of seven goals.

Notre Dame, 34; Michigan Agricul. College, 6.

On a soggy field and with a drizzling rain dripping from lowering skies, the Varsity on Thanksgiving afternoon defeated the representatives of the Michigan Agriculture College by a score of 34 to 6. The men from Michigan share with Chicago the honor of accomplishing that in which all our other opponents this year have failed—they scored on the Varsity. And they scored by good, hard football playing. Every man on their team played a good game, and Captain Baker and full-back Wells played exceptionally good ball. There was not the slightest quarrel—the game being played honestly by both sides. Referee Keep did his best; both he and Umpire McDonald gave satisfaction to both players and spectators.

For Notre Dame, Farley made the prettiest tackle seen here either this year or last. Schillo and Captain Mullen surpassed themselves, and Kegler's right leg was in the business all the time. Eggeman, Murray and Niezer held together bravely; Swonk was good and Lins at half was a success. The backs were strong on the offensive, but when M. A. C. had the ball they made big and frequent gains.

NOTRE DAME	THE LINE-UP:	M. A. C.
Farley	Left End	Baker (Capt.)
Niezer	Left Tackle	Price
Murray	Left Guard	Crane
Eggeman	Centre	Vanderstolpe
Swonk	Right Guard	Skinner
Schillo	Right Tackle	Williams
Mullen (Capt.)	Right End	Woodworth
Waters	Quarter-Back	Ranney
Lins	Left Half-Back	Brainerd
Fennessey	Right Half-Back	Fate
Kegler	Full-Back	Wells

Touchdowns: Lins (2), Kegler (2), Fennessey, Farley for Notre Dame; Wells for M. A. C. Goals from touchdowns: Farley (4), Waters (1). Time of halves, twenty-five minutes. Date and place: Notre Dame, Thanksgiving Day, 1897. Referee and Umpire: Keip, M. A. C.; McDonald, Notre Dame. Linesmen, Howell, Notre Dame.

CAPTAIN MULLEN

1898

Coach: Frank E. Hering
Captain: John I. Mullen

O.8	W	Illinois	5-0	A
O.15	W	Michigan State	53-0	H
O.23	L	Michigan	0-23	H
O.29	W	DePauw	32-0	H
N.11	L	Indiana	5-11	H
N.19	W	Albion	60-0	A

(4-2-0)   155-34

1898 LETTERMEN

J. I. Mullen (C)
A. M. Bennett
J. W. Eggeman
J. F. Farley
C. F. Fleming
A. C. Fortin
A. T. Hayes
G. W. Kuppler
G. J. Lins
A. D. McDonald
M. P. McNulty
W. P. Monahan
J. J. Murray
F. M. Winter

While the students were all comfortably resting in their cots last Friday night, a small party of husky young men from the southern part of the State quietly made their way into our grounds and brought with them a big surprise for Notre Dame. Their coming was no surprise, for that was expected; what occurred before they left was what took us off our feet. Indiana had played only one hard game this season and that resulted in a tie. Hence our men that had gone through battles with Illinois, Michigan and DePauw had expected to secure a victory from the Bloomington players. Saturday afternoon our team, minus its captain, went out of their training quarters and made ready to meet their rivals. At 2:30 the Indiana players filed out of Sorin Hall, all clad for the game, and wended their way toward the gridiron. When the heavy linemen and stocky little backs appeared, the crowd pressing against the side lines felt a shudder passing along their spinal columns, and it was evident that our men were up against a hard game. Captain Mullen was sadly missed, though we would not say that his presence might win the game. One or two fumbles and a blocked kick proved very disastrous to our side, and to this and the superior weight of the opposing team, is due the defeat that we sustained. The Indiana line averages up in weight better and more evenly than any line we faced this year. Murray retired in the second half in favor of Winter; Hayes filled Mullen's place at right end. Few end plays were tried, the visitors preferring to get their heavy guards back and hurl them at our line.

NOTRE DAME	THE LINE-UP:	INDIANA
Farley	Left End	McGooney
McNulty	Left Tackle	Neizer
Bennet	Left Guard	Sparks
Eggeman	Centre	Hurley
Winter	Right Guard	Pike
Murray		
Fortin	Right Tackle	Hubbard
Hayes	Right End	Dodge
Mcdonald (Capt.)	Quarter Back	Foster
Kuppler	Left Half-Back	Youtzler (C.)
Lins	Right Half-Back	Hunt
Monahan	Full Back	Halley

Umpire, Moore, C. A. C.; Referee, Wagner, C. A. C. 25 min. halves.

❧ THE NOTRE DAME PLAYERS. ❧

John Farley, left end, is 22 years old, 5ft. 9in. in height, and weighs 158 pounds. This is his third year on the 'Varsity. His home is at Paterson, New Jersey. He first played football on the Entre Nous team, an amateur team at Paterson. He was left fielder on the '98 'Varsity base ball team.

Earl Wagner, left tackle, is 24 years old, 5ft. 9in. in height and weighs 188 pounds. He played tackle on Purdue in '96. During '97 and '98 he played half-back and tackle on the South Bend Commercial Athletic Club team. His home is at South Bend. He is a post-graduate in chemistry. This is his first year on the 'Varsity.

F. W. Winters, left guard, is 20 years old, 5ft 8in. in height and weighs 210 pounds. He was substitute on the '98 'Varsity. His home is at Pittsburg.

D. K. O'Malley, left guard, is 22 years old, 6ft. 1in. in height and weight 198 pounds. This is his first year on the 'Varsity. His home is at Waunakee, Wisconsin.

J. W. Eggeman, centre, is 23 years old, 6ft. 5in. in height and weighs 248 pounds. This is his third year on the 'Varsity. He was a member of the '97 and '98 track teams, and at present is Manager of all the 'Varsity athletic teams for the coming year. His home is at Fort Wayne, Ind.

Michael McNulty, right guard, is 6ft. in height, 23 years old, and weighs 194 pounds. He first played on the Entre Nous team. His home is at Paterson, N. J.

Frank Hanley, right tackle, is 26 years old, 5ft. 10in. in height and weighs 186 pounds. He played tackle on the '96 'Varsity. In '97 and '98 he played tackle on the South Bend Commercial Athletic Club. His home is at South Bend.

A. D. McDonald, quarter-back, is 21 years old, 6ft. 1in. in height and weighs 178 pounds. He was substitute in '96 and quarter-back in '98. He plays first base on the 'Varsity nine. His home is at Austin, Texas.

John Mullen, (C) right end, is 24 years old, 5ft. 10in. in height and weighs 153 pounds. This is his fourth year on the 'Varsity.

A. T. Hayes, right half, is 19 years old, 6ft. in height and weighs 165 pounds. This is his first year on the 'Varsity. His home is at Cincinnati.

Ralph Glynn, left half, is 18 years old, 5ft. 10in. in height and weighs 157 pounds. This is his first year on the 'Varsity. He was a member of the '98 track team. His home is at Saginaw, Michigan.

G. W. Kuppler, left-half, is 20 years old, 5ft. 8in. in height and weighs 160 pounds. He was left-half on the '98 'Varsity. His home is at Seattle, Washington.

Ernest Duncan, full-back, is 20 years old, 5ft. 10in. in height and weighs 158 pounds. He played full-back on the '98 South Bend Commercial Athletic Club team. This is his first years on the 'Varsity.

Charley Daly, substitute quarter, is 22 years old, 5ft. 7in. in height and weighs 140 pounds. His home is at Paterson, N. J. This is his first year with the 'Varsity.

Charles Fleming, substitute quarter-back, is 23 years old, 5ft. 9in in height and weighs 145 pounds. He was quarter-back on the '98 'Varsity and has played for three years on the 'Varsity nine.

William Monahan, substitute end, is 5ft. 8in. in height, 20 years old, and weighs 150 pounds. He was substitute on '96 and '97 'Varsity and full-back on '98 'Varsity. His home is at Chicago.

A. G. Fortin, substitute tackle, is 18 years old, 5ft. 11in. in height and weighs 180 pounds. He was tackle on '98 'Varsity. His home is at Chicago.

J. S. Schneider, substitute center, is 20 years old, 6ft. in height and weighs 183 pounds. This is his first year with the 'Varsity. His home is at Menasha, Wisconsin.

	1899			
	Coach: James McWeeney			
	Captain: John I. Mullen			
S.27	W	Englewood H.S.	29-5	H
S.30	W	Michigan State	40-0	H
O.4	L	Chicago	6-23	A
O.14	W	Lake Forest	38-0	H
O.18	L	Michigan	0-12	A
O.23	W	Indiana	17-0	H
O.27	W	Northwestern (R)	12-0	H
N.4	W	Rush Medical	17-0	H
N.18	T	Purdue	10-10	A
N.30TH	L	Chicago Phys. & Surg.	0-5	H
	(6-3-1)		169-55	

Notre Dame vs. Englewood.

Last Wednesday over six hundred people passed through the gate leading to the new field to witness the first football game of the season of '99. The grounds were in good condition, and although the weather was a little warm for football it suited the spectators.

The Englewood High School team of Chicago were our opponents. The result of the game was somewhat of a surprise to Notre Dame enthusiasts; not one expected to see the men from Chicago score.

After Winters had succeeded in kicking goal after a touchdown in the first half, the ball was dropped to the centre of the field where Wishart, Englewood's full-back, sent it flying through the air for forty-five yards. Hayes caught the pig-skin, and by clever dodging succeeded in returning it fifteen yards. At this point the ball was fumbled and secured by one of the Englewood men who ran back to the twenty-yard line. A moment later the visitors were given ten yards for an off-side play. Captain Wishart signalled his men for a place kick. It was a wise move, for his team had not been able to make any gains through Notre Dame's heavy line. The ball was not passed properly; it went over the quarter-back's head and rolled along the ground to Wishart, who picked it up and sent it squarely over our goal from the fifteen-yard line, making a drop-kick which gave Englewood five points.

NOTRE DAME		ENGLEWOOD
Monahan and Duncan	L. E.	Buckhart
Wagner and Nalen	L. T.	Maxwell
O'Malley	L. G.	Sommers
Eggeman, Winters	C.	Lewis
McNulty	R. G.	Webster
Hanley, Fortin	R. T.	Indermile
Mullen	R. E.	Kennedy
Daly, Hayes, Fleming	Q. B.	Jenks, Stauch
Kuppler and Hayes	L. H.	Wishart
Weiss, Lins, Glynn	R. H.	Graver
Hayes and Duncan	F. B.	Rose

Umpire: Moore, Purdue. Referee: Van Fleck, Chicago. Touchdowns: Notre Dame, Kuppler, Lins, Hayes, Mullen, Farley. Goals: Winters (2), Fleming (2). Drop-kick, Englewood, Wishart.

THE Notre Dame Bands. NOV. 30 1899. FOOTBALL SOUVENIR.

❧ DESCRIPTION OF FOOTBALL ❧

FOR PERSONS UNACQUAINTED WITH THE GAME.

FOOTBALL is played on a field 330 feet long and 160 feet wide, enclosed by white lines and usually crossed by other white lines 5 yards apart; the latter are merely for the purpose of aiding the officials in determining distances. The shorter of the outside lines are the goal lines, and in the middle of these are the goal posts, 18½ feet apart, with a cross bar 10 feet above the ground.

A team is composed of 11 men—7 line men or rushers, and 4 backs—named according to the positions which they occupy in the line, or back of it—left end, left tackle, left guard, center, right guard, right tackle, right end, quarter back, left half-back, right half-back, and full-back.

The game, which consists of *two halves* of 35 minutes each, with a rest of 10 minutes between, is a struggle between the two teams to get the ball from the middle of the field over the goal line, and is begun by one side kicking the ball toward the other side, by one of whose players it will probably be caught. This man, protected by his fellows, will run as far forward as possible, and when he can go no further he will yell "down." The two teams will then range themselves opposite each other; the ball will be held on the ground by the center of the side to whom it temporarily belongs, until he hears a signal from captain (usually a string of figures, one or two of which indicate what is to be done, the superfluous ones being to hide the signal from the other team), when he will throw it, or "snap" it, as it is technically called, to the quarter-back, who will pass it to another player. As soon as the ball leaves the center's hands the eleven to whom it belongs immediately evolves itself into a certain formation and rush as fast as it can at the point of attack called for by the signal. The other side endeavors to break up the formation and to catch the man carring the ball. This mix-up is called a *scrim-mage*. As before stated, when the player carrying the ball can go no further, he calls "down," and the teams *line up* for another *scrimmage*.

The formation varies according to the part of the line attacked, and the player receives the ball for a run or a kick. All the players, except the center and quarter-back, can run with the ball from a *scrimmage*. Each play is directed at one of the spaces between the rushes, or outside the end men. A good team will have from 30 to 45 different plays, with a signal for each play. The side having possession of the ball must advance it 5 yards or retreat with it 20 yards in three trials, or surrender it to its opponents.

The men of the team which has the ball are not allowed to catch hold of their opponents with their hands; if any one does this it is called *holding*, and the team surrenders the ball as a penalty. The members of the other team may use their hands, The head, shoulder or hip is used when the hands are not allowed. When the teams face each other for a *scrimmage*, if any one steps over an imaginary line drawn through the center of the ball and between the two teams, he is *off side*, and this is punished by surrendering the ball, or losing several yards, according to which side has transgressed. Penalties are also inflicted for various other things, which can be found fully explained in the rules.

When the ball is carried by one team over its opponent's goal line, the result is called a *touchdown*, and counts five points. The victors bring the ball back into the field as far as they wish, and try to kick it over the cross bar and between the goal posts. If this is done the result is *goal*, which counts one point more.

If the ball is dropped on the ground and then kicked over the cross bar and between the goal posts. during the play, the result is a *goal from field*, and counts five points.

When the ball is held on the ground by one player and kicked by another of the same side it is called a *place kick*. If the ball goes over the bar and between the goal posts it counts five points.

A safety is made by the side which has possession of the ball touching it down behind their own goal line, to prevent opponents doing so, and counts two points for the opponents.

❧ SCORE CARD. ❧

182018

PLAYERS.	POS.	WT.	AGE		MADE BY	PTS.	PLAYERS.	POS.	WT.	AGE		MADE BY	PTS.
NOTRE DAME.							**PHYSICIANS AND SURGEONS.**						
Farley	L E	158	22				Dean	L E	160	20			
Wagner	L T	194	24	Touch Down (5 pts.)			Lockwood	L T	200	21	Touch Down (5 pts.)		
Winters	L G	210	20				Hassett	L G	185	22			
O'Malley	L G	193	22				Major	C	180	22			
Eggeman	C	248	23				Corry	C	180	24			
McNulty	R G	194	23	Goal (1 pt.)			Parry	R G	182	22	Goal (1 pt.)		
Hanley	R T	186	26				McCormick	R T	190	26			
Mullen	R E	153	24	Goal from Field (5 pts.)			Alward	R T	198	23	Goal from Field (5 pts.)		
McDonald	Q B	178	21				Dowdall	R E	170	24			
Hayes	R H	165	19				Turner	Q B	157	24			
Kuppler	L H	160	20				Bothne	R H	168	23			
Glynn	L H	157	18	Safety (2 pts.)			Comstock	L H	165	20	Safety (2 pts.)		
Duncan	F B	158	21				Flippin	F B	178	27			

Kicked off at.................P M   First Half ended...............P M   Time of game................hours.

Kicked off at.................P M   Second Half ended.............P M   Remarks:...................

Referee............................   Linesmen {...............................

Umpire.............................   Timers {...............................

VARSITY FOOTBALL ELEVEN, 1900.

1900 LETTERMEN

J. F. Farley (C)
C. J. Diebold
A. C. Fortin
J. F. Faragher
C. I. Gillen
R. L. Glynn
A. T. Hayes
G. W. Kuppler
G. J. Lins
H. J. McGlew
D. O'Malley
J. B. Pick
L. J. Salmon
C. L. Staudt
F. M. Winter

1900					
Coach: Pat O'Dea					
Captain: John F. Farley					
S.29	W	Goshen	55-0		H
O.6	W	Englewood H.S.	68-0		H
O.13	W	S.B. Howard Park	64-0		H
O.20	W	Cincinnati	58-0		H
O.25	L	Indiana	0-6		A
N.3	T	Beloit	6-6		H
N.10	L	Wisconsin	0-54		A
N.17	L	Michigan	0-7		A
N.24	W	Rush Medical (R)	5-0		H
N.29TH	W	Chicago Phys. & Surg.	5-0		H
	(6-3-1)		261-73		

Notre Dame Plays at Madison.

During the long history of athletics at Notre Dame never before was one of her teams so badly beaten as was our football eleven at Madison last Saturday. The Wisconsin players and supporters were greatly surprised at the way in which our eleven was pushed up and down the gridiron, and our fellows could not understand in the least how it all happened. The Madison team simply lined up, called their signal, and some cardinal player would be seen tearing around the end or hurdling the line for a good gain. Our fellows appeared to be out of the game altogether from the very start. To the unfairness of the officials Wisconsin owes a great deal of her big score. In the beginning of the game, when an advantage one way or the other counted for much, Notre Dame lost the ball on two occasions for holding in the line. To any unbiassed spectator the Wisconsin men appeared to be liable to such penalty much more frequently than our fellows did. But after every scrimmage the umpire invariably came up to one of our men and threatened to put him out of the game for holding. Not once did he speak to the Wisconsin boys, and they were guilty of holding in every line-up. The officials were either unfair or incompetent, but from their experience in this capacity we are inclined to think they ruled often with their eyes open.

But aside from the fact that we were given the worst of the decisions there are other things to account for our defeat. One other great advantage that Wisconsin had was a good set of cleats on every shoe. Our fellows were unusually slow in starting on the plays. The mud was so thick that it stuck to their shoes in clods and rendered their short cleats of no use whatever. The Wisconsin men on the other hand took a firm hold with their long cleats and started much faster than we did. But the principal reason that that horrible score was sent home from Camp Randall was that the Wisconsin eleven were somewhat superior to ours. We have some excellent individual players, and they had been coached well, but the Wisconsin men had the advantage of our fellows in some respects, and it may be in the knowledge of the game. Almost all the members of this year's team at Wisconsin have been at the University and trying for the eleven for three or more years. In this way they have had many opportunities to improve, and have had the advantage of the best possible coaching during that time.

Throughout the game our men appeared to do steady work, but we had the ball in our possession for so short a time that we can not tell what our men could have done on offensive play. John Farley was injured during the first ten minutes of the game and could not be expected to carry the ball. Kuppler plunged through a hole that Jim Farragher made against the great Curtis for four yards, and Fortin took advantage of Farragher's good work with Curtis to march through the same place for six yards. Give each of the backs another yard and two to Farragher and we have all the gains made against Wisconsin aside from Farley's punts. Cochems, Larsen, Curtis and Riordan ran between end and tackle with monotonous regularity, and Driver and Schrieber tore up the line without trouble.

The game was lost at the start. Winter drove the ball forty yards to Larsen, and the fast half-back skimmed down the field for twenty yards before he was downed. Larsen, Cochems, and Driver then carried the ball to the middle of the field in straight gains when Larsen fumbled the oval and we got it. Farley and Kuppler failed to gain, and Farley punted thirty-five yards to Cochems who returned the ball ten. Cochems was tried at right-end twice but failed, and Driver punted forty yards to Farley. Capt. John, to the surprise of Notre Dame supporters, fumbled the ball, and Curtis fell on it on our twenty-yard line. Driver, Curtis, Riordan and Larsen ran the ball to our five-yard line, and Cochems skirted right end for a touchdown. Tratt kicked the goal, and the game was Wisconsin's after ten minutes' play. Cochems made another touchdown at the end of the first half which Capt. Farley protested, but the protest did no good.

THE LINE UP.

WISCONSIN		NOTRE DAME
Abbot, Doar	L E	Sammon
Chamberlin, Schrieber	L T	Farragher, Cullinan
Riordan	L G	Gilman
Skow	C	Winter, O'Malley
Lerum	R G	Staudt
Curtis	R T	Fortin
Juneau	R E	Hayes
Tratt	Q B	Diebold
Cochems, Marshall	L H	Kuppler
Larsen, Crupp	R H	Farley, Glynn
Driver, Schrieber	F B	Lins

Touchdowns: Larson, 4; Cochems, 3; Juneau, 1; Marshall, 1. Goals from downs: Tratt, 6. Referee, Anderson. Umpire, Alexander. Linesmen, Powers and Senn. Time-keepers, McCowan and Yockey. Time of halves, 30 and 25 minutes.

1901 LETTERMEN

A. C. Fortin (C)
J. L. Doar
J. F. Faragher
C. I. Gillen
H. E. Kirby
G. J. Lins
F. J. Lonegan
H. J. McGlew
G. L. Nyere
D. O'Malley
E. J. Peil
J. B. Pick
L. J. Salmon
F. M. Winter

1901				
Coach: Pat O'Dea				
Captain: Albert C. Fortin				
S.28	T	South Bend A.C.	0-0	H
O.5	W	Ohio Medical U.	6-0	A
O.12	L	Northwestern (R)	0-2	A
O.19	W	Chicago Medical Col.	32-0	A
O.26	W	Beloit	5-0	A
N.2	W	Lake Forest	16-0	H
N.9	W	Purdue	12-6	H
N.16	W	Indiana (R)	18-5	H
N.23	W	Chicago Phys. & Surg.	34-0	H
N.28TH	W	South Bend A.C.	22-6	H
		(8-1-1)	145-19	

Northwestern, 2; Notre Dame, 0.

But two points were scored in the North western game, and these were made in the first half when Sammon was forced over our line for a safety.

We lost last Saturday's game; but there is no stigma to this defeat, for we felt that had the day been a dry one, our story might have a different ending. With a field that literally ran in mud and water, the team put up a magnificent defensive game in the first half, and a strong aggressive game in the second half, bringing the ball, by a series of rushes from their ten-yard line to Northwestern's three-yard line. We have no excuses to offer why we did not score, but we admire the strong defense put up by our opponents when we were within the shadow of their goal.

It was impossible to get a proper estimate of the ability of both teams, for the game was played for the greater part in the middle of the field, where the mud was four inches deep. So that after a few minutes of play it was impossible to distinguish one player from another. And though the ball was a mass of slime, but few fumbles marred the contest.

The playing was necessarily slow. McChesney found great difficulty in getting off his punts, being blocked twice, but the weight of the ball seemed to add more power to Sammon's leg. Owing to the ball being so slippery the Varsity backs played up close, and then began a series of rushes against Northwestern's heavy line. But these did not seem to avail much in the first half, so time and again Sammon was forced to punt. Our linemen at centre, Pick, Gillen and O'Malley, played a strong aggressive game; and Farragher and Fortin seemed to be mixed up in every Northwestern play. The playing of the ends was much in evidence, after the first few minutes of play. And our heavy half backs, Lins and Hannan, were under all scrimmage.

NORTHWESTERN		NOTRE DAME
Elliott	L. E.	Doran, Neerie
Fleager	L. T.	Farragher
Mauerman	L. G.	Gillen
Allen	C.	Pick
A. Baird	R. G.	O'Malley
Paddock	R. T.	Fortin
McChesney	R. E.	Lonergan
Johnson	Q. B.	McGlew
Ward	L. H. B.	Kirby, Hannan
G. O. Dietz	R. H. B.	Lins
Davidson	F. B.	Sammon

Referee, Fred Hayner, Lake Forest. Umpire, Everts Wrenn, Harvard. Timekeepers, Herbert and Koppelman. Linesmen, Collins and West. Time of halves, 25 min.

1902

Coach: James F. Faragher
Captain: Louis J. Salmon

S.27	W	Michigan State	33-0	H
O.11	W	Lake Forest	28-0	H
O.18	L	Michigan	0-23	N
O.25	W	Indiana	11-5	A
N.1	W	Ohio Medical U.	6-5	A
N.8	L	Knox	5-12	A
N.15	W	American Medical	92-0	H
N.22	W	DePauw	22-0	H
N.27TH	T	Purdue	6-6	A
		(6-2-1)	203-51	

N—at Toledo

1903

Coach: James F. Faragher
Captain: Louis J. Salmon

O.3	W	Michigan State	12-0	H
O.10	W	Lake Forest	28-0	H
O.17	W	DePauw (R)	56-0	H
O.24	W	American Medical	52-0	H
O.29	W	Chicago Phys. & Surg.	46-0	H
N.7	W	Missouri Osteopaths	28-0	H
N.14	T	Northwestern	0-0	A
N.21	W	Ohio Medical U.	35-0	A
N.26TH	W	Wabash	35-0	A
		(8-0-1)	292-0	

1902 LETTERMEN

L. J. Salmon (C)
J. J. Cullinan
W. W. Desmond
J. L. Doar
M. L. Fansler
N. R. Furlong
C. I. Gillen
F. J. Lonegan
E. W. McDermott
H. J. McGlew
G. L. Nyere
D. O'Malley
F. J. Shaughnessy
N. H. Silver
A. E. Steiner

1903 LETTERMEN

L. J. Salmon (C)
P. A. Beacom
J. J. Cullinan
R. W. Donovan
N. R. Furlong
F. J. Lonegan
H. J. McGlew
L. M. McNerney
G. L. Nyere
J. I. O'Phelan
F. J. Shaughnessy
C. J. Sheehan
N. H. Silver
A. E. Steiner

Captain Salmon

LOUIS J. SALMON (Capt. and Full-Back). Perhaps the most brilliant player Notre Dame has ever had is our captain and full-back, L. J. Salmon. Salmon is one of the wonders of the football world. His line bucking and punting this season were phenomenal. His work against the Champion Michigan team attracted the attention of every coach and critic in the country, and they were unanimous in declaring his playing marvellous. The *Chicago Daily News* picks him for half back on the All-Western Eleven, an honour which is denied him by the other papers because Notre Dame is not a member of the "big nine." In speaking of Salmon, the *News* says: "His ability to buck the line is something not seen in every football. In the game against Michigan, this player by the most indomitable perseverance carried the ball from Notre Dame's goal line far into Michigan territory. Man after man tackled him, but he shook off all the Wolverine stars." Salmon is twenty-two years of age, weighs 16? pounds and is five feet nine and a half inches.

Notre Dame vs. Northwestern.

Last Saturday on the American League Ball Grounds, Chicago, the football representatives of Notre Dame and Northwestern contended for supremacy in a game that resulted in a tie. Each team had an enviable record, and the prestige at stake, combined with the large number of followers both have in the Western metropolis, provoked unusual interest. In McCornack, Northwestern has one of the best football experts in the country, while Notre Dame, without any special coach, was tutored by Salmon, Holland and McWeeney.

That our men are made of the right material and well versed in football theory and practice was attested by their work on Saturday. It was generally conceded that no finer defensive exhibition was ever seen in the West, if indeed anywhere. Both teams played straight football almost throughout, and the sensational element was not lacking. Lonergan's end runs, McGlew's and O'Shaughnessy's tackling, Salmon's defense and the brilliant all-around work of Captain Fleager and Colton of Northwestern, gave the most fastidious spectator full value for his money.

Did we not know the disposition of our men we might deem it invidious to single out any one player, or set of players, for particular notice. The linemen — those too often overlooked in reports — never flinched and played a splendid game from start to finish. So too did our speedy little quarter-back, Silver; but why go further? Captain Salmon put the matter in a nutshell in his speech at the Sherman House when he said that all deserve equal credit; that if anyone acquitted himself less ably the battle was lost.

The team, accompanied by Manager Daly and Trainer Holland, arrived at the Victoria Hotel, Chicago, Friday evening, and at the appointed hour on Saturday set out for the scene of battle. They reached the League Ball Grounds just as the crowd was pouring in, and were lustily cheered and trumpeted by the good-humored spectators, amongst whom were several hundred students who had journeyed up from Notre Dame. The weather was clear and crisp, but owing to the car strike the attendance in the beginning was rather disappointing. Later, however, the benches filled, and here and there was a plentiful sprinkling of fair ones whose gaze seldom wandered from the knights on the gridiron. Ardent partisans they were, too, making the stands a riot of color with flags and ribands at every brilliant play.

THE LINE-UP.

NORTHWESTERN			NOTRE DAME
Weinberger	R E	L E	McGlew
Allen	R T	L T	Cullinan
Garrett, Bell	R G	L G	Beacom
Bell, Carlson	C	C	Sheehan
Phillips	L G	R G	Fansler, Furlong
Kafer	L T	R T	Steiner
Peckumn	L E	R E	Shaughnessy
McCann	Q B	Q B	Silver
Blair, Reuber	R H	L H	Lonergan
Colton	L H	R H	Nyere, McDermot
Fleager, C.; Wilson	F B	F B	Salmon, Capt.

Score—Northwestern, o; Notre Dame, o. Place and Date—American league-ball grounds, Nov. 14. Referee—Sheehan, Brown. Umpire—Hadden, Michigan. Linesman—McMillan, Chicago. Time of Halves—thirty-five minutes.
P.

*

OPINIONS OF THE GAME.

Prominent officials and players spoke as follows after the game:

Coach M'Cornack, Northwestern:—It was the hardest game we have played this season and the Notre Dame team is the best we have met. Their defense was as great an exhibition of football as I have ever seen.

Athletic Director Butterworth, Northwestern:—It was the hardest football game I have ever seen. The defense of both teams was great, and that of Notre Dame was almost a marvel. I think each team should be proud of the showing it has made.

Referee Sheehan:—It was the finest exhibition of football that I have seen this fall. The teams were equally matched. Notre Dame's defense on their one-yard line was superb; it has not, in my mind, been equalled this year. At times Northwestern's offense was irresistible and its defense was like a stone wall.

Captain Fleager, Northwestern:—I expected a hard game, but not as hard as the game turned out to be. Notre Dame's team played a defensive game at critical times that could not be beat.

1904				
Coach: Louis J. Salmon				
Captain: Frank J. Shaughnessy				
O.1	W	Wabash	12-4	H
O.8	W	American Medical	44-0	H
O.15	L	Wisconsin	0-58	N
O.22	W	Ohio Medical U.	17-5	A
O.27	W	Toledo A.A.	6-0	H
N.5	L	Kansas	5-24	A
N.19	W	DePauw	10-0	H
N.24TH	L	Purdue	0-36	A
		(5-3-0)	94-127	

N—at Milwaukee

1904 LETTERMEN

F. J. Shaughnessy (C)
P. A. Beacom
R. L. Bracken
D. Church
R. W. Donovan
W. A. Draper
M. L. Fansler
A. S. Funk
D. J. Guthrie
L. M. McNerney
D. L. Murphy
N. H. Silver
R. W. Waldorf

The Varsity of 1904.

IT was without regret that another page of Notre Dame's football history was turned down on Thanksgiving Day, for the record made by the Varsity of 1904 fell far below the standard set by the elevens of the past three years. But the poor showing made this year does not reflect in any way upon the ability of Coach Salmon, nor upon the pluck or ability of the men who made up the eleven. The whole cause of the disastrous season can be set down to two causes—the lack of material and the frequent injury of the players—neither of which was to have been foreseen by those in charge in time to have been avoided. Of the championship eleven of 1903 we lost our entire back-field, both tackles, an end and one guard. This in itself was a serious obstacle to overcome, and it was seen after the first week of practice, that there was a woeful lack of material from which to pick men to fill the vacant positions. Out of the squad of twenty-five there were but sixteen who were qualified by their classes to represent Notre Dame on the gridiron. Of the new men the majority were without previous experience and were very light, but Coach Salmon set to work to whip his men into shape for the season. It was at this stage that the injuries commenced and kept up during the rest of the season. In quick succession, McNerney, Guthrie, Healy, Silver, Shaughnessy and Church were injured so as to be forced to retire from the game. The lack of men forced Trainer Holland to put his cripples back in the game before they had recovered, and so our team always had one or more cripples in its line-up. And so with one or more of the best players in the college on the side-lines in every game it is no wonder that the Varsity was unable to put forth its best game. The loss of the Kansas contest at least can be laid to the number of cripples in our line-up, for it was not until after our subs had been put in the game that Kansas made their winning scores.

Coach Louis J. Salmon had a hard task before him and the complications which arose as the season advanced did not tend to lighten his burden. To his credit it must be said that he kept at work with the same spirit of perseverance that marked his playing during his four years on Notre Dame's teams and made his name famous in the annals of football from one coast to the other. The fact that the Varsity's team work and offensive play was developed to the speed and accuracy that was shown in the last few games speaks more for Salmon's ability than the record of an ordinary team with good luck on its side would have done. It is the hope of the entire student body that Salmon will return to Notre Dame next year, take charge of the team and bring Notre Dame back to the place she occupied when he was the pride of Notre Dame and the West.

1905
Coach: Henry J. McGlew
Captain: Patrick A. Beacom

S.30	W	N. Division H.S. (Chi.)	44-0	H
O.7	W	Michigan State	28-0	H
O.14	L	Wisconsin	0-21	N
O.21	L	Wabash	0-5	H
O.28	W	*American Medical	142-0	H
N.4	W	DePauw	71-0	H
N.11	L	Indiana	5-22	A
N.18	W	Bennett Med. Col. Chi.	22-0	H
N.24	L	Purdue	0-32	A
		(5-4-0)	312-80	

N—at Milwaukee

*After a 25-minute first half, with Notre Dame leading, 121-0, the second half was shortened to only 8 minutes to permit the "Doctors" time to eat before catching a train to Chicago. Notre Dame scored 27 touchdowns, but missed 20 extra points.

THE VARSITY FOOT BALL, 1905

ON the twenty-fourth of last November Notre Dame closed another foot ball season—one of pleasant surprises and disagreeable reverses. At the beginning of the year the men impressed everyone as being the best squad that ever represented the Gold and Blue. The work they did in their first game went beyond all expectations and our hopes consequently rose still higher. Praise came from all sides, both for the team and for the coach, and it was the general conviction that we were to have the greatest team in our foot ball history.

But soon there was a change; our surprises, at the excellent work of the early season, were followed by disappointments. Although the men had more practice and were better trained than any of our previous teams, they played without team-work, an absolute necessity for success. That every individual player did his best and fought to the utmost to win, can not be doubted. Nobody disliked losing a game so much as did the players themselves. The result of the various games, we can truly say, represented their best individual efforts.

Nor is Coach MacGlew in any way to blame for the meager success of this year's team. No coach ever worked harder or more unceasingly, none ever put forth more painstaking efforts than did Coach MacGlew. Some would call it our "off year," others a case of "hard luck." It was surely not the former; we had plenty of good big men who had had at least one year's experience in foot ball; men who were willing to work and who did work unflinchingly. In former years better teams have been picked from men who were not so well suited in every way for the work. If "hard luck" means fighting against fate, it indeed comes nearer the truth of the matter. We had the men who were practiced and trained; they had a coach who did his best, but the result was not what was expected, in fact it was the very opposite. We do not lay the blame on any individual, for coach, captain and players did all in their power to make the season a success.

LINE-UP

Ends—CALLICRATE, MacAVOY   Tackles—FUNK, M. DOWNS   Guards—BEACOM, DONOVAN

Center—SHEEHAN   Half-back—DRAPER, WALDORF, BRACKEN

Full-back—W. DOWNS   Quarter-backs—SILVER, MacNERNY

NOTRE DAME, 142; AMERICAN COLLEGE OF MEDICINE AND SURGERY, 0.

That looks good anyway. Rather relieves the feeling after the Wabash game. Although the Varsity had practically no opposition, they certainly had to go some to run up one hundred and forty-two points in thirty-three minutes of play. One hundred and forty-two is plenty, but had we kicked even a fair percentage of goals we would have twenty more points.

The halves were to have been twenty-five and twenty, but the last half was only eight minutes' long, as the "doctors" must eat before catching their train. And anyway the score suited them as it stood.

We were in good shape after the light work of the week before, and the men played the fastest game they have put up this year. The team work showed an improvement, and from the minute the whistle blew in the first half the only question the rooters could ask was: "How large will the score be?" On defence we had no chance to show what we could do as the "Medics" fumbled or mixed their signals so that they never gained an inch; in fact, lost ground every time they had the ball which, it must be mentioned in passing, was very seldom.

The game as a whole was a poor exhibition of football as it was played by only one team, the others simply filled in space. From two to four plays was all that was required for a touchdown. The most noticeable feature of the game was the speed of all, but especially the men who were drawn out of the line to carry the ball.

Notre Dame (142)		American Medicals (0)
Callicrate	L E	Behrendt
Munson	L T	Irwin
Beacom	L G	Sparr
Sheehan-Watkins	C	Ecle
Donovan	R G	Denny
M. Downs-Joyce	R T	Rouley
McAvoy	R E	Trombley
Silver	Q B	Wittenberg
Bracken-W. Downs	L H	Dean
Draper-M. Downs	R H	Newman
W. Downs-Sheehan	F B	Mooney

Touchdowns—Bracken, 3; Silver, 3; McAvoy, 3; Beacom, 2; W. Downs, 4; Callicrate, Munson, 2; Donovan, 2; M. Downs, 2; Sheehan, 3; Draper, 2. Goals from touchdown—M. Downs, 4; McAvoy, 2; Draper. Safety touchdown—Beacom. Umpire—Purdy. Referee—Studebaker. Time of halves—Twenty five and eight minutes.

※※

"Bill" Downs was the "touchdown man." Besides dashing through the line and around the ends for gains, ranging from ten to sixty yards he made four touchdowns.

※※

"Bud" Sheehan, centre for the past three years, had the honor of making his first touchdowns for Notre Dame. Three times Sheehan carried the ball over and planted it between the posts. The way he tore through the line and raced around the ends reminded one of a benzine buggy driven by a champion chauffeur.

※※

Probably the best feature of the game was the speed displayed by the Varsity; and if they can hit up a gait like that against Indiana and Purdue the state championship will come home with them.

NOTRE DAME, 71; DEPAUW, 0.

The scoring machine is still in working order, and the way McGlew's men waded through DePauw last Saturday makes things look good for us when we meet Indiana's team this afternoon. Although the Varsity outclassed DePauw in every department of the game, there was always "doings" of some kind by the blue-legged men. They were outweighed and outplayed, but they never quit, and a gamer bunch of little men has not been seen here in many years.

The new plays that Coach McGlew has been perfecting for the Indiana game were not tried against DePauw; so the rooters did not have a chance to see the new assortment of "touchdown makers" that McGlew is getting ready to hand Indiana.

Notre Dame,		DePauw
Callicrate	L E	Tucker
Munson	L T	Onely
Beacom	L G	M'Q'tter-Grider
Healy, Sheehan	C	Simkins
Donovan	R G	Law
M. Downs	R T	Shultz
McAvoy	R T	B. Hurst
Silver	Q B	Chester
Bracken, Waldorf	L H	Jewett
Draper	R H	Douglas
W. Downs	F B	Miller

Touchdowns—W. Downs, 6; McAvoy, Beacom, Donovan, 2; Waldorf, 2; Callicrate, 1. Goals from touchdowns—Draper, 6. Umpire—Talcott. Referee—Kilpatrick. Linesmen—Lathrop and Murray. Time of halves—Thirty minutes each.

※※

Coach "Jimmy" Sheldon of Indiana states that Notre Dame has more than ever a chance to defeat Purdue, and that there is a possibility of the local eleven beating his team at the State University. He said: "At the present time both Purdue and Indiana are ahead of Notre Dame on form, but McGlew has a great bunch of beef, and if it is developed there is no reason why the team can not more than hold its own in the big games.

※※

"Bumper" Waldorf made his first appearance Saturday. His line-bucking was easily the feature of the game.

※※

Callicrate showed the best form he has shown this season. In another year he ought undoubtedly be one of the best ends in the state.

※※

Donovan, Beacom, Downs and Draper played good ball and gained whenever called upon.

※※

Douglas and the Jewett brothers played brilliantly for DePauw.

※※

It has been almost impossible for Healy to get in shape this year. Healy went in at centre last Saturday, but he was nervous and repeatedly getting offside; McGlew took him out and will give him plenty of work in order to get him in shape for Indiana and Purdue.

※※

Sheldon sat in the bleachers Saturday and watched the game.

THOMAS BARRY, COACH.

The athletic board has been untiring in its efforts to secure a competent coach, and Mr. Thomas Barry, Brown '02, has been finally selected. For four years Barry played football on Brown's team and was the choice of many for the position of half back on the All American for 1902. He was also a star baseball player while at school, and later played with Buffalo and Montreal of the Eastern League. To his ability as an all-around athlete is added the experience that comes from having coached the star eleven of Brown University and Bowdoin College. Mr. Barry, who is athletic in mind too, is at present studying law at Harvard.

With a good coach and the material which always shows up at Notre Dame we are assured of a strong team. Several of the veterans will be back, and there is an abundance of promising material.

1906

Coach: Thomas A. Barry
Captain: Robert L. Bracken

O.6	W	Franklin	26-0	H
O.13	W	Hillsdale	17-0	H
O.20	W	Chi. Phys. & Surg.	28-0	H
O.27	W	Michigan State	5-0	H
N.3	W	Purdue	2-0	A
N.10	L	Indiana	0-12	N
N.24	W	Beloit (R)	29-0	H
		(6-1-0)	107-1	

N—at Indianapolis

Wearers of the N.D.

Football

ROBERT L. BRACKEN
DOMINIC L. CALLICRATE
PATRICK A. BEACOM
CLARENCE J. SHEEHAN
RUFUS W. WALDORF

FRANK E. MUNSON
FRED W. EGGEMAN
OSCAR D. HUTZELL
M. HARRY MILLER
SAMUEL M. DOLAN

RAYMOND J. SCANLON

NOTRE DAME, 29; BELOIT, 0.

The Varsity closed a successful season last Saturday by defeating Beloit, 29 to 0.

The game was a grand success of the new rules from the side team's standpoint. Captain Bracken and his men went through a variety of forward passes, quarter-back kicks, fake plays, long end runs, skin-tackle plays, and in fact everything in the calender. The outcome was never in doubt, but Beloit's defense was just strong enough to make the game an interesting one and one full of spectacular plays. As an Athletic Number of the SCHOLASTIC is to be published next week but a short account of the game is here printed.

The game, though one-sided in score, was exciting throughout. The Barryites received the ball on the kickoff, and by simply running the light visitors off their feet brought the pigskin to the Beloit one-yard line. Aided by a fifteen-yard penalty for holding, the visitors were able to ward off a touchdown for nearly twenty minutes. The local giants bumped the Beloit line hard and often and annexed many yards.

On the second kickoff Bracken caught the ball, and dodging through the entire Badger line-up ran 100 yards for a touchdown. The first half ended with the score 12 to 0 in Notre Dame's favor. Rain fell in torrents during the second half. Coach Barry sent in a score of substitutes, but notwithstanding the score ran higher than it did

in the first part of the game. Beacom started by pounding the line for a straight march to a touchdown. Callicrate got away for a ninety-yard run, and Beacom again went bounding through the line.

A sensational punting duel then took place between Johnson and Bracken, and when Beloit fumbled Notre Dame found itself within five yards of a touchdown. Sheehan went over for the last score. Armin twice tried a drop kick, but both attempts failed. Beacom and Sheehan, who have played for four years on Notre Dame's eleven, wound up their careers on the gridiron in a glorious manner. Beacom made two touchdowns and kicked three goals, and Sheehan's work was phenomenal.

After the game the two giants were carried on the rooters' shoulders from the field. Line-up:

Notre Dame (29).	Position.	Beloit (0)
Hutzell	L. E.	Mead
Beacom	L. T.	Horton
Eggeman	L. G.	Rowell
Sheehan	C.	Loos
Donovan	R. G.	Strang
Dolan	R. T.	Gleckler
Bervey	R. E.	Boger
Bracken	Q.	Armin
Callicrate	L. H.	Johnson
Waldorf	R. H.	Knudson
Diener	F.	Charters

Touchdowns—Dolan, Beacom, 2; Bracken, Sheehan. Goals from touchdowns—Beacom, 3; Umpire—O'Neal, Illinois. Referee—Studebaker, De Pauw. Time of halves—25 and 20 minutes.

The '07 Football Squad

1907

Coach: Thomas A. Barry
Captain: Dominic L. Callicrate

O.12	W	Chi. Phys. & Surg. (R)	32-0	H
O.19	W	Franklin	23-0	H
O.26	W	Olivet	22-4	H
N.2	T	Indiana	0-0	H
N.9	W	Knox	22-4	H
N.23	W	Purdue	17-0	H
N.28TH	W	St. Vincent's (Chi.)	21-12	A

(6-0-1)   137-20

1907 LETTERMEN

D. L. Callicrate (C)

J. F. Bertling

H. A. Burdick

S. M. Dolan

E. J. Lynch

P. A. McDonald

A. T. Mertes

M. H. Miller

F. E. Munson

R. E. Paine

W. R. Ryan

F. F. Wood

INDIANA, 0; NOTRE DAME, 0.

The game last Saturday in Indianapolis, between Notre Dame and Indiana, resulted in a tie, neither team scoring. The Varsity showed unexpected strength, especially the forwards who played Indiana's line to a stand-still. Both teams had a chance to score,—Indiana in the first half, and Notre Dame in the second,—but each team failed; and when the game was over, a tie truly represented the merits of the teams. Notre Dame supporters were inclined to think the Varsity should have won, but no doubt Indiana's backers thought the same thing about their team. Coach Sheldon of Indiana expressed himself after the game as "satisfied" and Coach Barry expressed the same opinion.

Every man on the team displayed the true Notre Dame spirit; they were all in the game every minute. Capt. Callicrate, Ryan, McDonald and Munson, and in fact, every man on the team, played a good game, but to give the credit where it truly belongs, notwithstanding the reports and newspaper accounts, "Red" Miller was without a doubt in a class by himself. It was Miller who blocked Indiana's punts; it was Miller who broke up Indiana's forward passes; it was Miller who tackled every other man on attempted end runs and cross tackle bucks; it was Miller who was in every play from the time the whistle blew at the beginning until the same whistle ended the game.

Notre Dame's strong defensive work was, at times, due in a large part to Miller's work backing up the line; the star of the game was easily the quiet "Red" Miller. Lynch, Paine and Mertes, all put up a great game in the line. McDonald played good ball behind them, and in fact each man was a star, with Miller playing the part of the Leading Man.

1908

Coach: Victor M. Place
Captain: M. Harry Miller

O.3	W	Hillsdale	39-0	H
O.10	W	Franklin	64-0	H
O.17	L	Michigan	6-12	A
O.24	W	Chicago Phys. & Surg.	88-0	H
O.29	W	Ohio Northern	58-4	H
N.7	W	Indiana	11-0	N
N.13	W	Wabash	8-4	A
N.18	W	St. Viator	46-0	H
N.26TH	W	Marquette	6-0	A

(8-1-0)   326-20

N—at Indianapolis

1908 LETTERMEN

M. H. Miller (C)
J. J. Collins
R. C. Dimmick
S. M. Dolan
J. F. Duffy
P. G. Dwyer
H. Edwards
D. M. Hamilton
L. L. Kelly
E. J. Lynch
P. A. McDonald
J. I. Maloney
R. L. Mathews
A. T. Mertes
G. W. Philbrook
U. Ruell
T. H. Sullivan
R. E. Vaughn
F. F. Wood

MICHIGAN, 12; NOTRE DAME, 6.

When Yost said "Michigan was lucky" he told the story of Saturday's battle. Not only did the Gold and Blue cross the Michigan line for the first time in her history, but our line flung back the terrific onslaughts of the Wolverine backs so effectively that they never scrimmaged within our twenty-five-yard line, and had it not been for fumbles at critical times Notre Dame might have emerged triumphant. It was not the machine of Yost, but the toe of Allerdice that brought victory to the Maize and Blue. Three times the Michigan star negotiated goals from the field, scoring all the points for his team after seeing his team-mates hurl their plays against the sturdy wearers of the Gold and Blue only to be shattered against our line or to be broken up by our speedy backs. When victory seemed within reach costly fumbles lost us the advantage, giving Allerdice the openings which he well knew how to utilize.

With the scare that Salmon and his warriors handed out in the famous battle of '02 still lingering in his mind, Yost expected a hard battle Saturday, and his expectations were realized. "Red" Miller and his men went into the fray with that dauntless spirit that has won Notre Dame such prestige in Western athletics, and after the first few minutes of play they had the better of the argument in every department except the punting.

To single out the stars would be a hard task, for every man played his game, which speaks volumes. However, the work of Hamilton, Vaughan, Dolan, and Matthews stood out especially prominent, and won frequent applause from the Michigan rooters.

In speaking of Hamilton's work the Detroit *News Tribune* said: "In running back punts, picking plays, and carrying the ball the Hoosier field general excelled his mates. He skirted the Michigan ends time after time for considerable gains, and carried back Allerdice's punts so far that he made up the difference between the rival punters." The other accounts also featured his phenomenal dodging, and the masterful manner in which he ran the team.

'08 on the Gridiron

COACH PLACE came to Notre Dame with the reputation of being a great coach, and he left with that reputation strengthened and enhanced. Compelled by injuries and other circumstances to develop practically two teams, he worked his material to the best advantage, and the results achieved testify how well he succeeded. For the second time since Notre Dame assumed prominence on the western gridiron its goal-line remained uncrossed until the end of the season, and the credit must go to Coach Place. He did not teach his men a bewildering variety of plays, but in those used he built up a concentrated offense that was irresistible, and a defense that proved impregnable before the fiercest onslaughts of the enemy. It is no exaggeration to say that, with perhaps one exception, Notre Dame this year had the strongest defensive team in her history, and certainly the best all-around team since the introduction of the new style of play. Place had every man in every play, and always with the ball, and it was this co-operative style of play that won such laurels for the Gold and Blue. Above all he taught a clean game, and let it be said to the credit of the men on the squad that his instructions in that line were faithfully carried out to the end. Coach Place was popular with the men, had their respect and co-operation which went far towards making the season a great success.

Coach Place was ably assisted by Joe Lantry, whose general knowledge of football, especially in the back-field department, proved a valuable asset to the team. Like Place, he won his spurs under the old game, but quickly mastered the new, and many a helpful suggestion was the result. He had charge of the Scrubs the entire season, and the many hard tussles they gave the varsity and the number of men who finally won berths on the regulars speak well for his ability. In addition to his wide knowledge of the game he possessed the confidence of the men, and had the faculty of communicating his own enthusiasm and spirit to those under him, which is one of the prime requisites of a successful coach. He worked hard, achieved results, and for that is entitled to a share in the gridiron honors of '08.

Asst. Coach Lantry

Coach Place

COLLINS DIMMICK DOLAN LYNCH KELLY PHILBROOK MATHEWS

LONGMAN MILLER HAMILTON EDWARDS RYAN VAUGHAN SCHMITT MALONEY

1909*

Coach: Frank C. Longman
Captain: Howard Edwards

O.9	W	Olivet	58-0	H
O.16	W	Rose Poly	60-11	H
O.23	W	Michigan State	17-0	H
O.30	W	Pittsburgh	6-0	A
N.6	W	Michigan (U)	11-3	A
N.13	W	Miami (Ohio)	46-0	H
N.20	W	Wabash	38-0	H
N.25TH	T	Marquette	0-0	A

(7-0-1)   236-14

*"The Notre Dame Victory March" was introduced this season.

NOTRE DAME, 6; PITTSBURG, 0.

This week we have practically the same story to tell as last week,—the story of a hard-fought and well-earned victory. And this week we are going to allow ourselves the luxury of a knock; a luxury which, had we lost the game, we would have to forego.

The umpire, Merriam or Merriman of Geneva, showed the most refreshing and naïve partiality towards Pittsburg we have ever heard of. We like to think that Mr. Merriam acted as he did, not that he loved Notre Dame less, but Pittsburg more. Whatever the case may be, he certainly did not handle us with kid gloves. Whenever he saw a chance to penalize he penalized, and when he saw no chance, he penalized us just the same.

There is no need of rehashing the same old dope,—no need of telling how every man on the team played the game of his life. We know the men who are supporting the Gold and Blue in football and we know that there is no loafing among them whenever there is work to be done.

Spectators of the game could name no individual stars. Of course Vaughan was in the limelight quite a little on account of his punting, as were the ends who covered the punts and received the forward passes. And Matthews earned the undying gratitude of all Notre Dame men when he slipped across Pittsburg's line with our only score. But it was the team who won the game, not one man, and to the twelve men who fought for Notre Dame in the contest, goes the credit for the victory.

Matthews	L. E.	Roe
Edwards	L. T.	Van Doren
Philbrook	L. G.	Blair
Lynch	C.	Galvin
Dolan	R. G.	Frankel
Dimmick	R. T.	Stevenson
Collins	R. E.	Lindsay
Hamilton	Q.	Budd
Miller	L. H.	Quailey
Dwyer	R. H.	Ent
Vaughan	F.	Richards

Touchdown—Matthews. Goal kicked from touchdown—Matthews. Substitutions—Peacock for Van Doren, Leahy for Blair, Bailey for Frankel, Budd for Lindsay, and Butler for Budd, W. Robinson for Budd at quarter, Fleightner for Quailey, A. Robinson for Ent and Ryan for Dwyer. Referee—Butler of Brown. Umpire, Merriman of Geneva. Head linesman—Rafferty of Yale.

NOTRE DAME, 17; M. A. C., O.

After all our fears and anxiety about the outcome of the M. A. C. game, we can now rest easy. The Aggies had as good a team as we expected, but Captain Edwards' men surpassed themselves and so far outclassed the farmers as to leave no doubt concerning their superiority. No element of 'uck figured in this game. It was good, old-fashioned, straight football that won.

Vaughan, Dimmick and Ryan, furnished the spectacular plays of the game, and every other man on the team aided these three in bringing victory to Notre Dame. Miller, though crippled, was in every play, forming interference, and when the runner was tackled Red was there to drag him on several yards farther. Dolan backed up the line in such fashion that when by-chance an "Aggie" happened to stray through an open place he got just as far as "Rosy," and then stopped—suddenly. Collins and Matthews were practically impregnable at the ends, and every other man on the team followed the ball and played the game as if his life were at stake.

Only one change was made in our line-up during the entire game. Pete Dwyer started at quarter, but as he was not fully recovered from injuries received in scrimmage earlier in the week, and as Coach Longman was afraid to risk further injury to him, Hamilton took his place toward the close of the first period. Don ran the team like a veteran, choosing his plays with all the good judgment in the world.

FOOTBALL CHAMPIONS

1910

Coach: Frank C. Longman
Captain: Ralph Dimmick

O.8	W	Olivet	48-0	H
O.22	W	Butchel (Akron)	51-0	H
N.5	L	Michigan State	0-17	A
N.12	W	Rose Poly	41-3	A
N.19	*W	Ohio Northern	47-0	H
N.24TH	T	Marquette	5-5	A
		(4-1-1)	192-25	

*Notre Dame's 100th victory

1910 LETTERMEN

R. C. Dimmick (C)
W. A. Clinnen
A. S. Clippinger
J. J. Collins
C. F. Crowley
Gus Dorais
T. F. Foley
L. L. Kelly
C. M. McGrath
W. C. Martin
R. L. Mathews
T. H. Oaas
G. W. Philbrook
J. T. Stansfield

THE CASE WITH MICHIGAN.

Michigan's cancellation of the Michigan-Notre Dame football game, which was to have been played at Ann Arbor last Saturday, has been the cause of much discussion here the past week. The trouble centered on our intention to play Dimmick and Philbrook, Michigan claiming that both these men were ineligible because of the fact that they had played out their time as collegiate football players. A review of the athletic career of both of these men shows that in 1904-'05 they were preparatory students in Tullatin academy and competed on teams there. The following year both men were students at Pearson's academy, an institution apart from Whitman college. In September, 1907, they registered at Whitman college, taking two freshman studies and three or four preparatory studies. Dimmick remained at Whitman until February, 1908, and Philbrook until June of the same year. Whitman college is not named in the list of conference colleges issued in September, 1907. Because of that it is only reasonable to presume these men as participating in preparatory athletics prior to their coming to Notre Dame. On these grounds we maintain that Philbrook and Dimmick are eligible and will continue to hold these grounds.

Last January when this game was arranged, Manager Curtis inquired as to whether we would be allowed to play these men in the game this fall, and Director of Athletics Bartelme gave his assurance that there would be no trouble on that score. Mr. Bartelme also assured Coach Longman to the same effect. The reason for Notre Dame's desire that this matter be settled was brought about by various reports which originated from the Michigan camp last fall, after the Notre Dame game, concerning the eligibility of these men.

The fact that Michigan sent down the names of Cole and Clarke as being eligible for this game leads to the one conclusion that they should consider Dimmick and Philbrook eligible, for Clarké and Cole, according to conference rules are ineligible, as Cole played the seasons of '05, '07, and '08 at Oberlin, and Clarke too has played his allotted time according to conference rule.

NOTRE DAME (51)		BUCHTEL (0)
Collins	L. E.	Wilcoyt
Philbrook	L. T.	Zimmerman
Kelly, Duffy	L. G.	Criss
Foley	C.	Selby
Stansfield	R. G.	Scott
Dimmick	R. T.	Conrad
Crowley	R. E.	Fleming
Matthews, Dorias	Q. B.	Gemis
Clinnin	L. H. B.	Akers
Ryan, McGinnis, Bergman	R. H. B.	Bethel
Clippinger, McGrath	F. B.	Jackson

Touchdowns—Philbrook (2), Clippinger (2), Dimmick (3), McGrath, Clinnin. Goals from touchdown—Matthews, 2; Dorias, 3.

100th N.D. WIN

OHIO NORTHERNERS UNINTERESTING.

The local football season was closed locally on Cartier field last Saturday when the Varsity walked off the field leading the Ohio Northerner's goat with a chain that had forty-seven links in its makeup. The day was favorable for the game, but the field was muddy and the going proved very poor. Despite this there were several spectacular runs made during the game for long gains. "Lee" Ryan started the spotlight going by taking the ball on the five-yard line and galloping down through the enemy's stamping ground like a house on fire. Dorias at another period grabbed the ball down near his own goal and brought it to the danger mark after much very effectual dodging and squirming. Then again Matthews got away on a run from about the twenty-five yard line and successfully planted the oval behind the enemy's lines.

NOTRE DAME (47).		OHIO NORTHERN (0)
Crowley, Martin	R. E.	Cox
Dimmick, Capt.	R. T.	Kohlburn, Capt
Kelly, Diebold	R. G.	Holliday
Foley	C.	Small
Diebold, Oaas	L. G.	Goringer
Oaas, Morgan	L. T.	Musante
Collins, Williams	L. E.	Fry
Dorias	Q. B.	Schules
Clinnin, McGinnis, Ryan	L. H.	Griggs
Matthews, Bergman	R. H.	Smith
Stansfield, Clippinger	F. B.	Peterson

Touchdowns—Matthews, 2; Ryan, 2; Dorias, 2; Bergman, Crowley. Goals from touchdowns—Dorias, 7. Time of quarters—15 minutes.

THE football season of 1910 at Notre Dame began most auspiciously. Miller, Dolan, Dwyer, Vaughan, Lynch, Ryan, Hamilton and A. Kelly of the championship eleven were graduated or left school, leaving Coach Longman a difficult task to accomplish. Developing new material to duplicate the record of '09 seemed to blast hopes, nevertheless, when the Olivet eleven left the field Notre Dame stock soared.

A bright future was predicted when the famed Buchtel team with goal line uncrossed was humbled to the tune of 51 to 0.

The team was beginning to display real form, similar to that of 1909, when a sad blow was dealt. On October 29th, at Lansing, Michigan, she was outplayed and beaten for the first time in two years. This slump aroused a fighting spirit, the players practiced faithfully intending to redeem themselves at Ann Arbor. Michigan evidently feared defeat because she cancelled the game the night before.

Again in old time form she met Rose Poly. The team returned with 41 points to Rose Poly's 3.

Players, 1911

L. E.	—Rockne, Mc-Ginnes
L. T.	—Philbrook
L. G.	—Oaas, Yund
C.	—Feeney, K. Jones

R. G.	—Harvat
R. T.	—Kelly (Capt.), Larson
R. E.	—Crowley, Dolan
Qu. B.	—Dorias, Lee
L. H. B.	—Berger, Bergman
R. H. B.	—Pliska, Kelleher
F. B.	—Eichenlaub, Mc-Grath

The Football Team of 1911

THE Football season of 1911 will go down in history as most satisfactory in its results. Although it would have been most gratifying to us to have won from Pittsburg and Marquette by a goodly score, we still believe that Notre Dame was virtual victor in both games. In both cases we were forced to tear up and down a muddy field, and that made impossible much of the fast work for which the team had been trained. Besides this, Pittsburg and Marquette were foes worthy of any team, and we have no little satisfaction in our holding them to scoreless ties. In the other games, our superiority was manifest. We piled up the big scores in true N. D. fashion.

One championship was added to our list. For the fourth consecutive year the Gold and Blue earned the title of State Champions. Our claim to it rests in our victory over Wabash. This game was fought stubbornly throughout, as the final score, 6-3, indicates. Our men showed their worth in the last quarter when the score was 3-0 against them. By splendid offensive playing, they carried the ball over for a touch-down. Wabash tried hard to regain the lead, but Notre Dame played safe, content to win the coveted honor even by a small margin.

**Football Schedule
1911**

Oct. 7	Notre Dame	32
	Ohio Northern	6
Oct. 14	Notre Dame	43
	St. Viateur	0
Oct. 21	Notre Dame	27
	Butler	0
Oct. 28	Notre Dame	80
	Loyola	0
Nov. 4	Notre Dame	0
	Pittsburg	0
Nov. 11	Notre Dame	34
	St. Bonaventure	0
Nov. 20	Notre Dame	6
	Wabash	3
Nov. 30	Notre Dame	0
	Marquette	0

1912			
Coach: John L. Marks			
Captain: Charles E. (Gus) Dorais			
O.5	W	St. Viator	116-7 H
O.12	W	Adrian	74-7 H
O.19	W	Morris Harvey	39-0 H
O.26	W	Wabash	41-6 H
N.2	W	Pittsburgh (S)	3-0 A
N.9	W	St. Louis	47-7 A
N.28TH	W	Marquette	69-0 N
		(7-0-0)	389-27

N—at Chicago

1912 LETTERMEN

Gus Dorais (C)
A. Berger
C. F. Crowley
R. J. Eichenlaub
A. G. Feeney
C. T. Finegan
F. Fitzgerald
F. W. Gushurst
P. J. Harvat
K. K. Jones
W. A. Kelleher
R. J. Lathrop
J. S. Pliska
Knute Rockne
W. S. Yund

VARSITY ATHLETICS.

Last Saturday Notre Dame opened the football season of 1912 in a game (so called) against St. Viator's College. The team from Kankakee was lighter, slower, and showed less training than the Varsity, and as a result the visitors were steam rollered, sat upon, and subjected to miscellaneous ill-treatment more appropriate in political conventions than in a football game. The St. Viator's line could not withstand the gold and blue backfield, and the St. Viator's backfield could not pierce the gold and blue line. Hence we have the score: Notre Dame, 116; St. Viator's, 7.

The visitors' score was made in the second quarter against the Varsity second string. Sherman recovered a punt on his own forty-yard line and raced away without opposition to the goal.

Although the game was too one-sided to be interesting as a contest, it proved so from other reasons. Every man on the squad was given an opportunity to display his ability, and the excellent work of the scrubs delighted not only the coach but the students as well. Besides this, the score of 116 sets a new mark for high football scores, superseding the 86 to 6 mark set in the Loyola game last year.

The fighting strength of Captain Dorais' men could not be adequately judged from Saturday's performance, but the terrific enslaughts of Eichenlaub and the fast work of Berger, Duggan and Larkin bid fair to pierce stronger and heavier lines.

Summary:

McGinnis, Metzger, Miller	L. E.	Magee.
Fitzgerald, Stevenson	L. T.	Dunn, Hicks.
Yund, Keefe, Munger	L. G.	Murray.
Feeney, McLaughlin	C.	Robeneau.
Harvat, Hicks, Cook	R. G.	Longer, Donnelly.
Jones, Duphy	R. T.	Fisher.
Dolan, Nowers, Morgan	R. E.	Sherman.
Dorias, Finnegan	Q. B.	Harrison.
Larken, Gargen	R. H.	Welch.
Eichenlaub, Dougherty	F. B.	Shafer.
Berger, Duggan	L. H.	Shea, Sullivan.

Touchdowns—Berger 5, Nowers 4, Eichenlaub 3, Duggan 3, Larkin, Finnegan, McLaughlin, Sherman. Goals from touchdowns—Dorais 3, Nowers, Metzger, McLaughlin, Harrison. Safety—Notre Dame. Referee Dunbar (Yale). Umpire—Callihan (Michigan). Head Lineman Philbrook (Notre Dame). Time of quarters, ten minutes.

MARQUETTE DOWNED AT LAST.

That tie with Marquette of three years' standing was not only broken Thanksgiving day at Comisky park, Chicago, it was smashed to smithereens when our own true Varsity piled up 69 points and allowed Marquette a sad one-eyed zero. Oh, for a diamond pen and golden ink and an orator's style to chronicle the game. And while we're wishing, we'll take a rubber stamp with Notre Dame on it and another with Dorais, and a third with Eichenlaub, for these names occur too often to pen.

The victory must be attributed to the team,—the splendid, magnificent, superb interference of the team, although the landslide of tallies that overwhelmed Marquette must be credited to Eichenlaub and Captain Dorais. The interference given our runners was the wonder and delight of all football fans who saw the game; and the work of Dorais and Eichenlaub,—well, it won the hearts of all non-partisan spectators and of some of the Marquette fans as well, and ten minutes after the game started the Milwaukee eleven didn't have a supporter who wasn't from Marquette.

In our enthusiasm over our team, we must not forget the coaches and the managers. Coaches Marks and Dunbar have developed what we confidently believe to be the best team in the West. The material was here to be sure, but the coaches cultivated it, and placed it where it produced the best results. For that reason the victory belongs to Coaches Marks and Dunbar as well as to the team. Then, too, Managers Cotter and O'Connell can not be too highly praised for negotiating the transfer of the game to Chicago. To team, to coaches, to managers, all thanks for the game that has meant more to us than any other since the Western Championship contest with Michigan.

NOTRE DAME [69]		MARQUETTE [0]
Crowley, Nowers	R. E.	Kelly
Harvat	R. T.	Vater
Fitzgerald	R. G.	McKusker (Capt.)
Feeney	C.	Krause
Yund, Lathrop	L. G.	Krebs
Jones	L. T.	Woodworth
Rockne, Cook	L. E.	Shubert
Dorais (Capt.)	Q. B.	Whalen, Slattery, Doyle
Pliska, Gushurst	R. H.	Lally, Prescott, Simmonet
Berger, Larkin	L. H.	Foley, Simmonet, Doyle
Eichenlaub, Finnegan	F. B.	Frawley, Johnson

Touchdowns—Pliska, Eichenlaub (4), Dorias (2), Finnegan, Berger, Gushurst. Goals from touchdown—Dorais (6). Goal from field—Dorias. Referee—Eckersall, Chicago. Umpire—Steffen, Chicago. Head linesman—Heneage, Dartmouth. Time of quarters—15 minutes. Attendance, 7,000.

Notre Dame Football Team, 1913

Back row: Edwards, Keefe, Eichenlaub, King, Fitzgerald, Finegan, Coach Harper. *Middle row:* Lathrop, Jones, Pliska, Capt. Rockne, Dorais, Gushurst, Feeney. *Front row:* Elward, Bergman, Cook, Larkin.

1913
Coach: Jesse C. Harper
Captain: Knute K. Rockne

O.4	W	Ohio Northern	87-0	H
O.18	W	South Dakota	20-7	H
O.25	W	Alma	62-0	H
N.1	W	Army (U)	35-13	A
N.7	W	Penn State (R)	14-7	A
N.22	W	Christian Bros. (St.L.)	20-7	A
N.27TH	W	Texas	30-7	A
		(7-0-0)	268-41	

DORAIS OUT-GENERALED.

Dorais, the great little general, was completely outdone last Monday. The football team was tendered a banquet at St. Mary's after which they were taken through the building by a prefect. In spite of Dorais' generalship the team never got nearer than a corridor's length to one of the St. Mary's students. The St. Mary's guide was some general. Attention Walter Camp.

DORAIS, Quarterback.

Dorais wrung recognition in the East and West as the foremost exponent of the forward pass ever developed. We quote from *Vanity Fair:* "Dorais is not only a sure catcher of punts, but he is also a master of the forward pass, a sure tackler, a good punter, an open-field runner with few equals, and altogether able to meet any emergencies of his position." And again, "The Notre Dame quarterback has shown more proficiency in throwing the forward pass than any other player." These qualities won him all-American quarterback, and we need add no more.

ROCKNE, Left End (Captain).

The team was very fortunate in its choice of captain. "Rock" is a born leader and an end extraordinary. A hard, sure tackler, very fast, and extra good at blocking tackles, an expert receiver of forward passes and very clever and shifty on his feet, he was a power on the team. He had no one specialty, but was unexcelled in all departments of the game. He was unanimous choice for all Western left end. His loss will be a severe one to the 1914 eleven.

NOTRE DAME CHAMPIONS WIDE-OPEN GAME.

More than one paper sees in the Varsity's victory over the Army a great triumph of Western over Eastern football methods. It is, we think, a great triumph of the new game over the old-style of play; but it is rather a triumph of Notre Dame's style of the progressive, wide-open game over the rest of the country's conservative attack than a victory of the West over the East. The forward pass was used with almost as much effect against South Dakota as it was against the Army. As a result of our splendid successes against both South Dakota and the Army the new game is admittedly a superior style of play to the old-fashioned line-plunging or even the semi-open game attempted heretofore. It is superior for ground-gaining purposes; it is less dangerous to the players; and it makes a prettier game to view from the side-lines.

ARMY (13)		NOTRE DAME (35)
Jouett	L. E.	Rockne (Capt)
Wynne	L. T.	Jones
Meacham	L. G.	Keefe
McEwan	C.	Feeney
Jones	R. G.	Fitzgerald
Weyand	R. T.	Lathrop
Merrillat	R. E.	A Gushurst
Pritchard	Q. B.	Dorais
Hoge	L. H.	Pliska
Hobbs	R. H.	Finnegan
Hodgson	F. B.	Eichenlaub

Referee—Morice (University of Pennsylvania). Umpire—Roper (Princeton.) Head linesman—Leurhing (Northwestern). Time of quarters—twelve and fifteen minutes. Scoring by the Army—Touchdowns—Hodgson, Pritchard. Goals from touchdown—Hoge. Notre Dame scoring: Touchdowns—Rockne, Eichenlaub (2), Pliska (2). Goals from touchdowns, Dorais (5).

Capt. Rockne

VARSITY SWAMPS TEXAS IN FINAL.

It was the greatest game ever seen in Texas. It was the greatest game in more ways than one. It is seldom that a Thanksgiving game is played between two teams, both of which have gone through the season without defeat, but such were the conditions last Thursday. Notre Dame went into the enemy's camp with a clean slate and more than an equal claim to the Championship of the West. Texas had not lost a game and were undisputed champions of the Southwest. No other eleven ever before played to such a crowd in the Southwest. No other eleven ever showed the finished article of football displayed by Notre Dame.

Texas played a fine game, played hard, and fought long, but they were simply outclassed. Simmons was their one big factor in keeping the Varsity from scoring more than they did. The big Longhorn back was fast and hard to tackle and more than once he broke through our team for thirty and forty yard gains. But in the pinches, our line strengthened, and with Dorais to do the open-work and Eichenlaub, Finnegan and Pliska to buck the line, we made consistent gains.

The game was the last for Dorais, Capt. Rockne and Gushurst. Dorais, in his farewell to football, played the best game of his life, throwing his passes far and accurately, even though the ball was wet; returning punts in a way never seen before in the South; dropkicking the slippery oval with telling accuracy; and generaling his team without an error. Our brilliant pair of ends, Rockne and Gushurst likewise gave noble account of themselves in their last fight for Notre Dame. The Texas team has been perfectly drilled in the end run. Simmons is a very hard man to get, and his interference has proved impregnable to other teams, but our ends managed to break up the strong interference and allow the backs to get the runner before many yards could be gained.

Final score, Notre Dame, 30; Texas, 7.

Gushurst, Mills	R. E.	Edmonds
Lathrop	R. T.	Charleton, Barry
Fitzgerald	R. G.	Jordan, Goodman, Birge
Feeney	C.	Dittmar
Keefe, Cook, King	L. G.	Birge, Murray
Jones	L. T.	Bass, Niblo
Rockne (C.), Elward	L. E.	Turner
Dorais	Q. B.	Barrett
Finnegan, Larkin	R. H.	Brown (Capt.)
Pliska, Bergman,		Daniels
Kelleher	L. H.	Simmons, Littlefield
Eichenlaub, Duggan	F. B.	Daniel, Simmons

Touchdowns—Dorais, Eichenlaub, Mills, Barrett. Goals from touchdowns—Dorais (2), Brown. Goals from field—Dorais (3). Referee—Van Riper (Wisconsin). Umpire Glaze (Dartmouth). Head linesman Utay (Texas Aggies).

TO COACH JESSE HARPER OF THE 1913 TEAM

By "Mal" Elward

A football team from Notre Dame
Left South Bend one day,
And travelled east to West Point
There the Army squad to play.

The Coach was Jesse Harper
An old Scotch-Irish name
And he led this team to victory
To fortune and to fame.

He had a secret weapon
Not used much by his class
No hidden ball or trick play
But the neglected forward pass.

Other coaches used it sparingly
In their repertoire of plays
But Jesse showed them how to score
In many different ways.

The Captain's name was Rockne
Of Norwegian-Irish strain
And the way he caught those passes
Drove the Army backs insane.

And when they covered Rockne
Joe Pliska caught the ball
And the vaunted Army defense
Just wasn't there at all.

The player calling signals
Was quarterback Dorais
No better passer you will see
On the gridirons of today.

No matter what the pattern
Long, short or buttonhook
The ball was waiting for you
When you turned to take a look.

And if the Army defense
Dropped back at given sign
An Irishman named Eichenlaub
Tore big holes in their line.

No two platoons were needed
In the football of that day
The players were all rugged
And went into the game to stay.

'Twas a big day for the Irish
The Swedes and Germans too
For Notre Dame is made up
Of the many Nations hue.

Many names upon that roster
Have passed beyond recall
But in my dreams I see them
And they still are playing ball.

I see Rock, Dorais and Pliska
And the others when I dream
They're All Americans up yonder
They are on St. Peter's team.

So here's to Jesse Harper
Old coach of Notre Dame
It's time that they should place you
In the Coaches' Hall of Fame.

They'll remember you at West Point
With distinction and with class
For the day you beat the Army
With your educated pass.

VARSITY DOWNS PENN STATE ON THEIR FIELD.

Although wearied by the long trip to West Point, the gruelling Army game, the homecoming and the almost immediate return into the East, the Varsity played a good brand of football at State College Friday, November 7, and succeeded in beating Penn State by a 14 to 0 score. The victory is particularly pleasing because it is the first that has ever been scored on Penn State on its home field since they began playing football there nineteen years ago.

Penn State has been beaten by Washington and Jefferson, Harvard, and Pennsylvania this year, and by larger scores than the Varsity beat them, but all three of Penn's previous losses were sustained in the enemy's territory and to teams unwearied by wearing travel.

Besides this, Penn had determined to make good for its previous poor record in its first big game at home. Furthermore, it was Penn Day—the big day for their college. But notwithstanding all Penn's incentive to fight, the Varsity went in to win, and succeeded in doing so, the final count being 14 to 0.

The game held particular interest because Dorais, who is acknowledged to be the best quarterback in the West, was pitted against Miller, the Penn quarterback, who was mentioned by several critics last year for All-American. We would naturally be inclined to consider our own man the better, and although we have no doubt of Dorais' superiority, we choose to bring in a non-partisan critic to state our convictions.

NOTES.

We have often wondered where Notre Dame would stow all her pennants if her football players showed as much strategy on the field as do the students when they "skive" to South Bend.—McEvoy in the Chicago Record-Herald.

1914 LETTERMEN

K. K. Jones (C)
C. W. Bachman
H. C. Baujan
A. Berger
A. J. Bergman
S. B. Cofall
E. D. Duggan
R. J. Eichenlaub
A. H. Elward
C. T. Finegan
F. Fitzgerald
G. N. Holmes
E. G. Keefe
W. A. Kelleher
A. B. Larkin
R. J. Lathrop
R. F. Mills
J. S. Pliska
L. J. Stephan

1914

Coach: Jesse C. Harper
Captain: Keith K. Jones

O.3	W	Alma	56-0	H
O.10	W	Rose Poly	103-0	H
O.17	L	Yale	0-28	A
O.24	W	South Dakota	33-0	N1
O.31	W	Haskell	20-7	H
N.7	L	Army	7-20	A
N.14	W	Carlisle	48-6	N2
N.26TH	W	Syracuse	20-0	A
		(6-2-0)	287-61	

N1—at Sioux Falls; N2—at Chicago

NOTRE DAME, 103; ROSE POLY, O.

With all due care and despatch, the team from Terre Haute was laid away to rest last Saturday, in the closing ceremonies of the Gold and Blue practice season. The visitors played the best game they knew, and it would hardly be considerate to call the event a track meet, as the score would indicate. They were completely outclassed, however, from the time the whistle blew to the very last moment, and it was a mercy to send the subs against them in the second. This didn't make so much difference, after all, as the scores came just as regularly, though not quite so fast. Nevertheless, the contest was very interesting to the local rooters, as it showed what a week of practice had done to weld the Notre Dame eleven into a composite, aggressive fighting machine.

NOTRE DAME, 103		ROSE POLY, 0
Mills, Baujan	Right End	Woodling
Sharp, Beh		Davis
	Right Tackle	
Ward, Voelkers		Piertle, Smock
	Right Guard	
Fitzgerald, O'Donnell		Cotton
	Centre	
Stephan, Keefe		Carter
	Left Guard	
Rausch, Jones		Woodward, Sommers
	Left Tackle	
Cofall, Bergman, Bush		Bush, Baxter
	Quarterback	
Pliska, Kelleher, Larkin		Goldsmith
	Right Halfback	
Kowalski, Finegan Matthews, Berger	Left Half back	Trimble
Eichenlaub, Duggan Miller.		J. Carter, Goldsmith Grope
	Full Back	

Touchdowns—Cofall, 4; Kelleher, 3; Finegan, 2; Duggan, 2; Miller, 2; Bergman, 2; Referee—Messick, Indiana; Umpire—Dunbar, Yale; Head lineman—Edwards, Notre Dame. Time of periods—15 minutes.

YALE VANQUISHES FOOTBALL INVADERS FROM NOTRE DAME

Old Eli Scores 28 to 0 Triumph Over Eleven From Catholic School.

FORWARD PASSES AND RUNS HELP EASTERNERS

Knowles Makes Long Dash for Touchdown—Guernsey Does Kicking.

NEW HAVEN, Ct., Oct. 17.—A long run by Knowles, together with the triple and forward passes by Wilson, Legore and Ainsworth, helped Yale to lower the Notre Dame colors here with unexpected ease today, the score being 28 to 0.

Cofall, the Cleveland boy playing quarter for Notre Dame, made several gains around the end, but the visitors were unable to follow up these advances.

The visiting eleven was slightly heavier, well balanced and fast. Its forward passing was brilliant and effective, but this play was discarded at critical moments in favor of old-fashioned line plunging, which the Blue forwards smothered. Errors in judgment in electing to rush the ball on the last down instead of punting proved fatal, for Yale held and took quick advantage.

Yale mixed plays well, working forward, double and triple passes with fair success. One of the prettiest plays was a forward pass from Legore to Higginbotham for twenty yards and a touchdown. Knowles made a spectacular thirty-two-yard run for a touchdown.

NOTRE DAME, 0.		YALE, 28.
Elward	L. E.	Higginbotham
Jones	L. T.	Talbott
Keefe	L. G.	Conroy
Fitzgerald	C.	Wiley
Bachman	R. G.	Walden
Lathrop	R. T.	Sheldon
Mills	R. E.	T. Wilson
Cofall	Q. B.	A. Wilson
Finegan	L. H.	Ainsworth
Pliska	R. H.	Knowles
Eichenlaub	F. B.	Legore

Touchdowns — Legore, Knowles, Higginbotham, Waite. Goals from touchdown — Legore, 3; Guernsey, 1. Substitutions—Weidman for Sheldon; Bergman for Cofall; Kelleher for Pliska; Baujan for Mills; Guernsey for Legore; MacLeish for Wilson; Waite for Ainsworth; Brann for Church; Cornell for Duryea; Druyea for Cornell; Schram for Higginbotham; Church for Wilson. Referee—Joseph Pendleton, Bowdoin; Umpire—Fred Murphy, Brown. Linesman—Wm. Morice, University of Pennsylvania. Field Judge—Michael Thompson, Georgetown. Time of periods—12 min.

Reprinted with permission from the
Cleveland Plain Dealer

TIME:—TURKEY DAY. PLACE:—SYRACUSE STADIUM, SYRACUSE, N. Y.

Thousands of spectators gathered from all corners of the old Empire State to witness the final intersectional battle of the year. The Orange, with a clear victory over one great Western team already to her credit, hoped to repeat and prove that her particular brand was just a little better than anything the West could produce. Notre Dame, after a season of mixed success, and two unsatisfactory invasions of the East, sought to demonstrate that an equal break of luck and a team playing with its full strength could do a great deal more than a crippled team working under a "jinx." Thursday's contest was in the nature of a vindication of the Gold and Blue in the East. After two defeats, there were many who began to think that last year's victory was an unusually fortunate break in luck, and that Notre Dame was not really in a class with big Eastern schools. But the whirlwind game that buried the Orange, banished such thoughts for good. Notre Dame is still a conspicuous spot on the football map, and must be taken into account when the leaders are picked.

The game not only grounded the reputation of the Gold and Blue in the East; it gave her a clear claim to the Western non-conference title. This year, almost anything can be proved by comparing scores, so often and so badly has the "dope" been upset. Direct comparisons, however, will always be valid, and on these we can bring good proof to back up the above assertion. Nebraska, Michigan, and Notre Dame are the three strongest teams outside the Conference. To go over old history—South Dakota played Nebraska 0—0, while Notre Dame soundly trounced the Dakotans by a margin of 33 points. Syracuse, in a decisive manner, conquered Michigan, 20-6; Notre Dame just as decisively defeated the Saltines, 20—0. The scores are not so close as to be the result of chance—they represent real values, and give Notre Dame the widest kind of a margin.

NOTRE DAME, 20		SYRACUSE,O
Elward	L. E.	Woodruff, Burns
Jones	L. T.	Schlacter
Keefe, Stephen	L. G.	McElligott, Meisner
Fitzgerald	C.	Shuffelt
Bachman	R. G.	White
Lathrop	R. T.	T. Johnson
Mills, Baujan	R. E.	Travis
Bergman, Larkin	Q.	Seymour, Johnson, Rafter
Cofall, Berger	L. H.	Wilkinson, Slater
Kelleher, Pliska	R. H.	Fose
Eichenlaub, Duggan	F.	Kingsley, Connell

Touchdowns—Cofall, Pliska, Bergman. Goals from touchdown—Cofall 1. Referee—Cross of Dartmouth. Umpire—Hinkey of Yale. Head linesman—Wathey of Syracuse. Time of periods—15 minutes.

Excursion to the Carlisle Game.

The Faculty have consented to permit the students of the University to attend the Notre Dame-Carlisle Game at Chicago, on Nov. 14. A special train will leave South Bend at 8:30 A. M., and returning will leave Chicago at 8:15 P. M. To make this trip written permission must be secured from home and presented to the Prefect of Discipline by November 12th.

No money will be advanced by the University. Money for expenses to the game must be sent specially for this purpose to the Students' Office or remitted directly to the student. The Lake Shore will make a rate of $3.50 for the round-trip. Admission to the game will be fifty cents for students of the University. A special rate will be secured for meals in a good hotel.

Left to right: First Row—Whipple, Malone, A. J. Bergman, Fitzgerald (Capt.), Elward, Baujan, Phelan.
Second Row—Harper (Head Coach), Cofall, Jones, Rydewski, McInerney, O'Donnell, Rockne (Assistant Coach).
Third Row—Stephan, Keefe, Bachman, J. Miller, King.

1915
Coach: Jesse C. Harper
Captain: Freeman C. Fitzgerald

O.2	W	Alma	32-0	H
O.9	W	Haskell	34-0	H
O.23	L	Nebraska	19-20	A
O.30	W	South Dakota	6-0	H
N.6	W	Army	7-0	A
N.13	W	Creighton	41-0	A
N.25TH	W	Texas	36-7	A
N.27	W	Rice	55-2	A
	(7-1-0)		230-29	

1915 LETTERMEN

F. Fitzgerald (C)
C. W. Bachman
H. C. Baujan
A. J. Bergman
S. B. Cofall
A. H. Elward
J. J. Jones
E. G. Keefe
H. E. King
A. M. McInerney
G. J. Malone
J. M. Miller
J. H. O'Donnell
M. J. Phelan
F. X. Rydzewski
L. J. Stephan
R. F. Whipple

Varsity Plays Wonderful Game.

Last Saturday afternoon, eight thousand cheering Nebraskans saw their football favorites snatch a one-point victory from what we are now proud to own as one of the greatest elevens that ever represented Notre Dame on the gridiron. The game was one of the most spectacular and hard-fought contests ever fought out in the West. The comparatively green Notre Dame team was pitted against an eleven, which, on advance dope, was so much stronger than the Varsity that even our own rooters realized that we had little chance to win. The Nebraska team excelled our own both in weight and experience. The Cornhuskers have not lost a football game since 1912. But the Notre Dame team went into the game with its heart set upon victory and full of the fighting qualities that have made Notre Dame's football teams justly famous, and, as one of the Omaha papers state: "It was pretty generally agreed that only the tender glances of Dame Fortune made it possible for Stiehm's men to register the victory."

Score: Notre Dame, 55; Rice, 2.

RICE	The line-up:	NOTRE DAME
Kalb	C	O'Donnell
McFarland	R G	Fitzgerald
Standish	R T	McInerny
Clark	R E	Baujan
Halton	L G	Keefe
Fulweiler	L T	Stephan
Coan	L E	Elward
Gripon	Q	Phelan
Brown	R H	Bergman
Stevens	L H	Cofall
Fendley	F	Bachman

Every Kick Is a Boost.

BY R. M. H.

Eight football games all in a row,
Alma gets biffed,—seven games to go.

Seven wee games still in the way,
Haskell snowed under,—six more to play.

Four games more,—we chuckle in glee,
Creighton we clean,—now there's only three.

Three games remain for N. D. U.
Army crocked,—so now there's but two.

Six little games now left by heck,
Nebraska and Ecky land on our neck!

Five little games all yet in store,
Coyotes defeated, now there's but four.

Two little games,—both good as won,
Texas croaks and that leaves but one.

One little game left,—Sis, boom, bah!
Rice digested,—Notre Dame, rah, rah, rah!

The Monogram Men

Captain Stanley B. Cofall, Cleveland, Ohio.
Captain-elect M. J. Phelan, Portland, Oregon.
Charles W. Bachman, Chicago, Illinois.
John M. Miller, Clinton, Illinois.
Harry C. Baujan, Beardstown, Illinois.
Gilbert J. Ward, Ottawa, Illinois.
Arthur J. Bergman, Peru, Indiana.
Frederick J. Slackford, Sandusky, Ohio.
George M. Fitzpatrick, Alpena, Michigan.
D. Chester Grant, South Bend, Indiana.

Ray F. Whipple, Elgin, Illinois.
John F. Meagher, Elgin, Illinois.
Arnold M. McInerny, South Bend, Indiana.
Frank E. Coughlin, Chicago, Illinois.
David Philbin, Portland, Oregon.
Frank A. Andrews, Rock Island, Illinois.
Walter B. DeGree, St. Cloud, Minnesota.
Frank X. Rydzewski, South Chicago, Illinois.
Thomas H. King, Thornton, Indiana.

The Men We Lose

Stanley Cofall
Charles Bachman
John Miller
Harry Baujan
Gilbert Ward

With Years to Play

James Phelan, one.
Arthur Bergman, one.
Frederick Slackford, one.
George Fitzpatrick, two.
Chester Grant, two.
Ray Whipple, one.
John Meagher, two.

Arnold McInerny, one.
Frank Coughlin, two.
Dave Philbin, one.
Frank Andrews, two.
Walter DeGree, two.
Frank Rydzewski, one.
Thomas King, one.

GOLD AND BLUE CAPTAINS AT 1916 COMMENCEMENT

	1916		
	Coach: Jesse C. Harper		
	Captain: Stan Cofall		
S.30	W Case Tech	48-0	H
O.7	W Western Reserve	48-0	A
O.14	W Haskell	26-0	H
O.28	W Wabash	60-0	H
N.4	L Army	10-30	A
N.11	W South Dakota	21-0	N
N.18	W Michigan State	14-0	H
N.25	W Alma	46-0	H
N.30TH	W Nebraska	20-0	A
	(8-1-0)	293-30	

N—at Sioux Falls

Football.

Last Saturday's 60 to 0 victory over Wabash brought the Varsity's seasonal score up to 182 against an aggregate of four ciphers to the credit of their opponents, and placed the Notre Dame fans in high hopes for to-day's game at Army, the result of which will have been learned before these lines are read.

Straight football was almost entirely responsible for Notre Dame's nine touchdowns. Scintillating end runs and off tackle smashes crumbled the visiting defense and dashed the hopes of those who had hoped that Wabash would give the Varsity a real contest. Even after Coach Harper had removed every one of his regulars, toward the end of the first half, Notre Dame had little difficulty in putting through long gains. In the second half, with the score 39 to 0, Harper sent back his first team, with the exception of McInerny, but removed them in the fourth period. Wabash failed to make a single first down during the game.

Between halves a trio of former N. D. football heroes were driven around the field for the edification of the spectators. The men were Gus Dorais, Art Bergman, and Joe Pliska. Royal Bosshard, president of the senior class, was the chauffeur. The crowd was the largest of the season, and a typical "big game" atmosphere surrounded the campus during the day.

The lineup and summary, with the numerous substitutions, are as follows.

NOTRE DAME, 60.

R.E.	King, Meagher, King, Meagher
R.T	McInerny, Philbin
R.G.	Degree, Ward, Degree, Ward
C.	Rydzewski, Jones, Rydzewski, Madigan
L.G.	Bachman, Franz, Ronchetti, Bachman
L.T.	Coughlan, Andrews, Coughlan, Andrews
L.E.	Baujan, Berkey, Baujan, Berkey
Q.	Phelan, Grant, Dorais, Pehlan, Grant
R.H.	Bergman, Malone, Fitzpatrick, Bergman, Fitzpatrick
L.H.	Cofall (Capt.), Fitzpatrick, W. Miller, Cofall, W. Miller
F.B.	J. Miller, Slackford, J. Miller, Slackford

WABASH, 0.

L.E.	O. G. Thomson, Heald
L.T.	Woodward, Thompson
L.G.	Caldwell (Capt.)
C.	Stonebreaker
R.G.	Michaels, Meal
R.T.	Hanicker
R.E.	Moses, Paulsen
Q.	Lindsey, Green
L.H.	Walker, Vermillion
R.H.	Coffing
F.B.	Bacon

Touchdowns—Cofall (2), Bergman (2), Fitzpatrick, Phelan, J. Miller, Dorais, Slackford. Goals from touchdowns Miller (3), Philbin (2), Cofall. Referee Van Riper, Wisconsin. Umpire—Hoffman, Chicago. Head linesman, —Coffins, Cornell.

The Army Game.

On our fourth visit to West Point, the Gold and Blue went down to defeat before the clever passing and toe work of Vidal and Oliphant, the two Army stars and two of the best backs in the East. The final score was 30 to 10, which was larger than any of the football critics in the country expected. The work of Cofall, Bergman, John Miller and Bachman was praised highly by eastern papers, as was also Notre Dame's perfection of every phase of the game—every phase except forward passing. It was through the aerial route that the West Pointers rode to victory, two of their touchdowns and one of their goals coming as a result of successful and phenomenal passes. It was by this department of the game, the one we taught them in 1913, that the Army beat us. It was a case of the pupil becoming more competent than the teacher.

ARMY, 30; NOTRE DAME, 10.

House	L. E	Baujan
Jones	L. T	Coughlan
Knight	L. G	Bachman
McEwan (Capt.)	C	Rydzewski
Meacham	R. G	De Gree
Butler	R. T	McInerny
Shrader	R. E	Whipple
Gerhardt	Q	Phelan
Vidal	L. H	(Capt.) Cofall
Oliphant	R. H	Bergman
Place	F	Miller

SCORE BY PERIODS:

Army		0	6	7	17 30
Notre Dame		3	0	7	0 10

Referee—A. C. Hann, Harvard. Umpire A. C. Tyler, Princeton. Head linesman E. Cochems, Wisconsin. Time of periods—12 minutes each. Army scoring: Touchdowns—Vidal 3. Goals from placement—Oliphant 2. Notre Dame Scoring: Touchdown—Bergman. Goal from touchdown Cofall. Goal from field—Cofall. Substitutions Army, Weems for McEwan, Stokes for Weems, McEwan for Stokes, Mullins for Shrader, Shrader for Mullins. Notre Dame, Grant for Phelan, Stackford for Miller.

1917

Coach: Jesse C. Harper
Captain: James Phelan

O.6	W	Kalamazoo	55-0	H
O.13	T	Wisconsin	0-0	A
O.20	L	Nebraska	0-7	A
O.27	W	South Dakota (R)	40-0	H
N.3	W	Army (U)	7-2	A
N.10	W	Morningside	13-0	A
N.17	W	Michigan State	23-0	H
N.24	W	Wash. & Jefferson	3-0	A
	(6-1-1)		141-9	

1917 LETTERMEN

J. Phelan (C)
W. Allison
F. Andrews
L. Bahan
J. Brandy
G. Gipp
D. Hayes
D. King
R. McGuire
E. Madigan
W. Miller
D. Pearson
D. Philbin
J. Ryan
F. Rydzewski
M. Smith
T. Spalding
B. Stanley
R. Stine
C. Zoia

COSTLY VICTORY OVER MORNINGSIDE.

There was no flavor in the Notre Dame victory at Sioux City, Iowa, last Saturday, when Morningside was humbled 13 to 0. The regrettable injury which incapacitated George Gipp for the remainder of the season marred the afternoon. When the big halfback from Calumet broke his leg early in the first quarter the players lost interest in the game. Not until the second quarter did they score.

"Big Frank" Rydzewski, whose interceptions are coming to be a part of every game, pulled a long Morningside forward pass out of the air, and sprinted forty yards for a touchdown. In the third quarter a combination of straight football and a sprinkling of forward passes enabled Notre Dame to score a second touchdown—the final one of the game.

NOTRE DAME vs. WISCONSIN.

Yale has her Bulldog, Princeton has her Tiger, other schools have their various ferocious animals, and they are welcome to the whole irrational kingdom as long as Notre Dame has her "fight'n Irish." Fight, the kind that gives overflowing measure for what it takes, never before protruded from every man of a Notre Dame eleven as it did on Camp Randall last Saturday when the Gold and Blue held the heavier Wisconsin team to a scoreless tie. With their goal menaced no less than six times on four occasions by attempted goals from the field and twice by incompleted forward passes over the goal line—Notre Dame kept defending and offending the Badgers until they played them to a standstill.

Notre Dame had not played a Conference eleven since 1908. Critics must have been impressed by the fighting spirit of the men from Hoosierdom who could hold the big Badgers at bay through a whole game, right on their own stamping ground. Many must have marvelled at the pluck and generalship of Capt. Phalen who trickled the last ounce of stamina out of his midget backfield, in a desperate though vain attempt to mathematically offset the avoirdupois of the men from the land of LaFollete. There came a tense moment in the expiring moments of the game, after all other means had failed, when the Notre Dame captain made ready to kick a field goal from his forty-one yard line. The ball sailed high and had the necessary momentum, but failed by inches when it struck the goal posts above the cross bar. Notre Dame had to be content with a moral victory.

Bahan, Brandy, and Walter Miller gave their all for Notre Dame. Fighting against odds seldom encountered by backfield men they tore into the heavy Wisconsin line time after time, never losing heart, always hoping and endeavoring for the "break" that did not come.

Dave Philbin also played like a wild man throughout the game. The big Oregonian has played some stellar games during his career at Notre Dame, but never did he assume such a determination to hold an opposing team at any cost as he did last Saturday. He and "Big Frank" Rydzewski were the stars of the defense. With three men hurling themselves at him throughout the game, Rydzewski managed to elude them and get into most every play. Once he caught a forward pass honestly intended for a Badger and made thirty-five yards towards the Wisconsin goal before he was downed.

Tom King and Dave Hayes, pitted against men way beyond their size, did exceptionally well. They are but typical of the rest of the team—they fight, then fight some more, and never quit. Madigan, Andrews, Stine and McGuire, did their parts well in the remaining positions of the line while Pierson got away for a fifteen-yard run when he was put into the game in the last quarter. Ryan also gave his best when injected into the fullback position in the same period.

The showing of Wisconsin should not be minimized. The men coached by Richards showed a lot of football, and probably their worst fault was that they entirely underestimated Notre Dame prior to the game. Capt. Hancock, Kelley, and Simpson were the Badger luminaries, and they kept things interesting for Notre Dame from whistle to whistle.

WISCONSIN (o)		NOTRE DAME (o)
Siever	L E	Hayes
Scott	L T	Stine
Kralovec	L G	Andrews
Carpenter	C	Rydzewski
Gallun	R G	Madigan
Hancock (Capt.)	R T	Philbin
Kelley	R E	King
Simpson	Q	Phalen (Capt.)
Davey	L H	Brandy
Gould	R H	Bahan
Jacobie	F	Miller

Summaries: Substitutions—Keyes for Kelley; Kelley for Gould, Starke for Kelley, Kelley for Keyes, McGuire for Stine, Ryan for Miller, Miller for Brandy, Pierson for Bahan.

Officials: Referee—Masker, Northwestern. Umpire—Birch, Wabash. Field Judge—Lipski, Chicago. Head linesman—Haines, Yale.

NEBRASKA GAME REAL BATTLE

Even the elastic language of the sport page fails ignobly when detailing the brilliant battle Notre Dame staged against the Nebraska Cornhuskers at Lincoln last Saturday. Anything that could be said here would be but a peurile portrayal of the pugnacious spirit which the gold and blue displayed on the western battleground one week ago.

After everyone had thought the zenith in fighting spirit had been reached at Wisconsin the week before, the Notre Dame warriors paused just long enough to get a good breath before curbing that spirit and hurling it at Nebraska. The story of the game with the Cornhuskers is an unabridged story of Notre Dame fight, the story of undiluted gameness that is even greater in defeat than in victory. Let mathematics show that Nebraska was the victor; many things often stick out between the lines of statistics.

When the heaviest team Nebraska has had in the last three years trotted on the field a few minutes before the game, the eye confirmed the lie of Lincoln papers that Notre Dame would not be outweighed. No judge of livestock was necessary to fathom the fact that the Cornhuskers outweighed the Hoosiers not less than fifteen pounds to the man. Eight regulars who faced Notre Dame the year before were in the Nebraska line up; two regulars of the 1916 game were on the side of Notre Dame. Everything pointed to an overwhelming defeat of the gold and blue.

It was not until the middle of the second quarter that Nebraska could puncture the wonderful Notre Dame defense for the lone score of the game. Quarterback Cook's 45 yard return of a punt, and Dobson's smash through the line for twelve yards, were important advances that brought the ball close to the Notre Dame goal and made it comparatively easy for the veteran Otoupalik to push it over. Notre Dame had her inning in the third quarter but lacked the offensive punch, once she was inside Nebraska's ten-yard line. After play upon play against the Cornhusker line failed of any material gain, a forward pass across the goal line fell into the hands of the tall Otoupalik, and Notre Dame's first and only real chance to score had gone awry.

Captain Jim Phelan, unmindful of his forced departure for an army camp an hour after the contest, played probably the best game of his career. It was Phelan who maintained the morale of the backfield after the light backs had been battered literally almost to a pulp. Bahan and Gipp, Pearson and Smith, along with Walter Miller backed up their captain as only fighting Notre Dame men can, and not till the struggle was over did they allow their tired bodies to feel the pain of battle overpower them.

NEBRASKA (7)		NOTRE DAME (o)
Rhodes	L E	Hayes
Duteau	L T	Andrews
Kositzky	L G	Zoia
Day	C	Rydzewski
Wilder	R G	Madigan
Shaw	R T	Philbin
Riddell	R E	King
Shellenberg	Q	Phelan
Cook	L H	Gipp
Dobson	R H	Bahan
Otoupalik	F	Miller

Substitutions by Nebraska—Munn for Duteau; Huba for Riddell; substitutions for Notre Dame—McGuire for Andrews, Stanley for Zoia, Smith for Gipp, Pearson for Bahan. Touchdown, Otoupalik. Goal from touchdown, Shaw. Time of periods 15 minutes. Officials: Masker, Northwestern, referee; Griffith, Drake, umpire; Anderson, Missouri, field judge; Wyatt, K. C. A. A., head lineman.

The King is Dead! Long Live the King!

FIVE years ago there came to Notre Dame a man who enjoyed a local reputation in the vicinity of Crawfordsville, Indiana, as a developer of more or less successful athletic teams. Today that man is known throughout the length and breadth of this land as one of the foremost coaches and directors intercollegiate athletics have ever produced. That man is Jesse C. Harper, the astute generalissimo of the Notre Dame athletic department, who has raised up Gold and Blue athletics till they now rest on a plane unsurpassed by any school East or West.

Harper has been such a success at Notre Dame because he is possessed of a vision that is tempered with good judgment and with a courage to do big things that admits of no obstacles. Before he had set foot on Notre Dame soil in the fall of 1913 he had arranged the most pretentious schedule the football world had ever known. Critics gasped, but they soon gasped again when he paraded his phantom-like eleven from the Hudson to the Rio Grande always in step with a victory march. Year-in and year-out he has done wonders with Notre Dame teams. Last fall he undermined the lie that he had to have men of Potsdam Guard proportions for his football teams by turning out a gridiron machine composed of youths averaging one hundred and sixty-six pounds. Army, and Washington and Jefferson, found out all too late that Harper was not a man to hide behind the fact that wholesale enlistments had depopulated his pigskin material.

Persistent, resourceful, and game to the core, Coach Harper stands for all that is good in athletics. Sportsmanship first, then victory or defeat second, has always been the way of Harper. Heads of athletic departments at other institutions have come to know Harper and Notre Dame, and to realize what the two stand for. No longer is Notre Dame knocking at the gate for desirable opponents. Now she is welcome in the best of athletic company because her athletes and her ideas of sportsmanship cannot be surpassed.

But Harper's career at Notre Dame is closed. Having reached the pinnacle of his profession at an early age he has decided to step down and follow the less precarious life of a farmer. If business sagacity is an asset in ranching, Western Kansas is about to behold her greatest cattleman. This announcement might be a dirge were it not that a man trained by Harper, slightly if any less capable than the master of the past five years, is to step to the athletic helm next fall.

Congratulations, Knute K. Rockne. No man in the days of modern intercollegiate athletics ever stepped into a desirable position better equipped for the job than the inimitable "Rock." Learned, liked, capable, inspiring, courageous, and resourceful, no one can see anything but undiluted success for the great 1913 football captain. In his own Alma Mater and in every other school with which Notre Dame competes he is a favorite. His popularity is in its infancy.

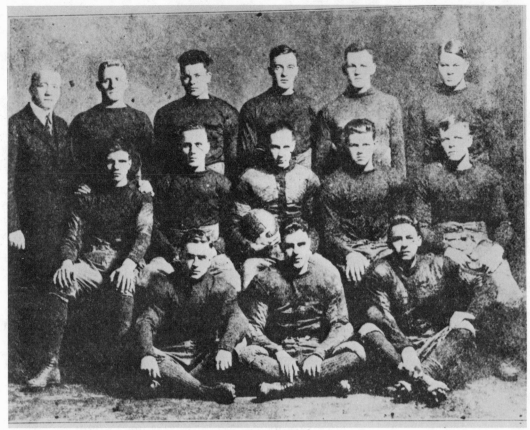

The Team of 1918

Front row: Lockard, quarterback; Barry, halfback; Mohn, quarterback. *Middle row:* E. Anderson, right end; Smith, right guard; Bahan, right half; Kirk, left end; H. Anderson, left guard. *Back row:* Coach Rockne; Crowley, right tackle; Lambeau, fullback; Gipp, halfback; Stine, left tackle; Larsen, center.

1918 LETTERMEN

L. Bahan (C)
E. Anderson
H. Anderson
N. Barry
C. Crowley
G. Gipp
P. Kirk
E. Lambeau
F. Larson
F. Lockard
W. Mohn
M. Smith
R. Stine

		1918		
		Coach: Knute K. Rockne		
		Captain: Leonard Bahan		
S.28	W	Case Tech	26-6	A
N.2	W	Wabash	67-7	A
N.9	T	Great Lakes	7-7	H
N.16	L	Mich. State (U) (R)	7-13	A
N.23	W	Purdue	26-6	A
N.28TH	T	Nebraska (S)	0-0	A
		(3-1-2)	133-39	

MICHIGAN STATE

Notre Dame was defeated last Saturday at Lansing by the Michigan Aggies, 13 to 7. The field was a quagmire of mud, and hence the speed of Bahan and Gipp did not in the least avail the gold and blue. The Aggies outweighed Notre Dame by at least 5 pounds to the man, but the lighter Notre Dame line was invulnerable inside of their 30-yd. line. Twice the Aggies, with their big negro fullback carrying the ball most of the time, took the oval to Notre Dame's 30-yd. line, but here the blue and gold line held; on both occasions the Aggies scored on forward passes. Rain fell all the time, which made passing of the ball very difficult, and Notre Dame attempted only three, two of which were successful, Bahan catching one and Kirk grabbing the other. Bahan was badly hurt in the first quarter and had to be taken out of the game. He suffered a wrenched shoulder and a badly torn knee. Gipp also was taken out in the third quarter, because of the rupture of a blood vessel on the left side of his face and other injuries. Stine, who went into the game with his left leg in a bad condition, came out none the better for the fray. It is very doubtful whether these three veterans, the only ones on the squad, will be seen in any more games this season. Their loss will be felt very heavily if they are incapacitated for the remainder of the season, as Gipp and Bahan are the main ground gainers and "Rollo" Stine is the mainstay of the line. In addition Bahan is captain.

In the fourth quarter Notre Dame showed her famous fighting spirit, when with Barry and Lombardo in the places of Bahan and Gipp, the team marched right down to the Aggies' 10-yd. line. Here the ball was lost on a penalty and the opportunity to tie the score was gone. It is hard to pick out an individual star from the Notre Dame team, as everyone played a great game. Lambeau deserves mention for his line plunging and Mohn used excellent headwork in the direction of the team's play.

Top row: Dooley, Shaw, Crowley, Kasper, Cudahy, Kiley, Coughlin, Trafton, Mehre, Voss, Wynn, Walsh. *Middle row:* H. Anderson, Slackford, Kirk, Bergman, Miller, Bahan (Capt.), Brandy, Hayes, Barry, E. Anderson, Pearson, O'Hara. *Bottom row:* Holton, Sexton, Donovan, Connors, Ambrose, Sanders, Payne, Prokop, Mohardt, Phelan. (Gipp, Smith, DeGree, Malone, and Madigan, five of the most prominent stars of the team, are unfortunately absent from the picture.)

Last Saturday Notre Dame's heart was for the first time gladdened by a great football crowd. The long east stands were full of color, heightened in its effect by the unique **A Stadium for** presence of the enthusiastic, **Notre Dame.** happy delegation from Saint Mary's. Throngs, unable to find seating room in the stands, were prevented from crowding on the field only by the strong arms and the commanding appearance of Notre Dame monogram men acting as "M. P.'s." The west bleachers were packed to overflowing, and a solid mass of students grouped themselves as close as possible about the cheering stands in order to help with the "Victory" song and the big "U. N. D's." Automobiles filled all available space in the field and many had difficulty in finding parking space within reasonable distance of the entrance gate. These great crowds, together with the spirited band and cheering delegation from the Michigan school which gave additional rivalry to the contest, provided all those picturesque and romantic incidentals so necessary to a "big" football game. And the enthusiastic cheers of encouragement from South Bend people throughout the game, warmed every Notre Dame man's heart. Notre Dame's wonderful record this year will without doubt secure for her an even more permanent place in the highest football circles. And why cannot Notre Dame bring the greatest teams of East and West to a new Cartier Field? In other words, let's have a stadium for Notre Dame.—L. L. W.

NOTRE DAME, 14; MORNINGSIDE, 6.

Before a large crowd of gridiron enthusiasts, who were not in the least discouraged by the inclement weather, Notre Dame humbled Morningside in a hotly contested game at Sioux City last Saturday, 14 to 6. Although Morningside furnished stiff opposition for Rockne's men, it may be safely said that the weather saved the Iowans from a much worse defeat. Notre Dame was slow in starting, and the Corn-State eleven, taking advantage, succeeded, with a series of brilliant end dashes by Hinkley and Wenig, in scoring a touchdown in the first five minutes of play. Captain Wenig failed at the kick for the goal.

Morningside's taste of triumph was very temporary. The Gold and Blue, roused into action by the apparent ease with which the Iowans had "put one over," took the aggressive. For the rest of the first quarter Morningside strove valiantly against the smashing attacks and the end-sprints of the Gold-and-Blue backs. The quarter ended with the ball on the enemy's twenty-yard line and the "Irish fairly rarin' to carry on." With Gipp and his crushing aids carrying the ball, the Morningside defense was brushed aside and the ball went over. Gipp added a mark with the old toe.

NOTRE DAME		MORNINGSIDE
Kiley	L. E.	Day
Coughlin	L. T.	Rorapaugh
H. Anderson	L. G.	Steele
Trafton	C.	Horney
Smith	R. G.	Beck
Degree	R. T.	Marcell
E. Anderson	R. E.	Wenig
Brandy	Q. B.	Lloyd
Gipp	L. H.	Davis
Bahan	R. H.	Gannt
Miller	F. B.	Hinkley

Substitutions: Notre Dame—Slackford for Miller; Barry for Bahan; Kirk for Kiley; Touchdowns: Notre Dame, 2; Brandy, Gipp; Morningside—Hinkley. Goals from touchdown: Gipp, 2. Morningside—none.

Football Facts.

The game with Morningside on Thanksgiving Day marked the close of Notre Dame's thirty-first football season. It was also her twenty-eighth consecutive season. The gridiron sport was inaugurated at Notre Dame back in 1887, when the Gold and Blue lost its first game to Michigan by a score of 8-0.

The "Fighting Irish" have participated in 211 contests, winning 159, losing 36, and tying 16.

The fact that Notre Dame has amassed a total of 5492 points against 1040 by her opponents forms a fine commentary on the chronic strength of her "pigskin jugglers."

This year's aggregation is the tenth Notre Dame team to go through a football season without a defeat.

In 1905 we administered our most crushing defeat on record by trouncing the American Medical College, by a total of 140 points, and holding them scoreless.

In 1904 Wisconsin gave us the worst drubbing in our gridiron history, when we bowed before her to the tune of 58-0.

FOOTBALL BANQUET.

Notre Dame formally ended the football season of 1919, the most successful in thirty years, on Sunday evening of December 14th, with the fifteenth annual football banquet, given by the Notre Dame Athletic Association to the men of the varsity and freshmen squads. The occasion was a fitting climax for the season. Covers were laid for more than sixty persons in the Turkish Room of the Oliver Hotel. Davis's Jazz Orchestra and the Varsity Quartet furnished the music and song. Coach Knute Rockne, presiding as toastmaster, called on the men who had finished their career for farewell remarks. These talks were the feature of the evening. The love, respect, and spirit of each man for Notre Dame was reflected in every speech and unanimous credit for the success of the season was given to the coaches. Every man wished that he might have accomplished more and each stated his determination to "carry on" for the University wherever he might be. Captain Bahan, Bergman, Barry, Miller, Slackford, Degree, Malone, Madigan, Smith, and George Hull were the speakers. Then followed the nomination and election of the captain for 1920. Frank Coughlin and George Gipp were the candidates. The ballot resulted in the election of George Gipp, of Laurium, Michigan. George is well known as one of the greatest all-around half-backs of the country and at the forward-pass as the greatest man in the game. He accepted the honor as the greatest of his life and pledged his best to the team of 1920. Frank Coughlin, after congratulating his rival, also pledged to George Gipp and to Notre Dame, his best efforts for the coming season, which will mean so much to the prestige of the Gold and Blue. In their talks Rockne and Dorais both declared the team of 1919 in every way the equal of any former Notre Dame eleven, and urged the necessity of constant physical care and preparation for next season. A round of cheers for the monogram winners closed the evening. The monogram winners as announced for the 1919 service on the gridiron are: Bahan, Brandy, Gipp, Miller, Bergman, Slackford, Barry, Malone, Madigan, Trafton, Dooley, Smith, R. Anderson, Coughlin, Degree, Shaw, Hayes, Kiley, E. Anderson, and Kirk.

1919—Notre Dame's Greatest Gridiron Season

K. K. ROCKNE, Coach   CHARLES DORAIS, Asst. Coach   LEONARD BAHAN, Captain

Varsity Record:

Oct. 4—Notre Dame, 14; Kalamazoo, 0; at Notre Dame.
Oct. 11—Notre Dame, 60; Mt. Union, 7; at Notre Dame.
Oct. 18—Notre Dame, 14; Nebraska, 9; at Lincoln.
Oct. 25—Notre Dame, 53; Western Normal, 0; at Notre Dame.
Nov. 1—Notre Dame, 16; Indiana U., 3; at Indianapolis.
Nov. 8—Notre Dame, 12; Army, 9; at West Point.
Nov. 15—Notre Dame, 13; Michigan Aggies, 0; at Notre Dame.
Nov. 22—Notre Dame, 33; Purdue, 13, at Lafayette.
Nov. 27—Notre Dame, 14; Morningside, 6; at Sioux City.

THE SEASON'S SUCCESSES

Notre Dame has not had equalled the successes of 1919 in all the previous thirty years of her gridiron history. Four other elevens have finished the season undefeated but tied once. Two elevens even won every game played, but none so successfully obtained nation-wide recognition in intercollegiate football as has the 1919 "Irish."

The State Championship is undisputedly theirs. Actually and comparatively there is no University eleven in the West with a clearer claim to the Western Championship, for Notre Dame is the only undefeated eleven in the section. Her claims to the National Collegiate title are at least as good as Harvard's and perhaps far broader. Far to the West and deep into the heart of the East the successes of the "Rockmen" extended. The "Irish" were never forced to the "last ditch" to win a game; their line smashing tactics and aerial tricks met no unfathomable opposition. On defense they were at ease, always confident of checking any charges that meant scores. They were veterans and played the safe game, never extending themselves unless conditions were advisable. When going at top speed their attack had no parallel in gridiron history. The forward pass attack was a "yardage riot" and the wing-sweeping end-rushes were usually invincible.

1920

Coach: Knute K. Rockne
Captain: Frank Coughlin

O.2	W	Kalamazoo	39-0	H	5,000
O.9	W	Western St. Nor.	42-0	H	3,500
O.16	W	Nebraska	16-7	A	9,000
O.23	W	Valparaiso	28-3	H	8,000
O.30	W	Army	27-17	A	10,000
N.6	W	Purdue (HC)	28-0	H	12,000
N.13	W	Indiana	13-10	N	14,000
N.20	W	*Northwestern	33-7	A	c20,000
N.25TH	W	Michigan State	25-0	A	8,000
			(9-0-0)	251-44	89,500

N—at Indianapolis
*George Gipp's last game. He contracted a strep
throat and died from complications of the disease on
December 14 at the age of 25.

1920 LETTERMEN

F. Coughlin (C)
E. Anderson
H. Anderson
N. Barry
J. Brandy
G. Carberry
P. Castner
E. DeGree
J. Dooley
A. Garvey
G. Gipp
C. Grant
D. Hayes
R. Kiley
F. Larson
H. Mehre
J. Mohardt
R. Phelan
L. Shaw
M. Smith
W. Voss
E. Walsh
C. Wynne

ARMY, 17; NOTRE DAME, 27.

A great chapter in Notre Dame's unparalleled football history has been completed; another, greater and more glorious, is about to be written. Seven continuous and successful years of eastern invasions have brought the reward of honest recognition to Notre Dame and the West.

THE PRESS BOWS.

Notre Dame's third consecutive victory over the Army at West Point Saturday has conclusively proved the contention that western football is the equal, if not the superior, of the eastern game. A score of coldly judging, later admiring and finally enthusiastic sport writers, gridiron experts and critics from the metropolitan press viewed the battle. They saw the Army team, admittedly the strongest, best coached and brilliant West Point machine in recent years, meet its defeat at the hands of the greatest combination of "football brains, speed and courage" seen in the east in a decade. A dozen of the great eastern papers carried the play-by-play story of the game, its wonders, revelations and lessons. Flaring headlines proclaimed All-American candidates, and long columns recorded and resounded with "Mr. George Gipp," "sons of old Notre Dame," "dazzling aerial attack," "keen generalship," "invincible line" and a hundred other phrases; all in just tribute to Coach Rockne's men, who have wrested the title of gridiron leadership from the east for the west.

BRILLIANT SETTINGS AND PLAYS.

Saturday was an off-day for eastern football. The press heralded the Army-Notre Dame game as "worthwhile" and a "true test of the undefeated Army." The trip up the Hudson, social features and brilliant company were all mentioned. For once the press did not fail. The occasion proved to be the most perfect socially and sensationally of the season.

Friday's rains ceased at nightfall; a keen breeze aided in drying the heavy field till the bright skies of morning took up the work. By noon the thousands of fashionable fans began to arrive and found the "Plains" at its best. The colorful autumn scenes of the Hudson and the towering battlements of the Academy lent every aid to brilliance. Motors large and small, trains, steamers and ferries poured hundreds of spectators upon the scene every hour.

Thousands of fashionable guests viewed the Cadets "on dress parade" and then settled in the stands to await the event of the day.

Nearly four hundred faithful followers and friends of Notre Dame massed in the east stands, and the score of writers and operators prepared to chronicle the clash of the undefeated east and west. The Cadet Corps with fife, drum and band swung into the west stands singing and cheering as they came. They had wagered their "all" and were confident of the returns. The tension was almost unbearable; something had to happen.

Something did. The Gold and Blue squad, led by "Little Willie" and Coach Rockne, trotted onto the field. Simultaneously the Cadet Corps in the west stands and the "gathered four hundred," from "Jimmy" Hoskins to "Rupe" Mills and "Red" Salmon in the east stands, rose and cheered. Brandy chased the first eleven smoothly up and down the field. Castner, Degree and Gipp entertained, each punting graceful forty, fifty and sixty yard spirals. "George" non-chalantly booted a few forty yard drop kicks over the bar. Then the Army's army of football men came. The Cadets in the west stands rose, hats off. They sang, cheered and shouted. An Army victory was demanded, it seemed impossible that anything else could happen. The Army team looked heavier, it was heavier than it looked, and they had a grim earnestness about them. The Army must win. The coaches had told them so, their brother cadets and visiting guests and West Point tradition demanded it. It was the even year; they had always beaten Notre Dame on the even year.

PIGSKIN PROSPECTS

Notre Dame will pry off the Seasons' lid by taking on the Kalamazoo College team today. This contest, which has been ordinarily looked upon as a mere formality, will assume all the aspects of a real contest owing to the recent surprise victory of the Celery City squad over Michigan Agricultural College. Furthermore it will furnish Rockne with a splendid opportunity to study the respective merits of the varsity candidates, each of whom is putting up a gritty fight for a regular position on the first squad.

The pronouncement of George Gipp's eligibility by the faculty board of control has, literally, furnished even the most pessimistic with barrels of happy meditation. Gipp has established an enviable reputation as a versatile, fearless and brilliant performer on the field. The big Wolverine broke into prominence in 1916 when he established a drop-kick record while a member of the Gold and Blue Frosh squad. As a varsity man his every performance has been marked by a superlative brand of play. It would be sheer nonsense to wonder at Rockne's broad smiles of assurance and contentment these days with Gipp cavorting around the backfield. With an even break in luck, Gipp should clinch many mythical honors.

THE HOME-COMING FRACAS

Notre Dame's Knights of the Gridiron marched "onward to victory" last Saturday afternoon, taking the measure of Scanlon's Boilermakers, 28 to 0, before a tremendous crowd that surged its way into every nook and cranny of Cartier Field. It was Home-coming Day and the day proved productive of everything that the word connotes. A tone of distinction was lent to the occasion of state by the presence of such a notable old-timer as "Red" Salmon,—Gold and Blue all-time fullback—and many other distinguished wearers of the monogram of past years. They were here to see Rockne's wonder eleven lauded by the press from coast to coast, in action, and they saw that eleven demonstrate with ease and power a faultless exhibition.

Purdue threatened but once and that was against the second string men who battled them to a standstill during all of the first and the greater part of the second quarter. Gipp's beautiful canter of eighty yards through the entire Boilermaker outfit to a touchdown, was just a bit more brilliant than the thrilling drive of Grant, quarterback of the second squadron, who covered fifty yards of Black and Brown territory and buried the oval behind the Purdue zero line for the game's first touchdown. Captain Coughlin, "Hunk" Anderson, Smith and Shaw fought like demons on the Varsity line, cutting wide deep gaps through which the backfield bullets whizzed. "Danny" Coughlin, Barry and Mohardt, "Chet" Wynne, Rockne's fullback sensation, and Castner, cavorted at will around ends and through every point in the line, advancing the ball in each instance for heavy gains.

George Gipp, than whom, perhaps, no performer in footballdom has received more well-earned recognition, was put into the game but a brief time by the "miracle man." Gipp was still considerably marred up as a result of the Army tilt, but he thrilled the eager stands with his best. He twisted and dodged through a maze of Purdue tacklers for a cross-country run of eighty yards from punt formation, he passed to Kiley and Anderson for one hundred-thirty yards, and his educated boot was good for three goal kicks.

NOTRE DAME, 33; NORTHWESTERN, 7.

In a slashing, lightning attack Rockne's all-conquering juggernaut dodged, dashed, and passed its way through the big Northwestern eleven last Saturday, 33 to 7. Flushed with confidence over the Purdue victory, the Purple entered the fight with an ambition to sweep through the Varsity to a victory.

Pandemonium broke loose when Gipp went into the fray at the beginning of the last quarter. On the second play the big half sent one of his famous passes to Kiley, who richocheted through the entire secondary defense of the opposition for the fourth touchdown. Grausnick, Patterson, and Palmer were hurled back on valiant attempts to gain, and the ball went over. Gipp again let fly a magnificent pass, addressed this time to Barry, who went twenty-five yards for another touchdown. A weak attempt was made by Northwestern to stem the stampede, and nothing but the final whistle prevented the Varsity from crushing through again. The game ended with the ball in Notre Dame's possession on Northwestern's sixteen-yard line.

Lineup and summary:

NOTRE DAME		NORTHWESTERN
Kiley	Left End	Sheron
Garvey	Left Tackle	H. Penfield
DeGree	Left Guard	G. Penfield
Larson	Center	Hathaway
Smith	Right Guard	Magnussen
Shaw	Right Tackle	Lassler
E. Anderson	Right End	Carney
Brandy	Quarterback	Palmer
Mohardt	Left Halfback	Grausnick
D. Coughlin	Right Halfback	Lane
Castner	Fullback	Patterson

Subs—Barry for D. Coughlin, Wynne for Castner; F. Coughlin for Garvey; H. Anderson for DeGree; Prokup for E. Anderson; Szold for Grausnick; Saunders for Sheron; Gibson for Szold; Lacount for Hathaway.

Touchdowns—Barry 2, E. Anderson 2, Kiley, Grausnick.

Goals after touchdown—DeGree, Shaw 2, Palmer.

Referee—Eckersall, Chicago.

Umpire—Hackett, West Point.

Headlinesman—Lipski, Chicago.

Field judge—DeGraves, Michigan.

Gipp of Notre Dame is Remarkable Half Back

Our first All-American candidate of the season is George Gipp, 172 pounds of remarkable halfback, whose work for Notre Dame was the biggest factor in the victory over the Army last Saturday. Gipp played the greatest individual game seen at West Point since the afternoon when Jim Thorpe of the Carlisle Indians defeated the Cadets single handed and single footed.

An idea of the great work done by Gipp may be gained from figures. He gained a total of 124 yards from scrimmage. We do not count the gains for which he was responsible with his throwing of the forward passes, which gave Notre Dame a total of 96 yards. Gipp ran back punts and kickoffs for a total of 112 yards. So in all he made 236 yards—quite a day's work. The Army could not stop this man.—*N. Y. Herald.*

GEORGE GIPP LOSES BATTLE FOR LIFE

Wonderful Notre Dame Football Player Dies From Throat Disease.

FAMED AS SEASON'S GREATEST PERFORMER

First Leaped Into Spotlight By His Sterling Work Against Army.

(Special to The Courant.)
South Bend, Ind., Dec. 14.

George Gipp, Notre Dame football player, died at twenty-three minutes after 3 o'clock this morning from streptococcic throat disease.

Gipp, whose splendid playing won him countrywide recognition and made him a choice for a position on an all-American eleven had been ill since the Notre Dame-Northwestern game on November 20.

Lacked the Stamina.

Pneumonia also helped to weaken the athlete. Specialists, called from Chicago, succeeded in ridding his system of pneumonia, but Gipp did not have the stamina left to ward off the poison resulting from the throat affection.

During the final hours of his fight for life Gipp was rational and was said to have shown remarkable grit as he gradually grew weaker, refusing to give in to the inevitable. His mother, brother and sister were at the bedside when he died. An ironclad determination to conquer his dreaded foe was the thread suspending the great Gipp from eternity for so long a time despite terrific odds. Doctors worked over the dying athlete all of yesterday in a desperate effort to prolong life. Gipp's mother, sister and Coach Rockne of Notre Dame and other personal friends were by his side soon after word

The ill-fated athlete would have been 26 years of age on February 18. He matriculated at Notre Dame four years ago after completing his high school course at Calumet, Mich.

Wonderful Athlete.

Famed the country over as the season's greatest college football player, Gipp had established a reputation unparalleled in the annals of Notre Dame athletics. In addition to his gridiron prowess he was a crack basketball performer, a billiard expert and a stellar ball player.

Gipp first jumped into the spotlight as an unusual football player when Notre Dame clashed with the Army eleven in 1919 when his kicking, forward passing, field running and generalship won him the plaudits of the Eastern football critics. One ray of happiness was brought into the athlete's few remaining hours when he was informed that he had been selected as a player on a mythical all-American eleven.

George Gipp not only was the individual star of the Notre Dame eleven but was generally conceded to be the most brilliant halfback of the season. The past season was his second on the team and both in 1919 and 1920 he was chosen by many writers for mythical All-American elevens.

Had Necessary Qualities.

In the opinion of football experts Gipp combined all the qualities necessary in an all-around star. A brilliant runner, he possessed an ability to sidestep, dodge and keep his feet, which frequently carried him many yards after he had apparently been brought to the ground. As a kicker he was adept both at punting at and booting field goals. While a freshman at Notre Dame he was credited with a sixty-two yard goal kick in a practice scrimmage.

Added to his ability to run and kick, Gipp was an almost perfect forward passer, either standing or running.

On the defense he seldom missed his man and his speed enabled him to range back and forth so that he was in every play. In this season's game against Army, Gipp went back despite an injured shoulder and won the contest for Notre Dame. In that game Gipp scored all his team's seventeen points and stamped himself as probably the greatest back of his day.

When Gipp was entered Notre Dame he had had little football experience. He did not even go out for the team, desiring only to make the baseball nine. One day, however, so the story goes, he was watching the team practice when a ball rolled over toward him. Gipp picked it up and drop kicked it between the goal posts from a distance of fifty yards. He immediately was "drafted" for the football team.

Hundreds of admirers of George Gipp viewed the remains which lay in state tonight. The student body of Notre Dame will accompany the body to the train tomorrow morning when the body will be shipped to Laurium, Mich., for burial. Several members of the Notre Dame football team will attend the funeral.

Reprinted with permission from the **Hartford Courant**

650 OFFERED BLOOD TO GIPP, DEAD STAR

According to Eddie Meehan of Philadelphia, former Notre Dame track star, 650 classmates of George Gipp, dead, Notre Dame athlete who will be buried tomorrow, offered their blood when a call for volunteers was made by physicians for a transfusion. Among those to give blood in efforts to save the life of their popular player were Larson, the varsity center, and Anderson, a halfback. It is said that Anderson, after giving up almost a pint, insisted on continuing practice that afternoon, but was ordered to the infirmary by the coach. Meehan was at one time a roommate of the ill-fated All-American selection for the fullback position.

Reprinted with permission from the **Hartford Courant**

In Memoriam

The glory of George Gipp's prowess had just begun to be re-echoed throughout the land when the knell of death cut short the swelling paen. December fourteenth marks a very important date in the student life of every Notre Dame man. It is on that day all our thoughts revert to George Gipp, to pay him respect and offer up prayers for his soul. He had brought to himself and to Notre Dame a wealth of glory and fame, he stepped into his grave, leaving but the memory of his flaring fame. Like a volcanic eruption, Gipp's fame flashed up before the masses, and almost within the twinkling of an eye it was quenched. His glory came in like the rushing waters of Niagara, and at once passed out in the pallor of death. The recollection of his life is as impressive as the flash of lightning. Upon him were showered the praises and honors that came to few men. He was proclaimed from coast to coast as the greatest player of all time. He was chosen on all the mythical elevens which were published at the close of the season of nineteen hundred and twenty. His name will never be forgotten, and to Notre Dame men especially he is an example. Words cannot contain our love and esteem for him. He was at all times a gentleman and a friend, of splendid character and high ideals. His name is one that will always command respect.

For George Gipp.

(Baptized on his deathbed)

STARS in their courses and twelve stars whose rays
But draw their beauty from Her circled brow
Fought in great peace to bring you, through what ways,
Where you are now.

There is a company about Her throne
Where all her knights are met in heaven's joys,
And you, the youngest, are not there alone
Among Her boys.

They have laid by the mail of many a field,
Out of a thousand climes, a thousand years,
To you, newcomer, welcome place they yield
Among your peers.

You wore Her armor, battling in Her name,
What though you scarcely knew its august power—
She knew Her knight and, fame beyond all fame,
Prepared this hour,

When with a kindness fitting such a Queen
She led you off, your tourney but begun,
With scutcheon bright and wreath of laurel green,
Your spurs quick-won.

For greaves may rust, and fame is but a breath
That blows or hot or cold beyond deserving,
But Honor lives immortal in this death,
Your name preserving.

Out of what far ways of the boundless skies
Fluttered the call that turned your footsteps here
Where over all our purpose shine Her eyes,
Her spirit near.

O Lady, you have taken of our best
To make a playmate for the Seraphim;
There on the wide sweet campus of the blest,
Be good to him.

GEORGE GIPP

Gipp came to Notre Dame not primarily for athletics. It was really an accident when the ever-diligent Rockne, observing his dexterity as he sported himself on the Brownson gridiron, signed him for the freshman squad. He was elected captain, and that year he set the record for distance drop-kicking, registering a 62 yard field-goal in the game with Kalamazoo. He was forced out of the game with a broken leg next season and it was not until 1919 that his name appeared again in the headlines. Notre Dame finished the season unconquered and Gipp was picked for All-Western. His name attached the highest possible honor in the world of sport following the classic contest at West Point this season. They called him Lochinvar of the West, and held him as a demi-god of Football. As he entered the field at Evanston, November 20, twenty thousand persons stood up to greet their idol. But he received his laurels carelessly, and while he was anticipating new fields to conquer the stroke of death cruelly took him off. Yet he was fortunate. He lived "as many a man has dreamed of living—for accomplishment; he died as many a man would be willing to die—in the flush of his fame".

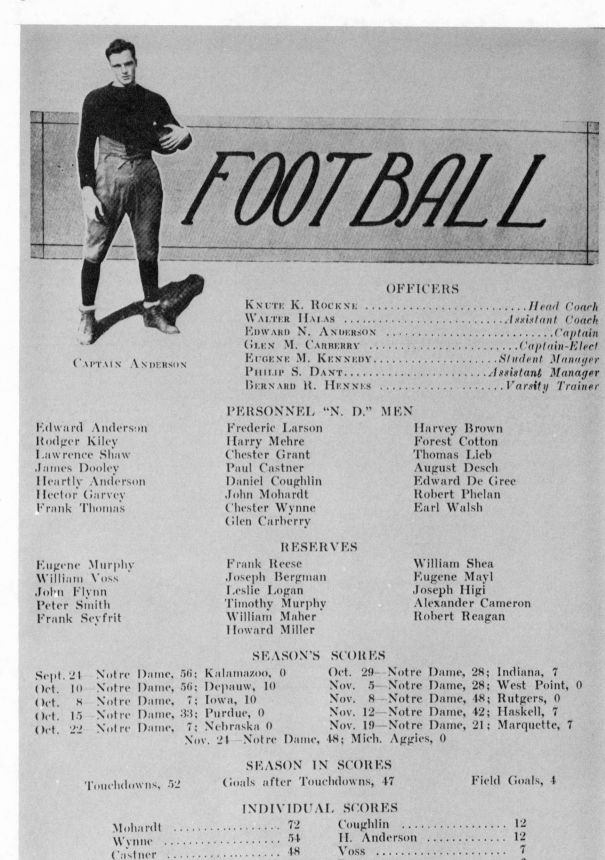

FOOTBALL

CAPTAIN ANDERSON

OFFICERS

KNUTE K. ROCKNE ....Head Coach
WALTER HALAS ....Assistant Coach
EDWARD N. ANDERSON ....Captain
GLEN M. CARBERRY ....Captain-Elect
EUGENE M. KENNEDY.........................Student Manager
PHILIP S. DANT.........................Assistant Manager
BERNARD R. HENNES ....Varsity Trainer

PERSONNEL "N. D." MEN

Edward Anderson	Frederic Larson	Harvey Brown
Rodger Kiley	Harry Mehre	Forest Cotton
Lawrence Shaw	Chester Grant	Thomas Lieb
James Dooley	Paul Castner	August Desch
Heartly Anderson	Daniel Coughlin	Edward De Gree
Hector Garvey	John Mohardt	Robert Phelan
Frank Thomas	Chester Wynne	Earl Walsh
	Glen Carberry	

RESERVES

Eugene Murphy	Frank Reese	William Shea
William Voss	Joseph Bergman	Eugene Mayl
John Flynn	Leslie Logan	Joseph Higi
Peter Smith	Timothy Murphy	Alexander Cameron
Frank Seyfrit	William Maher	Robert Reagan
	Howard Miller	

SEASON'S SCORES

Sept. 24—Notre Dame, 56; Kalamazoo, 0   Oct. 29—Notre Dame, 28; Indiana, 7
Oct. 10—Notre Dame, 56; Depauw, 10   Nov. 5—Notre Dame, 28; West Point, 0
Oct. 8—Notre Dame, 7; Iowa, 10   Nov. 8—Notre Dame, 48; Rutgers, 0
Oct. 15—Notre Dame, 33; Purdue, 0   Nov. 12—Notre Dame, 42; Haskell, 7
Oct. 22—Notre Dame, 7; Nebraska 0   Nov. 19—Notre Dame, 21; Marquette, 7
Nov. 24—Notre Dame, 48; Mich. Aggies, 0

SEASON IN SCORES

Touchdowns, 52   Goals after Touchdowns, 47   Field Goals, 4

INDIVIDUAL SCORES

Mohardt	72	Coughlin	12
Wynne	54	H. Anderson	12
Castner	48	Voss	7
Shaw	38	Rease	6
Kiley	30	Seyfrit	6
Desch	30	Mehre	6
Walsh	18	Lieb	2
Thomas	18		
E. Anderson	12	Total Points	371

1921 Notre Dame Varsity

Bottom: C. Wynne, R. Kiley, H. Anderson, Capt. E. Anderson, Mohardt, D. Coughlin, C. Grant. *Second row:* F. Larson, P. Castner, J. Dooley, L. Shaw, H. Garvey, E. Walsh. *Third row:* F. Thomas, A. Desch, G. Carberry, H. Mehre, E. DeGree, H. Brown. *Fourth row:* Coach Rockne, T. Lieb, F. Cotton, R. Phelan, Assistant Coach W. Halas.

Oct. 8—Iowa 10, Notre Dame 7.

And now—Iowa! The dope on Iowa was this: The Hawkeyes had a strong team. Devine, Slater and Belding were good men but the others were comparatively unknown. However, their record was good and they would offer a stiff battle.

But who had ever heard of Notre Dame losing? How could they lose? They had gone three years without dropping a game and just *loved* to pull a tough game out of the fire in the last quarter. So the team went to Iowa.

There were songs and friendly card games on the trip; and when the squad hit Iowa City a big truck carted the boys to the hotel. The small boy wanted to know which was Mohardt and Anderson. The town was Notre Dame. Everybody admitted that Rockne's team hadn't been beaten for three years and it was constantly drummed into the ears of local supporters that even Iowa people were betting on Notre Dame. There was more real doubt of defeat from Depauw than from Iowa to those on the grounds. The layout was glorious for a debacle—and it came. The game itself was a wonderful exhibition of the sport. Notre Dame was tolerantly confident—even when Iowa scored ten points in the first quarter. Other teams had done that—and no local man found cause for worry.

Iowa was an inferior eleven in power and skill—but fighting mad for a big stake. Every part of its emotional composition was adjusted to its physical make-up; and the result was sufficient to pile up ten points before Notre Dame woke up from its prepared bed of flattery. When Notre Dame did come to—when Mohardt circled the end and passed to Kiley for the first touchdown, Iowa abandoned its offense for a fighting resistance. Iowa had just enough prepared energy and determination to weather the strong attack that the powerful Notre Dame eleven now threw at it. Notre Dame fought and Iowa fought back.

Iowa was also fortunate, for a penalty stopped Notre Dame's first dash; then when Eddie had taken a pass to the five-yard line we plunged and were stopped—on the one-yard mark. Rodge Kiley did get by for our only touchdown, but the whistle blew at the end of the first half when three Notre Dame passes had gained 70 yards.

Again; we took the ball to the eight yard line and lost it. Castner missed a 50-yard drop-kick by five yards—Devine's winning kick was not so long. We brought the ball to the 14-yard line where a pass was intercepted; Kiley blocked a kick and the last man caught him by one leg; Mohardt passed to Eddie to the 8-yard line but another pass was intercepted; Castner ran the ball on a pass to the 17-yard line—and the game was over.

After the first quarter Notre Dame played rings around the Hawkeyes—what happened in the first quarter is probably explained somewhere in old Socrates!

MICHIGAN STATE GETS 0 FIRST DOWNS

Notre Dame in Easy Victory

Notre Dame, Ind.—Johnny Mohardt was the bright star of the Notre Dame 48 to 0 victory in the farewell performance of 13 letter men of the squad against the Michigan Aggies here Thursday. Mohardt went into the last game with a broken nose and, playing less than a half, scored three touchdowns by sensational open field running and throw passes good for 100 yards to Kiley and Capt. Anderson, both of whom completed their college careers in a blaze of glory.

Buck Shaw played a steady game at tackle and ran his season's string of goals to 41 out of 43 trials. Wynne, Notre Dame's plunging back, drove through the Aggie line consistently during the first quarter, after which he was taken from the game. Castner rivaled Mohardt's brilliant running by many gains, including a 65-yard return of a kickoff.

		1921				
		Coach: Knute K. Rockne				
		Captain: Edward N. Anderson				
S.24	W	Kalamazoo	56-0	H		8,000
O.1	W	DePauw	57-10	H		8,000
O.8	L	Iowa (U)	7-10	A		7,500
O.15	W	Purdue	33-0	A		7,500
O.22	W	Nebraska (HC)	7-0	H		14,000
O.29	W	Indiana	28-7	N1		10,000
N.5	W	Army	28-0	A		7,000
N.8	W	Rutgers	48-0	N2		12,000
N.12	W	Haskell	42-7	H		5,000
N.19	W	Marquette	21-7	A		11,000
N.24TH	W	Michigan State	48-0	H		15,000
		(10-1-0)	375-41			105,000

N1—at Indianapolis; N2—at Polo Grounds, New York City, on Election Day

OFFICERS

Knute K. Rockne	Head Coach
Roger Kiley	Asst. Coach
Glenn Carberry	Captain
Harvey Brown	Captain-Elect
Edward Lennon	Manager

PERSONNEL

Monogram Men

Carberry	Lieb	Brown	Regan
McNulty	Oberst	Degree	Walsh
Collins	Ed Miller	Kizer	Stuhldreher
Mayl	Stange	Flinn	Thomas
Vergara	Cotton	Weibel	Layden
Crowley	Maher	Don Miller	Bergman
Connell	Cerney	Livergood	Castner

Substitutes

Logan	Roux	Cook	Feltes
Gene Murphy	Griffin	Jerry Miller	Enright
Flynn	Coughlin	Voss	Kane
Hunsinger	Mixson	Reese	Tim Murphy
	Milbauer	Harmon	

WHAT'S WHAT IN ATHLETICS.
THE BAG OPENED.

When Rockne's Fighting Irish trotted out on Cartier Field last Saturday, the eyes of the football world were focused on them in doubt. After two hours Kalamazoo knew, and the world knew, that Rockne had again accomplished the impossible, and moulded a formidable team out of untried material. Our first victim fell by a score of 46 to 0. The game was not close, but Kazoo fought hard, and made our boys display some sterling football.

To those who have waited in suspense to see the results of Rock's grilling of green players, the game was a thrilling revelation. The work of the backs was sensational. Twice after kick-offs Paul Castner raced through the entire opposition for touchdowns, once from the 90 and again from the 95 yard line. Although his work was the feature of the backfield machine, Crowley, Don Miller, Layden, Kane, Maher and Stuhldreher also brought the stands to their feet.

1922

Coach: Knute K. Rockne
Captain: Glen Carberry

S.30	W	Kalamazoo	46-0 H	5,000
O.7	W	St. Louis	26-0 H	7,000
O.14	W	Purdue	20-0 A	9,000
O.21	W	DePauw	34-7 H	5,000
O.28	W	Georgia Tech	13-3 A	20,000
N.4	W	Indiana (HC)	27-0 H	c22,000
N.11	T	Army	0-0 A	15,000
N.18	W	Butler	31-3 A	12,000
N.25	W	Carnegie Tech (S)	19-0 A	30,000
N.30TH	L	Nebraska	6-14 A	16,000
		(8-1-1)	222-27	141,000

THE INVASION OF GEORGIA.

While 1500 cheering youths, et cetera, watching the game on the Gridgraph, nearly shook the gym from its foundations, the fighting men of Notre Dame went marching through Georgia Tech at Atlanta, dazzling 20,000 Southerners with their brilliant attack and stolid defense. For the first time in the history of football a northern invader has beaten the Yellow-jackets in their own stronghold.

Early in the second quarter Tech smashed its way to the Gold and Blue 30 yard line, where Brewster kicked a field goal. Then things hummed. Barron fumbled on a kick, and Cotton recovered on Tech's 22 yard line. Castner, Crowley and Miller took the ball to the four yard line, from which Stuhldreher heaved a pass to Castner for a touchdown. Biff!!

Again in the third quarter N. D. rushed the ball to the southerners' four yard line, but Tech held and took the ball on downs. But the close of the third quarter saw the opening up of Rockne's passes, until, after gains totalling 70 yards, Miller fumbled and lost the ball on Tech's five yard line. The fighting ire of eleven northerners had now been aroused, however, and after Tech punted N. D. again marched down the field through versatile football, and Stuhldreher wriggled over the line. Castner failed to kick goal.

No one Irishman stood alone in the spotlight, though Paul Castner was the biggest man of the day. He was used more than any other member of the backfield, gained constantly through the line, outpunted his opponents, and not only hurled passes, but also caught them. Talk about triple threat players is a bit overdone, but surely not when applied to Castner.

Georgia Tech

Verne Lewellen, No. 14, hits the line in the 1922 Nebraska-Notre Dame game. Nebraska won 14–6.

OFFICERS

KNUTE K. ROCKNE, *Head Coach* HARVEY BROWN, *Captain*
GEORGE KEOGAN, *Assistant Coach* ADAM WALSH, *Captain-elect*
JAMES SWIFT, *Student Manager*

The Players

COLLINS	NOPPENBERGER	VERGARA	CROWLEY	CERNEY
CROWE	BACH	KIZER	DON MILLER	ENRIGHT
MAYL	EDGAR MILLER	REAGAN	BERGMAN	LAYDEN
MURPHY	OBERST	WALSH	CONNELL	STANGE
HUNSINGER	BROWN	REESE	MAHER	LIVERGOOD
	WEIBEL	STUHLDREHER	HOUSER	

The Reserves

LAMONT	NEWMAN	BARRY	MILBAUER	FINCH
ARNDT	GLUECKERT	EATON	ROUX	WALLACE
FARRELL	JERRY MILLER	HARRINGTON	RIGALI	LA FOLLETTE
ROACH	MAGEVNEY	HARMON	EGGERT	RIGNEY
COUGHLIN	GLYNN	COOKE	McMULLEN	SULLIVAN
McGEE	McGRATH		FRISKE	MacNAB

1923

Coach: Knute K. Rockne
Captain: Harvey Brown

S.29	W	Kalamazoo	74-0	H	10,000
O.6	W	Lombard	14-0	H	8,000
O.13	W	Army	13-0	N	c30,000
O.20	W	Princeton	25-2	A	30,000
O.27	W	Georgia Tech	35-7	H	20,000
N.3	W	Purdue (HC)	34-7	H	20,000
N.10	L	Nebraska (U)	7-14	A	30,000
N.17	W	Butler	34-7	H	10,000
N.24	W	Carnegie Tech	26-0	A	30,000
N.29TH	W	St. Louis (R)	13-0	A	9,000
	(9-1-0)		275-37		197,000

N—at Ebbets Field, Brooklyn

WHAT'S WHAT IN ATHLETICS.

BY THOMAS COMAN.

THE KAZOO OPENER.

William "Red" Maher emblazoned his name in Notre Dame's football history as one of the most deceptive and shifty halfbacks that ever played with the "Fighting" Irish, when Notre Dame easily defeated Kalamazoo College, 74-0, on Cartier field yesterday afternoon.

Kalamazoo, while not providing any great amount of competition for the Rockmen, gave them a chance to display some of the best open field running that has ever been seen on the local gridiron. Beginning with Maher's snake dance from the 10-yard line to the Kazoo goal, for which almost perfect interference was provided, the fleet Irish backs continued to set the stands wild with excitement by long end runs and line smashes that completely broke down the resistance of the opposing eleven.

Not once during the entire game did Kalamazoo team make their first downs and of the three forward passes that they tried, not one of them was completed. The Irish backfield, masters of the passing game, are almost sure destruction to an opposing aerial attack.

One of the big factors in the success of the line smashing and end running game as played yesterday by the Rockmen, was the perfect coöperation of the linesmen in holding out the opposing line, thereby protecting their backfield men on punting, off-tackle smashes and end runs. The backfield's defence of the runner was a brilliant revelation, when time after time, the opposing ends and tackles were brushed aside to clear the path for the balltoters.

Crowley, Bergman, Miller, Connell and Hauser followed the pace set by Willie Maher, in turning the game into a track meet, with long runs of 50 to 60 yards. Enright at full, scored a touchdown in the second quarter, that was the direct result of an effective line charge. Cerney, opening the game at full-back, fairly destroyed the center of the Kalamazoo line by terrific plunging.

A fumble on the one yard line cost Notre Dame another touchdown, but it left Kalamazoo in a bad way for a few minutes, because the goal post was so close to the ball that the Kazoo backs did a circle dance around the post in order to buck the line for two yards.

Another Notre Dame touchdown was momentarily impeded, when the Kazoo safety man stopped Livergood, who had made a fast, hard drive through the center of the line an dbroke away from the secondary defence for 30 yards.

The Lombard scout, who attended the game, had something to think about before the final whistle blew. The plays were reeled off so fast that it was with di....culty that he kept track of the names of the loose-jointed backs that so easily wove their way through the Kalamazoo defence.

The exceptionally fine weather brought a large crowd of spectators, estimated at 3,500. The Kalamazoo eleven were the first on the field and proceeded to run signals. A wild outburst of cheering greeted the appearance of the Notre Dame team, who followed closely upon the field after the Celery City aggregation.

* * *

Kalamazoo defended the south goal. Captain Jacobs kicked off for Kalamazoo. Maher, receiving for Notre Dame, caught the ball on his 10-yard line and following perfect interference, raced 90 yards for the first touchdown. Bergman kicked goal.

Maher went round left end for 53 yards. Bergman hit tackle for 2 yards. Ball on Kalamazoo's 7-yard line. Maher went through tackle for a touchdown. Bergman kicked the goal. Score: Notre Dame, 14; Kalamazoo, 0.

Don Miller tore off 59 yards for a touchdown. Crowley made the goal kick, but Notre Dame was off-side.

Enright went through center 25 yards and crossed the line for a touchdown. Crowley made the kick. Score: 41-0.

Crowley received the kick-off and ran it back 28 yards, and then raced around the right end for 65 yards and a score. Crowley kicked goal. Score: 48-0.

Connell and McGrath crashed the center for a total of nine yards and Livergood tore through the middle of the line for a touchdown. Hauser failed to kick goal. Score: 54-0.

WHAT'S WHAT IN ATHLETICS.
THOMAS COMAN.
AMBLING THROUGH THE ARMY.

The Notre Dame football team decisively whipped the veteran West Point team, 13 to 0, on Ebbets field, Brooklyn, N. Y., Saturday, October 13.

Opening up a whirlwind attack that mixed passes with terrific off-tackle smashes, the Hoosiers' eleven, light and fast, drove their way through the Pointers' defense for two touchdowns.

The westerners' speed and deception in the execution of twenty-seven different plays from two formations was a revelation of premier football strategy to the 30,000 people that packed the stands of Palmer stadium in wild excitement for a glimpse of the Notre Dame football team in action.

Deception was the keynote of the attack and the downfall of the great Army eleven. The Irish scored their first tally in the second quarter, on the merits of this new form of gridiron warfare developed by Rockne, when Harry Stuhldreher passed to Layden, who received the toss over on the far side of the field with not an Army player within twenty feet of him.

The fake kick formation was another powerful medium by which the Rockmen made long gains through the line, as the Cadet tackles were being drawn out, anticipating a kick.

Going East to meet the Army team that had the year previous held the Rockmen to a scoreless tie, the Fighting Irish were on the low end of the betting odds which figured the Army to win. Eastern critics had proclaimed the Pointers from up the Hudson as the greatest and most powerful team in the East for the 1923 season and minus the services of such notable performers as Castner, Lieb, Carberry and Degree and Cotton, the experts held little hope for the Hoosier eleven.

Added to the already veteran Army machine was "Tiny" Hewitt, the plunging full back who had been the mainstay of the Pitt Panthers for the 1922 season. Breidster, the 225-pound tackle was graduated from the Army line but critics were of the opinion that Ellinger would hold down that position to the approval of the dopesters.

Behind the masterly offensive power of the Irish forward wall, Layden, Crowley and Don Miller ran, passed and kicked their way through the Army ranks till they had the ball down on the Pointers' 7-yard mark and Miller dove through the line for the second touchdown. Crowley failed to make the goal kick and the score stood, 13 to 0, in favor of Notre Dame.

Harry Stuhldreher, playing at the pilot position for his second year, gave a wonderful exhibition of defensive and offensive football. Displaying the keenest judgment, he outwitted the Army eleven by putting into play the unexpected.

In Elmer Layden, of Iowa, Rockne has a superb full back, in every sense of the word a triple-threat man and whose performance against the Pointers merited the attention of the football experts who for the past ten years have followed the fortunes of Rockne's football teams.

Don Miller, the fifth of the famous Miller brothers whose very name has booked defeat for some of the best football teams in the country during the past ten years, proved to the world that he is one of the greatest running backs in the history of the sport. Quick to pick holes in the line, Miller has the remarkable ability to elude tackler after tackler and once getting into the open field, his speed overcomes any difficulties offered by the opposition's secondary defense.

Jimmy Crowley, Rockne's Ace, as he has been called by eastern writers, was another stellar performer in the triple-threat department. Teams on the defense have experienced great difficulty in tackling Crowley because of his peculiar style of running which is executed with a quick side-step and a twisting motion that whirls him out of the arms of a would-be tackler.

Joe Bach, playing his first game at tackle for the Irish proved to be a brilliant find and the logical successor of "Buck" Shaw, Notre Dame's greatest tackle. Adam Walsh was a shining light at center and was the main factor in stemming the terrific drives of the mighty Hewitt, through the line.

NOTRE DAME-NEBRASKA GAME.

The biggest upset of the season occurred when Nebraska won over Notre Dame, 14 to 7, at Lincoln, Nebraska, Saturday, November 10, before a football frenzied throng that was estimated at 30,000.

Perhaps never before in the football history of the country did the defeat of a wonder team come with such surprise and unexpectedness. It was a case of the impossible taking on the folds of reality. Hundreds of thousands of football fans throughout the country were stunned by the untimely defeat of the brilliant Notre Dame football machine.

The Rockmen journeyed west, top heavy favorites to win over Nebraska, a team that had been beaten by Illinois and tied by several of the leading teams in their own conference. But Nebraska won by the margin of a touchdown and won by playing football on that memorable afternoon as they had never played the game before.

The Corn huskers played over their heads, played for the breaks and got them. And as the tide of the gruelling battle wended their way, the moleskin warriors from the wheat plains of Nebraska went wild with fight and played the game with the savage attack that had been smoldering in their hearts for many weeks.

Having seen how the Notre Dame football machine had swept three big intersectional teams and one conference team out of its way, the westerners held out little hope of being able to check the Hoosiers' steam roller. For weeks Coach Dawson had drilled, pointed and primed his men for the great objective, when they would meet the Fighting Irish. For weeks the mentor had goaded his players with the tempting bait, the glory of defeating Notre Dame, and when the hour of the game arrived, the Husker warriors were seething with that frenzied fighting temper, that has sent many a football machine to victory over great odds.

TAMING THE TIGER.

The Notre Dame grid warriors crushed the hopes of the Princeton colorful eleven, when the Irish defeated the Jungletown fighters at Palmer stadium, 25 to 2, Saturday, October 20.

With national honors at stake, the master mind of Rockne connived a mixed running and passing attack that completely blasted the championship aspirations of the Princeton school.

The Notre Dame-Princeton game was by far the most important attraction on the grid schedule for that day. Football critics from all over the country, awaiting the outcome of the now historic conflict, debated the merits of the two teams which so ably represented the standards of football as played by two different sections of the country.

Just a week previous, K. K. Rockne made his first invasion of the East when the Irish defeated the much-heralded West Point eleven at Ebbets field, New York. The remarkable work of the Rockmen on that occasion left an indelible impression on the minds of the football critics who saw the fleet Irish backs run circles around the heavy, slow-starting Army ball-toters. Eastern sport authorities, unable to account for this seemingly miraculous performance, eagerly anticipated the meeting of the Irish and the Princeton Tigers on the following Saturday. They waited not in vain.

Uncorking the most deceptive attack ever seen on an eastern gridiron, eleven men from the Hoosier school raced and passed their way to an overwhelming victory against a team of well-schooled football warriors that represented the championship hopes for thousands of Tiger followers.

Before the game, Coach Roper and his men were not as confident of stopping the Notre Dame attack, as were the great majority of the Princeton adherents. But the Tiger gridders went into the game determined to give their best and if possible beat Notre Dame with the very weapon that was conceived by Knute Rockne.

Princeton resorted to a passing game during almost the entire struggle only to arrive at a heart-breaking finish, when Layden, playing full back for Notre Dame, intercepted a Tiger pass and raced 48 yards for the last touchdown of the game just as the final whistle sounded.

Princeton, boasting of an intercollegiate fame for brilliant comebacks when the tide of the battle was crushing them down, met keen disappointment in the Irish conflict, when from the dead standstill to which they had been beaten, only one spark of hope flared up. Crum, at right half for the Jungletown eleven, scooped up Crowley's fumble on the Princeton 5-yard line and made a beautiful run through a broken field for 76 yards, only to be stopped within 19 yards of the goal, by Frank Reese, who made a long drive for his opponent and brought him down in a spectacular tackle.

The Officers of the 1924 Varsity

KNUTE K. ROCKNE .... *Head Coach*
TOM LIEB .... *Assistant Coach*
HARTLEY ANDERSON .... *Assistant Coach*
GEORGE KEOGAN .... *Freshman Coach*
GEORGE VERGARA .... *Assistant Freshman Coach*
ADAM WALSH .... *Captain*
LEO SUTLIFFE .... *Student Manager*

The Personnel

WALSH	WEIBEL	CERNEY	ROACH	HANOUSEK
CROWLEY	BACH	CONNEL	O'BOYLE	GLUECKERT
MILLER	E. MILLER	CROWE	HEARNDON	HARRINGTON
STUHLDREHER	COLLINS	EATON	REESE	McMANMON
LAYDEN	HUNSINGER	HARMON	HOUSER	BOLAND
KIZER	LIVERGOOD	SCHERER	EDWARDS	MAXWELL
G. MILLER				McMULLEN

The Reserves

KEEFE	COHEN	ANDERBERGER	SULLIVAN	GEBHARDT
RIGALI	REIDY	CANNY	DAHMAN	McCABE
C. REILLY	BIELLI	MULLIN	FRISKE	GISH
TRUCKNER	WHALEN	McNALLY	GORMAN	DIENHART
WHILTE	EGGERT	STACK	WYNNE	ARNDT
WALLACE	E. CROWE	COUGHLIN	BROWN	MURRIN
	MAYER	PRELLI	GENIESSE	

1924

Coach: Knute K. Rockne
Captain: Adam Walsh

O.4	W	Lombard	40-0	H	8,000
O.11	W	Wabash	34-0	H	10,000
O.18	W	Army	13-7	N1	c55,000
O.25	W	Princeton	12-0	A	40,000
N.1	*W	Georgia Tech (HC)	34-3	H	c22,000
N.8	W	Wisconsin	38-3	A	28,425
N.15	W	Nebraska	34-6	H	c22,000
N.22	W	Northwestern	13-6	N2	45,000
N.29	W	Carnegie Tech	40-19	A	35,000
	(9-0-0)		258-44		265,425

ROSE BOWL

Jan.1	W	Stanford	27-10	N3	c53,000

N1—at Polo Grounds; N2—at Soldier Field; N3—at Pasadena, Calif.

*Notre Dame's 200th victory

269,000 SAW NOTRE DAME.

Team Played Before Great Throngs During Season Just Closed.

SOUTH BEND, Ind., Dec. 1.—Two hundred and sixty-nine thousand persons saw Notre Dame's football team in action during the season which it closed Saturday against Carnegie Tech at Pittsburgh, according to records compiled here.

The attendance figures for games in which Notre Dame participated are believed to set a new record for Middle Western football. Michigan during the past season played before 262,000, according to figures announced at Ann Arbor. This total was a new high mark for Conference football.

The Notre Dame-Army game at the Polo Grounds in New York drew the largest crowd—55,000—of all the games in which Coach Rockne's team shared honors.

Notre Dame	40
Carnegie Tech.	19

The season of 1924 will go down in the annals of football as one of upsets and surprising consequences. Until the Tech victory, Notre Dame was undefeated but the football world feared for the outcome of Notre Dame's final game. However, the four Horsemen treated the 35,000 fans to such an exhibition of dazzling football that there remained no doubt as to which was the nations greatest football team.

Rockne, following the custom of preceding games, sent in his shock team consisting of Crowe and Eaton, ends; McMullen and McManmon tackles; Glueckert and Hanousek, guards; Maxwell at center; the backfield included Edward's, O'Boyle, Connell and Livergood. But the Rockmen were confronted with a team of tearing, smearing, fighting Tartans who refused to be subdued until Kristoff blocked a punt and raced thirty-five yards for a touchdown. At this point, Rock stood up and signalled to Walsh to lead his team on the field. Once the regulars got warmed up there was no doubt as to the outcome, though the battlers of Carnegie Tech were by no means easily tamed.

Layden was unable to play because of an injury but Livergood and Cerney, alternating at fullback, played a game which will be long remembered. Don Miller went over for the first touch-down on a pass from his room-mate Stuhldreher; Cerney, who had replaced Livergood, was the next to counter, and the half ended with the score tied at 13-13.

In the second half the Tartan defense weakened and Livergood went over for two touch-downs; Crowley and Stuhldreher added each another one to make the score tally unanimous in the backfield. Bede for Carnegie Tech, added a third touch-down against the Notre Dame "shock troops," who had relieved the regulars.

In the Tech game, Notre Dame successfully completed twelve consecutive passes, a new world's record.

NOTRE DAME'S 200th VICTORY

NOTRE DAME IS 34 TO 3 VICTOR

Georgia Tech Shows Fight Against Odds.

SOUTH BEND, Ind., Nov. 1.—The Golden Tornado of Georgia Tech unleashed all its fury against the University of Notre Dame in their intersectional gridiron classic, but the Rocknemen turned it back and for the third successive year defeated the southerners today by a score of 34 to 3.

Tech took defeat in glory and left the name of Douglas Wycoff, its driving fullback emblazoned on the football roll in Notre Dame's archives. Wycoff's tearing, running, plunging attacks, always in the face of stubborn resistance was considered the outstanding individual performance of the game. The final gun robbed him of a possible sensational climax when, after racing forty-seven yards to Notre Dame's one-yard line, time was called.

Coach Knute K. Rockne started his second string against the Georgians. After a few moments had elapsed Wycoff tore off forty yards in a pretty scamper through the line. Williams, left half, after working the ball to Notre Dame's 42-yard line, booted a beautiful drop kick for his team mates' only score.

The Notre Dame regulars opened the second quarter and then the superiority of Rockne's team exerted itself. Right half Don Miller, receiving a pass from Crowley, took it over for Notre Dame's first touchdown. Layden placed it behind Tech's goal for Rockne's second score, shortly after which the second team again took the field.

Reprinted with permission from the **Cleveland Plain Dealer**

GRANTLAND RICE
(New York Times.)

POLO GROUNDS, New York, October 18, 1924.—Outlined against a blue, gray October sky the Four Horsemen rode again.

In dramatic lore they are known as famine, pestilence, destruction and death. These are only aliases. Their real names are: Stuhldreher, Miller, Crowley and Layden. They formed the crest of the South Bend cyclone before which another fighting Army team was swept over the precipice at the Polo Grounds this afternoon as 55,000 spectators peered down upon the bewildering panorama spread out upon the green plain below.

A cyclone can't be snared. It may be surrounded but somewhere it breaks through to keep on going. When the cyclone starts from South Bend where the candle lights still gleam through the Indiana sycamores those in the way must take to the storm cellars at top speed. The cyclone struck again as Notre Dame beat the Army 13 to 7 with a set of backfield stars that ripped and rushed through a strong Army defense with more speed and power than the warring Cadets could meet.

Notre Dame won its eighth game in eleven starts through the driving power of one of the greatest backfields that ever churned up the turf of any gridiron in any football age. Brilliant backfields may come and go but in Stuhldreher, Miller, Crowley and Layden, covered by a fast and charging line Notre Dame can take its place in front of the field.

Coach McEwan sent one of his finest teams into action, an aggressive organization that fought to the last play around the first rim of darkness, but when Rockne rushed his four horsemen to the track they rode down everything in sight.

It was in that 1400 gray clad cadets pleaded for the Army line to hold. The Army line was giving all it had but when a tank tears in with the speed of a motorcycle, what chance had flesh and blood to hold? The Army had its share of stars in action, such stars as Garbisch, Farwick, Wilson, Wood, Elinger and many others, but they were up against four whirlwind backs who picked up top speed from the first step as they swept through scant openings to slip on by the secondary defense. The Army had great backs in Wilson and Wood, but the Army had no such quartet who seemed to carry the mixed blood of the tiger and the antelope.

Rockne's light and tottering line was just about as tottering as the Rock of Gibraltar. It was something more than a match for the Army's great set of forwards who had earned their fame before, yet it was not until the second period that the first big thrill of the afternoon set the great crowd into a cheering whirl and brought about the wild flutter of flags that are thrown to the wind in exciting moments. At the game's start, Rockne sent in almost entirely the second string cast. The Army got the jump and began to play most of the football. It was the Army attack that made three first downs before Notre Dame had caught its stride.

The South Bend cyclone opened like a zephyr and then, in the wake of a sudden cheer, out rushed Stuhldreher, Miller, Crowley and Layden, the four star backs who helped best the Army a year ago. Things were to be a trifle different now. After a short opening flurry in the second period the cloud in the west at this point was no larger than a football. There was no sign of a tornado starting, but it happened to be at just this spot that Stuhldreher decided to put on his attack and begin the long and dusky hike.

On the first play the fleet Crowley peeled off 15 yards and the cloud from the west was now beginning to show signs of lightning and thunder. The fleet, powerful Layden got six yards more and then Don Miller added 10. A forward pass from Stuhldreher to Crowley added 12 yards and a moment later Don Miller ran 20 yards around the Army's right wing. He was on his way to glory when Wilson, hurtling across the right of way, nailed him on the 10 yard line and threw him out of bounds.

Crowley, Miller and Layden—Miller, Layden and Crowley—one or the other, ripping and crashing through as the Army defense threw everything it had in the way to stop this wild charge that had now come 70 yards. Crowley and Layden added five yards more and then on a split play Layden went 10 yards across the line as if he had just been fired from the black mouth of a Howitzer.

Speed Beat West Point.

It was speed that beat the Army, speed plus interference. And when a back such as Harry Wilson finds few chances to get started you figure upon the defensive strength that is barricading the road. Wilson is one of the hardest backs in the game to suppress, but he found few chances yesterday to show his broken field ability. You can't run through a broken field until you get there.

One strong feature of the Army play was its head long battle against heavy odds. Even when Notre Dame had scored two touchdowns and was well on its way to a third, the army fought on with fine spirit, until the touchdown chance came at last, and when this chance came in the fourth quarter coach McEwan had the play ready for the final march across the line.

The Army has a better team than it had last year. So has Notre Dame. We doubt that any team in the country could have beaten Rockne's yesterday afternoon, east or west. It was a great football team brilliantly directed, a team of speed, power and team play. The Army has no cause for gloom over its showing. It played first class football against more speed than it could match.

Those who have tackled a cyclone can understand.

Stuhldreher, Layden, Crowley, Miller.

NOTRE DAME RACES TO 27-10 VICTORY

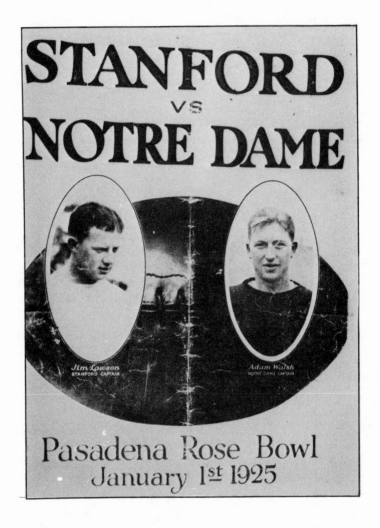

1925 ROSE BOWL — Notre Dame 27, Stanford 10				
Notre Dame 0		13	7	7 — 27
Stanford 3		0	7	0 — 10
Attendance: 53,000				

Team	Score S-ND	Qtr.	*Time Left	Play
Stanford	3-0	1	8:00	Cuddeback 27 FG
ND	3-6	2	13:30	Layden 3 run (Crowley kick failed)
ND	3-13	2	8:00	Layden 78 interception (Crowley kick)
ND	3-20	3	5:00	Hunsinger 20 fumble return (Crowley kick)
Stanford	10-20	3	1:00	Shipkey 7 pass from Walker (Cuddeback kick)
ND	10-27	4	0:30	Layden 70 interception (Crowley kick)

*Time approximate

STANFORD UNABLE TO HALT HORSEMEN

Huge Western Linesmen Outcharge Visitors Responsible For Scoring.

BUT NOTRE DAME LIVES UP TO RECORD

Great Middle West College Team Plays Great Game of Football.

Pasadena Rose Bowl, Cal., Jan. 1.— (By The Associated Press).—A typhoon of speed swirled out of South Bend, Ind., and landed here today, swamping Stanford University's football team under a 27 to 10 score. Notre Dame had the speed.

The famous "four horsemen" were pitted against Ernie Nevers, of Stanford and the gallant Cardinal, although he covered himself and his Alma Mater with glory, could not offset their repeated charges.

Rose Bowle is Packed.

At that, the hugh red-shirted Stanfords out-charged the squat blue jerseyed linemen of Notre Dame and it was owing to their work that the Palo Alto institution was able to register ten points in the face of the fierce galloping of the cavalry of the Indianians.

Notre Dame added to its list of honors that of having scored the first victory for the East in four intersectional games played on the Pacific coast this season.

For the first time in a number of years the Rose Bowl was packed to capacity and it was estimated that upwards of 52,000 watched the contest.

At every moment throughout the four periods the Notre Dame men lived up to their reputation for speed in foot and head.

The start was inauspicious for the easterners. Coach Rockne sent in his second string men to open the fight, but Stanford, strong, aggressive and beefy, shoved them steadily down field. Then Rockne called on his stars and the real battle was on. Stanford's errors, which might not have been very costly against other opponents, were fatal when pulled in the face of Notre Dame. When the Cardinal foot slipped, the South Bend hard was there to take it.

Stanford Starts Scoring.

Stanford started the scoring by a placement kick off Cuddeback's toe in the first period.

In the second period for the only time during the game, Notre Dame was able to gain consistently through the big Red line. A prolonged drive ended when Layden scored through left guard three yards to a touchdown.

A few minutes later, Layden came to the front again, pulled Never's pass out of the air and sprinted seventy yards for the second South Bend touchdown. Crowley converted it. In the third period occurred one of Stanford's expensive errors. Solomon fumbled a punt on his own 20-yard line. He stooped to recover when he might have played safely, falling on the ball. Huntsinger swooped down on him, shoved Solomon aside, grabbed the pigskin and ran unopposed to a touchdown. Crowley again converted.

Stanford Gets Touchdown.

Later in the period, Notre Dame, defying rule and fate, boldly attempted a forward pass within its 20-yard line, and Nevers pulled it down. Then followed a series of line bucks, nearly all of them featuring the hefty Nevers, who savagely shoved, heaved and ground his way to Notre Dame's eight yard line.

The Horsemen from the East were set for another back, but it did not come. Walker passed over the line to Ted Shipkey, and Stanford chalked up a touchdown. Cuddeback kicked goal for extra point. That ended Stanford's scoring.

In the fourth period Stanford had another opportunity. An intercepted forward pass on Notre Dame's 35-yard line put the ball in Baker's hands.

Nevers was called on and in a succession of plunges carried the sphere to Notre Dame's 8 inch line. The stands thought it was a touchdown for Stanford, but when Referee Thorpe unscrambled the heap of players he found the goal mark had not been crossed.

Layden to Front Again.

The last scoring play of the contest gave Layden another chance to show his speed. He intercepted a pass from Nevers' hands and led a chase all the way for thirty-five yards across the Stanford chalk mark. Crowley's toe did the rest.

The four horsemen cantered, trotted and galloped with all the abandon expected of them. Harry Stuhldreher's play was handicapped when he twisted his left ankle early in the opening period and it slowed up his play during the remainder of the game although at no moment did it appear that any Cardinal back could match any South Bend backfield man in point of speed.

Layden and Crowley were the most effective carriers for Notre Dame. Don Miller performed well, but his mark did not quite reach the high mark set by his teammates.

Nevers Shines Brilliantly.

No one of the field today performed more brilliantly than the blonde giant fullback, Nevers, who was subjected to an unmerciful beating. Two broken ankles early in the season prevented Nevers getting into as good shape as his teammates, and today saw him play his first full game in more than a year.

Except on the one occasion when he halted on the eight inch line, the Notre Dame line was unable to halt the terrific smashes that carried the force of every ounce of his 200 pounds.

Statistics Favor Loses.

Rockne made frequent substitutions at guard and tackle, the points at which the Stanford attacks were centered. The statistics of the game nearly all favor the losers. Stanford gained 164 yards from scrimmage as compared with Notre Dame's 134. The Cardinals registered seventeen first downs, ten more than the South Benders. Stanford completed twelve out of seventeen attempted forward passes and Notre Dame three out of seven. The horsemen's aerial attack resulted in a gain of forty-eight while the Cardinals gained 146 yards.

Rockne's men were penalized four times for a total of thirty yards while a single fifteen yard penalty was inflicted against Stanford. Notre Dame made one fumble, by Harry Stuhldreher on the first play and it was the only bobble made by Notre Dame players, while three misplays were registered by Pop Warner's charges. Notre Dame intercepted five forwarded passes and Stanford two.

The lineup and summary:

Notre Dame		Stanford
Crowe	le	T. Shipkey
Boland	lt	H. Shipkey
Hanousek	lg	Swan
Maxwell	c	Baker
Glueckert	rg	Neill
McManmen	rt	Johnson
Eaton	re	Lawson
Scharer	qb	Solomon
O'Boyle	lhb	Cuddeback
Hearndon	rhb	Walker
Cerney	fb	Nevers

Score by periods:

Notre Dame	0	13	7	7—27	
Stanford	3	0	7	0—10	

Notre Dame scoring: Touchdowns, Layden (sub for Cerney), 3; Huntzinger (sub for Eaton); points from try after touchdown, Crowley, 3.

Stanford scoring: Touchdowns, T. Shipkey; points from try after touchdown, Cuddeback; field goal, Cuddeback.

Referee, Thorpe, Columbia; umpire, Quigley, Kansas; head linesman Eckersall, Chicago; field judge, Morris, Washington; time of periods, 15 minutes each.

1925

Coach: Knute K. Rockne
Captain: Clem Crowe

S.26	W	Baylor (R)	41-0	H	13,000	
O.3	W	Lombard	69-0	H	10,000	
O.10	W	Beloit	19-3	H	10,000	
O.17	L	Army	0-27	YS	c65,000	
O.24	W	Minnesota	19-7	A	c12,000	
O.31	W	Georgia Tech (R)	13-0	A	12,000	
N.7	T	Penn State (R)	0-0	A	c20,000	
N.14	W	Carnegie Tech (HC)	26-0	H	c27,000	
N.21	W	Northwestern	13-10	H	c27,000	
N.26TH	L	Nebraska (U)	0-17	A	c45,000	
		(7-2-1)	200-64		278,000	

FOOTBALL PROGRAM

Price Twenty-Five Cents

Notre Dame vs. Northwestern
November 21 at Cartier Field

NOTRE DAME COMES BACK TO OUTSCORE NORTHWESTERN TEAM

South Bend, Ind., November 21.—(Associated Press.)—Overcoming in ten minutes a lead of ten points amassed against it in the first half, Notre Dame today defeated Northwestern 13 to 10. Two downfield marches at the start of the third quarter netted the pair of touchdowns which erased the visitors' margin and brought victory.

Both touchdowns were the result of straight football, without a single forward pass to interrupt the steady punch of smashes and the sweep of wide end runs with which the Rockne-men earned their conquest.

The first half of the game had given Northwestern a substantial lead. Lewis kicked a goal from placement at thirty-five yards in the opening quarter and Captain Tim Lowry, Purple center, grabbed Edwards's fumble in the second period and scrambled eight yards across the Notre Dame goal for a touchdown, to which Lewis added the extra point. Virtually all the play in the half was on Notre Dame's half of the gridiron.

ROCKNE'S FAMOUS HALFTIME SPEECH "FIGHTING IRISH"

80,000 See Army Beat Notre Dame

By HARRY CROSS

An Army football team which is not only powerful but also smart and alert defeated Notre Dame at the Yankee Stadium yesterday afternoon, by a score of 27 to 0, to the cheers of 80,000 spectators, New York's greatest football gathering. West Point has been waiting a good long time for a chance like this, for Rockne's gridiron pupils have handed the Cadets many an unhappy afternoon in by-gone years.

In the vast gathering which was banked on all sides of the stadium gridiron were thousands who had come expecting to see Notre Dame take away another victory. The reputation of Rockne and his Notre Dame elevens has aroused interest in college football among spectators who have never had the opportunity to watch it before.

But Rockne did not have one of his great teams this time. He can hardly be expected to have them all the time. West Point has a superior eleven, one which promises to give a great account of itself when it clashes with the Navy at the season's end.

The Cadets scored four touchdowns, two in the second period and two in the fourth. The line of soldiers rode rough shod over the Notre Dame wall of forwards throughout the game, outplaying them so thoroughly that West Pointers were charging through the line upsetting Notre Dame backs before they could get started.

Rockne groped about all afternoon trying to find some surprise to spring on the Cadets but he also found them watchful. He rushed in reserves by the score. He shuffled up his squad like a pack of cards and hoped that at some time or another he might draw another four of a kind as he held last year with his talented Four Horsemen and other quartets which have carried his fame over many a football field.

Army had the satisfaction of scoring the first touchdown on speedy, businesslike football tactics. As the linemen opened great gaps in the Notre Dame forwards, Wilson, Yoemans at quarter and Hewitt, who had succeeded Buell, worked the ball down to the four yard line where big Jack Smith, the Hoosier left guard, unceremoniously shoved Wilson out of bounds. When the teams lined up on the four-yard mark, Wilson, taking the ball faked his run toward Notre Dame's right end, which was in

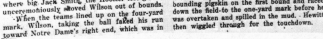

the path to the goal posts. The whole Notre Dame line leaned to that direction when Wilson hurled himself through a big hole which Sprague and Captain Baxter had made for him.

The unusual crowd had looked upon the proceeding up to this point with much surprise. They had expected the Hoosiers to turn loose volleys of aerial passes and had expected evidences of the close compact team work for which the Notre Dame elevens have ever been noted.

There were only a handful of Cadets at the game, just a few score who were fortunate to get the week-end away from the Point. There were, however, many army officers there and they had plenty of their friends with them. All the Notre Dame alumni in the east enlisted their friends, but they could make little impression with their enthusiasm compared with the demonstration the Army folks started after the first touchdown and continued throughout the game.

There was some hard grueling scrimmaging in the third period. The players on both teams got many hard knocks which necessitated many delays and brought the rubbers and trainers scurrying from the side lines with their water buckets. The Army tackling was quick and decisive and the Notre Dame tackling was heavy but slow.

Notre Dame made frantic efforts to get an overhead attack going in the fourth period. O'Boyle and Scharer was one combination which tried in vain, and Roach and Voedisch was another. The alert Army ends and secondary defense were usually outguessing the Hoosiers in their efforts to execute their forward passes.

Early in that fourth period Hewitt's attempt to kick was thwarted by Jack Smith, who blocked the kick and recovered the ball. Prelli jammed through the Army line for a couple of yards, but another attempted forward pass failed miserably, the Cadet line smashing through to upset the combination. O'Boyle was tired again and Roach came back into the game. When he attempted to punt, Saunders, Army's right tackle, broke through, blocked the kick, and Born, who was at his side, clutched the bounding pigskin on the first bound and raced down the field to the one-yard mark before he was overtaken and spilled in the mud. Hewitt then wiggled through for the touchdown.

Gray's Mighty Toe Stops Rock's Clan in Drizzle of Rain

STATE COLLEGE, Pa.—Butchered by the Army in its first invasion of the East, the Lochinvars of Notre Dame in the vestments of football came back to the terrain of the effete East today to battle a scoreless tie with the cubs of the famed and mythical Lion of Old Nittany.

Twenty-two thousand sat through a drizzle and downpour that changed the velvet turf of Beaver Field into a morass and quagmire to see Penn State, a fighting clan, dauntless in spirit, if unsuccessful in quest, fight the foes from the land of the Hoosier to a stalemate. Eleven years ago the College that sits atop that hill in South Bend sent its warriors here to overthrow and spoil a triumphant season of the Blue and White. Since that day the defeat has rankled in the hearts of the Lions' cubs, the iron has lodged in the souls of the gladiators who bear her colors into the arena each season.

Determined to thwart this second invasion of Center County, whose battling youngsters, fighting in the strength of an unconquerable spirit, went out on the rain-soaked battlefield and fought with every inch of their being, every ounce of their might. No moral victories are ever hailed with jubilation and glee by the stalwarts who battle for Bezdek and their alma mater, but today's renewal of that ancient feud might well be viewed in such a light.

Two golden opportunities to score came one to each eleven, and the fight and the power of the rival stopped the conquest.

Third Period a Thriller.

Notre Dame held the leash the greater part of the time, but once aroused and Penn State could not be downed or forced to surrender or capitulate.

The Aerial Game.

Flanagan, a titan on the offense, swept into the line and was spilled nine yards from the line of scrimmage. The ball rested on State's sixteen-yard line. Enright, on a split play, shot ahead for three yards more. A first down on the thirteen-yard line came now, the West to bask in glory by a splendid achievement. The Hoosiers elected to go into the air, hoping that victory would wing its flight out of the ozone.

Backward went Edwards, a lanky Hoosier,

reminiscent of Slim Harris of the Mackmen. As the ball came to him the Indianan dropped back several yards to throw a forward pass. He swept the field with his eyes, selected his eligible man, but tarried too long. Through the line came a thundering end, Weston of the Lions. He bore down upon Edwards like a Hussar in a charge. He chased the Hoosier backward, and as Edwards drew back his arm to fling the cowskin, Weston tore into him, flung his arms around the Notre Dame man's knees. Down he went in the slime and muck of a morass. Twenty yards had Notre Dame lost on this thrilling feat by Weston.

As the State cohorts broke into a roar that resounded over the hills tinged with autumn foliage, their plaudits died in a groan. For as Edwards tried to forward pass again to Voedisch an impetuous State man flung himself at the receiver, roughing him and a penalty resulted. It was the Hoosiers' ball at the point where the error was committed, a first down and only eight yards for a touchdown.

Then came that fighting spirit of the Lions' whelps to throttle the invader in one of the finest defensive fights that ever Beaver Field has known. Flanagan swerved toward the end to collide with a horde of State tacklers. Two yards gained now. Enright tried to mob the center. A scant two yards more his reward.

Back to the thirteen-yard mark roamed Enright, before him knelt a colleague to hold the ball for a placement kick. The ball came back perfectly, the toe met the cowskin with a resounding thump, but the oval veered away. Notre Dame's golden opportunity was lost.

One Philadelphian cloaked himself in glory. He was Joe Boland, the behemoth at tackle, who once made history at Catholic High in the Quaker City.

Flanagan, a mighty son of Texas, also shone resplendently in the Hoosier attack.

Rockne uncovered one of the finest ends that we have seen this season. His name is Voedisch, and he became a combatant when Captain Crowe was injured so badly that he was withdrawn early in fray. The field leader was not missed, his substitute covering the wing in exemplary fashion.

Thomas F. Hearden
Eugene H. Edwards
Captains

John P. Smith
Capt. Elect

Peter A. Bee	John E. Hogan	Joseph S. Morrissey
Joseph F. Benda	Richard T. Hogan	Timothy A. Moynihan
Arthur B. Boeringer	Bernard J. Hugger	Edward J. Murphy
Joseph M. Boland	James Hurlburt	George P. Murrin
James M. Brady	William A. Hurley	Joseph H. Nash
James F. Bray	William B. Jones	John A. Niemiec
Francis F. Brown	William J. Judge	Harrington J. Noon
John W. Carberry	Francis J. Keefe	Harry W. O'Boyle
John E. Chevigney	Marshall F. Kizer	Francis A. O'Toole
George F. Cogan	Dave Krembs	Arthur E. Parisien
Frederick L. Collins	John B. Law	Robert E. Plummer
Edmund A. Collins	George E. Leppig	Robert K. Polley
John T. Colrick	Henry G. Le Strange	John Poliskey
John J. Corcoran	Brendon V. McAdams	James T. Quinn
Francis A. Crowe	Harold T. McCabe	Thomas J. Qualters
Bernard P. Crowley	Francis P. McCarthy	John W. Roach
Raymond J. Dahman	Charles B. McDermott	Charles C. Riley
John C. Doarn	John E. McGrath	Joseph Reedy
Richard J. Doyle	Charles J. McKinney	Anthony J. Ransavage
John A. Dudas	John V. McManmon	John W. Reilly
Paul Dunculovic	Vincent A. McNally	Hebert Schulz
A. Wortham Duperier	John McSorley, Jr.	William V. Snell
John J. Elder	Raymond C. Marelli	Robert E. Shields
Raymond D. Ernst	Francis G. Mayer	Edwin A. Stein
Christie J. Flanagan	Joseph W. Maxwell	Harry M. Vezie
William G. Fitzpatrick	Francis M. Metrailer	John J. Wallace
John Frederick	Frederick C. Miller	Charles F. Walsh
Robert L. Gavin	Daniel A. Moore	Elmer T. Weibel
Albert J. Gebert		Elmer B. Wynne

1926

Coach: Knute K. Rockne
Co-Captains: Eugene Edwards and Thomas Hearden

O.2	W	Beloit	77-0	H	8,000
O.9	W	Minnesota	20-7	A	c48,648
O.16	W	Penn State (R)	28-0	H	18,000
O.23	W	Northwestern	6-0	A	c41,000
O.30	W	Georgia Tech (R)	12-0	H	11,000
N.6	W	Indiana	26-0	H	20,000
N.13	W	Army	7-0	YS	c63,029
N.20	W	Drake (HC) (S)	21-0	H	20,000
N.27	L	Carnegie Tech (U)	0-19	A	c45,000
D.4	W	So. Calif. (2:00)	13-12	A	c74,378
	(9-1-0)		210-38		349,055

Rockne's Team Saves Game With Four Minutes To Play

Trailing 7 to 12, South Benders Score on Two Forward Passes by Parisien, Last of Four Quarterbacks to Direct Hoosiers—Kaer Forced Out

Los Angeles Coliseum, Cal., Dec. 4.—(AP.)—Speed on the breaks, headwork in the pinches, ability to kick goal when it was needed and baffling strategy gave the Notre Dame football team a 13 to 12 victory over Southern California here today.

The Trojans lost the first of the five intersectional games they have played primarily because there apparently was not a single toe that could kick the extra goal point after touchdown.

Ball Tipped Over.

Notre Dame failed to do this once, but made good on its other try. An unstretched Trojan hand, there in an attempt to block the kick, tipped the pigskin just enough to send it over the bar.

The South Bend, Ind., team came to Troy's backyard smarting under a defeat at the hands of Carnegie Tech last week. It headed for home tonight with the mythical title of second place national champion.

With the exception of the last four minutes of play the battle was a grim scramble between two evenly matched football machine skeyed up to near perfect playing pitch. There was one fumble, that by Hearndon of Notre Dame, but he recovered the ball himself.

The last four minutes, with twilight falling and Parisien's generalship functioning in high, brought the South Benders to the top of their form and in that brief period of action Southern California went down before a momentarily superior football aggregation.

Parisien Turns Tide.

Rockne had pulled his last quarterback out of the reserve list when he sent Parisien to do the trick of victory. Riley, Edwards and McNally had preceded him and har shone but Parisien was dazzling. He shot a 25-yard pass to Niemic on Southern California's 28-yard line. Then his unerring hand heaved another to Leppig, who went over for the touchdown that won.

Morton Kaer, Troy's great groundgainer, lived up to his reputation for long advances, but he went out of the game in the third period after a hard tackle out of bounds.

The lineup

Notre Dame		U. S. C.
Voedisch	le	Badgro
Miller	lt	Hibbs
J. Smith	lg	Taylor
Boeringer	c	Cravath (c)
Mayer	rt	Gorrell
McManmon	rg	Cox
Maxwell	re	Behrendt
Riley	qb	Kaer
Niemic	lh	Drury
Dahman	rh	L. Thomas
Wynne	fb	Larenta

Score by periods
Notre Dame ...... 0 7 0 6—13
U. S. C. ...... 0 6 0 6—12

Notre Dame scoring touchdowns, Riley, Leppig (sub for Mayer.) Points from try after touchdown, O'Boyle.

U. S. C. scoring: touchdown, Kaer, William (sub for Kaer.)

Officials: referee, Birch, Earlham; umpire, McCord, Illinois; head linesman, Wyatt, Missouri; field judge, Badenoch, Chicago.

Outplayed All The Way, Notre Dame Bows To Carnegie Tech Warriors 19-0

Pittsburgh Team Rips Way To Decisive Win

Rockne's Team Held On One-Half Yard Line—Donohue Stars in Winners' Running Attack—Harpster Kicks Two Field Goals

Forbes Field, Pittsburgh, Pa., Nov. 27.—(AP.)—Notre Dame bowed in defeat on the gridiron here today, Carnegie Tech winning from the South Bend outfit, 10 to 0, in one of the most startling upsets of the football season.

Carnegie outplayed the visitors from start to finish. The Tartans ripped through the Notre Dame line at will and time and again broke up the Rockne men's passes. In the final period, Notre Dame advanced to within one half yard of the Carnegie goal line, only to lose the ball on downs.

Horsemen Outclassed.

The second edition of Rockne's famous "Four Horsemen" of 1924, was completely outclassed in every department of play by the Skibos. Notre Dame conquered eight previous opponents this season, including Army, while Carnegie tasted defeat at the hands of New York University and Washington and Jefferson.

Chrissy Flanagan, flashy Notre Dame halfback, who rose to great heights with a long run to beat the Army, was stopped by Carnegie every time he carried the ball or attempted to turn the tide with forward passes. Hearden, his mate, bore the brunt of what little opposition was offered by the Rocknemen.

Threaten But Once.

Only once did the Rockne clan threaten the Carnegie goal. That was in the fourth period, when the visitors yard line, with the aid of a forward worked the ball to the Skibos' one half pass. Carnegie's defense braced and held Notre Dame for downs.

Little Bill Donohue, fleet halfback of the Skibos, circled Notre Dame's terminals and battered the line almost at will. Sharing honors with him was Letzelter, Mefort and Harpster. The latter drop kicked two beautiful field goals in the third period.

Statistics of the battle showed that Carnegie outplayed the Rockneman in all departments. Carnegie made eleven first downs against six for Notre Dame. Four Carnegie forward passes completed out of ten tries netted 54 yards. Notre Dame succeeded four times in the air out of 18 attempts gaining 52 yards.

Punting Duel

The first period resolved itself into a punting duel after Carnegie blocked a punt and downed the ball on Notre Dame's 30-yard stripe. Forward passing by both teams met with little success.

Notre Dame's first string men—Flanagan, O'Boyle, Hearden, et al—were sent in at the start of the second period.

The line was unable to stem the rushes of the Skibos' backfield and the ball was soon in Notre Dame's territory. After a pass, Harpster to Donohoe, had netted 18 yards, the latter ran wide around left end for a touchdown. Letzelter failed to kick goal.

Benefitted by a break, when Mefort blocked a punt and recovered the ball on Notre Dame's 18, Letzelter carried the ball over for another touchdown. He added the extra point.

The third period had just begun, when Yoder intercepted a Notre Dame pass on the latter's 33-yard line. On the next play, Harpster drop-kicked a field goal from the 38. Carnegie kicked to Notre Dame, which lost the ball on a fumble on its own 30. Harpster stepped back 5 yards and drop-kicked another field goal.

Battling with their backs against the wall, the Rocknemen worked the ball to the Carnegie one-half-yard line in the final period, only to be repulsed.

Summary:

Carnegie Tech.		Notre Dame.
Mefort	le	Walsh
Mielziner	lt	Hogan
Cowan	lg	Leppig
Manby	c	Frederick
Anderson	rg	Mariellie
Yoder	rt	Poliski
Sweet	re	Benda
Harpster	qb	Riley
Donohoe	lhb	Nemic
Goodwin	rhb	Dahlman
Letzelter	fb	Wynne

Score by periods:
Carnegie Tech. ...... 0 13 6 0—19

Carnegie scoring: Touchdowns, Donohoe, Letzelter; point after touchdown, Letzelter (placement); field goals, Harpster 2 (drop kicks); officials: Referee, O'Brien (Tufts); umpire, Daugherty (W. and J.); linesman, Lipski (Chicago); field judge, Lambert (Ohio State).

NOTRE DAME 1927 FOOTBALL SQUAD

ROCKNE TEACHING BABE RUTH ABOUT FOOTBALL

		1927			
		Coach: Knute K. Rockne			
		Captain: John P. Smith			
O.1	W	Coe (R)	28-7	H	10,000
O.8	W	Detroit	20-0	A	c28,000
O.15	W	Navy	19-6	N1	45,101
O.22	W	Indiana	19-6	A	16,000
O.29	W	Georgia Tech	26-7	H	17,000
N.5	T	Minn. (S) (1:00-M)	7-7	1'	25,000
N.12	I	Army	0-18	YS	c65,678
N.19	W	Drake	32-0	A	8,412
N.26	W	So. California	7-6	N2	*c120,000
		(7-1-1)	158-57		335,191

*Paid attendance: 99,573
N1—at Baltimore; N2—at Soldier Field

Notre Dame 19
Navy - - 6

They used to call him General Rockne, but it's Admiral Rockne from now on. Admiral Rockne brought his small fleet of Cruisers to Baltimore, the home port of the Navy, and despite the presence of many of Uncle Sam's greatest strategists succeeded in out-maneuvering the Naval Fleet.

The contest was more even than the score indicates. The midshipmen were leading the Fighting Irish by a score of 6 to 0 at the end of the first half, and at no time was Notre Dame absolutely sure of victory.

Rock started the second team, and the future admirals promptly pushed over a touchdown after a splendid march from midfield. The regulars were then pressed into action, but the Navy held them in check for the rest of the half.

In the third quarter Frederick broke through the line, blocked the kick, and cut down Lloyd as the latter started to recover the ball which was bounding back down the field. The ever alert Chile Walsh scooped up the ball, and raced across the goal line, tying the score.

Chris Flanagan then started to function, and ran the Navy ends ragged bringing the ball to the Navy's goal line. Charley Riley made a few mysterious passes with the ball; finally taking it himself and scooting around right end for Notre Dame's second score.

Chris retired from the game and Niemiec replaced him. The midshipmen were surprised to find that Niemiec was the equal of Flanagan and had the same peculiar knack of shaking off ambitious tacklers and sprinting for long gains. Late in the fourth quarter he passed thirty yards to Chile Walsh, and on the next play smashed through tackle for the last Irish touchdown of the day.

The battle was a magnificent clash, courageously fought between two evenly matched elevens. Both teams were possessed of powerful lines and strong backfields. Both were well fortified with practically the same type of offense, the aerial game and wide flank sweeps.

Riley's cunning and the well drilled Notre Dame team were too much for the Navy, and they were at sea most of the afternoon. Navy backs found the Notre Dame line impenetrable; and with Miller, Smith, Fredericks and Poliskey breaking through on defense the Navy backs had a busy afternoon.

Notre Dame was far superior to the Navy in every department of the game and illustrated the old maxim that "a good team makes its own breaks." There was precision in Notre Dame's attack. Eleven men moved as one, and the blocking and tackling was extremely accurate.

The game was hard fought but clean from the kickoff to the last play. This was Notre Dame's first game with the Naval Academy, and Irish supporters are confident that the same cordial relations that have existed between the Army and Notre Dame will exist with the other branch of the service.

Notre Dame 7
Minnesota 7

Irish eyes were smiling as the last few minutes of the final quarter ticked away. Notre Dame was in the lead, 7 to 0; and the Irish had just held Minnesota for downs in the shadow of the Irish goal posts. Niemiec dropped back to punt formation; and Riley called a line play to use up the remaining time which he understood from the officials to be 15 seconds. The backfield misunderstood the signals, and the ball was lobbed halfway between the center and Niemiec. Before Niemiec had a chance to dart up and get it, Nagurski the Gopher guard, broke through and recovered the ball on the fifteen yard line.

Three times the "Northern Thunderbolt" Joesting, smashed the Irish line, and three times he was repulsed for no gain. On the fourth down, he drifted back and hurled a forward pass. Out of the dusk came the ball; hurled from Notre Dame's 22-yard line, it sped with bullet-like swiftness into the arms of Walsh, the Gopher right end. Doc Spears then inserted Pharmer, who promptly booted the ball between the uprights to give Minnesota a tie.

From the kickoff to the last play, there was no let-up in this thrill-packed battle. The old guard was unanimous in saying that it was the most spectacular football game ever staged on historic Cartier Field.

Notre Dame scored in the first quarter when the Minnesota safety man fumbled a punt which was recovered by Captain "Clipper" Smith. On the next play Niemiec scooted 18 yards around right end for a touchdown and then added the extra point.

From this point until Minnesota scored, the two teams battled up and down the chalk lined field on even terms. Neither team could gain consistently through the line. Notre Dame stopped Joesting, and Minnesota stopped Chris Flanagan except for one 30 and another 15-yard gallop. The statistics show that Flanagan outgained All American Joesting.

The Minnesota Daily claimed a victory on first downs, but first downs in deciding the outcome of a football game are like foul balls—they go for ten cents a thousand. Quoting from the official football rules we find that: "The game shall be decided by the final score at the end of the four periods."

In 1924 when Notre Dame won the National Championship by defeating Stanford 27 to 10, "Pop" Warner was showing "Rock" how Stanford had really won the game on first downs when "Rock" interrupted with: "I hear they are going to decide the world's series next year by the number of men left on bases."

Notre Dame supporters are so accustomed to winning that they consider a tie game as a lost game. The game will be played over and over this winter in the Hot Stove League, but regardless of all arguments advanced pro and con the fact remains that the classic ended with each team having seven points and it will go down on the football records as a tie game.

Army - 18
Notre Dame 0

Scoring a greater number of first downs but lacking in its usual style of smart football, Notre Dame lost its fourth game out of fourteen starts to the seasoned veterans of the Army at the Yankee before a maddening crowd of 75,000 people.

The Army drew blood in the early few moments of the game when after an exchange of punts, Cagle broke through the primary Notre Dame defense and with splendid interference evaded the secondary defense and ran half the distance of the field for the first touchdown.

The try for point was missed, and then Coach Rockne yanked the shock troops who had failed in their purpose to hold the Army team and take the first knocks. From that point until the termination of the second quarter the play was rather uncertain for both teams.

Notre Dame flashed its nationally known style of straight football toward the end of the second quarter when it marched a distance of seventy yards toward the Army goal line. However, here the team differed from other Irish teams in that it was unable to punch the ball across for the six point tally, and consequently lost the ball on downs.

The commencement of the third period found the Irish rooters certain of a reversal of form for their favorites.

However, due perhaps to the powerful Minnesota outfit that had been met the previous Saturday, and due to the fact that all the breaks of the game were going in the direction of the Army, the Irish continued holding their own and in straight football were able to out-score the Army in first downs.

In the third quarter, with the ball about in mid-field, Nave, the Army quarterback, intercepted an Irish forward pass and raced the remainder of the field for the second touchdown; and again Army missed the try for point. In the final quarter of the game, Cagle intercepted one of the many passes that were being hurled and raced about 30 yards for the third and final touchdown of the game.

The final score, 18 to 0, in justice to both Army and Notre Dame, does not indicate the closeness of this struggle. Much could be said about individual stars: the sterling work of Captain Smith who played the entire game; the work of Colerick, Walsh, Miller, Riley, Brady, and Collins. However, by saying that the entire team as a whole played the Army on even terms in one phase of the game; and outplayed the Army in another phase of the game would be placing credit where credit is due.

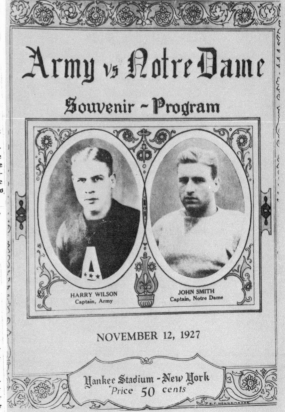

Army vs Notre Dame

Souvenir ~ Program

HARRY WILSON
Captain, Army

JOHN SMITH
Captain, Notre Dame

NOVEMBER 12, 1927

Yankee Stadium - New York
Price 50 cents

The Varsity Roster

No.	Name	Position	Prep School	Age	Wt.	Ht.	
82	Acers, Julian	L. Half	Campion, Wis., Prep	19	170	5 ft. 11 in.	
29	Bailie, Roy	R. End	Hollywood High	20	163	5 ft. 11 in.	
38	Barlow, Austin	Full	Mt. Carmel, Chicago	21	167	5 ft. 11 in.	
87	Bee, Peter	R. Guard	Textile High, N. Y. C.	22	192	5 ft. 10 in.	
25	Bondi, Gus	R. Guard	Dixon, Ill., High	21	175	5 ft. 9 in.	
57	Brady, James	Quarter	Pocatello, Idaho, High	21	140	5 ft. 7 in.	
42	Brannon, Bob	L. Half	Denison, Iowa	20	155	5 ft. 9 in.	
20	Bray, James	L. Half	Kansas City High	21	170	5 ft. 11 in.	
43	Cannon, Jack	L. Guard	Aquinas Columbus, Ohio	20	193	5 ft. 11 in.	
55	Cannon, Dan	R. Half	Aquinas Columbus, Ohio	21	163	5 ft. 11 in.	
71	Carberry, Jack	R. End	Ames, Iowa, High	22	175	6 ft.	1
24	Carideo, Frank	Quarter	Dean Academy	20	172	5 ft. 7 in.	0
15	Cassidy, Wm.	L. Guard	St. Stanislaus	22	172	5 ft. 9 in.	0
12	Chevigny, John	R. Half	Hammond, Ind., High	22	168	5 ft. 9 in.	2
83	Christianson, Carl	R. Guard	Mishawaka High	22	169	5 ft. 9 in.	0
56	Christman, Bill	Quarter	Green Bay, Wis.	19	152	5 ft. 7 in.	0
27	Collins, Ed.	L. End	St. Ignatius, Chicago	22	169	6 ft.	0
1	Collins, Fred	Full	Columbia, Portland, Ore.	24	170	5 ft. 8 in.	2
17	Colrick, John	L. End	St. Benedict, N. J.	21	175	6 ft.	1
30	Conley, Thomas	R. End	Roman Catholic, Phila.	20	170	5 ft. 11 in.	0
70	Conelley, Frank	L. Tackle	Charleston High, Mass.	23	180	6 ft.	0
19	Conway, Pat.	Full	Warren, Ohio, High	21	162	5 ft. 10 in.	0
76	Cronin, Carl	R. Half	St. Rita, Chicago	20	155	5 ft. 7 in.	0
58	Covington, W.	Full	Senn High, Chicago	21	165	5 ft. 11 in.	0
49	Culver, Al	R. Tackle	St. Thomas, St. Paul	22	212	6 ft. 2 in.	0
46	Dailey, Frank	Full	D. L. S., Joliet	21	180	5 ft. 9½ in.	0
73	Deegan, Harry	R. Half	Hartford, Conn.	21	157	5 ft. 9 in.	0
31	Dew, Wm.	R. Half	Fond du Lac, Wis.	20	169	5 ft. 10 in.	1
39	Doarn, John	R. Tackle	Omaha Tech.	22	200	5 ft. 11 in.	2
45	Donogohue, Richard	L. Tackle	Auburn, New York, High	20	220	6 ft. 2 in.	0
72	Donogohue, Bernard	L. Half	Auburn, New York, High	18	161	5 ft. 10½ in.	0
84	Elder, John	L. Half	Lebanon, Ky., High	21	165	5 ft. 8 in.	1
68	Fitch, George	R. Half	Central, Pittsburgh	21	159	5 ft. 9 in.	0
50	Gebert, Al.	Quarter	Jacksonville, Ill.	21	160	5 ft. 8 in.	0
48	Guadnola, Jos.	L. Tackle	Garfield, Colo., High	21	172	6 ft.	0
28	Greer, Walter	L. Guard	Carey, Ohio, High	22	172	5 ft. 9 in.	0
77	Grisanti, Al.	R. End	Catholic Latin, Cleveland	19	155	5 ft. 9 in.	0
37	Herwit, Norm	L. Guard	Senn High, Chicago	19	185	5 ft. 9 in.	0
4	Jones, Bill	R. Guard	Trinity, Sioux City	21	183	5 ft. 10 in.	1
92	Judge, Bill	L. End	Broklyn, Man.	23	159	6 ft.	1
9	Kassis, Tom	Center	Casper, Wyo., High	20	185	5 ft. 11 in.	0
15	Kersjes, Frank	L. End	Central High, Kalamazoo	21	180	5 ft. 11 in.	0
10	Kenneally, Thomas	Quarter	Crosby High, Wat. Conn.	20	145	5 ft. 7 in.	0
32	Kosky, Frank	R. End	Yonkers Prep	18	174	6 ft.	0
78	Kosky, Ed.	Quarter	Yonkers Prep	21	158	5 ft. 10 in.	0
64	Law, John	R. Guard	Yonkers High, N. Y.	22	163	5 ft. 9 in.	1

The Varsity Roster

No.	Name	Position	Prep School	Age	Wt.	Ht.	Years on Squad
69	Leahy, Bernard	L. Half	St. Mel, Chicago	20	178	5 ft. 11 in.	0
26	Leahy, Frank	L. Tackle	Winer High, S. Dak.	20	183	5 ft. 11 in.	0
97	Lennon, Charles	L. Guard	D. L. S., Joliet	20	168	5 ft. 7 in.	0
41	Leppig, George	L. Guard	East High, Cleveland, O.	21	180	5 ft. 9 in.	2
22	Locke, Joseph	L. Guard	St. Rita, Chicago	22	165	5 ft. 10 in.	0
112	Listzwan, Tom	Full	Proctor, Vermont, High	21	158	5 ft. 8 in.	0
34	Lyons, Jim	R. Guard	Holyoke High	21	170	5 ft. 11 in.	0
59	Massey, Robt.	L. Guard	Bloomfield High, N. J.	20	165	5 ft. 10 in.	0
6	Mahoney, Gene	R. Tackle	Jamestown, N. Y., High	21	192	6 ft.	0
75	Malek, John	R. Half	Bellaire, Ohio, High	22	162	5 ft. 8½ in.	0
34	McManmon, Art.	R. Tackle	Lowell High, Lowell, Mass.	20	201	6 ft. 2 in.	0
8	McGrath, John	R. Tackle	Glenville High, Cleveland	23	195	6 ft.	1
67	Metzger, Bert	L. Guard	Loyola, Chicago	19	165	ft. 9 in.	0
44	Miller, Fred	L. Tackle	Mil. Day School	22	200	6 ft.	2
23	Montroy, Jack	R. Half	Cath. Cent. Grand Rapids	22	175	5 ft. 10 in.	0
2	Morrissey, Jos.	Quarter	Danville, Ill., High	24	166	5 ft. 10 in.	1
7	Moynihan, Tim	Center	Rawlings, Wyo., High	23	195	6 ft. 1 in.	1
21	Mullins, Larry	Full	So. Pasadena, Calif., High	20	175	6 ft.	0
11	Murphy, Thomas	R. End	Baptist High, Conn.	20	185	6 ft. 1 in.	0
60	Nash, Jos.	Center	Mt. Carmel, Chicago	22	177	5 ft. 10½ in.	0
18	Niemiec, John	L. Half	St. Edwards, Texas	23	170	5 ft. 7½ in.	2
81	Nichols, John	Quarter	Lakewood, N. Y., High	20	151	5 ft. 7½ in.	0
89	O'Brien, Ed.	L. Half	D. L. S., Chicago	19	172	5 ft. 10 in.	0
47	O'Brien, John	L. End	Los Angeles High	21	180	6 ft. 2 in.	0
64	O'Connor, Paul	Full	N. Walpole, N. H., High	20	175	5 ft. 9 in.	0
51	Griffin, Jim	L. End	St. Ignatius, Chicago	21	178	6 ft. 1 in.	0
61	Premdergast, John	Center	Harrisburg Tech., Pa.	19	165	5 ft. 11 in.	0
33	Provisserio, P.	L. Guard	Paterson, N. J., High	21	194	5 ft. 8 in.	0
36	Ransavage, Jerry	R. Tackle	Columbia, Ore., Prep	28	182	5 ft. 11½ in.	2
35	Reilly, Jack	R. Half	Morristown High, N. J.	21	165	5 ft. 8 in.	1
98	Reiman, Fred	Center	La Crosse, Cent. Wis.	21	186	6 ft. 2 in.	0
54	Savoldi, Jos.	Full	Three Oaks High, Mich.	20	192	5 ft. 11 in.	0
62	Schwartz, Chas.	L. Tackle	Naperville, Ill., High	20	195	6 ft. 3 in.	0
40	Shay, George	Full	Hatford, Conn., High	21	160	5 ft. 9 in.	0
65	Stephan, Jos.	L. Half	Cath. Acad. D. M. Ia.	20	159	6 ft.	0
95	Smith, Howard	R. Half	Dean Academy	21	147	5 ft. 6 in.	0
6	Struve, Otto	L. Tackle	Yonkers High, N. Y.	21	178	5 ft. 11 in.	0
99	Sylvester, Harry	R. Half	Broklyn, Man.	20	165	5 ft. 10 in.	0
68	Thorton, Jos.	R. Tackle	St. James, Haverill	22	182	5 ft. 9½ in.	0
32	Twomey, Ted	R. Tackle	Duluth Catholic High	22	195	6 ft.	0
9	Vezie, H. M.	R. End	McDonald, Pa., High	22	175	6 ft.	0
16	Vlk, George	R. End	Holy Name High, Cleve.	20	170	6 ft.	0
94	Walker, Jack	Full	Fordham Prep	21	169	5 ft. 11 in.	0
86	Wilhemly, Chris	L. Half	St. Ignatius, Cleveland	22	167	6 ft.	1
14	Yarr, Thomas	Center	Chinacum Prep Wash.	20	185	5 ft. 10 in.	0
79	Yelland, John	Center	West High, Minn.	20	173	6 ft.	0

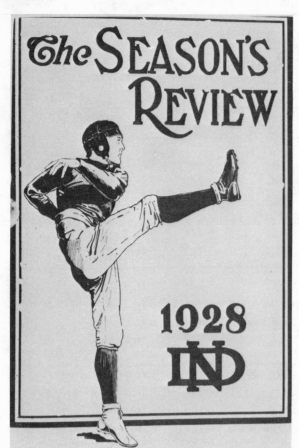

1928

Coach: Knute K. Rockne
Captain: Frederick Miller

S.29	W	Loyola (N.O.)	12-6	A	15,000
O.6	L	Wisconsin	6-22	A	29,885
O.13	W	Navy	7-0	N1*c	120,000
O.20	L	Georgia Tech	0-13	A	c35,000
O.27	W	Drake	32-6	H	12,000
N.3	W	Penn State (R)	9-0	N2	30,000
N.10	W	Army (U) (2:30)	12-6	YS	c78,188
N.17	L	Carnegie Tech (R)	7-27	H†	c27,000
D.1	L	So. California	14-27	A	c72,632
	(5-4-0)		99-107		419,705

*Paid attendance: 103,081
†First defeat at home since 1905
N1—at Soldier Field; N2—at Philadelphia

Pass, Niemiec to Colrick, Wins Game

By Warren Brown

Notre Dame's revamped football team gained enough yards at Soldier Field to defeat three football teams. They gained enough points to defeat but one, and by a score of 7 to 0. The stand of "Navy Bill" Ingram's Middies before a crowd of 120,000 persons was all in vain.

Only for a few moments, in the gathering darkness, of what was a long, drawn-out afternoon, did the Middies have a look-in in that ball game. And even then it required the employment of high-powered glasses to discover that.

From start to finish, Knute Rockne's ramblers outrushed them, outpassed them, and, in the first few minutes of the fourth period, shoved over the touchdown that outscored them.

Casting about for the heroes of the hard fought combat — hard fought and winning for the Irish, harder fought, because it was losing, for the Middies —one strikes upon the names of Johnny Niemiec and John Chevigny.

Niemiec Passes to Colrick

Long after the work of the stalwart linemen and the supporting cast of the backfield is forgotten, the Notre Dame adherents, and their number today was legion, will be talking about the onslaught of those Johnnies, Niemiec and Chevigny.

They cantered on tackle. They slipped around the ends. They, or rather Niemiec, passed, by way of variety, and—when all else had failed—he passed by way of a touchdown.

It was his slanting toss over to the left side of his line, just out of the reach of some frantically clutching Midshipmen, that landed in the outstretched paws of Colrick, shortly after the final period had begun.

Carideo Kicks Goal

As Colrick happened to be standing on the right side of the Navy line at that time, there was nothing much to be done about it. It was the touchdown that Notre Dame has awaited all afternoon and the touchdown that 120,000 spectators had just about despaired of ever seeing.

Carideo kicked the goal, just to pick up the

extra point, and the ball game was over, though Navy, fighting to the last, opened up a belated rush that carried the Middies' cause down close enough to Notre Dame's goal line to make the Irish following uncomfortable for the first and last time in the afternoon.

Up until this last despairing effort, most of the ground covered by Navy was in the wrong direction. But even at that, they were as close, for all practical purposes, to scoring for three periods as were the Irish, though the latter, with marches of sixty-five and fifty-six yards, one of thirty-two and a pair of twenty-eight yards, were gaining practically all the territory encompassed in the gray walls of Soldier Field.

The twenty-eight yard march, and the last one, at that, was the one that materialized in the touchdown.

Irish Penalized 65 Yards

Some of the early efforts were neutralized by the infliction of penalties, some sixty-five yards of these being charged against the Irish, compared with twenty-five yards of the same irritating decisions against the Navy. In the course of the competition, Notre Dame rolled up something like 268 yards to Navy's 93, and much of the latter yardage wasn't compiled until after Notre Dame had scored. In fact, in the first half, and a goodly portion of the second, Navy was inside Notre Dame territory just twice, and then across the line that marks midfield.

Coach Rockne, who can always be depended upon to do the unexpected, started what amounts to his first team, and the "shock troops" were conspicuous by their absence.

Only One Fumble In The Game

The lads that started for Notre Dame hung on until they were physically unable to continue, and Chevigny, one of the two heroic figures of the victorious cause, remained on the job until he had to be carried from the field. But before he left, Notre Dame had seven points and Navy had none.

The Lineup

Notre Dame		Navy
Collins	L. E.	Moret
Miller (c)	L. E.	Wilson
Leppig	L. G.	Eddy
Moynihan	C.	Hughes
Law	R. G.	Burke (c)
Twomey	R. T.	Giese
Vezie	R. E.	Beans
Brady	Q. B.	Whelchel
Bray	L. H.	W. Bauer
Chevigny	R. H.	Castree
Dew	F. B.	Clifton

Georgia Tech Thrusts Back Notre Dame Invaders, 13 To 0

Golden Tornado Gets Jump on Rockne Machine With Air Attack—Then Hold Niemic and Mates At Bay

Atlanta, Oct. 20.—(AP.)—The golden tornado of Georgia Tech blew out on Grant Field today and swept the football forces of Notre Dame to defeat for the first time in seven years of this intersectional rivalry.

Striking the invading ramblers of Knute Rockne before they had time to get their bearings, the Tech tornado whirled out in front in the opening period, successfully withstood the counter thrusts of the Hoosiers; and emerged with a triumphant last period flourish. The final score was 13 to 0. The victory aroused some 30,000 Georgians to a delirious demonstration as the South added another scalp to its growing gridiron collection.

Tech stole its rivals' thunder at the outset, by completing two long passes, one for 14 yards and the other for 11, to pave the way for a dash through tackle by Warner Mizell, versatile halfback, for the first touchdown. Mizell, whose running, passing and kicking were outstanding features of the game, received the first pass from Durant and hurled the second one to Thomason, who made a fine running catch on Notre Dame's three-yard line. It took only two plunges from there for the Tech star to tally.

Tech clung grimly to this slim margin until the closing moments of the game, when Lumpkin, sensational sophomore fullback, plucked one of Johnny Niemiec's passes out of the air and raced 28 yards to the Hoosier 3 yard mark. This time Randolph took the ball over and Mizell added the final point of the game with his toe.

Notre Dame		Georgia Tech.
Colrick	le	Holland
Miller	lt	Maree
Law	lg	Westbrook
Moynihan	c	Pund
Twomey	rg	Drennon
Lepping	rt	Speer
Vezie	re	Waddy
Brady	qb	Durant
Niemeic	lhb	Mizell
Chevigny	rhb	Thomason
Dew	fb	Randolph

Score by periods:
Georgia .... 6 0 0 7—13
Notre Dame .... 0 0 0 0— 0

Touchdowns: Mizell, Randolph; points after touchdown, Mizell (placement).

Referee, Virch, Chicago; umpire, Powell, Wisconsin; field judge, Streithn, Auburn; head linesman, Wyatt, Chicago.

Carnegie Upsets Notre Dame Tradition Wins, 27 to 7

By Arch Ward
Chicago Tribune Press Service

NOTRE DAME, IND., Nov. 17—Never did a football team fight harder than Notre Dame on the mud and water of Cartier Field today. But all the fight and all the courage the Irish could develop was inadequate and they went down in defeat before a big, powerful team from Carnegie. 27 to 7.

The Scotch from Carnegie made history in their victory over the Irish. They are the first to defeat Notre Dame on its home field in 23 years. This is the first Rockne coached eleven that ever has been on the losing end three times in one season.

Game Settled at Once

Notre Dame, apparently suffering from anti-climaxities, following its victory over the Army, found out early in the first quarter that Carnegie was every bit as good as the scouts had reported. Notre Dame kicked off to Carnegie's 30-yard line and after two line plays, failed. Harpster flipped a pass to Rosenzweig who raced down the right side of the field to Notre Dame's 21 yard line where he was downed. The play was timed perfectly, Rosenzweig, playing left, cut across behind the Notre Dame line, outsped the Irish secondary and caught the ball at his finger tips. On the next play Letzelter crashed off left tackle for a touchdown. Harpster's kick was low.

Even this whirlwind attack caused no consternation in the Notre Dame stands. But the situation became serious a moment later when Eyth of Carnegie intercepted Niemiec's long pass on Notre Dame's 38-yard strip. Eyth and Karcis made it first down on the 21-yard line and again the Scotch were hammering at the Irish goal.

Capt. Miller of Notre Dame stopped Karcis but on the next play Letzelter raced to the five-yard line. Karcis crashed to the one-yard mark and on the next play Harpster scored. He also kicked goal and it was Carnegie, 13; Notre Dame, 0.

End Around Scores Again

The first quarter was hardly over before Steffen's men again were menacing Notre Dame's goal. The goalward march started when Harpster caught a punt on his 28-yard line. It didn't end until Rosenzweig planted the ball behind the line for a touchdown. It was an end 'round play with Rosenzweig carrying the ball that brought the score. That play had been fooling the Irish all the way. Harpster kicked goal and when the teams left the field for the half, Carnegie was out in front, 20 to 0.

That score would have discouraged almost any band of athletes. But not Notre Dame. The team's indomitable fighting spirit made it appear for moment in the third quarter like it might come back.

Moon Mullins, a substitute half-back, on the third play of the third quarter, scooped up the ball which Karcis had let slip from his hands and sped 10 yards to the goal. Niemiec kicked the extra point.

Mullins, a moment later, fell on another fumble and Notre Dame started a march down field that seemed to have continuity. It ended on the 25-yard line in a vain attempt to score through the air.

Carnegie Scores Again

Carnegie's final touchdown was the result of a wide pass, Harpster to Letzelter, that caught Rockne's men napping. Letzelter had a clear field in his 23-yard sprint to the goal.

Elder, sprinter, who replaced Bray in the Notre Dame lineup, added a final thrill by breaking away for a 65-yard run shortly before the game ended. Johnny O'Brien, who caught the pass that beat the Army, was rushed into the battle in time to share a toss that put the ball on Carnegie's 3-yard line. Here it was that Carnegie showed its defensive strength. Reilly fumbled and recovered. Elder was held for no gains. An attempted pass was knocked down and Notre Dame's last chance to score ended when a pass sailed straight into the arms of Harpster, who downed it behind the goal line for a touchback.

Irish Gloom

Notre Dame		Carnegie
Colrick	L. E.	Rosenzweig
Miller	L. T.	Schmidt
Leppig	L. G.	Lovewell
Moynihan	C.	Mielzener
Law	R. G.	Dreshar
Twomey	R. T.	Highberger
Vezie	R. E.	Sweet
Brady	Q. B.	Harpster
Niemiec	L. H.	Eyth
Chevigny	R. H.	Letzelter
Collins	F. B.	Karcis

Notre Dame Stops Army By 12 To 6

John O'Brien Hero As Rockne Strategy Beats West Point Power in Sensational Game

Army Misses Tie By Only Two Feet

Greatest Crowd to See Football Game in East, 86,000, At Yankee Stadium Battle

BY LESLIE A. YOUNG.

New York, Nov. 10.—New York today hailed a new Caesar—Knute Rockne of Notre Dame.

He came East with his Notre Dame football warriors, saw 87,000 seated in the Yankee Stadium awaiting the fray, and conquered the great Army of the Hudson, 12 to 6, in one of the most sensational battles in all the history of gridiron warfare. Strategy beside which the wooden horse of Trojan days stands as ordinary won the day for the gallant "Fighting Irish" and their "miracle men" and snatched from West Point all chance for a national title.

A long forward pass hurled by the magnificent Christian "Red" Cagle of the Soldiers to Ed Messinger, Army end, and a series of terrific smashes at the Notre Dame line by Cagle and "Hertz" Murrel had given West Point a touchdown in the third period and a 90-yard drive down the field by Notre Dame, only once interrupted briefly, had tied the score before the sage of South Bend resorted to the strategy for which he is famous.

That Unsung Substitute.

It was the fourth period with not so many minutes left for action and to all intents and purposes the Irish had decided to play defensively in hope of a deadlock. When Billy Dew replaced the injured Chevigny, few suspected that Rockne was doing other than making a necessary substitution. Immediately there was a forward pass by Frank Carideo, Notre Dame substitute quarterback, over the right flank of the Army, but it fell in "no man's land."

Then from the Rockne bench scurried a tall, gangling youth to rush out upon the field and relieve the faltering John Colerick, with the ball 28 yards from the Army goal. Again Carideo took the pass from center and stepped backward as the Army forwards flung themselves at him, and again he hurled the ball, this time to the right. As the ball was heaved the tall, slim lad who had substituted for Colerick was heading boldly for the goal line. Fifteen yards away he turned, stretched out his long arms and grasped the flying oval. It bounded upward but the long arms pursued it, hugged it again and John O'Brien of Los Angeles hurtled over the goal line to beat his team's greatest foe.

Center of Jubilation.

Then John O'Brien departed from the contest and his mates on the bench milled around him to do honor to a hero for the first time since that day two years ago when Christy Flannagan of Notre Dame slipped past the lunging Hammack and raced 71 yards to defeat this same team, 6 to 0.

For the first time this season Army faced defeat. There were very few minutes left, but there came over the Soldiers a fierce determination to carry on to that national title they had so coveted. Carrideo of Notre Dame kicked off and the quartet which always is part of the Army formation to receive a kickoff, actually stepped aside to permit the bounding ball to reach the arms of Cagle.

Taking the ball on his 15-yard mark, the doughty "Red" was off down the field, knees flying high, right arm bowling over tacklers, until his interference had been smeared by Notre Dame. Then he went alone, dodging, whirling, diving until he reached the enemy's 30-yard line and was forced outside by Fred Collins. Spectators were on their feet and a steady roar such as the Yankee Stadium never before has heard arose from the crowded stands.

Long Pass Fails.

Notre Dame, amazed by the charge of "the Red," called for time out and took too much of it, to be penalized five yards for delaying the game, and Army was only 25 yards from a touchdown and possible victory. Cagle, from far behind the line, essayed the play that scored against Harvard, feinting a pass to his right, then hurtling it far to the left. Ed Messinger was out there to receive it on the three-yard mark but Carideo cut down the ball to make the pass incomplete.

Again Cagle went far back, received the ball and poised to throw but instead he speeded around the Notre Dame left and behind good interference to a first down on the 10-yard mark.

"Biff" Jones, coach of the Army, must have been thinking of what Rockne had done only a few minutes before, for he ordered Hutchinson to warm up, then told him to sit down again. It was evident that Jones was about to resort to strategy in a last desperate effort to win. Delay cost the Army five yards and perhaps the victory at this point. Then Cagle dropped back and hurled another pass, which grounded.

Hutchinson again was off the bench and this time he rushed upon the field to take the place of Cagle, while the crowd looked on in astonishment. His first effort was a pass and Army went back to the 20-yard line as penalty for two incomplete forwards. Then Hutchinson shot the ball straight over the center of the line and Gibner, racing across the field, grasped and held it as Fred Collins bore him down on the Notre Dame four-yard mark. Quickly the Army host lined up again and Hutchinson this time leaped headlong into the mass of humanity that blocked the way.

And Notre Dame Wins.

The whistle that ended the game was blowing as the referee untangled that heap of arms and legs and when the ball had been uncovered it lay two feet from the goal line and Notre Dame had conquered Army.

Thus did Army and Notre Dame entertain the greatest throng that ever viewed a football game in the East, a conflict that will be discussed for seasons to come. Jones spoke wisdom the night before the game when he said that Army never underrated the teams of Knute Rockne.

The Soldiers were outplayed, except in the first period—there can be no doubt of that. "Butch" Niemiec was a better kicker than "Mule" Murrel, the West Bend booter sending many beautiful shots down the gridiron to keep his team from danger. A perfectly placed kick, which rolled outside at Army's two-yard mark, put Notre Dame in a strategic position early in the second period and three times Niemiec sent long boots over the Army goal line.

Summary:

Notre Dame		Army
E. Collins	le	Carlmark
Twomey	lt	Sprague
Law	lg	Hammack
Moynihan	c	Hall
Leppig	rg	Humber
Miller	rt	Perry
Vezie	re	Messinger
Brady	qb	Nave
Niemiec	lhb	O'Keefe
Chevigny	rhb	Cagle
F. Collins	fb	Murrel

Score by periods:

Notre Dame	0	0	6	6—12
Army	0	0	6	0— 6

Touchdowns, Ehevigny, Murrel, O'Brien. Referee, Walter Eckersoll, Chicago; umpire, Tom Thorp, Columbia; linesman, F. W. Murphy, Brown; field judge, N. E. Kearns, DePaul. Time, 15 minute quarters.

Substitutions: Notre Dame, Colerick for E. Collins, Cannon for Leppig, Carides for Brady, Dew for Chevigny, O'Brien for Colerick; Army, Parkham for Sprague, Maxwell for Hammack, Dilb for Humber, Lynch for Messinger, Gibner for Nave, Hutchinson for Cagle, Piper for Murrel, Allan for O'Keefe, Walsh for Dibb.

THIS IS THE FAMOUS "FOR THE GIPPER" GAME

Record Breakers—The "Zepp" and Notre Dame

From stern to stem: Savoldi, F. Leahy, Kassis, O'Connor, Moynihan, Metzger, Gebert, Nash, Elder, Kaplan, O'Brien, Colrick, Locke, Brill, Schwartz, Donoghue, Bondi, Howard, Koken, Shay, Kenneally, Culver, McNamara, Vlk, Twomey, Murphy, B. Leahy, Cannon, Yarr, McManmen, Mullins, Collins, Conley, Carideo, Vezie, Capt. Law. Below, left to right: Trainer Abbott, Managers Conroy and Quinn, Assistant Coaches Jones, Voedisch, Chevigny, Mills, and Lieb, Head Coach Rockne.

1929 Coaching Staff

K. K. Rockne	*Head Coach*	John Voedisch	*Assistant Coach*
Thomas Lieb	*Assistant Coach*	John Chevigny	*Assistant Coach*
Thomas F. Mills	*Assistant Coach*	William Jones	*Freshman Coach*

Varsity Personnel

John B. Law, *Captain*	Albert Gebert	Tim Moynihan
August Bondi	Norman Herwit	Lawrence Mullins
Martin Brill	Nordoff Hoffman	Thomas Murphy
John Cannon	Al Howard	Joseph Nash
Frank Carideo	Clarence Kaplan	John O'Brien
William Cassidy	Thomas Kassis	Paul O'Connor
William Christman	Thomas Kenneally	Fred Reiman
Edmond Collins	Bernard Leahy	Joseph Savoldi
John Colrick	Frank Leahy	Marchmont Schwartz
Thomas Conley	Joseph Locke	George Shay
Carl Cronin	Arthus McManmon	Ted Twomey
Al Culver	Regis McNamara	H. Manfred Vezie
Richard Donoghue	Bertram Metzger	George Vlk
John Elder		Thomas Yarr

1929†

Coach: Knute K. Rockne
Captain: John Law

O.5	W	Indiana	14-0	A	16,111
O.12	W	Navy	14-7	N1	c64,681
O.19	W	Wisconsin	19-0	N2	90,000
O.26	W	Carnegie Tech	7-0	A	c66,000
N.2	W	Georgia Tech	26-6	A	22,000
N.9	W	Drake	19-7	N2	50,000
N.16	W	So. California	13-12	N2*	c112,912
N.23	W	Northwestern	26-6	A	c50,000
N.30	W	Army	7-0	YS	c79,408
	(9-0-0)		145-38		551,112

†No home games; Notre Dame Stadium was under construction
*Paid attendance: 99,351
N1—at Baltimore; N2—at Soldier Field

Notre Dame - - - - - 7
Carnegie Tech - - - - - 0

JUDGE WALTER STEFFAN
Carnegie Tech Coach

We at Carnegie Tech are proud of our relationship with Notre Dame and we are proud that we were able to hold Notre Dame to a 7 to 0 score in our game this year. Your 1929 team is a great team. I wish to congratulate the national champions and Coach Rockne.

JOHN DRESHAR
Carnegie Tech Captain

The Notre Dame team we played this year was, without doubt, the best we met all season. I have never seen any team show such remarkable improvement in a year's time as the Notre Dame eleven did from 1928 to 1929. Although made up of the same men, the line this year was far superior to the one last season.

"Twenty-seven to seven"! "Twenty-seven to seven"! This is the cry that rang across Cartier practice field the week before Coach Rockne pitted his fighting men against the powerful Carnegie Tech machine, and when the starting whistle sounded, at Pittsburgh, Notre Dame was in a rare fighting mood.

Twenty-seven to seven was the score of the 1928 game when the towering Skibos ground 23 years of cherished tradition into the mud of Cartier field, and the mere mention of these two apparently harmless figures was to inflame to fighting pitch every man on this year's squad.

There were other incentives, too. For example, there was "Rock" helpless in his wheel-chair on the sidelines after leaving a sickbed and making the effort that was to keep him away from the next two games. There was also the game of 1926, when the hardy Scots knocked Notre Dame out of a national championship.

But these were avenged before the greatest crowd that ever turned out for a sports spectacle in Pittsburgh. The great Karcis, who had plunged the 1928 eleven to destruction, was stopped by a dauntless line led by the inspired Jack Cannon. The only serious threat Carnegie made all afternoon was in the last quarter when Judge Steffan's club was stopped (by Cannon) 20 yards out.

The Notre Dame touchdown was a marvel to watch. Carideo had taken a punt from McCurdy on the 50-yard line. Jack Elder, still unstopped by any man's ball team, scrambled to the 17-yard line; Marty Brill crashed to the eight-yard stripe; then Joe Savoldi took the situation in hand. Three times he flung himself bodily at the stubborn Plaid line to put the ball on the one-yard stripe. On the fourth down, he again dived fearlessly into the air and sailed to rest in the end zone for victory and revenge.

But why shouldn't Notre Dame men fight? The picture of their greatest friend, Knute K. Rockne, huddled in his wheel-chair near the Notre Dame bench in excruciating pain—fighting for them—was reason enough.

No greater compliment can be paid to the great Carnegie team than the tribute the players themselves made after the game: "Carnegie was the hardest team we've played this year."

But a team fighting for a national championship, for its revenge, and above all for its Rockne, could not be stopped.

ELDER OFF ON HIS 97 YARD RUN AGAINST THE ARMY IN 1929

Notre Dame - - - - - 7
Army - - - - - 0

"BIFF" JONES
Army Coach

While probably lacking in the finesse of the 1924 team, Notre Dame's eleven this year was one of the greatest I have ever seen. The line stopped every Army drive and the pass defense was excellent. I am sorry I did not see them under better playing conditions. No team can match Notre Dame's 1929 record.

"CHRIS" CAGLE
Army Captain

The Army-Notre Dame game this year was one of the greatest I have ever had the pleasure to take part in during my college career. I am thankful that I had the opportunity to play against men who could execute their assignments so well on that frozen field and glad that we were a real barrier before the national champions, for it may be years before another team has such a successful season.

The 1929 renewal of the Army-Notre Dame game, which has become THE classic of football, saw a glorious climax to a glorious Notre Dame season.

The Cadets rose far above anything they had done previously and battled to the end like true soldiers in a vain attempt to overcome the lone score of the day made on Jack Elder's brilliant run in the second quarter.

Both lines were in there fighting as they had never battled before, Army with its Perry and Messinger and Notre Dame with its Cannon and Twomey standing out head and shoulders above the two struggling masses. Army was great that day. Chris Cagle, Army's valiant captain, outdid even himself with his determined offensive and defensive tactics in this last Notre Dame game of his remarkable career.

The power and alertness of Notre Dame's great club, however, was too much for the best that West Point could offer. Every fresh march through the line or around the ends was stopped by Tom Lieb's powerful forwards, and every Army pass was either incomplete or intercepted. Some said Elder's run was a break of the game, but they must remember that three other of Cagle's desperate tosses were intercepted by vigilant Notre Dame backs.

John Colrick, Ted Twomey, Jack Cannon, Joe Nash, Capt. Johnny Law, and Jack Elder, playing their last game for the Blue and Gold, performed, if possible, better than in any other battle during the rigorous season. Frank Carideo's excellent judgment in playing safe after scoring, Marty Brill's great blocking and defensive work, Larry Mullins' determined plunging, and the work of Frank Leahy, Dick Donoghue, Tom Conley, Eddie Collins, and Al Culver in the line was close to perfection.

The shock troop backs, Al Gebert, March Schwartz, Joe Savoldi, and Bucky O'Connor, who made four first downs in the first quarter also share in the great victory.

Notre Dame's claim to a national title, made by the press and fans, rather than by the team itself, certainly seems justified after the last great ride of the New Four Horsemen. What other team in the country could play nine major games, six of them without their coach, and not crack? Notre Dame couldn't have without the excellent work of "Rock's" three former pupils, Tom Lieb, Jack Chevigny, and Ike Voedisch.

NOTRE DAME *named* NATIONAL CHAMPION
By Nation's Sports Writers

To Notre Dame goes the first National Collegiate Football Championship and to its coach, Knute Rockne, goes the Albert Russel Erskine Award for 1929. Presentation of the Erskine Award, symbolical of football supremacy, to the Ramblers' mentor is the result of a nation-wide poll of opinions of the most prominent sports writers made under the direction of W. O. McGeehan, sports editor of the New York Herald Tribune and chairman of the Erskine Award Committee.

The final ballot showed Rockne's team leading with 179 votes, Pittsburgh second with 41 votes, and Purdue third with two votes. The vote of the committee of award, composed of nationally known patrons of football, gave Notre Dame 11 additional votes, making her grand total 190, Pittsburgh and Purdue received no votes in the committee of award. The vote of Theodore Roosevelt, a member of the committee, was cabled from Porto Rico by way of the War Department in Washington.

The Notre Dame team will receive a huge silver cup signifying the football title, to be held for one year. The final act in the drama will be the presentation of a President Eight to Knute Rockne, the coaching wizard of Notre Dame.

With the announcement of final results, Robert O. Delin of New York City, the certified public accountant who verified results for

This cup, emblematic of the national title, remains in possession of the Notre Dame team until 1931 when it will be presented to the 1930 champion.

the committee of award, revealed the details of all the balloting. In the preliminary ballot, which served to select the teams to be voted for on the final ballot, each member of the jury named three teams.

Valuing the votes at 5 for first place, 3 for second and 1 for third, this first ballot produced the following results:

Notre Dame, 777; Pittsburgh, 442; Purdue, 210; St. Mary's, 48; Tulane, 22; Southern California, 21; Texas Christian, 10; Tennessee, 8; Yale, 2; Dartmouth, 2; North Carolina, 2; Colgate, 2; Utah, 1; Stanford, 1.

Analyzing the jury's voting by States, it is found that the majority in every State except six voted on the first ballot for Notre Dame. These six were Missouri and Nebraska, for Pittsburgh; Alabama and Kansas, which were both divided between Notre Dame and Pittsburgh; New Mexico, which split between Notre Dame and St. Mary's, and Oregon, which hesitated between Notre Dame, St. Mary's and Purdue. On the final ballot, however, every State turned its majority to Notre Dame.

"Reception of the Erskine Award in this, its first year, has been so enthusiastic on the part of both football experts and the public at large that it has been decided to renew it in 1930," states W. O. McGeehan, chairman of the committee. "It fills a very real need."

1930 Notre Dame University Varsity Football Roster

No.	Name	Position	Preparatory School	Age	Wt	Ht.	Years on Squad
1	Jaskwich, Chas.	Quarter	Kenosha High	19	164	5-11	0
2	Metzger, Bert	R. Guard	Loyola Academy, Chicago	21	155	5-8½	1
3	Murphy, Emm't	Quarter	De LaSalle, M. C. Mo.	22	154	5-7½	0
6	Grisanti, Al	R. End	Cathedral, Latin, Cleveland	21	160	5-8	0
7	Mahoney, Dick	R. End	Cathedral Latin, Cleveland	21	175	5-11	0
8	Koken, Mike	L. Half	South High, Youngstown, Ohio	21	162	5-8	0
9	Christman, Norbert	Quarter	East H. S., Green Bay, Wis.	21	168	5-9½	1
10	Conley, Tom (Capt.)	R. End	Roman Catholic H. S., Phila.	22	175	5-11	2
11	Host, Paul	L. End	LaCrosse Central	20	173	5-10	0
12	Brill, Martin	R. Half	Penn Charter	22	190	5-10½	1
13	Connolly, John	L. Half	St. John's, Toledo, Ohio	20	160	5-9	1
15	Vlk, George	R. End	Holy Name, Cleveland, Ohio	21	175	6	2
16	Kaplan, Clarence	R. Half	Owatonna, Minn.	23	156	5-8	1
17	Bailie, Roy	L. End	Fairfax, Hollywood, Calif.	21	173	6-0	0
18	Schwartz, Marchmont	L. Half	Bay St. Louis, Miss.	21	170	5-11½	1
19	O'Brien, Ed.	Quarter	De LaSalle, Chicago, Ill.	21	172	5-10	0
24	Carideo, Frank	Quarter	Dean Acad., Mt. Vernon, N. Y.	22	175	5-7	2
26	Cronin, Carl	Quarter	St. Rita's, Chicago, Ill.	21	155	5-7	1
27	Bice, Leonard	L. End	Hollywood, California, H. S.	20	172	6-½	0
28	Manley, John	L. Tackle	Dyersville, Ia.	21	170	6	0
29	Morrow, Thomas	Fullback	Regis, N. Y.	18	172	5-11	0
31	Mullins, Larry	Fullback	South Pasadena High	22	175	6	2
32	Greeney, Norman	L. Guard	J. Marshall, Cleveland, Ohio	22	185	5-11	0
33	Leahy, Bernard	L. Half	St. Mel's, Chicago, Ill.	22	175	5-11	1
34	Kosky, Edwin	L. End	Yonkers, N. Y., High	20	182	5-11½	0
35	Capter, Albert	Fullback	Central, Paterson, N. J.	20	185	6	0
36	McNamara, Regis	L. Tackle	Binghamton High, New York	22	192	6-1½	1
37	O'Connor, Paul	R. Half	East Orange, N. J.	21	180	5-10	2
38	Harriss, James	L. Guard	Linsley, Bellaire	21	185	5-9	0
39	Sheeketski, Joe	R. Half	Shadyside, O., High	21	165	5-7	0
40	Terlaak, Robert	R. Guard	Marshall, Cleveland, Ohio	21	180	5-10	0
41	O'Brien, John	L. End	Los Angeles, Calif., High	23	185	6-2	2
42	Cavanaugh, Vincent	Center	St. Ignatius, Chicago, Ill.	20	175	5-10½	0
43	Howard, Al	Fullback	Alhambra, Calif., H. S.	21	170	5-10	1
45	Holman, Currier	L. End	Shattuck Military, Ia.	19	180	6	0
46	Goldstein, Sam	L. Tackle	Marshall, Chicago, Ill.	21	178	5-10	0
48	Savoldi, Joe	Fullback	Three Oaks, Mich.	21	192	5-11	2
49	Van Rooy, William	L. Guard	Cathedral Latin, Cleveland	20	190	5-10½	0
50	Tobin, John	R. Half	Janesville, Wis., High	20	180	5-7	0
51	Gorman, Thomas	Center	St. Phillip's, Chicago, Ill.	20	194	6-1	0
52	Kerjes, Frank	R. Guard	Kalamazoo High	22	192	5-10	0
53	Pierce, William	L. Guard	Sherman, Texas	21	185	5-8	0
55	Staab, Fred	Fullback	Madison, Wis., Central	20	178	5-11	0
56	Zoss, Oscar	Guard	South Bend High	20	184	5-11	0
57	Brancheau, Ray	R. Half	Monroe, Mich., H. S.	20	180	5-11½	0
58	Carberry, Jack	R. End	Ames, Ia., H. S.	22	175	6	2
59	Whelan, Vincent	L. Guard	Grantwood, N. J.	20	175	5-8	0
60	Bloemer, Bernie	R. Guard	St. Xavier, Louisville	21	180	5-9	1
61	Coughlan, Tom	L. Guard	Whiting, Ind., H. S.	22	180	5-10½	1
62	Massey, Robert	L. Guard	Bloomfield, N. J.	21	170	5-11	0
63	Herwit, Norman	L. Guard	Senn, Chicago, Ill.	20	185	5-9	2
64	Rogers, John	Center	Alexis, Ill., High	20	170	5-8	0
65	Bassett, Charles	R. Tackle	Stratford High	20	180	6	0
66	Kurth, Joseph	R. Tackle	Madison East	23	197	6-1½	0
67	Hoffman, Frank	R. Tackle	St. Martin's, Seattle, Wash.	20	198	6-2	0
68	Agnew, Edward	Center	Loyola, Chicago, Ill.	21	178	6	0
69	Kassis, Tom	R. Guard	Casper, Wyo., High	20	185	5-11	2
70	Butler, Frank	Center	Tilden Tech., Chicago, Ill.	19	202	6-2	0
71	Leahy, Frank	L. Tackle	Winer, S. D., High	21	183	5-11	2
72	Wunsch, Harry	R. Guard	South Bend High	19	200	5-11	0
76	Yarr, Tom	Center	Chinacum Prep., Wash.	21	195	5-10½	1
77	Vyaral, Edward	R. Tackle	Lindbloom, Chicago, Ill.	20	215	6-4	0
78	Carmody, James	R. Tackle	Mt. Carmel, Chicago, Ill.	20	200	6	0
79	McManmon, Art	R. Tackle	Lowell, Mass., High	21	202	6-2½	1
80	Donoghue, Richard	R. Tackle	Auburn, N. Y., H. S.	22	215	6-3¼	2
81	Culver, Alvin	L. Tackle	St. Thomas, St. Paul	23	212	6-2½	1
	Kremer, Theodore	Fullback	Woodsfield, O., High	20	175	5-9½	0
	Rohrs, George	R. End	Fordham Prep	18	164	5-8½	0
	Nichols, John	Quarter	Lakewood, Ashville, N. Y.	22	155	5-7	0
	Hanley, Daniel	Fullback	Butte Central	21	195	6-1½	0
	Thornton, Joe	R. Tackle	St. James, Haverhill	23	182	5-9½	0
	Kreuz, Paul	R. Guard	Menominee High	20	185	5-11	0
	Dilling, Leo	R. Half	Emerson, Gary, Indiana	22	166	5-11	0
	Banas, Steve	L. Half	Hammond, Indiana, H. S.	20	18.	5-11	0
	Beirne, Roger	L. End	Peddie, N. J.	19	170	6-2	0
	Lukats, Nicholas	L. Half	Froebel, Gary	19	178	6	0
	Cousino, Bernard	R. Tackle	St. John's, Toledo, Ohio	20	170	6	0
	Leding, Michael	L. Tackle	South Bend High	20	177	6-1	0

Cardeo, Brill, Mullins, Schwartz
Capt. Conley, Kurth, Metzger, Yarr, Kassis Culver, Kosky

THE NOTRE DAME STADIUM

1930					
Coach: Knute K. Rockne					
Captain: Thomas Conley					
O.4	W	S.M.U. (4:00)	20-14	H	14,751
O.11	W	Navy†	26-2	H	40,593
O.18	W	Carnegie Tech	21-6	H	30,009
O.25	W	Pittsburgh	35-19	A	c66,586
N.1	W	Indiana	27-0	H	11,113
N.8	W	Pennsylvania	60-20	A	c75,657
N.15	W	Drake	28-7	H	10,106
N.22	W	Northwestern	14-0	A	c44,648
N.29	W	Army (R-S) (3:30)	7-6	N1°	c110,000
D.6	W	So. California (U)	27-0	A	c73,967
		(10-0-0)	265-74		477,430

†Dedication of Notre Dame Stadium
°Paid attendance: 103,310
N1—at Soldier Field

THE Notre Dame University stadium is built on the most advanced lines of study in stadia. The plans and structures of the other large universities in the United States were carefully studied, it being the hope of the Notre Dame stadium committee to embody all the good points into the stadium at Notre Dame.

The length of the stadium is 670 feet and the width is 480 feet. The distance around the outside wall is about 2000 feet. The structure is designed strictly for football. The curved stand, a new idea in stadium construction, gives the maximum amount of seats between the goal posts. It also faces everybody toward the center of the field than at right angles to it, as in the case of other rectangular stands. In the stadium proper there are sixty rows of seats set about thirty feet from the playing field, and are behind the 244 boxes which accommodate six people in each box.

There is provided in the stadium a total seating capacity for fifty four thousand four hundred people, exclusive of the players and of the press reporters' seats. There are thirty six portals around the stand to provide entrances. Underneath the stands, long gently sloping ramps bring the spectators quickly to their seats. The entire stadium can be emptied of a capacity crowd without confusion in fifteen minutes.

The structural portion of the building, comprising the seat banks and their supports is of reinforced concrete. The exterior is enclosed by a brick wall with stone trim, through which open embrasures in the upper portion give direct light and air to all the passageways in the

stands. In this wall, there are twenty three large doors, serving for entrance and exit to and from a concourse or passageway entirely around the structure. This concourse is cindered and will be available for a practice track for the track team.

Underneath the stands on the north sides are the teams lockers, trainers and coaches' rooms, officials' dressing rooms, and all the needed facilities for both the home and visiting teams. Other facilities provided for under the stands include concession stands, manager's room, a first aid hospital room and provisions for the future installation of a number of handball and squash courts. All rooms under the stand may be heated and are provided with electric lights.

The seats in the stadium are provided with ample foot room, giving each patron plenty of space.

Provision is made in the stadium to care for pageants and processionals. This is provided for by a depressed ramp descending from the exterior grade at the northern end into and under the stand and the concourse out onto the field.

Above the stands both at the north and south ends of the stadium, scoreboards, modern in every detail, are built into the structure. They are operated by direct telephone control from the playing field.

The Notre Dame stadium was designed by the Osborn Engineering Company of Cleveland and was constructed by the Ralph Sollitt and Sons Construction Company of Chicago and South Bend.

| Notre Dame | - - - - - | 20 |
| Southern Methodist | - - - | 14 |

RAY MORRISON
S. M. U. Coach

My boys, though defeated, enjoyed their trip to South Bend. They will long remember the courtesies shown them by Notre Dame students and officials, and their one desire is to repay these courtesies; and perhaps the defeat, in the near future.

BILL SKEETERS
S. M. U. Captain

I have much respect for Notre Dame's football team and coach. Their blocking was far superior to any I had previously seen, and on defense their tackling could not help being effective. Rockne's 1930 team is the best I have ever played against.

Not over-rated was the fighting band of Mustangs Coach Ray Morrison brought to Notre Dame to open unofficially a new era in Notre Dame football history. Their record of winning three Southwest conference championships in three years and their reputation as perhaps the leading exponent of the forward pass made them a team to be feared when they stepped into the newly opened Notre Dame stadium.

Admittedly they had been pointing for Notre Dame since the game was scheduled in the fall of 1929 and it was not long before the fact became apparent that they were out to win. Playing in midseason form against an Irish band that was fighting but that had not yet hit its stride, they carried the battle to Notre Dame's shock troops with their reckness, vicious attacks.

Undaunted by the fact that their regular quarter-back, Bob Gilbert, was on the sidelines, they played smart, heads-up football with Bruce Kattman, rubber-armed ball heaver, tossing the swineskin all over the Cartier sod. Every year, coaches divide their time between developing an attack and forming a defense. Coach Rockne in three short weeks, had not much of a chance to work out any plan to stop the glorified basketball used Southern Methodists' red-jersied warriors, but he met Morrison's strategy with some of his own.

Morrison's theory is that if enough passes are thrown, the law of averages will work to the completion of some of them. Rockne added that by the same omen, a number would be intercepted. His strategy lay, however, in meeting passes with passes not so many of Notre Dame's were intercepted.

Highlights were Mason's pass to Kattman to put the ball on the two-yard line in the first quarter and Hopper's ensuing plunge for the touchdown; Joe Savoldi's return of the next kick-off; Ed Kosky's steady work at end; Joe Kurth's brilliant tackle of Mason who was runing full tilt in the open field; Kattman's 38-yard pass to Koontz for a touchdown, Carideo's return of a Mustang punt from the 39 to the 11-yard line from which Notre Dame scored in two attempts; Larry Mullins' 60-yard run that was called back; and Carideo's pass to Kosky for 25 yards which set the stage for the winning touchdown in the last quarter.

Rockne was thankful because his team had survived its baptism of fire and had proved itself capable of stopping passes, and because it fought to the last ditch and proved itself, thereby, a representative Notre Dame team.

IRISH SWAMP NAVY IN DEDICATORY TILT, 26 TO 2

South Bend, Ind., Oct. 11.—The first hero in the lore of Notre Dame's $750,000 stadium is none less than the renowned hod carrier from Three Oaks, Mich., "Galloping Joe" Savoldi.

Piercing through the Navy's defense when all the rest of Knute Rockne's famous "shock troops" failed, Savoldi made the dedication ceremonies for the new stadium a perfect one by leading Notre Dame to a 26-to-2 victory over the Middies.

Three times did "Galloping Joe" crash through and around the Navy wall for touchdowns, and many more times did he back up a staggering line with a brand of unbeatable defensive play.

The rest of the Irish, at last with a new home of their own, did their share and two others joined in the scoring, but Savoldi stood out of the fight like a man mountain. Forty thousand fans, who came to cheer Rockne and the stadium he built, turned their cheers for Savoldi. He was the first hero of the new stadium.

Navy's best chance came late in the final period, when a bad punt by Koken traveled only fifteen yards to Notre Dame's 20-yard line. Gannon and Kirn punched their way to the seven-yard line, but were stopped.

Nearly 50,000 people crowded into the new stadium to see the warriors of the Green open a new era in their football history.

DEDICATION NOTRE DAME STADIUM
NAVY vs NOTRE DAME
OCTOBER 11, 1930   50¢
OFFICIAL PROGRAM

Reprinted from the
Baltimore Sunpapers
with permission.

Schwartz slices off right tackle for five yards and Notre Dame's second touchdown.

Notre Dame - - - - - 7
Army - - - - - - 6

MAJ. RALPH SASSE
Army Coach

After every Army-Notre Dame game, win, loss or draw, the fine relations built up during the past 17 years are strengthened. We hope that the game will continue to be the football classic of the season.

CHARLES HUMBER
Army Captain

The Army football squad sends its heartiest congratulations to Captain Conley and his team. Aside from the weather we all enjoyed the game more than any other of the entire season.

When Charles (Gus) Dorais, quarter-back, threw passes to Knute Rockne, end, in 1913 on the Army Plains at West Point in 1913 and surprised the Cadets with a 35 to 13 victory, there started a rivalry which has become the most colorful that football knows today. Playing every year with the exception of 1918, when the World War intervened, Army and Notre Dame have won the attention of the football world with their hard-fought games, many of which have gone into history as real classics. Punctuating the long rivalry is the fact that the under dog as often as not has won.

The game always had been played in New York or at West Point, and when it was moved to Chicago this year, 110,000 persons braved snow, sleet, mud, and rain to see, in a dogged, determined fight at Soldier Field, perhaps the two best teams the two schools have ever turned out.

Notre Dame had won all of its games but Army, although tied once, was confident. Maj. Ralph Sasse, their new coach, had won the respect of the Cadets and this confidence was reflected in their defiant attitude as they took their places in the half-frozen slime of an impossible field. With both attacks slowed by most unfavorable footing, there started a punting duel which saw Fields and Frentzel staying off Notre Dame scoring threats time and again. Army, it was apparent, was content to play for a tie and its strong powerful line and accurate punts kept every Irish scoring threat in the category of threats.

Each discouraging set-back, however, only spurred Field General Carideo on as he kept plugging away with Schwartz and Mullins off tackle. Finally, the perfect play came, the one Carideo had been trying all afternoon, with Schwartz driving off his right tackle to run 54 yards on a bee-line for the goal with every Army man blocked out cleanly and securely. Mullins, who proved to be the best mudder of the day, got King, the Army end, Capt. Con-ley drove in the tackle, and Carideo, Metzger, and Brill swarmed through the hole to mow down the secondary and to leave the path clear for Marchy. Carideo added his twenty-fifth extra point of the year out of 30 attempts.

Army's blocking and recovering of Carideo's punt for a touchdown a moment later proved only a gesture when Broshus' drop-kick for the extra point was blocked. A great Army eleven had bowed to an unbeatable Notre Dame band of real fighters who never failed to start out anew on a scoring drive against most discouraging odds; and another chapter had been added to the vivid history of a great rivalry.

FIGHTING IRISH WIN NATIONAL TITLE

Rockmen Trim Southern Cal., 27-0; Nineteenth Straight Victory

NOTRE DAME'S Fighting Irish, "the greatest team in the history of football," closed their second consecutive undefeated season with a 27-0 victory over the Trojans of the University of Southern California. The game was played before 90,000 spectators in the Los Angeles Coliseum, a fitting place, for what could be more like the massacres of ancient Rome than the crushing defeat of the Southern California warriors? Notre Dame's victory gives them their second successive national championship and permanent possession of the Rissman Intercollegiate trophy, symbolical of three national football championships within a decade.

The Fighting Irish, like the Greeks of old, stormed successfully the walls of Troy; but it took the Greeks ten years to penetrate the Trojan defense, while the Fighting Irish required only ten minutes. Carideo, a Napoleon without a Waterloo, was uncanny in his selection of plays. Notre Dame worked double passes, double laterals, double reverses, double spinners, in fact everything but the wooden horse trick, in their spectacular and methodical devastation of the Trojans.

Aided by a 25-yard pass, Schwartz to Captain Conley, the Rockets advanced 60 yards from the opening kickoff. They lost the ball on an incompleted pass into the end zone, recovered a Trojan fumble on the next play, and scored on the next. Schwartz flipped a short pass to Carideo, who scampered ten yards to the goal line for the initial score. Carideo place-kicked the extra point.

Was this a football team, or a cyclone that so violently disrespected the mighty Trojans, standard bearers of western football? The coast team was bewildered; they made a futile effort to retaliate. After a first down resulting from a penalty, they were stopped. A bad pass from center was responsible for the only noteworthy Trojan play of the game. Duffield, field marshall of the Californians, found himself trapped 23 yards behind the line of scrimmage and got off an incredibly quick punt that rolled over the Notre Dame goal line.

The Fighting Irish took possession of the ball on the 20-yard line and went to work. One play into the line netted no gain, and then Schwartz tossed a lateral to O'Connor, who went through right tackle, broke into the clear, sidestepped Duffield, Apsit, and Musick who ran him to the sidelines, and galloped to a touchdown.

Southern California was demoralized, the spectators dumbfounded, and the Fighting Irish cool and mercilessly confident. The Westerners were finding that they had underrated this "worn-out" team from the east. They had failed to respect the generalship of Carideo, the master mind; the faultlessness of Brill, the all-time blocking halfback; the elusiveness of Schwartz, the phantom ball carrier. They were amazed when their line was outplayed from end to end by the Fighting Irish forwards, when their power plays through Baker, 215-pound guard, were smeared by the midget Metzger, but what awed them most of all was this wild man, O'Connor, who changed from a second team halfback to a varsity fullback in two days.

Notre Dame sent in an almost entirely new team in the second quarter. They scored once on a 25-yard pass, Carideo to Hanley, but it was nullified by a penalty. The Trojans tried everything in this quarter but failed to chalk up even a first down.

Moon Mullins, Notre Dame's great fullback, received a big ovation when he limped on to the gridiron to start the second half. A single minute of play constituted his football swan song.

The Fighting Irish scored their third touchdown in one devastating sweep, advancing 70 yards in seven plays. Schwartz contributed two runs of 12 and 37 yards, Brill got 5 yards, and O'Connor went 8 yards on a lateral pass from Schwartz to score. Carideo converted.

The remainder of the game was a run away for Notre Dame. Smearing Trojan plays, intercepting passes, advancing on wide open spectacular plays, the Fighting Irish tramped on the ruins of fallen Troy. Schwartz ran wild; a forward pass followed by a lateral, Schwartz to Kosky to Carideo, was good for 40 yards and almost a touchdown. O'Connor went all the way to the 7-yard line. Penalties cost the Irish two touchdowns.

Notre Dame did their final scoring late in the game. Hanley intercepted a Trojan pass on the 21-yard line, carried the ball 7 yards in two plunges, and then Lukats, substitute halfback, went through tackle for the remaining distance. Jaskwich added the extra point.

Notre Dame's victory gave them undisputed possession of the national championship. This is the third year that the Rockets have won that title, and the fifth season that they have been undefeated since Rockne took charge. They won their first national championship six years ago when the immortal Four Horsemen journeyed to California to conclude an undefeated season by trampling the Stanford university eleven 27-10 in the Rose Bowl. Last year the new Four Horsemen romped to the title. Just after the end of the War, in 1919 and 1920, "Rock" accomplished his first two undefeated seasons when in his second and third years as head coach.

STATISTICS OF THE GAME

FIRST DOWNS:
Notre Dame, 16.
Southern California, 8.

YDS. GAINED FROM SCRIMMAGE:
Notre Dame, 356.
Southern California, 94.

FORWARD PASSES COMPLETED:
Notre Dame, 4 of 13 for 77 yards.
Southern California, 4 of 16 for 46 yards.

PENALTIES:
Notre Dame, 35 yards.
Southern California, 5 yards.

Knute Rockne, Notre Dame Coach, and 7 Others Killed As Plane Crashes in Kansas

COTTONWOOD FALLS, Kan., March 31.—Knute Rockne of Notre Dame, wizard of football, reached the end of his dynamic career in the crash of an air transport plane near here today which carried seven others to death.

The cause of the tragedy was unexplained tonight, although eye-witnesses seemed agreed the air liner of the Transcontinental & Western Air, Inc., lost a wing as it roared through muggy weather en route from Kansas City to California. Ice is believed to have formed on the wing, tearing it away.

Spinning down through fog and clouds the crippled ship hit with tremendous force on a farm eleven miles southwest of here, near the village of Bazaar.

The six passengers and two pilots met death instantly. Five bodies were thrown from the plane and the others, broken and mutilated, were found in the wreckage of the transport, which did not catch fire.

The dead, in addition to Rockne, are:

H. J. CHRISTEN, Chicago.
J. H. HOOPER, Chicago.
W. B. MILLER, Hartford, Conn.
SPENCER GOLDTHWAITE, New York.
C. A. ROBRECHT, Wheeling, W. Va.
ROBERT FRY, pilot, Los Angeles.
JESS MATHIAS, pilot, Los Angeles.

The bodies were brought to a morgue here. It was planned to start Rockne's body back to Notre Dame on a train leaving early tomorrow.

The plane with its six passengers and two operators left the Municipal Airport at Kansas City at 9:15 this morning. It had been delayed 45 minutes in a wait for air mail bound for Wichita, southern points and Los Angeles. As it took off it flew into a fine mist. An hour later it was a mass of twisted debris in the spot where it crashed on the Seward Baker farm four miles from Bazaar.

It was apparent that weather conditions became worse as Pilot Fry headed his craft over the Kansas flint hill district for Wichita. The mist formed and ice stuck to the plane. Witnesses who arrived on the scene shortly after the craft crashed said ice was on the ship when they reached it.

Just Misses Seeing Sons.

Rockne was bound for Hollywood to complete arrangements for the making of a feature talking picture and several short subjects.

By a margin of minutes he missed seeing his sons, Knute, jr., 14, and Billy, 11, who arrived in Kansas City where they are students at Pembroke School at 8:15 a. m. They were returning from a visit with their mother at Coral Gables, Fla.

Rockne was forced to leave the station twenty minutes before their arrival in order to reach the airport in time for his plane's scheduled departure at 8:30. It was then held up 45 minutes by delayed mails.

Carry Away Souvenirs.

From miles around farmers came to view the wreckage and carry away souvenirs. Many rode cow ponies. Half a hundred automobiles were stalled in the mud in the vicinity.

After viewing the body of Rockne, a close friend, Dr. D. M. Nigro of Kansas City, telephoned Mrs. Rockne in Florida. She instructed him to make arrangements to return the body to South Bend, Ind., immediately.

Dr. Nigro planned to leave with the remains on a Santa Fe train departing at 4:34 a. m. tomorrow. The train will reach Chicago at 7:45 tomorrow night and the final stage of the trip will be over the New York Central on a train reaching South Bend at 11:20 p. m. The Rockne boys will accompany Dr. Nigro, president of the Notre Dame Club of Kansas City.

A preliminary inquest was called for tonight so the bodies of the victims could be released promptly. Further testimony will be taken tomorrow.

Sons Fight Back Sobs.

When Dr. Nigro told the coach's sons their father was dead, they sobbed for a few minutes on his shoulder. He comforted them. They fought back the tears and became more composed when asked to "take it like sports—the sons of a great man."

"I'm going to be a coach like my father," Knute, jr., said.

Leonard Jurdon, Department of Commerce inspector, and his assistant, B. M. Jacobs, arrived tonight from Kansas City and were followed by John Collings of New York, assistant operations manager of the Transcontinental Air Transport, and Jerry Bridges, Kansas City traffic manager of the air line. They announced they would start their investigation in the morning.

Coaches and athletic directors from near-by colleges and schools came to pay tribute to the great gridiron mentor. Among them were H. W. (Bill) Hargiss, football coach of the University of Kansas, and Mike Getto, assistant coach; Frank McDonald, director of athletics at Haskell Indian Institute, and head coach, William H. (Lone Star) Dietz, and A. N. (Bo) McMillin, football coach of Kansas State College.

The transport landed on a hilltop. The wing descended several seconds later on another hilltop three-eighths of a mile away. One motor of the tri-motor ten-passenger ship buried itself four feet in the ground. It was necessary to use horses to pull the engine out in order to remove the bodies of three of the victims.

Inspected Two Days Ago

Los Angeles, Calif.—(AP)—Anthony Fokker, airplane designer, left by air Wednesday to investigate the crash of the Fokker airplane which carried Knute Rockne to his death. Bad weather conditions, he said, undoubtedly caused the accident. "It is out of the question to consider that the airplane itself was defective," he said. "I inspected it personally two days ago and found it in perfect condition."

Hears News Bravely

Coral Gables, Fla.—(AP)—Mrs. Knute Rockne sped northward Wednesday from her winter residence here to South Bend, Ind., for the funeral of her husband. She was accompanied by her daughter, Mary Jean, 10, and her son, Jackie 5. Mrs. Rockne received the news of her husband's death bravely and helped members of her household with their packing for the trip.

Reprinted with permission from the **Cleveland Plain Dealer**

'Irish' Coach Was Adviser to His Players

'Can't Explain Bond Between Great Man and His Players,' Says Elmer Layden

BY THE ASSOCIATED PRESS

TRIBUTES to the memory of Knute Rockne today painted the portrait of a personality and a friend in harmony with his place in the realm of collegiate sports as the foremost football coaching genius.

Other football coaches did not stress his admitted ability in the game as much as they did his ideals and the heritage of true sportsmanship which he left.

Don Miller, backfield coach at Ohio State university, and one of the famous four horsemen of 1924, sounded

Hanley's Luck

Chicago, Ill.—(AP)—Chance kept Dick Hanley from taking the fatal plane in which Knute Rockne died Tuesday.

The Northwestern university football coach had been planning to join Rockne on the trip to Los Angeles, but at the last minute his wife fell ill and he decided to remain in Chicago.

the keynote of the estimate of Rockne voiced by scores after word of his death in an airplane accident was received.

"He was a lovable character whose beautiful personality made him legions of friends," Miller said.

He was the idol of millions who had never seen him.

His death was taken as a personal loss not only by his friends and associates but by thousands who knew him only as a molder of football teams that came, saw and conquered.

Boys Lose Intimate Friend

That football had lost its dominating figure was secondary to the fact that his boys had lost an intimate and beloved friend. They took all their troubles to him, even their love affairs.

KNUTE K. ROCKNE
(1888–1931)

✛

Whose life has inspired American Youth with the finest ideals of sportsmanship; and whose teaching has ever-placed the ventures of intelligence, courage and fair play above the achievements of brute strength. ☞ ☞ ☞ ☞

Body on Way Home
Kansas City, Mo. —(AP)— The body of Knute Rockne was escorted to Kansas City Wednesday by his two sons, Knute, jr., 12, and William, 15.

The boys, accompanied by Dr. D. M. Nigro, Notre Dame alumnus, went to Cottonwood Falls, Kas., Tuesday, upon receiving news of the gridiron mentor's death. They are students in the Pembroke school here.

The body was met here by Father Michael Mulcaire, vice president of Notre Dame; Jack Chevigny, assistant Notre Dame coach; "Hunk" Anderson, another assistant coach; Edward Halpin, manager of the Notre Dame team, and Earl King and Howard Edwards.

The party boarded the train which took the remains of the gridiron genius on toward Chicago and South Bend, Ind.

Rockne's Road to Death

WHERE EIGHT WERE KILLED— Map shows route of Western Air Express plane which crashed yesterday at Bazaar, Kan., killing eight persons, including Knute.

Rockne Letter to Schoolboy Puts Veto on Tobacco

MANNINGTON, W. Va., April 2 (AP).—One of Knute Rockne's last letters was written to a Mannington school boy who wanted to know the great coach's opinion on the use of tobacco by athletes.

Daniel Hanley Sturm, sixth grade student, is the possessor of the prized letter. He wrote to Rockne while fellow students were writing to other athletic leaders concerning the use of tobacco. The famous coach did not delay in replying to Daniel. The reply, dated last Thursday, was:

"Dea. Daniel:

"My experience has shown that tobacco shows up the reflexes of the athletes, lowers their morale and does nothing constructive.

"Athletes who smoke are the careless type and do not have the best interests of their team at heart.

"Yours sincerely,
"K. K. ROCKNE
"Director of Athletics."

A Requiem for Rockne

BY JEAN BOSQUET
[Associated Press Staff Writer]

The tolling bells of stricken Notre
Dame
Gave ringing voice to requiem
profound,
And, penned in gold, a new immortal name
Within valhalla's corridors is
found.

Let ring the bells, and bow each
rev'rent head
Where chivalry and honor count
for most—
The Rock, the old Rock loved by
all, is dead,
And silence grips an unbelieving
host.

The Rock against which thund'rous
waves were spent
In vain onslaught that died in
futile spray,
Is vanished from the Irish battlement,
Where once it turned the conflict's tide away.

The stalwart band that scaled the
crested height,
Fair victors on the throng encircled field,
Were nurtured by their Viking
chieftain's might,
And like their Rock knew naught
of how to yield.

Gird well the raiders for the battle's
shock,
Without the guidance of the
master hand—
Take up the gauntlet of the mighty
Rock,
Who watches from valhalla's distant land.

Play hard the game he loved, but
clean and fair,
As he would play who filled his
destiny;
His place upon the vacant bench is
there—
Hold high the fallen master's
memory.

Athletic World Mourns | Death of Knute Rockne

Most of Ship Carried Away for Souvenirs

Rumor of Half Million Aboard Heard After Disaster That Killed Eight Men

Cottonwood Falls, Kas.—(AP)—A coroner's jury was told Wednesday that the Transcontinental & Western Air Transport plane apparently was in distress for some minutes, with its motors backfiring, before it hurtled from the clouds Tuesday to carry Knute Rockne and seven others to death in a pasture near Bazaar, Kas.

Robert Z. Blackburn, stockman, who witnessed the tragic crash, said he had drawn this conclusion from the sound of the craft's engines.

"I heard the plane above the clouds. Then I ceased to hear it," he testified. "After a lapse of five minutes, perhaps, I heard it again.

"It seemed to linger in my hearing some time. Then I heard the engines backfire for some time. I was of the opinion then something was wrong.

Came Out of Clouds

"The sound attracted the attention of my cattle. Then I saw the plane coming out of the clouds at an angle of 45 degrees. I watched it until it went out of sight behind a hill. I heard a crash."

The cattle raiser testified that it had not rained in the vicinity Tuesday and there was no mist at the time of the accident.

"When I heard the crash I got in my car, but finally had to abandon it and go afoot," he said. "The wreckage had headed down in the ground. The bodies of passengers were strewn about the ground. Three or four were near the plane. The main portion of the wreckage was in a radius of 300 feet.

"The wing broken from the plane came down a quarter of a mile away. It was broken off rather square across. The edge looked ragged. It landed upside down. The glass in one of the plane's lights was unbroken."

Inspect Ships Regularly

Blackburn said he noticed no ice on the wreckage, saw some spilled gasoline, but no evidence of fire.

Jack Frye, vice president of Western Air, testified that the company's planes were inspected as a matter of routine every 28 hours. He said the ill fated craft had been in service a little more than a year. It is common in Europe, Frye said, for such ships to remain in service nine years.

It came to light during the inquest that one of the 18 pouches of mail carried by the plane was found beneath the broken wing, which fluttered to earth a quarter of a mile from the main wreckage. Other pouches were scattered about the ground.

Other witnesses to be heard by Dr. Jacob Hinden, Chase county coroner, were Edward Baker, son of Steward H. Baker, upon whose ranch the plane fell, and Clarence H. McCracken, ranchman who saw the liner hurtle to earth from a cloudy sky.

Fokker Is Expected

Dr. Hinden said other witnesses would be called, among them Harris Hanshue, of Transcontinental & Western Air Express, Inc., owner of the ill fated plane, and a department of commerce aviation inspector.

The inspector, who has viewed the wreckage is Leonard Jurdon, Kansas City. Anthony Fokker, designer of the craft, was expected to arrive here Wednesday.

1931 University of Notre Dame Varsity Football Roster

No.	Name	Position	Home City	Preparatory School	Age	Wt.	Ht.	Yrs. on Squad
1	Jaskwhich, Charles	Q.B.	Kenosha, Wis.	Kenosha High	20	174	5:11	1
2	Millheam, Duke	R.H.	Beloit, Wis.	Beloit High	20	156	5:7	0
3	Murphy, Emmett	Q.B.	Duluth, Minn.	De LaSalle, K. C., Mo.	22	153	5:8	1
4	Foley, Joe	Q.B.	Jacksonville, Fla.	Robt. E. Lee	21	158	5:7	0
5	Vejar, Laurie	Q.B.	Hollywood, Cal.	Hollywood High	21	168	5:7	0
6	Rohrs, George	R.E.	New York City, N. Y.	Fordham Prep	20	168	5:10	0
7	Mahoney, Dick	R.E.	Cleveland, Ohio	Cath. Latin	20	175	5:10	1
8	McGuff, Al	Q.B.	Chicago, Ill.	St. Mel's	20	170	5:10	0
9	Christman, Norb	Q.B.	Green Bay, Wis.	E. Green Bay	21	172	5:9	2
10	Sheeketski, Joe	R.H.	Shadyside, Ohio	Shadyside High	21	172	5:9	1
11	Host, Paul	L.E.	LaCrosse, Wis.	LaCrosse High	21	175	5:11	1
12	Brancheau, Ray	R.H.	Monroe, Mich.	Monroe High	21	180	5:10	0
13	Connelly, John	L.H.	Toledo, Ohio	St. John's High	21	165	5:10	0
14	Franklin, Randolph	R.E.	Youngstown, Ohio	South High	21	174	5:11	0
15	Canale, Frank	L.E.	Memphis, Tenn.	Catholic High	20	190	6:	0
16	Mahaffey, Tom	L.G.	Indianapolis, Ind.	Cathedral High	21	170	5:9	0
17	LaBorne, Frank	L.H.	Brooklyn, N. Y.	Brooklyn Prep	21	163	5:10	0
18	Schwartz, Marchmont	L.H.	Bay St. Louis, Miss.	St. Stanislaus	22	170	5:11	2
20	Bice, Leonard	L.E.	Hollywood, Cal.	Hollywood High	21	175	6:	0
21	Burke, Vince	Q.B.	Pittsburgh, Pa.	Sacred Heart High	19	152	5:9	0
22	Koken, Mike	L.H.	Youngstown, Ohio	South High	22	170	5:9	1
23	Krusiec, E. F.	F.B.	Chicago, Ill.	De LaSalle	20	180	5:8	0
24	Boland, Raymond	Q.B.	Chicago, Ill.	De LaSalle	20	160	5:7	0
25	Bolger, Charles	L.E.	Chicago, Ill.	De LaSalle	20	170	6:1	0
26	Cronin, Carl	R.H.	Chicago, Ill.	St. Rita's	22	157	5:7	2
29	Hagen, Lowell	F.B.	Monroe City, Mo.	Holy Rosary High	19	170	6:	0
30	Melinkovich, George	F.B.	Tooele, Utah	Tooele High	20	180	5:11	0
32	Greeney, Norman	L.G.	Cleveland, Ohio	John Marshall	22	185	5:11	1
33	Leahy, Bernie	R.H.	Chicago, Ill.	St. Mel's	22	175	5:10	2
34	Leonard, James	F.B.	Podricktown, N. J.	St. Joseph's	20	190	6:	0
35	Captor, Albert	F.B.	Paterson, N. J.	Central	21	185	6:	0
36	McNamara, Regis	R.T.	Pittsburgh, Pa.	Binghampton, N. Y., HS.	23	190	6:1	2
38	Harriss, James	L.G.	Bellaire, Ohio	Linsley (Bellaire)	22	187	5:9	1
40	Rouland, Ray	R.E.	Reedsburg, Wis.	Reedsburg High	21	182	6:2	0
41	Schumacher, Al	L.H.	Shawano, Wis.	Shawano High	21	171	6:	0
42	Cavanaugh, Vincent	R.G.	Chicago, Ill.	St. Ignatius	21	175	5:10	0
43	Beirne, Roger	L.E.	Fairfield, Conn.	Peddie	20	175	6:1	0
44	Kosky, Edwin	L.E.	Yonkers, N. Y.	Yonkers High	21	185	6:	1
45	Witucki, Bernard	C.	South Bend, Ind.	South Bend High	20	175	5:11	0
47	Alexander, Benjamin	C.	San Marino, Cal.	So. Pasadena High	22	185	6:	0
48	Lukats, Nick	F.B.	Gary, Ind.	Froebel	20	178	6:	1
49	Barstow, Fred	R.T.	Menominee, Mich.	Menominee High	19	207	6:2	0
50	Tobin, John	R.H.	Janesville, Wis.	Janesville High	21	180	5:9	0
51	Gorman, Tom	C.	Chicago, Ill.	St. Phillip's	21	187	6:	0
52	Leding, Mike	L.T.	South Bend, Ind.	South Bend High	21	180	6:1	0
53	Pierce, Bill	R.G.	Sherman, Tex.	Sherman High	22	185	5:8	1
54	Grundeman, Reuben	F.B.	Merrill, Wis.	Merrill High	20	183	5:11	0
56	Zoss, Oscar	C.	South Bend, Ind.	South Bend High	20	175	5:11	0
57	DeVore, Hugh	R.E.	Bloomfield, N. J.	St. Benedict's	20	180	6:	0
58	Kreuz, Paul	R.G.	Menominee, Mich.	Menominee High	20	180	5:8	0
59	Whelan, Vincent	C.	Grantwood, N. J.	St. Benedict's	21	175	5:8	0
60	Banas, Steve	F.B.	East Chicago, Ind.	Cath. Cent. Hammond	22	188	5:11	0
61	Jehle, Frank	L.T.	Detroit, Mich.	Western High	20	195	6:1	0
62	Acers, Julian	L.H.	Chicago, Ill.	Campion	21	175	5:11	0
63	Halpin, Robert	C.	New Haven, Conn.	New Haven High	20	178	6:	0
64	Rogers, John	C.	Alexis, Ill.	Alexis High	21	175	5:8	1
65	Flynn, Jack	R.T.	Quincy, Ill.	Quincy High	19	196	6:	0
66	Kurth, Joe	R.T.	Los Angeles, Cal.	Madison, Wis., High	21	200	6:1	1
67	Gildea, Hubert	L.E.	New Haven, Conn.	Milford & Hillhse.	20	188	6:1	0
68	Pivarnik, Joe	L.G.	Bridgeport, Conn.	Harding High	19	195	5:9	0
69	Krause, Ed.	L.T.	Chicago, Ill.	De LaSalle	19	210	6:3	0
70	Cousino, Bernard	R.T.	Toledo, Ohio	St. John's	21	175	6:	0
72	Wunsch, Harry	L.G.	South Bend, Ind.	South Bend High	20	200	5:11	0
73	Schrenker, Paul	L.G.	Elwood, Ind.	Elwood High	19	185	5:11	0
74	Hoffman, Frank Nordy	R.G.	Seattle, Wash.	St. Martin's	21	204	6:2	1
75	Kozak, George	R.T.	Cleveland, Ohio	Holy Name High	22	198	6:2	0
76	Yarr, Tom (Capt.)	C.	Dabob, Wash.	Chimacum Prep	22	197	5:11	2
77	Vyzral, Edward	R.T.	Chicago, Ill.	Lindblom	21	209	6:4	1
78	Carmody, James	R.T.	Chicago, Ill.	Mt. Carmel	21	210	6:1	0
79	Mariani, H.	L.T.	Pearl River, N. Y.	Pearl River High	20	193	5:11	0
81	Culver, Alvin	L.T.	Wilmette, Ill.	St. Thos., St. Paul	23	212	6:2	2

SHEEKETSKI   MELINKOVICH   SCHWARTZ
JASKWHICH
DEVORE   KURTH   HOFFMANN   CAPT YARR   HARRIS   KRAUSE   KOSKY

They Carried On!

1931†

Coach: Heartley W. (Hunk) Anderson
Captain: Thomas Yarr

O.3	W	Indiana	25-0	A	12,098
O.10	T	Northwestern (R)	0-0	N1	65,000
O.17	W	Drake	63-0	H	23,835
O.24	W	Pittsburgh	25-12	H	37,394
O.31	W	Carnegie Tech	19-0	A	42,271
N.7	W	Pennsylvania	49-0	H	39,173
N.14	W	Navy	20-0	N2	56,861
N.21	L	So. Calif. (U)(1:00)	14-16	H	*50,731
N.28	L	Army (U)	0-12	YS	c78,559
		(6-2-1)	215-40		405,922

*First capacity crowd in Notre Dame Stadium
N1—at Soldier Field; N2—at Baltimore
†Coach Knute K. Rockne, 43, and seven other persons were killed in a plane crash near Bazaar, Kansas, on March 31, 1931.

Notre Dame Power Wrecks Drake Bulldogs, 63 To 0

Irish Cyclone Overwhelms Rivals by Most Top-Heavy Score of Series—Ramblers Gain 636 Yards From Scrimmage

South Bend, Ind., Oct. 17.—(AP.)—The pent-up fury of Notre Dame's big football army fell on the valiant but out-classed Bull Dogs from Drake today and submerged them under a one-sided score of 63 to 0, the largest count against them since they started playing the "Fighting Irish."

Smarting under the criticism received for failing to score against Northwestern in the mud of Soldiers' Field last week, the touchdown makers of Notre Dame paraded up and down the field with monotonous regularity from the middle of the first period on. The game wasn't even interesting except to the scouts of rival teams, who confessed they had never seen a greater running attack.

Fifty-seven players, two more than five complete teams, were used.

Notre Dame gained 636 yards from the line of scrimmage to 60 for Drake. Of the 28 first downs scored, Notre Dame collected 23 to Drake's 5.

Notre Dame		Drake
Host	le	Briley
Culver	lt	Blanck
Pierce	lg	Bowers
Gorman	c	Robertson
Harriss	rg	Olson
Kozak	rt	Kokjohn
Mahoney	re	Cless
Vejar	qb	Goodwin
Koken	lhb	Lindstrom
Cronin	rhb	Wieland
Banas	fb	Lansrud

Notre Dame ....7 20 21 15—63
Drake ....0 0 0 0— 0

Notre Dame touchdowns: Koken 3; Melinkovich (sub for Cronin) 2; Shetketski 1; Leahy (sub for Shetketski) 1; Laborne (sub for Koken) 1; Leonard (sub for Shetketski) 1.

Points after touchdown: Koken 4; Murphy (sub for Vejar) 2; Jaskwhich (sub for Vejar) 1.

Safety: Drake (Ross).

Referee, Ed Cochrane (Kalamazoo); umpire, Dr. F. A. Lambert (Ohio State); field judge, M. P. Ghee (Dartmouth); head linesman, H. L. Ray (Illinois).

NOTRE DAME, 0

On October 10, for the first time since 1928, Notre Dame failed to cross its opponent's goal. Played in a downpour, on a rain-soaked gridiron, the Notre Dame-Northwestern game was not an indication of the strength of either team. A fast and varied attack was out of the question; both teams relied on punting and watching for breaks.

Frequent fumbles in the first quarter kept the Irish on the defense deep in their own territory and only Schwartz's magnificent punting staved off Northwestern drives. On three occasions Schwartz punted out of danger from behind his own goal line. The Notre Dame attack never had a chance to function as a result of repeated fumbles but late in the second quarter one of Schwartz's long kicks forced the Wildcats back to their 20-yard line.

From here they were compelled to punt and the Irish attack began to click. Sheeketski and Schwartz punctured the line for first downs. In spite of the insecure footing, the Notre Dame backs drove down the field. Another fumble, however, stopped the march when it appeared as if the Wildcat defense was giving way.

For the rest of the period Northwestern fought stubbornly against determined Irish drives. The mud made it impossible for the Notre Dame blocking backs to reach the Northwestern secondary in time; the Irish offense was accordingly smothered.

Olson's kicking helped Northwestern out of tough spots. One of his long punts traveled to the Notre Dame 30-yard line late in the second period, where a costly fumble on the first play gave the Wildcats the ball.

But their threat was stopped cold. Krause, who was playing a whale of a game at tackle, broke through twice to throw ball carriers for losses and Northwestern lost the ball on downs.

Notre Dame couldn't get going and again Schwartz was forced to punt. Three line plays gave Northwestern a first down, but Olson was soon thrown for a three-yard loss and Rentner failed to gain. Olson kicked to the Irish 25-yard line as the half ended.

NORTHWESTERN, 0

Notre Dame started the second half with a rush. Schwartz and Banas made a first down on the Irish 40-yard line. Here the Wildcats held and Schwartz kicked.

An exchange followed with neither team able to keep up a sustained drive. Once Schwartz cut through tackle and appeared to be in the clear on one of his remarkable long runs but he slipped in the mud. Notre Dame was soon forced to punt.

Rentner's long pass was immediately knocked down and Olson kicked back. A spinner resulted in a fumble which Riley recovered for Northwestern. A long pass was smothered by Schwartz in the end zone and the Irish took the ball on their 20-yard line. Schwartz, entirely at ease, got off a long spiral.

Finding the Irish line impenetrable, Rentner tried a pass which was intercepted by Captain Yarr on his 30-yard line. Two line-plays gained eight yards but Banas just failed to make a first down. Again Schwartz got off a long punt.

Olson failed to gain and a fumble gave Notre Dame the ball on the Wildcats' 35-yard line. Schwartz got seven yards in two plays but a penalty for holding forced the Irish to punt.

As the last period opened an exchange of kicks gave Notre Dame the ball on their 40-yard line. Melinkovich, who went in for Banas, reeled off a pretty 15-yard run through center but slipped with a clear field in front of him and was brought down from behind by Potter.

Northwestern held and Schwartz kicked. Olson tried a return punt but his kick was blocked and Krause recovered on the Northwestern 20-yard line. Northwestern held for downs and the game ended shortly afterward, with the Irish in possession of the ball on their 40-yard line.

Though mud stopped the powerful offenses of both teams, Notre Dame had the edge on its rivals in first downs and in rushing, making six first downs to Northwestern's three and gaining 106 yards from rushing to Northwestern's 81 yards.

NOTRE DAME, 19

Notre Dame gained its third consecutive victory over Carnegie Tech in a 19 to 0 triumph at Pittsburgh. All the scoring came in the first half; in the second half honors were fairly even.

The Irish experienced trouble in getting started during the first period. Three marches which seemed destined to end in touchdowns were stopped by penalties and fumbles. The first score came as a result of one of Schwartz's long runs.

With the ball on his 33-yard line, Melinkovitch hit center for nine yards and on the next play Schwartz broke through left tackle and zig-zagged 58 yards for a touchdown. Jaskwich kicked the point.

The second score came at the beginning of the second quarter. After receiving the kick-off, the Skibos decided to punt but Hoffmann and Harris crashed in to block Armentrout's kick on the nine-yard line, where Harris recovered.

A 15-yard penalty for holding set the Irish back but Leahy made up the distance by making a first down on the 10-yard line. Leahy then took the ball to the four-yard marker; on the next play he cut in through right guard to score the second touchdown. Fletcher blocked Jaskwich's attempted kick and the score stood, 13 to 0.

Late in the second period, Notre Dame scored again. When Koken replaced Schwartz, he and Leahy ran the ball to Carnegie's 20-yard line. After two line plays and a pass had failed to gain, however, the Skibos took the ball on downs. Armentrout and Kavel gained only six yards in two tries and Armentrout kicked to Jaskwich at mid field.

Koken made a first down around right end. Eight yards more through center and then Leahy's five brought another first down.

Koken took the ball to the 11-yard line on a spinner. From here Koken passed laterally to Leahy and the fullback ran the rest of the way for the third touchdown. The kick was wide. Shortly after Carnegie received the kick-off the half ended with the Irish holding a 19 to 0 lead.

CARNEGIE TECH, 0

Carnegie came back fighting at the beginning of the second half with Armentrout and Kavel hitting the line for consistent gains. At mid field, Notre Dame stopped the advance and Armentrout punted to Murphy, who was brought down in his tracks.

Koken made five yards on the first play but then the Skibo line stiffened and Koken kicked to Dueger. Carnegie kicked back and again their line stopped the Irish backs. A punting duel between Armentrout and Koken followed with neither team able to keep up a sustained drive.

Starting on their 20-yard line, Carnegie began another offensive march. After two penalties had stopped the Skibos on their 35-yard line, Armentrout kicked to Murphy, who ran the ball back to his 40-yard line before Ducanis brought him down.

Two passes were grounded by the Carnegie secondary and Koken kicked to Bevenino. A long pass intended for Stewart was intercepted by Murphy on the Tech 48-yard line. On the next play a fumble gave Tech possession of the ball.

Armentrout made seven yards in two plays but a fake reverse met with disaster when Pierce broke through to spill Kavel for a six-yard loss. Armentrout then kicked over the goal for a touchback, making it first down and ten for the Irish on their 20-yard line as the period ended.

Notre Dame found the going tough through the Skibo line and had to punt. The ball see-sawed back and forth for the rest of the period, and though both teams showed offensive flashes, the defensive line play balked the running attacks. Apparently content to hold a 19-point lead, Notre Dame concentrated on stopping Carnegie's belated passing attack. The game ended with the ball at mid field in possession of the Irish.

Schwartz was the outstanding star of the contest. He made a total of 188 yards from scrimmage, which was 80 yards more than the Carnegie aggregate. The lead which Notre Dame piled up in the first half was apparently a safe one. Even during the second half Carnegie was unable to push the ball past the Irish 45-yard line.

NOTRE DAME
VERSUS
SOUTHERN
CALIFORNIA

PRICE

OFFICIAL
PROGRAM
NOVEMBER 21, 1931

NOTRE DAME
STADIUM

NOTRE DAME, 14

In a savagely fought contest on November 21, Southern California broke a three-year string of Notre Dame triumphs with a 16 to 14 victory. A place kick in the last minute of play was the deciding factor in the game. An apparently inexplicable let down on the part of the Irish in the last quarter enabled the Trojans to score two touchdowns and a place kick to overcome the 14-point lead which Notre Dame held. It was a titanic struggle, a game packed with all the thrills that an afternoon of football can offer.

Notre Dame received the kick-off and on the third down Schwartz punted to the Trojan 45-yard line. From here the Southern Cal offense started off with a rush. Aided by three offside penalties inflicted on the Irish, the Trojans marched down to the two-yard line. But here the Notre Dame line stiffened; as Musick was thrown back for a loss; he fumbled and Kurth recovered for the Irish.

After Schwartz punted out of danger, the Trojans began another drive which was stopped on the 15-yard line. For the first time in the game the Notre Dame offense got under way and a series of off-tackle plays carried the ball to the 40-yard line, where Schwartz kicked. An exchange of kicks followed and then a long Southern Cal pass was intercepted by Schwartz on his 37-yard line.

The Irish touchdown drive began. Schwartz went around right end for 12 yards. Banas made another first down. A long pass, Schwartz to Jaskwich, was good for a first down on the Trojan 18-yard line. Brancheau made eight yards on a delayed buck and Marchy made another first down on the four-yard line. Banas drove through center to the one-yard line and then dove over the line for a touchdown. Jaskwich's kick from placement was good.

The Trojans then took to the air after receiving the kick-off. But Mohler was thrown for a 15-yard loss in attempting to pass and the next long toss was intercepted by Jaskwich, who ran the ball back to the Southern Cal 18-yard line as the half ended.

SOUTHERN CALIFORNIA, 16

Southern Cal received the kick-off at the beginning of the second half and was soon forced to punt. Schwartz took the kick and raced back to his 37-yard line. In four plays, Notre Dame had scored a second touchdown. Brancheau made nine yards on a lateral. Marchy swung wide around right end for 15 yards. On the next play Banas took a lateral from Schwartz, raced through the Trojan secondary, shaking off tacklers as he went, and was finally brought down on the three-yard line. Then Marchy took the ball through right tackle for a touchdown. Again Jaskwich's place kick was good and the score stood 14 to 0.

Receiving the kick-off, Southern Cal made two first downs, with Sparling and Mohler carrying the ball. They were soon forced to punt. Notre Dame kicked back. As a long Southern Cal forward pass was ruled completed because of interference, the third quarter ended with the Trojans in possession of the ball on the Irish 14-yard line. Three plays took the ball to the one-foot line. With inches to go for a touchdown, Shaver catapulted himself over for the score. Kurth blocked the try for the extra point.

Southern Cal kicked off and after two line plays, Schwartz punted. Shaver dropped back and threw a long pass which was knocked down. But again the officials gave the Trojans the ball on interference. Mohler and Shaver took the ball to the Irish 10-yard line. From here Shaver scored on a lateral pass. Baker made good his try for the extra point.

On the third play after receiving the kick-off, Schwartz punted. Southern Cal failed to gain but the Irish were penalized 15 yards, giving the Trojans a first down. A long pass was completed on the Notre Dame 17-yard line. Mohler gained only one yard in two plays.

With a minute left, Baker dropped back in place kick formation and sent the ball squarely between the uprights. Score: U. S. C. 16, Notre Dame 14.

The gun went off a few seconds later with Notre Dame trying desperately to score. The game marked the first defeat in three years for Notre Dame, but what a battle!

1932 UNIVERSITY OF NOTRE DAME VARSITY FOOTBALL ROSTER

No.	Name	Position	Home City	Preparatory School	Age	Wt.	Ht.	Yrs. on Squad
1	Jaskwhich, Charles J.	Q.B.	Kenosha, Wis.	Kenosha H. S.	21	164	5:11	2
2	Millbearn, Curtis K.	R.H.	Beloit, Wis.	Beloit H. S.	21	160	5:7	1
3	Murphy, Emmett F.	Q.B.	Duluth, Minn.	De LaSalle, K. C., Mo.	23	153	5:8	2
4	Foley, Joseph M.	Q.B.	Jacksonville, Fla.	Robert E. Lee H. S.	21	155	5:7	1
5	Vejar, Laurie	Q.B.	Hollywood, Calif.	Hollywood H. S.	22	150	5:6	1
6	Bohrs, George H.	R.E.	New York City, N. Y.	Fordham Prep	21	187	5:10	1
7	Boland, Raymond J.	Q.B.	Chicago, Ill.	De LaSalle	21	165	5:7	0
9	McGuff, Albert L.	L.H.	Chicago, Ill.	St. Mel	21	171	5:10	0
10	Sheeketski, Joseph L.	R.H.	Shadyside, Ohio	Shadyside H. S.	23	170	5:8	2
11	Host, Paul A. (Capt.)	R.E.	LaCrosse, Wis.	LaCrosse Central	22	175	5:11	2
12	Brancheau, Raymond J.	R.H.	Monroe, Mich.	Monroe H. S.	22	185	5:10½	1
13	Davis, Irwin V.	R.E.	Ponchatoula, La.	Ponchatoula H. S.	18	180	5:11	0
14	Carideo, Angelo, Jr.	Q.B.	Mt. Vernon, N. Y.	Mt. Vernon H. S.	19	165	5:8	0
15	Freschi, William J.	L.H.	Webster Groves, Mo.	Webster Groves H. S	20	170	5:8	0
17	LaBorne, Frank H.	L.H.	Brooklyn, N. Y.	Brooklyn Prep	22	168	5:11	1
18	Daigle, Thos. F.	L.H.	New Orleans, La.	Jesuit H. S.	22	160	5:10	0
19	Canale, Frank S.	L.E.	Memphis, Tenn.	Catholic H. S.	21	190	6:	0
20	Rascher, Norbert H.	R.E.	Cedar Lake, Ind.	St. Viator Acad.	21	188	6:1	0
21	Burke, James V.	Q.B.	Pittsburgh, Pa.	Sacred Heart H. S.	20	145	5:8	1
22	Koken, Michael R.	L.H.	Youngstown, Ohio	South High	23	168	5:9	2
25	Weidner, Fred W.	R.G.	LaPorte, Ind.	LaPorte H. S.	21	172	5:9	0
26	Vairo, Dominic M.	L.E.	Calumet, Mich.	Calumet H. S.	18	192	6:	0
27	Meyer, Robert J.	F.B.	Jersey City, N. J.	St. Peter's Prep	20	195	5:9½	0
28	Witucki, Bernard F.	C.	South Bend, Ind.	Central H. S.	21	175	5:11	0
29	Hagan, Lowell L.	F.B.	Monroe City, Mo.	Holy Rosary H. S.	20	180	6:	0
30	Melinkovich, George J.	F.B.	Tooele, Utah	Tooele H. S.	21	180	6:	1
31	Albosta, Anthony V.	R.E.	Saginaw, Mich.	St. Mary's	20	170	6:	0
32	Greeney, Norman J.	L.G.	Cleveland, Ohio	John Marshall H. S.	23	190	6:	2
33	Tobin, John E.	R.H.	Janesville, Wis.	Janesville H. S.	21	178	5:7½	0
34	Leonard, James R.	F.B.	Pedrickstown, N. J.	St. Joseph, Phila.	21	190	6:	1
35	Gaul, Frank J.	Q.B.	Waterville, Me.	Waterville H. S.	19	170	5:10	0
36	Hafron, Charles F.	L.E.	South Bend, Ind.	Central H. S.	21	160	5:11	0
37	Esser, Carl F.	L.T.	Aurora, Ill.	West Aurora H. S.	20	190	6:2	0
38	Harris, James M.	L.G.	Bellaire, Ohio	Linsley, Wheeling	23	188	5:10½	2
39	Dilling, Leo T.	R.H.	Gary, Ind.	Emerson H. S.	22	175	5:11½	1
41	Winterbottom, John R.	R.H.	Alhambra, Calif.	Alhambra H. S.	19	185	5:11	0
42	Becker, Harry P.	L.T.	Louisville, Ky.	St. Xavier H. S.	21	185	6:1	0
44	Kosky, Edwin S.	L.E.	Yonkers, N. Y.	Yonkers High	22	185	6:	2
45	Bonar, Reyman E.	Q.B.	Bellaire, Ohio	Bellaire H. S.	21	160	5:8	0
46	Quinlan, Harold F.	L.E.	Needham, Mass.	Needham H. S.	19	180	6:	0
47	Alexander, Benjamin F.	C.	San Marino, Cal.	So. Pasadena H. S.	22	181	6:	1
48	Lukats, Nicholas P.	L.H.	Perth Amboy, N. J.	Froebel, Gary, Ind.	21	185	6:	1
49	Barstow, Fred A.	L.T.	Menominee, Mich.	Menominee H. S.	20	200	6:2	1
50	Nabicht, Ferdinand C.	L.T.	South Bend, Ind.	Central H. S.	19	195	6:2	1
51	Gorman, Thos. A.	C.	Chicago, Ill.	St. Philip's H. S.	22	190	6:1	1
52	Leding, Michael J.	L.T.	South Bend, Ind.	Central H. S.	21	180	6:2	0
53	Pierce, William C.	R.G.	Sherman, Tex.	Sherman H. S.	22	180	5:8	2
54	Carideo, Fred, Jr.	F.B.	Mt. Vernon, N. Y.	Mt. Vernon H. S.	21	180	5:10½	0
55	Staab, Fred Edwin	F.B.	Madison, Wis.	Central H. S.	22	180	5:11	1
56	Costello, Albert T.	R.H.	Akron, Ohio	North H. S. Akron	21	185	5:9	0
57	DeVore, Hugh J.	R.E.	Newark, N. J.	St. Benedict's	21	181	6:	1
59	Kennedy, Kenneth S.	L.T.	Papillion, Nebr.	Papillion H. S.	20	196	6:1	0
60	Banas, Stephen P.	F.B.	E. Chicago, Ind.	Cath. Cent. Hammond	22	185	5:11	1
61	Jehle, Frank J.	L.T.	Detroit, Mich.	Western H. S.	21	204	6:2	0
62	Young, John R.	L.H.	Houston, Tex.	St. Thomas H. S.	20	180	6:1	
64	Fulnecky, Karl D.	C.	Frankfort, Ind.	Frankfort H. S.	19	195	6:	0
65	Flynn, John J.	R.G.	Quincy, Ill.	Quincy Col. Academy	20	190	6:1	1
66	Kurth, Joseph J.	R.T.	Madison, Wis.	East Side H. S.	22	204	6:1½	2
67	Gildea, Hubert F.	L.E.	New Haven, Conn.	Hillhouse and Milford	21	182	6:1	0
68	Pivarnik, Joseph J.	R.G.	Bridgeport, Conn.	Harding H. S.	20	195	5:9	1
69	Krause, Edward W.	L.T.	Chicago, Ill.	De LaSalle	19	220	6:3	0
70	Cousino, Bernard L.	R.T.	Erie, Mich.	St. John, Toledo	22	178	6:	1
71	Schiralli, Rocco V.	L.G.	Gary, Ind.	Emerson H. S.	20	175	5:10	0
73	Schrenker, Paul E.	L.G.	Elwood, Ind.	Elwood H. S.	20	185	5:11	1
74	Solari, Fred C.	C.	Pembroke, Mass.	Commerce H. S., Bost.	19	205	6:2	0
75	Lesko, Paul J.	R.G.	Homestead, Pa.	Homestead H. S.	19	185	6:	0
76	Robinson, John J.	C.	Huntington, N. Y.	Georgetown Prep, Md.	19	200	6:3	0
77	Vyzral, Edward F.	R.T.	Chicago, Ill.	Lindblom H. S.	22	210	6:4	0
79	Mariani, Hector J.	L.T.	Pearl River, N. Y.	Pearl River H. S.	21	193	6:	0
81	Roach, Thomas G.	R.T.	Grand Rapids, Mich.	Catholic Central	23	205	6:1½	0
82	Pfefferle, Richard J.	L.T.	Appleton, Wis.	Campion Prep, Wis.	19	196	6:2	0
84	Wunsch, Harry F.	R.G.	South Bend, Ind.	Central H. S.	21	212	5:11	1

Brancheau   Jaskwhich   Melinkovich   Koken

Capt. Host   Kurth   Greeney   Alexander   Harris   Krause   Kosky

1932

Coach: Heartley W. (Hunk) Anderson
Captain: Paul A. Host

O.8	W	Haskell	73-0	H	8,369
O.15	W	Drake	62-0	H	6,663
O.22	W	Carnegie Tech	42-0	H	16,015
O.29	L	Pittsburgh (U)	0-12	A	55,616
N.5	W	Kansas	24-6	A	18,062
N.12	W	Northwestern	21-0	H	31,853
N.19	W	Navy	12-0	N	61,122
N.26	W	Army	21-0	YS	c78,115
D.10	L	So. California	0-13	A	93,924
	(7-2-0)		255-31		369,739

N—at Cleveland

NORTHWESTERN
VERSUS
NOTRE DAME

OFFICIAL
PROGRAM

25c

NOVEMBER, 12
1932

NOTRE DAME STADIUM

MICHAEL KOKEN
Left Halfback

"Even Pittsburgh papers had deserted their team. Forecasts ran as high as 31 to 0 for the Irish. Too much power, experience, versatility. Hadn't a green Ohio team tied Pitt the week before, after pushing them around for three quarters? There would be nothing to it. The boys exuded confidence as they ate their steaks in the Pittsburgh A. C. They looked great out on that field before the game in their green jerseys and gleaming gold pants. Big leaguers. And they played like big leaguers between the 20-yard stripes. But then.

Pitt's pants may not have fitted them so nicely around the knees nor did they have a sweet hike cadence as did the Irish, but they stuck in there all along the line and made it tough for the boys when down around their goal line. Finally, in the fourth period, Sebastien, who had been tossed around, along with the rest of the Pittsburgh attack like so much hay all afternoon, started around his own left end, moved through half a dozen tacklers waving at him, and trundled 45 yards to the Notre Dame goal, six points, and a win, not fast, you understand but steady. A moment later, just to settle all doubts about the matter, Ted Dailey, one of those crashing ends, plucked off a Notre Dame pass and really roared down across the line—nothing of that Pitt backfield about him.

There is no doubt that Pittsburgh played a great defensive game. Any team that can take the awful pushing around they took for three quarters and then come plowing back up the field to win in the fourth has something great. The two ends, Skladany and Dailey, were the best pair that Notre Dame faced all year, and that goes for Southern California, too. Hogan played a tough, consistent game, as did Captain Heller, the master of understatement.

Notre Dame's second team backfield opened the game and pushed down to the Pittsburgh 25-yard line. Sheeket-

JOSEPH SHEEKETSKI
Right Halfback

ski just missed a touchdown pass and the quarter ended with the ball in Pitt's possession on their own 20-yard line. Jaskwhich took a long pass to the 24-yard line, from where it was booted back to the Irish 8. The half ended with the Irish moving up to their 45. Later they marched to the Pitt 10 and missed first down by inches. In the fourth quarter they tackled Hogan on his one-foot line but he kicked out from behind goal through the hands of Krause and Kurth and this was just a little too much for the boys. Followed the Pitt touchdowns and then, in the Associated Press Story: "Notre Dame fell apart like an expensive toy dropped from a considerable height with the mainspring tightly wound." With all confidence gone, no rhythm in the shift, and but a few minutes of fierce hope left, the dazed Irish threw pass after pass, which the jubilant Panthers batted down feverishly. The gun sounded with the ball in Notre Dame territory.

NICHOLAS LUKATS
Left Halfback

NOTRE DAME   0
SO. CALIFORNIA   13

"A tide of Trojans flows and fills the place
And lifts the Trojan glory to the skies."

—HOMER.

■ Thus wrote the old Homer about a victory at the old Troy...

"Southern California 13, Notre Dame 0." That is the writing of a new Homer. And the victory is that of a new Troy. It was not an aged, blind, wandering bard who carved out the newest pinnacle of Trojan glory. Rather it was a whirling, racing, gridiron dervish, 190 pounds of skilled, speedy youth, Homer Griffith, Howard Jones' great quarterback.

Following the formula of his most famous namesake, Griffith guided the undefeated U. S. C. eleven through the air and over the land to its nineteenth consecutive victory. And the victory was no less glorious than any of the other eighteen.

"Hunk" Anderson looked at the game's result as a victory "for the better team." His Irish, so he said, were out-played. When defeat comes that way, there is no need for explanation, much need for tribute to the superior machine.

Following the peculiar rites of their cult, the betting public had made the Irish the favorites. The "why" of that choice is hard to discover. At their peak for the Army game, two weeks previous, there was little reason to expect Notre Dame to stay at its best form for the U. S. C. clash. That they were below that form is in no way an attempt to dim the glory of Troy, once again "lifted to the skies." It is merely a statement of an evident and an expected fact.

Two days before the game, Anderson picked the Trojans to win by 13 to 0. Coming from the man closest to the Irish situation, the prophecy bore much weight. In the light of the ultimate result, it was a startling forecast. But all in all, it was a common sense outlook by a sound gridiron expert who realized that the greatest heights are reached only once. And nothing short of the greatest perfection could stop the Trojans.

As the Trojans outscored the Irish, they smashed an eight year tradition of the Notre Dame crew. Not since Nebraska's Cornhuskers turned back Notre Dame in 1922 and 1923 has a team defeated the Irish twice in as many years. Notre Dame had been the perfect football team to prevent Army from turning the trick; their sub-perfection could not withstand the Trojans.

INDIVIDUAL YARDAGE			
	Attempts	Total	Average
Koken	105	375	3.6
Lukats	89	477	5.3
Melinkovich	88	536	6.0
Branchau	48	137	2.9
Sheeketski	45	252	5.6
Banas	71	401	5.6
Leonard	30	136	4.5
Tobin	12	93	7.8
Laborne	9	69	7.7
McGuff	14	47	3.3
Hagen	10	80	8.0
Costello	8	22	2.7
Jaskwhich	5	33	6.6
Murphy	1	3	3.0
Kosky	3	11	3.2

	TOTALS								Carn.												
	N.D.	Opp.	N.D.	Hask.	N.D.	Drake	N.D.	Tech.	N.D.	Pitt.	N.D.	Kans.	N.D.	N.U.	N.D.	Navy	N.D.	Army	N.D.	U.S.C.	
First downs	137	46	23	3	8	3	20	4	16	6	11	7	10	8	20	4	16	5	13	6	
First downs rushing	115	33	21	3	7	4	17	2	11	5	11	3	6	3	17	1	13	3	7	5	
First downs passing	20	9	2	0	1	2	3	2	3	0	0	3	3	1	2	3	1	6	1		
Total yardage gained	3285	912	673	50	396	61	466	79	237	193	407	189	216	82	310	92	355	100	225	148	
Total yardage rushing	2632	659	578	50	331	41	369	48	153	147	407	97	136	30	272	71	273	61	119	117	
Total yards passing	678	368	125	0	65	20	97	31	90	40	0	92	80	52	38	21	82	39	113	13	
Forwards attempted	103	90	7	5	8	5	11	11	29	3	4	9	10	20	7	11	10	18	17	8	
Forwards completed	41	22	4	0	3	2	6	5	10	0	0	4	4	4	2	2	5	4	7	1	
Forwards intercepted	18	7	1	0	2	0	1	0	2	2	1	1	4	1	4	1	3	0	0	2	
No. of punts	60	91	2	11	6	9	3	9	5	7	7	12	11	9	5	8	8	13	14	13	
Yardage of punts	2339	3286	60	337	169	235	96	375	275	229	313	441	401	359	216	320	379	551	339	339	
Average yards of punts	40	35.1	30	31.6	28	26	32	41	46	39	44.7	36.7	36	40	43	40	47	42	33	33	
Punts returned, yards	404	109	95	0	95	0	106	13	17	5			34	0	9	0	40	9	3	72	
Kickoffs returned, yards	385	503	47	114	78	89	0	117	59	0			99	76	6	80	40	27	59		
Fumbles	21	18	3	1	3	1	1	2	2	2	3	4	3	2	2	2	3	2	1	2	
Fumbles recovered—own	8	11	2	1	2	0	0	1	1	1	1	3	0	1	1	2	0	0	0	2	
Fumbles recovered—opp.	6	14	0	1	1	1	0	1	1	1	1	2	1	3	0	1	2	3	0	2	
No. of penalties	65	30	10	1	10	4	7	2	10	7	5	5	6	5	6	3	4	5	1	1	
Yards lost on penalties	540	245	70	5	110	30	60	30	50	45	65	45	60	55	50	20	50	25	5	10	

Official 1933 University of Notre Dame Football Roster

No.	Name	Position	Home City	Preparatory School	Age	Wt.	Ht.	Yrs. on Squad
1	McFadden, Daniel T.	Q.B.	Allentown, Pa.	Allentown H. S.	20	170	5:10	0
2	Church, August J.	C.	N. Plainfield, N. J.	N. Plainfield H. S.	19	160	5:7	0
3	Moriarty, George J.	Q.B.	Lynn, Mass.	Clark (Hanover, N. H.)	20	150	5:8	0
5	Harper, Mell C.	Q.B.	Wichita, Kans.	Wichita H. S. North	19	170	5:10	0
7	Beach, Joseph D.	R.H.	New Orleans, La.	Holy Cross Col. H. S.	20	172	5:10	0
9	Fromhart, Wallace L.	Q.B.	Moundsville, W. Va.	Moundsville, H. S.	20	178	5:11	0
10	Alworth, Sam R.	Q.B.	Tooele, Utah	Tooele H. S.	20	172	5:11	0
11	Layden, Francis L.	R.H.	Davenport, Ia.	Davenport H. S.	20	179	6:1	0
12	**Brancheau, Raymond J.	R.H.	Monroe, Mich.	Monroe H. S.	23	190	5:11	2
13	Davis, Irwin V.	R.E.	Ponchatoula, La.	Ponchatoula H. S.	19	177	5:11	1
17	*LaBorne, Frank H.	L.H.	Brooklyn, N. Y.	Brooklyn Prep.	23	165	5:11	2
19	Canale, Frank S.	L.E.	Memphis, Tenn.	Catholic H. S.	22	190	6:	2
20	*Rascher, Norbert H.	R.E.	Cedar Lake, Ind.	St. Viator (Ill.)	22	184	6:1	2
21	Shamla, Richard J.	R.G.	Glencoe, Minn.	Glencoe H. S.	20	188	5:10	0
22	Ream, William E.	R.E.	Hollywood, Calif.	Hollywood H. S.	20	190	6:2	0
24	Caldwell, Edwin G.	Q.B.	Hudson, Ohio	Ponce de Leon, Fla. H. S.	22	163	5:9	1
25	Weidner, Fred W.	R.G.	LaPorte, Ind.	LaPorte H. S.	21	170	5:9	1
26	*Vairo, Dominic M.	L.E.	Calumet, Mich.	Calumet H. S.	19	188	6:	1
27	Smith, William R.	R.G.	Hackettstown, N. J.	St. Benedict's (Newark)	20	173	5:10	0
28	Martin, James R.	R.G.	Concord, N. H.	Concord H. S.	20	176	5:11	0
29	Hagan, Lowell L.	F.B.	Monroe City, Miss.	Holy Rosary H. S.	21	180	6:	2
31	*Hanley, Daniel J.	F.B.	Butte, Mont.	Central H. S.	22	188	6:2	1
32	Pilney, Andy E.	L.H.	Chicago, Ill.	Harrison H. S.	20	170	5:11	0
33	Tobin, John E.	R.H.	Janesville, Wis.	Janesville H. S.	22	177	5:8	2
34	**Leonard, James R.	L.G.	Pedricktown, N. J	St. Joseph, Phila.	22	187	6:	2
35	Gaul, Frank J.	Q.B.	Waterville, Me.	Waterville H. S.	19	167	5:10	0
36	McMahon, Joseph P.	L.G.	Chicago, Ill.	St. Philip H. S.	18	178	5:11	0
37	Esser, Carl F.	L.T.	Aurora, Ill.	West Aurora H. S.	20	190	6:2	1
38	Millner, Wayne V.	L.E.	Salem, Mass.	Villanova, Pa., Prep.	21	189	6:1	0
39	Mazziotti, Anthony J.	Q.B.	Elmsford, N. Y.	White Plains H. S.	19	190	5:7	0
40	Dunn, Edward R.	C.	Chicago, Ill.	Campion (Wis.)	19	190	5:11	0
41	Pojman, Henry F.	C.	Chicago, Ill.	Harrison H. S.	19	188	6:	0
42	Becker, Harry P.	R.T.	Louisville, Ky.	St. Xavier H. S.	22	188	6:1	1
43	Fulnecky, Karl D.	R.G.	Frankfort, Ind.	Frankfort H. S.	20	196	6:	1
44	Peters, Martin J.	R.E.	Peoria, Ill.	Spalding Institute	20	187	6:2	0
45	Bonar, Reyman E.	Q.B.	Bellaire, Ohio	Bellaire H. S.	21	170	5:8	1
46	Allen, Donald L.	R.E.	Chicago, Ill.	St. Mel H. S.	18	186	6:2	0
47	Young, John R.	R.H.	Houston, Tex.	St. Thomas H. S.	21	177	6:1	0
48	**Lukats, Nicholas P.	L.H.	Perth Amboy, N. J.	Froebel, Gary, Ind.	22	185	6:	2
49	Scafati, Orlando M.	R.E.	Dedham, Mass.	Hopkins (New Haven)	20	194	6:1	0
50	Miller, Stephen C.	F.B.	Rock Island, Ill.	St. Joseph H. S.	18	180	6:	0
51	**Gorman, Thomas A.	C.	Chicago, Ill.	St. Philip H. S.	23	190	6:1	2
53	Thernes, Matthew J.	L.E.	Cincinnati, Ohio	Roger Bacon H. S.	19	189	6:1	0
54	Carideo, Fred J., Jr.	F.B.	Mt. Vernon, N. Y.	Mt. Vernon H. S.	22	180	5:10	0
56	*Costello, Albert T.	R.H.	Akron, Ohio	North H. S.	22	180	5:9	1
57	**Devore, Hugh J.	R.E.	Newark, N. J.	St. Benedict's	22	179	6:	2
60	**Banas, Stephen P.	F.B.	East Chicago, Ind.	Cath. Cent. (Hammond)	23	185	5:11	2
61	Solari, Fred C.	C.	Pembroke, Mass.	Commerce H. S. (Boston)	20	198	6:2	0
63	Shakespeare, William V.	L.H.	Staten Island, N. Y.	Port Richmond H. S.	20	179	5:11	0
68	**Pivarnik, Joseph J.	R.G.	Bridgeport, Conn.	Harding H. S.	21	195	5:9	2
69	**Krause, Edward W.	L.T.	Chicago, Ill.	De LaSalle H. S.	20	217	6:3	2
71	*Schiralli, Rocco V.	L.G.	Gary, Ind.	Emerson H. S.	21	172	5:10	1
73	Schrenker, Paul E.	R.G.	Elwood, Ind.	Elwood H. S.	21	183	5:11	1
75	Dunn, Thomas J.	C.	Christopher, Ill.	Christopher H. S.	19	201	6:2	0
76	Cronin, Arthur D., Jr.	R.T.	Detroit, Mich.	U. of Detroit H. S.	19	211	6:	0
77	Kopczak, Frank G.	R.T.	Chicago, Ill.	Harrison H. S.	19	207	6:	0
78	Stilley, Kenneth L.	L.T.	Clairton, Pa.	Clairton H. S.	20	210	6:1	0
79	Sullivan, Joseph G.	R.T.	Belle Harbor, N. Y.	St. John (Brooklyn)	20	195	6:	0
80	Elser, Donald L.	F.B.	Gary, Ind.	Horace Mann	20	215	6:3	0
81	*Roach, Thomas G.	R.T.	Grand Rapids, Mich.	Catholic Central	23	198	6:1	2
82	Katz, Arthur S. J.	L.T.	Chicago, Ill.	Western Military	20	241	5:9	0
83	Michuta, John F.	R.T.	Detroit, Mich.	Holy Name Institute	20	207	6:1	0
84	**Wunsch, Harry F.	L.G.	South Bend, Ind.	Central H. S.	22	197	5:11	2

* denotes major monogram

1933				
Coach: Heartley W. (Hunk) Anderson				
Co-captains: Hugh J. Devore and Thomas A. Gorman				
O.7	T	Kansas	0-0	H	9,221
O.14	W	Indiana	12-2	A	15,152
O.21	L	Carnegie Tech (U)	0-7	A	45,890
O.28	L	Pittsburgh	0-14	H	16,627
N.4	L	Navy	0-7	N	34,579
N.11	L	Purdue	0-19	H	27,476
N.18	W	Northwestern	7-0	A	31,182
N.25	L	So. California	0-19	H	25,037
D.2	W	Army (U)	13-12	YS	c73,594
		(3-5-1)	32-80		278,758
N—at Baltimore					

N.D. SCORES AFTER 4 CONSECUTIVE SHUTOUTS!!

Notre Dame 7
Northwestern 0

When Northwestern and Notre Dame met at the Dyche Stadium, the public was ready to expect anything. The records of the Wildcats and the Irish were almost identical. Each team in six starts had succeeded in defeating only weak Indiana.

One flash of brilliant aggressive football at the opportune moment, when the Fates finally smiled, gave the Irish a 7-0 victory over the Wildcats. Ed Krause, Kitty Gorman and Andy Pilney were directly responsible for the sudden and successful thrust at Northwestern's goal. Krause started the onslaught when he blocked one of Ollie Olson's punts on the Wildcat 10 yard line. Kitty Gorman recovered for the Irish. On the second play thereafter, Andy Pilney scurried 11 yards around right end for the third Irish score of the season. Tony Mazziotti placekicked the extra point.

During the remainder of the game, Notre Dame played a strictly defensive game to protect its single score. Northwestern was able to make but one first down during the entire game through the stubborn Notre Dame defense. The Irish outclassed the Wildcats in every department of the game and well deserved their victory. The brand of football Notre Dame displayed in defeating Northwestern was, however, far inferior to that they displayed while being defeated by Pittsburgh, Navy and Purdue.

The Irish giant did exist. He was alive. But he was not awake. Somnolently, he had again brushed away a fly.

FINISH WORST SEASON IN MODERN N.D. HISTORY

Notre Dame 13
Army 12

The first three quarters of the Army game were just like the first three quarters of every other game Notre Dame played this fall. A dropped pass threw away an Irish touchdown; a fumble nullified a sixty yard march; another fumble gave the Army its first scoring chance; a desperate pass, when there was no need to be desperate, was intercepted and put the Cadets in scoring position for the second time. The alert Army team took advantage of both these breaks and by hard, heady football pushed over two touchdowns.

But suddenly, with but sixteen minutes of the game left, something happened. The Irish giant who had been slumbering all season finally awoke. With one huge hand, which looked suspiciously like Moose Krause, he pushed forward to block Buckler's punt. With his other hand, which clenched up fist-like appeared to be the low charging Nick Lukats, he shoved aside the entire Army team and stamped down the field for a gain of 15 yards. The march was on. Lukats led. Fifteen yards, ten yards, nine yards and finally Nick crashed across the last two for a touchdown after an astounding 52 yard march. Ray Bonar threw off his helmet, kicked the point that meant the margin of victory.

Some five minutes later Army was forced back to their eight yard line by Lukats' prodigious 72 yard punt. Simon went back of his own goal line to kick the Cadets out of danger. He never got the ball away. Wayne Millner crashed through and jumped in front of it just as it left his foot. The ball struck his chest and bounded over the goal line. Millner pounced on it. Players pounced on top of him. Officials untangled the mass. The referee raised his hands. It was a touchdown. Notre Dame was ahead 13-12. The Army, dazed, beaten, discouraged, could do nothing about it.

Notre Dame had come back.

The roar heard in the stadium was really the laughter of the Irish giant.

OFFICIAL 1934 UNIVERSITY OF NOTRE DAME FOOTBALL ROSTER

No.	Name	Position	Home City	Preparatory School	Age	Wt.	Ht.	Yrs. on Squad
1	*Bonar, Reyman Edward	Q.B.	Bellaire, Ohio	Bellaire H. S.	22	170	5:8	1
2	Caldwell, Geo. Edwin	Q.B.	Hudson, Ohio	Hudson H. S.	22	165	5:9	2
3	Moriarty, George Jos.	Q.B.	Lynn, Mass.	Clark (Hanover, N. H.)	21	150	5:8	1
5	*Gaul, Francis Jos.	Q.B.	Waterville, Maine	Waterville H. S.	21	175	5:8	0
8	Bruno, William Ben	Q.B.	Asbury Park, N. J.	Asbury Park H. S.	21	180	5:10	1
9	Fromhart, Wallace Leo	Q.B.	Moundsville, W. V.	Moundsville H. S.	21	175	5:11	1
10	Alworth, Samuel Ross	Q.B.	Tooele City, Utah.	Tooele H. S.	22	178	6:1	1
11	Layden, Francis Louis	L.H.	Davenport, Iowa	Davenport H. S.	21	170	6:	0
12	Wilke, Robert Edward	L.H.	Hamilton, Ohio	Catholic H. S.	19	170	6:	0
13	Saffa, William Paul	R.H.	Dumright, Okla.	Dumright H. S.	19	170	5:10	0
14	Marr, John Harold	R.E.	Waltham, Mass.	Boston College H. S.	18	180	6:	2
15	Canale, Frank Sturla	L.E.	Memphis, Tenn.	Catholic H. S.	22	190	6:	0
16	Zwers, Jos. Bernard	R.E.	Grand Rapids, Mich.	Cath. Central H. S.	19	185	6:	1
17	Schroder, Wm. Henry	R.E.	Atlanta, Ga.	Georgetown Prep.	20	180	6:	0
18	Church, August Joseph	L.G.	N. Plainfield, N. J.	N. Plainfield H. S.	20	159	5:7	0
19	Wojcihovski, Victor	R.H.	Weston, W. Va.	Weston H. S.	20	182	6:	0
20	Ronzone, Matthew Mike	F.B.	Elkhart, Ind.	Elkhart H. S.	23	180	5:10	1
21	Shamla, Richard Jos.	L.G.	Glencoe, Minn.	Glencoe H. S.	21	183	5:10	0
22	Beach, Joseph DePaul	R.H.	New Orleans, La.	Holy Cross Col. H. S.	21	170	5:9	1
23	Marek, Max Anthony	F.B.	Chicago, Ill.	Lindblom H. S.	20	180	5:10	0
24	Hickey, Louis Joseph	L.E.	South Bend, Ind.	Central H. S.	19	165	6:	0
25	Weidner, Fred Wm.	R.G.	LaPorte, Ind.	LaPorte H. S.	22	170	5:9	1
26	Hack, James Gorman	L.G.	Chicago, Ill.	Culver Military Acad.	19	180	5:9	0
27	Smith, Wm. Robert	R.G.	Hackettstown, N. J.	St. Benedict	22	170	5:10	1
28	Mueller, Arthur Casey	C.	New York City, N. Y.	Lowell, San Fran.	23	185	5:10	1
29	*Davis, Irwin Vincent	R.E.	Ponchatoula, La.	Ponchatoula H. S.	20	177	5:11	2
30	**Melinkovich, Geo. Jos.	R.H.	Tooele, Utah	Tooele H. S.	23	180	6:	2
31	*Hanley, Daniel Joseph	R.H.	Butte, Mont.	Central H. S.	23	188	6:2	2
32	*Pilney, Andy James	L.H.	Chicago, Ill.	Harrison Tech.	21	170	5:10	1
33	*Mazziotti, Anthony Jos.	R.H.	Elmsford, N. Y.	White Plains H. S.	20	190	5:8	1
34	Zenner, Elmer John	R.T.	Racine, Wis.	St. Catherine H. S.	20	190	6:	0
35	McCarthy, Wm. Patrick	L.E.	Glen Cove, L. I., N. Y.	Glen Cove H. S.	21	185	6:	0
36	McMahon, Joseph Pat.	L.G.	Chicago, Ill.	St. Philip H. S.	20	185	5:11	0
37	Esser, Carl Francis	L.T.	Aurora, Ill.	W. Aurora H. S.	21	190	6:2	1
38	*Millner, Wayne Vernal	L.E.	Salem, Mass.	Villanova Prep.	22	185	6:	1
39	Quinlan, Harold Francis	R.E.	Needham, Mass.	Needham H. S.	20	172	5:11	1
40	Dunn, Edward Reardon	C.	Chicago, Ill.	Campion Academy	20	190	6:	1
41	McGuire, James Francis	L.E.	Anaconda, Mont.	Anaconda H. S.	19	176	5:10	0
42	Becker, Harry Pelle	R.T.	Louisville, Ky.	St. Xavier H. S.	22	188	6:1	1
43	Fulnecky, Karl Dwyer	C.	Frankfort, Ind.	Frankfort H. S.	21	190	6:	0
44	Van Wagner, Gerald Jos.	L.H.	Staten Island	Curtis H. S.	22	178	6:1	0
45	Schrenker, Paul Eugene	R.G.	Elwood, Ind.	Elwood H. S.	22	190	5:11	2
46	Shea, Wm. Stephen	R.T.	New York City, N. Y.	Xavier H. S.	22	210	5:7	0
47	Young, Leighton F.	R.H.	Houston, Texas	St. Thomas H. S.	20	175	6:	0
48	O'Neill, Jos. Ignatius	L.E.	Phoenixville, Pa.	LaSalle, Phila.	20	182	6:2	0
49	Scafati, Orlando Mike	L.H.	Dedham, Mass.	Hopkins Prep.	22	195	6:2	1
50	Miller, Steve Christian	F.B.	Rock Island, Ill.	St. Joseph H. S.	19	180	6:	1
51	Pojman, Henry Frank	C.	Chicago, Ill.	Harrison Tech.	20	192	6:	1
52	**Vairo, Dominic Martin	R.E.	Calumet, Mich.	Calumet H. S.	21	196	6:2	2
53	Thernes, Matthew Jno.	L.E.	Cincinnati, Ohio	Bacon H. S.	20	190	6:1	0
54	*Carideo, Fred Joseph	F.B.	Mount Vernon, N. Y.	Mount Vernon H. S.	22	187	5:10	1
55	Hoctor, Joseph Francis	L.H.	New York City, N. Y.	Iona, New Rochelle	20	175	5:11	0
56	*Costello, Albert Thos.	R.H.	Akron, Ohio	North H. S.	22	185	5:10	2
57	Levicki, John Joseph	R.E.	Manayunk, Pa.	Perkiomen Prep.	21	205	6:3	0
58	*Peters, Martin Joseph	R.E.	Peoria, Ill.	Spalding Institute	21	187	6:2	1
59	Conner, Jos. George	R.G.	W. Springfield, Mass.	Cathedral H. S.	21	195	5:9	0
60	Paul, Peter Vincent	R.G.	Zanesville, Ohio	St. Nicholas	22	185	5:11	0
61	*Solari, Fred Charles	C.	Pembroke, Mass.	Commerce H. S.	21	205	6:2	1
62	Ely, Eugene James	L.T.	Auburn, Nebr.	Auburn H. S.	19	185	6:1	0
63	Shakespeare, Wm. Valen.	L.H.	Staten Island	Port Richmond	21	180	5:11	1
64	Martin, James Richard	L.G.	Concord, N. H.	Dean Academy	21	188	5:11	1
65	Moreau, Louis Steve	R.T.	Port Arthur, Tex.	Allen Academy	22	185	6:	0
67	Kopczak, Frank Gregory	R.T.	Chicago, Ill.	Harrison Tech. H. S.	20	196	6:	0
68	Mundee, Fred William	C.	Youngstown, Ohio	South H. S.	21	190	6:1	0
69	Steinkemper, Wm. Jos.	L.T.	Chicago, Ill.	DePaul Academy	20	215	6:1	0
70	*Pfefferle, Richard Jos.	L.T.	Appleton, Wis.	Campion Academy	22	195	6:2	1
71	**Schiralli, Rocco V.	L.G.	Gary, Ind.	Emerson H. S.	22	170	5:9	2
72	Lauter, John Paul	L.G.	Moundsville, W. V.	Moundsville H. S.	22	190	6:1	0
73	Barstow, Fred Adolph	R.T.	Menominee, Mich.	Menominee H. S.	20	198	6:1	1
74	Cronin, Arthur D., Jr.	R.T.	Detroit, Mich.	U. of Detroit H. S.	20	201	6:	0
75	Schilling, Jos. Valentine	R.T.	Pleasantville, N. Y.	Dwight Prep.	22	206	6:2	0
76	*Robinson, John Joseph	C.	Huntington, N. Y.	Georgetown Prep.	21	200	6:3	1
78	Stilley, Kenneth Len.	L.T.	Clairton, Pa.	Clairton H. S.	22	209	6:1	1
79	Sullivan, Jos. Geo.	L.T.	Belle Harbor, N. Y.	St. John's, Brooklyn	21	210	6:	1
80	*Elser, Don Lewis	F.B.	Gary, Ind.	Horace Mann	21	215	6:2	1
81	Danbom, Laurence Edw.	F.B.	Calumet, Mich.	Calumet H. S.	19	188	6:	0
83	*Michuta, John Francis	R.T.	Detroit, Mich.	Holy Name Institute	21	207	6:1	1
84	Nabicht, Ferdinand	L.T.	South Bend, Ind.	Central H. S.	20	195	6:1	1

*Indicates major monogram.

LAYDEN ASSUMES NOTRE DAME POST

Refuses to Make Any Glowing Predictions as He Takes Over Rockne's Office.

TO ATTEND MEETING HERE

His First Official Act Will Be to Represent University at Football Rules Session.

By The Associated Press.

SOUTH BEND, Feb. 1.—Elmer Layden sat down at Knute Rockne's famous old desk under the golden dome today and began his active campaign to bring Notre Dame back to its former glory in the football world.

Back on the grounds where he gained fame as fullback on the immortal Four Horsemen eleven, Layden officially took charge of Notre Dame's athletic destinies as director of athletics and head football coach.

Brings Aide With Him.

Layden, who won national renown as a football player under Rockne and a reputation as a fine football coach at Duquesne University, brought one new assistant with him as he took over the offices, previously held by Jess Harper and Heartly (Hunk) Anderson. The newcomer was Joe Boland, who played on Notre Dame's football teams in 1925 and 1926 and who will be Layden's chief gridiron assistant.

Tom Conley, captain of the undefeated 1930 team, was the only survivor of the 1933 football coaching staff, being retained as end coach. One more assistant, to be named later, will be hired.

Working with Layden in other departments were George Keoghan, basketball coach, and John Nicholson, track mentor. They are the only members of the entire coaching staff who are not Notre Dame graduates, Keogan coming from Minnesota and Nicholson from Missouri.

His Chief Concern.

Scholarly looking, quiet and unassuming, Layden refused to make any glowing predictions for his coaching régime today. He said he was concerned over the probable ineligibility of several members of the football squad.

"I can promise you one thing, though," he said as a smile spread over his face, "we won't lose a single game this year—in Spring practice."

Layden's first official act will be to represent Notre Dame at the football rules meeting at New York Saturday. He will be accompanied by Noble Kizer, Purdue football coach and one of his former team-mates.

		1934			
		Coach: Elmer F. Layden			
		Captain: Dominic M. Vairo			
O.6	L	Texas	6-7	H	20,353
O.13	W	Purdue	18-7	H	34,263
O.20	W	Carnegie Tech (R)	13-0	H	11,242
O.27	W	Wisconsin	19-0	H	25,354
N.3	L	Pittsburgh	0-19	A	56,556
N.10	L	Navy (R)	6-10	N	54,571
N.17	W	Northwestern	20-7	A	38,413
N.24	W	Army (4:00)	12-6	YS	c78,757
D.8	W	So. California	14-0	A	45,568
		(6-3-0)	108-56		365,077

N—at Cleveland

CAPTAIN "JOE" SULLIVAN

In March of 1935, Joseph G. Sullivan, varsity right tackle and Captain-elect of the football team, died in New York. To Notre Dame men everywhere, and particularly to Joe's friends, his death was a personal loss.

No greater tribute can be paid a man than to say, "He was loved by his fellow men." Joe Sullivan was—dearly, by his friends. No greater tribute can be paid a Notre Dame man than to call him a REAL Notre Dame man—a son of Mary. If Notre Dame has ever harbored a man worthy of carrying her banner that man was Joe Sullivan. Strength of physique was equally matched by strength of character; his worth on the gridiron paralleled his worth in life. It is easy to write in glowing terms of a man like Joe Sullivan—so easy that any account of him to an outsider must seem like an imaginative ideal of a young man. That was Joe Sullivan—an exemplar youth living an exemplar life.

Official 1935 University of Notre Dame Football Roster

NO.	NAME	POSITION	HOME CITY	PREPARATORY SCHOOL	AGE	WT.	HT.	YRS. ON SQUAD
1	Puplis, Andrew Joseph	Q.B.	Chicago, Ill.	Harrison Tech H. S.	20	169	5:8	0
2	McKenna, James Arthur	Q.B.	St. Paul, Minn.	Crotin H. S.	19	169	5:10½	2
3	Moriarty, George Joseph	Q.B.	Lynn, Mass.	Clark, Hanover, N. H.	22	145	5:7½	2
4	Megin, Bernard Edward	Q.B.	Concord, Mass.	Bridgton, Me., Acad.	21	168	5:10	1
5	**Gaul, Francis Joseph	Q.B.	Waterville, Maine	Waterville H. S.	21	167	5:9½	2
6	Gleason, Joseph Thomas	Q.B.	Chicago, Ill.	Leo H. S.	21	181	6:	0
7	O'Reilly, Charles Wm.	Q.B.	St. Mary's, Ohio	Memorial H. S.	21	170	5:8	0
8	Bruno, Wm. Benjamin	Q.B.	Asbury Park, N. J.	Asbury Park H. S.	21	175	5:8	1
9	*Fromhart, Wallace Leo	Q.B.	Moundsville, W. Va.	Moundsville H. S.	22	183	5:11	2
11	*Layden, Francis Louis	R.H.	Davenport, Ia.	Davenport H. S.	22	177	6:1	2
12	Wilke, Robert Edward	L.H.	Hamilton, Ohio	Hamilton Catholic	20	165	6:	1
14	Marr, John Harold	R.E.	Waltham, Mass.	Boston College H. S.	19	178	6:	1
15	Crotty, Irwin Patrick	R.H.	Storm Lake, Ia.	Storm Lake H. S.	22	180	5:10½	1
16	Zwers, Joseph Bernard	R.E.	Grand Rapids, Mich.	Catholic Central H. S.	19	178	6:	0
17	Schloemer, Bertrand Aug.	L.E.	Cincinnati, Ohio	Xavier H. S.	20	185	5:11	0
18	*Church, August Joseph	L.G.	N. Plainfield, N. J.	N. Plainfield H. S.	21	153	5:7	2
19	Wojichovski, Victor Jos.	R.H.	Weston, W. Va.	Weston H. S.	21	179	6:	1
20	McCormick, Nevin Francis	R.H.	Livermore, Calif.	Livermore H. S.	21	167	5:8	0
21	Schrader, Walter Lang	R.G.	Weston, W. Va.	Danville, Va., Mil.	20	168	5:9	0
22	Borowski, Chas. Casimir	L.H.	South Bend, Ind.	Central H. S.	20	170	5:11	0
23	McGrath, Robert Arthur	F.B.	Oak Park, Ill.	Fenwick H. S.	19	179	6:1½	0
24	Hickey, Louis Joseph	L.E.	South Bend, Ind.	Central H. S.	21	179	6:	1
25	Chanqwicz, Stanley Jos.	R.T.	Philadelphia, Pa.	West Catholic H. S.	20	197	6:1	0
26	Rack, James Gorman	L.G.	Chicago, Ill.	Loyola, & Culver, Ind.	21	187	5:10	1
27	Elliott, Francis Joseph	R.E.	New Rochelle, N. Y.	New Rochelle H. S.	21	195	6:2	0
28	Arboit, Ennio Benjamin	R.H.	Oglesby, Ill.	St. Bede, Peru Ill.	17	180	5:10½	0
29	Clifford, Jeremiah Jos.	L.E.	Chicago, Ill.	Mt. Carmel H. S.	20	190	6:1	0
30	Kovalcik, George John	L.H.	Donora, Pa.	Donora H. S.	20	188	5:11	0
31	Darcy, John Francis	L.H.	Boston, Mass.	Mission H. S. Roxbury	22	180	6:	1
32	**Pilney, Andy James	L.H.	Chicago, Ill.	Harrison Tech H. S.	22	175	5:11	2
33	**Mazziotti, Anthony Jos.	R.H.	Elmsford, N. Y.	White Plains H. S.	21	193	5:8	2
34	Zenner, Elmer John	R.G.	Racine, Wis.	St. Catherine H. S.	21	181	6:	1
35	McCarthy, Wm. Patrick	R.E.	Glen Cove, L. I., N. Y.	Glen Cove H. S.	22	187	6:1	1
36	McMahon, Joseph Patrick	L.G.	Chicago, Ill.	St. Phillip H. S.	21	178	5:11½	1
37	Jackowski, Ralph George	R.H.	Chicago, Ill.	St. Rita Col. Acad.	20	183	5:10	0
38	**Millner, Wayne Vernal	L.E.	Salem, Mass.	Salem H. S.	22	184	6:	2
39	McCarthy, Jack Gregory	L.H.	Glencoe, Ill.	Loyola Acad., Chicago	19	177	6:	0
40	Dunn, Edward Reardon	C.	Chicago, Ill.	Campion, Wis.	21	195	6:2	2
41	McCarty, Patrick Francis	C.	Toledo, Ohio	Cent. Catholic H. S.	19	201	6:2½	0
42	*Becker, Harry Pelle	R.G.	Louisville, Ky.	St. Xavier H. S.	22	182	6:	1
43	DiMatteo, Jos. Angelo	F.B.	Pittsburgh, Pa.	Perry H. S.	20	178	5:9	0
44	Van Wagner, Gerard Jos.	L.H.	W. Brighton, S. I., N. Y.	Curtis H. S.	21	177	6:1½	1
45	Emanuel, Dennis George	L.T.	Iowa City, Ia.	St. Patrick H. S.	19	194	6:1	0
46	Hauck, John Booth	R.G.	Donora, Pa.	Donora H. S.	19	182	5:10½	0
47	Sweeney, Charles Alex.	R.E.	Bloomington, Ill.	Trinity H. S.	20	187	5:11½	0
48	O'Neill, Jos. Ignatius, Jr.	L.E.	Phoenixville, Pa.	LaSalle H. S., Phila.	20	186	6:2	1
49	Schilling, Jos. Valentine	R.T.	Pleasantville, N. Y.	Dwight, N. Y. City	21	198	6:2½	1
50	*Miller, Stephen Christian	F.B.	Rock Island, Ill.	St. Joseph H. S.	20	183	6:	1
51	*Pojman, Henry Frank	C.	Chicago, Ill.	Harrison Tech H. S.	21	193	5:11	2
52	Skoglund, Leonard Howard	L.E.	Chicago, Ill.	Nicholas Senn H. S.	19	187	6:1	0
53	*Themes, Matthew John	L.T.	Cincinnati, Ohio	Roger Bacon H. S.	21	188	6:1	2
54	**Carideo, Fred Joseph, Jr.	F.B.	Mt. Vernon, N. Y.	Mt. Vernon H. S.	22	180	5:10½	2
55	Snell, Edward William	L.H.	Erie, Pa.	Academy H. S.	21	186	6:1	0
56	Kuharich, Jos. Lawrence	R.G.	South Bend, Ind.	Riley H. S.	18	188	5:11	0
57	Levicki, John Joseph	R.T.	Philadelphia, Pa.	St. John Baptist H. S.	21	198	6:3	1
58	**Peters, Martin Joseph	R.E.	Peoria, Ill.	Spalding Institute	22	205	6:3	2
59	Connor, Joseph George	R.G.	W. Springfield, Mass.	Cathedral H. S.	20	195	5:9	0
60	Winsauer, Paul Vincent	C.	Peoria, Ill.	Spalding Institute	20	189	6:	1
61	**Solari, Fred Charles	C.	Pembroke, Mass.	Commerce H. S., Boston	22	205	6:2	2
62	Marshall, Walter Michael	R.G.	Philadelphia, Pa.	Gratz H. S.	20	184	5:10½	0
63	**Shakespeare, Wm. Valentine	L.H.	Staten Island, N. Y.	Port Richmond H. S.	22	179	5:11	2
64	Martin, James Richard	L.G.	Concord, N. H.	Dean Acad., Mass.	21	181	5:11	1
65	Kelly, John Grog	R.E.	Chicago, Ill.	St. George, Evanston	19	181	6:1	0
66	Murphy, John Patrick	R.E.	South Bend, Ind.	Central H. S.	20	175	5:11	0
67	Kopczak, Frank Gregory	R.T.	Chicago, Ill.	Harrison Tech H. S.	21	198	6:	1
68	Mundee, Fred William	C.	Youngstown, Ohio	South H. S.	21	187	6:1½	1
69	*Steinkemper, Wm. Jacob	L.T.	Chicago, Ill.	DePaul Academy	21	209	6:2	1
70	**Pfefferle, Richard Jos.	L.T.	Appleton, Wis.	Campion Prep, Wis.	22	205	6:2	2
71	Race, Adrian Joseph	R.G.	Milwaukee, Wis.	Pio Nono H. S.	20	183	5:10½	0
72	*Lautar, John Paul	L.G.	Moundsville, W. Va.	Moundsville H. S.	21	185	6:1	1
73	Ruetz, Joseph Hubert	L.G.	South Bend, Ind.	Central H. S.	19	187	5:11½	0
74	Cronin, Arthur Dennis, Jr.	R.T.	Detroit, Mich.	U. of Detroit H. S.	21	203	6:	0
75	Fogel, John Nick	C.	Chicago, Ill.	Mt. Carmel H. S.	20	185	5:10	0
76	Robertson, Robt. Samuel	C.	Peru, Ind.	Peru H. S.	20	197	6:2	0
78	*Stilley, Kenneth Leonard	L.T.	Clairton, Pa.	Clairton H. S.	22	210	6:1	2
79	Schwartz, Wm. Spencer	R.E.	Bay St. Louis, Miss.	St. Stanislaus Col.	19	185	6:2	0
80	**Elser, Donald Lewis	F.B.	Gary, Ind.	Horace Mann H. S.	22	220	6:3	2
81	Danbom, Laurence Edwin	F.B.	Calumet, Mich.	Calumet H. S.	20	192	6:	1
82	Belden, Wm. Hinchliffe	R.T.	Canton, Ohio	Phillips Exeter, N. H.	20	205	6:2	2
83	**Michuta, John Francis	R.T.	Detroit, Mich.	Holy Name Inst.	22	198	6:1½	2
84	Foster, Harvey Goodson	L.G.	South Bend, Ind.	Highland Pk. H. S. Dtrt.	21	185	6:	0

*Indicates major Monogram.

NOTRE DAME DOWNS PITTSBURGH 9 - 6; AS ACCURATE KICKING FEATURES GAME

By Gene Vaslett

The Irish of Notre Dame served tice to the country at large and ,000 spectators in particular that y are once more on the march to otball greatness, last Saturday when y conquered the Panther of Pittsgh in a stirring game that kept

FRED SOLARI
Pitt felt his pressure.

e spectators in constant upr ar om the opening whistle to the closg gun. The Notre Dame team not ly avenged themselves for three evious defeats at the hands of the wing Panthers but made it doubly tisfying by coming from behind in e second period and forging ahead th but three minutes to play to iumph by the score of 9-6.

A great Pittsburgh team came out of the Smoky City to do battle with the sons of Notre Dame anticipating a duplication of the past three years but did not reckon with the right foot of Marty Peters or the stalwartness of the revised Irish line. Led by Randour and LaRue, backs who seemingly refused to be stopped, the Panthers determinedly went about the task of trying to subdue the Irish for the fourth successive year.

It looked very much as though the Panther would turn the trick once more when Bob LaRue slipped around left end midway in the first quarter and headed for the Irish goal eighty yards away with four Pitt men in front of him and only Wally Fromhart in position to stop him. Fromhart, however, frustrated this attempt by running along with the interference and on the 20 yard line feinting the four men out of position and allowing Fred Carideo to make the tackle from behind on the 18 yard line. Fromhart's play on this 62 yard run was the outstanding defensive performance of the game. On the 18 yard line the Panthers could gain but four yards in three plays, and on the fourth down Patrick dropped back to attempt a field goal but the kick

went wide and the first Pitt threat was stopped.

The first quarter ended with the ball on the Irish 48 yard line in Pitt's possession. Then Randour, Stapulis, Patrick, and Shedloskey pushed the ball to the Irish two yard line, and Patrick went over for the first score of the game. Wayne Millner blocked the attempted conversion.

Then came the break of the game for the Notre Dame team. Following the kick-off by Pitt the Irish were unable to gain, and Bill Shakespeare dropped behind the goal line to kick. He sent a booming punt far over the head of the Pitt safety man which was finally downed on the Pitt 17 yard line. The ball had traveled more than 90 yards before being touched by a Pitt man. The Panthers were unable to gain and Greene dropped back to kick. His punt landed on the 15 yard line but bounced back and back to the Pitt 20 yard marker and it was the Irish ball. A Notre Dame fumble lost four yards then Carideo in three plays crashed his way to the five yard line and Shakespeare slid through right tackle for five yards and the first Irish score against Pitt since 1931. The place kick of Fromhart was no good and the score was tied 6-6 when the half ended.

The third quarter found the same Irish team that had started and played throughout the first half without replacements, take the field once more. The play see-sawed back and forth during the quarter and neither team seemed to have the advantage in play. Coach Layden made the first substitutions of the game late in the third quarter when he sent the second team into the fray and gave his regulars a much needed rest. The quarter ended with the ball in the possession of Notre Dame on their own 48 yard line.

The final period saw the first team return after five minutes of play had ensued. With but five minutes of the game remaining Fromhart returned a Pitt punt 18 yards to the Pitt 34 yard line, and Shakespeare and Carideo collaborated in taking the ball to the Pitt 19 yard line. Three plays gained nothing, and with the precious seconds ticking away the remaining two and a half minutes Fromhart called upon acting captain Peters to attempt a field goal, seldom used in Notre Dame play, from the 26 yard line. Fromhart held the ball as Peters' foot swung back and met it. The upraised arms of the referee and the bedlam in the South stands conveyed the news that the kick was good and that Notre

Dame had defeated the Pittsburgh Panther for the first time in four years. Jubilant students and teammates acclaimed Marty Peters as the man of the hour with cheers that were deafening.

Then followed a wild two minutes of play with Pitt desperately trying to score and the Notre Dame supporters yelling for the gun, that would signify Irish victory, to be shot. Pitt attempted double laterals and passes but to no avail, and the game ended with Fred Solari intercepting a Pitt pass.

The entire Irish first team led by Shakespeare, Carideo, Peters, and Millner played great football reminiscent of the Rockne era when a Notre Dame team wouldn't be beaten. Pressmen acclaim the team as the greatest Irish squad since Rockne, and the Pitt performance last Saturday only added more force and truth to the statement.

The lineup:

Notre Dame (9)		Pittsburgh (6)
Millner	LE	Souchak
Pfefferle	LT	Matisi
Lautar	LG	Glassford
Solari	C	Klisskey
Martin	RG	Dalle Tezze
Kopczak	RT	Detzel
Peters	RE	Shaw
Fromhart	QB	Michelosen
Shakespeare	LH	Randouer
Wojcihovski	RH	La Rue
Carideo	FB	Patrick

Touchdowns—Patrick, Shakespeare; field goal—Peters (placement).

Referee—Frank Lane (Cincinnati), Umpire—Frank Birch (Earlham), Field Judge—J. S. Gethell (St. Thomas); Head Linesman—W. D. Knight (Dartmouth).

1935					
Coach: Elmer F. Layden					
Captain: *Joseph G. Sullivan					
S.28	W	Kansas	28-7	H	11,102
O.5	W	Carnegie Tech	14-3	A	27,542
O.12	W	Wisconsin	27-0	A	19,863
O.19	W	Pittsburgh (3:00)	9-6	H	39,989
O.26	W	Navy	14-0	N	c57,810
N.2	W	Ohio St. (U) (0:32)	18-13	A	c81,018
N.9	L	Northwestern (R) (U)	7-14	H	34,430
N.16	T	Army (0:29-ND)	6-6	YS	c78,114
N.23	W	So. California	20-13	H	38,305
		(7-1-1)	143-62		388,173

*Died from complications of pneumonia, March, 1935
N—at Baltimore

NOTRE DAME AND ARMY FIGHT TO TIE AS IRISH STAGE LAST MINUTE RALLY

BUCKEYES WITHER UNDER IRISHERS' LATE PASSING ATTACK TO LOSE THRILLER

By Gene Vaslett

By Arch Gott

A wild screaming throng of 80,000 saw in Yankee Stadium last Saturday, a battle which left them gasping for air and limp in their seats at its conclusion. Only twice did the little scoring bug enter the conflict and he chose to land once on each team. After leading 6-0 for the first 59 minutes of the game, the Army was forced to yield a touchdown to an awakened Notre Dame juggernaut that crashed relentlessly down the field 85 yards terminating in a shattering smash across the goal by Larry Danbom

TONY MAZZIOTTI
Off side kicker deluxe.

with a scant ten seconds to play. The "greatest finish team in history" had unleashed its fury again and tied up the count in a game that appeared to be hopelessly lost but a few seconds before. With fire in their hearts and victory within their grasp the Irish under their valiant leader, Wally Fromhart, tried for the point after touchdown which meant so much to them—but the scoring bug had flown and the kick was wide by inches ending the game at 6-6.

Eighty-one thousand people sat in the huge Ohio Stadium at Columbus two weeks ago and watched an inspired, fighting Notre Dame football team overcome seemingly impossible odds and defeat the highly touted

FRANK KOPCZAK
"Bearskin's my uncle."

Ohio State juggernaut, 18-13. Few people who saw the game will ever forget the unbelievable last quarter finish when Andy Pilney ran wild and paved the way for all three of the touchdowns that spelled victory for the Irish team that had been hopelessly outclassed in the first half.

Some sort of magic must have entered the Notre Dame locker room between the halves and something surely went out of the Ohio State dressing room at the same time because when the two teams met in the second half Notre Dame had found itself and Ohio State was floundering. It seemed only a matter of time before the Irish would triumph. No one will ever know what happened to Ohio State while their band was waving green handkerchiefs at the Irish stands between the halves but one can contemplate what took place in the Irish locker room at the same time. The Spirit of Notre Dame was born anew and the team took the field with new hope and fight born in them.

As a result of this game there will be one name that will go down in Irish history as one of the greatest football players that ever wore a Notre Dame uniform on a gridiron. That name is Andy Pilney. It was Pilney who returned an Ohio State punt 27 yards to the Buckeye 12 yard line as the third quarter ended and a few plays later, in the fourth quarter, tossed a pass to Frank Gaul on the one yard line. Then Steve Miller plunged over for the first Irish touchdown. Then it was Pilney again who

looped a pass to Mike Layden from the Ohio State 15 yard line for the second touchdown. But when Fromhard missed the extra point and the score stood 13-12 with but one minute to play Irish supporters thought the game was gone. But hope revived when Hank Pojman fell on an Ohio State fumble on the Irish 49 after the kickoff. Andy Pilney was called upon again to pass but this time with all his receivers covered Andy decided to run. He sprinted, slipped and scrambled to the Ohio State 19 yard line where he was tackled so viciously that he had to retire from the game. But Andy had set the stage for the last Irish touchdown. Bill Shakespeare replaced him and two plays later dropped back to the 30 yard line and looped a pass to Wayne Millner in the end zone who caught it for the winning touchdown over the heads of two Ohio State defensive backs. Jubilant teammates swarmed over Wayne as he lay in the end zone with the ball in his arms.

Although Notre Dame dominated the second half the Ohio State team was plainly the superior in the first two periods. The lateral offensive employed by the Bucks completely confused the Irish and it looked as though it would be an Ohio State rout. The first quarter was not five minutes old when Antenucci intercepted a pass from Layden and immediately lateralled it to Boucher who

raced 70 yards the west side line for the first touchdown of the game. The place kick was good and the Scarlet Scourge led 7-0. Later in the same quarter Pincura intercepted an Irish pass on the 50 yard line and started a drive for the second touchdown. Six plays later the Bucks had the ball on the Irish 15 yard line and the quarter ended. With the resumption of play the Bucks sustained their drive and Jumping Joe Williams slid across the goal line for the second touchdown from the four yard line. The kick was bad and Ohio State led the Irish 13-0. The remainder of the quarter saw no scoring and the half ended with the Irish trailing 13-0 and seemingly headed for certain defeat.

The miracle of the locker room happened and the third quarter found a rejuvenated Irish team on the field and although neither team scored during this period it was evident that the Irish were gaining power with every play. Midway in this period Miller raced 30 yards from the Ohio State 40 yard line and Notre Dame was in scoring position for the first time. But the Bucks were successful in holding the Irish on downs and prevented a score.

Notre Dame couldn't be denied in the fourth quarter and Pilney's great playing behind the second team line won for the Irish the game that will go down in football history as the greatest contest ever played.

A factor that was of prime importance to the victory of the Irish was the excellent treatment received by the squad from the seminarians of the Seminary of St. Charles Borromeo. Columbus was football mad on the eve of the game and the seminary was a sanctuary to the Notre Dame players who wished to be removed from the contagious football fever that swept the Ohio town the night before the Ohio game. The team stayed at the seminary prior to the game and returned to it immediately following.

It mattered not that Marty Peters' attempted conversion was wide, the game had but a few seconds to go and the greatest Irish victory was assured.

Official 1936 University of Notre Dame Football Roster

NO.	NAME	POSITION	HOME CITY	PREPARATORY SCHOOL	AGE	WT.	HT.	YRS. ON SQUAD
1	Puplis, Andrew Joseph	Q.B.	Chicago, Ill.	Harrison Tech H. S.	21	168	5:8½	1
2	Crowe, Emmett Hoste	Q.B.	Lafayette, Ind.	Jefferson H. S.	19	163	5:8	0
3	Hofer, Willard Clair	Q.B.	Rock Island, Ill.	Rock Island H. S.	20	180	5:11½	0
4	Megin, Bernard Edward	Q.B.	Concord, Mass.	Bridgton Acad., Me.	22	168	5:10	2
5	Sullivan, Daniel Francis	Q.B.	Chicago, Ill.	St. Ignatius	21	170	5:9	0
7	O'Reilly, Chas. Wm.	Q.B.	St. Mary's, Ohio	Memorial H. S.	22	160	5:8	1
8	Bruno, Wm. Ben	Q.B.	Asbury Park, N. J.	Asbury Park H. S.	23	166	5:8	2
9	*Ruetz, Joseph Hubert	Q.B.	South Bend, Ind.	Central H. S.	19	190	5:11	1
10	Sadowski, Ed. Marion	L.E.	Westfield, Mass.	Westfield H. S.	21	170	5:11	0
11	*Gleason, Joseph Thomas	R.H.	Chicago, Ill.	Leo High School	22	175	6:0	1
12	*Wilke, Robert Edward	L.H.	Hamilton, Ohio	Hamilton Catholic H. S.	21	158	6:0	2
13	Theisen, Chas. John	C.	St. Joseph, Mich.	St. Joseph's Catholic	20	215	6:4	0
14	Marr, John Harold	R.E.	Waltham, Mass.	Boston Coll. H. S.	20	164	6:0	1
15	McMahon, John Edward	L.H.	Indianapolis, Ind.	Cathedral H. S.	18	164	5:11	0
16	*Zwers, Joseph Bernard	L.G.	Grand Rapids, Mich.	Catholic Central H. S.	20	171	6:0	1
17	Bossu, August Francis	L.G.	Monongahela, Pa.	Monongahela H. S.	20	185	5:10	0
18	Kennedy, Leo Raymond	R.G.	Cleveland, Ohio	Holy Name H. S.	20	175	5:10½	0
19	*Wojcihovski, Victor Joseph	R.H.	Weston, W. Va.	Weston H. S.	21	180	6:½	2
20	McCormick, Nevin Francis	R.H.	Livermore, Calif.	Livermore H. S.	22	159	5:8	1
21	Nickel, Russell Laurence	L.H.	Hamilton, Ohio	Hamilton Cath. H. S.	18	155	5:10½	0
22	Borowski, Chas. Casimer	L.H.	So. Bend, Ind.	Central H.. S.	21	170	5:11	1
23	McGrath, Robert Arthur	F.B.	Oak Park, Ill.	Fenwick H. S.	20	166	6:2	1
24	Hickey, Louis Joseph	L.E.	South Bend, Ind.	Central H. S.	22	171	6:1	2
25	Brown, Earl Melvin, Jr.	L.E.	Benton Harbor, Mich.	Benton Harbor H. S.	21	171	6:0	0
26	Hack, James Gorman	L.G.	Chicago, Ill.	Loyola & Culver Acad.	23	190	5:10	2
27	Rogenski, Steven John	C.	Moline, Ill.	Moline H. S.	19	186	6:1	0
28	Arboit, Ennio Benjamin	R.H.	Oglesby, Ill	St. Bede, Peru, Ill.	19	175	5:11	1
29	Clifford, Jeremiah Joseph	L.E.	Chicago, Ill.	Mt. Carmel H. S.	21	169	6:1½	1
30	Kovalcik, George John	L.H.	Donora, Pa.	Donora H. S.	21	190	6:0	0
31	Darcy, John Francis	L.H.	Boston, Mass.	Mission H. S., Roxbury	23	176	5:11	1
32	Saffa, William Paul	R.H.	Drumwright, Okla.	Drumwright H. S.	22	185	5:10½	1
33	Horan, Wm. Cornelius	L.H.	Chicago, Ill.	St. Ignatius Academy	19	169	5:11	0
34	*Zenner, Elmer John	R.G.	Racine, Wis.	St. Catherine's H. S.	22	184	6:½	2
35	McCarthy, Wm. Patrick	R.T.	Glen Cove, L. I., N. Y.	Glen Cove H. S.	23	180	6:1	2
36	McMahon, Joseph Patrick	L.G.	Chicago, Ill.	St. Philip H. S.	21	170	5:11½	1
37	Fox, Harry Francis	R.G.	Cleveland Hts., Ohio	Cleveland Hts. H. S.	20	168	5:8	1
38	O'Loughlin, Wm. Anthony	L.E.	Toledo, Ohio	Central Catholic H. S.	19	177	6:0	0
39	McCarthy, Jack Gregory	L.H.	Glencoe, Ill.	Loyola Acad., Chicago	20	172	6:0	1
40	Burnell, Herman Joseph	L.H.	Duluth, Minn.	Duluth Cathedral H. S.	21	166	5:11	0
41	McCarty, Pat. Francis	C.	Toledo, Ohio	Central Catholic H. S.	20	198	6:2½	1
42	Hoppel, Leo Theodore	R.H.	Evansville, Ind.	Reitz Memorial H. S.	21	180	5:11½	1
43	DiMatteo, Joseph Angelo	F.B.	Pittsburgh, Pa.	Perry H. S.	21	171	5:9½	1
44	Morrison, Paul Edward	R.H.	Jersey City, N. J.	Lincoln H. S.	21	179	5:10	0
45	Emanuel, Dennis George	L.T.	Iowa City, Iowa	St. Patrick H. S.	21	198	6:2	1
46	Schrader, Walter Lang	R.G.	Weston, W. Va.	Weston H. S.	21	160	5:7½	0
47	Sweeney, Chas. Alexander	R.E.	Bloomington, Ill.	Trinity H. S.	22	179	6:0	1
48	*O'Neill, Joseph Ignatius, Jr.	L.E.	Phoenixville, Pa.	LaSalle H. S., Phila.	22	186	6:2	2
49	Schilling, Joseph Valent.	R.T.	Pleasantville, N. Y.	Dwight Prep.	22	198	6:3	2
50	**Miller, Stephen Christ.	F.B.	Rock Island, Ill.	St. Joseph H. S.	21	181	5:11¾	2
51	Longhi, Edward John	C.	Torrington, Conn.	Torrington H. S.	20	195	6:2	0
52	Skoglund, Leonard Howard	L.E.	Chicago, Ill.	Senn H. S.	20	182	6:1½	1
53	Broscoe, Ed. Michael	R.E.	Youngstown, Ohio	Dickinson Seminary	21	178	5:11	0
54	McGovern, Geo. Washington	R.T.	Lynbrook, N. Y.	Fishburne Milit., Va.	22	197	6:2½	1
55	Snell, Edward William	L.H.	Erie, Penn.	Academy H. S.	22	173	6:1	1
56	*Kuharich, Jos. Lawrer	R.G.	South Bend, Ind.	James W. Riley H. S.	19	182	5:11½	1
57	Levicki, John Joseph	L.T.	Philadelphia, Pa.	St. John Baptist H. S.	24	200	6:3	2
58	Tonelli, Mario George	F.B.	Chicago, Ill.	DePaul Academy	19	189	6:0	0
59	McGoldrick, James Joseph	L.G.	Philadelphia, Pa.	W. Phila. Catholic H. S.	19	184	5:11½	0
60	Winsouer, Paul Vincent	C.	Peoria, Ill.	Spalding Institute	21	182	6:½	2
61	Mulcahey, James Lane	R.G.	Taunton, Mass.	Taunton H. S.	20	190	5:8½	0
62	Marshall, Walter Michael	R.G.	Philadelphia, Pa.	Gratz H. S.	21	188	5:11	1
63	Gallagher, Francis Joseph	L.E.	Scranton, Pa.	St. John's H. S.	20	162	5:10	1
64	*Martin, James Richard	L.G.	Concord, N. H.	Dean Acad., Franklin	21	185	5:11	2
65	Kelly, John Greg	R.E.	Chicago, Ill.	St. George H. S.	20	184	6:0	0
66	Murphy, John Patrick	R.E.	South Bend, Ind.	Central H. S.	21	176	5:11	1
67	*Kopczak, Francis Gregory	R.T.	Chicago, Ill.	Harrison Tech	22	196	6:0	2
68	Mundee, Fred William	C.	Youngstown, Ohio	South H. S.	23	185	6:½	2
69	**Steinkemper, Wm. Jacob	L.T.	Chicago, Ill.	DePaul Academy	22	210	6:2	2
70	Cavalier, John Michael	L.T.	Middlebranch, Ohio	Middlebranch H. S.	20	200	5:11	0
71	Race, Adrian Joseph	R.G.	Milwaukee, Wis.	Pio Nono H. S.	21	185	5:10½	1
72	**Lautar, John Paul (Capt.)	L.G.	Moundsville, W. Va.	Moundsville H. S.	23	184	6:1	2
73	Beinor, Jos. Edward	L.T.	Harvey, Ill.	Thornton Twp. H. S.	19	197	6:2	0
74	*Cronin, Arthur Dennis, Jr.	R.T.	Detroit, Mich.	U. of Detroit H. S.	22	210	6:0	2
75	Fogel, John Nicholas	C.	Chicago, Ill.	Mt. Carmel H. S.	21	185	5:10	0
76	Ely, Eugene James	C.	Auburn, Nebraska	Auburn H. S.	21	185	6:1¾	0
78	Kell, Paul Ernest	R.T.	Niles, Mich.	Niles H. S.	21	209	6:2	0
79	Binkowski, Benedict F.	F.B.	Chicago, Ill.	St. Bede, Peru, Ill.	20	181	6:1	0
80	Simonich, Edward Francis	F.B.	Ironwood, Mich.	Luther L. Wright H. S.	20	200	6:1¾	0
81	*Danbom, Laurence Edwin	F.B.	Calumet, Mich.	Calumet H. S.	21	192	6:2	2
82	Shellogg, Fred. Richard	L.T.	New Castle, Pa.	New Castle H. S.	20	213	6:1½	0
83	Shellogg, Alec Regis	R.T.	New Castle, Pa.	New Castle H. S.	20	204	6:½	0
84	Foster, Harvey Goodson	L.G.	So. Bend, Ind.	Highland Park, Detroit	21	178	6:0	1
	*Smith, Wm. Robert (Capt.)	R.G.	Hackettstown, N. J.	St. Benedict's, Newark	23	165	5:10	2

* Indicates major Monogram.

NOTRE DAME, 1936

Line: Joe Zwers (RE), Frank Kopczak (RT), Joe Kuharich (RG), Fred Mundee (C), Capt. John Lauter, Bill Steinkemper, Joe O'Neill. *Backfield:* Vic Wojcihovski (RHB), Steve Miller (FB), Andy Puplis (QB), Bob Wilke (LHB).

1936

Coach: Elmer F. Layden
Captain: °William R. Smith—John P. Lautar

O.3	W	Carnegie Tech	21-7	H	15,673
O.10	W	Washington (St. L.)	14-6	H	9,879
O.17	W	Wisconsin (R)	27-0	H	16,423
O.24	L	Pittsburgh	0-26	A	c66,622
O.31	W	Ohio State (R)	7-2	H	50,017
N.7	L	Navy (U)	0-3	N	51,126
N.14	W	Army	20-6	YS	c74,423
N.21	W	Northwestern (U)	26-6	H	52,131
D.5	T	So. California	13-13	A	71,201
		(6-2-1)	128-69		407,495

°Captain-elect. Smith resigned his captaincy because of illness and Lautar was elected Acting Captain.
N—at Baltimore

AP POLL

1936

1. Minnesota
2. L.S.U.
3. Pittsburgh
4. Alabama
5. Washington
6. Santa Clara
7. Northwestern
8. NOTRE DAME
9. Nebraska
10. Pennsylvania

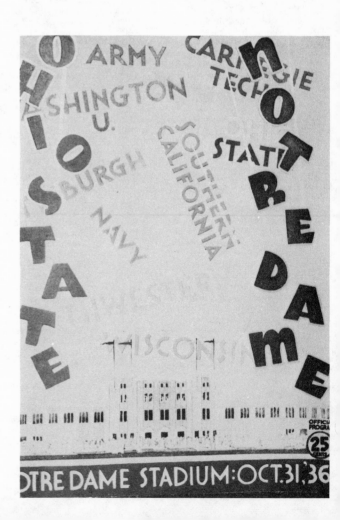

IRISH BEAT BUCKEYES IN THRILLING GAME BY 7-2 SCORE

●

By Al Bride

The largest crowd ever to push its way into the local stadium witnessed an alert Notre Dame team triumph, 7-2, over the tricky ball-handling outfit from Ohio State. Led by California's speedy "Bunny" McCormick and the hard driving sophomore full-back Simonich the Fighting Irish dominated the Ohioans in every de-

RUETZ   CRONIN

partment with the exception of punting.

Rain which showered at intervals did not dim the enthusiasm of the capacity crowd which was brought to its feet in the closing minutes by a determined Ohio State drive that was reminiscent of last year's contest. Taking the ball deep in its own territory Ohio State passed its way to the Irish 12 yard line before losing the ball on two incomplete passes into the end zone.

Ohio State scored first, capitalizing on a fumble early in the second period. From near his own goal line Miller, on a fake kick, broke through the line only to lose the ball when he was tackled hard by the Scarlet secondary. Ohio State registered a first down, but was then stopped with a touchdown in sight. A safety was good for two points, and the Irish were trailing, 2-0.

After an exchange of kicks the Laydenmen started to move. A pass to McCormick was good on the two yard line, and on the next play McCormick started swiftly to the left, cut in sharply over tackle, and dashed into the end zone for a touchdown. Wojcihovski was rushed in to hold the ball for Danbom, who booted a perfect placement to make the score 7-2.

The second half found Ohio State

using every trick in its "razzle dazzle" in an attempt to break loose for a score, but the hard charging Irish line broke up most of the plays before they could get under way. In the closing minutes red shirted receivers managed to elude the Notre Dame secondary, and several completed passes brought the ball to the Irish 12 yard line. In a desperate attempt to score before the gun went off the Ohioans threw two passes into the end zone, both of which were incomplete. According to the new rules Notre Dame received the ball, and for the remaining seconds they held on to it.

One of the features of the game was the performance of Simonich. This husky 200 pounder was given his chance, and he came through in a manner that ought to give the other fullbacks something to worry about. Time after time he crashed through the powerful Ohio line for gains. When not advancing the ball through sheer power this second year man was clearing the way with some of the best blocking displayed by an Irish player to date.

NOTRE DAME'S "PERFECT PLAY" OF 1936

AS SEEN IN NORTHWESTERN-NOTRE DAME GAME OF 1936

● Bob Wilke (12) is shown outspeeding Northwestern's defense to score the first of four touchdowns the Irish made, two of them by Wilke, in defeating the 1936 Western Conference champions, 26 to 6. The defeat knocked Northwestern out of a national title

● Notre Dame players shown in the picture include Bill Steinkemper (69), Larry Danbom (81), Capt. John Lautar (72), 1937 Capt. Joe Zwers (16), Fred Mundee (68), Andy Puplis (1), and Nevin (Bunny) McCormick (20). Joe Kuharich is blocking Leon Fuller

OFFICIAL 1937 NOTRE DAME FOOTBALL ROSTER

NO.	NAME	POSITION	HOME CITY	PREPARATORY SCHOOL	AGE	WT.	HT.	YRS. ON SQUAD
1	*Puplis, Andrew Joseph	Q.B.	Chicago, Ill.	Harrison Tech H. S.	22	168	5:8	2
2	Crowe, Emmett Hoste	Q.B.	Lafayette, Ind.	Jefferson H. S.	20	165	5:9	1
3	Hofer, Willard Clair	Q.B.	Rock Island, Ill.	Rock Island H. S.	21	180	5:11	1
4	Kelleher, John Charles	Q.B.	Lorain, Ohio	Lorain H. S.	19	158	5:8	0
7	*O'Reilly, Charles Wm.	Q.B.	St. Mary's, Ohio	Memorial H. S.	22	165	5:8	2
8	Sitko, Steve Joseph	Q.B.	Ft. Wayne, Ind.	Central H. S.	20	173	6:0	0
9	Archer, Clyde William	Q.B.	Parkersburg, W. Va.	Parkersburg H. S.	20	179	5:11	0
10	Fitzgerald, Raymond Chas.	R.G.	Detroit, Mich.	St. Catherine's H. S.	20	175	5:11	0
11	**Gleason, Joseph Thomas	R.H.	Chicago, Ill.	Leo H. S.	22	173	6:0	2
12	Sheridan, Benjamin Mason	L.H.	Havana, Ill.	Havana H. S.	20	75	5:8½	0
13	Sullivan, John Edward	L.H.	Chicago, Ill.	St. Mel H. S.	21	182	6:1	0
14	Borer, Harold William	R.H.	Little Neck, L. I.	Blair Prep, N. J.	20	175	5:10	0
15	McMahon, John Edward	L.H.	Indianapolis, Ind.	Cathedral H. S.	20	175	5:11½	1
16	**Zwers, Joseph Bernard (C)	R.E.	Grand Rapids, Mich.	Catholic Central H. S.	22	183	6:0	2
17	Bossu, August Francis	L.G.	Monongahela, Pa.	Monongahela H. S.	21	187	5:10	1
18	Kelly, John Francis	R.E.	Rutherford, N. J.	Pennington Prep, N. J.	21	189	6:2	0
19	Tuck, Frank Sweeney	L.H.	Hayden, Arizona	Hayden H. S.	19	170	5:9	1
20	*McCormick, Nevin Francis	R.H.	Livermore, Calif.	Livermore H. S.	22	159	5:8	2
21	Finneran, John Clement	C.	Columbus, Ohio	Columbus H. S.	19	190	6:0	0
22	Borowski, Charles Casimir	L.H.	South Bend, Ind.	Central H. S.	22	170	5:11	2
23	Zontini, Louis Rogers	L.H.	Whitesville, W. Va.	Sherman (Seth, W. Va.)	19	175	5:9	0
24	Biagi, Frank Walter	L.E.	St. Paul, Minn.	Mechanical Arts H. S.	19	183	5:11½	0
25	Brown, Earl Melvin, Jr.	L.E.	Benton Harbor, Mich.	Benton Harbor H. S.	21	178	6:½	1
26	Corgan, Michael Henry	R.H.	Alma, Mich.	Alma H. S.	19	183	5:10	0
27	Zuendel, Joseph Charles	L.G.	Des Moines, Ia.	Dowling H. S.	20	183	5:11	1
28	Arboit, Ennio Benjamin	R.H.	Oglesby, Ill.	St. Bede (Peru, Ill.)	20	178	5:10½	2
29	Clifford, Jeremiah Joseph	L.E.	Chicago, Ill.	Mt. Carmel H. S.	22	184	6:2	2
30	*Kovalcik, George John	R.H.	Donora, Pa.	Donora H. S.	22	190	6:0	1
31	Kennedy, Maurice James	L.H.	Ogden, Utah	Ogden H. S.	22	187	6:½	2
32	Stevenson, Harry, Jr.	L.H.	East Orange N. J.	East Orange H. S.	20	185	6:1	0
33	Thesing, Joseph Roger	F.B.	Cincinnati, Ohio	Elder H. S.	19	190	5:11	0
34	Mandjiak, Michael	R.H.	Kalamazoo, Mich.	St. Augustine's H. S.	19	185	6:0	0
35	Brennan, Thomas Joseph	L.F	Chicago, Ill.	Leo H. S.	19	183	6:2	0
36	Karr, James Joseph	L.G.	Milwaukee, Wis.	Pio Nono H. S.	19	189	5:11	0
37	Fox, Harry Francis	R.G.	Cleveland Hts., Ohio	Cleveland Hts. H. S.	21	175	5:8	2
38	O'Loughlin, William Anthony	L.E.	Toledo, Ohio	Central Catholic	20	178	6:0	1
39	*McCarthy, Jack Gregory	L.H.	Glencoe, Ill.	Loyola Acad. (Chicago)	21	175	6:0	2
40	Burnell, Herman Joseph	L.H.	Duluth, Minn.	Duluth Cathedral	21	178	5:11	1
41	*McCarty, Patrick Francis	C.	Toledo, Ohio	Central Catholic H. S	22	200	6:2½	2
42	Kerr, William Howard	L.E.	Newburgh, N. Y.	Newburgh Academy	20	187	6:1	0
43	Sullivan, Robert Edwin	R.E.	Helena, Mont.	St. Charles H. S.	20	195	5:11	0
44	Morrison, Paul Edward	R.H.	Jersey City, N. J.	Raymond Riordan Prep	22	176	5:10	1
45	Emanuel, Dennis George	L.T.	Iowa City, Ia.	St. Patrick's H. S.	22	203	6:2	2
46	Lynn, Bradley Nicholas	R.H.	San Francisco, Calif.	Santa Cruz H. S.	20	180	5:10	0
47	*Sweeney, Charles Alexander	R.E.	Bloomington, Ill.	Trinity H. S.	22	188	6:0	2
48	Sullivan, Daniel Francis	R.H.	Chicago, Ill.	St. Ignatius H. S.	21	175	5:8	1
49	Gottsacker, Harold Alfred	F.B.	Sheboygan, Wis.	Sheboygan H. S.	20	187	6:0	1
50	Riffle, Charles Francis	F.B.	Warren, Ohio	Warren H. S.	19	195	6:0	0
51	Longhi, Edward John	C.	Torrington, Conn.	Torrington H. S.	21	195	6:2	1
52	*Skoglund, Leonard Howard	L.E.	Chicago, Ill.	Senn H. S.	21	189	6:1½	2
53	Broscoe, Edward Michael	R.E.	Youngstown, Ohio	Dickinson Sem. (Pa.)	21	180	5:11	1
54	Hollendoner, Francis Joseph	R.T.	Chicago, Ill.	De LaSalle Academy	19	203	6:3	0
55	DeFranco, Joseph Francis	L.G.	Weirton, W. Va.	Weirton H. S.	21	175	5:7	0
56	**Kuharich, Joseph Lawrence	R.G.	South Bend, Ind.	James W. Riley H. S.	20	193	5:11½	2
57	Arboit, Peter Samuel	L.E.	Oglesby, Ill.	St. Bede (Peru, Ill.)	18	187	6:0	0
58	Tonelli, Mario George	F.B.	Chicago, Ill.	DePaul Academy	20	190	5:11	1
59	McGoldrick, James Joseph	L.G.	Philadelphia, Pa.	W. Philadelphia H. S.	20	180	5:11	1
60	Adamonis, Stanley Charles	C.	Ambridge, Pa.	St. Veronica H. S.	20	198	6:1	0
61	Mulcahey, James Lane	R.G.	Taunton, Mass.	Taunton H. S.	21	185	5:8½	1
62	*Marshall, Walter Michael	R.G.	Philadelphia, Pa.	Gratz H. S.	22	189	5:10¾	2
63	Saffa, Farris Paul	L.H.	Drumwright, Okla.	Drumwright H. S.	19	183	5:11½	0
64	Albert, Francis Joseph, Jr.	R.T.	Covington, Va.	Covington H. S.	21	210	5:10	0
65	Kelly, John Greg	R.E.	Chicago, Ill.	St. George (Evanston)	21	185	6:0	2
66	*Murphy, John Patrick	R.E.	South Bend, Ind.	Central H. S.	22	178	5:11	2
67	Brew, Francis Joseph	L.T.	Superior, Wis.	Cathedral (Duluth) H. S.	19	208	6:1	0
68	McIntyre, John Aloysius	C.	Providence, R. I.	LaSalle Academy	20	188	6:1	0
69	**Ruetz, Joseph Hubert	L.G.	South Bend, Ind.	Central H. S.	21	184	5:11½	2
70	Harvey, Thaddeus Harrison	L.T.	Wilmette, Ill.	New Trier H. S.	19	207	6:2	0
71	Race, Adrian Joseph	R.G.	Milwaukee, Wis.	Pio Nono H. S.	22	188	5:10½	2
72	McDonough, Joseph James	R.T.	Chicago, Ill.	De LaSalle H. S.	20	177	6:0	0
73	*Beinor, Joseph Edward	L.T.	Harvey, Ill.	Thornton Twp. H. S.	20	200	6:2	1
74	O'Neill, Robert Francis	L.T.	Phoenixville, Pa.	LaSalle (Philadelphia)	20	195	6:0	0
75	Fogel, John Nicholas	C.	Chicago, Ill.	Mt Carmel H. S.	22	190	5:10	2
76	Ely, Eugene James	L.T.	Auburn, Nebr.	Auburn H. S.	21	198	6:1½	2
78	*Kell, Paul Ernest	R.T.	Princeton, Ind.	Niles (Mich.) H. S.	21	209	6:1	1
79	Binkowski, Benedict F.	F.B.	Chicago, Ill.	St. Bede (Peru, Ill.)	20	181	6:1	1
80	*Simonich, Edward Francis	F.B.	Ironwood, Mich.	L. L. Wright H. S.	21	205	6:2	1
81	Mooney, Alan Brendan	F.B.	Hartford, Conn.	Bulkeley H. S.	19	185	6:2	0
82	Shellogg, Frederick Richard	L.T.	New Castle, Pa.	New Castle H. S.	21	215	6:1½	1
83	*Shellogg, Alec Regis	R.T.	New Castle, Pa.	New Castle H. S.	21	209	6:½	1
84	Foster, Harvey Goodson	L.G.	South Bend, Ind.	Highland Park (Detroit)	23	183	6:0	2

*Indicates Major Monogram.

1937

Coach: Elmer F. Layden
Captain: Joseph B. Zwers

2	W	Drake	21-0	H	14,955
9	T	Illinois	0-0	A	42,253
16	L	Carnegie Tech (U)	7-9	A	30,418
23	W	Navy (S) (2:00)	9-7	H	45,000
30	W	Minnesota (U)	7-6	A	c63,237
6	L	Pittsburgh	6-21	H	c54,309
13	W	Army (R)	7-0	YS	c76,359
20	W	Northwestern	7-0	A	42,573
27	W	So. California (1:45)	13-6	H	28,920
		(6-2-1)	77-49		398,024

STUBBORN ILLINOIS DEFENSE HOLDS IRISH TO SCORELESS TIE IN DULL BATTLE

By Nick Lamberto

The Fighting Illini from Illinois surprised the Fighting Irish from Notre Dame by holding them to a scoreless tie last Saturday afternoon in Memorial Stadium at Champaign before 50,000 fans. The green Illinois team made up for what they lacked in experience by showing an aggressive fighting spirit throughout the game.

Notre Dame's attack was stopped cold by the charging Illini line. At spasmodic intervals McCormick, Zontini, or McCarthy would reel off a good gain, but a coordinated goalward march was sadly lacking. The only Irish scoring threat came in the second period when they reached the Illini 12-yard line. The threat soon fizled out on three incomplete passes and an unsuccessful reverse.

Illinois, on the other hand, had the Notre Dame adherents in a state of grave apprehension on two occasions. In the first period Illinois advanced to Notre Dame's 14-yard line. The threat ended when Brewer's attempted place kick was low. Again in the fourth period Brewer attempted a field goal, this time from the 34-yard line, but the kick was short.

Illinois won the toss and elected to kick off. Berner, the Illinois punter, set the Irish back on their heels with his accurate punts. Spurgeon's returns of Notre Dame punts also helped to keep the ball deep in the Irish territory. The Irish finally penetrated into Illinois territory in the second quarter. Puplis returned a punt to midfield and the Irish second string went in. In three line plays the ball was advanced to the Illinois 39. A pass to Brown put the ball on the 24. A five-yard penalty and three thrusts by Simonich gave Notre Dame a first down on the Illini 12. Then the Irish launched their unsuccessful aerial attack and lost the ball on downs.

The remainder of the game found the Illini displaying their superior advantage in punting, and the Irish exhibiting some sloppy ball handling. Fumbles at strategic moments took the heart out of the Irish attack but they went down fighting to the end. Once in the fourth quarter Brown almost snared a pass for a touchdown, but the ball trickled from his hands.

The stars for Illinois were Spurgeon, Brewer, Castelo, and Klemp. Spurgeon, the Illini captain, led his team on both offense and defense. Klemp and Castelo were two smashing, vicious ends and broke up a major portion of Notre Dame plays. Brewer, a sophomore guard, showed the Notre Dame line that All-American rating is not merited by last season's play.

Bunny McCormick was the usual elusive rabbit. He gained nearly 50 yards in five plays. Had he been used more he might have bettered his good average. Chuck Sweeney, playing before a home town delegation, gave a good exhibition of offensive and defensive end play. Pat McCarty backed up the Irish line in superior fashion. The two left halfs, Zontini and McCarthy, both gave good accounts of themselves. Both had good gains nullified by penalties.

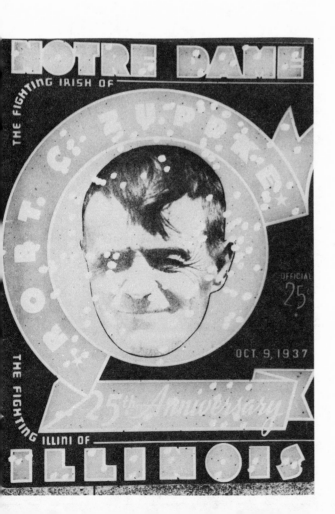

1938 UNIVERSITY OF NOTRE DAME FOOTBALL ROSTER

No.	Name	Position	Yrs. on Squad	Age	Weight	Height	Home Address
60	Adamonis, Stanley Charles	Center	1	21	195	6:1	Ambridge, Pa.
64	Albert, Francis Joseph	Left Guard	1	22	210	5:10	Covington, Va.
46	Ames, Richard Francis	Right Guard	1	23	180	5:10	Mt. Vernon, Ill.
9	Archer, Clyde William	Quarterback	1	21	180	5:10½	Parkersburg, W. Va.
39	Barber, Robert Anthony	Right End	1	21	178	6:1	Erie, Pa.
56	Bechtold, Joseph Hubert	Right Tackle	0	19	207	6:2	Sioux Falls, S. D.
75	Beinor, Joseph Edward**	Left Tackle	2	21	207	6:2	Harvey, Ill.
41	Berta, William	Right End	0	20	190	6:2	South Bend, Ind.
24	Biagi, Frank Walter	Left End	1	20	180	6:0	St. Paul, Minn.
79	Binkowski, Benedict Francis	Fullback	2	21	187	6:1	Chicago, Ill.
14	Borer, Harold Wilbur	Right Halfback	1	20	187	5:10	Little Neck, L. I.
17	Bossu, August Francis	Right Guard	2	22	188	5:10	Monongahela, Pa.
35	Brennan, Thomas Joseph	Right End	1	20	187	6:2	Chicago, Ill.
67	Brew, Francis Joseph	Left Tackle	1	20	205	6:1	Superior, Wis.
53	Broscoe, Edward Michael	Right End	2	25	185	5:11	Youngstown, Ohio
25	Brown, Earl Melvin, Jr.*	Left End	2	25	178	6:0	Benton Harbor, Mich.
40	Burnell, Herman Joseph	Right Halfback	2	25	180	5:11	Duluth, Minn.
19	Cassidy, Thaddeus Donald	Right Halfback	0	19	170	5:9	Altoona, Pa.
26	Corgan, Michael Henry	Right Halfback	1	20	185	5:10	Alma, Mich.
2	Crowe, Emmett Hoste	Quarterback	2	21	170	5:8	Lafayette, Ind.
55	DeFranco, Joseph Francis	Left Guard	1	22	175	5:7	Weirton, W. Va.
62	Doody, Frank Arthur	Right Halfback	0	18	180	5:10½	Oak Park, Ill.
21	Finneran, Jack Clement	Center	1	20	190	6:1	Columbus, Ohio
82	Frost, Robert Joseph	Right Tackle	1	20	195	5:11	Hicksville, L. I.
84	Gallagher, Thomas Charles	Left Tackle	0	21	204	6:1	Chicago, Ill.
49	Gottsacker, Harold Alfred	Fullback	2	21	195	6:1	Sheboygan, Wis.
66	Gubanich, John Aloysius	Right Guard	0	19	170	5:10	Phoenixville, Pa.
70	Harvey, Thaddeus Harrison	Right Tackle	1	20	215	6:2	Wilmette, Ill.
28	Heath, Clifford Edward	Right Guard	0	20	180	5:10	Flint, Mich.
3	Hofer, Willard Clair	Quarterback	2	22	190	5:11	Rock Island, Ill.
54	Hollendoner, Francis Joseph	Left Tackle	1	20	208	6:5	Chicago, Ill.
36	Karr, James Joseph	Right Guard	1	21	190	5:11	Milwaukee, Wis.
78	Kell, Paul Ernest**	Right Tackle	2	25	209	6:2	Niles, Mich.
4	Kelleher, John Charles	Quarterback	1	20	160	5:9	Lorain, Ohio
18	Kelly, John Francis	Right End	1	22	186	6:2	Rutherford, N. J.
57	Kelly, Peter Mullen	Left Guard	0	20	185	5:9½	Chicago, Ill.
42	Kerr, William Howard	Left End	1	22	190	6:1	Newburgh, N. Y.
7	Koch, Robert James	Quarterback	0	19	170	5:10	Calumet City, Ill.
61	Korth, Howard Joseph	Right Tackle	0	19	190	6:1	Saginaw, Mich.
30	Kovalcik, George John*	Right Halfback	2	25	190	6:0	Donora, Pa.
76	Larkin, Edward Joseph	Right End	0	19	180	6:5	Peoria, Ill.
37	Lee, Albert Bush	Fullback	0	20	190	5:10	Carlinville, Ill.
10	Leonard, Robert John	Fullback	0	21	190	6:1	Cincinnati, Ohio
51	Longhi, Edward John*	Center	2	22	195	6:2	Torrington, Conn.
45	Maloney, John Malachi	Center	0	21	185	6:2	Boise, Idaho
11	Marquardt, Clarence William	Right Halfback	0	19	175	6:0	Oak Park, Ill.
6	Masterson, Bernard James	Quarterback	0	21	160	5:8	Oak Park, Ill.
22	Matthews, Edward Eugene	Right Tackle	1	20	215	6:0	New Straitsville, Ohio
72	McDonough, Joseph James	Right Guard	1	21	177	6:0	Chicago, Ill.
63	McGannon, William Vincent	Left Halfback	0	19	170	5:9	Evansville, Ind.
59	McGoldrick, James Joseph (Capt.)*	Left Guard	2	21	175	5:11	Philadelphia, Pa.
68	McIntyre, John Aloysius	Center	1	21	186	6:1	Providence, R. I.
15	McMahon, John Edward	Left Halfback	2	21	175	5:11	Indianapolis, Ind.
81	Mooney, Alan Brendan	Center	1	21	190	6:5	Hartford, Conn.
44	Morrison, Paul Edward	Right Halfback	2	25	185	5:10	Jersey City, N. J.
52	Mortell, John Edwin	Center	0	20	180	6:0	Kankakee, Ill.
47	O'Brien, John Dennis	Right End	0	20	188	6:0½	Swissvale, Pa.
38	O'Loughlin, William Anthony	Left End	2	21	180	6:0	Toledo, Ohio
1	O'Meara, Walter Charles	Quarterback	0	20	165	5:8	Stamford, Conn.
74	O'Neill, Robert Francis	Left Tackle	1	21	205	6:0	Phoenixville, Pa.
85	Papa, Joseph John	Left Tackle	0	20	208	6:1	Pittsburgh, Pa.
71	Piepul, Milton John	Fullback	0	20	207	6:1	Thompsonville, Conn.
29	Plain, George Frederick, Jr.	Left End	1	21	190	6:1	East Orange, N. J.
69	Rassas, George James	Left End	0	22	196	6:5	Stamford, Conn.
50	Riffle, Charles Francis	Right Guard	1	20	205	6:0	Warren, Ohio
51	Rogenski, Steven Joseph	Center	2	22	205	6:1	Moline, Ill.
34	Saggau, Robert Joseph	Left Halfback	0	18	185	6:0	Denison, Iowa
65	Schrenker, Henry Pershing	Left Guard	1	20	190	5:10	Elwood, Ind.
12	Sheridan, Benjamin Mason	Left Halfback	1	21	171	5:9	Havana, Ill.
48	Sheridan, Philip Francis	Left End	0	21	181	6:2	Rutherford, N. J.
80	Simonich, Edward Francis**	Fullback	2	22	205	6:2½	Ironwood, Mich.
8	Sitko, Steven Joseph	Quarterback	1	21	185	6:0	Fort Wayne, Ind.
32	Stevenson, Harry, Jr.	Left Halfback	1	21	190	6:1	Bloomfield, N. J.
13	Sullivan, John Edward	Left Halfback	1	22	180	6:2	Chicago, Ill.
43	Sullivan, Robert Edward	Right Guard	1	21	197	5:11	Helena, Mont.
73	Theisen, Charles John	Left Tackle	2	22	225	6:4	St. Joseph, Mich.
33	Thesing, Joseph Robert*	Fullback	1	20	190	5:11	Cincinnati, Ohio
58	Tonelli, Mario George*	Fullback	2	21	188	5:11	Chicago, Ill.
16	Tuck, Frank Sweeney	Left Halfback	2	20	175	5:10	Hayden, Ariz.
20	Williams, Theodore Patrick	Right Halfback	0	21	180	5:11	Gloucester, Mass.
23	Zontini, Louis Rogers*	Right Halfback	1	20	175	5:11	Whitesville, W. Va.
27	Zuendel, Joseph Charles	Left Guard	2	21	185	5:11	Des Moines, Iowa

* Indicates Major Monogram.

1938				
Coach: Elmer F. Layden				
Captain: James J. McGoldrick				
O.1	W	Kansas	52-0	H	25,615
O.8	W	Georgia Tech	14-6	A	26,533
O.15	W	Illinois	14-6	H	29,142
O.22	W	Carnegie Tech	7-0	H	25,934
O.29	W	Army	19-7	YS	c76,338
N.5	W	Navy (R)	15-0	N	58,271
N.12	°W	Minnesota	19-0	H	c55,245
N.19	W	Northwestern	9-7	A	c46,348
D.3	L	So. California (U)	0-13	A	c97,146
		(8-1-0)	149-39		440,572

N—at Baltimore
°Notre Dame's 300th victory

ND's 300th WIN

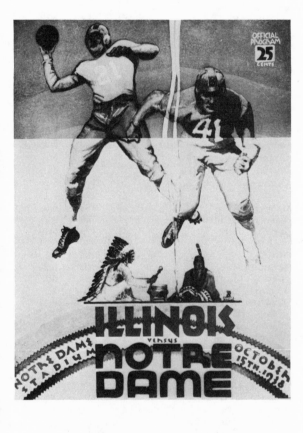

MIGHTY MINNESOTA BECOMES NO. 7

Minnesota came, they saw, and were conquered. Out of the northwest came the so-called "powerful" Golden Gophers, to meet a team of the opportunist variety. Three quick thrusts were all that Notre Dame team needed to preserve its perfect record and hang up a 19-0 win.

The Gophers slashed their way up and down between the two 40-yard lines to amass a total of 6 first downs, while the Irish, holding themselves in check most of the game, made only two.

The first few minutes of the first quarter went by with little happening. With the ball on the Notre Dame 16 yard line, a smash by Bob Saggau failed to gain. Then Zontini, behind almost perfect interference, broke off right tackle, danced his way to the sidelines, and raced 84 yards for the score. After regaining his breath he stepped back and booted the ball for the extra point. Minnesota, stunned for the moment by the devastating suddenness of the play, fought back with all the power and fury they could master, but to no avail. At the end of the first quarter, Notre Dame led 7-0.

In the second quarter, like the first, Minnesota kept driving toward the Irish goal, but whenever they seemed to get started Notre Dame braced, and stopped the attack. There were but five minutes of play remaining in the second quarter when Notre Dame again struck with lightning-like swiftness. With the ball on the Gopher 47 yard stripe, Bob Saggau faded back and lofted a pass to Earl Brown, who had outdistanced the secondary. Without slackening his stride Brown glanced back, took the ball in his arms, and raced 15 yards to the goal. This time Zontini failed to convert.

In the closing minutes of the game Notre Dame made her final score, climaxing a drive of 37 yards through the air. After completing a pass to Zontini, Saggau heaved an 18 yard throw to Kelly in the end zone, and the score was 19-0.

THE U.S.C. GAME

Dec. 3—After halting eleven successive teams during the past two seasons, Notre Dame's National Championship-bound gridders were upset by the sturdy Trojans of Southern California, 13 to 0, before 100,000 spectators at Los Angeles.

Ollie Day, unknown reserve for highly-touted Grenville and Mickey Anderson, assumed the starring rôle for the victors by hurling a 33-yard pass to Al Krueger for the initial Troy marker with but four seconds remaining in the first half. Lou Zontini, Notre Dame back, tackled Krueger but the latter had dived successfully into the end zone. The placekick attempt was wide.

In the first half the Irish penetrated to the Trojan 16-yard line but a pair of passes which went awry when the passer was rushed nullified a dangerous touchdown threat. In the last quarter, Notre Dame marched from its own 32-yard line 52 yards to the Trojan 16 before Jones intercepted a Saggau pass.

In the fourth quarter, Southern California capitalized on a Notre Dame fumble to count the second touchdown—thus becoming the only team to accomplish the feat this season.

JOSEPH R. THESING

OFFICIAL 1939 NOTRE DAME FOOTBALL ROSTER

NO.	NAME	POSITION	HOME TOWN	PREPARATORY SCHOOL	AGE	WGT.	HT.	EXP.
1	O'Meara, Walter Charles	Q.B.	Stamford, Conn.	Stamford H. S.	21	155	5:8	1
2	Hayes, Clarence William	Q.B.	Atchison, Kansas	Maur Hill H. S.	21	164	5:9	0
3	Hargrave, Robert Webb	Q.B.	Evansville, Ind.	Reitz Memorial H. S.	19	185	5:11	0
4	Kelleher, John Charles	Q.B.	Lorain, Ohio	Lorain H. S.	21	156	5:9	2
7	Koch, Robert James	Q.B.	Calumet City, Ill.	Cath. Cent., Hammond	20	165	5:10	1
8	*Sitko, Steven Joseph	Q.B.	Fort Wayne, Ind.	Central H. S.	22	183	6:0	2
11	Rockne, Knute Kenneth, Jr.	R.H.	South Bend, Ind.	Miami, Fla., Mil. Acad.	21	155	5:9	0
12	*Sheridan, Benjamin Mason	L.H.	Havana, Ill.	Havana H. S.	22	160	5:9	2
13	Stelmaszek, Edward Thos.	L.G.	Chicago, Ill.	Mt. Carmel H. S.	22	175	5:8	0
14	Schmid, Charles William	R.T.	Detroit, Mich.	De LaSalle H. S.	21	180	5:10	1
15	Juzwik, Steven Robert	R.H.	Chicago, Ill.	De Paul Academy	21	182	5:8½	0
16	Bagarus, Stephen, Jr.	R.H.	South Bend, Ind.	Washington H. S.	20	155	5:11½	0
17	Laiber, Joseph	R.G.	South Bend, Ind.	Washington H. S.	19	165	5:10	0
18	*Kelly, John Francis (Capt.)	R.E.	Rutherford, N. J.	St. Mary's H. S.	23	190	6:2	2
20	Marko, Peter Joseph	L.H.	South Bend, Ind.	Washington H. S.	19	155	5:10	0
21	Finneran, John Clement	C.	Columbus, Ohio	Rosary H. S.	21	189	6:1	2
23	**Zontini, Louis Rogers	R.H.	Whiteville, W. Va.	Sherman, Seth, W. Va.	21	181	5:8½	2
24	Biagi, Frank Walter	L.E.	St. Paul, Minn.	Mech. Arts H. S.	21	176	5:11	2
25	Petschel, Howard Kenneth	R.E.	St. Paul, Minn.	Washington H. S.	20	176	6:1	0
26	Corgan, Michael Henry	R.H.	Alma, Mich.	Alma H. S.	21	186	5:10	2
27	Kristoff, Walter William	R.H.	Chicago, Ill.	De LaSalle Acad.	21	163	5:10	1
28	Chlebeck, Andrew John	F.B.	St. Paul, Minn.	St. Thomas H. S.	20	180	6:0	0
29	Kovatch, John Geo., Jr.	R.E.	South Bend, Ind.	Washington H. S.	19	173	6:2	0
30	McCabe, George Jos., Jr.	L.H.	Davenport, Ia.	St. Ambrose Academy	19	155	5:11	0
31	Leonard, Robert John	F.B.	Cincinnati, Ohio	St. Xavier H. S.	22	192	6:	1
32	**Stevenson, Harry, Jr.	L.H.	Bloomfield, N. J.	E. Orange, N. J., H. S.	22	189	6:1	2
33	**Thesing, Joseph Roger	F.B.	Cincinnati, Ohio	Elder H. S.	21	192	5:11	2
34	*Saggau, Robert Joseph	L.H.	Denison, Iowa	Denison H. S.	19	188	6:0	1
36	Maloney, John Malachi	C.	Boise, Idaho	St. Teresa's Academy	22	189	6:3	
37	Lee, Albert Bush	F.B.	Carlinville, Ill.	Carlinville H. S.	21	178	5:10	1
38	Bairley, Roy James	R.T.	Monroe, Mich.	Monroe H. S.	19	200	5:11	1
39	Barber, Robert Anthony	R.E.	Erie, Penna.	Erie H. S.	22	180	6:1	2
40	Hogan, Donald John	L.H.	Chicago, Ill.	St. Ignatius H. S.	18	193	6:2	[illegible]
41	Rively, Clair Michael	L.T.	Altoona, Penna.	Altoona Cath. H. S.	20	188	6:1	0
42	*Kerr, William Howard	L.E.	Newburgh, N. Y.	Newburgh Free Acad.	24	194	6:1	2
43	Sullivan, Robert Edwin	R.G.	Helena, Montana	St. Charles H. S.	22	185	5:11	2
44	Crimmins, Bernard Anthony	R.H.	Louisville, Ky.	St. Xavier H. S.	20	188	5:11	0
45	O'Reilly, Martin Gordon	C.	Chicago, Ill.	Mt. Carmel H. S.	19	180	6:2	0
46	Ames, Richard Francis	R.G.	Mt. Vernon, Ill.	Mt. Vernon H. S.	24	167	5:9½	2
47	*O'Brien, John Dennis	R.E.	Swissvale, Penna.	Swissvale H. S.	21	186	6:0½	1
48	Sheridan, Philip Francis	L.E.	Rutherford, N. J.	St. Mary's H. S.	22	183	6:1½	1
49	Maddock, Robert Charles	R.G.	Santa Ana, Calif.	Santa Ana H. S.	19	204	5:11½	0
50	Riffle, Charles Francis	R.G.	Warren, Ohio	Warren H. S.	21	200	6:0	2
51	Osterman, Robert Thomas	C.	Detroit, Mich.	St. Theresa's H. S.	20	205	6:3	1
52	Pepelnjak, Nicholas Frank	L.H.	Virginia, Minn.	Roosevelt H. S.	19	175	5:10	0
53	Prokop, Joseph Michael	R.H.	Cleveland, Ohio	Cathedral Latin H. S.	19	195	6:1	0
54	Robinson, Angus	L.T.	Stamford, Conn.	Greenwich, Conn., H. S.	20	225	6:2	0
55	*DeFranco, Joseph Francis	L.G.	Weirton, W. Va.	Weir H. S.	23	188	5:7	2
56	Ebli, Raymond Henry	L.E.	Ironwood, Mich.	St. Ambrose H. S.	20	204	6:2	0
57	Kelly, Peter Mullen	L.G.	Chicago, Ill.	Fenwick, Oak Park	21	190	5:10	1
58	Arboit, Peter Samuel	L.E.	LaSalle, Ill.	St. Bede, Peru, Ill.	20	188	6:0	1
59	Bereolos, Hercules	L.G.	Hammond, Ind.	Hammond H. S.	20	198	5:11	0
61	Korth, Howard Joseph	R.G.	Saginaw, Mich.	Saginaw H. S.	20	178	[illegible]:1	1
63	McGannon, William Vincent	L.H.	Evansville, Ind.	Reitz Memorial H. S.	20	174	5:9	1
64	Albert, Francis Joseph	L.T.	Covington, Va.	Covington H. S.	23	204	5:10	2
65	Schrenker, Henry Pershing	L.G.	Elwood, Ind.	Elwood H. S.	21	187	5:10½	1
66	*Gubanich, John Aloysius	R.G.	Phoenixville, Pa.	Phoenixville H. S.	20	160	5:9	1
67	Ford, James Brendan	C.	Binghamton, N. Y.	Allentown, Pa., Prep.	21	204	6:0	0
68	*McIntyre, John Aloysius,	C.	Providence, R. I.	LaSalle Academy	22	196	6:1	2
69	Rassas, George James	L.E.	Stamford, Conn.	Stamford H. S.	22	185	6:3	1
70	*Harvey, Thaddeus Harrison	R.T.	Wilmette, Ill.	New Trier, Winnetka	21	217	6:2	2
71	*Piepul, Milton John	F.B.	Thompsonville, Conn.	Enfield H. S.	21	204	6:1	1
72	Ostroski, Edward Adam	R.G.	Shamokin, Penna.	Shamokin H. S.	20	196	5:9½	0
73	Brutz, James Charles	L.T.	Warren, Ohio	Warren H. S.	20	217	6:0	0
74	O'Neill, Robert Francis	R.T.	Phoenixville, Pa.	LaSalle, Phila.	22	200	6:0	2
75	Lillis, Paul Bernard	R.T.	Mt. Vernon, N. Y.	Bennett, Buffalo, N. Y.	18	205	6:2	0
76	Larkin, Edward Joseph	R.E.	Peoria, Ill.	Spalding Institute	20	177	6:2	1
78	Brosey, Henry Clifford	R.T.	Ozone Park, N. Y.	Brooklyn Tech, N. Y.	20	235	6:1	0
79	Sullivan, Edward Joseph	L.G.	Belle Harbor, N. Y.	St. John's, Brooklyn	19	196	5:9½	0
80	McNeill, Charles Edward	F.B.	Midland, Penna.	Lincoln H. S.	20	195	6:1¼	0
81	*Mooney, Alan Brendan	C.	Hartford, Conn.	Bulkeley H. S.	22	184	6:3	2
83	Papa, Joseph John	L.T.	Pittsburgh, Penna.	Kiski, Saltburg, Pa.	21	220	6:1	1
84	*Gallagher, Thomas Chas.	L.T.	Chicago, Ill.	Leo H. S.	22	202	6:1	1

*—Indicates number of monograms won.

1939

Coach: Elmer F. Layden
Captain: John F. Kelly

S.30	W	Purdue	3-0	H	31,341
O.7	W	Georgia Tech	17-14	H	17,322
O.14	W	S.M.U.	20-19	H	29,730
O.21	W	Navy	14-7	N	c78,257
O.28	W	Carnegie Tech (S)	7-6	A	c61,420
N.4	W	Army	14-0	YS	c75,632
N.11	L	Iowa (U)	6-7	A	c42,380
N.18	W	Northwestern (3:30)	7-0	H	49,204
N.25	L	So. California	12-20	H	c54,799
			(7-2-0)	100-73	440,085

N—at Cleveland

AP POLL

1939

1. Texas A&M
2. Tennessee
3. U.S.C.
4. Cornell
5. Tulane
6. Missouri
7. U.C.L.A.
8. Duke
9. Iowa
10. Duquesne
13. NOTRE DAME

Notre Dame Defeats SMU In Thriller

Mustangs Give Irish Wild Ride Before Bowing Out, 20 to 19; Milt Piepul Stars

Notre Dame-SMU Game Statistics

South Bend, Ind., Oct. 14.—(AP.) —Statistics of the Southern Methodist-Notre Dame football game:

	S.M.	N.D.
First downs	10	13
Yards gained rushing (net)	96	205
Forward passes attempted	17	7
Forward passes completed	7	4
Yards gained by forward passes	98	96
Yards lost, attempted forward passes	0	0
Forward passes intercepted by	1	1
Yards gained, run-back of int. passes	3	2
Punting average (from scrimmage)	33	36
xTotal yards, all kicks returned	84	52
Opponents fumbles recovered	3	1
Yards lost by penalties	20	45

x—Includes punts and kick offs.

South Bend, Ind., Oct. 14.—(AP.) — The Mustangs of Southern Methodist University took Notre Dame for a wild ride today, but at the finish the Irish held the whip hand, 20-19.

Notre Dame "backed into" the hard won victory, SMU missing a tie in the final minute of play. Jack Sanders, big lineman, failed to make the extra point on a touchdown scored after a blocked Notre Dame punt had given the invaders possession on the Irish two yard line. Seconds later Notre Dame had its third straight victory of the season in the books and Southern Methodist its first defeat.

The finish of the furiously fought battle matched its start, both teams scoring touchdowns in the first seven minutes of play. Each added another touchdown and missed the try for point in the second period to enter the last half deadlocked at 13-13. Then, after a comparatively quiet third quarter, Notre Dame smashed through for a touchdown and an extra point and Southern Methodist made its gallant but futile bid to escape defeat as the clock ticked away the Mustang hopes.

Lineups:

S. METHODIST		NOTRE DAME
Tunnell	le	Kerr
Sanders	lt	Gallagher
Bailey	lg	Defranco
Echols	c	McIntyre
Bianchi	rg	Riffle
Curik	rt	Harvey
Baccus	re	J. Kelly
Miller	qb	Sitko
Johnston	lh	Stevenson
Crouch	rh	Zontini
Bearden	fb	Thesing

Score by periods:

Notre Dame ....7 6 0 7—20
Southern Methodist .....7 6 0 6—19

Southern Methodist scoring: touchdowns, Johnston (2) Mallouf (sub for Johnston); point from try after touchdown, Sanders; Notre Dame scoring; touchdown, Zontini, Piepul (2) (sub for Thesing); point from try after touchdown, Zontini, Kelleher (sub for Sitko). Southern Methodist substitutions: ends, Maddox, Goss, Keeton, Collins, Meyers; tackles, Harris, Barnett; guards, Duvall, Baker, Fawcett, Simes; center, Pope; quarterbacks, Young, Mangrum, Clinton; halfbacks, Belville, Norte Dame substitutions, ends, Biagi, Obrien; tackles, Brutz, Lillis; guards, P. Kelly, Gubanich; center, Finneran; quarterbacks, D. F. Kelleher; halfbacks, Saggau, Sheridan, Crimmins, Bagarus; fullback, Piepul.

Rockne MEMORIAL

On Saturday, June 3, 1939, the Knute Rockne Memorial Field House was dedicated in the presence of some 3,000 persons. This impressive program was broadcast over the coast-to-coast facilities of the Mutual Network. Among the speakers were Arch Ward, Charles "Gus" Dorais, Elmer Layden, and the Rev. John F. O'Hara, C.S.C.

OFFICIAL 1940 NOTRE DAME FOOTBALL ROSTER

NO.	NAME	POSITION	HOME TOWN	PREPARATORY SCHOOL	AGE	WGT.	HGT.	EXP.
1	O'Meara, Walter Charles	Q.B.	Stamford, Conn.	Stamford H. S.	22	165	5:8	2
2	Hayes, John William	Q.B.	Atchison, Kansas	Maur Hill Prep	22	164	5:9	1
3	*Hargrave, Robert Webb	Q.B.	Evansville, Ind.	Reitz Memorial H. S.	20	172	5:11	2
4	Doody, Frank Arthur	Q.B.	Oak Park, Ill.	Fenwick H. S.	20	178	5:11	1
5	Patten, Paul Edward	Q.B.	Canton, N. Y.	Canton H. S.	20	169	5:8	2
7	Koch, Robert James	Q.B.	Calumet City, Ill.	Cath. Cent., Hammond	21	168	5:10	0
9	Girolami, Anthony Gregory	Q.B.	Chicago, Ill.	Crane Tech H. S.	19	193	6:0	0
12	Peasenelli, John Joseph	L.H.	Rochester, Pa.	Rochester H. S.	20	173	5:11	2
14	Schmid, Charles Willic~	R.T.	Detroit, Mich.	De LaSalle H. S.	22	180	5:9½	1
15	Juzwik, Steve Robert	R.H.	Chicago, Ill.	DePaul Academy	22	185	5:8½	1
16	Bagarus, Stephen Michael	R.H.	South Bend, Ind.	Washington H. S.	21	160	5:11	0
17	Laiber, Joseph James	R.G.	South Bend, Ind.	Washington H. S.	20	172	5:10	0
18	Murphy, George Edward	R.E.	South Bend, Ind.	Central H. S.	20	170	6:1	0
20	Callahan, Thomas Francis	L.E.	Stamford, Conn.	Stamford H. S.	19	172	6:0	0
21	Lanahan, John Francis	C.	Jacksonville, Fla.	Immaculate Conception	19	189	6:1½	0
23	Evans, Frederick Owen, Jr.	L.H.	South Bend, Ind.	Riley H. S.	19	174	5:11	0
26	Earley, William Joseph	R.H.	Parkersburg, W. Va.	Parkersburg H. S.	21	176	6:0	1
28	Chlebeck, Andrew John	F.B.	St. Paul, Minn.	St. Thomas Military	20	177	6:3	1
29	Kovatch, John George	R.E.	South Bend, Ind.	Washington H. S.	23	197	6:1	0
31	Leonard, Robert John	F.B.	Cincinnati, Ohio	St. Xavier H. S.	19	175	5:9½	2
32	Warner, John Andrew, Jr.	L.H.	New Haven, Conn.	Cheshire Academy	19	175	6:2½	0
33	O'Brien, Richard Charles	R.E.	Peoria, Ill.	Spalding Institute	20	189	6:0	0
34	Saggau, Robert Joseph	L.H.	Denison, Iowa	Denison H. S.	20	173	5:11	2
36	Michels, Andrew Jacob	L.G.	Mishawaka, Ind.	Mishawaka H. S.	22	180	6:0	0
37	Lee, Albert Bush	F.B.	Carlinville, Ill.	Carlinville H. S.	19	181	6:1	2
39	Perko, Thomas William	L.E.	Chisholm, Minn.	Chisholm H. S.	20	189	6:2	0
40	Hogan, Donald John	L.H.	Chicago, Ill.	St. Ignatius H. S.	21	193	6:1	1
41	Rively, Clair Michael	L.T.	Altoona, Pa.	Altoona Catholic H. S.	19	188	6:2	1
42	Dove, Robert Leo	L.E.	Youngstown, Ohio	South H. S.	20	182	6:1	0
43	Creevy, Richard Cassell	R.H.	Chicago, Ill.	Mt. Carmel H. S.	21	185	5:11	0
44	*Crimmins, Bernard Anthony	F.B.	Louisville, Ky.	St. Xavier H. S.	20	179	6:2	1
45	O'Reilly, Martin Gordon	C.	Chicago, Ill.	Mt. Carmel H. S.	19	174	5:8½	1
46	Barry, Norman John, Jr.	R.E.	Chicago, Ill.	Fenwick, Oak Park	22	187	6:½	0
47	**O'Brien, John Dennis	R.E.	Swissvale, Pa.	Swissvale H. S.	23	180	6:2	2
48	Sheridan, Philip Francis	L.E.	Rutherford, N. J.	St. Mary's H. S.	20	204	6:0	2
49	Maddock, Robert Charles	L.G.	Santa Ana, Calif.	Santa Ana H. S.	21	197	5:11	1
50	Walsh, Robert Michael	L.G.	Springfield, Ill.	Cathedral H. S.	21	202	6:3	0
51	Osterman, Robert Thomas	C.	Detroit, Mich.	St. Theresa's H. S.	20	196	6:1	2
53	Prokop, Joseph Michael	R.H.	Cleveland, Ohio	Cathedral Latin H. S.	19	214	6:2	1
54	Peterson, Elmer John	R.T.	Chicago, Ill.	Crane Tech H. S.	21	184	6:0	0
55	Wright, Harry Charles	F.B.	Hempstead, L. I., N. Y.	Chaminade, Mineola	21	205	6:2	1
56	Ebli, Raymond Henry	L.E.	Ironwood, Mich.	St. Ambrose H. S.	22	184	5:10	0
57	*Kelly, Peter Mullen	L.G.	Chicago, Ill.	Fenwick, Oak Park	19	180	6:1	1
58	Miller, Thomas Seeay	L.E.	Wilmington, Del.	Alexis I. DuPont H. S.	21	193	5:11	0
59	Bereolos, Hercules	R.G.	Hammond, Ind.	Hammond H. S.	19	189	5:9½	1
60	Webb, Robert Bailey	R.G.	Santa Ana, Calif.	Santa Ana H. S.	21	179	6:1	0
61	Korth, Howard Joseph	R.G.	Saginaw, Mich.	Saginaw H. S.	20	172	5:10	2
62	Kelly, James Lavelle	L.G.	Peoria, Ill.	Spalding Institute	21	172	5:9	0
63	McGannon, William Vincent	L.H.	Evansville, Ind.	Reitz Memorial H. S.	20	236	6:1½	2
64	Neff, Robert Hudkins	R.T	Buckhannon, W. Va.	Buckhannon-Upshur	22	193	5:11	0
65	Schrenker, Henry Pershing	L.G.	Elwood, Ind.	Elwood H. S.	21	161	5:9	2
66	**Gubanich, John Aloysius	R.G.	Phoenixville, Pa.	Phoenixville H. S.	22	196	6:0	2
67	Ford, James Brendan	C.	Binghamton, N. Y.	Allentown, Pa., Prep.	20	188	6:1	1
68	Brock, Thomas James	C.	Columbus, Neb.	Kramer H. S.	24	182	6:3	1
69	Rassas, George James	L.E.	Stamford, Conn.	Stamford H. S.	21	223	6:4	2
70	Rymkus, Louis	L.T.	Chicago, Ill.	Tilden H. S.	22	206	6:1	0
71	**Piepul, Capt. Milton John	F.B.	Thompsonville, Conn.	Enfield H. S.	21	219	6:2	2
72	Sullivan, Lawrence Patrick	L.T.	Brockton, Mass.	Brockton H. S.	21	209	6:0	0
73	*Brutz, James Charles	L.T.	Warren, Ohio	Warren H. S.	21	225	6:3	1
74	Ziemba, Walter John	R.T.	Hammond, Ind.	Hammond H. S.	19	210	6:2	0
75	*Lillis, Paul Bernard	R.T.	Mt. Vernon, N. Y.	Bennett, Buffalo, N. Y.	21	234	6:1	1
78	*Brosey, Henry Clifford	R.T.	Ozone Park, L. I., N. Y.	Brooklyn Tech.	20	188	5:10	1
79	Sullivan, Edward Joseph	L.G.	Belle Harbor, N. Y.	St. John's, Brooklyn	19	201	6:3	1
81	McHale, John Joseph	C.	Detroit, Mich.	Cath. Central H. S.	20	185	5:11	0
82	Postupack, Joseph Victor	F.B.	McAdoo, Pa.	McAdoo H. S.	22	220	6:1	1
83	Papa, Joseph John	L.T.	Pittsburgh, Pa.	Kiski Prep	23	208	6:1	2
84	**Gallagher, Thomas Charles	L.T.	Chicago, Ill.	Leo H. S.				

—Indicates number of monograms won.

Juzwik Day at Yankee Stadium. The movie camera clicks off Steve's 83 yard dash through Army

Notre Dame 7; Army 0

A great Notre Dame team lost most of its lustre as a greatly inspired Cadet eleven pushed them all over Yankee Stadium, outdoing them in everything but the scoring. Near the end of the first period Steve Juzwik snatched an intended Army touchdown pass out of the air on his own 19-yard line and streaked down the sideline, outstepping would be Cadet tacklers, to payoff territory. Captain Piepul added the extra point and the Irish defense did the rest as Army racked up 16 first downs to four for the Irish, and out-gained the winners by 175 yards. Thus did Notre Dame gain her 20th victory of the 38-year-old series over "the weakest Army team in history."

1940

Coach: Elmer F. Layden
Captain: Milt Piepul

O.5	W	Col. of Pacific	25-7	H	22,670
O.12	W	Georgia Tech	26-20	H	32,492
O.19	W	Carnegie Tech	61-0	H	29,515
O.26	W	Illinois	26-0	A	c68,578
N.2	W	Army (R)	7-0	YS	c75,474
N.9	W	Navy (4:00)	13-7	N	c61,579
N.16	L	Iowa (5:00) (U)	0-7	H	45,960
N.23	L	Northwestern	0-20	A	c46,273
D.7	W	So. California	10-6	A	85,808
	(7-2-0)		168-67		468,349

N—at Baltimore

Layden Resigns As Football Coach, Athletic Director At Notre Dame

Becomes Commissioner Of Pro Football With Five Years Contract

Chicago, Feb. 3.—(AP.)—Elmer Layden resigned today as head coach and athletic director at Notre Dame to accept a five-year contract as commissioner of professional football.

The contract, effective March 1, calls for an annual salary of $20,000. Layden's contract at Notre Dame expired last Saturday.

His duties as boss of the National Football League and several minor circuits will be comparable to those of Kenesaw M. Landis, czar of baseball.

Leaving Good Job.

In accepting the new post, Layden is leaving one of the best coaching positions in the collegiate sports world. The choice of his successor was a matter of wide conjecture, especially in view of the suddenness of Layden's departure.

The deal by which the rapidly growing professional sport obtained Layden was completed two days ago.

Club owners of the National Football League, which sponsored the hiring of a commissioner, met here several weeks ago to consider several persons for the job but Layden had not been mentioned previously as a possibility.

Layden's contract at Notre Dame expired last Saturday.

An all-America star as one of the famed "four horsemen" of Notre Dame in the early twenties, Layden became head coach there is 1934. In seven years his Irish elevens won 46 games and lost only 14. His best season was in 1938 when Notre Dame won eight of nine games.

Leahy Becomes Athletic Director And Head Football Coach At Notre Dame

Takes Job Left Open By Layden

Released From Five-Years Contract by Boston College; Keeps Present Assistants

South Bend, Ind., Feb. 1.—(AP.) —Frank Leahy, 33-years-old Boston College coach, is going back home to Notre Dame.

Father John Cavanaugh, vice president of Notre Dame, announced tonight that Leahy had accepted the post as athletic director and head football coach, a vacancy created 11 days ago when Elmer Layden resigned to become pro football commissioner.

Leahy will sign a long-term contract tomorrow in the office of the Rev. Hugh O'Donnell, C. S. C., school president.

The youthful, affable college mentor said in Boston that going back to Notre Dame would be "just like going home to me." Leahy played under the immortal Knute Rockne through 1930, being a lineman on the old master's last Irish machine and the last undefeated eleven at the school.

Salary Not Revealed.

His salary at Notre Dame was not disclosed, but Leahy implied he was making a financial sacrifice in order to take the job.

"The financial element does not figure in my decision to return to Notre Dame," he said, adding that he would never have considered leaving Boston College for any job except this one.

Leahy, a native of Winner, S. D., carved out a brilliant record in his two years as a head coach. Boston College signed him in 1939 and in two seasons his teams won 19 of 20 games, finishing an undefeated 1940 campaign with a spectacular victory over Tennessee in the Sugar Bowl.

After graduating from Notre Dame in 1931, Leahy took a job as line coach at Georgetown, later serving in a similar capacity at Michigan State under Jimmy Crowley. He stayed with Crowley when the latter became head coach at Fordham, coaching the line there until Boston College hired him.

"I am going to take along all of my assistants—Ed McKeever, backfield coach; John Druze, end coach and Joe McArdle, line coach," Leahy said as soon as the news of his appointment leaked out prematurely in Boston. "We will start spring practice about March 7.

"I deeply regret that I am leaving Boston College but I consider it my duty to return to Notre Dame. Every Notre Dame man would welcome a chance to go back as head coach, for it is the greatest honor that can come to any of us."

Keeps Same Staff.

His decision to keep his Boston College staff intact means the release at Notre Dame of Layden's aides—line coach Joe Boland, backifeld coach Chet Grant, end coach Joe Benda and "B" squad coach William J. Cerney.

Leahy was signed to a new five-year contract at Boston College on Feb. 3. A few hours after Layden quit at Notre Dame. But when approached about succeeding Layden, the Boston coach obtained release from his contract there.

Notre Dame's best season under Layden was in 1938 when the team won eight of nine games.

OFFICIAL 1941 NOTRE DAME FOOTBALL ROSTER

NO.	NAME	POSITION	HOME TOWN	PREPARATORY SCHOOL	AGE	WEIGHT	HEIGHT	EXP.
1	Earley, William Joseph	Q.B.	Parkersburg, W. Va.	Parkersburg H. S.	20	177	5:10	1
2	Creevy, Thomas Edwin	Q.B.	Chicago, Ill.	Mt. Carmel H. S.	19	185	5:11	0
3	Hargrave, Robert Webb	Q.B.	Evansville, Ind.	Reitz Memorial H. S.	21	165	5:11	2
4	Wright, Harry Charles	Q.B.	Hempstead, L. I., N. Y.	Chaminade Prep, Mineola	21	188	6:0	1
5	Patten, Paul Edward	Q.B.	Canton, N. Y.	Canton H. S.	20	172	5:8	2
9	Girolami, Anthony Gregory	Q.B.	Chicago, Ill.	Crane Tech H. S.	20	186	6:1½	1
15	Juzwik, Steve Robert	R.H.	Chicago, Ill.	DePaul Academy	23	185	5:8½	2
17	Laiber, Joseph James	R.G.	South Bend, Ind.	Washington H. S.	21	175	5:10	2
18	Murphy, George Edward	R.E.	South Bend, Ind.	Central H. S.	20	176	6:0	1
20	Kudlacz, Stanley Adam	C.	Chicago, Ill.	DePaul Academy	19	182	5:9	0
21	Lanahan, John Francis	C.	Jacksonville, Fla.	Immaculate Conception H. S.	20	182	6:1½	1
23	Evans, Frederick Owen, Jr.	F.B.	South Bend, Ind.	Riley H. S.	21	78	5:11	1
28	Riordan, Wilbur Eugene	R.G.	Sioux City, Iowa	East H. S.	22	180	5:10½	1
29	Kovatch, John George	R.E.	South Bend, Ind.	Washington H. S.	21	181	6:2½	2
30	Chlebeck, Andrew John	F.B	St. Paul, Minn.	St. Thomas Military Acad.	21	182	6:0	2
31	Tessaro, Edward Alexander	R.H.	Greensburg, Pa.	F.-Marshall Academy	21	175	5:11½	0
32	Warner, John Andrew, Jr.	L.H.	New Haven, Conn.	Cheshire Academy	20	174	6:0	1
33	O'Brien, Richard Charles	R.E.	Peoria, Ill.	Spalding Institute	20	178	6:2	1
35	McGinnis, John James	R.E.	Chicago, Ill.	St. George H. S., Evanston	19	179	6:2	0
36	Peasenelli, John Joseph	R.H.	Rochester, Pa.	Rochester H. S.	21	176	5:10½	1
37	Miller, Creighton Eugene	F.B.	Wilmington, Del.	Alexis I. DuPont H. S.	18	187	6:1	0
40	Hogan, Donald John	L.H.	Chicago, Ill.	St. Ignatius H. S.	20	189	6:2	2
42	Dove, Robert Leo	L.E.	Youngstown, Ohio	South H. S.	20	197	6:1½	1
43	Creevy, Richard Cassell	R.H.	Chicago, Ill.	Mt. Carmel H. S.	20	182	6:1	1
44	Crimmins, Bernard Anthony	R.G.	Louisville, Ky.	St. Xavier H. S.	22	185	5:11	2
45	O'Reilly, Martin Gordon	C.	Chicago, Ill.	Mt. Carmel H. S.	20	185	6:2	2
46	Barry, Norman John	R.E.	Chicago, Ill.	Fenwick H. S., Oak Park	19	184	5:8½	1
47	McBride, Robert James	L.G.	Lancaster, Ohio	Logan H. S.	18	192	6:0	0
48	Bertelli, Angelo Bortolo	L.H.	W. Springfield, Mass.	Cathedral H. S.	20	170	6:½	0
49	Maddock, Robert Charles	L.G.	Santa Ana, Calif.	Santa Ana H. S.	21	189	6:0	2
50	Walsh, Robert Michael	R.G.	Springfield, Ill.	Cathedral H. S.	22	188	5:11	1
51	Bolger, Matthew Joseph	L.E.	Newark, N. J.	St. Benedict's Prep	21	190	6:1½	0
52	Filley, Patrick Joseph	L.G.	South Bend, Ind.	Central H. S.	19	178	5:8	0
53	Prokop, Joseph Michael	F.B.	Cleveland, Ohio	Cathedral Latin H. S.	21	196	6:1	2
54	Ellefsen, Charles Robert	R.E.	Ironwood, Mich.	Wright H. S.	20	183	6:1	0
55	Ashbaugh, Russell Gilman	L.H.	Youngstown, Ohio	South H. S.	20	173	5:9	0
56	Ebli, Raymond Henry	L.T.	Ironwood, Mich.	St. Ambrose H. S.	21	197	6:2	2
57	McLaughlin, David Tennant	R.G.	So. Orange, N. J.	Columbia H. S.	18	186	5:11	0
58	Miller, Thomas Seeay	R.H.	Wilmington, Del.	Alexis I. DuPont H. S.	20	183	6:1	1
59	Bereolos, Hercules	R.G.	Hammond, Ind.	Hammond H. S.	22	205	5:11	2
60	Webb, Robert Bailey	R.G.	Santa Ana, Calif.	Santa Ana H. S.	20	184	5:10	1
64	Neff, Robert Hudkins	L.T.	Buckhannon, W. Va.	Buckhannon-Upshur H. S.	21	216	6:1½	1
66	Smyth, William Krantz	L.E.	Cincinnati, Ohio	Roger Bacon H. S.	19	199	6:3	0
67	Hines, Michael Leo	R.T.	Kewanna, Ind.	Kewanna H. S.	21	208	6:3	2
68	Brock, Thomas James	C.	Columbus, Neb.	Kramer H. S.	21	190	6:1½	1
70	Rymkus, Louis	R.T.	Chicago, Ill.	Tilden H. S.	21	225	6:4	1
72	Sullivan, Lawrence Patrick	R.T.	Brockton, Mass.	Tilton Prep, N. H.	21	204	6:2	1
73	Brutz, James Charles	L.T.	Niles, Ohio	Warren, Ohio, H. S.	22	209	6:0	2
74	Ziemba, Walter John	C.	Hammond, Ind.	Hammond H. S.	22	228	6:2½	1
75	Lillis, Capt. Paul Bernard	R.T.	Chicago, Ill.	Bennett H. S., Buffalo, N. Y.	20	218	6:2	2
79	Sullivan, Edward Joseph	L.G.	Belle Harbor, N. Y.	St. John's Prep, Brooklyn	21	181	5:9½	2
80	McNeill, Edward Charles	F.B.	Midland, Pa.	Lincoln H. S.	22	193	6:1½	2
82	Postupack, Joseph Victor	F.B.	McAdoo, Pa.	McAdoo H. S.	21	190	6:0	2

—Indicates number of monograms won.

THE FIGHTING IRISH

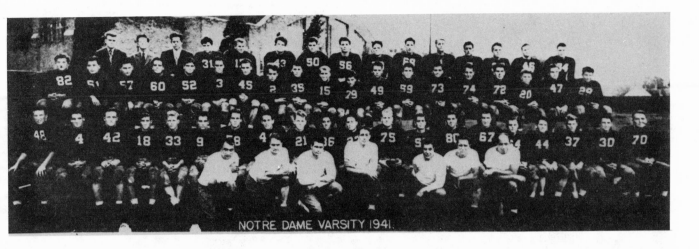

NOTRE DAME VARSITY 1941.

Top Row: WALSH. BERMINGHAM. STEW. AT. TESSARO. LAIBER. R. CREEVY. WALSH. EBLI. RIORDAN. BROCK. EARLEY. PATTEN. WARNER. BARRY. ELLEFSEN. 3RD Row: POSTUPACK. BOLGER. McLAUGHLIN. WEBB. FILLEY. HARGRAVE. O'REILLY. T. CREEVY. McGINNIS. JUZWIK. E. SULLIVAN. MADDOCK. BEREOLOS. BRUTZ. ZIEMBA. L. SULLIVAN. KUDLACZ. McBRIDE. KOVATCH. 2ND Row: BERTELLI. WRIGHT. DOVE. MURPHY. O'BRIEN. GIROLAMI. T. MILLER. HOGAN. LANAHAN. PEASENELLI. EVANS. Capt. LILLIS. ASHBAUGH. McNEILL. HINES. NEFF. CRIMMINS. C. MILLER. CHLEBECK. RYMKUS. FRONT Row: SCHRENKER. CERNEY. SULLIVAN. FRANK LEAHY, Head Coach. ED. McKEEVER. JOE McARDLE. and JOHN DRUZE. Coaches.

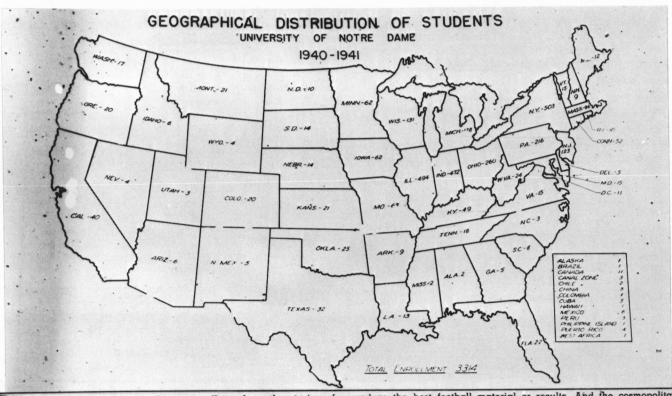

GEOGRAPHICAL DISTRIBUTION OF STUDENTS
UNIVERSITY OF NOTRE DAME
1940-1941

TOTAL ENROLLMENT 3314

World travelers are surprised occasionally to hear the strains of the "Notre Dame Victory March" float to their ears from radios, band platforms, record playing machines and the like in such far-flung spots as the Orient, and the countries of Europe and South America.

A glance at the accompanying chart shows that the fame of Notre Dame has spread wide, not alone through her football teams, but also through her own graduates. Every state in the Union, along with 14 foreign countries, were represented in the student enrollment last year. A comparable mark is being made this year.

The remark is heard occasionally that "Notre Dame should have good athletic teams. Its players come from all over the country." Increase of intersectional warfare has shown more and more in the past decade, however, that no one section of the country may be said to produce the best football material or results. And the cosmopolitan makeup of the Fighting Irish football squad is merely an accurate reflection of the student body as a whole. The 54 members of this year's squad hail from 35 cities and towns in 16 states. Illinois leads with 13 men from three towns, 11 of the boys from Chicago. Indiana is next with nine from four towns, and the neighboring state of Ohio takes third with six men from five towns. New York and Pennsylvania have five and four men, respectively, from as many towns. There are two from Michigan, Massachusetts, New Jersey, West Virginia, Delaware, and California; one each from Connecticut, Iowa, Florida, Nebraska, and Kentucky.

Another interesting point in this connection is found in the fact that a survey of the student body as of 50 years ago would show largely the same widespread distribution, although a much smaller total of students than the present enrollment of approximately 3,000 a year.

1941

Coach: Frank Leahy
Captain: Paul B. Lillis

S.27	W	Arizona	38-7	H	19,567
O.4	W	Indiana (R)	19-6	H	34,713
O.11	W	Georgia Tech	20-0	A	c28,986
O.18	W	Carnegie Tech (R)	16-0	A	17,208
O.25	W	Illinois	49-14	H	34,896
N.1	T	Army (R)	0-0	YS	c75,226
N.8	W	Navy	20-13	N	c62,074
N.15	W	Northwestern	7-6	A	c46,211
N.22	W	So. California	20-18	A	c54,967
		(8-0-1)	189-64		373,848

N—at Baltimore

Frank Leahy Named Coach of the Year

New York, Nov. 29.—(AP).—Frank Leahy of Notre Dame has been voted "coach of the year" in the seventh annual poll of the nation's football mentors conducted by the World-Telegram.

Of 274 coaches who participated in the contest, 58 cast their ballots for Leahy, who did not suffer a defeat in his first year at South Bend. Bernie Bierman, whose Minnesota team has piled up 17 straight victories, ran a close second with 54 votes.

Earl Blaik of Army placed third with 27, while Paul Brown, Ohio State's youthful new mentor, was fourth with 18. Homer Norton of Texas A&M landed 15, and Dana X. Bible of Texas and Dick Harlow of Harvard each polled 12. In all, 3* coaches figured in the voting.

It was the closest race in the seven-year history of the event. Clark Shaughnessy of Stanford was the overwhelming choice last year, with 253 votes to Bierman's 33.

Notre Dame 0 — Army 0

With student spirit on the upsurge as a result of the Illinois rout, the Fighting Irish scrambled through the cheering students at the Circle to make their way to a special train to New York. Speeding eastward, they carried the appeal for revenge on a Cadet eleven that in 1940, with the exception of Steve Juzwik's brilliant touchdown run from a pass interception, had drubbed all the fight out of a high-riding Irish eleven.

A hard rain that began falling in New York on Friday night virtually washed out all these appeals and dampened the spirits of both Cadet and Irish elevens. Saturday afternoon the rain was still falling as seventy-six thousand onlookers huddled under umbrellas and newspapers, and watched the two teams wade up and down the field for two hours.

It was a fierce, hard-hitting game in which both teams were forced to the monotonous procedure of two or three attempts for muddy gains on the line and then a punt. It was Army's Mazur who kept the Irish sliding in the mud with his seemingly-impossible end runs and amazing cutbacks over the line and his booming punts. Early in the first quarter, Mazur slid around left end behind an army of blockers to the Irish 25. From there Maupin and Hatch moved the ball to the Notre Dame 10 where, despite the mud, the Irish line braced and threw the Cadets back. Harry Wright tried to shake Evans or Juzwik loose around the ends, but Army's ends could not be taken out of play. Evans' kicks were long but Mazur's were longer, and the Irish were forced to do most of their mudding in their own back yard. Late in the second quarter the slimy pigskin rolled off the side of Mazur's foot on the Army 45. Notre Dame took it up there and with Juzwik sweeping the ends

and Evans ploughing for short gains at center, moved to the Cadet 17 where the Army line closed in and the Cadets took the ball on downs.

With Evans and Mazur dueling with third down punts, the two teams fought through the third quarter. The Irish went down to the Army 28 on the strength of Creighton Miller's smashing gains at tackle and Bill Earley's dashes inside the right end. There the Notre Dame backs lost their footing and Army took over the ball. The Cadets sent Ralph Hill inside the Irish right end and Hatch around guard to bring the ball down to the Irish 25; there the tackles and guard closed and the Cadets made but a yard as the Irish forwards cut them down.

With less than two minutes left in the final quarter the Irish machine churned over the Army line and the ticking seconds sped by while the Army line gave ground slowly. On the Cadet 20 yard line with seven seconds remaining, Harry Wright, moved out on the right flank along with Steve Juzwik and Angelo Bertelli for a final try at the Boston College famous triple-flanker, the last chance for the Irish to come out of the Cadet clash clean and undefeated. The muddy ball came up from center in a wobbling spin, and sailed through Evans' arms as he chased it, picked it up, evaded two tacklers only to be tackled and splashed out of bounds as the game ended.

AP POLL

1941

1. Minnesota
2. Duke
3. NOTRE DAME
4. Texas
5. Michigan
6. Fordham
7. Missouri
8. Duquesne
9. Texas A&M
10. Navy

COMPLETE SUMMARY OF GAME STATISTICS

PLAYER and POSITION	RUSHING				FORWARD PASSING						TOTAL OFFENSE		RECEIVING		INT. RETURNS		PUNTING			PUNT RETURNS		K.O. RETURNS		SCORING			
	Times Carried	Yards Gain	Yards Loss	Net Gain	No. Att.	No. Comp.	Had Inter.	Yards Gain	Yards Loss	Net Gain	Total Plays	Net Gain	No. Caught	Yards Gain	No. Inter.	Yards Return	Times Kicked	Yards Kicked	Had Blocked	Number Returns	Yards Return	Number Returns	Yards Return	Touch downs	C'vert Att.	C'erts Made	Field Goals
Bertilli	41	116	60	56	123	70	10	1028	1	1027	164	1083			1	0						1	17	0	3	3	0
Juzwik	101	432	56	376							101	376	17	305	3	29				23	290	1	20	8	19	13	0
Evans	141	549	69	480	1	1	0	0	11	-11	142	469	9	132	2	57	66	2569	1	9	106	9	206	11	1	1	0
Warner	24	101	15	86	15	6	2	96	0	96	39	182					13	403						0	2	1	0
Earley	30	92	41	51							30	51	5	106	3	51				2	13	1	21	2	0	0	0
C. Miller	59	206	23	183							59	183					4	197						1	0	0	0
Murphy													13	130										1	0	0	0
Kovatoh													3	41													
Wright													9	108	2	29						2	18				
McBride													2	0													
Hargrave													1	7								6	61				
Patten																						1	9				
Crimmins													4	12													
Hogan	10	28	13	15	7	3	1	59	0	59	17	74			1	0	2	42	21					1	2	0	8
R. Creevy	3	19	0	19	1	1	0	41	0	41	4	60												0	1	1	1
T. Miller	1	1	0	1							1	1	2	68										2	0	0	12
Dove													15	187										1	0	0	6
Bolger													8	135										1	0	0	6
Ashbaugh																											
Laiber													1	15						1	1						
Riordan													1	3													
McNeill	6	15	0	15							6	15	1	3													
Maddock													1	18													
Ziemba													2	51						safety							2
Brutz																				1	0						
Team Totals	416	1559	277	1282	147	81	13	1224	12	1212	563	2494	81	1212	25	275	85	3211	1	43	480	15	295	28	28	19	0	193
Opp. Totals	395	1032	432	600	141	48	25	680	0	680	536	1280	48	680	13	207	94	3511		39	390	21	401	10	10	4	0	

OFFICIAL 1942 NOTRE DAME FOOTBALL ROSTER

NO.	NAME	POSITION	HOME TOWN	PREPARATORY SCHOOL	AGE	WEIGHT	HEIGHT	EXP.
1	Earley, William Joseph	R.H.	Parkersburg, W. Va.	Parkersburg H. S.	21	173	5:10	2
2	Creevy, Thomas Edwin	Q.B.	Chicago, Ill.	Mt. Carmel H. S.	20	185	5:11	1
4	Wright, Harry Charles	R.G.	Hempstead, L. I., N. Y.	Chaminade, Mineola	22	190	6:0	2
5	Creevy, John Francis	Q.B.	Clawson, Mich.	Clawson H. S.	19	205	6:2	0
15	O'Connor, William Joseph	R.G.	Tulsa, Okla.	Subiaco, Ark., Acad.	19	185	6:0	0
17	Tobin, George Edward	R.G.	Arlington, Mass.	Marianapolis Acad.	21	191	5:10	0
18	Murphy, Capt. George Edward	R.E.	South Bend, Ind.	Central H. S.	21	170	6:0	2
20	Kudlacz, Stanley Adam	C.	Chicago, Ill.	DePaul Academy	20	187	5:9	1
21	Lanahan, John Francis	C.	Jacksonville, Fla.	Immaculate Conception	21	188	6:1½	2
23	**Evans, Frederick Owen, Jr.	L.H.	South Bend, Ind.	Riley H. S.	21	175	5:11	2
25	Piccone, Cammille William	L.H.	Vineland, N. J.	Vineland H. S.	20	186	6:0	0
29	Cusick, Francis Michael	L.E.	Providence, R. I.	La Salle Academy	20	180	6:2	0
30	Limont, Joseph Paul	R.E.	New Orleans, La.	Jesuit H. S.	19	190	6:2	0
31	Frawley, George Michael	R.H.	Los Angeles, Calif.	Mt. Carmel H. S.	21	177	6:0	0
33	Krupa, Edward Harry	R.H.	Flint, Mich.	Flint Northern H. S.	20	182	5:11	0
35	McGinnis, John James	R.E.	Chicago, Ill.	St. George, Evanston	20	185	6:2	1
36	Peasenelli, John Joseph	R.H.	Rochester, Pa.	Rochester H. S.	22	176	5:10½	2
37	*Miller, Creighton Eugene	R.H.	Wilmington, Del.	Alexis I. DuPont	20	188	6:0	1
39	David, Robert Joseph	F.B.	Dalton, Ill.	Mt. Carmel, Chicago	21	205	6:0	0
40	Livingstone, Robert Edward	L.H.	Hammond, Ind.	Hammond H. S.	20	175	6:0	0
42	**Dove, Robert Leo	L.E.	Youngstown, Ohio	South H. S.	21	195	6:1½	2
43	Creevy, Richard Cassell	L.H.	Chicago, Ill.	Mt. Carmel H. S.	21	182	6:1	2
44	Coleman, Herbert Edward	C.	Chester, W. Va.	Chester H. S.	19	195	6:1	0
45	Szymanski, Francis Stanley	R.T.	Detroit, Mich.	Northeastern H. S.	19	205	5:11½	0
47	*McBride, Robert James	L.G.	Lancaster, Ohio	Logan H. S.	20	198	6:0	1
48	*Bertelli, Angelo Bortolo	Q.B.	W. Springfield, Mass.	Cathedral H. S.	21	171	6:½	1
49	Meter, Bernard James	L.G.	Cleveland, Ohio	Cathedral Latin	18	190	5:10½	0
51	Dwyer, Eugene Joseph	R.E.	Chicago Hts., Ill.	Mt. Carmel, Chicago	20	190	6:½	0
52	Filley, Patrick Joseph	R.G.	South Bend, Ind.	Central H. S.	20	178	5:8	1
53	Cowhig, Gerard Finbar	F.B.	Dorchester, Mass.	Marianapolis, Acad.	21	205	6:2	0
54	Huber, William Wendell	R.E.	Tuscola, Ill.	Tuscola H. S.	19	197	6:3	0
55	Ashbaugh, Russell Gilman	Q.B.	Youngstown, Ohio	South H. S.	2	178	5:9	1
58	Miller, Thomas Seeay	L.H.	Wilmington, Del.	Alexis I. DuPont	21	183	6:1	2
60	Webb, Robert Bailey	L.G.	Santa Ana, Calif.	Santa Ana H. S.	21	190	5:10	2
63	Hecht, Daniel Jerome	R.G	Peoria, Ill.	Spalding Institute	19	197	5:11	0
64	*Neff, Robert Hudkins	R.T.	Buckhannon, W. Va.	Buckhannon-Upshur	22	215	6:1½	2
65	Mello, James Anthony	F.B.	West Warwick, R. I.	W. Warwick Sr. H. S.	21	188	5:11	0
68	*Brock, Thomas James	C.	Columbus, Nebr.	Kramer H. S.	22	195	6:½	2
69	Clatt, Corwin Samuel	F.B.	East Peoria, Ill.	E. Peoria Community	18	198	6:0	0
70	*Rymkus, Louis	L.T.	Chicago, Ill.	Tilden H. S.	22	218	6:4	2
71	White, James Joseph	L.T.	Edgewater, N. J.	All Hallows, N.Y.C.	21	210	6:1½	0
72	Sullivan, Lawrence Patrick	R.T.	Brockton, Mass.	Tilton, N. H., Prep	22	205	6:2	2
73	Brutz, Martin Michael	L.G.	Niles, Ohio	McKinley H. S.	19	190	5:11	0
74	**Ziemba, Walter John	C.	Hammond, Ind.	Hammond H. S.	23	225	6:2½	2
75	Higgins, Luke Martin	R.T.	Edgewater, N. J.	Cliffside H. S.	21	210	6:0	0
76	Czarobski, Sigismunt Peter	L.T.	Chicago, Ill.	Mt. Carmel H. S.	20	205	6:0	0
78	King, James Francis	F.B.	Internat'l. Falls, Minn.	Falls Senior H. S.	19	215	6:0	0
80	Adams, John William	L.T.	Charlestown, Ark.	Subiaco, Ark. Acad.	20	225	6:7	0
82	Yonakor, John Joseph	L.E.	Dorchester, Mass.	Mechanic Arts. H. S.	21	222	6:4	0

*—Indicates number of monograms won.

	1942			
	Coach: Frank Leahy			
	Captain: George E. Murphy			
S.26	T	Wisconsin	7-7	A	22,243
O.3	L	Georgia Tech (U)	6-13	H	20,545
O.10	W	Stanford	27-0	H	22,374
O.17	W	Iowa Pre-Flight (U)	28-0	H	26,800
O.24	W	Illinois	21-14	A	43,476
O.31	W	Navy (R)	9-0	N1	66,699
N.7	W	Army	13-0	YS	c74,946
N.14	L	Michigan	20-32	H	c54,379
N.21	W	Northwestern	27-20	H	26,098
N.28	W	So. California	13-0	A	94,519
D.5	T	Great Lakes (S)	13-13	N2	19,225
		(7-2-2)	184-99		472,304

N1—at Cleveland; N2—at Soldier Field

AP POLL

1942
1. Ohio State
2. Georgia
3. Wisconsin
4. Tulsa
5. Georgia Tech
6. NOTRE DAME
7. Tennessee
8. Boston College
9. Michigan
10. Alabama

Notre Dame .. 27
Stanford .. 0

NOTRE DAME, IND.

With Coach Frank Leahy stricken and in the Mayo Clinic and Dippy Evans watching from the bench, Notre Dame struck four times through the air to win their first game humbling the Stanford Indians, 27-0.

The battle began peacefully with neither team making a threat towards scoring. Harry Wright had relieved Angelo Bertelli of the job of calling signals, and the pass-slinging quarterback returned to his old form, much to the discomfiture of the Palo Alto boys. Corwin Clatt, replacing injured Jim Mello, set up Bert's first touchdown fling. Throwing from the 45, Angelo hit Bob Dove and the Irish had their first lead of the year, increased to 7-0 by Bertelli's conversion. On the next series of plays, the Indians fumbled on fourth down and the boys in the green shirts went to work again. Pete Ashbaugh picked up nineteen yards around end; Bertelli then threw from the 16 to Paul Limont in the end zone, and came up to add another extra point.

"Marchy" Schwartz, former Irish all-American of the Rockne undefeated years, brought the Indians out for a game second half; they threatened twice, but lacked scoring power. Meantime, Angelo was hitting his receivers with consistency. Opening the third quarter, Bob Dove snapped a Bertelli special and raced to the Stanford 26 for a forty-yard gain. On the next play, Captain George Murphy caught touchdown pass number three.

Leading 20-0, Notre Dame again moved down the field and added another touchdown on a pass from Bertelli to Livingstone. Bertelli added the extra point. Acting coach Ed McKeever watched the boys play out the game, and wondered if the rejuvenation would last through the following Saturday. The Irish were not the same team which was beaten by Georgia Tech; they tackled low and hard, and Harry Wright was calling daring plays from his guard position, but the undefeated Iowa Seahawks were bearing down.

The first dash of fire came in the Stanford game, as Angelo Bertelli threw four touchdown passes to beat Stanford, 27-0. Paul Limont grabs one of them in the end zone, while Capt. George Murphy catches another before being stopped.

Notre Dame .. 13   Great Lakes .. 13

CHICAGO, ILL.

The spirited fire of Notre Dame's Fighting Irish and the cold crush of Great Lakes power were pointed on the sod of Soldier Field's half-forgotten battles for sixty minutes, and from the pulsating pattern of run, pass, kick, and tackle, of green and white shirts on a frozen field, came a 13-13 tie that will flood back to the thoughts of football men.

Great Lakes, pre-game favorite, rode into the game on the push of six straight wins in which they were not scored upon. They kept the push going for the first half, and piled up fourteen first downs as Bruce Smith, Sweiger, and Bellachick bulled through the ribbon of Irish line for long gains. And the Irish, in their eleventh and last hard game, left the field stunned by the power of line and backs and trailing by a 13-0 score.

A different-spirited Notre Dame team started the second half. On the first play from scrimmage, the Irish sprung loose Corwin Clatt for a brilliant 82-yard run for a touchdown. Seconds later, they took the ball on their own 28-yard line, and Creighton Miller broke through the line, cut away to the side and went 72 yards for another score.

John Creevey kicked the tying point as four minutes of the half had elapsed. In the remaining 26 minutes both teams surged up and down the field, were held, pushed back, and broke loose again. Clatt recovered a fumble on the Sailor 29, and the Irish drove to the 20 and were held. Bob Dove partially blocked a Great Lakes kick and Notre Dame took over on the 39 and moved down field but could not score. Mucha kicked long to the Irish 15, but passes by Bertelli to Dove and Murphy and the flash running of C. Miller and Livingstone rocked the ball back to the Great Lakes 21, where the Sailors took over on downs. Four times the Sailors drove down the field and were slowed; each time Bob Nelson came out to try for a field goal, and each time he missed. The Irish fought back with the passing of Bertelli; the running of C. Miller, Clatt, Livingstone; and the knifing line play of seniors Dove, Murphy, Ziemba, Wright, Filley, Brock, Rymkus, and Neff. With 59 seconds left and 80 yards to go, Bertelli passed to C. Miller who fought to the Sailor 40; C. Miller broke loose to the 28 and, as the gun went off, John Creevey's try for field goal fell short. The game ended the Notre Dame season at seven wins, two losses, and two ties against the toughest schedule in their long history.

OFFICIAL 1943 NOTRE DAME FOOTBALL ROSTER

NO.	NAME	POSITION	HOME TOWN	MILITARY STATUS	AGE	WEIGHT	HEIGHT	PREVIOUS EXPERIENCE
1	Earley, J. Frederick	R.H.	Parkersburg, W. Va.	U.S.N.R.	18	165	5:7	0
2	Terlep, George	Q.B.	Elkhart, Indiana	U.S.N.R.	20	165	5:8	0
4	Dancewicz, Frank J.	Q.B.	Lynn, Mass.	Civilian	18	173	5:10	0
9	Waldron, Ronayne	Q.B.	Silver Springs, Md.	17 yr. old	17	170	5:10	0
15	Angsman, Elmer J.	L.H.	Chicago, Ill.	17 yr. old	17	185	5:11	0
17	Rellas, Chris S.	R.E.	Nashua, N. H.	U.S.N.R.	21	183	6:0	0
18	Flanagan, James	L.E.	W. Roxbury, Mass.	U.S.N.R.	20	175	6:1/2	0
20	Rykovich, Julius A.	F.B.	Gary, Indiana	U.S.M.R.C.	20	190	6:1/2	0
21	Statuto, Arthur J.	C.	Saugus, Mass.	U.S.N.R.	18	190	6:2	0
30	Limont, J. Paul	L.E.	Hyannis, Mass.	U.S.N.R.	20	185	6:2	1
31	Davis, Raymond	L.H.	Spokane, Wash.	U.S.M.R.C.	23	170	5:10	3 (Idaho)
32	Lujack, John	L.H.	Connellsville, Pa.	U.S.N.R.	18	180	6:0	0
33	Krupa, Edward Harry	R.H.	Flint, Mich.	U.S.M.R.C.	21	178	5:11	1
35	Lyden, Michael P., Jr.	C.	Youngstown, Ohio	17 yr. old	17	188	6:2	0
37	Miller, Creighton	L.H.	Wilmington, Del.	1C	21	185	6:0	2
39	Snyder, James	F.B.	Taff, California	17 yr. old	17	188	5:5	0
44	Coleman, Herbert E.	C.	Chester, W. Va.	U.S.N.R.	20	198	6:1	1
45	Szymanski, Francis S.	C.	Detroit, Mich.	U.S.N.R.	20	197	6:0	1
46	Palladino, Robert F.	R.H.	Natick, Mass.	U.S.N.R.	18	175	5:10	0
47	Berezney, Peter, Jr.	L.T.	Jersey City, N. J.	Civilian	19	215	6:1	2
48	Bertelli, Angelo B.	Q.B.	W. Springfield, Mass.	U.S.M.R.C.	22	173	6:1	2
49	Meter, Bernard	R.G.	Cleveland, Ohio	U.S.M.R.C.	19	185	5:10	1
50	Ganey, Michael	R.T.	Chicago, Ill.	17 yr. old	17	194	6:0	0
51	Hanlon, Robert S.	F.B.	Chicago, Ill.	U.S.N.R.	19	185	6:1	0
52	Filley, Capt. Patrick J.	L.G.	South Bend, Ind.	U.S.M.R.C.	21	175	5:8	2
53	Cibula, George	L.T.	Chicago, Ill.	17 yr. old	18	197	5:11	0
54	Sullivan, George A.	L.T.	Walpole, Mass.	17 yr. old	17	205	6:2 1/2	0
55	Todorovich, Marko S.	R.E.	St. Louis, Mo.	U.S.M.R.C.	20	205	6:1	1 (Wash. U.)
56	Zilly, John L.	R.E.	Southington, Conn.	N.R.O.T.C.	21	188	6:2	1
57	Perko, John F.	L.G.	Ely, Minn.	U.S.M.R.C.	22	200	5:11	1 (Minn.)
60	Trumper, Edward	R.E.	St. Paul, Minn.	U.S.M.R.C.	23	208	6:2	1 (Minn.)
62	Mieszkowski, Edward T.	L.T.	Chicago, Ill.	17 yr. old	17	205	6:1	0
63	Ruggiero, Frank A.	L.T.	Orange, N. J.	Civilian	20	215	5:8 1/2	0
64	Renaud, Charles	L.G.	Fort Worth, Texas	17 yr. old	17	185	5:8	0
65	Mello, James A.	F.B.	W. Warwick, R. I.	U.S.N.R.	21	185	5:11	1
66	Kuffel, Raymond	L.E.	Milwaukee, Wis.	U.S.M.R.C.	21	210	6:5	1 (Marq.)
69	Kulbitski, Victor J.	F.B.	St. Paul, Minn.	U.S.M.R.C.	22	205	5:11	2 (Minn.)
71	White, James J.	L.T.	Edgewater, N. J.	U.S.N.R.	22	208	6:2	1
74	Signaigo, Joseph	R.G.	Memphis, Tenn.	U.S.M.R.C.	20	200	6:0	0
75	Urban, Gasper G.	L.G.	Lynn, Mass.	U.S.M.R.C.	20	190	6:0	0
76	Czarobski, Zygmont	R.T.	Chicago, Ill.	U.S.M.R.C.	21	212	6:0	1
80	Adams, John W.	R.T.	Charlestown, Ark.	Civilian	21	212	6:7	1
82	Yonakor, John J.	L.E.	Dorchester, Mass.	U.S.M.R.C.	22	215	6:4	1

THE FIGHTING IRISH OF 1943

Front Row: Left to Right—Szymanski, Earley, Snyder, Mello, Lujack, Hanlon, McQuire, Welch, Waldron, Rellas. 2nd Row: Left to Right—Flanagan, Palladino, Yacobi, Renaud, Ellsperman, Skinner, Kelly, Perko, Cibula, Ganey, Sullivan, G., Manzo—Coach Leahy. 3rd Row: Left to Right—Comdr. Malcomson, Coach Krause, Coach Devore, Kuffel, Skat, Curley, Todorovich, Czarobski, Statuto, Berezney, Yonakor, Bertelli, Miezskowski, Parnum, Paulian, Cannon, Adams, Meter, Coleman, Coach McKeever, Boss. 4th Row: Left to Right—Toczylowski, Rykovich, Layden, Dancewicz, Atkins, Terlep, Magglioli, Sullivan, Angsman.

	1943		
	Coach: Frank Leahy		
	Captain: Patrick J. Filley		

S.25	W	Pittsburgh	41-0	A	43,437
O.2	W	Georgia Tech	55-13	H	26,497
O.9	W	Michigan	35-12	A	c86,408
O.16	W	Wisconsin	50-0	A	16,235
O.23	W	Illinois (R)	47-0	H	24,676
O.30	W	Navy	33-6	N	c77,900
N.6	W	Army	26-0	YS	c75,121
N.13	W	Northwestern	25-6	A	c49,124
N.20	W	Iowa Pre-Flight	14-13	H	39,446
N.27	L	Gt. Lakes (U) (0:33)	14-19	A	c23,000
		(9-1-0)	340-69		461,844

N—at Cleveland

AP POLL

1943
1. NOTRE DAME
2. Iowa Pre-Flight
3. Michigan
4. Navy
5. Purdue
6. Great Lakes
7. Duke
8. Del Monte P
9. Northwestern
10. March Field

Team Statistics for 1943 Season

Player	Carried Times	Gained Net Yds.	Average	T.D.	P.A.T.	Pts.
Miller, LH	151	911	6.03	13	0	78
Mello, FB	137	714	5.21	5	0	30
Rykovich, RH	66	339	5.13	8	0	48
Earley, LH	22	121	5.50	3	10	28
Palladino, RH	20	190	6.78	3	0	18
Lujack, QB	46	191	4.15	4	3	27
Hanlon, FB-RH	40	142	3.55	1	0	6
Kelly, RH	38	119	3.13	3	0	18
Kulbitski, FB	48	265	5.52	0	0	0
Bertelli, QB	14	22	1.58	4	21	45
Mazzioli, RH	4	34	8.50	0	0	0
Krupa, RH	4	13	3.25	0	0	0
Davis, LH	18	55	3.05	0	0	0
Skat, QB	1	15		0	0	0
Danceyicz, QB	1	6		0	0	0
Yonakor, RE				4	0	24
Sullivan, LT				1	0	6
Lyden, C				1	0	6

Great Lakes Rob Irish of Perfect Slate in Last 40 Seconds of Great Season

BY JOHN POWER

Pandemonium reigned during four quarters last Saturday as 22,000 Sailors saw a persistent Great Lakes eleven defeat a never-say-die Notre Dame team 19-14 on Ross Field. The Fighting Irish, a great comeback team, marched 80 yards for their final score, only to have victory snatched from them on a touchdown pass from Steve Lach to Paul Anderson with but 25 seconds to play. Emil Sitko, a former Notre Dame boy, and Dewey Proctor spearheaded the Great Lakes attack.

Notre Dame received the kickoff on the 33 and garnered their first touchdown in 17 plays on thrusts by Creighton Miller, Jim Mello, and a plunge by John Lujack. Fred Earley converted and it was 7-0, Notre Dame. Rykovich kicked out of bounds on the 35, Jones picked up 18, Proctor fumbled, and Miller recovered for the Irish on the 38. Notre Dame failed to gain and Lujack kicked to Jones, who returned to the 23. The Bluejackets moved to the 41 as the quarter ended.

Resuming play the Sailors picked up 26 yards, fumbled and Notre Dame recovered. The game then became a stalemate as each team was forced to punt. As the half ended Great Lakes had possession of the ball on its own 33.

Great Lakes received on the 26 and Sitko and Proctor proceeded to tote the pigskin to midfield. Proctor plowed to the 36, and Anderson picked up ten more. Sitko darted around left end for 26 yards and a touchdown, but Juzwik's placement was blocked—Notre Dame 7; Great Lakes 6. The Irish received, picked up 16 yards on a dash by Miller, but were finally forced to kick to the "Lakes" on the eleven. An exchange of punts took place and Great Lakes then went into action on the 20. Proctor rammed his way to the 43, and Sitko made it midfield. The Bluejackets then took the lead as Proctor went over the left side, shook himself loose from would-be tacklers, and scored standing up. Juzwik's conversion was wide and Great Lakes led 12-7.

With but eight minutes remaining in the final period Notre Dame tramped 80 yards for a touchdown, without once relinquishing possession of the ball. Mello, Miller, and Kelly collaborated in toting the ball to the one, where Miller plunged for the score. Earley's placement was perfect and the Irish were out in front

14 to 12. A minute and six seconds remained to play as Great Lakes received on the 38. A pass by Lach was completed to Pirkey on the 46. Lach faded back to pass, the Irish line charged, but he ducked away from them, ran to the left, and tossed a long pass to Anderson who scored with 25 seconds remaining in the ball game. Juzwik converted as Great Lakes handed Notre Dame its first and only defeat 19-14.

Bertelli Runs Away With Heisman Trophy; Takes Place Beside Recent Grid Greats

Marine Angelo Bortolo Bertelli ran away with the Heisman Trophy awarded annually to the outstanding college football player of the year. Notre Dame's All-American quarterback, who played but six games this campaign, polled 648 (two digits of which were his jersey number) points to walk away from his nearest competitors, Bob Odell from Pennsylvania with 177; Northwestern's Otto Graham, with 140, and

He duplicated the award-winning vote piled up by Frankie Sinkwich of Georgia in 1942. The selection terminated what is probably the outstanding three-year performance in the history of the award. Bertelli was runner up to Tom Harmon as a sophomore in 1941, and finished fourth in 1942.

Notre Dame's great halfback, Creighton Miller, was a strong fourth. Son of a Notre Dame immortal, Creightie was the talk of the midwest with his payoff gallops that broke close contests wide open. The most dangerous runner on the squad his seasonal play won him well deserved All-American award.

The third Fighting Irishman to make the list of leaders was tackle Jim White, who finished ninth. Jim had the distinction of being the only lineman to receive mention. His spirited play won plaudits from all, coaches and reporters alike.

OFFICIAL 1944 NOTRE DAME FOOTBALL ROSTER

NO.	NAME	POSITION	HOME TOWN	PREP SCHOOL	AGE	WEIGHT	HEIGHT
1	Cadieux, Roger	Q.B.	Springfield, Mass.	Cathedral H. S.	18	160	5:9
4	*Dancewicz, Frank J.	Q.B.	Lynn, Mass.	Lynn H. S.	19	177	5:10
8	Clasby, Edward	Q.B.	Natick, Mass.	Natick H. S.	18	175	6:0
9	Ratterman, George	Q.B.	Cincinnati, Ohio	St. Xavier	17	160	6:0
13	Franklin, Raymond	L.H.	Claremont, N. H.	Stevens H. S.	21	175	6:0
15	Angsman, Elmer J., Jr.	F.B.	Chicago, Ill.	Mt. Carmel H. S.	18	190	5:11½
17	Manzo, Michael B., Jr.	L.T.	Medford, Mass.	Medford H. S.	23	200	6:0
18	Skoglund, Robert W.	R.E.	Chicago, Ill.	Loyola Academy	19	194	6:1
19	Cash, Anthony	R.E.	New Orleans, La.	Holy Cross Coll. H. S.	20	185	6:0
20	Nemeth, Steve J.	R.H.	South Bend, Ind.	Riley H. S.	21	166	5:10½
21	Statuto, Arthur J.	C.	Saugus, Mass.	Saugus H. S.	19	190	6:2
22	Lebrau, John	L.H.	Baltimore, Md.	Calvert Hall	20	165	5:9
23	*Kelly, Robert J.	R.H.	Chicago, Ill.	Leo H. S.	19	182	5:9½
25	O'Connor, William F.	R.E.	Ft. Montgomery, N. Y.	Mt. St. Michael	18	208	6:4
29	Dailer, James H.	L.G.	Wheeling, W. Va.	Central Catholic	17	180	5:9
30	Terlep, George R.	L.H.	Elkhart, Indiana	Elkhart H. S.	21	166	5:8
31	McGurk, James S.	F.B.	Montclair, N. J.	Montclair H. S.	18	190	5:1
32	Marino, Nunzio R.	R.H.	Windber, Pa.	Windber H. S.	18	160	5:8
34	Limont, Mark	L.E.	Pittsfield, Mass.	Yarmouth H. S.	18	190	6:3
37	Burke, Francis	R.H.	New York, N. Y.	Mt. St. Michael	18	165	5:11
38	Guthrie, Thomas F., Jr.	L.E.	Newark, N. J.	Seton Hall Prep	17	200	6:4½
39	Parry, Thomas	L.T	Arnold, Pa.	Arnold H. S.	18	198	5:11
40	Ruggerio, Frank A.	R.H.	Orange, N. J.	Orange H. S.	21	200	5:8
41	Iliff, Robert	L.H.	Montclair, N. J.	Montclair H. S.	18	185	5:11
42	Rovai, Fred Joseph	R.G.	Hammond, Ind.	Hammond H. S.	21	198	6:0
43	Endress, Frank	F.B.	Evansville, Ind.	Reitz Memorial	17	195	6:0
44	Waybright, Douglas G.	R.H.	Saugus, Mass.	Saugus H. S.	17	178	5:11½
45	Chandler, William	L.H.	Chicago, Ill.	Amundsen H. S.	17	172	5:9½
46	Ray, John William	C.	South Bend, Ind.	John Adams H. S.	18	188	6:0
47	Berezney, Peter, Jr.	L.T.	Jersey City, N. J.	Dickinson H. S.	20	215	6:2
48	Gasparella, Joseph R.	Q.B.	Vandergrift, Pa.	Vandergrift H. S.	17	203	6:3
50	Ganey, Michael J.	L.G.	Chicago, Ill.	Leo H. S.	18	187	6:0
51	Scott, Vince	F.B.	LeRoy, N. Y.	LeRoy H. S.	19	190	5:8
52	*Filley, Capt. Patrick J.	L.G.	South Bend, Ind.	Central H. S.	2.	182	5:8
53	Lanigan, John	R.G.	Cleveland, Ohio	Holy Name	17	175	5:10
54	*Sullivan, George A.	L.T.	East Walpole, Mass.	Walpole H. S.	18	212	5:2½
55	Davlin, Michael F.	L.E.	Omaha, Nebraska	Creighton Prep	16.	180	6:1
56	Fitzgerald, Arthur	R.H.	Ridgefield Park, N. J.	Ridgefield Park H. S.	18	185	5:11
57	Archer, Arthur	L.G.	Chicago, Ill.	Proviso H. S.	18	180	5:9½
59	Fay, Edward	R.G.	Pittsburgh, Pa.	Central Catholic	21	190	5:11
60	Maggioli, Achille F.	L.H.	Mishawaka, Ind.	Mishawaka H. S.	22	180	5:10½
61	Stewart, Ralph	C.	St. Louis, Mo.	McKinley H. S.	20	186	5:10
62	Mieszkowski, Edward T.	L.G.	Chicago, Ill.	Tilden Tech	18	205	6:2
63	Martz, George	L.G.	East St. Louis, Ill.	Central Catholic	17	200	6:0
64	Glaab, John	R.T.	Long Beach, Calif.	Woodrow Wilson H. S.	18	190	6:1½
65	Krall, Rudolph A.	F.B.	Gary, Indiana	Lew Wallace	19	190	5:11
66	Bush, Roy Alvin	L.E.	Davenport, Iowa	St. Ambrose Acad.	17	180	6:1
67	Bernhardt, Richard	C.	Toledo, Ohio	Central Catholic	18	192	6:1
68	Fallon, John J.	R.G.	Alton, Ill.	Marquette H. S.	17	205	6:1½
69	D'Alonzo, Alfred	L.G.	Orange, N. J.	Orange H. S.	18	190	5:10
70	Kelly, Joseph	L.T.	Akron, Ohio	Akron North H. S.	20	220	6:7
71	Welch, Robert F.	L.T.	Wauwatosa, Wis.	Wauwatosa H. S.	18	220	6:1
72	Schuster, Kenneth R.	R.T.	Chicago, Ill.	St. Rita	17	215	6:2
73	Mergenthal, Arthur	R.G.	Bellevue, Ky.	Bellevue H. S.	22	210	6:2
74	Corbisiero, John V.	F.B.	Medford, Mass.	Medford H. S.	18	180	5:10½
75	Mastrangelo, John B.	R.G.	Vandergrift, Pa.	Vandergrift H. S.	18	200	6:0
76	Schreiber, Thomas	C.	Detroit, Mich.	St. Martin H. S.	20	212	6:3
80	*Adams, John W.	R.T.	Charleston, Ark.	Subiaco, Ark.	22	218	6:7

*Indicates Lettermen.

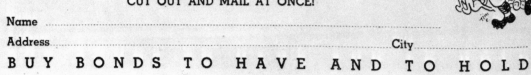

1944

Coach: Edward C. McKeever
Captain: Patrick J. Filley

S.30	W	Pittsburgh	58-0	A	46,069
O.7	W	Tulane	26-0	H	32,909
O.14	W	Dartmouth (R)	64-0	N1	c38,167
O.21	W	Wisconsin	28-13	H	36,086
O.28	W	Illinois	13-7	A	57,122
N.4	L	Navy	13-32	N2	c60,938
N.11	L	Army	0-59	YS	c75,142
N.18	W	Northwestern	21-0	H	39,701
N.25	W	Georgia Tech	21-0	A	28,662
D.2	W	Great Lakes	28-7	H	36,900

	(8-2-0)	272-118			451,696

N1—at Fenway Park, Boston; N2—at Baltimore

Notre Dame 58; Pittsburgh 0

Operating in the same "T" formation that carried the Blue and Gold banner to the top of the 1943 pigskin throne, the Fighting Irish of Notre Dame, with Coach Ed McKeever in the driver's seat, hit on all cylinders as they completely demolished the Pitt Panthers before 60,000 spectators at Pitt Stadium in the Steel City. The Irish opening eleven was supposed to have quite a struggle on its hands in the form of the experienced Panther squad, but it took only one half to deflate the buoyant hopes of the Pittsburgh eleven.

The heavy Red and White forward wall received a thorough going over from the hard-charging Irish linemen and the fast flying Notre Dame backs. The well diversified Irish attack kept the courageous Pitt eleven on the defense most of the game and frequent fumbles brought on by the pile-driving tackles of the green-clad defenders hurt the Pitt cause no end.

Notre Dame quarterbacks, Frank "Boley" Dancewicz and Big Joe Gasparella, threw pigskin lightning at the Panther defense, pitching five passes that were good for six-pointers. Bob Kelly, the sensational right half from last year's champs, crossed the double stripe four times and added two extra points to count for 26 points in the 35 minutes he played, and established himself as one of the nation's leading backs. George Sullivan and John "Tree" Adams played two terrific games at the tackles, the "Massachusetts Marvel" proving a bulwark on defense and Big John opening up gaping holes in the left side of the Red and White line for the Irish backs.

Captain Pat Filley, Fred Rovai, and Johnny Mastrangelo plugged up the guard posts in every capable fashion, and Bill O'Connor and Bob Skoglund performed well as flankmen. In the backfield, besides Dancewicz, Kelly, and Gasparella, "Chick" Maggioli and Elmer Angsman, at left half and fullback, respectively, turned in some fancy runs to show future promise.

The 1944 season was only ten minutes old when Bob Kelly took a 14 yard pass from Dancewicz and scampered 22 yards for the initial Irish tally. For the remainder of the period the score stood at 6-0, but in the second quarter Kelly crossed the Panther goal two more times. The first score was a result of a 13 yard Dancewicz to Kelly aerial and the second came when the Chi Flyer carried over from the 5 to climax an 81 yard march. Kelly's conversion brought the halftime lead to 19-0 and the rest of the contest proved to be a Pitt nightmare.

In the third canto Kelly broke over right tackle and raced 85 yards to touchdown territory. Then Dancewicz hit O'Connor in the end zone from the Pitt 8 and Gasparella and George Terlep hooked up in a 65 yard touchdown pass. The fourth TD of the period came when Gasparella quarterback-sneaked over from the Panther one. The final two markers were chalked up on Steve Nemeth's one yard plunge and Gasparella's 22 yard pass to Mark Limont.—*George Krauser*

Navy 32; Notre Dame 13

Baltimore and the U. S. Naval Academy played host to the Irish, Saturday, November 4, and a fatal day it was for an unbeaten Notre Dame eleven. Facing our young linemen were seasoned and muscular giants who stopped any running play sent their way, and for its own offensive strength, Navy had many backs who seemed to be able to romp any place they had a mind to go.

Before 63,000 astonished people in Baltimore's largest athletic plant, the 1944 edition of Annapolis football power ran through and around an outclassed Irish line to the tune of 32 to 13. This was the greatest number of points that any Navy team in 18 attempts, ever scored against any Notre Dame team. The Navy pounced early to score twelve points in the first quarter and kept the scoring kettle boiling by notching three more touchdowns before the afternoon was over.

Only in the second touchdown drive did such a modern weapon as the forward pass intrude. The other four came by the straight football route, behind blocking that was primitive in its savagery. That truthfully measures the difference in the ability of the two lines, and explains how Navy dashed the hopes of any National Championship residing in South Bend this year.

Hardly had the game got under way when Navy lived up to its pregame reputation as a fumbling team, when Bill Barron, one of the many Navy backs, fumbled a Kelly punt on his own 38, and Elmer Angsman recovered it after some pursuit on the Navy twenty yard stripe. Notre Dame went that twenty yards to score a touchdown with the ball under Angsman's arms. The referee saw Notre Dame's backfield in motion, so the play was promptly nullified and the penalty assessed and the ball was soon lost on downs. For the rest of the half, it was all Navy. Taking the ball on Notre Dame's 32 after an exchange of kicks, Bill Barron, on a reverse, ate up 27 of the remaining yards and then the strongest Navy back of the day, Clyde Scott, behind wicked blocking, bulldozed his way over the Irish line and scored the first Navy touchdown with Bob Kelly hanging on. Not much later Scott went over for his second score and that was that for the half. The second half opened with Navy marching down the field in twelve or fifteen yard spurts to score another touchdown and Fred Earley, formerly a Notre Dame extra point specialist, kicked the point.

It was at this point that Boley Dancewicz started throwing strikes. He completed four rifle like passes to bring the ball to the Navy five, where Bob Kelly plowed through a thicket of enemy arms for the first Irish score. Navy came back to score again, making the scoreboard read 25-7. But the Irish, still not beaten, came back on the strength of the right arm of Frank Dancewicz. Marching 78 yards on passes and remarkable catches by O'Connor and Guthrie, the ball was taken to the Navy three where Kelly went over for his second score.

The Navy line told the whole story of that sad day. This wall of flesh would tear such holes in the immature Notre Dame line, that the Navy backs could run yards into the secondary before a finger would touch them. Kelly, despite his poor yardage, stood out as the best back on the field, and it wasn't often that the Navy would attempt to puncture Sullivan's side of the line. Yet this youthful team was never beaten, no matter how badly it was hurt, and one sportswriter said.

They sent a boy out on a man's errand, and the boy came back with abrasions, contusions and just plain lumps."—*Hank Slamin*

AP POLL

1944

1. Army
2. Ohio State
3. Randolph Field
4. Navy
5. Bainbridge
6. Iowa Pre-Flight
7. U.S.C.
8. Michigan
9. NOTRE DAME
10. 4th AAF

Army 59; Notre Dame 0

Army had planned year after year, till they had run the count to thirteen and then let loose with a ground and aerial attack never before paralleled in football history. It might be common to see a score of 59-0 in these days of football, but for a Notre Dame team to lose by that margin—well, that just "ain't" in the everyday books—but that's what they did—gave the Irish their worst defeat in 56 seasons of football.

After five successful attempts, the kids who reside within the shadows of the Golden Dome got their first taste of defeat against Navy and now they had to mess around with Army on the following week. No matter what paper figures said, this was still the game of the year in everyone's book. But the Cadets in the highlands of the Hudson were more than an even match for any college team composed of 17-, 18-, and 19-year-olds. Their impressive record of one-sided wins over North Carolina, Brown, Pittsburgh, Coast Guard Academy, Duke, and Villanova was highly indicative of their offensive strength.

Ed McKeever was making no excuses on the local scene for the poor showing of the team against the Middies but concentrated on an attack that might hamper the Grey and Gold. Coach Earl Blaik was taking no chances in losing this one. He knew that Notre Dame was inexperienced and that a crew of seasoned veterans could run circles around them, but then, that undefined factor called "the Spirit of Notre Dame" might pop up at any time and spoil a pleasant afternoon, and so Col. Blaik definitely decided not to speculate with any of his maneuvers—everyone was to be a potential pay-off play—and it turned out that nine of them were.

After 76,000 gridiron fans crowded subways, taxis and sidewalks in making good their path to Yankee Stadium, then reclining in the seats provided and some not provided, the opening kickoff took place. After receiving the opening kickoff on their own 13, the Irish fell a yard short of first down and kicked to the Army on the Irish 45. A sustained drive carried to the five but there in four plays the Cadets were seemingly halted. However, a penalty to the Irish one gave Doug Kenna the initial opportunity to crash over on the fourth down for the first of a flood of touchdowns.

Before the period had ended, the Irish goal had been crossed two additional times and a 20-0 margin prevailed. From here on, Army showed no mercy and Notre Dame felt the full blows of three great Cadet teams. Only once did the Irish offense move and that advance was halted with Notre Dame on the Army 15 as the first half ended. Six interceptions were, throughout the sequence of events, converted into scores. Punt runbacks were a constant menace as the soldiers struck again and again.

STATISTICS

	Pitt. Ats.Yds.	Tulane Ats.Yds.	Dart. Ats.Yds.	Wis. Ats.Yds.	Ill. Ats.Yds.	Navy Ats.Yds.	Army Ats.Yds.	North. Ats.Yds.	Te. Ats.Yds.	Gt.La. Ats.Yds.	Total Ats.Yds.
Kelly	11-136	13-77	10-89	11-80	18-44	15-31	10-11	....	26-111	19-97	133-676
Dancewicz	4-10	5-13	3-3	5-39	5-13	6-(−8)	12-29	6-64	8-28	15-39	69-230
Angsman	9-16	11-80	10-41	10-70	13-49	9-17	3-3	....	3-7	....	58-273
Brennan	....	....	....	....	....	3-16	....	15-120	16-93	4-(−8)	38-231
Maggioli	7-41	10-85	4-11	5-22	8-26	....	....	....	....	....	34-185
Marino	....	....	4-73	5-25	.....	1-0	5-31	16-24	2-5	....	33-162
Wendell	....	....	....	....	....	....	....	9-36	13-22	9-24	31-82
Nemeth	13-47	5-35	4-71	4-15	....	....	....	....	....	2-(−4)	28-164
Terlep	6-15	3-9	8-75	3-7	....	3-(−4)	....	....	....	....	23-110
Gasparella	3-2	....	1-21	1-1	....	....	....	....	15-71	....	21-97
Corbisiero	3-24	1-2	2-10	5-22	....	....	....	....	....	....	11-58
Fitzgerald	2-15	....	3-11	....	....	....	....	....	....	....	5-26
McGurk	....	....	3-15	....	....	....	....	....	....	....	3-15
Clasby	....	....	2-10	....	....	....	....	....	....	....	2-10
Chandler	....	....	....	....	....	....	1-1	1-1	....	....	2-2
LeBrew	....	....	....	....	....	....	....	....	2-2	....	2-2
Ruggerio	2-9	....	....	....	....	....	....	....	....	....	2-9

Av. yd per try

		Av. yd per try
Kelly	133-676	5.1
Dancewicz	69-230	3.3
Angsman	58-273	4.7
Brennan	38-231	6.1
Maggioli	34-185	5.4
Marino	33-162	4.9
Wendell	31-82	2.8
Nemeth	28-164	5.9
Terlep	23-110	4.8
Gasparella	21-97	4.6
Corbisiero	11-58	5.3
Fitzgerald	5-26	5.2
McGurk	3-15	5.0
Clasby	2-10	5.0
Chandler	2-2	1.0
LeBrew	2-2	1.0
Ruggerio	2-9	4.5

PASSING RECORD

	Ats.	C.	I.	Yds.	Pct.
Dancewicz	153	72	10	999	.471
Gasparella	28	13	5	240	.464
Clasby	1	0	0	000	.000
Kelly	1	0	1	000	.000

OFFENSIVE RECORD

(Yards Rushing)

Pit.	Tul.	Dar.	Wis.	Ill.	Navy	Army	NW	GT	Gt.L.	Total
315	301	418	281	132	52	70	335	268	148	2321

(Yards Passing)

Pit.	Tul.	Dar.	Wis.	Ill.	Navy	Army	NW	GT	Gt.L.	Total
184	237	114	90	102	170	100	47	123	72	1239

In 678 offensive plays—Total 3560

Yards gained overall per play, 5.25

POINTS SCORING

	TD	PAT	PTS.
Kelly	13	6	84
Brennan	4	0	24
Maggioli	4	1	25
Nemeth	2	12	24
Terlep	3	4	22
Angsman	3	0	18
Dancewicz	2	0	12
Gasparella	2	0	12
Clasby	1	1	7
Corbisiero	1	0	6
Limont	1	0	6
Marino	1	0	6
O'Connor	1	0	6
Skoglund	1	0	6
Waybright	1	0	6
Wendell	1	0	6
Mergenthal (safety)	0	0	2
	41	24	272

OFFICIAL 1945 NOTRE DAME FOOTBALL ROSTER

N	NAME	POSITION	HOME TOWN	PREP SCHOOL	AGE	WEIGHT	HEIGHT
1	Cadieux, Roger E.	Q.B.	Springfield, Mass.	Cathedral H. S.	19	160	5:10½
4	*Dancewicz, Capt. Francis J.	Q.B.	Lynn, Mass.	Lynn Classical H. S.	21	180	5:10
9	Ratterman, George W.	Q.B.	Cincinnati, Ohio	St. Xavier H. S.	19	157	6:0
15	*Angsman, Elmer J., Jr.	R.H.B.	Chicago, Ill.	Mt. Carmel H. S.	20	185	5:11½
17	Agnone, John J., Jr.	L.H.B.	Youngstown, Ohio	Raven H. S.	21	165	5:9½
18	*Skoglund, Robert W.	L.E.	Chicago, Ill.	Loyola Academy	20	188	6:1
19	Zehler, William D.	L.H.B.	Rutledge, Pa.	Ridley Township H. S.	19	185	6:1
22	LeBrou, John F.	L.H.B.	Baltimore, Md.	Calvert Hall	21	155	5:9
23	Gompers, William G.	R.H.B.	Wheeling, W. Va.	Central Catholic H. S.	17	175	6:1
25	O'Connor, Philip	R.E.	Indianapolis, Ind.	Cathedral H. S.	19	190	6:1½
29	Colella, Philip J.	L.H.B.	Rochester, Pa.	Rochester H. S.	20	170	5:9
30	Heman, Richard D.	R.H.B.	Bowling Green, Ky.	Bowling Green H. S.	17	185	6:1
31	McGurk, James S.	F.B.	Montclair, N. J.	Montclair H. S.	19	190	6:1
33	Maryanski, Matthew S.	R.T.	Bloomfield, N. J.	Bloomfield H. S.	26	185	6:1
34	Opela, Bruno P.	L.E.	Chicago, Ill.	Lane Technical H. S.	22	196	6:1
35	White, Robert T.	L.E.	Chicago, Ill.	St. Philip H. S.	19	185	6:2
36	Malec, Robert	R.H.B.	Blawnox, Pa.	Aspinwall H. S.	20	180	5:10
37	Brennan, Terence P	L.H.B.	Milwaukee, Wis.	Marquette H. S.	17	180	5:11
38	Cronin, Richard M.	L.E.	River Forest, Ill.	Fenwick H. S.	19	205	6:3
39	Oracko, Stephen F.	L.G.	Lansford, Pa.	Lansford H. S	18	193	6:0
40	Ruggerio, Frank A.	F.B.	Orange, N. J.	Orange H. S.	22	200	5:8
41	Flynn, William J. P.	L.E.	Gary, Indiana	Horace Mann H. S	18	190	6:1
42	*Rovai, Fred J.	R.G.	Hammond, Ind.	Hammond H. S.	22	198	6:0
43	Potter, Thomas A.	R.G.	Kearny, N. J.	St. Benedict's Prep	23	202	5:10
44	Leonard, William	R.E.	Youngstown, Ohio	East H. S.	18	195	6:2
46	Walsh, William H.	C.	Phillipsburg, N. J.	Phillipsburg H. S.	18	212	6:2½
47	*Berezney, Peter, Jr.	R.T.	Jersey City, N. J.	Dickinson H. S.	22	215	6:2
48	*Gasparella, Joseph R.	Q.B.	Vandergrift, Pa.	Vandergrift H. S.	18	210	6:3
49	Pantera, Leroy P.	L.G.	Evanston, Ill.	St. George H. S.	18	195	6:1½
51	Scott, Vincent J.	L.G.	LeRoy, N. Y.	LeRoy H. S.	20	195	5:8
52	Grothaus, Walter J., Jr.	C.	Cincinnati, Ohio	Purcell H. S.	19	205	6:3
53	Virok, Ernest S.	C.	Trenton, N. J.	Trenton Catholic H. S.	18	190	5:10
55	Stanczyak, Alphonse	C.	Bridgeport, Conn.	Warren Harding H. S.	22	190	6:0
56	Stelmazek, Edward T.	R.G.	Chicago, Ill.	Mt. Carmel H. S.	27	185	5:8
57	Slovak, Emil	R.H.B.	Elliston, Ohio	Oak Harbor, Ohio H. S.	22	158	5:6
59	Fay, Edward J.	L.G.	Pittsburgh, Pa.	Central Catholic H. S.	22	190	5:10
61	Russell, Willmer	L.T.	Omaha, Nebraska	Omaha Technical	19	215	6:1
62	Mieszkowski, Edward T.	L.T.	Chicago, Ill.	Tilden Tech	20	205	6:2
63	Kurzynske, James R.	R.T.	Fond du lac, Wis.	Fond du lac H. S.	18	200	6:1
64	Glaab, John P.	R.T.	Long Beach, Calif.	Woodrow Wilson H. S.	19	190	6:1½
65	Panelli, John R.	R.H.B.	Morristown, N. J.	Cheshire Academy	19	200	5:11
66	Bush, Roy A.	R.E.	Davenport, Iowa	St. Ambrose Academy	19	180	6:1
68	Fallon, John J.	R.G.	Alton, Ill.	Marquette H. S.	18	205	6:1
70	DeBuono, Richard F.	L.T.	Port Chester, N. Y.	Port Chester H. S.	18	205	6:2
71	Vainisi, Jack A.	R.T.	Chicago, Ill.	St. George H. S.	18	220	6:1
72	Fischer, William	L.T.	Chicago, Ill.	Lane Technical H. S.	18	200	6:2
73	Schmid, Alfred L.	F.B.	Trenton, N. J.	Trenton Catholic H. S.	18	200	6:1
74	Kane, Charles J.	F.B.	Brooklyn, N. Y.	Power Memorial Academy	18	210	6:2
75	*Mastrangelo, John B.	L.G.	Vandergrift, Pa.	Vandergrift H. S.	19	200	6:0
76	Schreiber, Thomas P.	C.	Detroit, Mich.	St. Martin H. S.	21	215	6:1½

* Indicates Lettermen.

1945

Coach: Hugh J. Devore
Captain: Frank J. Dancewicz

S.29	W	Illinois	7-0	H	41,569
O.6	W	Georgia Tech	40-7	A	30,157
O.13	W	Dartmouth	34-0	H	34,645
O.20	W	Pittsburgh	39-9	A	c57,542
O.27	W	Iowa	56-0	H	42,841
N.3	T	Navy	6-6	N	c82,020
N.10	L	Army	0-48	YS	c74,621
N.17	W	Northwestern	34-7	A	c46,294
N.24	W	Tulane	32-6	A	51,368
D.1	L	Great Lakes	7-39	A	c23,000
		(7-2-1)	255-122		484,057

N—at Cleveland

AP POLL

1945

1. Army
2. Alabama
3. Navy
4. Indiana
5. Oklahoma State
6. Michigan
7. St. Marys
8. Pennsylvania
9. NOTRE DAME
10. Texas

Notre Dame 0, Army 48

It was a gray and gloomy day in the Bronx on November 10. Threatening skies were overhead, and a huge tarpaulin covered the gridiron below in Yankee Stadium. Yet 75,000 of New York celebrated subway alumni and mixed partisans from points north, west and south occupied every available seat of the spacious arena. They were all there for a common purpose—to see what the grid-ders of Notre Dame could do in the way of avenging the stinging 59-0 blow dealt them by the golden-helmeted juggernaut from the plains of West Point. Few experts anywhere conceded Notre Dame victory; the Pointers were at least a four-touchdown favor-ite. Army was bidding for its 16th consecutive victory over a span of two years. Before coming up to the Notre Dame game, it had run roughshod over all comers—P. D. C. (Ky.), Wake Forest, Duke, Melville Navy, Michigan, and Villanova.

As the 75,000 spectators filed out of the stadium that after-noon, they were convinced that here was an Army team which was no fluke, having just witnessed them combine air and ground maneuvers to blitzkrieg a plucky and stubborn Notre Dame eleven, 48 to 0, for their seventh victory of the 32 meetings between the two schools. The Irish, only the week previous, had thoroughly outplayed Navy at Cleveland, but had to settle for a bitter 6-6 tie. Consequently, we were not at top strength, the Navy game having taken its toll in injuries. Ruggerio received a gash on his chin requiring 13 stitches, but played briefly in the Army game, using a mask for protection. Colella and Angsman, too were injured in that hotly disputed Navy game, yet both started the Army game. But the Cadets from up the Hudson were distinctly the superior team. It was the old story of Felix (Doc) Blanchard and Glenn Davis, the Mr. Inside and Mr. Outside of the West Point attack. They did everything and they seemed to be taking turns doing it. And when it wasn't Blanchard and Davis, it would be Short McWilliams, Arnold Tucker, or Stuart—all less publicized but very effective backs.

The game was only a minute old when Elmer Angsman fum-bled on the third play after the opening kick-off. Army recovered on the Notre Dame 30 yard line and after Blanchard picked up three on a plunge, Davis, the elk-like Californian, sped 27 yards off tackle for Army's first score. Dick Walterhouse converted and the touchdown parade was on. The Irish fought back gallantly after Army's initial tally, as it always does when the opponent

scores first. In successive order Ruggerio and Colella charged for first downs. Then Angsman, N.D.'s leading ground gainer for the season, ripped 20 yards off-tackle, bringing Irish rooters to their feet. But Army, as they proved all afternoon whenever the Devore Boys neared the pay-off stripe, would dig in as if to say, "That's all, brother!"

The only other real Notre Dame opportunity for a score came late in the third period. Dancewicz had engineered a successful, sustained drive down to the Army one foot line. Gompers, trying for the TD off-tackle, fumbled and before anyone knew what happened Stuart had recovered the fumble before it hit the ground and raced it back to the Army 27 yard line where he was tackled by Boley Dancewicz. Incidentally "tackled by Dancewicz" was a familiar sound on the public address system all afternoon. Time and again he brought down Blanchard and Davis in the open field to prevent scores. Other defensive stars were Johnny Mastrangelo, Dick Cronin, Terry Brennan, and Bob Skoglund, who left a couple of molars on the Yankee Stadium turf, tackling Blanchard. For the Cadets, Tucker, particularly, was a hawk on pass defense, coming out of nowhere to bat down sure clicking passes out of the waiting clutches of Phil Colella, Bob Skoglund, and Billy Leonard.

There will be a day of reckoning for Army on the gridiron, and every Notre Dame man will want to see it. For the present, however, we'll string along with the words of Captain Boley Dancewicz when he addressed the entire student body who had come to Union Station to greet the squad on its return: "They're the greatest team I ever played against. They had Class."

Individual Statistics for the 1945 Season

Players	TD	PAT	PTS	TC	NYG	Avg	PA	PC	I	NYG
Angsman	7	0	42	87	616	7.0	0	0	0	0
Agnone	3	0	18	22	131	6.2	0	0	0	0
Brennan	2	0	12	57	252	4.4	1	0	1	0
Colella	4	0	24	63	317	5.0	0	0	0	0
Dancewicz	0	0	0	12	12	1.0	88	32	5	539
Earley	0	1	1	1	3	3.0	0	0	0	0
Gasparella	0	0	0	2	10	5.0	4	1	0	50
Gompers	3	0	18	36	185	5.1	0	0	0	0
Heman	0	0	0	3	3	1.0	0	0	0	0
Krivik	1	23	29	9	39	4.8	0	0	0	0
Leonard	1	0	6	0	29	9.8	0	0	0	0
McGee	0	0	0	3	29	9.8	0	0	0	0
McGurk	1	0	6	11	29	2.5	0	0	0	0
Panelli	2	0	12	18	115	6.3	0	0	0	0
Potter	0	0	0	2	6	3.0	0	0	0	0
Ratterman	0	0	0	8	8	1.0	30	9	5	203
Ruggerio	4	0	24	79	279	3.5	0	0	0	0
Simmons	1	0	6	14	42	3.0	0	0	0	0
Slovak	2	0	12	24	92	4.0	0	0	0	0
Skoglund	1	1	7	0	0	0	1	1	0	21
Tripucka	0	0	0	2	8	4.0	1	1	0	21
Traney	1	0	6	4	37	9.2	0	0	0	0
Van Sumner	0	0	0	7	13	1.8	0	0	0	0
Virok	1	0	6	0	0	0	0	0	0	0
Yonto	2	0	12	13	53	4.4	0	0	0	0
Zehler	2	0	12	15	122	8.1	0	0	0	0
Safety (Iowa)				2						
	38	25	255	492	2401	4.8	124	43	11	813

KEY TO ABBREVIATIONS: TD—Touchdowns. PAT—Points After Touchdowns. PTS—Points. TC—Times Carried. NYG—Net Yards Gained. Avg.—Average. PA—Passes Attempted. PC—Passes Completed. I—Intercepted.

OFFICIAL 1946 NOTRE DAME FOOTBALL ROSTER

NO.	NAME	POSITION	HOME TOWN	SERVICE	AGE	WEIGHT	HEIGHT	YRS. OF EXP.
1	*Farley, Fred	Right Halfback	Parkersburg, W. Va.	Navy	21	165	5:7	2
3	Brown, Roger	Quarterback	Chicago, Illinois	None	18	185	5:11	0
6	Heywood, William	Quarterback	Providence, R. I.	Army	22	190	6:0	0
7	Begley, Gerald	Quarterback	Yonkers, N. Y.	None	17	165	6:1	0
8	Tripucka, Frank	Quarterback	Bloomfield, N. J.	None	18	180	6:0	1
9	*Ratterman, George	Quarterback	Cincinnati, Ohio	Navy	19	165	6:0	2
10	*Creevey, John	Fullback	Clawson, Mich.	Army	23	215	6:2	1
11	*Brennan, James	Right Halfback	Milwaukee, Wis.	Navy	20	165	5:8	1
12	*Ashbaugh, Russell	Quarterback	Youngstown, Ohio	Army	25	175	5:9	2
14	Sitko, Emil	Right Halfback	Fort Wayne, Ind.	Navy	22	185	5:10	0
15	*Agnone, John	Left Halfback	Youngstown, Ohio	None	22	170	5:8	1
16	*Skoglund, Robert	Left End	Chicago, Illinois	Navy	21	198	6:1	2
17	*Tobin, George	Guard	Arlington, Mass.	Navy	25	195	5:10	1
18	*Flanagan, James	Right End	W. Roxbury, Mass.	Navy	23	187	6:1	1
20	*Smith, William L.	Left Halfback	Lebanon, Ky.	Army	23	165	5:11	0
21	Statuto, Arthur	Center	Saugus, Mass.	Navy	21	215	6:1	1
22	McNichols, Austin	Center	Chicago, Illinois	Navy	19	193	6:0	0
23	*Kelly, Robert	Left Halfback	Chicago, Illinois	Navy	21	181	5:9	2
24	Coutre, Lawrence	Right Halfback	Chicago, Illinois	None	18	175	5:8	0
25	*O'Connor, William (Zeke)	Left End	Ft. Montgomery, N.Y.	Navy	20	215	6:4	1
26	McGehee, Ralph	Right Tackle	Chicago, Illinois	None	18	210	6:1	0
27	Espenan, Ray	Left End	New Orleans, La.	Navy	20	195	6:2	0
28	*O'Connor, William (Bucky)	Left Guard	Tulsa, Okla.	Army	23	195	6:0	1
30	*Gompers, William	Right Halfback	Wheeling, W. Va.	None	18	180	6:1	1
31	*McGurk, James	Fullback	Montclair, N. J.	Navy	19	195	6:1	2
32	*Lujack, John	Quarterback	Connellsville, Pa.	Navy	21	180	6:0	1
33	Kosikowski, Frank	Right End	Milwaukee, Wis.	Navy	19	205	6:0	0
34	*Limont, Paul	Left End	Pittsfield, Mass.	Navy	23	200	6:2	2
36	Frampton, John	Left Guard	Pomona, Calif.	Navy	22	190	5:11	0
37	*Brennan, Terence	Left Halfback	Milwaukee, Wis.	None	17	175	6:0	1
38	Martin, James	Left End	Cleveland, Ohio	Marines	22	205	6:2	0
40	*Livingstone, Robert	Left Halfback	Hammond, Ind.	Army	24	175	6:0	1
41	Connor, Charles	Left Guard	Chicago, Illinois	Navy	22	200	5:10	0
42	*Rovai, Fred	Right Guard	Hammond, Ind.	None	23	200	6:0	2
43	*Potter, Thomas	Left Guard	Kearney, N. J.	Army	23	190	5:10	1
44	LeCluyse, Leonard	Fullback	Kansas City, Mo.	Navy	21	188	5:11	0
46	*Walsh, William	Center	Phillipsburg, N. J.	None	18	210	6:2	1
47	*McBride, Robert	Right Guard	Lancaster, Ohio	Army	23	205	6:0	2
48	*Gasparella, Joseph	Quarterback	Vandergrift, Pa.	None	19	205	6:3	2
49	*Meter, Bernard	Right Guard	Cleveland, Ohio	Marines	23	190	5:11	2
50	Walsh, Robert	Left End	Chicago, Illinois	Navy	21	200	6:2	0
51	*Scott, Vincent	Left Guard	LeRoy, N. Y.	None	20	210	5:8	
53	*Cowhig, Gerald	Left Halfback	Dorchester, Mass.	Army	25	211	6:3	1
54	*Sullivan, George	Right Tackle	E. Walpole, Mass.	Navy	20	210	6:3	2
55	Swistowicz, Michael	Right Halfback	Chicago, Illinois	None	19	190	5:11	0
56	*Zilly, John	Right End	Southington, Conn.	Navy	24	200	6:2	2
57	*Slovak, Emil	Right Halfback	Eliston, Ohio	None	20	155	5:7	2
58	*Wendell, Martin	Center	Chicago, Illinois	Navy	19	200	5:9	1
59	Zmijewski, Al	Right Tackle	Newark, N. J.	None	18	215	6:1	0
60	Strohmeyer, George	Center	McAllen, Texas	Navy	22	195	5:9	0
61	*Russell, Wilmer	Left Tackle	Omaha, Nebraska	None	19	220	6:4	1
62	Simmons, Floyd	Right Halfback	Portland, Ore.	Navy	21	195	6:0	1
63	*Hanlon, Robert	Left Halfback	Chicago, Illinois	Navy	22	180	6:1	1
64	*Urban, Gasper	Tackle	Lynn, Mass.	Marines	23	215	6:1	1
65	*Mello, James	Fullback	West Warwick, R. I.	Navy	25	185	5:10	2
66	Vangen, Willard	Center	Bell, Calif.	Navy	26	205	6:1	0
67	*Panelli, John	Fullback	Morristown, N. J.	None	19	190	5:11	1
68	*Fallon, John	Right Tackle	Alton, Illinois	None	19	210	6:0	2
69	*Clatt, Corwin	Fullback	E. Peoria, Illinois	Army	22	200	6:0	1
70	Schuster, Kenneth	Left Tackle	Chicago, Illinois	Navy	19	215	6:2	1
71	*Higgins, Luke	Right Guard	Edgewater, N. J.	Army	25	208	6:0	1
72	*Fischer, William	Left Guard	Chicago, Illinois	None	19	225	6:2	1
73	Brutz, Martin	Right Guard	Niles, Ohio	Army	23	208	5:11	1
74	*Signaigo, Joseph	Left Guard	Memphis, Tenn.	Navy	23	200	6:0	1
75	*Mastrangelo, John	Right Guard	Vandergrift, Pa.	None	20	210	6:1	2
76	*Czarobski, Zygmont	Right Tackle	Chicago, Illinois	Navy	23	213	6:0	2
80	Cifelli, August	Left Tackle	Philadelphia, Pa.	Marines	21	225	6:4	0
81	Connor, George	Left Tackle	Chicago, Illinois	Navy	21	225	6:3	0
82	Hart, Leon	Right End	Turtle Creek, Pa.	None	18	225	6:4	0
83	Wightkin, William	Right End	Detroit, Mich.	Co. Gd.	19	200	6:2	1

*Indicates Lettermen.

AP POLL

1946
1. NOTRE DAME
2. Army
3. Georgia
4. U.C.L.A.
5. Illinois
6. Michigan
7. Tennessee
8. L.S.U.
9. North Carolina
10. Rice

1946
Coach: Frank Leahy
New Captain Each Game

S.28	W	Illinois	26-6	A	c75,119
O.5	W	Pittsburgh	33-0	H	50,350
O.12	W	Purdue	49-6	H	c55,452
O.26	W	Iowa	41-6	A	52,311
N.2	W	Navy	28-0	N	c63,909
N.9	T	Army	0-0	YS	c74,121
N.16	W	Northwestern (R)	27-0	H	c56,000
N.23	W	Tulane	41-0	A	65,841
N.30	W	So. California	26-6	H	c55,298
	(8-0-1)		271-24		548,401

N—at Baltimore

ARMY STARTING LINE-UP

LEFT END	LEFT TACKLE	LEFT GUARD	CENTER	RIGHT GUARD	RIGHT TACKLE	RIGHT END
89	79	61	56	65	73	81
Poole	Biles	Steffy	Enos	Gerometta	Bryant	Foldberg

LEFT HALFBACK	QUARTERBACK	RIGHT HALFBACK
41	17	22
Davis	Tucker	Fuson

FULLBACK
35
Blanchard

NOTRE DAME STARTING LINE UP

LEFT END	LEFT TACKLE	LEFT GUARD	CENTER	RIGHT GUARD	RIGHT TACKLE	RIGHT END
38	81	72	60	42	76	56
Martin	Connor	Fischer	Strohmeyer	Rovai	Czarobski	Zilly

LEFT HALFBACK	QUARTERBACK	RIGHT HALFBACK
40	32	14
Livingstone	Lujack	Sitko

FULLBACK
65
Mello

Notre Dame 0 – Army 0

On Nov. 9, 1946, undefeated Notre Dame met undefeated Army in a football classic that will go down as one of the greatest sports spectacles of modern times. Never in the annals of football had a single contest attracted such world-wide interest. The sports writers had termed it the "Game of the Century" and for once they were correct.

The human interest behind the game was far-reaching. During the two previous seasons a power-laden Army eleven had soundly thrashed the youthful Irish team. Now the Notre Dame stars of previous years were back from the wars and grimly determined to turn the tables. On the other hand Glen Davis and Doc Blanchard, the mighty "touchdown twins," were gracing the Army gridiron for the last year. Army's unbroken string of 25 victories was in jeopardy. The national championship was at stake.

What could be the answer? What would happen when two such football titans met? Surely one would have to topple from its pinnacle of renown. And yet, curiously enough, neither did; for at the end of sixty minutes of bruising, shocking, bone-crushing football, of gallant, intrepid, lion-hearted play, of a thousand exultant thrills, each team trudged off the field still undefeated. They had played to a dramatic 0-0 tie.

The battle of the century was over, a scoreless tie. What of the answers to those great pre-game questions? The only forthcoming answer was the one already known. These two gridiron machines were the greatest in the nation.

Neither team had won, but both had covered themselves with glory. The Irish line accomplished what had previously been regarded as the impossible, completely throttling the vaunted charges of Glen Davis and Doc Blanchard. Johnny Lujack, Notre Dame's All American quarterback, performed brilliantly despite the handicap of a bad ankle. Meanwhile, the Army defenders, inspired by their own great quarterback, Arnold Tucker, withheld an attack that had not failed to produce at least four scores in each of its preceding games.

In the second quarter the Irish staged their most serious threat marching to the Army four yard line only to be held on downs, while throughout the game the Cadets were completely unable to capitalize on the scoring opportunities frequently offered them.

In a sense, by snapping Army's victory string and breaking the power of Blanchard and Davis, Notre Dame did gain a moral victory. But then moral victories aren't real victories nor are they entered in the books. One thing, however, stood out as significant . . . at the close of the struggle it was the Black Knights of the Hudson who were quick-kicking for a tie while the sons of the Golden Dome were still driving for that win.

The play that didn't make it— Hank Foldberg preparing to stop Bill Gompers on Army's 4 yd. line.

Notre Dame 26
So. California 6

The sports question of the century which was to have been settled in the Yankee Stadium Nov. 9th was finally answered. Notre Dame 26—Southern Cal. 6 . . . Army 21—Navy 18 . . . and the rest is history.

The Ramblers, in a style smacking of exhibitionism, strutted off the football stage just as they had entered it at the beginning of the season against Rose Bowl-bound Illinois . . . that is, on the top end of another 26-6 score which itself failed to reveal the thoroughness of their victory. The Irish had "lowered the boom" so convincingly upon the hapless Trojans, however, that the 56,000 fans on hand were not left with any doubt that the team performing before them was one of the best in the history of Notre Dame.

No doubt the tidal wave unleashed by the Kelly-greens (referred to in statistics as "yards gained") made the gold rush of '49 seem like a Strauss waltz to the sun-kissed boys of Southern Cal. It was no cause for wonder . . . after Jackrabbit McGee, Steamroller Simmons, and that sleight-of-hand artist, Ratterman had begun their performance . . . that several Southern Cal. visor-wearing substitutes used their sun-visors as blinders instead.

A week later the sons of the golden dome were again the possessors of the crown that Army had stolen from them during the war—the national Championship.

INDIVIDUAL STATISTICS

Nine Games—Final Statistics

Player	Touch Downs	Points After Touchdown	Points	Times Carried	Net Yds Gained	Average
Sitko	3	0	18	54	346	6.407
Simmons	2	0	12	36	229	6.361
Gompers	3	0	18	51	279	5.3
Mello	6	0	36	61	307	5.0
Cowhig	2	0	12	40	199	5.0
Livingstone	2	0	12	40	191	4.8
Lujack	1	0	6	23	108	4.7
T. Brennan	6	0	36	74	329	4.4
Panelli	4	0	24	58	265	4.6
Swistowicz	0	0	0	41	186	4.5
McGee	3	0	18	21	250	11.9
Clatt	2	0	12	28	105	3.8
Ratterman	0	0	0	4	24	6.0
LeCluyse	0	0	0	3	−9	−3.0
Zalejski	2	0	12	14	154	11.0
Smith	0	0	0	6	39	6.5
McGurk	0	0	0	4	7	1.8
Tripucka	0	0	0	1	−6	−6.0
Ashbaugh	0	0	0	2	−10	−5.0
Agnone	0	0	0	5	13	2.6
J. Brennan	0	0	0	1	1	1.0
Coutre	0	0	0	2	11	5.5
Slovak	1	0	6	1	18	18.0
Zilly	1	0	6	0	0	0.0
Skoglund	1	0	6	0	0	0.0
Hart	1	0	6	0	0	0.0
Earley	0	31	31	0	0	0.0
TOTALS	40	31	271	570	3036	5.3

Player	Passes Attempt.	Passes Compl.	Passes Had Int.	TD Passes	Pct.	Net Yds. Gained	Passes Rec'd	Net Yds. Gained	Passes Int. By	Yds. Gained on Int.
Lujack	100	49	8	5	.490	778	0	0	2	31
Ratterman	18	8	2	1	.444	114	0	0	1	1
Tripucka	5	1	0	0	.200	19	0	0	0	0
T. Brennan	0	0	0	0	.000	0	10	154	3	18
Zilly	0	0	0	0	.000	0	8	152	0	0
Skoglund	0	0	0	0	.000	0	6	76	1	7
Hart	0	0	0	0	.000	0	5	107	0	0
Swistowicz	0	0	0	0	.000	0	4	70	0	0
Cowhig	0	0	0	0	.000	0	4	42	0	0
Martin	0	0	0	0	.000	0	4	37	0	0
Sitko	0	0	0	0	.000	0	3	55	2	3
Livingstone	0	0	0	0	.000	0	3	38	0	0
Mello	0	0	0	0	.000	0	2	40	0	0
Simmons	0	0	0	0	.000	0	2	43	1	8
Zalejski	0	0	0	0	.000	0	2	24	1	20
Limont	0	0	0	0	.000	0	2	7	0	0
Gompers	0	0	0	0	.000	0	1	35	0	0
Ashbaugh	0	0	0	0	.000	0	1	29	1	38
Kosikowski	0	0	0	0	.000	0	1	2	0	0
Strohmeyer	0	0	0	0	.000	0	0	0	3	19
Brown	0	0	0	0	.000	0	0	0	1	2
TOTALS	123	58	10	6	.471	911	58	911	16	147

1947

...National Champions

Notre Dame Roster—1947

No.	Name	Pos.	Age	Ht.	Wt.	Hometown	Yr. Pt. at N.D.
1	EARLEY, Fred	HB	22	5'8	170	Parkersburg, W. Va.	3
3	BROWN, Roger	QB	19	5'11	180	Chicago, Ill.	1
7	BEGLEY, Gerald	QB	18	6'1	170	Yonkers, N. Y.	1
8	TRIPUCKA, Frank	QB	19	6	178	Bloomfield, N. J.	2
11	BRENNAN, James	RH	21	5'8	160	Milwaukee, Wisc.	2
12	ASHBAUGH, Russell	QB	25	5'9	175	Youngstown, O.	2
14	SITKO, Emil	RH	23	5'8	175	Ft. Wayne, Ind.	1
15	O'CONNOR, Wm. (Bucky)	RG	24	5'11	196	Tulsa, Okla.	2
16	LESKO, Alex	E	20	6	180	Homestead, Pa.	2
17	COUCH, Leo	G	25	5'9	200	South Bend, Ind.	0
18	JOHNSON, Frank	E	20	5'11	185	Cincinnati, O.	0
19	McGEE, Coy	LH	21	5'9	165	Longview, Texas	2
20	SMITH, Lancaster	LH	24	5'10	165	Lebanon, Ky.	1
21	STATUTO, Arthur	C	22	6'2	200	Saugus, Mass.	2
22	GAY, William	HB	19	5'10	180	Chicago, Ill.	0
24	COUTRE, Lawrence	HB	19	5'8	170	Chicago, Ill.	1
25	O'CONNOR, Wm. (Zeke)	E	21	6'4	200	Ft. Montgomery, N.Y.	2
26	McGEHEE, Ralph	LT	19	6'1	211	Chicago, Ill.	1
27	ESPENAN, Raymond	E	21	6'2	189	New Orleans, La.	1
28	SPANIEL, Frank	HB	18	5'10	180	Vandergrift, Pa.	0
29	DAILER, James	G	20	5'9	180	Wheeling, W. Va.	1
30	GOMPERS, William	RH	20	6'1	175	Wheeling, W. Va.	2
31	FALLON, Joseph	G	20	5'11	190	Alton, Ill.	2
32	LUJACK, John	QB	22	6	180	Connellsville, Pa.	3
33	KOSIKOWSKI, Frank	RE	21	6	202	Milwaukee, Wisc.	1
34	SAGGAU, Thomas	HB	18	6	170	Dennison, Iowa	1
36	FRAMPTON, John	G	23	5'11	190	Pomona, Calif.	2
37	BRENNAN, Terence	LH	19	6	173	Milwaukee, Wisc.	2
38	MARTIN, James	LE	23	6'2	205	Cleveland, O.	1
39	ORACKO, Steve	G	20	6	193	Lansford, Pa.	2
40	LIVINGSTONE, Robert	LH	25	6	168	Hammond, Ind.	2
41	CONNOR, John	G	19	6	185	Chicago, Ill.	1
42	WAYBRIGHT, Douglas	E	21	6	180	Saugus, Mass.	1
43	LeCLUYSE, Leonard	FB	22	5'11	188	Kansas City, Mo.	1
44	LEONARD, William	E	20	6'2	190	Cleveland, O.	1
45	MICHAELS, William	E	19	6'1	190	Girard, O.	1
46	WALSH, William	C	19	6'3	205	Phillipsburg, N. J.	2
47	HELWIG, John	T	19	6'2	198	Los Angeles, Cal.	0
49	HUDAK, Edward	C	19	6'2	200	Bethlehem, Pa.	0
51	CARTER, Donald	C	19	6'3	200	Detroit, Mich.	0
52	GROTHAUS, Walter	C	21	6'2	197	Cincinnati, O.	1
53	HELWIG, Joseph	G	20	6'2	200	Los Angeles, Cal.	0
54	SULLIVAN, George	RT	21	6'3	206	E. Walpole, Mass.	3
55	SWISTOWICZ, Michael	HB-FB	20	5'11	175	Chicago, Ill.	1
56	BURNETT, Albert	E	21	6'2	195	Irvington, N. J.	0
57	LALLY, Robert	G	18	6	185	South Euclid, O.	1
58	WENDELL, Martin	LG	20	5'10	198	Chicago, Ill.	2
59	ZMIJEWSKI, Alfred	T	19	6'1	200	Newark, N. J.	1
60	STROHMEYER, George	C	23	5'9	195	McAllen, Texas	2
61	RUSSELL, Wilmer	T	20	6'4	200	Omaha, Nebr.	2
62	SIMMONS, Floyd	FB	22	6	195	Portland, Ore.	2
63	BUDYNKIEWICZ, Theodore	RT	24	6	205	Chicopee, Mass.	2
64	URBAN, Gasper	T-G	24	6	200	Lynn, Mass.	1
65	McCARTY, Thomas	FB	19	6'1	185	Trenton, N. J.	1
67	PANELLI, John	FB	20	5'11	190	Morristown, N. J.	2
69	CLATT, Corwin	FB	23	6	200	E. Peoria, Ill.	2
70	SCHUSTER, Kenneth	T	20	6'3	210	Chicago, Ill.	0
71	WILKE, Clifford	HB	18	6	190	Hamilton, O.	2
72	FISCHER, William	LG	20	6'2	230	Chicago, Ill.	2
73	GAUL, Frank	T	21	5'10	200	Cleveland, O.	2
74	SIGNAIGO, Joseph	RG	24	6'1	205	Memphis, Tenn.	3
76	CZAROBSKI, Ziggy	RT	24	6	213	Chicago, Ill.	3
80	CIFELLI, August	T	22	6'4	225	Philadelphia, Pa.	1
81	CONNOR, George (Capt.)	LT	22	6'3	220	E. Chicago, Ill.	1
82	HART, Leon	RE	18	6'4	216	Turtle Creek, Pa.	1
83	WIGHTKIN, William	RE	20	6'2	205	Santa Monica, Cal.	1
84	CIECHANOWICZ, Emil	T	20	6'4	230	Chicago, Ill.	1

Head Coach—FRANK W. LEAHY
Assistant Coaches
Edward Krause, Joseph McArdle, John Druze, Bernard Crimmins,
William Earley, Walter Ziemba.

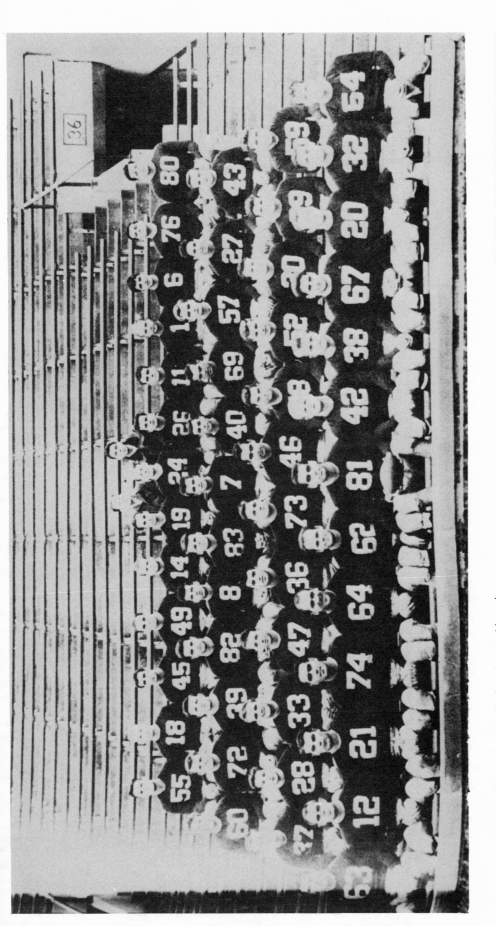

Left to Right (First Row) Budynkiewicz, Ashbaugh, Statuto, Signaigo, Urban, Simmons, Connor (captain), Waybright, Martin, Panelli, Smith, Lujack, Sullivan. (Second Row) T. Brennan, Spaniel, Kosikowski, Helwig, Frampton, Gaul, Walsh, Wendell, Grothaus, Gompers, Dailer, Zmijewski. (Third Row) Strohmeyer, Fischer, Oracko, Hart, Tripucka, Wightkin, Begley, Livingstone, Clatt, Lally, Espenan, LeCluyse. (Fourth Row) Swistowicz, Johnson, Michaels, Hudak, Sitko, McGee, Coutre, McGehee, J. Brennan, Earley, Skall, Czarobski, Cifelli. (Fifth Row) Leo Costello (associate manager), Larry Ryan (senior manager).

1947

Coach: Frank Leahy
Captain: George Connor

O.4	W	Pittsburgh	40-6	A	c64,333
O.11	W	Purdue	22-7	A	42,000
O.18	W	Nebraska	31-0	H	c56,000
O.25	W	Iowa	21-0	H	c56,000
N.1	W	Navy	27-0	N	c84,070
N.8	W	Army	27-7	H	c59,171
N.15	W	Northwestern (R)	26-19	A	c48,000
N.22	W	Tulane	59-6	H	c57,000
D.6	W	So. California	38-7	A	c104,953
	(9-0-0)		291-52		571,527

N–at Cleveland

NOTRE DAME 27

ARMY 7

ARMY MULE

AIN'T WHAT SHE USED TO BE----

TERRY BRENNAN'S 97-yard touchdown run on the opening kickoff was the keynote of the devastating attack employed by Notre Dame as they whipped Army, 27 to 7, in Notre Dame stadium November 8. A record crowd of 59,171 saw the historic rivalry between the two schools come to a thrilling end amidst flurries of snow and chilling breezes.

After Jack Mackmull's first kickoff for Army had gone out of bounds, Brennan snared Mackmull's second kickoff over his shoulder, turned on the Irish 3, and sprinted 97 yards for a touchdown. Fred Earley converted and the Irish were off to gain revenge for those war time trouncings suffered at the hands of Army. Brennan's once-in-a-lifetime score was the first Irish touchdown against Army since 1943.

Later in the first quarter, the Irish pounded out 80 yards for their second touchdown. Brennan scored from the 3. Bob Livingstone went over from the 6 in the third quarter and Larry Coutre registered the fourth touchdown in the final period on a 12 yard trip.

Army roared back after the third Notre Dame touchdown and went 56 yards into the end zone with Rip Rowan scoring. Captain Joe Steffy kicked the extra point.

OFFICIAL PROGRAM · 50c
NOTRE DAME STADIUM
NOVEMBER 8 · 1947

NOTRE DAME 38

SOUTHERN CALIFORNIA 7

THE NATIONAL CHAMPIONSHIP was won by the Irish football team for the second consecutive year as they subdued the Trojans of Southern Cal, 38-7, before the largest football crowd of the year.

Notre Dame scored first when Fred Earley kicked a field goal from the seven, five minutes after the opening of the game. Emil Sitko capped an 87-yard drive early in the second period by forcing through from the one. Earley converted. A Lujack pass was intercepted, and Southern Cal roared back to score 7 points in the last three minutes of the first half.

Sitko took the ball on the first play of the second half and ran 76 yards behind vicious blocking for the next score. Earley made it 17-7. Another drive headed by Sitko was climaxed when John Panelli went over from the 5. Another extra point was made by Earley. A few plays later N.D. took over on their 8. On the first play Bob Livingstone galloped 92 yards for another 6 points, with excellent blocking by George Connor and Jim Martin. Earley again converted.

The subs took over, and with 15 seconds to go Al Zmijewski reserve right tackle intercepted a Trojan pass and traveled 34 yards for a score. Earley made it six consecutive kicks, and ended the day with eight points. The Irish ended their first unbeaten season in 17 years and their third National Championship in the last five years of play.

Complete 1947 Individual and Team Statistics

Player	Touch-downs	Points After Touchdown	Field Goals	Points	Times Carried	Net Yds. Gained	Average Gain
Lujack	1	0	0	6	12	139	11.1
Martin	1	0	0	6	10	86	8.6
Gompers	1	0	0	6	20	136	6.8
Sitko	5	0	0	30	60	426	7.1
Smith	2	0	0	12	13	70	5.3
Swistowicz	1	0	0	6	58	257	4.4
McGee	2	0	0	12	36	158	4.4
T. Brennan	11	0	0	66	87	404	4.6
Clatt	1	0	0	6	11	49	4.4
J. Brennan	1	0	0	6	4	18	4.5
Coutre	2	0	0	12	34	127	3.7
Panelli	4	0	0	24	72	254	3.5
Spaniel	0	0	0	0	4	13	3.3
Gay	0	0	0	0	12	36	3.0
Le Cluyse	0	0	0	0	3	9	3.0
Wightkin	0	0	0	0	1	3	3.0
Livingstone	4	0	0	24	45	242	5.5
Simmons	1	0	0	6	23	35	1.5
Brown	0	0	0	0	2	3	1.5
Tripucka	0	0	0	0	5	—36	—7.2
Hart	3	0	0	18	0	0	0.0
Waybright	2	0	0	12	0	0	0.0
Earley	0	26	1	29	0	0	0.0
Oracko	0	1	1	4	0	0	0.0
Zmijewski	1	0	0	6	0	0	0.0
Totals (Team)	43	27	2	291	512	2429	4.7

Player	Passes Attemp.	Passes Compl.	Passes Had Int.	TD Passes	Pct.	Net Yds. Gained	Passes Rec'd	Net Yds. Gained	Passes Int. by	Yds. Int. Ret.
Tripucka	44	25	1	3	.567	422	0	0	0	0
Lujack	109	61	8	9	.559	777	0	0	3	53
Brown	1	0	0	0	.000	0	0	0	0	0
T. Brennan	0	0	0	0	.000	0	16	191	1	36
Martin	0	0	0	0	.000	0	13	170	0	0
Wightkin	0	0	0	0	.000	0	11	149	0	0
Hart	0	0	0	0	.000	0	9	158	0	0
McGee	0	0	0	0	.000	0	7	92	0	0
Coutre	0	0	0	0	.000	0	4	87	1	5
Sitko	0	0	0	0	.000	0	4	48	0	0
Waybright	0	0	0	0	.000	0	4	47	0	0
Simmons	0	0	0	0	.000	0	4	32	0	0
Livingstone	0	0	0	0	.000	0	3	73	2	45
Swistowicz	0	0	0	0	.000	0	2	37	1	18
Gay	0	0	0	0	.000	0	2	20	0	0
Smith	0	0	0	0	.000	0	1	37	1	6
Leonard	0	0	0	0	.000	0	1	15	0	0
Espenan	0	0	0	0	.000	0	1	15	0	0
Panelli	0	0	0	0	.000	0	3	27	0	0
Gompers	0	0	0	0	.000	0	1	1	1	0
J. Brennan	0	0	0	0	.000	0	0	0	1	30
Zmijewski	0	0	0	0						
Totals	154	86	9	12	.558	1199	86	1199	11	193

Lujack To Receive Heisman Trophy

New York, Dec. 1 (AP)—Johnny Lujack, field general of Notre Dame's all-conquering football team, today added the Heisman Memorial Trophy to his long list of honors for gridiron prowess.

The 22-year-old quarterback from Connellsville, Pa., received a total of 742 points in the downtown A.C.'s annual poll of sportswriters and broadcasters to determine the nation's outstanding college football player.

An all-America back last year and a virtual certainty to duplicate the feat this year, Lujack will personally receive the gleaming prize at the sponsoring club's dinner here December 10.

A great passer as well as an able strategist, Lujack won easily over Michigan's Bob Chappuis who collected 555 points. Doak Walker, of Southern Methodist, was third with 196, followed by Charley Conerly, Mississippi, 186; Harry Gilmer, Alabama, 115; Bobby Layne, Texas, 74; Charley Bednarik, Pennsylvania, 65, and Bill Swiacki, Columbia, 61. The first six are all backs. Bednarik is a center and Swiacki an end.

A senior, who is being pursued by pro scouts, Lujack follows in the steps of Army's Glenn Davis, winner of the 1946 award. Doc Blanchard, Davis's teammate at West Point, won the trophy in 1945.

Notre Dame Roster—1948

No.	Name	Pos.	Age	Ht.	Wt.	Hometown	Service	Yrs. Pl. N.D.
4	CARTER, Thomas	QB	21	5'11	173	Los Angeles, Cal.	None	0
7	BEGLEY, Gerald	QB	20	6'1	175	Yonkers, N. Y.	None	2
8	TRIPUCKA, Francis	QB	20	6'2	176	Bloomfield, N. J.	None	3
9	WILLIAMS, Robert	QB	18	6'1	180	Baltimore, Md.	None	0
12	ZALEJSKI, Ernest	LH	22	5'11	180	South Bend, Ind.	Army	1
14	SITKO, Emil	RH	25	5'8	179	Ft. Wayne, Ind.	Navy	2
15	SMITH, Eugene	RH	18	5'9	177	LaCrosse, Wis.	None	0
16	LESKO, Alexander	E	21	6'0	180	Homestead, Pa.	None	2
18	JOHNSON, Frank	G	21	6'0	190	Cincinnati, O.	Army	1
19	McGEE, Joy Coy	LH	21	5'9	147	Longview, Texas	Army	2
20	SMITH, Lancaster	HB	25	5'11	158	Lebanon, Ky.	Army	2
21	CONNOR, John	G	20	6'0	190	Chicago, Ill.	None	1
22	GAY, William	HB	20	5'11	170	Chicago, Ill.	Army	1
23	DICKSON, George	QB	25	5'11	171	S. Pasadena, Cal.	Army	0
24	COUTURE, Lawrence	RH	20	5'9	170	Chicago, Ill.	None	2
25	KROLL, Leonard	HB	21	5'10	165	Boys Town, Neb.	None	0
26	McGEHEE, Ralph	LT	20	6'1	195	Chicago, Ill.	None	2
27	ESPENAN, Charles	E	22	6'2	188	New Orleans, La.	Navy	2
28	SPANIEL, Frank	FB	20	5'10	180	Vandergrift, Pa.	None	1
29	DAILER, James	G	21	5'9	185	Wheeling, W. Va.	Army	2
30	LANDRY, John	HB	22	6'1	180	Rochester, N. Y.	None	0
31	FALLON, Joseph	G	19	5'11	180	Alton, Ill.	None	1
34	SAGGAU, Thomas	HB	19	6'0	177	Denison, Iowa	None	1
36	FRAMPTON, John	LG	24	5'11	190	Pomona, Cal.	Navy	1
37	BRENNAN, Terence	LH	20	6'0	170	Milwaukee, Wis.	None	3
38	MARTIN, James	LE	24	6'2	204	Cleveland, O.	Marines	2
39	ORACKO, Stephen	G	21	5'11	195	Lansford, Pa.	Army	2
40	McKILLIP, Wm.	HB	19	5'10	175	McCook, Neb.	None	0
41	FLYNN, William	E	21	6'2	190	Gary, Ind.	Marines	1
42	WAYBRIGHT, Douglas	E	21	6'1	187	Saugus, Mass.	Army	2
43	KUH, Richard	G	22	6'0	198	Chicago, Ill.	Army	0
44	LEONARD, William	E	21	6'1	188	Youngstown, O.	Army	2
46	WALSH, William	C	21	6'3	205	Phillipsburg, N. J.	None	3
47	HELWIG, John	G	20	6'2	190	Los Angeles, Cal.	None	1
48	WALLNER, Frederick	FB	20	6'2	198	Greenfield, Mass.	None	0
49	HUDAK, Edward	T	20	6'2	200	Bethlehem, Pa.	None	1
50	JEFFERS, John	C	19	5'11	195	Phoenixville, Pa.	None	1
51	COTTER, Richard	FB	19	6'1	185	Austin, Minn.	None	0
52	GROTHAUS, Walter	C	22	6'2	192	Cincinnati, O.	Army	2
53	FEIGEL, Charles	C	19	6'1	190	Chicago, Ill.	None	0
54	CANTWELL, Philip	E	22	6'2	194	Los Angeles, Cal.	Army	0
55	SWISTOWICZ, Michael	FB	21	5'11	195	Chicago, Ill.	None	2
56	YANOSCHIK, Philip	C	23	6'0	195	Conemaugh, Pa.	Army	0
57	LALLY, Robert	RG	19	6'0	185	Cleveland, O.	None	1
58	WENDELL, Martin	RG	21	5'11	198	Chicago, Ill.	Navy	3
59	ZMIJEWSKI, Alfred	T	20	6'1	200	Newark, N. J.	None	2
60	GROOM, Jerome	C	19	6'3	210	Des Moines, Iowa	None	0
63	BUDYNKIEWICZ, Theodore	T	25	6'0	205	Chicopee, Mass.	Army	2
67	PANELLI, John	FB	22	5'11	185	Morristown, N. J.	None	3
68	FALLON, John	RT	21	6'0	194	Alton, Ill.	None	2
69	O'NEIL, John	FB	19	6'0	185	Aurora, Ill.	Marines	0
70	MAHONEY, James	T	21	6'1	195	Erie, Pa.	M. Marines	0
72	FISCHER, William (Capt.)	LG	21	6'2	233	Chicago, Ill.	None	3
73	GAUL, Francis	T	22	5'11	210	Cleveland, O.	None	1
74	THOMAS, Deane	T	19	6'2	197	Chicago, Ill.	None	0
75	PALMISANO, Frank	G	19	5'11	190	Vandergrift, Pa.	None	0
76	STE. MARIE, Vincent	G	19	6'0	197	Klondike, Wis.	None	0
78	SCHWARTZ, Phillip	T	18	6'4	198	Madison, Wis.	Marines	0
79	CIFELLI, August	T	23	6'4	212	Philadelphia, Pa.	Marines	2
80	HART, Leon	RE	19	6'4	228	Turtle Creek, Pa.	None	2
82	WIGHTKIN, William	E	21	6'2	198	Culver City, Cal.	C. Guard	2
83	CIECHANOWICZ, Emil	T	20	6'4	220	Chicago, Ill.	None	1

Head Coach—FRANK W. LEAHY

Assistant Coaches

Edward Krause, Joseph McArdle, John Druze, Bernard Crimmins,
William Earley, Walter Ziemba, Frederick Miller.

Notre Dame Beats Michigan State

South Bend, Ind., Oct. 9.—(AP.) —Notre Dame put on another victory march today—26 to 7—against a tough Michigan State team.

A crowd of 58,126 saw the Irish score in every period on parades of power that went 70, 96, 80 and 20 yards.

Michigan State landed the first punch in the opening quarter. Horace Smith set up the opportunity when he intercepted a pass on the Irish 21. Lynn Chandnois went around his left end to the six, and Leroy Crane crashed over for a touchdown. Smtih kicked the extra point.

Notre Dame rallied and drove 70 yards on running and passing plays. Frank Tripucka tossed four yards to Leon Hart for the score. Steve Oracko's attempted conversion was wide.

Notre Dame, from that point on, made efficient use of its bigger and better line. The Irish put on a 96-yard attack that put them out in front.

1948

Coach: Frank Leahy
Captain: William Fischer

S.25	W	Purdue	28-27	H	c59,343
O.2	W	Pittsburgh	40-0	A	c64,000
O.9	W	Michigan State	26-7	H	c58,126
O.16	W	Nebraska	44-13	A	c38,000
O.23	W	Iowa	27-12	A	c53,000
O.30	W	Navy	41-7	N	c63,314
N.6	W	Indiana (R)	42-6	A	c34,000
N.13	W	Northwestern	12-7	H	c59,305
N.27	W	Washington	46-0	H	50,609
D.4	T	So. Cal.(0:35-ND)	14-14	A	c100,571
		(9-0-1)	320-93		580,268

N—at Baltimore

Notre Dame 14
So. California 14

The Irish will not quit!

One hundred thousand spectators and the Southern California football team found this out, Dec. 4, when the Fighting Irish of Notre Dame staged a desperation last-second rally to tie the Trojans, 14-14.

With the score 14-7 against Notre Dame and time running out, Bill Gay grabbed a Southern California kickoff on his one-yard line, picked up a horde of determined blockers, and blazed 87 yards before being downed on the Trojan 13-yard line. Bob Williams, subbing for the injured Frank Tripucka, fired two passes. The first was incomplete, but interference was called on the second. That put the ball on the one. John Panelli was stopped. Then Emil Sitko crashed the last foot and Notre Dame had come from nowhere to within a point of Southern California. With the game resting on his shoulders, Steve Oracko calmly booted the ball between the uprights. Notre Dame had come from behind again.

Broken was the Irish consecutive winning streak and gone were her hopes for a perfect season. The reason was an inspired Trojan team which played tremendous football against a team rated its superior by three touchdowns. Their strong forward wall checked the Irish running attack and their precision punters kept the Irish deep in their own territory for part of the game.

Southern Cal was aided by an outbreak of Irish fumbles. Before the afternoon was over Notre Dame had handed over the ball six times to the Trojans. Only a great Irish line led by All-Americans Hart and Fischer prevented those bobbles from developing into enemy touchdowns.

Notre Dame drew first blood. After a bruising but scoreless first quarter, the Notre Dame ground attack put together two first downs in a row. Then Frank Tripucka hit Hart with a pass on the Trojan 39. Big Leon bulled his way over and through the enemy secondary with unbelievable power and scored standing up. Oracko notched the point.

After a first half drive had failed on the Irish one, the Trojans struck for keeps in the fourth period. Jake Kirby intercepted a Williams' pass on the Irish 42 and Bill Martin smacked over from the two yard line just a few plays later. Soon the Trojans had the ball again and again they could not be stopped. Dill, Kirby, and Martin again teamed for what looked like the winning seven points.

Then Mr. Gay stepped in!

Another season was ended and another great Notre Dame team had taken its place in sports history. Once more men of Notre Dame had lived up to their name: the Fighting Irish.

Bill Gay throws block that set off the season's most spectacular run. Hart scores first Irish touchdown in second period.

TEAM STATISTICS
10 Games

Notre Dame		Opponents
153	First downs	112
3194*	Yards gained rushing	1036
105	Passes attempted	216
61	Passes completed	86
770	Yards gained passing	1013
16	Passes intercepted by	13
904	Yards all kicks returned	1265
20	Opp. fumbles recovered	20
842	Yards lost by penalties	335

* Breaks all-time Notre Dame rushing record of 3137 yards set in the 10-game schedule of 1943.

"Cheer, Cheer, for Old Notre Dame"

BY CARL APONE

(Condensed from Catholic Digest)

"Cheer, cheer, for old Notre Dame!
Wake up the echoes cheering her name!
Send a volley cheer on high—
Shake down the thunder from the sky!"

These familiar lyrics Jack Shea wrote in 1909 to a "Victory March" composed by his brother. The brother-composer was Rev. Michael J. Shea, later a student at the Pontifical School of Music in Rome, and then just Mike Shea, —graduate student,—Notre Dame. The brothers had often arranged Notre Dame words to songs from eastern colleges, but decided to write an original school song while watching an Indiana-Notre Dame football game.

A week later on an old piano in Sorin Hall, Mike played a "tune that had been running through his head," and overnight Jack wrote lyrics to the music. The next day the Sheas returned to try their work in Sorin Hall, but finding the recreation room too noisy they went instead to the organ in the campus Sacred Heart Church, the student Chapel at Notre Dame, and there for the first time the words and music of the "Victory March" were sung and played.

The Notre Dame bandmaster at that time received their work coolly, and for a long time refused to play it. However, after much persuasion he agreed to try their music; and the Victory March had its first public performance at Notre Dame on Washington's birthday, 1909. It was an instant success. In fact, a friend voted to hearing it in the Soviet Union. A Notre Dame student said that the famous Chinese merchants who roamed the streets of Tientsin, China, selling Chinese model violins demonstrated their instruments by playing the "Victory March". An article in the Chicago Tribune told of the time that Fred Snite, Jr., the famous man in the iron lung and a Notre Dame graduate, was in China and heard the familiar strains echoing from an inn. He investigated but couldn't understand a word of the lyrics—the chorus was all Chinese.

This music which has inspired "Fighting Irish" greats from George Gipp to Johnny Lujack has also stirred the fighting men on the battlefields of the recent war. In the official navy film "Appointment in Tokyo", the marines can be heard singing the Victory March while going in for a beach-head landing. When the 36th division hit the beaches at Salerno, several national magazines wrote about the troops singing the march while waiting to land.

The music even reached the prisoner-of-war camps. In a recently released letter sent to the Reverend John J. Cavanaugh, C.S.C., President of Notre Dame, Captain Trevor E. Hughes of the British 51st Highland Division told of hearing the Victory March in a prisoner-of-war camp at Lodz, Poland. "When the allies invaded Normandy", he writes, "the German commandant granted our request for a gramophone. Though we were not allowed to play our national songs, I thought you might be very happy to know that we began and ended each program with the Notre Dame Victory March." Captain Hughes wrote to thank Notre Dame for the inspiration the Victory March had given the thousands of homesick British prisoners.

Among the many alumni and friends of Notre Dame who have heard the Victory March in the remote corners of the world, is Frank Leahy, head football coach at the University. In 1944 Lieutenant Leahy, U. S. N., was on the tiny Pacific island of Myrtle off Majuro in charge of recreation for submarine crews. "The natives of Myrtle Island", he said, "entertained our men with programs of native songs and dances. On one of these programs a native spokesman announced that as a special attraction the natives were going to sing an American song, which they had heard over the radio. You can imagine our surprise when instead of 'The Star Spangled Banner' or some other universally known music, the natives sang the Notre Dame Victory March."

In appreciation of his music Father Shea was awarded a major athletic monogram on November 23, 1935, at the N. D.-So. Cal. game. It was an award which he prized highly. Jack had won a baseball monogram at Notre Dame.

Upon leaving Notre Dame, Father Shea taught theology at St. Joseph's seminary, Dunwoodie, Yonkers, New York. From there he went to St. Augustine's Church in Ossining, New York, where he died at the age of 55 on August 21, 1940. Jack Shea became a state senator in Massachusetts and is now a businessman in Holyoke, Massachusetts.

"What though the odds be great or small?
Old Notre Dame will win over all,
While her loyal sons are marching
Onward to victory."

THE 25 YEAR TEAM

Quarterbacks

John Lujack .... Notre Dame 23

Lujack of Notre Dame has no stronger admirer than Bierman of Minnesota. Following the Shriners East-West game at San Francisco, Bernie Bierman, coaching the East team remarked: "You don't have to worry about a team with Lujack in charge. Just turn the reins over to him and relax." And George Halas, his current employer, says that completely stripped of all his amazing football talents Lujack is still indispensable for one thing — his poise! In three years at Notre Dame with every opponent primed for the Irish, Lujack, calm, deliberate, unhurried and unruffled was in every emergency or crisis, the personification of poise.

The preliminary vote by the sportswriters gave Lujack a safe lead as the 25-year quarterback and the final vote by the coaches confirms the verdict. A special quarterback ballot was submitted to the 48 coaches, listing Kinnick (Iowa); Albert (Stanford); Carideo and Lujack (Notre Dame); and Friedman (Michigan).

Nile Kinnick, lost at sea in the war, was the football player of the year in 1939 and like Frankie Albert, following him at Stanford, Kinnick was endowed with football intuition, rare judgment and a quick mind, and both received a heavy vote in the 25-year All America balloting from writers and coaches alike. In 1935 Frank Carideo was the overwhelming choice for quarterback in a 10-year All America selection and in his prime, under Rockne, Carideo had no close competitor.

But the highest vote for Quarterback went to John Lujack, whose collegiate career provided many climax moments, with the West Point Cadets providing the back-drop for his best shows. As a green, unknown Sophomore, substituting for the brilliant Bertelli, in the 1943 Army game, Lujack took charge right from the kick-off and engineered a 26 to 0 victory with all the poise and finesse of a veteran. Three years later in the historic deadlock with a powerful Army team, Lujack downed mighty Doc Blanchard three times when the human pile-driver was heading for a touchdown. Lujack, injured, played the full 60 minutes of that bruising contest.

Reprinted with permission from *College Football and All American Review* by Christy Walsh (House-Warren, Publishers, 1951).

RUSHING

	Times Carried	Yds. Gained	Avg.
Hart	4	39	9.8
Wightkin	4	32	8.0
Panelli	92	692	7.5
Spaniel	24	174	7.3
L. Smith	4	28	7.0
Gay	64	382	6.0
Brennan	48	284	5.9
Sitko	129	742	5.8
Coutre	27	152	5.6
Zalejski	7	34	4.9
Swistowicz	41	172	4.2
Landry	80	309	3.9
McKillip	26	96	3.7
Cotter	9	33	3.7
Wallner	11	37	3.1
McGee	2	5	2.5
Williams	6	11	1.9
Martin	5	0	0.0
Tripucka	16	—28	—1.7
	599	3194	5.3

SCORING

	TD	PAT & FG	Points
Sitko	9	0	54
Panelli	8	0	48
Landry	6	0	36
Oracko	0	*29	*31
Hart	5	0	30
Gay	4	0	24
Wightkin	3	0	18
Spaniel	2	0	12
L. Smith	2	0	12
Brennan	2	0	12
Coutre	2	0	12
Swisotwicz	2	0	12
McKillip	1	0	6
Martin	1	0	6
Zmijewski	1	0	6
Tripucka	0	1	1
	48	*30	320

*Includes one field goal.

PASSING

	Att.	Comp.	TD Passes	Yds. Passes	Pct.
Tripucka	91	53	11	660	.582
Williams	14	8	0	110	.571
	105	61	11	770	.581

	Rec'd	Yds. Gained	Intrcptd By	Intrcptn Ret'd.
Hart	16	231	0	0
Martin	14	98	0	0
Gay	10	131	6	74
Sitko	7	70	0	0
Brennan	5	102	1	1
Wightkin	4	112	0	0
Coutre	2	—1	1	41
Lesko	1	14	0	0
Landry	1	10	0	0
Spaniel	1	3	2	33
L. Smith	0	0	3	37
Swistowicz	0	0	1	5
Zmijewski	0	0	1	5
Groom	0	0	1	2
	61	770	16	198

Notre Dame's 1949 National Champions

Left to right: Front row: Steve Oracko, George Dickson, Ed Hudak Frank Johnson, Gus Cifelli, Leon Hart, Ray Espenan, Gerry Begley, Ralph McGehee, Bob Lally. Second row: William Kramer, Larry Coutre, Frank Spaniel, Bill Gay, Mike Swistowicz, Paul Burns, Don Huml, Bill Barrett, Jerry Groom, Johnny Helwig, Jim Mutscheller, Chet Ostrowski, Joe Caprara. Third row: Marty Kiousis, Jim Bartlett, Jim Hamby, Frank Johnston, Tom Huber, Bill Flynn, John O'Neil, Jack Nusskern, Ernie Zalejski, Jim Mahoney, Ernie Knapik, Doug Waybright, Jack Connor, Fred Wallner. Fourth row: Jim Funari (Mgr.), Ed Smith, John Zancha, Bob Dolmetsch, Byron Boji, Bob Toneff, Bill Whiteside, Dan Modak, Art Perry, Jack Bush, Bill Higgins, Emil Sitko, Dick Cotter, Jim Dailer. Fifth row: Don Lueck (Mgr.) John O'Hara, John Mazur, Bob Williams, Gene Smith, Bob Kapish, Bill Hovey, John Petitbon, Del Gander, Walt Grothaus, Tony Zambroski, Dave Koch, Jack Daut, Jack Finnegan (Mgr.). Jim Martin was missing when the picture was taken.

1949 - Notre Dame Football Squad - 1949

BACKS

No.	Name	Wt.	Ht.	Age	Home Town
1	Mazur, John E.	185	6-1	19	Plymouth, Pa.
3	Whiteside, William A.	172	5-10	20	Philadelphia, Pa.
6	Dickson, George C.	170	5-11	26	S. Pasadena, Cal.
7	Begley, Gerald C.	175	6-1	21	Yonkers, N.Y.
9	Williams, Robert A.	180	6-1	19	Baltimore, Md.
12	Zalejski, Ernest R.	185	5-11	23	South Bend, Ind.
14	Sitko, Emil M.	180	5-8	26	Fort Wayne, Ind.
22	Gay, William T.	168	5-10	21	Chicago, Ill.
23	Petitbon, John E.	180	5-11	18	New Orleans, La.
24	Coutre, Lawrence E.	170	5-9	21	Chicago, Ill.
26	Bush, John L.	185	6-0	19	Davenport, Iowa
28	Spaniel, Francis J.,	184	5-10	20	Vandergrift, Pa.
30	Landry, John W.	180	6-1	23	Rochester, N.Y.
37	Barrett, William C.	179	5-8	19	Chicago, Ill.
40	McKillip, Leo	175	5-10	20	McCook, Neb.
41	Caprara, Joseph A.	198	6-0	19	Turtle Creek, Pa.
44	Swistowicz, Michael P.	195	5-11	22	Chicago, Ill.
47	Gander, Fidel J.	190	6-1	19	Chicago, Ill.
48	Cotter, Richard A.	178	6-1	20	Austin, Minn.

CENTERS

No.	Name	Wt.	Ht.	Age	Home Town
50	Groom, Jerome P.	210	6-3	20	Des Moines, Iowa
51	Boji, Byron	190	5-11	19	Chicago, Ill.
52	Grothaus, Walter J.	192	6-2	23	Cincinnati, Ohio
54	Bartlett, James J.	196	6-3	20	Cincinnati, Ohio
55	Hamby, James H.	195	6-1	18	Caruthersville, Mo.
57	Feigl, Charles	185	6-1	20	Chicago, Ill.

GUARDS

No.	Name	Wt.	Ht.	Age	Home Town
39	Kiousis, Martin J.	190	5-11	19	Lakewood, Ohio
49	Helwig, John F.	194	6-2	21	Los Angeles, Cal.
60	Lally, Robert J.	185	6-0	20	Cleveland, Ohio
61	Johnson, Frank A.	195	6-0	22	Cincinnati, Ohio
62	Oracko, Stephen F.	185	6-0	22	Lansford, Pa.
63	Wallner, Frederick W.	208	6-2	21	Greenfield, Mass.
64	Burns, Paul E.	205	6-2	20	Athens, Pa.
65	Modak, Daniel	197	6-1	22	Campbell, Ohio
66	Perry, Arthur R.	198	5-11	19	Davenport, Iowa
67	Johnston, Frank A.	184	5-8	20	Chicago, Ill.
68	Higgins, William P.	180	5-11	22	Chicago, Ill.
69	Zambroski, Anthony J.	196	5-11	19	Erie, Pa.

TACKLES

No.	Name	Wt.	Ht.	Age	Home Town
38	Martin, J. E., (Co-Capt.)	204	6-2	25	Cleveland, Ohio
71	Cifelli, August B.	230	6-4	24	Philadelphia, Pa.
72	Hudak, Edward J.	200	6-2	21	Bethlehem, Pa.
73	Nusskern, Jack	215	6-2	24	West View, Pa.
74	McGehee, Ralph W.	202	6-1	21	Chicago, Ill.
75	Toneff, Robert	232	6-1	19	Barberton, Ohio
76	Zancha, John D.	195	5-10	19	Chicago, Ill.
78	Zmijewski, Alfred A.	200	6-1	21	Newark, N.J.

ENDS

No.	Name	Wt.	Ht.	Age	Home Town
80	Waybright, Douglas G.	186	6-1	22	Saugus, Mass.
81	Flynn, William J.	197	6-2	22	Gary, Ind.
82	Hart, Leon J. (Co-Capt.)	245	6-4	20	Turtle Creek, Pa.
83	Wightkin, William J.	204	6-2	22	Culver City, Cal.
84	Espenan, Ray	188	6-2	22	New Orleans, La.
85	Mutscheller, James F.	194	6-1	19	Beaver Falls, Pa.
86	Jonardi, Raymond C.	188	6-2	19	Pittsburgh, Pa.
87	Ostrowski, Chester C.	196	6-1	19	Chicago, Ill.
88	Dolmetsch, Robert E.	195	6-2	19	Chicago, Ill.

AP POLL

1949
1. NOTRE DAME
2. Oklahoma
3. California
4. Army
5. Rice
6. Ohio State
7. Michigan
8. Minnesota
9. L.S.U.
10. College Pacific

1949

Coach: Frank Leahy

Co-Captains: Leon J. Hart and James E. Martin

S.24	W	Indiana	49-6	H		53,844
O.1	W	Washington	27-7	A	c	41,500
O.8	W	Purdue	35-12	A	c	52,000
O.15	W	Tulane	46-7	H	c	58,196
O.29	W	Navy	40-0	N	c	62,000
N.5	W	Michigan State	34-21	A	c	51,277
N.12	W	North Carolina	42-6	YS	c	67,000
N.19	W	Iowa	28-7	H	c	56,790
N.26	W	So. California	32-0	H	c	57,214
D.3	W	S.M.U.	27-20	A		75,457
		(10-0-0)	360-86			575,278

N—at Baltimore

OFFICIAL PROGRAM • THIRTY-FIVE CENTS

INDIANA

NOTRE DAME

NOTRE DAME STADIUM   SEPTEMBER 24 ★ 1949

Notre Dame 40
Navy 0

Middies Are No Match for Rampant Irish as Williams Stars for Home Town Fans

For the first four minutes in Baltimore's packed Babe Ruth Stadium the fleet was sailing high, wide and handsome toward the Irish goal, but the ND dreadnought, in its first Eastern appearance, launched a mythical Flying Dutchman in surprise starter Ernie Zalejski who took charge as the Midwesterners racked up a 40-0 scuttling of the Navy.

Irish speed, power and deception behind a water-tight defense and under the smooth navigation of Commodore Bob Williams was too much for the sailors who found Zalejski alone scoring three times.

Williams Takes Over

Performing before his home-town fans, Williams steered the Irish powerhouse to a score a few plays after the Green clads' defense had stopped the opening Middy thrust uncomfortably close to the Irish goal. A 23 yard toss from Williams to Zalejski was scooped in on the Navy 25 and Ernie had his first score four and a half minutes from the opening whistle. Twice more after Oracko had made

the score 7-0 for the Irish the Navy drove within the ND 20 only to have the shifting, deceptive Irish defense, spike the big guns of the fleet, with Mutscheller and Burns sparking the action.

The early minutes of the second frame found the Irish in possession on their own 14. Coutre lost five yards over Navy's left tackle, then on the next play roared 91 yards through the same spot for the second Irish tally, and again Oracko converted.

Five plays later, with Emil Sitko carrying on two of them, the Redhead bored through center for 16 yards and the third TD of the day. After Oracko made it 21-0, the Middies tried again, this time reaching only their own 46 before surrendering to the Irish. Two Williams' aerials to Zalejski covered the distance neatly and Ernie carried the last on his second visit to the Navy end zone. This time Oracko's effort was wide and the Irish sported a 27-0 half time lead.

Statistics

N. D.		Navy
9	First downs	15
352	Net yards rushing	141
7	Forward passes attempted	21
5	Forward passes completed	8
159	Yards gained passing	100
1	Passes intercepted by	0
2	Yards gained on interceptions	0
41.8	Punting average	40.1
58	Total yards, kicks returned	134
1	Opponents fumbles recovered	2
55	Yards lost on penalties	45

Notre Dame 32
S. California 0

Four Horsemen See Hart at Fullback; Trojans' Passing Fails as Irish Take No. 37

Notre Dame's Fighting Irish re-emphasized their claim to the National Championship today as they methodically and spectacularly carved out the 37th notch in their four-year undefeated skein 32-0 at the expense of an outclassed Southern California.

While a capacity crowd suffered from the cold the Irish drove for two tallies in the opening frame, then added a score in each succeeding quarter while holding the Westerners scoreless.

The famed Four Horsemen were guests on their twenty-fifth anniversary and saw an exhibition of speed and power second to none in their experience, with Leon Hart briefly making his debut in the fullback slot.

Statistics

N. D.		So. California
17	First downs	9
316	Net yards rushing	17
23	Forward passes attempted	36
7	Forward passes completed	16
112	Yards gained passing	148
3	Passes intercepted by	2
16	Yards gained on interceptions	2
36	Punting average	37
26	Total yards, kicks returned	114
1	Opponents fumbles recovered	1
50	Yards lost on penalties	15

NEW NOTRE DAME HUDDLE: Bob Williams (foreground), Notre Dame quarterback, faces his teammates in the new huddle formation to be used by Notre Dame this season. Under game conditions Williams will have his back to the line of scrimmage, while the rest of the team will be facing the opponents. (Line of scrimmage on this picture would be off the lower left hand corner).

DIAGRAM OF FORMATION: E   B   B   B   E
                          T   G   C   G   T
                                QB
        - - - - Line of Scrimmage - - - - - -

Irish Take 10th after SMU Scare

Dallas, Texas, Dec. 3.—Mighty Notre Dame battled against Southern Methodist for its championship life today, and, like a champion, it won.

Powering 56 yards on the ground to break a 20-all fourth period tie and then stand off a furious Mustang drive on their own four-yard line, the Irish defeated SMU, 27-20, in the biggest thriller of the 1949 season.

The 75,428 who sat in the drizzling rain at the Cotton Bowl here expected Coach Frank Leahy's team to roll to an easy win. Instead, they saw Matty Bell's aroused Texans give Notre Dame its toughest contest in an unbeaten string that now stands at 38 games. Notre Dame has gone four consecutive seasons without losing and Coach Leahy's record stands at 60 wins, three losses and five ties.

When the Kyle Rote-led Mustangs tied the score at 20-20, there were less than 6 minutes to play. Left half Frank Spaniel ran the kickoff back all the way to the ND 46. Emil Sitko, All-American senior, and soph star, Bill Barrett, took the ball to the 26 in five plays. Then, other All-American, end Leon Hart, moved to the fullback post and slammed to the 20. Barrett followed with six yards. Bill Gay with six more and Barrett with another two. The SMU line couldn't hold the ND backs and Barrett swung wide on the next play, chugged for the corner and went over. Steve Oracko's third conversion practically assured the Irish of at least a tie.

But SMU hadn't given up all afternoon and they didn't this time either. Rote ran and passed the Texans to the 28. Kyle was momentarily hurt, but Benners came in and threw to H. Russell on the five. Here the great Irish line held, and Rote's fourth down jump-pass was grabbed by both Jerry Groom and Bob Lally, two tremendous

By RALPH WRIGHT

line backers all afternoon. The Irish moved out of danger, punted and the game ended shortly thereafter.

The first half was a tea party compared to the second 30 minutes. Both Notre Dame's first half scores came on Williams passes. One went to Bill Wightkin who got behind Rote, caught the pass and ran 10 more yards to complete a 42 yard play. The other TD pass

"Notre Dame met their match in Rote and Southern Methodist but fought back in champion style to a hard-earned victory."—Paul Neville, South Bend "Tribune."

was caught by Ernie Zalejski on a play that started from the SMU 35. An opponent reflected the ball, but Ernie was behind him and caught it in the end zone.

John Petitbon set up the first scoring drive by intercepting a pass on his 27. Gay started the second by spearing another stray Mustang pass and running 20 yards to the home team's 35.

SMU's only first half threat was Rote. After ND's first touchdown, sawed-off Johnny Champion threw to end Zohn Milam for 78 yards and a first down on the six. However, four Rote rushes at the line left SMU a foot shy.

If the first half was like a tea party, the second half resembled a barroom brawl. Notre Dame's attack looked sharp and twice they marched toward the SMU only to lose the ball on Zalejski fumbles—once on the 12 and once on the 38. The second muff gave the Mustangs the life needed.

Rote, now running like a madman, streaked for 18, then for 23 more. Then he handed off to little Champion who

squirmed all the way to the three-yard line. Rote hit the line for one and followed with a touchdown plunge.

ND crossed the goal again in a hurry. Soph Jim Mutscheller intercepted Rote's toss on the 22 and, in four plays, the Irish were on the three. Barrett made the first of his game-winning touchdowns by jamming through right tackle.

Less than a minute later, Champion ran a Rote pass all the way to the ND one and hard-running Kyle smashed over.

A 15-yard penalty pushed the Irish back to their one-yard line shortly after the kickoff, and Bill Richards ran Williams' punt down on the 14. In three plays, Rote bounded into the end zone for the third time. Bill Sullivan, who kicked the first two extra points, booted again, but Groom burst through to block the attempt and keep SMU from going ahead.

This afternoon there were heroes all over the place. ND's whole line, especially Hart, Groom and Lally did a tremendous job. In the defensive backfield, Petitbon was sensational until he had to leave the game with injuries. On offense, Bob Williams connected on 11 passes to break an ND record for passes completed in one season—83. And Barrett, Larry Coutre, Sitko, Spaniel and Hart stood out among the ball-carriers.

Grover Walker, Franklin and I. D. Russell played their hearts out for the Mustang defensive unit, but the man of the hour was Rote. The 190-pound San Antonio junior ran for 115 yards on the ground and passed for 168 more. The injured All-American, Doak Walker, couldn't have been better—it was impossible.

These Irish won this season with non-chalance, but, when they had to fight, they did. They're the Fighting Irish and they're still winning.

Hart Is Coy To Offers By Pro Elevens

Notre Dame Captain Asks Off-Season Job Plus Huge Salary

New York, Dec. 7. — (AP.)— College football's "player of the year," big Leon Hart of Notre Dame, may command the highest price ever paid a collegian to turn pro.

"I don't intend to play unless I get the right offer—a better one than I've received so far," the six-foot-four, 260-pound Irish end said today.

Hart is in town to receive the Heisman trophy, awarded yearly to the player voted the outstanding performer of the season in a national poll of sports writers and broadcasters.

He discussed his future plans at an informal luncheon for the press and radio crowd at the Downtown Athletic Club, donor of the handsome bronze plaque.

Asked what it might take to lure him into money ranks, the boyish giant from Turtle Creek, Pa., winked impishly and replied, "Well, you might say $25,000 a year as a starter."

The Detroit Lions of the National League and the Baltimore Colts of the All-America Conference have draft rights to the Irish co-captain, whose brilliant all-around play was largely responsible for Notre Dame's fourth unbeaten season.

The Lions' coach Bo McMillin, main speaker at the presentation ceremonies tonight, has already fit Hart into his 1950 plans. The Irish husky will be his fullback, McMillin says.

Hart said he has been approached by the pros but hasn't heard an offer "substantial enough to grab at it."

"It's not only the salary I'm interested in but some sort of off-season job security," he added.

The word is that several big automobile manufacturers in the motor city are eager to hire the handsome Pennsylvanian, who is a top engineering student at the South Bend institution.

The dough Hart is demanding in salary plus that offered for engineering services probably surpasses anything ever dangled under the nose of a prospective pro hireling.

Statistics Prove ND Might

SCORING

	TD	PAT	Points
Sitko	9	0	54
Barrett	9	0	54
Spaniel	7	0	42
Coutre	7	0	42
Oracko	0	38	38
Hart	6	0	36
Zalejski	5	0	30
Swistowicz	2	0	12
Wightkin	2	0	12
Gay	2	0	12
Landry	2	0	12
Williams	1	0	6
Petitbon	1	0	6
	53	38	360*

*Includes two safeties

PASSING

	Att.	Comp.	TD Passes	Yds. Passes	Pct.
Williams	147	83	16	1374	.565
Mazur	5	2	2	36	.400
Barrett	1	1	0	24	1.000
Whiteside	1	0	0	0	.000
	154	86	18	1434	.558

RUSHING

	Times Carried	Yards Gained	Avg.
Sitko	120	712	5.9
Coutre	102	645	6.3
Spaniel	80	496	6.2
Barrett	75	359	4.8
Zalejski	29	171	5.9
Landry	37	147	4.0
Hart	18	73	4.1
Cotter	16	64	4.0
Williams	34	63	1.9
Swistowicz	11	53	4.8
Gander	10	52	5.2
Gay	14	47	3.4
Wightkin	3	14	4.7
McKillip	1	11	11.0
Bush	2	11	5.5
Begley	4	7	1.8
Dickson	2	3	1.5
Smith	1	3	1.0
Espenan	1	0	0.0
Mazur	2	0	0.0
Whiteside	1	−8	−8.0
Petitbon	3	−9	−3.0
	566	2914	5.1

PUNTING

	Kicks	Yards	Avg.
Williams	42	1621	38.6
Barrett	8	344	43.0
Mazur	2	54	27.0
	52	2019	38.8

PASS-RECEIVING

	Caught	Yards Gained	TD Passes
Wightkin	17	309	2
Coutre	13	271	0
Hart	19	257	5
Spaniel	16	212	3
Zalejski	5	151	4
Barrett	6	125	3
Gay	5	60	1
Mutscheller	2	27	0
Sitko	2	15	0
Flynn	1	7	0
	86	1434	18

PASS INTERCEPTION

	Int. By	Yards Ret'd.
Swistowicz	1	84
Gay	4	80
Petitbon	3	62
Helwig	1	41
Groom	2	16
Mutscheller	1	5
Cotter	1	3
Whiteside	1	3
Hamby	1	2
Begley	1	2
	16	298

PUNT RETURNS

	Ret'd	Yards	Avg.
Gay	19	254	13.4
Spaniel	3	32	10.7
Sitko	1	23	23.0
Begley	1	18	18.0
Cotter	1	13	13.0
Petitbon	2	8	4.0
Williams	1	5	5.0
Barrett	1	0	0.0
Gander	1	0	0.0
	30	353	11.8

KICKOFF RETURNS

	Ret'd	Yards	Avg.
Sitko	4	89	22.5
Spaniel	5	70	14.0
Swistowicz	1	55	55.0
Coutre	4	48	12.0
Wightkin	3	30	10.0
Gay	1	24	24.0
Zalejski	1	23	23.0
Flynn	1	16	16.0
Barrett	1	8	8.0
Hart	1	8	8.0
	22	371	16.9

Notre Dame Roster — 1950

No.	Name	Pos.	Age	Ht.	Wt.	Hometown	Class
1	MAZUR, John E.*	QB	20	6'1	190	Plymouth, Pa.	Jr.
3	WHITESIDE, William A.	QB	21	5'10	172	Philadelphia, Pa.	Sr.
4	CARTER, Thomas	HB	23	5'11	173	Los Angeles, Cal.	Sr.
5	GAUDREAU, William L.	QB	19	6'1	178	Baltimore, Md.	So.
6	WISE, John T.	QB	19	6'2	185	Cleveland, Ohio	So.
7	SMITH, Edward	QB	21	5'10	160	Pueblo, Colo.	Sr.
8	CASEY, Daniel	QB	20	6'0	175	Lafayette, Ind.	So.
9	WILLIAMS, Robert A.**	QB	20	6'1	185	Baltimore, Md.	Sr.
12	MARCHAND, Gerald H.	FB	19	5'8	175	Baton Rouge, La.	So.
15	SMITH, Eugene F.	HB	20	5'9	170	LaCrosse, Wis.	Sr.
17	WHELAN, John D.	HB	19	5'11	180	Miami, Fla.	So.
22	GAY, William T.**	HB	22	5'11	175	Chicago, Ill.	Sr.
23	PETITBON, John E.*	HB	19	5'11	190	New Orleans, La.	Jr.
24	PAOLONE, Ralph N.	HB	19	6'0	195	New Castle, Pa.	So.
25	BUCZKIEWICZ, Edward G.	HB	19	6'0	182	Chicago, Ill.	So.
26	BUSH, John L.	HB	20	6'0	190	Davenport, Iowa	Jr.
27	HOVEY, William	HB	24	5'10	175	Lake Placid, N. Y.	Jr.
29	JOHNSON, Murray E.	HB	19	6'2	195	Gary, Ind.	So.
30	LANDRY, John W.**	FB	24	6'1	180	Rochester, N. Y.	Sr.
32	FLOOD, David M.	HB	21	5'10	185	Pittsburgh, Pa.	Jr.
37	BARRETT, William C.*	HB	20	5'8	180	Chicago, Ill.	Jr.
40	McKILLIP, Leo*	HB	21	5'10	175	McCook, Neb.	Sr.
43	DAVID, Joseph	HB	19	5'10	175	New Orleans, La.	So.
47	GANDER, Fidel J.*	FB	20	6'1	190	Chicago, Ill.	Jr.
48	COTTER, Richard A.**	HB	22	6'1	180	Austin, Minn.	Sr.
49	CAPARA, Joseph A.	FB	20	6'0	192	Turtle Creek, Pa.	Jr.
50	GROOM, Jerome P. (Capt.)**	C	21	6'3	215	Des Moines, Iowa	Sr.
51	FLYNN, David M.	C	19	6'3	195	Gary, Ind.	So.
52	ALESSANDRINI, James F.	G	19	5'11	198	Charleston, W. Va.	So.
54	BARTLETT, James J.*	C	21	6'3	202	Cincinnati, Ohio	Jr.
55	HAMBY, James H.*	C	19	6'1	200	Caruthersville, Mo.	Jr.
57	FEIGL, Charles	C	21	6'1	200	Chicago, Ill.	Sr.
60	BOJI, Byron B.*	G	19	5'11	198	Chicago, Ill.	Jr.
61	STROUD, Clarke	G	19	6'1	200	Casper, Wyo.	So.
62	SEAMAN, Thomas	G	20	5'11	200	Canton, Ohio	So.
63	WALLNER, Frederick W.**	G	22	6'2	212	Greenfield, Mass.	Sr.
64	BURNS, Paul E.*	G	20	6'2	208	Athens, Pa.	Jr.
65	CARTER, Daniel J.	G	19	6'1	200	Chicago, Ill.	So.
66	PERRY, Arthur R.*	G	19	5'11	198	Davenport, Iowa	Jr.
67	JOHNSTON, Frank A.	G	20	5'8	184	Chicago, Ill.	Jr.
68	HIGGINS, William P.	G	23	5'11	180	Chicago, Ill.	Sr.
69	EPSTEIN, Frank	G	18	5'8	205	Chicago, Ill.	So.
70	MODAK, Daniel	T	23	6'1	205	Campbell, Ohio	Jr.
71	DUNLAY, James F.	T	18	6'2	205	Oakmont, Pa.	So.
72	ZAMBROSKI, Anthony J.	G	20	5'11	196	Erie, Pa.	Jr.
73	MAHONEY, James	T	23	6'1	206	Erie, Pa.	Sr.
74	FLYNN, William J.***	T	23	6'2	197	Gary, Ind.	Sr.
75	TONEFF, Robert*	T	20	6'1	235	Barberton, Ohio	Jr.
76	ZANCHA, John D.	T	20	5'10	195	Chicago, Ill.	Jr.
77	WEITHMAN, James T.	T	20	6'1	195	Bucyrus, O.	So.
78	MURPHY, Thomas	T	19	6'1	210	Chicago, Ill.	So.
79	BARDASH, Virgil J.	T	19	6'0	210	Gary, Ind.	So.
80	KELLY, Robert J.	E	19	6'2	200	Duluth, Minn.	So.
81	MESCHIEVITZ, Vincent A.	E	19	6'4	215	Chicago, Ill.	So.
82	BENSON, Robert A.	E	20	6'5	195	Omaha, Neb.	So.
83	CZAJA, Walter C.	E	21	6'2	205	Niagara Falls, N.Y.	So.
84	KAPISH, Robert J.	E	20	6'0	187	Barberton, Ohio	Jr.
85	MUTSCHELLER, James F.*	E	20	6'1	194	Beaver Falls, Pa.	Jr.
86	JONARDI, Raymond	E	21	6'2	188	Pittsburgh, Pa.	Sr.
87	OSTROWSKI, Chester C.*	E	20	6'1	196	Chicago, Ill.	Jr.
88	DOLMETSCH, Robert E.	E	20	6'2	195	Chicago, Ill.	Jr.
89	HELWIG, John F.**	E	22	6'2	194	Los Angeles, Calif.	Sr.
90	FRENCH, William P.	E	19	6'2	190	Murphysboro, Ill.	So.
91	KOCH, David A.	E	20	6'2	190	Wayzata, Minn.	Jr.
92	MURPHY, Charles H.	E	20	6'1	205	Eureka, Calif.	So.

* INDICATES MONOGRAM WINNER.

1950

Coach: Frank Leahy
Captain: Jerome P. Groom

S.30	W	No. Carolina (2:40)	14-7	H	c56,430	
O.7	L	Purdue (U) (R)	14-28	H	c56,746	
O.14	W	Tulane	13-9	A	73,159	
O.21	L	Indiana (U)	7-20	A	c34,000	
O.28	L	Michigan State	33-36	H	c57,866	
N.4	W	Navy (R-S)	19-10	N	71,074	
N.11	W	Pittsburgh	18-7	H	c56,966	
N.18	T	Iowa	14-14	A	c52,863	
D.2	L	So. California	7-9	A	70,177	

(4-4-1) 139-140 529,281

N—at Cleveland

1950 EDITION OF NOTRE DAME'S FIGHTING IRISH

First Row: Bob Williams, John Mazur, Jim Mutscheller, John Helwig, Fred Wallner, Bill Gay, Capt. Jerry Groom, Bill Barrett, Byron Boji, Leo McKillip, Bob Kapish, Dan Modak, Lee Getsschow, Ray Jonardi; Second Row: Joe Caprara, Gerry Marchand, Ed Smith, Bill Vernasco, Bill French, Bill Whiteside, Gene Smith, Ralph Paolone, Tony Zambroski, Jim Bartlett, Jack Bush, Chuck Feigl, Joe David, Murray Johnson; Third Row: Bob Dolmetsch, Jim Weithman, Ed Buckiewicz, Bob Kelly, Jack Wise, Tom Murphy, Frank Epstein, Bill Spieler, Fred Banicki, Clarke Stroud, Vince Meschievitz, Art Perry, Len Wolniak;

Fourth Row: Dick Cotter, Tom Carter, Bill Higgins, Lou Emerick, Dave Koch, Jack Daut, Bob Benson, Dan Casey, Ernie Knapick, Jack Alessandrini, Bill Gaudreau, Dave Flynn, Bill Flynn, Charlie Doud; Fifth Row: Bob Raymond (Mgr.), Jack Whelan, Tom Seaman, Virgil Bardash, Jim Hamby, Ed Whelan, Paul Burns, Bill Hovey, John Petitbon, Del Gander, Dan Carter; Sixth Row: Al Guarnieri (Mgr.), Matt O'Donnell (Mgr.), Bob Toneff, Dave Flood, Frank Johnston; Missing: Chet Ostrowski, Jack Landry, and Jim Dunlav.

— Photo by Bruce Harlan

Notre Dame 14   Purdue 28

UNDER A DRIZZLING CANOPY of clouds, Notre Dame's bid for a 40th consecutive game without defeat was drowned beneath a downpour of Boilermaker passes. A capacity crowd of 56,746 incredulous spectators sat huddled in the rain-soaked Notre Dame Stadium as the top-ranked Fighting Irish fell before a fast, powerful Purdue eleven by a 28-14 score.

It was a sad day for Notre Dame. Injuries and penalties hobbled the Irish performance, but the ND spirit was far from crippled, as three goal line stands clearly indicated. In the words of Coach Frank Leahy: "We were out-played and out-coached, but not out-fought."

STATISTICS

Notre Dame		Purdue
17	First downs	18
237	Net yards rushing	201
46	Passing yardage	158
22	Passes attempted	21
7	Passes completed	9
3	Passes had intercepted	1
3	Punts	4
31	Punting average	42
2	Fumbles lost	1
108	Yards penalized	47

Action as Purdue Ended Notre Dame's Streak — 28-14

Jim Mutscheller (85), who is setting a modern record in pass-catching, grabs one early in the Boilermaker contest.

Notre Dame 7   Southern California 9

As if the Irish had not had enough ill luck thus far, the season's finale against Southern Cal brought a new series of mishaps and bad breaks. The fact that Coach Leahy was confined to bed with a case of the flu might well have been the first suggestion of what was to befall the Irish gridders in the land of sunshine.

It was not until the second period that Notre Dame was able to break into the scoring column, with a one yard plunge by Williams capping a 54-yard drive. Meschievitz added the extra point to make it 7-0, and it looked like the Irish were on their way.

But, just 20 seconds later, a glance at the scoreboard showed a 7-7 count. The Trojan's Jim Sears had taken the N.D. kickoff on his own six and carried it 94 yards to paydirt. Gifford's kick had tied the score.

During the first half, the Irish had surprised Jeff Cravath's boys by shifting into the old Notre Dame box formation. But, Petitbon, the tailback and key man in the box, was carried off the field in the second quarter, thus eliminating the surprise offense.

It was during the second half, however, that the fortunes of the Irish skidded to a new low. One by one, Barrett, Johnson, Flood and Gay had to be carried off the field. And shortly afterwards, Williams' punt from his own 10 was blocked, only to roll out of bounds in the end zone, thereby giving the Trojans a safety and a 9-7 lead. For the second time this year, a blocked N.D. punt was to spell defeat for the Irish.

Early in the fourth period, Notre Dame's great All-American, Bob Williams, was carried from the gridiron. The Irish offensive line had been weak all afternoon, and Williams had absorbed quite a going-over. It was on the same field two years ago that Williams replaced Tripucka, who had sustained a back injury. Now, Williams himself was victimized by a back injury and had to be replaced.

Before the fray was over, Notre Dame's other All-American, Captain Jerry Groom had to leave the game. The iron man of the Irish squad had entered the battle with a badly bruised shoulder, but he gave everything he had right up to the final few minutes of the game.

Throughout the long afternoon, John Williams, playing safety for the Trojans, had been the chief cog in the S. C. defense. But the dynamic play of Notre Dame's Bob Toneff more than made up for the alert defensive wizardry of the Trojan. Time and again, Toneff roared into the Southern Cal backfield, as he lived up to pre-season expectations for the first time this year.

This was a game in which the Irish tried everything, but they just didn't seem to have enough. They switched from the "T" to the box; Petitbon reversed the usual procedure and passed to Williams; the ever-brilliant Baltimore Bob ran successfully from a fourth down punt formation; even the statistics heavily favored the Irish   but, despite all this, Notre Dame incurred its fourth defeat of the season, against one tie and four wins.

But in spite of these losses, it was a season that will long be favorably remembered by Irish rooters throughout the land. For one thing, it was a year of records: Jim Mutscheller garnered two pass-catching marks, while Bob Williams finished his great career with six out of eight single and multi-season Notre Dame passing records. Then, too, it was a year that found Jerry Groom and Bob Williams nominated for All-American honors. But, most important of all, it was a year of unparalleled spirit. Starting with Coach Frank Leahy, and continuing down through the assistant coaches, to the injury-riddled players like Billy Gay who just wouldn't quit, and finally right down to the student body   fighting spirit was the keynote at the school of Our Lady.

Jerry Groom, center

STATISTICS		
Notre Dame		So. California
13	First downs	1
145	Net yards rushing	70
104	Passing yardage	4
30	Passes attempted	2
12	Passes completed	1
3	Passes had intercepted	0
9	Punts	11
37.5	Punting average	39
2	Fumbles lost	2
110	Yards penalized	51

Facts About the 1950 Season

SCORING

	TD	PAT	Points
Mutscheller	7	0	42
Petitbon	5	0	30
Landry	2	0	12
Williams	2	0	12
Gander	2	0	12
Caprara	0	10	10
Ostrowski	1	0	6
Marchand	1	0	6
Gay	1	0	6
Meschievitz	0	3	3

PASSING

	Mazur	Williams	Petitbon	Barrett
Attempted	24	210	2	1
Completed	13	99	0	0
Had Intercepted	1	15	0	1
TD Passes	2	10	0	0
Yardage	177	1035	0	0
Percentages	.542	.471	.000	.000

RUSHING

	Times Carried	Yardage	Average
Petitbon	65	388	6.0
Landry	109	491	4.5
Barrett	41	171	4.2
Cotter	28	111	4.0
Gander	25	77	3.1
Gay	21	63	3.0
Flood	11	33	3.0
Johnson	13	33	2.9
Williams	40	115	2.9
Paolone	14	35	2.5
Marchand	21	38	1.6
Mazur	2	—7	—3.5
Mutscheller	1	6	6.0

STATISTICS FOR 1950

ND		Opp.
139	POINTS SCORED	140
137	FIRST DOWNS	109
82	Rushing	67
53	Passing	35
3	Penalties	7
1547	YARDS RUSHING	1404
391	Times Carried	392
4.0	Yards-per-try	3.6
1212	YARDS PASSING	868
237	Passes Attempted	142
112	Passes Completed	66
.473	Completion Percentage	.465
9	Passes Intercepted By	17
128	Yards Interception Returned	326
2759	TOTAL OFFENSE	2272
44	PUNTS	48
1710	Total Yardage	1693
38.9	Average Length	35.3
122	Yards Punts Returned	356
13	FUMBLES	22
9	Ball Lost	14

PASS RECEIVING

	No. Caught	Yds.	TDs
Mutscheller	35	426	7
Petitbon	18	269	2
Ostrowski	26	221	1
Gay	7	57	1
Landry	7	57	0
Marchand	4	52	1
Gander	4	44	0
Barrett	4	24	0
Johnson	4	27	0
Paolone	1	11	0
Kapish	1	8	0
Cotter	1	6	0

PASS INTERCEPTIONS

	Number Intercepted	Yards Returned
Flood	4	28
Burns	1	45
McKillip	1	36
Bush	1	17
Helwig	1	2
Petitbon	1	0

PUNT RETURNS

	Number Returned	Yards Returned
Gay	14	96
Petitbon	1	14
Flood	2	7
Barrett	1	5

PUNTING

	Number	Yardage	Average
Williams	42	1648	39.2
Barrett	1	39	39.0
Caprara	1	23	23.0

KICK-OFF RETURNS

	Number Returned	Yards Returned
Landry	11	195
Petitbon	2	69
Flood	3	44
Gay	2	42
Gander	1	30
Barrett	2	28
Bush	2	17
Williams	1	15
Mutscheller	1	12

1950 All-Opponent Team

Ends: Bob Carey, Michigan State
Clifton Anderson, Indiana
Chris Warriner, Pittsburgh

Tackles: *John Beletic, Purdue
*Don Coleman, Michigan State

Guards: John Yocca, Michigan State
Dennis Doyle, Tulane

Center: Irvin Holdash, No. Carolina

Backs: Dale Samuels, Purdue
Everett Grandelius, Michigan State
Al Carmichael, So. Calif.
*John Kerestes, Purdue

* These men were also chosen on the 1949 All-Opponent Team
(12 man team because of a tie between Anderson and Warriner at end position)

No.	Name	Pos.	Age	Ht.	Wt.	Hometown	Class
1	MAZUR, John E.**	QB	21	6'2	198	Plymouth, Pa.	Sr.
2	CAREY, Thomas F.	QB	18	5'10	175	Chicago, Ill.	Fr.
3	GUGLIELMI, Ralph V.	QB	18	6'0	180	Columbus, Ohio	Fr.
4	BUCCI, Donald	QB	18	6'0	180	Youngstown, Ohio	Fr.
5	GAUDREAU, William L.	QB	20	6'1	180	Baltimore, Md.	Jr.
6	MARTIN, Robert L.	QB	20	6'2	185	Davenport, Ia.	So.
7	BUCZKIEWICZ, Edward G.	QB	20	6'0	177	Chicago, Ill.	Jr.
10	PATERRA, Francis F.	HB	19	5'11	180	McKeesport, Pa.	So.
14	LATTNER, John J.	HB	18	6'1	188	Chicago, Ill.	So.
17	WHELAN, Jack D.	HB	20	5'11	180	Miami, Fla.	Jr.
18	REYNOLDS, Paul R.	HB	18	6'0	180	Springfield, Ill.	Fr.
20	CARRABINE, Eugene P.	HB	18	6'1	178	Gary, Ind.	Fr.
23	PETITBON, John E.**	HB	20	6'0	185	New Orleans, La.	Sr.
24	JOSEPH, Robert	HB	20	5'9	165	Martins Ferry, O.	So.
26	BUSH, Jack*	HB	21	6'1	190	Oak Park, Ill.	Sr.
27	HOVEY, William	HB	25	5'10	170	Lake Placid, N. Y.	Sr.
28	SARNA, Edward	HB	21	5'11	175	South River, N. J.	So.
29	DUNLAY, James*	T-G	19	6'2	215	Oakmont, Pa.	Jr.
30	McHUGH, Thomas L.	FB	19	6'1	190	Toledo, O.	So.
31	BUBICK, Raymond	T	18	6'4	222	South Bend, Ind.	So.
32	FLOOD, David*	HB	24	5'10	185	Pittsburgh, Pa.	Jr.
33	SHANNON, Daniel J.	FB	18	6'0	190	Chicago, Ill.	Fr.
37	BARRETT, William C.**	HB	22	5'8	180	River Forest, Ill.	Sr.
40	BIANCO, Donald J.	HB	19	5'11	185	Great Neck, N. Y.	Fr.
42	HEAP, Joseph L.	HB	19	5'11	175	Covington, La.	So.
44	ARRIX, Robert J.	FB	18	5'10	188	Teaneck, N. J.	Fr.
45	RIGALI, Robert J.	HB	19	5'8	172	Oak Park, Ill.	So.
47	GANDER, Fidel J.	FB	21	6'1	196	Chicago, Ill.	Sr.
48	WORDEN, Neil J.	FB	20	5'11	187	Milwaukee, Wis.	So.
49	CAPRARA, Joseph	FB	22	6'0	195	Turtle Creek, Pa.	Sr.
50	HUNTER, Arthur J.	C	18	6'3	222	Akron, O.	So.
51	BOJI, Byron B.**	C	21	6'0	200	Chicago, Ill.	Sr.
52	SZYMANSKI, Richard F.	C	18	6'2	210	Toledo, O.	Fr.
53	SCHRADER, James L.	C	19	6'2	203	Carnegie, Pa.	So.
55	HAMBY, James H.*	C	20	6'2	205	Caruthersville, Mo.	Sr.
56	BECKER, John J.	C	18	6'0	203	Fort Wayne, Ind.	Fr.
57	FRASOR, Richard	C	18	5'11	190	Blue Island, Ill.	Fr.
60	VARRICHIONE, Frank J.	G	19	6'0	207	Natick, Mass.	Fr.
61	TAYLOR, Robert H.	G-T	18	6'2	200	Pekin, Ill.	Fr.
62	SEAMAN, Thomas J.	G	21	5'11	198	Canton, O.	Jr.
63	OSTROWSKI, Chester C.**	G	21	6'1	197	Chicago, Ill.	Sr.
64	BURNS, Paul E.**	G	21	6'2	196	Athens, Pa.	Sr.
65	LEE, John P.	G	19	5'11	190	Medford, Mass.	Fr.
66	ROBST, Paul K.	G	18	5'11	195	Chicago, Ill.	So.
67	PALUMBO, Samuel	G	19	6'0	195	Cleveland, O.	Fr.
68	ALESSANDRINI, Jack F.	G	20	5'11	198	Charlestown, W. Va.	Jr.
70	KELLY, Robert J.*	T	21	6'2	203	Duluth, Minn.	Jr.
71	MAVRAIDES, Menil	T-E	19	6'1	202	Lowell, Mass.	So.
72	ZAMBROSKI, Anthony J.*	T	21	6'0	200	Erie, Pa.	Sr.
73	BUSH, Joseph R.	T	19	6'3	203	Oak Park, Ill.	So.
74	READY, Robert	T	19	6'3	208	Lowell, Mass.	Fr.
75	TONEFF, Robert**	T	21	6'2	230	Barberton, O.	Sr.
76	POEHLER, Frederick C.	T	21	6'4	210	Jackson, Mich.	So.
77	McCARTHY, William	T	20	6'3	210	Pittsburgh, Pa.	Jr.
78	MURPHY, Thomas L.	T	20	6'1	210	Chicago, Ill.	Jr.
79	BARDASH, Virgil	T	20	6'0	206	Gary, Ind.	Jr.
80	WEITHMAN, James C.	E-T	21	6'0	190	Bucyrus, Ohio	Jr.
81	KOHANOWICH, Albert J.	E	21	6'1	189	Hempstead, N. Y.	Jr.
82	O'NEIL, Robert	E	20	6'2	195	Bridgeville, Pa.	Jr.
83	PENZA, Donald F.	E	19	6'1	200	Kenosha, Wis.	So.
84	KAPISH, Robert J.	E	21	6'0	187	Barberton, O.	Sr.
85	MUTSCHELLER, James F. (C)**	E.	21	6'1	198	Beaver Falls, Pa.	Sr.
86	MANGIALARDI, Fred	E	18	6'1	197	Chicago, Ill.	So.
87	HALL, William L.	E.	19	6'5	205	Cincinnati, O.	So.
88	CABRAL, Walter K.	E.	19	6'3	198	Honolulu, Hawaii	Fr.
89	GOMOLA, Stephen T.	E	18	6'0	180	Delancey, Pa.	Fr.
90	MATZ, Paul A.	E	18	6'1	191	Chicago, Ill.	Fr.
91	KATCHIK, Joseph	E	20	6'9	255	Plymouth, Pa.	So.
92	CYTERSKI, Leonard J.	E	18	5'11	188	Erie, Pa.	Fr.

* DENOTES MONOGRAMS WON
Gander, Barrett and Hamby Won Monograms in 1949 But Not in 1950.

1951
Coach: Frank Leahy
Captain: Jim Mutscheller

S.29	W	Indiana	48-6	H	55,790
O.5	W	Detroit (Nt)	40-6	N1	52,331
O.13	L	S.M.U. (U)	20-27	H	c58,240
O.20	W	Pittsburgh	33-0	A	c60,127
O.27	W	Purdue	30-9	H	c57,890
N.3	W	Navy	19-0	N2	44,237
N.10	L	Michigan State	0-35	A	c51,296
N.17	°W	North Carolina	12-7	A	c44,500
N.24	T	Iowa (0:55-ND)	20-20	H	40,685
D.1	W	So. California (R)	19-12	A	55,783

(7-2-1) 241-122 520,879

N1—at Briggs Stadium, Detroit; N2—at Baltimore
°Notre Dame's 400th victory

S * M * U
vs
NOTRE DAME
NOTRE DAME STADIUM ★ OCTOBER 13 ★ 1951

OFFICIAL PROGRAM ★ THIRTY-FIVE CENTS

NOTRE DAME'S 400TH WI

notre dame 12

north carolina . . 7

Chapel Hill, N. C., Nov. 17—Fighting to the end, an aroused North Carolina eleven came within a hand's breadth of victory before bowing to the University of Notre Dame in a 12-7 thriller.

Freshman Gene Carrabine batted away a fourth down Carolina pass in the end zone late in the final period to save the game, which was played before 44,500 Rebel fans in Kenan Memorial Stadium.

The Tarheels were definitely "up" as they went all out to win one for Coach Carl Snavely, under fire for the team's disastrous season.

STATISTICS

North Carolina		Notre Dame
12	First downs	22
144	Rushing yardage	278
68	Passing yardage	118
14	Passes attempted	23
4	Passes completed	10
3	Passes had intercepted	3
6	Punts	8
37.3	Punting average	30.4
2	Fumbles lost	3
25	Yards penalized	90

1951 Season Statistics

SCORING

	TD	PAT	FG	Points
Worden	8	0	0	48
Lattner	6	0	0	36
Barrett	5	0	0	30
Petitbon	4	0	0	24
Mavraides	0	19	1	22
Mazur	3	0	0	18
Reynolds	3	0	0	18
Mutscheller	2	0	0	12
Heap	2	0	0	12
Ostrowski	1	0	0	6
Guglielmi	1	0	0	6
Gander	1	0	0	6
Joseph	0	3	0	3

PASSING

	Carey	Guglielmi	Lattner	Mazur	Heap	Petitbon
Attempted	11	53	2	110	3	1
Completed	7	27	1	48	0	0
Had Intercepted	0	4	0	12	0	0
TD Passes	0	0	0	5	0	0
Yardage	61	438	23	645	0	0
Percentages	.636	.510	.500	.436	.000	.000

RUSHING

	Times Carried	Yardage	Average
Joseph	2	11	5.5
Paterra	19	98	5.2
Lattner	68	341	5.0
Petitbon	48	227	4.7
Heap	38	166	4.4
McHugh	7	29	4.1
Reynolds	93	375	4.0
Gander	11	42	3.8
Worden	181	676	3.7
Barrett	69	210	3.0

PASS RECEIVING

	No. Caught	Yards	TDs
Mutscheller	20	305	2
Ostrowski	15	204	1
Worden	12	111	0
Lattner	8	157	0
Barrett	8	136	2
Petitbon	8	105	0
Reynolds	6	80	0
Heap	2	25	0
Mavraides	2	17	0
Toneff	1	21	0
Penza	1	6	0

PASS INTERCEPTIONS

	Number Intercepted	Yards Returned
Lattner	5	66
Gaudreau	4	52
Szymanski	3	5
Carrabine	2	3
Petitbon	2	3
Shannon	2	0
Alessandrini	1	

STATISTICS FOR 1951

Notre Dame		Opponents
241	POINTS SCORED	122
166	FIRST DOWNS	120
112	Rushing	72
49	Passing	43
5	Penalties	5
2090	YARDS RUSHING	1294
593	Times Carried	414
3.4	Yards-per-try	3.1
1167	YARDS PASSING	1235
180	Passes Attempted	220
83	Passes Completed	95
.461	Completion Percentage	.432
19	Passes Intercepted By	16
129	Yards Interception Returned	228
3257	TOTAL OFFENSE	2529
66	PUNTS	71
2281	Total Yardage	2498
34.6	Average Length	35.2
401	Yards Punts Returned	140
29	FUMBLES	36
8	Ball Lost	22

PUNT RETURNS

	Number Returned	Yards Returned
Petitbon	14	189
Lattner	10	91
Barrett	5	107
Whelan	1	9
Heap	1	5

PUNTING

	Number	Yardage	Average
Barrett	40	1440	36.0
Lattner	26	841	32.4

KICK-OFF RETURNS

	Number Returned	Yards Returned
Flood	6	88
Reynolds	5	84
Barrett	4	86
Petitbon	3	115
Heap	2	50
Ostrowski	2	13
Mutscheller	1	13

1951 ALL-OPPONENT TEAM

Ends:
    *Bob Carey, Michigan State
    Darrell Brewster, Purdue

Tackles: Fritz Davis, Navy
    **Don Coleman, Michigan State

Guards:
    Herschel Forester, Southern Methodist
    Pat Cannamella, Southern California
    Joe Skibinski, Purdue

Center:
    Dick Hightower, Southern Methodist

Backs:
    Al Dorow, Michigan State
    Fred Benners, Southern Methodist
    Frank Gifford, Southern California
    Bill Reichardt, Iowa

* These men were chosen on the 1950 All-Opponent Team.
** Coleman was named to the All-Opponent squad in 1949 also.
(Twelve man team because of a tie between Cannemella and Skibinski at guard position.)

FIRST ROW—(left to right): Les Traver, George Williams, John Powers, Frank Grau, Roger Wilke, Nick Buoniconti (Co-Capt.), Norb Roy, (Co-Capt.), Joe Carollo, Bob Bill, George Sefcik, Angelo Dabiero, Tom Hecomovich, Gene Viola. SECOND ROW — (left to right): David Steube (Manager), Gerry Gray, Clay Schulz, Jim Loula, Tom Liggio, Dick Naab, Bill Snyder, Jim Mikacich, Bill Ford, Joe Perkowski, Bill Ahern, Steve Kolski, Ed Hoerster, Wally Dant (Manager). THIRD ROW—(left to right): Nick DePola, Dennis Murphy, Joe Kantor, Leo Caito, Norb Rascher, Dan Kolasinski, Ed Rutkowski, Charlie O'Hara, Dennis Phillips, Daryle Lamonica, Mike Lind, Joe Maxwell, Frank Minik, Bill Kutzavitch, John Slafkosky, John Zimmer (Manager). FORTH ROW—(left to right): Jim Sherlock, Dan Reardon, George Bednar, Dave Humenik, Bob Secret, Mickey Bitsko, Marty Olosky, Bill Pfeiffer, Denis Szot, Jim Kelly, Tom MacDonald, Frank Budka, Bill Burns, Pat Keneally, Glen Pierson, Brian Boulac. FIFTH ROW—(left to right): Bob Lehmann, Paul Costa, Jim Snowden, Warren Stephens, Mike DiCarlo, Jon Prusmack, Harold Vogel, Greg Divis, Don Candido, John Anton, John Dow, Boyd Jajesnica, John Simon, John Barnard, Joe Farrell, Jack Cullen, John Murray, Phil Kienast, Ed Burke. SIXTH ROW—(left to right): John Geraghty, Lionel Rodgers, Bill Mundee, Nick Etten, Wayne Zdanowicz, Mike Minnig, Tom Meagher, Greg Wood, Tom Finneran, Frank Fee, Ron Vomero, Bob Lesko, Nick Muller, Joe Monahan, Wayne Allen, Tom Goberville, Lou Lucas

1952

Coach: Frank Leahy
Captain: James F. Alessandrini

S.27	T	Pennsylvania	7-7	A	c74,518
O.4	W	Texas (U)	14-3	A	c67,666
O.11	L	Pittsburgh (U)	19-22	H	45,507
O.18	W	Purdue	26-14	A	49,000
O.25	W	North Carolina	34-14	H	54,338
N.1	W	Navy	17-6	N	61,927
N.8	W	Oklahoma (U)	27-21	H	c57,446
N.15	L	Michigan State	3-21	A	c52,472
N.22	W	Iowa	27-0	A	46,600
N.29	W	So. California (U)	9-0	H	c58,394
	(7-2-1)		183-108		567,868

N—at Cleveland

AP POLL

1952

1. Michigan State
2. Georgia Tech
3. NOTRE DAME
4. Oklahoma
5. U.S.C.
6. U.C.L.A.
7. Mississippi
8. Tennessee
9. Alabama
10. Texas

UPI POLL

1952

1. Michigan State
2. Georgia Tech
3. NOTRE DAME
4. Oklahoma
5. U.S.C.
6. U.C.L.A.
7. Mississippi
8. Tennessee
9. Alabama
10. Wisconsin

UNIVERSITY OF NOTRE DAME
SQUAD

No.	Name	Pos.	Age	Ht.	Wt.	Hometown
2	Carey, Thomas F. * '55	QB	19	5-10	175	Chicago, Ill.
3	Guglielmi, Ralph V. * '55	QB	19	6-0	180	Columbus, O.
4	Bucci, Donald '55	QB	19	6-0	180	Youngstown, O.
6	Martin, Robert L. '54	QB	20	6-2	185	Davenport, Ia.
7	Buczkiewicz, Edward '53	QB	21	6-0	177	Chicago, Ill.
8	Bigelow, James '55	QB	18	5-11	170	Glenshaw, Pa.
9	Galvin, Patrick J. '55	QB	18	6-0	185	Detroit, Mich.
10	Paterra, Francis F. * '54	HB	20	5-11	190	McKeesport, Pa.
14	Lattner, John J. * '54	HB	19	6-1	190	Chicago, Ill.
15	Callaghan, Leo P. '55	HB	19	6-1	185	Passaic, N. J.
16	Morrissey, Rockne J. '54	HB	20	5-9	165	Cincinnati, O.
17	Whelan, Jack D. * '53	HB	21	5-11	180	Miami, Fla.
18	Reynolds, Paul R. * '55	HB	19	6-0	180	Springfield, Ill.
19	Getschow, Lee E. '53	HB	20	6-0	175	Kenilworth, Ill.
20	Carrabine, Eugene * '55	HB	19	6-1	178	Gary, Ind.
24	Joseph, Robert '54	HB	21	5-9	165	Martins Ferry, O.
28	Sarna, Edward '54	HB	22	5-11	175	South River, N. J.
29	Galardo, Armando '54	HB	20	5-10	170	Watertown, N. Y.
30	McHugh, Thomas L. '54	FB	20	6-1	190	Toledo, Ohio
32	Flood, David ** '53	HB	24	5-10	185	Pittsburgh, Pa.
33	Shannon, Daniel J. * '55	FB	19	6-0	190	Chicago, Ill.
42	Heap, Joseph L. * '55	HB	20	5-11	175	Covington, La.
44	Arrix, Robert J. '55	FB	19	5-10	188	Teaneck, N. J.
45	Rigali, Robert J. '54	HB	20	5-8	172	Oak Park, Ill.
48	Worden, Neil J. * '54	FB	21	5-11	185	Milwaukee, Wis.
49	Stephens, Jack '55	HB	19	6'2	190	Chicago, Ill.
52	Szymanski, Richard * '55	C	19	6-2	210	Toledo, O.
53	Schrader, James L. * '54	C	20	6-2	206	Carnegie, Pa.
54	Nowack, Arthur C. '54	C	21	6-1	208	Rochester, N. Y.
56	Cook, Edward J. '55	C	19	6-1	210	Philadelphia, Pa.
60	Varrichione, Frank * '55	T-G	20	6-0	207	Natick, Mass.
62	Seaman, Thomas J. * '53	G	22	5-11	198	Canton, O.
63	Frasor, Richard '55	G-C	19	5-11	190	Blue Island, Ill.
65	Lee, Jack * '55	G	20	5-11	190	Medford, Mass.
66	Robst, Paul K. '54	G	20	5-11	195	Chicago, Ill.
67	Palumbo, Samuel * '55	G	20	6-0	195	Cleveland, O.
68	Alessandrini, Jack * (C) '53	G	21	5-11	197	Charleston, W. Va.
69	Bardash, Virgil * '53	G-T	22	6-0	206	Gary, Ind.
71	Taylor, Robert H. '55	T	20	6-2	200	Pekin, Ill.
73	Bush, Joseph R. * '54	T	20	6-3	206	Oak Park, Ill.
74	Ready, Robert * '55	T	20	6-3	208	Lowell, Mass.
75	Pasquesi, Anthony L. '55	T	19	6-4	212	Chicago, Ill.
76	Poehler, Fred * '54	T	22	6-4	210	Jackson, Mich.
78	Murphy, Thomas F. ** '53	T	22	6-1	210	Chicago, Ill.
79	Weithman, James C. † '53	T	22	6-0	190	Bucyrus, O.
80	Hunter, Arthur * '54	E	19	6-3	221	Akron, O.
81	Kohanowich, Albert '53	E	22	6-1	189	Hempstead, N. Y.
82	O'Neil, Robert * '53	E	21	6-2	195	Bridgeville, Pa.
83	Penza, Donald * '54	E	20	6-1	200	Kenosha, Wis.
85	Mavraides, Menil * '54	G	19	6-1	205	Lowell, Mass.
86	Mangialardi, Fred * '54	E	19	6-1	195	Chicago, Ill.
88	Cabral, Walter K. * '55	E	20	6-3	205	Honolulu, Hawaii
90	Matz, Paul A. '55	E	19	6-1	191	Chicago, Ill.

*—Denotes Monogram Won.

Notre Dame	14	6	0	6	26
Purdue	7	0	0	7	14

STATISTICS

Notre Dame		Purdue
16	First downs	10
195	Rushing yardage	63
116	Passing yardage	196
12	Passes attempted	30
7	Passes completed	13
4	Passes had intercepted	0
4	Punts	6
35	Punting average	29
3	Fumbles lost	8
103	Yards penalized	60

Lafayette, Ind., Oct. 19—Taking a special liking to the role of underdog, an alert Notre Dame squad shrugged off the odds for the second time in three weeks to upset the Big Ten's top-ranking Purdue Boilermakers 26-14 here today before 52,000 Ross-Ade Stadium fans.

The tale is told in the fumble column. There were 21 juggles in all, the tally reading 11-10 for Purdue. But the score on fumbles recovered read 15-6 for the Irish and that was the ball game.

This was the 24th annual renewal of the hard-fought intra-state rivalry, with the Irish running their edge to 17-5-2 in the overall series. The last Boilermaker defeat was one year and seven games ago—to this same Notre Dame squad.

Jackie Lee, rugged sophomore middleguard, won himself "Lineman of the Week" honors with three enemy fumbles to show for his afternoon's work. Alert offensive guard Tom Seaman recovered two of the Irish miscues.

The Irish took the lead on the fourth play of the afternoon. Lee didn't waste any time making his first recovery; it came on the kickoff on the 24. Heap and Lattner teamed to take it into paydirt. Lattner fumbled taking it across, but tackle Joe Bush was on the alert and recovered the six points rolling around loose in the end zone. Mavraides converted and Purdue was wondering what happened.

The Boilermakers retaliated midway through the period with a 28-yard Samuels to Flowers pass to knot it at 7-7. The Irish turned around and came back downfield in twelve plays, with Carey at the helm. After Notre Dame shifted Purdue offsides for the second time on the 2, Worden banged over and Mavraides again made it good.

As time was running out in the first half, the Irish tallied again. A recovered fumble set the stage for Guglielmi's desperation 47-yard scoring pass to Lattner, and the Irish left the field with a 20-7 half-time lead.

The third period was scoreless and saturated with fumbles. Midway through the last quarter the Boilermakers recovered an Irish fumble on the Notre Dame 35. On the second play Flowers caught another scoring pass, this one from Evans, and Samuels' PAT made it 20-14 with 7:30 to play. Things were getting tight when Carey, with a third and fifteen situation on his own 32, came through with a 41-yard strike to Art Hunter. Lattner and Worden bulled to the Boilermaker 12, Carey hit Penza on the 3 with a jump pass, and Worden barreled over. Purdue was beaten, and the clock ran out.

And the Irish had gotten off the floor against the top team in the Big Ten. They now looked homeward, scene of their first defeat, with no little consternation. For Coach Carl Snavely's polio-ridden but perennially-difficult Carolina Tarheels were on the Notre Dame arena.

Notre Dame, Ind., Nov. 8—Here's the score-by-score account of the first meeting between Oklahoma and Notre Dame on the gridiron. This initial meeting will go down in history, and if this is any indication of what is yet to come, break out the record books and stand back out of the way!

FIRST QUARTER: A Lattner punt took a bad bounce and Oklahoma took over on the ND 27 with less than 3 minutes left in the period. Quarterback Eddie Crowder found halfback Billy Vessels open along the left sideline and hit him with a 27-yard scoring pass. Leake converted, 7-0, at 12:40.

SECOND QUARTER: After O'Neil's recovery, the Irish moved 60 yards in 9 plays, Guglielmi zeroing Heap with a 17-yard scoring pass at 11:03. Arrix matched Leake, and it was 7-7. One minute and a half later, Vessels broke off tackle and went 62 yards to score. Leake made it 14-7 at halftime.

THIRD QUARTER: Lattner intercepted a Crowder pass and rammed it back to the Sooner 8. Three plays later, at 8:57, Worden bulled over from a yard out. Arrix sweated it out, but matched Leake again, 14-14.

Two minutes later Vessels was at it again, cracking off tackle for 47 yards to score. Leake automatically made it 21-14.

FOURTH QUARTER: Worden bucked over 35 seconds after the start, carrying the ball seven straight times to cap a 79-yard march. Arrix clicked, 21-21. On the ensuing kickoff, Kohanowich recovered after Shannon's earth-shaking tackle on the Sooner 24. Lattner went through for 17; a penalty put the ball on the 2. Worden got to the 1, and then Carey dove over to give the Irish the lead for the first time, with better than 13 minutes left to play. Arrix's extra point try was blocked, and it was 27-21. Better than 13 minutes later, it was still 27-21.

———————————

And the Irish had pulled it off. The first half of the murderous 1-2 assignment was successfully completed. Next week was another big one . . . Could the Irish stay up?

	First	Second	Third	Fourth	Final
Notre Dame	0	7	7	13	27
Oklahoma	7	7	7	0	21

STATISTICS

Notre Dame		Oklahoma
23	First Downs	13
219	Rushing Yardage	313
135	Passing Yardage	44
22	Passes Attempted	10
13	Passes Completed	2
1	Passes Had Intercepted	1
8	Punts	5
38	Punting Average	37
2	Fummbles Lost	5
70	Yards Penalized	37

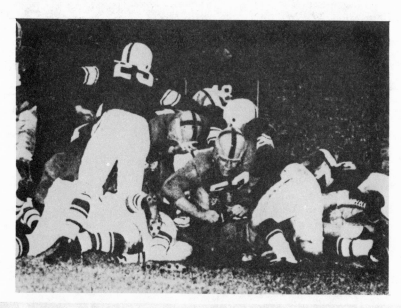

WINNING TOUCHDOWN is scored by Carey, somewhere behind Mavraides (left of center), Schrader (55), and Seaman (on bottom).

| Notre Dame | 0 | 0 | 3 | 0 | 3 |
| Mich. State | 0 | 0 | 14 | 7 | 21 |

STATISTICS

Notre Dame		Michigan State
13	First Downs	11
147	Rushing Yardage	128
150	Passing Yardage	41
21	Passes Attempted	21
10	Passes Completed	5
1	Passes Had Intercepted	1
7	Punts	9
37	Punting Average	45
7	Fumbles Lost	1
89	Yards Penalized	55

East Lansing, Mich., Nov. 15—A dream which had been taking shape for a week was turned into a nightmare in the short space of 20 minutes here this afternoon as seven heart-breaking fumbles flung Notre Dame down from the crest she almost scaled and handed Michigan State a 21-3 gift. Some 53,000 fans packed Macklin Field to watch the Irish try to pull off the biggest 1-2 upset in football history on succeeding weekends, only to have Leahy's game youngsters become the 22nd victims in a long State undefeated string.

The neighborhood rivalry now stands at 15-5 in favor of the Irish, who last won in 1949.

An omen of what was in store came on the first play from scrimmage after the State kickoff. Quarterback Tom Carey fumbled on the Notre Dame 34 and State recovered. But State didn't score that time, nor did the powerful Spartans score on the two other Irish fumbles in the first half. With the defensive line of O'Neil, Palumbo, Lee, Ready, and Matz completely throttling the high-stepping Spartan offense, backed up by Szymanski, Shannon, Flood, Alessandrini, and Lattner, who took care of anybody that managed to wander into the secondary, an upset was still highly possible as the teams left the field at the half in a scoreless deadlock.

On the first series of downs after the second half kickoff, State momentarily caught the fumbling bug and Lattner recovered on the Spartan 11. Between the tough State defensive line and the whistle-happy officials, the Irish only got to the 6 in the next three plays. But on fourth down, Bob Arrix broke the scoring ice and temporarily shoved the Irish out in front, 3-0, as he booted a 17-yard field goal.

Everything stayed the same for the next 8 minutes, with Lattner and State quarterback Yewcic still batting punts back and forth like a ping pong ball. Then, with 5 minutes to go in the third period, the proverbial roof fell in. The Irish fumbled on their own 33, and State recovered. Lattner's interception on the 10 interrupted the Spartan "drive."

The defensive platoon had no sooner sat down, however, when State linebacker Dick Tamburo made his third straight recovery on the 13, and back they went. The Spartans still couldn't do anything, so the Irish were penalized back to the 1, from where State finally took the hint and scored. McAuliffe's touchdown and Slonac's conversion added up to a 7-3 Spartan lead.

Notre Dame took the kickoff and promptly fumbled on the 10 on the first play. The defensive line held though, and took over on the 21. So what happened on the next play? You guessed it, and a minute later another penalty had the ball on the Irish 1 again. McAuliffe stumbled over and Slonac made it 14-3. Paced by Lattner's 38-yard run early in the fourth period, the Irish put together their last real threat, but Guglielmi was hung up heart-breaking inches short of a first down on the Spartan 1. With four minutes left an interception set up the final State score from the Notre Dame 24. Slonac, evidently sick of kicking extra points, carried the ball around right end for one of the longer Spartan runs of the day, and, after he converted, it was 21-3.

They might have done it, but fate wouldn't have it that way. Yet the Irish had gone down fighting, in keeping with their great tradition. And there could be no backward glances, not with the Iowa jinx team on deck next week.

SCORING

PLAYER	TD	PAT	FG	POINTS
Worden	10	0	0	60
Lattner	5	0	0	30
Heap	5	0	0	30
Arix	0	10	3	19
McHugh	2	6	0	12
Mavraides	0	6	0	6
Hunter	1	0	0	6
Guglielmi	1	0	0	6
Carey	1	0	0	6
Bush	1	0	0	6
O'Neil	0	0	0	*2

*Safety

RUSHING

PLAYER	TC	YDS.	AVE.	TD
Lattner	148	734	4.9	2
Worden	150	504	3.4	1
Heap	89	383	4.3	1
Paterra	28	130	4.6	0
McHugh	32	124	3.9	0

PASSES CAUGHT

PLAYER	NC	YDS.	TD
Heap	29	407	4
Lattner	17	252	0
Hunter	16	246	1
Worden	16	80	0
Penza	11	164	0

PASSING

PLAYER	ATTEMPTED	COMPLETED	HAD INTERCEPTED	YARDAGE	PCT.
Guglielmi	142	61	9	683	.429
Carey	41	20	3	250	.489
Heap	13	7	1	130	.538

PASS INTERCEPTIONS

PLAYER	NUMBER	YARDS
Lattner	4	58
Whelan	4	35

KICKOFF RETURNS

PLAYER	NUMBER	YARDS	TD
Heap	6	145	1
Reynolds	5	94	0
Worden	5	75	0

PUNTING

PLAYER	NUMBER	YARDS	AVE.
Lattner	64	2345	36.6

PUNT RETURNS

PLAYER	NUMBER	YARDS	TD
Heap	10	126	1
Reynolds	10	104	0
Lattner	7	113	1

OPPONENT'S FUMBLES RECOVERED: Flood (5), Lattner (3), Shannon(3), O'Neil (3), Lee (3).   BLOCKED PUNT: Lee.

1953 NOTRE DAME FOOTBALL ROSTER, ALPHABETIZED

No.	Name	Pos.	Age	Ht.	Wt.	Hometown	High School	Class
62	Biscegia, Patrick G.	g	22	5-10	190	Worcester, Mass.	Commerce	So.
73	**Bush, Joseph R.	t	20	6-3	208	Oak Park, Ill.	St. Ambrose (Davenport, Ia.)	Sr.
88	*Cabral, Walter K.	e	20	6-3	205	Honolulu, Hawaii	St. Louis	Jr.
2	**Carey, Thomas F.	qb	20	5-10	175	Chicago, Ill.	Mt. Carmel	Jr.
	Dumas, Jack	e	18	6-3	190	Grand Rapids, Mich.	Catholic Central	So.
82	Edmonds, Wayne	e-t	19	6-0	195	Canonsburg, Pa.	Canonsburg	So.
32	Fitzgerald, Richard P.	fb	20	5-11	190	Chicago, Ill.	St. George	So.
63	Frasor, Richard	c-g	20	5-11	190	Blue Island, Ill.	Mt. Carmel	Jr.
34	Gaffney, John J.	fb	19	6-1	190	Chicago, Ill.	St. Ignatius	So.
81	George, Donald H.	e	19	6-4	205	Dunbar, Pa.	Dunbar	So.
3	**Guglielmi, Ralph V.	qb	19	6-0	180	Columbus, Ohio	Grandview	Jr.
42	**Heap, Joseph L.	hb	21	5-11	180	Abita Springs, La.	Holy Cross (New Orleans)	Jr.
49	Hendricks, Richard J.	hb	19	6-1	180	Danville, Ill.	Schlarman	So.
80	**Hunter, Arthur	t	20	6-3	226	Akron, Ohio	St. Vincent	Sr.
89	Kapish, Eugene B.	e	18	6-1	193	Barberton, O.	Barberton	So.
78	Kegaly, John A.	t	19	6-3	207	Chicago, Ill.	St. Ignatius	So.
40	Keller, Richard W.	hb	18	6-0	175	Toledo, Ohio	Central Catholic	So.
79	Lasch, Robert W.	t	18	6-3	212	Clairton, Pa.	Clairton	So.
14	**Lattner, John J.	hb	20	6-1	190	Chicago, Ill.	Fenwick	Sr.
65	**Lee, Jack	g	21	5-11	190	Medford, Mass.	Malden Catholic	Jr.
72	Lemek, Raymond E.	t	18	6-1	207	Sioux City, Ia.	Heelan	So.
86	**Mangialardi, Fred	e-g	19	6-1	195	Chicago, Ill.	St. Phillip	Sr.
70	Martell, Eugene J.	t	19	6-3	211	Midland, Pa.	Lincoln	So.
90	*Matz, Paul A.	e	19	6-1	191	Chicago, Ill.	Mt. Carmel	Jr.
85	**Mavraides, Menil	g	20	6-1	205	Lowell, Mass.	Lowell	Sr.
30	*McHugh, Thomas F.	fb	20	6-1	195	Toledo, Ohio	Central Catholic	Sr.
61	McMullan, John G.	g	19	5-10	203	Hoboken, N. J.	Demerest	So.
51	Mense, James J.	c	18	5-11	205	Hamilton, Ohio	Hamilton Catholic	So.
77	Nicula, George D.	t	19	6-2	204	Warren, Ohio	Harding	So.
67	**Palumbo, Samuel	g	20	6-0	203	Cleveland, Ohio	Collinwood	Jr.
75	Pasquesi, Anthony L.	t	19	6-4	212	Chicago, Ill.	St. Phillip	Jr.
83	**Penza, Donald (Capt.)	e	21	6-1	200	Kenosha, Wis.	St. Catherine (Racine)	Sr.
37	Raich, Nicholas S.	fb	19	5-10	185	Milwaukee, Wis.	Marquette	So.
74	**Ready, Robert	t	20	6-3	212	Lowell, Mass.	Lowell	Jr.
9	Schaefer, Donald T.	qb	19	5-11	185	Pittsburgh, Pa.	Central Catholic	So.
53	**Schrader, James L.	c	20	6-2	210	Carnegie, Pa.	Scott Twp.	Sr.
33	**Shannon, Daniel J.	fb	19	6-0	190	Chicago, Ill.	Mt. Carmel	Jr.
52	**Szymanski, Richard F.	c	20	6-2	212	Toledo, Ohio	Libbey	Jr.
60	**Varrichione, Frank	t	21	6-0	205	Natick, Mass.	Natick	Jr.
41	Washington, Richard M.	hb	18	6-1	195	Vanderbilt, Pa.	Dunbar Twp.	So.
38	Wilson, George A.	hb	19	5-11	185	Polo, Ill.	Community	So.
48	**Worden, Neil J.	fb	21	5-11	185	Milwaukee, Wis.	Pulaski	Sr.
84	Zajeski, Benedict J.	e	19	6-3	204	Chicago, Ill.	Mt. Carmel	So.

*Denotes Monograms Won

1953

AP POLL

1. Maryland
2. NOTRE DAME
3. Michigan State
4. Oklahoma
5. U.C.L.A.
6. Rice
7. Illinois
8. Georgia Tech
9. Iowa
10. West Virginia

UPI POLL

1953

1. Maryland
2. NOTRE DAME
3. Michigan State
4. U.C.L.A.
5. Oklahoma
6. Rice
7. Illinois
8. Texas
9. Georgia Tech
10. Iowa

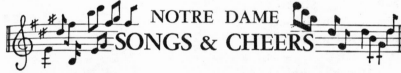

NOTRE DAME SONGS & CHEERS

NOTRE DAME, OUR MOTHER

Notre Dame, our Mother,
Tender, strong and true.
Proudly in the heavens,
Gleams the gold and blue,
Glory's mantle cloaks three,
Golden is thy fame,
And our hearts forever,
Praise thee, Notre Dame.
And our hearts forever,
Love thee, Notre Dame.

VICTORY MARCH

Rally, sons of Notre Dame;
Sing her glory and sound her fame,
Raise her Gold and Blue
And cheer with voices true:
Rah, rah, for Notre Dame (U rah, rah)
We will fight in ev-ry game,
Strong of heart and true to her name
We will ne'er forget her
And we'll cheer her ever
Loyal to Notre Dame
    (Chorus)
Cheer, cheer for old Notre Dame.
Wake up the echoes cheering her name,
Send a volley cheer on high,
Shake down the thunder from the sky.
What though the odds be great or small?
Old Notre Dame will win over all,
While her loyal sons are marching
Onward to victory.

NEW LOCOMOTIVE

Rah, Rah, Rah, Rah
Not-re Dame U!
(Repeat three times increasing speed)

WHEN IRISH BACKS GO MARCHING BY

Rah! Rah! Rah!
Up! Notre Dame men! Answer the cry,
Gathering foemen fling to the sky.
Fight! Fight! Fight!
Brave hosts advancing challenge your name
Rah! Rah! Rah!
    (Chorus)
And when the Irish backs go marching by
The cheering thousands shout their battle cry:
For Notre Dame men are marching into the game,
Fighting the fight for you, Notre Dame,
And when that Irish line goes smashing through,
They'll sweep the foemen's ranks away;
When Notre Dame men fight for Gold and Blue,
Then Notre Dame men will win that day.

HIKE SONG

The march is on, no brain or brawn
Can stop the charge of fighting men.
Lou rings the cry of grim defy
Of hard attack let loose again.
Oh, it's the hike, hike of victory.
The call, to rise and strike.
For Notre Dame men are winning
When Notre Dame hears hike, hike, hike.
    (Chorus)
Hark to the cheering song rising high,
Hark to the roar as the ranks go marching by;
Shoulder to shoulder chanting her glorious name.
Burn high your fires and swing along for Notre Dame.

DOWN THE LINE

On down the line! beside the glory of her name,
On down the line! beneath the colors of an ancient fame,
On down the line; another day for her proclaim;
Go down the line for Notre Dame!

SPELL IT OUT!

N-O-T-R-E D-A-M-E
Notre Dame! Notre Dame!
Notre Dame!

YEA BO

Y——E——A (Slowly)
BO
Notre Dame, Let's Go!

THUNDERCLAP

Clap hands slowly at start in unison, following cleerleaders for increase of speed. At signal, yell:

NOTRE DAME

BIG U.N.D.

U.N.D. Rah, Rah
U.N.D. Rah, Rah
Hoo-Rah, Hoo-Rah
U.N.D. Rah, Rah
Team, Team, Team.

SKYROCKET

Ssssssssssss
BOOM
Aaaaaaaaaaa
(Whistle)
NOTRE DAME

HE'S A MAN

He's a Man!
Who's a Man?
He's a Notre Dame Man!
————, ————, ————

1953

Coach: Frank Leahy
Captain: Donald Penza

S.26	W	Oklahoma	28-21	A	c59,500
O.3	W	Purdue	37-7	A	49,135
O.17	W	Pittsburgh	23-14	H	c57,998
O.24	W	Georgia Tech	27-14	H	c58,254
O.31	W	Navy	38-7	H	c58,154
N.7	W	Pennsylvania	28-20	A	c74,711
N.14	W	North Carolina	34-14	A	c43,000
N.21	T	Iowa (0:06-ND)	14-14	H	c56,478
N.28	W	So. California	48-14	A	97,952
D.5	W	S.M.U.	40-14	H	55,522
	(9-0-1)		317-139		610,704

NOTRE DAME ENDS GEORGIA TECH STREAK 27-14

Joe Heap breaks away in the first quarter for 33 yards to set up the first Notre Dame touchdown. Ray Lemek (72) and Neil Worden (48) lead the Irish blockers.

Notre Dame, Ind., Oct. 24 — The Notre Dame cyclone struck again under a dark sky and out of the wreckage came the shattered remnants of Georgia Tech's 31-game victory streak. Before 58,254 onlookers the Fighting Irish wrote a 27-14 finis to the Engineers' success story. The Southerners were tough but not tough enough. The classy Irish backs, operating behind a line which provided them with ample opportunities, tore out huge chunks of yardage while the dangerous Georgia Tech ball-carriers were grounded by the brilliant Notre Dame line.

NOTRE DAME		PENN
18	First downs	16
234	Rushing yardage	131
95	Passing yardage	157
16	Passes attempted	18
5	Passes completed	10
1	Passes had intercepted	3
24.0	Punting average	38.0
1	Fumbles lost	0
80	Yards penalized	11

Philadelphia, Pa., Nov. 7 — A Penn team which was nearly run off snowbound Franklin Field in the first half returned from the half-time chat with Coach George Munger to give Notre Dame an anxious afternoon before finally allowing the Irish to leave town with a shaky 28-20 win.

Quite likely a sterling exhibition by John Lattner was all that saved the greenshirts from their first disaster of the season. Lattner raced all over the turf with the pigskin and was an absolute marvel on the receiving end of kicks. His heroics helped to offset fine performances by Penn's Ed Gramigna, Joe Varaitis, and Dick Shanafelt.

The upstart Pennsylvanians scored the first time they had the ball, but the lead lasted about nine seconds, or as long as it took Lattner to race back 93 yards with the kickoff.

The first play of the second period found the befuddled Quakers on the short end of a 21-7 score and apparently going downhill after touchdowns by Guglielmi and Schaefer.

It was still a 21-7 affair until Penn took the second half kickoff and hit pay dirt in twelve plays. Lattner, working overtime, bounced back 56 yards with the kick to set up the winning touchdown, a 23 yard pitch from Guglielmi to Heap. However, Gramigna still had a touchdown drive in the bag as he out-maneuvered a faltering Irish defense for the last score of the game.

STATISTICS

NOTRE DAME		IOWA
21	First downs	10
229	Rushing yardage	189
129	Passing yardage	9
30	Passes attempted	12
12	Passes completed	3
3	Passes had intercepted	1
37.1	Punting average	33.4
0	Fumbles lost	1
65	Yards penalized	60

Notre Dame, Ind., Nov. 21—No coach anywhere could ever be prouder of his team than Frank Leahy on this day. In a fitting ending, a bruised and battered Irishman by the name of Daniel Shannon picked a football thrown by Ralph Guglielmi out of the foggy air as he ran into the Iowa end zone with six seconds left in the combat. The ensuing kick by Don Schaefer gave Notre Dame a 14-14 tie with an Iowa squad which played as no team had ever played against Notre Dame this season. The 56,478 spectators sat amazed as the Iowans overcame almost all obstacles in the path to victory. One they could not overcome. That was the fierce tenacity with which the Irish fought and conquered imminent disaster.

Dusty Rice's interception midway of the first period set the Hawkeyes up in business on their 29. Eight plays later Ed Vincent galloped 12 yards for the initial score and Notre Dame trailed, 7-0.

The Iowans' stout defensive play preserved the shaky lead until the Irish started racing the clock towards the end of the half. With a mere two seconds left, Shannon crept into the end zone and received a pitch from Guglielmi. Schaefer's boot produced a stalemate as the half ended.

A savage scoreless battle of the lines occupied the spotlight throughout the third quarter and part of the final stanza until the Hawkeyes parlayed a stray aerial into a 14-7 margin with two minutes remaining.

Neil Worden lugged back the kickoff 21 yards to the Notre Dame 42, from where the Irish set about picking up the broken pieces of an undefeated season. Heap passed to Lattner, Guglielmi threw to Lattner, to Heap, to Lattner again, and finally located Shannon in the end zone just six seconds before it was all over. Too late Iowa had discovered what Frank Leahy already knew—the Irish will not quit.

Notre Dame's Johnny Lattner Meets And Conquers Famed Four Horsemen

NEW YORK, Dec. 8 (P)—Johnny Lattner met the Four Horsemen, and vice versa, today and by a 4-1 vote it was decided that Johnny is a good enough football player to make anyone's team. The two generations of Notre Dame stars were brought together as Lattner received the Heisman Trophy, awarded annually by the Downtown Athletic Club to the outstanding college football player of the year.

They were Lattner, a poised, 21-year-old who has earned All-America honors twice and led Notre Dame to an undefeated 1953 season, and the four great backs of 1924-25 — Harry Stuhldreher, Jim Crowley, Elmer Layden and Don Miller — who were known as the "Four Horsemen."

Lattner was the only one who expressed any doubt about his ability.

"You want to know how good he is?" demanded the stubby, balding Stuhldreher, now good will ambassador for a Pittsburgh steel company. "Well, I saw him when he was playing end for Fenwick High School in Oak Park, Ill., and I still was coach at Wisconsin. We wanted him — I can't tell you how much. He's a really good all-around player, and you haven't seen many of them in the past few years."

Game Is Different

"A real good player," asserted Layden, the slim Chicago transportation man, while Miller, the Cleveland lawyer, nodded agreement. "You ask how he'd go with us? You might ask how we'd go with him. We only had two weak side plays — reverses. The game is different."

"He's a right half, isn't he?," asked the portly Scranton, Pa., television man, Crowley. "He'd make our team al right. Of course, he wouldn't make it at left half." That was Crowley's position.

Without being unduly modest, Latner would like to try pro football for a couple of years after graduation just to find out how good he is. But he's expecting to be in the Air Force for the next couple of years if he gets a commission.

"I'd like to try pro ball for a while to see if I could play it," Johnny said. "It's like the jump from high school to college. Just because you're a bigshot in college doesn't mean you're going to be a bigshot in the pros."

Prefers Chicago

Lattner doesn't care particularly what clubs seek his service. He's willing to play with whatever club draws his name in the pro draft. Or if Canadian clubs make him a better offer, he'll listen too. He'd prefer one of the Chicago clubs, of course, since they're nearer home, but he never has followed them closely.

"The Bears and Cardinals always played on Sunday and as a parochial high school we played Sunday games, too," he explained. "But I used to watch the Rockets and the Hornets in the All America Conference."

1953 SEASON STATISTICS

ND	TEAM	OPP.
317	Points Scored	139
206	First Downs	119
155	Rushing	65
47	Passing	46
4	Penalties	8
2881	Yards Rushing	1207
616	Times Carried	394
4.7	Yards-per-try	3.1
958	Yards Passing	1032
137	Passes Attempted	181
63	Passes Completed	66
.460	Completion Percentage	.365
17	Passes Intercepted By	7
166	Yards Int. Returned	60
3839	Total Offense	2239
40	Punts	59
1372	Total Yards	2157
34.3	Average Length	36.6
315	Yards Punts Returned	273
37	Fumbles	37
19	Ball Lost	22

RUSHING

	TC	YDS.	AVG.
Worden	145	859	5.9
Lattner	134	651	4.9
McHugh	67	341	5.1
Heap	62	314	5.0
Fitzgerald	56	254	4.5
Schaefer	23	100	4.8
Keller	15	91	6.1
Washington	18	78	4.3
Guglielmi	60	74	1.2
Carey	21	57	2.7
Raich	8	42	5.3
Rigali	4	11	2.8
Bigelow	1	6	6.0
Markowski	1	2	2.0
Galardo	1	1	1.0

PASSES CAUGHT

	NO.	YDS.	TD
Heap	22	336	5
Lattner	14	204	1
Shannon	7	138	2
Penza	7	113	0
Matz	5	61	0
Schaefer	1	42	0
Washington	1	16	0
Kapish	1	15	0
George	1	14	0
Keller	1	8	1
Worden	1	8	0

SCORING

	TD	PAT	FG	PTS.
Worden	11	0	0	66
Lattner	9	0	0	54
Heap	7	0	0	42
Guglielmi	6	5	0	41
Mavraides	0	24	1	27
McHugh	3	0	0	18
Schaefer	2	6	0	18
Shannon	2	0	0	12
Washington	1	0	0	6
Hunter	1	0	0	6
Keller	1	0	0	6
Carey	1	0	0	6
Bisceglia	1	0	0	6
Varrichione	1	0	0	6
*Safety against Pitt				*2
Lee	0	1	0	1

PASS INTERCEPTIONS

	NO.	YDS.	TD
Guglielmi	5	47	1
Lattner	4	4	0
Lemek	2	67	0
Heap	2	2	0
Carey	2	0	0
Schaefer	1	37	0
Szymanski	1	9	0

KICKOFF RETURNS

	NO.	YDS.	TD
Lattner	8	321	2
Worden	8	164	0
Heap	4	76	0
McHugh	1	26	0
Guglielmi	2	15	0
Keller	1	8	0
Shannon	1	3	0
Matz	1	2	0
Galardo	1	2	0

PUNT RETURNS

	NO.	YDS.	TD
Heap	7	143	1
Lattner	10	103	0
Fitzgerald	4	36	0
Washington	1	27	0
Schaefer	1	6	0
Guglielmi	1	0	0

PUNTING

	NO.	YDS.	AVG.
Lattner	29	1014	35.0
McHugh	6	189	31.5
Schaefer	4	136	34.0
Gaffney	1	33	33.0

PASSING

	ATT.	COMP.	HAD INT.	YDS.	TD	PCT.
Guglielmi	113	52	5	792	8	.460
Lattner	2	1	0	55	0	.500
Heap	6	4	1	48	0	.667
Schaefer	8	3	1	39	0	.375
Carey	7	3	0	24	1	.429
Fitzgerald	1	0	0	0	0	.000

Opponents' Fumbles Recovered: Penza 5, Hunter 3, Matz 2, Palumbo, Schrader, Lemek, Worden, Heap, Washington, Lattner, Mangialardi, Bisceglia, Varrichione, Mavraides, Shannon. Blocked Punts: Varrichione, Kapish.

THE FRANK LEAHY ERA

By KEN MURPHY

Perhaps there had been an inkling of what was coming back as early as October 17, although no one realized it at the time. It had been here at Notre Dame Stadium, that Pitt had given the Irish such a tough game before finally bowing out. Afterwards Coach Frank Leahy had been quoted: "It's been a long, hard afternoon."

Then, hard on the heels of this inconspicuous statement, had come the coach's collapse between halves of the Georgia Tech game on the following Saturday ... and the nation knew that Frank Leahy was a sick man.

And yet, through a grim determination—the same grim determination which had brought him from the Dakota prairies to the height of football coaching fame—Leahy was back with his team two weeks later at Philadelphia against Penn. That had been another hard game, and at the conclusion Leahy said: "I've never been so tired and completely exhausted in my life."

Somehow he managed to last out the season, but the picture of him in the papers toward the end of the campaign showed a tired man—old at the age of 46.

It should have been expected, and yet, that radio bulletin at 4:30 p.m. on Sunday, January 31st, which told of the resignation of Coach Frank Leahy, stunned the nation. The story rated the front page in newspapers across the country and grabbed off the headlines in most of them.

"It certainly came as a great surprise to me," said Coach Earl Blaik of Army, whose teams had been perennial challengers to Notre Dame's national ranking. "The college coaching profession has certainly lost one of its most capable and colorful members."

"One of the great coaches in the history of football ... his loss leaves a void in our ranks that cannot be filled," uttered Bud Wilkinson of Oklahoma, who now has the best record among active coaches.

The rest of them were unanimous in their reactions ... "great loss to intercollegiate football" ... "best coach of his generation."

Eighty-seven times in his eleven seasons of coaching Notre Dame's Fighting Irish, Frank Leahy's teams had won the good fight. Only eleven times had they been defeated; and on nine other occasions had they been held to ties. Six seasons they were unbeaten; four times they were national champions. Leahy himself had been singled out for individual honors as "Coach of the Week" on innumerable occasions, as "Coach of the Year" four times, and as "Football Man of the Year" at the conclusion of the 1949 season.

The local reaction to the resignation was summed up by grizzled old Joe Dierickx, Stadium caretaker and brother-in-law of Rockne, on the next morning. Standing in the middle of his workshop in the bottom of the Stadium, amid the dusty, discolored photos and newspaper clippings of great Irish teams of bygone eras, he muttered: "It was different with Rock—he was killed. But the reaction is the same—the same stunned atmosphere."

The baptismal records in St. Patrick's Church, O'Neill, Nebraska, show that on August 27, 1907, a son was born to Mr. and Mrs. Frank Leahy—one of eight children whom Leahy's father tried to support on the meager earnings of a restaurant keeper. Some have intimated that Leahy fits romantically into the Notre Dame picture since his forebears

A new coach...

Coach Terry Brennan completed his initial season as head football mentor by piloting the Irish gridders to a very successful 9 wins and 1 loss record. This was the best first year record that any football coach has ever turned in including the great Knute Rockne and Brennan's predecessor, Frank Leahy.

The only blemish on Terry's record was a 27-14 loss to a fired up Purdue team. However, under his guidance the Irish bounced back to run over Pittsburgh 33-0. This rebound showed the same kind of spirit that Brennan himself displayed in his famous 97-yard opening kickoff return for a touchdown against Army in 1947.

After graduating from Notre Dame in 1948 with a Bachelors degree in Pre-Law, he took over the head football coaching duties at Chicago's Mount Carmel High School. He led this team to three city championships before taking over the reins as Freshman Coach here at Notre Dame in 1953. Two of the ballplayers who played for Brennan at Mount Carmel were co-captains Dan Shannon and Paul Matz.

1954
Coach: Terry Brennan
Co-Captains: Paul A. Matz and Daniel J. Shannon

S.25	W	Texas	21-0	H	c57,594
O.2	L	Purdue (U)	14-27	H	c58,250
O.9	W	Pittsburgh	33-0	A	c60,114
O.16	W	Michigan State (R)	20-19	H	c57,238
O.30	W	Navy	6-0	N	c60,000
N.6	W	Pennsylvania	42-7	A	61,189
N.13	W	North Carolina	42-13	H	55,410
N.20	W	Iowa	34-18	A	c56,576
N.27	W	So. Calif (R) (5:57)	23-17	H	c56,438
D.4	W	S.M.U.	26-14	A	c75,501
	(9-1-0)		261-115		598,310

N—at Baltimore

AP POLL

1954
1. Ohio State
2. U.C.L.A.
3. Oklahoma
4. NOTRE DAME
5. Navy
6. Mississippi
7. Army
8. Maryland
9. Wisconsin
10. Arkansas

UPI POLL

1954
1. U.C.L.A.
2. Ohio State
3. Oklahoma
4. NOTRE DAME
5. Navy
6. Mississippi
7. Army
8. Arkansas
9. Miami, Florida
10. Wisconsin

University of Notre Dame 1954 Varsity Alphabetical Roster

No.	Name and Position	Age	Ht.	Wt.	Hometown	Class
71	Beams, Byron, T	19	6-4	214	Ada, Okla.	So.
8	Bigelow, James, QB	20	5-11	170	Glenshaw, Pa.	Sr.
79	Bihn, Joseph, T	19	6-2	208	San Jose, Calif.	So.
62	Bisceglia, Pat, G*	23	5-10	190	Worcester, Mass.	Jr.
48	Bosse, Joseph, T	19	6-2	205	Lawrence, Mass.	So.
4	Bucci, Donald, QB	21	6-0	180	Youngstown, Ohio	Sr.
88	Cabral, Walter, E**	21	6-3	205	Honolulu, Hawaii	Sr.
15	Callaghan, Leo, HB	21	6-1	185	Passaic, N. J.	Sr.
2	Carey, Thomas, QB***	21	5-10	180	Chicago, Ill.	Sr.
53	Carrabine, Luke, C	19	6-1	205	Gary, Indiana	So.
6	Cooke, Larry, QB	18	6-0	185	Ennis, Texas	So.
56	Cook, Edward, C	21	6-1	210	Philadelphia, Pa.	Sr.
55	Coyne, Robert, C	18	6-1	200	Joliet, Ill.	So.
64	Cunningham, Thomas, G	19	6-0	200	Pomona, Calif.	So.
47	Davin, David, T	19	6-4	203	Chicago, Ill.	So.
87	Dumas, Jack, E	19	6-3	190	Grand Rapids, Mich.	Jr.
82	Edmonds, Wayne, G*	20	6-0	205	Canonsburg, Pa.	Jr.
32	Fitzgerald, Richard, FB*	21	5-11	190	Chicago, Ill.	Jr.
63	Frasor, Richard, C	21	5-11	190	Chicago, Ill.	Sr.
34	Gaffney, John, FB	20	6-1	190	Chicago, Ill.	Jr.
81	George, Donald E*	20	6-4	205	Dunbar, Pa.	Jr.
21	Gerami, Gerald, HB	19	5-9	178	Lafayette, La.	So.
76	Groble, George, T	18	6-2	212	Chicago, Ill.	So.
3	Guglielmi, R., QB***	20	6-0	185	Columbus, Ohio	Sr.
42	Heap, Joseph, HB***	22	5-11	180	Abita Springs, La.	Sr.
57	Hedrick, Eugene, G	18	6-0	190	Canton, Ohio	So.
49	Hendricks, Richard, HB	20	6-1	180	Danville, Ill.	Jr.
5	Hornung, Paul, QB	18	6-2	190	Louisville, Ky.	So.
24	Hughes, Thomas, FB	18	6-0	190	Portland, Ore.	So.
89	Kapish, Eugene, E	19	6-1	190	Barberton, Ohio	Jr.
78	Kegaly, John T	20	6-3	207	Chicago, Ill.	Jr.
40	Keller, Richard, HB*	19	6-0	175	Toledo, Ohio	Jr.
58	King, Jack, G	18	5-10	200	Weirton, W. Va.	So.
91	Lasch, Robert, T	19	6-3	212	Clairton, Pa.	Jr.
65	Lee, Jack, G***	21	5-11	190	Medford, Mass.	Sr.
72	Lemek, Raymond, G*	19	6-1	205	Sioux City, Ia.	Jr.
85	Loncaric, Louis, C	18	6-3	190	Battle Creek, Mich.	So.
43	Markowski, Joseph, FB	20	6-0	185	Hamilton, Ontario	Jr.
70	Martell, Eugene, T	19	6-3	212	Midland, Pa.	Jr.
90	Matz, Paul (C-C), E**	20	6-1	190	Chicago, Ill.	Sr.
11	McDonnell, John, HB	19	5-11	175	Sterling, Ill.	Jr.
61	McMullan, John, G	20	5-10	200	Hoboken, N. J.	Jr.
51	Mense, James, C	19	5-11	205	Hamilton, Ohio	Jr.
19	Milota, James, HB	19	5-11	170	Park Ridge, Ill.	So.
73	Mondron, Robert, T	19	6-3	210	Charleston, W. Va.	So.
17	Morse, James, HB	19	5-11	180	Muskegon, Mich.	So.
80	Munro, James, E	18	6-0	195	Chicago, Ill.	So.
39	Murphy, Ed., G	19	6-2	200	Lansing, Mich.	Jr.
68	Nakfoor, Patrick, E	20	6-4	205	Phoenix, Ariz.	So.
77	Nicula, George, T	19	6-2	205	Warren, Ohio	Jr.
50	Noznesky, Pete, E	19	6-0	180	Lansdowne, Pa.	So.
67	Palumbo, Samuel, T***	21	6-1	208	Cleveland, Ohio	Sr.
75	Pasquesi, Anthony, T	20	6-4	215	Chicago, Ill.	Sr.
41	Pinn, Frank, FB	19	5-10	190	Chicago, Ill.	So.
37	Raich, Nicholas, FB	20	5-10	185	Milwaukee, Wis.	Jr.
74	Ready, Robert, T**	21	6-3	212	Lowell, Mass.	Sr.
59	Regan, Michael, E	19	6-2	200	Buffalo, N. Y.	Jr.
18	Reynolds, Paul, FB**	21	6-0	180	Springfield, Ill.	Jr.
16	Rigali, William, HB	19	5-10	175	Chicago, Ill.	So.
83	Scannell, Robert, E	19	6-0	190	South Bend, Ind.	So.
9	Schaefer, D., FB-HB*	20	5-11	185	Pittsburgh, Pa.	Jr.
86	Schramm, Paul, T	18	6-2	212	Cincinnati, Ohio	So.
33	Shannon, D. (C-C), E***	20	6-0	190	Chicago, Ill.	Sr.
12	Sipes, Sherrill, HB	19	6-0	185	Louisville, Ky.	So.
69	Stanitzek, Francis, G	19	5-10	200	Grand Rapids, Mich.	So.
22	Studer, Dean, HB	18	5-11	180	Billings, Mont.	So.
52	Szymanski, R., C***	21	6-2	215	Toledo, Ohio	Sr.
60	Varrichione, Frank, T***	21	6-0	210	Natick, Mass.	Sr.
38	Wilson, George, FB	20	5-11	185	Polo, Ill.	Jr.
28	Williams, Donald, FB	21	5-10	180	Montrose, Calif.	So.
20	Witucki, Jack, HB	19	6-1	185	Tulsa, Okla.	So.
84	Zajeski, Benedict, G	20	6-3	205	Chicago, Ill.	Jr.
66	Zervas, Thomas, G	19	6-1	205	Lakewood, Ohio	So.

* Denotes Monograms Won

Purdue Passes Down Irish 27-14

Len Dawson, Purdue's sensational sophomore, re-enacted Dale Samuels' 1950 performance and led a tired up Boilermaker squad to a 27-14 upset victory. Notre Dame's winning streak was snapped at 13 games.

The Irish started off in the hole by fumbling the first play from scrimmage. Murakowski, Purdue's fullback, cracked for 8 yards and three plays later Springer scooted to a first down on the 6. A Dawson to Kerr touchdown pass capped the 32 yard drive.

Notre Dame failed to gain after the kickoff and a poor punt gave Purdue possession on the Irish 42. On third down Dawson again found a gap in Irish defense and his pass to Brock resulted in a 14-0 lead for the Boilermakers.

The first Irish score came when Brock was tackled in the end-zone by Lemek and Palumbo. A few seconds later Notre Dame scored when Hornung took the ensuing kickoff and raced 60 yards to the Purdue 1 where Raich plunged over for the touchdown.

The Irish reached their peak in the third quarter. In a time-consuming display of ball control and power football, Notre Dame ground out 91 yards and a score tying TD.

Dawson, however, quickly dispelled Notre Dame's hope for victory. A 73 yard pass play from the crafty quarterback to giant 6-7 Lamar Lundy gave Purdue the lead for good.

In the final quarter Purdue added an insurance touchdown on a screen pass from Dawson to Murakowski, who ran 38 yards to end the scoring.

	STATISTICS	
N.D.		Purdue
15	First Downs	13
91	Rushing Yardage	94
179	Passing Yardage	224
33	Passes Attempted	15
15	Passes Completed	9
0	Passes Intercepted	1
5	Punts	4
32.8	Punting Average	31.5
2	Fumbles Lost	0
60	Yards Penalized	15

Irish Slip By State 20-19

A gallant Fighting Irish team marched to victory in a heavy rain over Michigan State 20-19 with the winning margin being provided by a missed extra point.

Michigan State struck like lightning the first time they had the ball with Clarence Peaks going over from the one. The ensuing Irish drive was halted on the State 35 yard line from where State started their second scoring drive. The tally came on a 35 yard pass from Morrall to Lewis. The extra point was good and the Spartans had taken an early 13-0 lead.

After receiving the kick-off the Irish marched 69 yards in 11 plays to score with Joe Heap going over from the one. Schaefer's P.A.T. was good and the Irish left the field at half time trailing 13-7.

Midway through the third quarter Dick Szymanski intercepted a pass at mid-field and the Irish could not be denied. In eleven plays Notre Dame had taken the lead with Heap going over from the 16. This set the stage for a very dramatic finish which kept the rain-soaked Notre Dame partisans in their seats until the final whistle.

With 3 minutes remaining to play, Paul Reynolds dashed 9 yards around left end to provide the Irish with what proved to be the winning margin. However the Spartans marched right back to score, as Bert Zagers ran 14 yards to score. Jerry Planutis, who had previously missed two field goal attempts, missed the extra point and the Irish had won a well deserved battle.

	STATISTICS	
N.D.		Mich. State
18	First Downs	12
276	Rushing Yardage	142
38	Passing Yardage	149
8	Passes Attempted	16
3	Passes Completed	8
1	Passes Intercepted	0
2	Punts	2
45	Punting Average	38
1	Fumbles Lost	1
110	Yards Penalized	25

Irish Corral Mustangs 26-14

1954 Season Statistics

Notre Dame finished their 1954 season at the Cotton Bowl in Dallas as they triumphed over S.M.U. 26-14 and ended the season with a 9-1 record.

Two quick first quarter touchdowns seemed to presage a close, high-scoring battle. First Notre Dame marched 59 yards with Heap slanting off tackle for the final four. Then S.M.U. came back with a 53 yard drive of their own. Roach got the last ten on a keep it play and Barnet's kick gave the Mustangs a 7-6 edge.

The S.M.U. squad then came up with its best defensive performance of the day, as they stopped two Irish thrusts. Eventually power shots into the line wore down the Mustang defenders and Guglielmi went over tackle for three yards and a score. This time Schaefer didn't miss and Notre Dame led 13-7.

With only 2:51 left in the half, Brennan gave the regulars a rest and the second stringers took over. When Bob Scannell blocked Roach's punt, overtook the bounding pigskin and carried it twenty yards into the S.M.U. end zone, The Fighting Irish had an unexpected 19-7 lead.

With the help of over 100 yards in penalties assessed against the visitors from South Bend, the Mustangs managed to match the Irish second half scoring.

Notre Dame's only score of the second half came near the end of the third period. Heap swung wide around end and eluded four would-be tacklers as he threaded his way 89 yards down the sidelines. Schaefer's placement was good. In the final quarter, S.M.U. matched the Notre Dame touchdown on John Marshall's 76 yard scoring romp.

STATISTICS

N.D.		S.M.U.
23	First Downs	7
321	Rushing Yardage	51
156	Passing Yardage	49
18	Passes Attempted	15
11	Passes Completed	6
1	Passes Intercepted	1
2	Punts	9
37.5	Punting Average	37.3
2	Fumbles Lost	1
175	Yards Penalized	45

PUNT RETURNS

	NO.	YDS.	TD
Studer	6	62	0
Heap	8	37	0
Morse	4	31	0
Reynolds	2	25	0
Fitzgerald	2	20	0
Hornung	1	6	0
Guglielmi	1	4	0
Hendricks	1	2	0
Scannell	1	20	1

KICKOFFS RETURNED

	NO.	YDS.	TD
Heap	7	143	0
Morse	5	166	0
Schaefer	5	82	0
Carey	2	68	0
Studer	2	46	0
Hornung	1	58	0
Hendricks	1	31	0
Bigelow	1	18	0
Guglielmi	1	10	0
Shannon	1	8	0
Reynolds	1	62	0

PASS INTERCEPTIONS

	NO.	YDS.
Guglielmi	5	51
Hornung	3	94
Heap	2	22
Schaefer	1	5
Carey	1	3
Lemek	1	3
Szymanski	1	2
Pinn	1	0

RUSHING

	TC	YDS.	AVG.
Schaefer	141	766	5.4
Heap	110	594	5.4
Morse	68	345	5.0
Hornung	23	159	6.9
Studer	30	151	5.0
Reynolds	29	113	3.9
Guglielmi	79	95	1.1
Witucki	9	39	4.3
Raich	11	29	2.6
Sipes	10	28	2.8
Carey	19	25	1.3
Fitzgerald	13	26	2.0
Pinn	5	15	3.0
Milota	1	4	4.0
Gaffney	2	3	1.5
McDonnell	1	1	1.0

SCORING*

	TD	PAT	FG	PTS.
Heap	8	0	0	48
Schaefer	3	22	0	40
Morse	5	1	0	31
Guglielmi	5	0	0	30
Shannon	3	0	0	18
Hornung	2	6	0	18
Studer	2	0	0	12
Munro	2	0	0	12
Sipes	1	0	0	6
Reynolds	1	0	0	6
Pinn	1	0	0	6
Raich	1	0	0	6
Witucki	1	0	0	6
Matz	1	0	0	6
Kapish	1	0	0	6
Scannell	1	0	0	6

* plus two safeties

PASSES CAUGHT

	NC	YDS	TD
Heap	18	369	0
Matz	16	224	1
Morse	15	236	3
Shannon	11	215	3
Scannell	5	63	0
Kapish	4	79	1
Reynolds	4	51	0
Schaefer	3	60	0
Munro	3	32	2
Sipes	2	38	1
Fitzgerald	2	37	0
Studer	1	47	0
Noznesky	1	11	0
Witucki	1	10	0
George	1	1	0
Szymanski	1	1	0
Raich	1	—16	0

PASSING

	ATT.	COMP.	HAD INT.	YDS.	TD	PCT.
Guglielmi	127	68	7	1160	6	.535
Carey	17	9	1	172	4	.529
Hornung	19	5	0	36	0	.263
Heap	3	3	0	32	1	1.000
Studer	1	1	0	10	0	1.000
Reynolds	2	1	1	20	0	.500
Bigelow	4	2	1	28	0	.500
Morse	3	0	0	0	0	.000
Keller	1	0	0	0	0	.000
Sipes	1	0	0	0	0	.000

OPPONENTS' FUMBLES RECOVERED—Varrichione 4, Lee 2, Guglielmi 2, Raich 2, Heap 2, Matz 2, Szymanski, Bisceglia, Hornung, Carey, Schaefer, Scannell. BLOCKED KICK—Scannell.

PUNTING

	NO.	YDS.	AVG.
Hornung	6	234	39
Schaefer	8	217	27
Heap	10	265	26.5
Morse	4	124	31
Raich	2	79	40
Cooke	1	24	24
Witucki	1	33	33

University of Notre Dame 1955 Varsity Alphabetical Roster

No.	Name and Position	Age	Ht.	Wt.	Home Town	Class
71	Beams, Byron, T	22	6-4	220	Ada, Okla.	Jr.
79	Bihn, Joseph, T	20	6-2	210	San Jose, Calif.	Jr.
92	Bill, Joseph, T-E	20	6-5	230	Garden City, N. Y.	Sr.
62	**Bisceglia, Pat, G	25	5-10	190	Worcester, Mass.	Sr.
74	Bosse, Joseph, T	21	6-2	207	Lawrence, Mass.	Jr.
6	Cooke, Larry, QB	20	6-0	190	Ennis, Texas	Jr.
55	Coyne, Robert, C	19	6-1	200	Joliet, Ill.	Jr.
45	Cunningham, Thomas, G	19	6-0	200	Pomona, Calif.	Jr.
2	De Nardo, Ronald, QB	19	6-3	195	Bloomington, Ill.	So.
64	Djubasak, Paul, G	19	6-0	200	Cleveland, Ohio	So.
46	Dolan, Patrick, T	20	6-3	210	Throop, Pa.	So.
56	Dumas, Jack, E	20	6-3	195	Grand Rapids, Mich.	So.
82	**Edmonds, Wayne, T	22	6-0	210	Cannonsburg, Pa.	Sr.
32	**Fitzgerald, Dick, HB-FB	22	5-11	190	Chicago, Ill.	Sr.
63	Francis, Al, G-C	19	6-0	210	San Jose, Calif.	So.
68	Gaydos, Robert, G	20	6-0	200	Donora, Pa.	So.
21	Gerami, Gerald, HB	20	5-9	173	Lafayette, La.	Jr.
16	Gormley, James, HB	20	5-10	185	Indianapolis, Ind.	Jr.
76	Groble, George, T	19	6-2	212	Chicago, Ill.	Jr.
8	Hebert, Carl, QB	19	5-11	170	Lafayette, La.	So.
65	Hedrick, Eugene, G	19	6-0	190	Canton, Ohio	Jr.
49	Hendricks, Richard, FB	21	6-1	180	Danville, Ill.	Sr.
5	*Hornung, Paul, QB	19	6-2	205	Louisville, Ky.	Jr.
67	Hughes, Thomas, G	20	6-0	190	Portland, Ore.	Jr.
90	Kane, Thomas, G	19	6-1	185	Coeur d'Alene, Idaho	So.
89	*Kapish, Gene, E	20	6-1	190	Barberton, Ohio	Sr.
78	Kegaly, John, G	21	6-3	210	Chicago, Ill.	Sr.
40	*Keller, Richard, HB	21	6-0	175	Toledo, Ohio	Sr.
4	Kennedy, John, QB	19	5-10	170	Tacoma, Wash.	So.
20	Kiley, Roger Jr., HB	19	5-11	178	Chicago, Ill.	So.
58	King, Jack, G	19	5-10	195	Weirton, W. Va.	Jr.
54	Kuchta, Frank, C	19	6-1	205	Cleveland, Ohio	So.
72	**Lemek, Ray (Capt.), G-T	21	6-1	205	Sioux City, Ia.	Sr.
23	Lewis, Aubrey, HB	19	6-0	185	Montclair, N. J.	So.
48	Lima, Charles, FB	19	6-2	190	Cincinnati, Ohio	So.
85	*Loncaric, Louis, C-T	20	6-3	190	Battle Creek, Mich.	Jr.
25	Lynch, Richard, HB	19	6-0	185	Clinton, N. J.	So.
70	*Martell, Gene, T-G	21	6-3	215	Midland, Pa.	Sr.
11	McDonnell, John, HB-QB	20	5-11	175	Sterling, Ill.	Jr.
75	McGinley, John, T	18	6-2	195	Indianapolis, Ind.	So.
61	McMullan, John, G	22	5-10	203	Hoboken, N. J.	Sr.
51	*Mense, James, C	20	5-11	206	Hamilton, Ohio	Sr.
26	Miller, Richard, FB	19	5-11	190	Medford, Wis.	So.
19	Milota, James, HB	20	5-10	165	Parkridge, Ill.	Jr.
73	Mondron, Robert, T	20	6-3	210	Charleston, W. Va.	Jr.
17	*Morse, James, HB	20	5-11	175	Muskegon, Mich.	Jr.
42	Mugford, John, E	19	6-2	185	Chelsea, Mass.	So.
80	Munro, James, E	20	6-0	193	Chicago, Ill.	Jr.
77	*Nicula, George, T	21	6-2	210	Warren, Ohio	Sr.
50	Nozensky, Pete, E	21	6-0	180	Lansdowne, Pa.	Jr.
81	Owens, William, E	19	6-2	190	Lafayette, La.	So.
87	Prendergast, Dick, E	18	6-2	195	Homewood, Ill.	So.
29	Quinlan, William, HB	19	5-11	165	Mt. Pleasant, Mich.	So.
37	*Raich, Nicholas, G	21	5-10	188	Milwaukee, Wis.	Sr.
59	Regan, Michael, E	20	6-2	212	Buffalo, N. Y.	Jr.
18	***Reynolds, Paul, HB	22	6-0	182	Springfield, Ill.	Sr.
57	Salvino, Robert, T	20	6-3	210	Chicago, Ill.	Jr.
83	*Scannell, Robert, E	20	6-0	190	South Bend, Ind.	Jr.
9	**Schaefer, Don, FB	21	5-11	190	Pittsburgh, Pa.	Sr.
86	Schramm, Paul, E	20	6-2	200	Cincinnati, Ohio	Jr.
28	Scott, Frank, FB	19	5-8	175	Carnegie, Pa.	So.
39	Shulsen, Richard, G	19	6-0	190	Salt Lake City, Utah	So.
12	*Sipes, Sherrill, HB	20	6-0	185	Louisville, Ky.	Jr.
69	Stanitzek, Francisc, G	20	5-10	205	Grand Rapids, Mich.	Jr.
22	*Studer, Dean, HB	19	5-11	180	Billings, Mont.	Jr.
52	Sullivan, Edward, C-T	20	6-0	190	McKeesport, Pa.	Jr.
91	Sullivan, James, G	19	6-3	200	Santa Rosa, Calif.	So.
7	Trapp, Harold, QB	19	6-0	180	Sycamore, Ill.	So.
35	Ward, Robert, HB	20	5-8	160	Lamberton, Pa.	Jr.
30	Wetzel, Gerald, E	20	6-2	190	Miami Beach, Fla.	Jr.
33	Wilkins, Richard, FB-HB	21	5-11	190	Duncan, Okla.	So.
84	Wilson, George, E	21	5-11	190	Polo, Ill.	Sr.
88	Zajeski, Ben, E	21	6-3	205	Chicago, Ill.	Sr.
66	Zervas, Thomas, G	20	6-1	205	Lakewood, Ohio	Jr.

* Denotes Monograms Won.

AP POLL

1955

1. Oklahoma
2. Michigan State
3. Maryland
4. U.C.L.A.
5. T.C.U.
6. Ohio State
7. Georgia Tech
8. NOTRE DAME
9. Mississippi
10. Auburn

UPI POLL

1955

1. Oklahoma
2. Michigan State
3. Maryland
4. U.C.L.A.
5. Ohio State
6. T.C.U.
7. Georgia Tech
8. Auburn
9. NOTRE DAME
10. Mississippi

1955

Coach: Terry Brennan
Captain: Raymond E. Lemek

S.24	W	S.M.U.	17-0	H	c56,454
O.1	W	Indiana	19-0	H	c56,494
O.7	W	Miami (Fla.) (Nt)	14-0	A	c75,685
O.15	L	Michigan State	7-21	A	c52,007
O.22	W	Purdue	22-7	A	c55,000
O.29	W	Navy (R)	21-7	H	c59,475
N.5	W	Pennsylvania	46-14	A	45,226
N.12	W	North Carolina	27-7	A	38,000
N.19	W	Iowa (2:15)	17-14	H	c59,955
N.26	L	So. California (U)	20-42	A	94,892
		(8-2-0)	210-112		593,188

INDIANA
NOTRE DAME

41.6 yd. Average on Receptions by Morse

Notre Dame 20 — So. California 42

On November 26, 1955, the Fighting Irish invaded sun-bleached California only to be dealt a disastrous defeat which will be remembered for years to come as "the ambush in the Coliseum." A stunned crowd of 94,899 looked on.

The opening period was a preview of things to come as the Trojans went 68 yards in 11 plays for the score; Ellsworth Kissenger scoring and Jon Arnett converting. The Irish countered immediately, Hornung scoring and converting.

Southern Cal then struck two lightning blows, one by fullback C. R. Roberts, and one by Arnett, and Arnett's two placements were true.

With the score 21-7 and the half coming to a close, Paul Hornung pitched a long one to halfback Jimmy Morse, who legged the remaining distance, the play covering 78 yards. Paul's kick was wide, and the score remained 21-13.

The third stanza saw no score as Notre Dame's bid failed when Schaefer fumbled in the end zone. The Irish, still fighting, scored to open the fourth quarter. Hornung passed to Morse, for 60 yards, and Paul bulled over from the one. His kick was good and the score stood at 21-20. It looked as if a storybook finish was in store. But that was the last chance Irish eyes had to smile. Two pass interceptions and a fumble set up three TD's for the westerners and when the smoke cleared the score board read 42-20.

Thus the season ended on a rather dismal note and Southern Cal gained an extremely rewarding revenge victory. However, Notre Dame's fine 8-2 record had provided an irrefutable reply to the pre-season prognosticators and merited ninth place in the national rankings. It was the sixteenth time in twenty years that the Irish had fought their way into the top ten.

N.D.		So. Cal.
18	First Downs	17
238	Rushing Yardage	252
283	Passing Yardage	146
23	Passes Attempted	11
11	Passes Completed	7
5	Passes Intercepted	1
2	Punts	4
28.5	Punting Average	39.2
2	Fumbles Lost	2
46	Yards Penalized	55

Morse downed from behind.

FINAL STATISTICS
1955

TEAM

Notre Dame		Opponents
210	Points Scored	112
190	First Downs	137
153	by Rushing	80
35	by Passing	50
2	by Penalties	7
2727	Yards Rushing	1469
601	Times Carried	398
4.5	Yards per Try	3.7
846	Yards Passing	1011
121	Passes Attempted	171
51	Passes Completed	83
.421	Completion Percentage	.485
17	Passes Intercepted by	12
246	Yards Interceptions Returned	28
3573	TOTAL OFFENSE	2480
38	Punts	40
1320	Total Yards Punts	1544
34.8	Punting Average	38.6
171	Yards Punts Returned	202
22	Fumbles	30
17	Ball Lost	19

SCORING

	TD	PAT	FG	Pts.
Hornung	6	5	2	47
Morse	6	0	0	36
Schaefer	3	16	0	34
Kapish	3	0	0	18
Lewis	3	0	0	18
Prendergast	2	0	0	12
Studer	2	0	0	12
Fitzgerald	1	0	0	6
Lynch	1	0	0	6
Reynolds	1	0	0	6
Wilson	1	0	0	6
Loncaric	1	0	0	6
Ward	0	1	0	1
Safety vs. Purdue				2

PASSING

	Att.	Comp.	Had Int.	Yds.	TD	Pct.
Hornung	103	46	10	743	9	.446
Studer	4	2	0	37	0	.500
Hebert	1	1	0	24	1	1.000
Reynolds	1	1	0	18	0	1.000
Cooke	4	0	2	0	0	.000
Morse	3	0	0	0	0	.000
Lewis	3	0	0	0	0	.000
Schaefer	2	1	0	0	0	.500

RUSHING

	TC	Yds.	Avg.
Schaefer	145	638	4.4
Morse	92	404	4.4
Studer	88	440	5.0
Hornung	92	474	5.2
Lewis	56	222	3.9
Fitzgerald	45	218	4.8
Lynch	24	121	5.0
Ward	21	111	5.3
Cooke	18	60	3.3
Sipes	8	20	2.5
Wilkins	4	2	0.5
Lima	2	6	3.0
McDonnell	1	4	4.0
Reynolds	5	14	2.8

PUNTS RETURNED

	No.	Yds.	TD
Studer	6	92	0
Morse	6	26	0
Reynolds	1	21	0
Lynch	1	19	0
Ward	2	13	0
Cooke	1	0	0

KICKOFFS RETURNED

	No.	Yds.	TD
Hornung	6	109	0
Lewis	4	91	0
Studer	5	116	0
Morse	5	88	0
Fitzgerald	3	47	0
Lima	1	19	0
Schaefer	1	27	0
Sipes	1	15	0
Ward	1	24	0

PASSES CAUGHT

	No.	Yds.	TD
Morse	17	424	3
Kapish	11	142	3
Prendergast	8	105	2
Schaefer	6	36	2
Scannell	2	21	0
Lewis	1	32	1
Wilson	1	24	1
Studer	2	32	0
Schramm	1	18	0
Fitzgerald	2	12	0

UNIVERSITY OF NOTRE DAME
1956 VARSITY FOOTBALL ROSTER

No.	Name	Pos.	Ht.	Wt.	Class	Hometown	High School
77	Ciesielski, Richard	T	5-11	210	Soph.	South Bend, Ind.	St. Joseph
6	*Cooke, Larry	QB	6-0	190	Sr.	Ennis, Texas	Ennis
40	Costa, Donald	FB	5-10	195	Soph.	Ellwood City, Pa.	Lincoln
46	Dolan, Patrick	T	6-3	210	Jr.	Throop, Pa.	Scranton Tech
1	Dugan, Mike	QB	6-1	181	Soph.	Omaha, Neb.	Creighton Prep
60	Ecuyer, Al	G	5-10	195	Soph.	New Orleans, La.	Jesuit
68	*Gaydos, Robert	G	6-0	200	Jr.	Donora, Pa.	Donora
66	Geremia, Frank	T-G	6-3	215	Soph.	Sacramento, Cal.	C. K. McClatchy
76	Groble, George	T	6-2	212	Sr.	Chicago, Ill.	St. Ignatius
65	*Hedrick, Gene	G	6-0	190	Jr.	Canton, Ohio	Central Catholic
5	**Hornung, Paul	QB	6-2	205	Sr.	Louisville, Ky.	Flaget
44	Just, James	FB-HB	6-1	190	Soph.	Milwaukee, Wisc.	Don Bosco
54	Kuchta, Frank	C	6-1	205	Jr.	Cleveland, Ohio	Benedictine
72	Lawrence, Donald	T	6-1	215	Soph.	Cleveland, Ohio	Cathedral Latin
23	*Lewis, Aubrey	HB	6-0	185	Jr.	Montclair, N. J.	Montclair
48	Lima, Charles	FB	6-2	190	Soph.	Cincinnati, Ohio	Purcell
85	**Loncaric, Louis	C	6-3	195	Sr.	Battle Creek, Mich.	St. Philip
25	*Lynch, Richard	HB	6-0	185	Jr.	Clinton, N. J.	Phillipsburg Cath.
90	Manzo, Louis	E	6-2	205	Soph.	Old Forge, Pa.	Old Forge
11	McDonnell, John	HB	5-11	175	Sr.	Sterling, Ill.	Newman Catholic
78	Meno, Charles	T-G	6-0	200	Soph.	Gillespie, Ill.	Gillespie
19	Milota, James	HB	5-10	170	Sr.	Park Ridge, Ill.	Fenwick
17	**Morse, James (Capt.)	HB	5-11	175	Sr.	Muskegon, Mich.	St. Mary's
79	Mosca, Angelo	T-G	6-4	230	Soph.	Waltham, Mass.	Waltham
80	Munro, James	E	6-0	195	Sr.	Chicago, Ill.	St. George
82	Myers, Gary	E	6-1	195	Soph.	Spokane, Wash.	Gonzaga Prep
70	Nagurski, Bronko	T	6-1	215	Soph.	Inter. Falls, Minn.	International Falls
50	Noznesky, Pete	C	6-0	180	Sr.	Lansdowne, Pa.	LaSalle Military
18	Odyniec, Norman	FB	5-11	180	Soph.	Greensboro, N. C.	Greensboro
49	Pietrosante, Nick	FB	6-2	205	Soph.	Ansonia, Conn.	Notre Dame
87	*Prendergast, Dick	E	6-2	200	Jr.	Homewood, Ill.	Mt. Carmel
27	Reynolds, Frank	HB	5-11	170	Soph.	Oak Park, Ill.	Fenwick
84	Royer, Richard	E	6-2	190	Soph.	Cincinnati, Ohio	Elder
29	Salsich, Pete	HB	5-10	175	Soph.	St. Louis, Mo.	St. Louis U.
83	**Scannell, Robert	E	6-0	190	Sr.	South Bend, Ind.	Central
62	Schaaf, James	G	6-0	195	Soph.	Erie, Pa.	Cathedral Prep
86	*Schramm, Paul	T	6-2	200	Sr.	Cincinnati, Ohio	Purcell
28	Scott, Frank	FB	5-8	175	Jr.	Carnegie, Pa.	Scott Twp.
88	Seaman, Neil	E	6-1	198	Soph.	Power Hill, Pa.	Scott Twp.
10	Selcer, Richard	QB	5-9	173	Soph.	Cincinnati, Ohio	Elder
39	Shulsen, Richard	G	6-0	190	Jr.	Salt Lake City, U.	West
12	Sipes, Sherrill	HB	6-0	185	Sr.	Louisville, Ky.	Flaget
22	**Studer, Dean	FB-HB	5-11	180	Sr.	Billings, Mont.	Central
52	Sullivan, Ed	C	6-0	190	Jr.	McKeesport, Pa.	McKeesport
43	Toth, Ron	E	6-1	205	Soph.	E. Cleveland, Ohio	Cathedral Latin
35	*Ward, Robert	HB	5-8	160	Sr.	Lamberton, Pa.	German Twp.
89	Wetoska, Robert	T	6-3	215	Soph.	Minneapolis, Minn.	DeLaSalle
9	Williams, Robert	QB	6-2	185	Soph.	Wilkes-Barre, Pa.	G.A.R.

*Denotes Monograms Won

1956

Coach: Terry Brennan
Captain: James A. Morse

S.22	L	S.M.U. (U) (Nt)		A	61,000
		(1:50)	13-19		
O.6	W	Indiana	20-6	H	c58,372
O.13	L	Purdue	14-28	H	c58,778
O.20	L	Michigan State	14-47	H	c59,378
O.27	L	Oklahoma	0-40	H	c60,128
N.3	L	Navy (R)	7-33	N	57,773
N.10	L	Pittsburgh	13-26	A	c58,697
N.17	W	No. Carolina (1:16)	21-14	H	c56,793
N.24	L	Iowa	8-48	A	c56,632
D.1	L	So. California	20-28	A	64,538
	(2-8-0)		130-289		592,089

N—at Baltimore

Heisman Award Won By Hornung

NEW YORK, Dec. 4 (P)—Paul Hornung, Notre Dame quarterback, today was awarded the Heisman Trophy given by the Downtown Athletic Club as the outstanding college football player of 1956.

Hornung becomes the 22nd winner of the trophy, established in 1935 in honor of John W. Heisman, famed coach. Jay Berwanger of the University of Chicago was the first winner, and Howard "Hopalong" Cassady, Ohio State halfback, was chosen for the 1955 trophy.

The Notre Dame star received a total of 1,006 points in the poll conducted among 1,318 registered electors over the nation.

Johnny Majors Second

Johnny Majors, fine Tennessee back, was second in the balloting with 994 points, making it the closest finish in years.

Twelve players were listed in the voting, with two Oklahomans ranking third and fourth, respectively. Tommy McDonald, speedy Sooner halfback, received 973 points to press Majors for runnerup honors, and Jerry Tubbs, center on the unbeaten Oklahoma team, polled 724.

Others receiving votes were Jimmy Brown, Syracuse, 561; Ron Kramer, Michigan, 518; John Brodie, Stanford, 281; Jim Parker, Ohio State, 248; Kenny Ploen, Iowa, 150; Jon Arnett, Southern California, 128; Joe Walton, Pittsburgh, 97, and Jim Swink, Texas Christian, 84.

The choice of Hornung continues an almost uninterrupted monopoly by backfield men of the honor. Only twice have linemen—both ends—been honored. Larry Kelley, Yale wingman, won in 1936, and Leon Hart, Notre Dame, was chosen in 1949.

Notre Dame Bows 47-14 To Spartans

SOUTH BEND, Ind., Oct. 20 (P) — Dennis (The Menace) Mendyk, bursting 62 and 68 yards on touchdown runs, today featured unbeaten Michigan State's production line use of three sets of backs in overwhelming Notre Dame's worn-down football forces, 47-14.

In pumping more points against the Irish than at any time since the series was inaugurated in 1897, the No. 2 ranking Spartans blasted six touchdowns in the second half after the teams had battled to a 7-7 standstill.

The key play came in the first 2½ minutes of the third period when Mendyk, 183 - pound senior left half from St. Charles, Mich., streaked 62 yards on a quick opener.

John Matsko booted the first of his three extra points and the Spartans were off to their greatest victory over the Irish since blanking them 35-0 in 1951.

The triumph, before an overflowing throng of 59,378 fans, was MSU's fourth over the Irish in their last five meetings and gave coach Terry Breannan's young team its third loss in four starts this season.

Mich. State	0 7 14 26—47	
Notre Dame	0 7 0 7—14	

Michigan State scoring: touchdowns, Wilson (1, plunge); Mendyk 2 (62, run, 68, run), Gilbert (2, plunge); Peaks (2, plunge); Harding (38, interception); Arend (65, run). Conversions, Matskos, Panitch 2.

Notre Dame scoring: touchdowns, Reynolds (5, run); Sipes (2, plunge). Conversions, Hornung 2.

The eager fresh battalions — led by quarterbacks Pat Wilson, Ninowski and Panitch; halfbacks Peaks and Mendyk and fullbacks Gilbert, Arend and sophomore Bob Handloser — slammed through the Irish for 396 yards rushing and 125 more passing.

1956 Season Statistics

ND	TEAM	OPP.
130	POINTS SCORED	289
142	FIRST DOWNS	193
92	by RUSHING	147
46	by PASSING	40
4	by PENALTIES	6
1708	YARDS RUSHING	2791
431	Times Carried	548
4.0	Yards-per-try	5.0
1264	YARDS PASSING	935
167	Passes Attempted	135
87	Passes Completed	66
.521	Completion Percentage	.489
9	Passes Intercepted by	18
160	Yards Int. Returned	357
2972	TOTAL OFFENSE	3726
39	PUNTS	31
1433	Total Yards	1219
36.7	Average	39.3
129	Yards Punts Returned	173

PASSES CAUGHT

PLAYER	NUMBER	YARDS	TD
Morse	20	442	1
Lewis	11	170	1
Lima	7	105	0
Royer	7	85	1
Ward	6	77	1
Wetoska	5	57	1
Lynch	5	54	0
Reynolds	4	63	0
Myers	4	39	0
Toth	3	49	0
Prendergast	3	29	0
Hornung	3	26	0
Just	3	25	0
Sipes	3	24	0
Studer	2	3	0
Munro	1	16	0

SCORING

PLAYER	TD	PAT	POINTS
Hornung	7	14	56
Ward	3	0	18
Lewis, Reynolds	2	0	12
Morse, Royer, Sipes, Williams, Wetoska	1	0	6
Safety (with Iowa)	0	0	2

PUNTING

PLAYER	NUMBER	YARDS	AVG.
Hornung	33	1242	37.6
Cooke	4	155	38.8
Morse	1	36	36.0

TACKLES: (leaders only and includes assists):

Sullivan 79; Hornung 55; Nagurski 52; Ecuyer 46; Lewis 44; Hedrick 41; Shulsen 37; Geremia 35; Reynolds 26; Wetoska 25; Morse, Gaydos and Lima 23; Myers and Just 22; Mosca 21; McGinley and Royer 18; Ward 14; Williams 13.

PUNTS RETURNED

PLAYER	NUMBER	YARDS	TD
Hornung	4	63	0
Lewis	5	46	0
Morse	1	12	0
Lynch	2	8	0

KICKOFFS RETURNED

PLAYER	NUMBER	YARDS	TD
Hornung	16	496	1
Ward	9	195	1
Lewis	6	167	0
Morse	4	72	0
Lynch	2	53	0
Williams	3	45	0
Lima	3	36	0
Reynolds	2	33	0
McDonnell	1	27	0
Wetoska	1	19	0
Just	1	17	0
Milota	1	14	0

PASS INTERCEPTIONS

PLAYER	NUMBER	YARDS	TD
Lewis	3	39	0
Hornung	2	59	0
Williams	1	30	0
Shulsen	1	12	0
Sullivan	1	11	0
Ward	1	1	0
Lawrence	0*	5	0

*On lateral from Hornung

PASSES BROKEN UP: (leaders only) Hornung 7; Lynch, Morse, Reynolds, Ward and Lewis 2.

RUSHING

PLAYER	TC	YARDS	AVG.
Hornung	94	420	4.5
Lewis	59	292	4.9
Ward	38	170	4.5
Lima	39	157	4.0
Morse	48	148	3.0
Milota	25	99	4.0
Just	27	96	3.6
Reynolds	20	76	3.8
Studer	18	63	3.5
Williams	22	46	2.0
Royer	0*	39	0.0
Pietrosante	8	27	3.4
Sipes	5	20	4.0
Odyniec	6	19	3.3
McDonnell	2	10	5.0
Cooke	4	10	2.5
Lynch	14	10	0.7
Selcer	2	6	3.0

*On run with recovered fumble

PASSING

PLAYER	ATT.	COMP.	INT.	YDS.	TD.	PCT.
Hornung	111	59	13	917	3	.532
Williams	31	16	4	197	1	.516
Morse	7	5	1	68	0	.714
Cooke	12	6	0	63	1	.500
Milota	2	1	0	19	0	.500
Lewis	3	0	0	0	0	.000
Ward	1	0	0	0	0	.000

NOTRE DAME 1957 Varsity Alphabetical Roster

No.	Name	Pos.	Age	Ht.	Wt.	Hometown	High School	Cl.
67	ADAMSON, KENNETH	G	19	6-2	200	Atlanta, Ga.	Marist	So.
51	BESCHEN, RICHARD	C	20	6-1	190	Philadelphia, Pa.	St. Thomas More	Jr.
53	BURKE, KEVIN	C	20	6-2	200	Richland, Wash.	Columbia	Jr.
41	COLOSIMO, JAMES	E	20	6-1	198	Eveleth, Minn.	Eveleth	Jr.
69	CORSON, ROBERT	C	20	6-3	205	Manistique, Mich.	Manistique	Jr.
40	COSTA, DONALD	G	20	5-11	195	Ellwood City, Pa.	Lincoln	Jr.
24	CROTTY, JAMES	HB	19	5-10	185	Seattle, Wash.	Intern'l Falls, Minn.	So.
2	DeNARDO, RONALD	FB	21	6-3	195	Bloomington, Ill.	Trinity	Sr.
64	DJUBASAK, PAUL	G-T	21	6-0	200	Cleveland, Ohio	Benedictine	Sr.
46	DOLAN, PATRICK	T	21	6-3	210	Throop, Pa.	Scranton Tech	Sr.
32	DOYLE, PATRICK	HB	19	6-0	190	Sioux City, Ia.	Heelan	So.
1	DUGAN, MICHAEL	QB	20	6-1	180	Omaha, Nebraska	Creighton Prep	Jr.
60	*ECUYER, ALLEN	G	20	5-10	195	New Orleans, La.	Jesuit	Jr.
83	FLOR, OLIVER	E	19	6-2	202	Seattle, Wash.	Seattle Prep	So.
38	FREDERICK, CHARLES	E	21	6-0	187	Ft. Thomas, Ky.	Newport (Ky.) Cath.	Jr.
68	**GAYDOS, ROBERT	G	21	6-0	200	Donora, Pa.	Donora	Sr.
66	*GEREMIA, FRANK	T	20	6-3	215	Sacramento, Cal.	C. K. McClatchy	Jr.
78	GORHAM, MICHAEL	T	19	6-3	215	Wilkes Barre, Pa.	G. A. R.	So.
22	HEALY, PATRICK	HB	21	6-1	212	Baltimore, Md.	Loyola	So.
7	HEBERT, CARL	QB	21	5-11	170	Lafayette, La.	Cathedral	Sr.
37	HICKMAN, WILLIAM	HB	20	5-11	190	Oak Park, Ill.	Oak Park	Jr.
50	HURD, DAVID	C	19	6-2	215	Three Rivers, Mich.	Three Rivers	So.
3	IZO, GEORGE	QB	19	6-2	205	Barberton, Ohio	Barberton	So.
44	*JUST, JAMES	HB	20	6-1	188	Milwaukee, Wis.	Don Bosco	Jr.
54	*KUCHTA, FRANK	C	21	6-1	205	Cleveland, Ohio	Benedictine	Sr.
72	*LAWRENCE, DONALD	T	20	6-1	212	Cleveland, Ohio	Cathedral Latin	Jr.
23	**LEWIS, AUBREY	HB	21	6-0	185	Montclair, N. J.	Montclair	Sr.
48	*LIMA, CHARLES	FB	21	6-2	190	Cincinnati, Ohio	Purcell	Sr.
74	LODISH, MICHAEL	E-T	19	6-0	210	Detroit, Mich.	Detroit U. (H.S.)	So.
31	LOOP, PAUL	G	19	6-1	208	Tulsa, Okla.	Cascia Hall	So.
25	**LYNCH, RICHARD	HB	21	6-0	185	Bound Brook, N. J.	Phillipsburg Cath.	Sr.
90	MANZO, LOUIS	T	19	6-2	205	Old Forge, Pa.	Old Forge	Jr.
73	McALLISTER, DONALD	T	19	6-3	225	Louisville, Ky.	St. Xavier	So.
75	*McGINLEY, JOHN	G	20	6-2	195	Indianapolis, Ind.	Cathedral	Sr.
16	McGINN, DOUGLAS	FB	19	6-2	195	Sterling, Ill.	Newman Catholic	So.
82	*MYERS, GARY	E	20	6-1	195	Spokane, Wash.	Gonzaga Prep	Jr.
63	MUEHLBAUER, MICHAEL	G	19	5-10	200	Buffalo, N. Y.	Canisius	So.
70	*NAGURSKI, BRONKO	T	19	6-1	230	Intern'l Falls, Minn.	Intern'l Falls, Minn.	Jr.
86	NEBEL, EDWARD	E	19	6-2	195	Mt. Clemens, Mich.	St. Mary's	So.
76	NICOLAZZI, ROBERT	T	19	6-2	215	Kenosha, Wis.	Mary D. Bradford	So.
18	ODYNIEC, NORMAN	FB	20	5-11	180	Greensboro, N. C.	Greensboro	Jr.
81	OWENS, WILLIAM	E	21	6-2	190	Lafayette, La.	Cathedral	Sr.
49	PIETROSANTE, NICK	FB	20	6-2	205	Ansonia, Conn.	Notre Dame (W. Haven)	Jr.
61	PIETRZAK, ROBERT	G	19	6-2	215	Hamtramck, Mich.	Cath. Central	So.
87	**PRENDERGAST, RICHARD	E	21	6-2	205	Homewood, Ill.	Mt. Carmel (Chicago)	Sr.
33	PRING, LARRY	G	19	5-9	190	Salisbury, N. C.	Boyden	So.
57	PUNTILLO, CHARLES	T	20	6-2	205	East Chicago, Ind.	Roosevelt	Jr.
27	REYNOLDS, FRANK	HB	20	5-11	170	Oak Park, Ill.	Fenwick (Chicago)	Jr.
21	RINI, THOMAS	HB	19	5-9	185	Cleveland, Ohio	Benedictine	So.
84	ROYER, RICHARD	E	20	6-2	190	Cincinnati, Ohio	Purcell	Jr.
65	SABAL, ALBIN	G	19	5-11	205	Chicago, Ill.	Mendel Cath.	So.
29	SALSICH, PETER	HB	20	5-10	175	St. Louis, Mo.	St. Louis U. (H.S.)	Jr.
62	SCHAAF, JAMES	G	20	6-0	195	Erie, Pa.	Cathedral Prep	Jr.
55	SCHOLTZ, ROBERT	C	19	6-2	225	Tulsa, Okla.	Marquette	So.
58	SEAMAN, NEIL	T	20	6-1	198	Bower Hill, Pa.	Scott Twp. (Carnegie)	Jr.
10	SELCER, RICHARD	HB	20	5-9	173	Cincinnati, Ohio	Elder	Jr.
39	SHULSEN, RICHARD	G	20	6-0	190	Salt Lake City, Utah	Catholic Cent.	Sr.
26	STECKLER, GARY	G	19	5-10	200	Ville Platte, La.	Ville Platte	So.
80	STICKLES, MONTY	E	19	6-4	215	Poughkeepsie, N. Y.	Poughkeepsie	So.
52	SULLIVAN, EDWARD	C	22	6-0	195	McKeesport, Pa.	McKeesport	Sr.
13	TOTH, RONALD	FB	20	6-1	205	E. Cleveland, Ohio	Cathedral Latin	Jr.
35	*WARD, ROBERT	HB	22	5-8	156	Lamberton, Pa.	German Twp.	Sr.
91	WEBER, PAUL	E	19	6-2	196	Cascade, Iowa	Campion, Wis.	So.
89	*WETOSKA, ROBERT	E	20	6-3	215	Minneapolis, Minn.	De LaSalle	Jr.
6	WHITE, DONALD	QB	19	5-11	190	Haverhill, Mass.	Haverhill	So.
4	WILKE, HENRY	QB	19	6-0	200	Hamilton, Ohio	Hamilton Cath.	So.
9	*WILLIAMS, ROBERT	QB	20	6-2	190	Wilkes Barre, Pa.	G. A. R.	Jr.

* Denotes Monograms Won

Comeback Team of 1957

1st Row, left to right: Tom Gozdecki (associate senior manager), Dick Shulsen, Pat Dolan, Dick Lynch, Bob Gaydos, Dick Prendergast, Ed Sullivan, Wade Aubrey Lewis, Chuck Lima, Frank Kuchta, John McGinley, Mart Allen (head manager of football).

2nd Row: John McFadden (associate senior manager), Frank Reynolds, Dick Royer, Gary Myers, Al Ecuyer, Ron DeNardo, Bill Owens, Carl Hebert, Dubasek, Bronko Nagurski, Bob Wetoska, Bob Williams, Frank Geremia, Mike Muehlbauer.

3rd Row: Pete Salsich, Mike Dugan, Bill Hickman, Kevin Burke, Neil Seaman, Jim Colosimo, Charlie Puntillo, Don Lawrence, Norm Odyniec, Jim Koeth, Ken Toth, Nick Pietrosante, Dick Selcer.

4th Row: Mike Gorham, Ollie Flor, Mike Lodish, Bob Pietrzak, Pat Doyle, Dick Beschen, Don Costa, Charlie Fredericks, Lou Manzo, Dave Hurd, Ken Adamson, Pat Heady, George Izo, Monty Stickles, Don White.

5th Row: Tom Rini, Doug McGinn, Bob Nicolazzi, Bob Nicolazzi, Don McAllister, Paul Weber, Larry Pring, Jim Crotty, Ed Nebel, Bob Corson, Henry Wilke, Paul Bob Scholtz, John Quinn, Al Chonko, Gary Steckler, Al Sabal, John Harczlak.

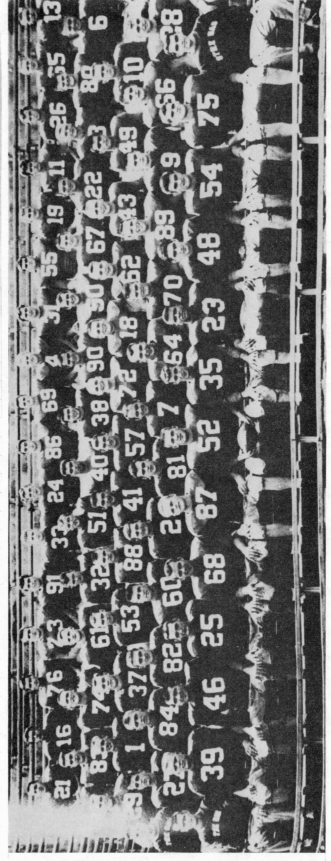

1957 Season Statistics

No.	TEAM	OPP.
200	POINTS SCORED	136
153	FIRST DOWNS	145
104	by RUSHING	98
44	by PASSING	38
5	by PENALTIES	9
1915	YARDS RUSHING	1859
520	TIMES CARRIED	466
3.7	Yards-per-try	4.0
1055	YARDS PASSING	933
166	Passes Attempted	176
79	Passes Completed	73
.476	Completion Percentage	.415
16	Passes Intercepted by	13
158	Yards Int. Returned	71
2970	TOTAL OFFENSE	2792
52	PUNTS	56
1888	Total Yards	1954
36.3	Average	34.9
122	Yards Punts Returned	226
28	FUMBLES	37
13	Ball Lost	15

RUSHING

PLAYER	TC	YARDS	AVG.
Pietrosante	90	449	5.0
Lynch	77	287	3.7
Toth	49	214	4.4
Reynolds	66	191	3.0
Just	36	169	4.7
Williams	62	144	2.3
Doyle	16	120	7.5
Lima	34	100	3.0
Selcer	12	85	7.0
Crotty	14	69	5.0
Odyniec	11	62	5.6
White	14	47	3.4
Lewis	11	20	1.8
Hickman	2	10	5.0
Wilke	1	2	2.0
Hebert	1	1	1.0
Dugan	2	—2	—1.0
Ward	1	—12	—12.0
Izo	21	—41	—2.0

PASSES CAUGHT

PLAYER	NO.	YDS.	TD
Lynch	13	128	0
Stickles	11	183	3
Wetoska	8	141	0
Prendergast	8	129	1
Colosimo	7	103	0
Reynolds	7	68	1
Royer	6	69	0
Myers	4	40	0
Pietrosante	4	5	0
Lewis	2	96	1
Selcer	2	29	0
Just	2	12	0
Odyniec	1	20	0
Doyle	1	16	0
Ward	1	11	0
Lima	1	5	0
Toth	1	—2	0

PUNTING

PLAYER	NO.	YDS.	AVG.
Pietrosante	39	1444	39.6
Lynch	1	38	38.0
Izo	8	204	25.5
Williams	4	102	25.5

PUNTS RETURNED

PLAYER	NO.	YDS.	AVG.
Lynch	4	43	10.8
Reynolds	3	30	10.0
Lewis	2	27	13.5
Just	3	12	4.0
Doyle	1	9	9.0
Scholtz	1	1	1.0

SCORING

PLAYER	TD	PAT	FG	PTS.
Stickles	3	11	1	32
Lynch	5	0	0	30
Williams	4	0	0	24
Toth	3	0	0	18
Doyle	3	0	0	18
Pietrosante	2	0	0	12
Reynolds	2	0	0	12
Lima	2	0	0	12
Odyniec	2	0	0	12
Lewis	1	1	0	7
Just	1	0	0	6
Crotty	1	0	0	6
Prendergast	1	0	0	6
White	0	5	0	5

Opponents' Fumbles Recovered: Pietrosante and Scholtz, 2; Hurd, Izo, Lynch, Lewis, Williams, Reynolds, Toth, Puntillo, Kuchta, McGinley, Nagurski and Ecuyer, 1.

Passes Broken Up: Lynch and Just, 6; Pietrosante, 5; Scholtz, Reynolds and Crotty, 3; Stickles, 2; Williams, Selcer, Sabal, Izo, Hebert, DeNardo, Colosimo, Schaaf, Hurd, Odyniec, White, Nagurski and Lima, 1.

PASS INTERCEPTIONS

PLAYER	NO.	YDS.	TD
Williams	3	28	0
Doyle	2	28	0
Izo	2	6	0
Lewis	1	36	0
Just	1	15	0
Lynch	1	13	0
Ecuyer	1	12	0
Reynolds	1	9	0
Lima	1	6	0
Odyniec	1	7	0
Pietrosante	1	0	0
Kuchta	1	0	0

KICKOFFS RETURNED

PLAYER	NO.	YDS.	TD
Lynch	6	163	0
Doyle	2	114	1
Williams	6	102	0
Reynolds	4	92	0
Crotty	2	91	0
Just	3	60	0
Lewis	1	21	0
Pietrosante	1	18	0
Wetoska	1	13	0

Defensive Statistics: Tackles—Schaaf and Ecuyer, 88; Scholtz, 60; Lawrence, 48; Royer, 46; Puntillo, 45; Pietrosante and Reynolds, 37; Nagurski, 34; Lynch, 28; Stickles, 27; Wetoska, 26; Kuchta, 23; Toth, 22; Just and Williams, 20; Djubasak and Sabal, 19; Geremia, 17; Prendergast, 15; Lima, 14; Hurd, 13; Gaydos, 12; Myers, Adamson and Selcer, 11; Izo, 9; Lewis and Crotty, 7; Sullivan and Dolan, 6; Hebert, White and Colosimo, 5; Muehlbauer, Doyle and Ward, 3; Odyniec and Seaman, 2; Dugan, DeNardo and Hickman, 1.

PASSING

PLAYER	ATT.	COMP.	INT.	YDS.	TD.	PCT.
Williams	106	53	5	559	3	.500
Izo	37	17	4	367	3	.459
Reynolds	8	4	2	58	0	.500
Dugan	2	2	0	29	0	1.000
Lynch	5	2	1	26	0	.400
White	2	1	1	10	0	.500
Lewis	2	0	0	0	0	.000
Selcer	2	0	0	0	0	.000
Just	2	0	0	0	0	.000

1957

Coach: Terry Brennan
Co-Captains: Richard Prendergast and Edward A. Sullivan

S.28	W	Purdue	12-0	A	52,108
O.5	W	Indiana	26-0	H	54,026
O.12	W	Army	23-21	N	95,000
O.26	W	Pittsburgh	13-7	H	c58,775
N.2	L	Navy (R)	6-20	H	c58,922
N.9	L	Michigan State	6-34	A	c75,391
N.16	W	Oklahoma (U) (3:50)	7-0	A	c63,170
N.23	L	Iowa	13-21	H	c58,734
N.30	W	So. California (S)	40-12	H	54,793
D.7	W	S.M.U.	54-21	A	51,000
	(7-3-0)		200-136		621,919

N—at Philadelphia

NOTRE DAME 1958 Varsity Alphabetical Roster

No.	Name	Pos.	Age	Ht.	Wt.	Hometown	High School	Cl.
67	*ADAMSON, KENNETH	G	20	6-2	200	Douglas, Ariz.	Marist (Atlanta, Ga.)	Jr.
85	BAER, MICHAEL	E	18	6-2	205	Dunkirk, N. Y.	Cardinal Mindszenty	So.
51	BESCHEN, RICHARD	C	21	6-1	190	Philadelphia, Pa.	St. Thomas Moore	Sr.
54	BOYLE, RICHARD	C	19	6-1	200	Chicago, Ill.	Leo High	So.
53	BURKE, KEVIN	C	21	6-2	200	Richland, Wash.	Columbia	Sr.
2	CASTIN, JOHN	QB	19	6-0	175	Okmulgee, Okla.	Okmulgee	So.
77	*CIESIELSKI, RICHARD	T	21	5-11	210	South Bend, Ind.	St. Joseph	Jr.
25	CLARK, WILLIAM	HB	19	5-11	175	Youngstown, O.	East	So.
40	COSTA, DONALD	G	21	5-11	195	Ellwood City, Pa.	Lincoln	Sr.
24	*CROTTY, JAMES	HB	20	5-10	180	Seattle, Wash.	Int. Falls, Minn.	Jr.
81	DEIGERT, DANIEL	E	19	6-3	195	Flint, Mich.	St. John Vianney	So.
32	*DOYLE, PATRICK	HB	20	6-0	180	Sioux City, Ia.	Heelan	Jr.
1	DUGAN, MICHAEL	QB	21	6-1	180	Omaha, Neb.	Creighton Prep	Sr.
15	EASELEY, GEORGE	HB	19	6-2	200	Lincoln, Neb.	St. Pius X	So.
14	EATINGER, HAROLD	FB	20	6-1	200	Dundee, Ill.	St. Edward's (Elgin)	So.
60	**ECUYER, ALLEN (Co-Capt)	G	21	5-10	205	New Orleans, La.	Jesuit	Sr.
83	FLOR, OLIVER	T	20	6-2	200	Seattle, Wash.	Seattle Prep	So.
92	GARGIULO, FRANK	FB	19	6-0	190	North Bergen, N. J.	St. Joseph (W.N.Y.,N.J.)	So.
66	**GEREMIA, FRANK	T	21	6-3	225	Sacramento, Calif.	C. K. McClatchey	Sr.
87	GRANEY, MICHAEL	E	19	6-5	225	Chesterton, Ind.	Bishop Noll (Hammond)	Jr.
46	GRIFFITH, DANIEL	FB	19	5-10	185	River Forest, Ill.	Fenwick	So.
7	HENNEGHAN, WILLIAM	QB	19	6-2	190	Detroit, Mich.	DeLaSalle	So.
47	HOFFMAN, CHARLES	QB	19	6-1	190	Northampton, Pa.	Northampton	So.
50	*HURD, DAVID	C	20	6-2	215	Three Rivers, Mich.	Three Rivers	Jr.
3	*IZO, GEORGE	QB	20	6-2	205	Barberton, Ohio	Barberton	Jr.
44	**JUST, JAMES	HB	21	6-2	190	Milwaukee, Wis.	Don Bosco	Sr.
28	KANE, JAMES	G	19	5-6	170	Bloomington, Ill.	Holy Trinity	So.
68	KORECK, ROBERT	T	19	6-2	210	Philadelphia, Pa.	Northeast Catholic	So.
72	**LAWRENCE, DONALD	T	21	6-1	220	Cleveland, Ohio	Cathedral Latin	Sr.
74	LODISH, MICHAEL	E	20	6-0	210	Detroit, Mich.	Detroit U. High School	Jr.
31	LOOP, PAUL	T	20	6-1	210	Tulsa, Okla.	Cascia Hall	So.
5	LUECKE, DANIEL	QB	19	6-0	175	Los Angeles, Cal.	Notre Dame (S. Oaks)	So.
23	MACK, WILLIAM	HB	21	6-0	175	Allison Park, Pa.	Hampton Twnshp.	So.
58	MONAHAN, THOMAS	E	20	6-2	185	Arcola, Ill.	Arcola	So.
63	MUEHLBAUER, MICHAEL	G	20	5-10	200	Buffalo, N. Y.	Canisius	Jr.
82	**MYERS, GARY	E	21	6-1	195	Spokane, Wash.	Gonzaga Prep	Sr.
70	**NAGURSKI, BRONKO	T	20	6-1	225	Int. Falls, Minn.	International Falls	Sr.
86	NEBEL, EDWARD	E	20	6-3	195	Mt. Clemens, Mich.	St. Mary's	Jr.
76	NICOLAZZI, ROBERT	T	20	6-2	215	Kenosha, Wis.	Mary D. Bradford	Jr.
69	NISSI, PAUL	G	19	6-0	205	Haverhill, Mass.	Haverhill	So.
18	ODYNIEC, NORMAN	FB	21	5-11	180	Greensboro, N. C.	Greensboro	Sr.
48	O'LEARY, RICHARD	FB	19	6-0	180	Terre Haute, Ind.	Schulte	So.
42	PENTZ, WILLIAM	G	19	6-0	190	Charleroi, Pa.	Charleroi	So.
49	*PIETROSANTE, NICHOLAS	FB	21	6-2	215	Ansonia, Conn.	Notre Dame (W. Haven)	Sr.
61	PIETRZAK, ROBERT	T	20	6-3	215	Hamtramck, Mich.	Cath. Central (Detroit)	So.
75	POTTIOS, MYRON	C	19	6-2	215	VanVoorhis, Pa.	Charleroi	So.
57	*PUNTILLO, C. (Co-Capt)	T	21	6-2	200	E. Chicago, Ind.	Roosevelt	Sr.
35	RATKOWSKI, RAYMOND	HB	19	6-1	185	Ridgewood, N. Y.	St. Francis Prep (Brk.)	So.
27	*REYNOLDS, FRANK	HB	21	5-11	170	Oak Park, Ill.	Fenwick	Sr.
91	RIGALI, DONALD	E	19	5-10	190	Oak Park, Ill.	Fenwick	So.
21	RINI, THOMAS	HB	20	5-9	185	Cleveland, Ohio	Benedictine	Jr.
36	RIORDAN, MICHAEL	T	20	6-0	220	Chicago, Ill.	Leo	So.
73	ROMANOWSKI, THEOD'RE	T	20	6-3	240	Albany, N. Y.	Schuyler	So.
59	ROTH, RICHARD	T	20	6-5	225	Toledo, Ohio	Mt. Carmel Seminary	So.
84	ROYER, RICHARD	E	21	6-2	190	Cincinnati, Ohio	Elder	Sr.
65	SABAL, ALBIN	G	20	5-11	210	Chicago, Ill.	Mendel Catholic	Jr.
52	SACHER, CHARLES	C	19	5-10	185	Miami, Fla.	St. Theresa (C. Gables)	So.
29	SALSICH, PETER	HB	21	5-10	175	St. Louis, Mo.	St. Louis U. High School	Sr.
30	SANFILIPPO, ANTHONY	HB	20	6-0	180	North East, Pa.	North East	So.
37	SCARPITTO, ROBERT	HB	19	5-11	180	Rahway, N. J.	Rahway	So.
62	SCHAAF, JAMES	G	21	6-0	203	Erie, Pa.	Cathedral Prep	Sr.
55	*SCHOLTZ, ROBERT	C	20	6-2	225	Tulsa, Okla.	Marquette	Jr.
79	SCIBELLI, JOSEPH	T	19	6-0	235	Springfield, Mass.	Cathedral	So.
88	SEAMAN, NEIL	T	21	6-1	200	Bower Hill, Pa.	Scott Twp. (Carnegie)	Sr.
10	*SELCER, RICHARD	HB	21	5-9	173	Cincinnati, Ohio	Elder	Sr.
39	*SHULSEN, RICHARD	G	21	6-0	200	Salt Lake City, Utah	West	Sr.
80	*STICKLES, MONTY	E	20	6-4	225	Poughkeepsie, N. Y.	Poughkeepsie	Jr.
43	*TOTH, RONALD	FB	21	6-1	205	E. Cleveland, Ohio	Cathedral Latin	Sr.
89	WETOSKA, ROBERT	E	21	6-3	200	Minneapolis, Minn.	DeLaSalle	Sr.
6	*WHITE, DONALD	QB	20	5-11	190	Haverhill, Mass.	Haverhill	Jr.
4	WILKE, HENRY	E	20	6-0	195	Hamilton, Ohio	Hamilton Catholic	Jr.
9	**WILLIAMS, ROBERT	QB	21	6-2	190	Wilkes-Barre, Pa.	G. A. R.	Sr.

* Denotes Monograms Won.

1958

Coach: Terry Brennan
Co-Captains: Allen J. Ecuyer and
Charles F. Puntillo

S.27	W	Indiana	18-0	H	49,347
O.4	W	S.M.U.	14-6	A	61,500
O.11	L	Army	2-14	H	c60,564
O.18	W	Duke	9-7	H	c59,068
O.25	L	Purdue (R)	22-29	H	c59,563
N.1	W	Navy	40-20	N	c57,773
N.8	L	Pittsburgh (0:11)	26-29	A	55,330
N.15	W	North Carolina	34-24	H	c56,839
N.22	L	Iowa	21-31	A	c58,230
N.29	W	So. California	20-13	A	66,903
		(6-4-0)	206-173		585,117

N—at Baltimore

Notre Dame Edges Duke On Stickles' Field Goal

SOUTH BEND, Ind. (P)—Monty Stickles, 225-pound end, snagged an 8-yard scoring pass and booted a 23-yard field goal for all of penalty-bogged Notre Dame's scoring in a tough 9-7 football triumph over Duke's spry Blue Devils today.

In the first gridiron meeting between the two schools, Notre Dame—a two-touchdown favorite —trailed 7-6 until Stickles booted his perfect three-pointer midway in the third period.

Irish Quarterback Bob Williams, who tossed the touchdown shot to Stickles early in the first quarter, also held the ball for the field goal.

Duke Scores On Pass

Duke's touchdown came later in the first quarter. Quarterback Bob Brodhead looped a neat 4-yard pass to Halfback Dane Lee in the end zone. The Blue Devils went ahead 7-6 when Wray Carlton booted the extra point.

Notre Dame had a whopping assessment of 135 yards in penalties, compared with only 10 for Duke which was an alert, scrappy foe all this sunny, pleasant football afternoon.

Irish Rush 266 Yards

The Irish, rolling to 266 yards from rushing with Sophomore Red Mack carrying the hod, bounced back from last week's 14-2 setback by Army for a 3-1 season record.

Duke, winning its last two starts over Illinois and Baylor after losing to South Carolina and Virginia, now has a 2-3 mark.

Notre Dame started in complete charge of the game, controlling the ball the first 4½ minutes and scoring on a 57-yard drive in five plays.

Prior to Williams' clever aerial shot to Stickles for the game's first score, Mack had scampered 64 yards for a Notre Dame touchdown which was recalled because of Irish holding.

Then Mack started the Irish scoring drive rolling with a 45-yard run to Duke's 13. Four plays later came the payoff toss from Williams to Stickles.

Notre Dame's gamble for two points after its opening touchdown failed.

Nick Pietrosante tried to shoot a pass to Bob Wetoska but Duke defenders batted it down.

Duke's brisk attack quickly retaliated in the first period for a touchdown in a 60-yard strike in 10 plays. The score came on Brodhead's clean flip to Lee from the 4-yard line.

The Blue Devils moved ahead 7-6 on Wray Calrton's extra point boot. That's the way the first half ended, although Notre Dame had a 30-yard run from Bob Scarpitto to Duke's 46 and a 52-yard run, nullified by Irish clipping, by Bob White to Duke's 25.

Duke	7	0	0—7	
Notre Dame	6	0	3	0—9

Notre Dame - Stickles 8 pass from Williams (pass failed).

Duke - Lee 4 pass from Brodhead (Carlton kicked).

Notre Dame (P) Stickles 23 field goal.

ARMY

MAJOR C. D. DALY
1913 Army Coach

BENJAMIN F. HOGE
1913 Army Captain

OFFICIAL PROGRAM

October 11, 1958
NOTRE DAME STADIUM

FIFTY CENTS

JESSE C. HARPER
1913 Notre Dame Coach

KNUTE ROCKNE
1913 Notre Dame Captain

NOTRE DAME

1958 Season Statistics

TEAM

Notre Dame		Opponents
206	Points Scored	173
194	First Downs	141
120	by Rushing	85
66	by Passing	61
8	by Penalties	6
2136	Yards Rushing	1441
512	Times Carried	434
4.2	Yards-per-try	3.3
1561	Yards Passing	1217
198	Passes Attempted	183
93	Passes Completed	85
.470	Completion Percentage	.464
18	Passes Intercepted by	22
119	Yards Int. Returned	185
3697	TOTAL OFFENSE	2658
39	Punts	52
1305	Total Yards	2026
33.5	Average	39.0
405	Yards Punts Returned	85
39	Fumbles	34
23	Ball Lost	13

PASSES CAUGHT

Player	Number	Yards	TD
Stickles	20	328	7
Mack	8	227	1
Wetoska	12	210	1
Myers	9	177	1
Scarpitto	6	155	1
Crotty	13	137	0
Royer	7	122	1
Pietrosante	10	78	0
Odyniec	3	49	0
Doyle	2	47	1
Toth	3	16	0
Wilke	1	15	0

SCORING

Player	TD	PAT	SAF.	FG	Pts.
Stickles	7	15	0	1	60
Mack	6	0	0	0	36
Pietrosante	4	1 (pass)	0	0	26
Izo	4	0	0	0	24
Williams	4	0	0	0	24
Doyle	1	0	0	0	6
Royer	1	0	0	0	6
Myers	1	0	0	0	6
Scarpitto	1	0	0	0	6
Wetoska	1	0	0	0	6
Crotty	0	1 (pass)	0	0	2
Team	0	0	2	0	4

KICKOFFS RETURNED

Player	No.	Yds.	TD
Crotty	9	228	0
Mack	5	94	0
Williams	4	55	0
Izo	3	39	0
Rini	1	24	0
Reynolds	1	22	0
Doyle	2	21	0
Just	1	19	0
Pietrosante	1	17	0
Scarpitto	2	16	0
Stickles	1	5	0

RUSHING

Player	TC.	Yds.	Avg.
Pietrosante	117	556	4.8
Mack	71	429	6.0
Crotty	67	315	4.7
Odyniec	58	273	4.7
Scarpitto	28	149	5.3
Williams	44	140	3.2
Toth	32	111	3.5
Just	15	88	5.9
Doyle	28	74	2.6
Reynolds	7	32	4.6
Rini	4	17	4.3
White	17	17	1.0
Dugan	2	4	2.0
Selcer	1	2	2.0
Izo	21	-59	-2.8

PASS INTERCEPTIONS

Player	No.	Yds.	TD
Just	1	30	0
Hurd	2	18	0
Wetoska	1	17	0
Ecuyer	2	16	0
White	1	12	0
Izo	4	11	0
Scholtz	1	8	0
Royer	1	6	0
Williams	3	1	0
Pottios	1	0	0
Crotty	1	0	0

PUNTING

Player	No.	Yds.	Avg.
Odyniec	3	130	43.3
Scarpitto	8	273	34.1
Pietrosante	26	877	33.7
Reynolds	1	15	15.0
Williams	1	10	10.0

PUNTS RETURNED

Player	No.	Yds.	Avg.
Scarpitto	4	142	35.5
Mack	3	103	34.3
Crotty	5	64	12.8
Doyle	7	64	9.1
White	2	22	11.0
Rini	1	6	6.0
Odyniec	1	4	4.0

DEFENSIVE STATISTICS

Tackles

Ecuyer 78; Adamson 53; Scholtz 51; Mack 48; Pietrosante 44; Lawrence 43; Geremia 39; Crotty, Wetoska, and Hurd 38; Royer and Shulsen 36; Pottios 32; Odyniec and Stickles 31; Puntillo and Sabal 28; Schaaf 26; Williams and Scibelli 23; Izo and Myers 21; Toth 18; Scarpitto 12; Reynolds, Doyle, and Nagurski 11; Dugan 9; White and Just 8; Rini 7; Loop and Pietrzak 4; Burke 3; Lodish and Muehlbauer 1.

Passes Broken Up

Crotty 4; Williams, Mack, Doyle, and Pietrosante 3; Stickles, Scarpitto, and Hurd 2; Just, Burke, White, Lawrence, Toth, Wetoska, Schaaf, Odyniec, Rini, and Sabal 1.

Opponents Fumbles Recovered

Stickles, Hurd and Lawrence 2; Izo, Pottios, Crotty, Nagurski, Scholtz, Odyniec and Ecuyer 1.

PASSING

Player	Att.	Comp.	Had Int.	Yds.	TD	Pct.
Izo	118	60	11	1067	9	.508
Williams	65	26	9	344	4	.400
White	10	4	2	82	0	.400
Dugan	3	2	0	36	0	.666
Pietrosante	1	1	0	32	0	1.000
Mack	1	0	0	0	0	.000

Notre Dame Fires Terry Brennan

Kuharich Looms As Successor

SOUTH BEND. Ind. (P)—Terry Brennan said Sunday night he has been fired as head football coach of Notre Dame.

The boy wonder who took over as Irish head coach five years ago and succeeded the ailing Frank Leahy said he knew of no reason for his dismissal except that "they wanted a change."

Brennan said he had no idea whom his successor would be but the Associated Press learned from an excellent source that Joe Kuharich would take over.

Kuharich, former Notre Damer, recently signed a five-year contract to continue as head coach of the professional Washington Redskins.

"I knew about this thing a couple of days ago." said Brennan. "The announcement was to have been made tonight but I guess it leaked out. These things usually do."

Brennan said the decision was made by the Notre Dame Board of Athletic Control. Brennan's five year record at Notre Dame was 32 victories and 18 defeats.

Great Irish Player

Brennan said he did not know whom his successor would be but added "I can only say it will not be someone at Notre Dame."

That, apparently knocked out the possibility of any of Brennan's assistants—Bill Fischer, Bill Walsh, Bernie Witucki, Jack Zilly, Bernie Crimmins, Hugh Devore and Hank Stram—getting the job. (Zilly hails from Southington, Conn.)

Brennan played varsity football at Notre Dame for four years from 1945 through 1948. A great player, his finest performances came against Army in a scoreless tie in 1946 and the following year his 97-yard touchdown runback of the opening kickoff sparked the Irish to a 27-7 triumph.

Brennan went on to coach high school at Mt. Carmel High School of Chicago. where his teams won an unprecedented three successive city titles. In 1953. Leahy brought him to Notre Dame as freshman football coach.

Less than a year later Leahy resigned for reasons given as ill health and Brennan was named head coach on Feb. 1, 1954. Brennan was 25 at the time.

No Time To Think

Asked what his plans are, Brennan said:

"It all happened so fast, I haven't had time to reflect. I'll think about it for a couple of days and decide after that."

Hard Core Drive To Provide Talent Equal To Opponents

SOUTHBEND, Ind., (P) — A hard-core recruiting program with enough athletic scholarships to provide talent equal to any of Notre Dame's future football opponents — that is the picture indicated Tuesday by the Irish's new head coach, Joe Kuharich.

Kuharich returnd to his South Bend home and his alma mater, where he played for Elmer Layden 20 years ago, as successor to 30-year-old Terry Brennan. Brennan was released for not winning enough football games. He had a 32-18 record in five years.

Understanding of Minds

Kuharich, who since 1954 has been coach of the professional Washington Redskins, said "I've had an understanding of the minds" with Notre Dame officials in regard to scholarships. He added:

"This is going to be a tough job, but all coaching jobs are tough. The number of scholarships that we give out to prospective athletics will be flexible and adequate and in the same proportion in comparison with the football teams we will meet."

The 41-year-old Kuharich, whose last collegiate coaching experience was in guiding the University of San Francisco to an undefeated season in 1951, declined to comment on the actual number of scholarships to be available. But he seemed satisfied that he had enough to go out and try to get the material he wants.

Stepped Up Emphasis

He also refused to be put on the spot by estimating how many games he would have to win a season to satisfy what appears to be a return to stepped-up football emphasis at Notre Dame.

"That is one question I will not answer, and it shouldn't even be asked," said Kuharich, who has signed a four-year contract at a figure which might be close to $15,000 annually.

"I think so much of Notre Dame," he continued, "that even if the Redskins had won the pro title this last season, I still would have wanted to return to Notre Dame if given opportunity."

Kuharich's Redskins had a 4-7 mark in the National Football League this season. He was released from four years of a five-year contract by Washington President George Preston Marshall so he could accept the Notre Dame position.

NOTRE DAME Alphabetical Roster

No.	Name	Pos.	Age	Ht.	Wt.	Hometown	High School	Cl.
67	**ADAMSON, KEN (Capt.)	G	21	6-2	205	Colo. Springs, Colo.	Marist (Atlanta, Ga.)	Sr.
87	AUGUSTINE, CHARLES	E	19	6-3	205	San Rafael, Calif.	Marin	So.
71	BILL, ROBERT	T	18	6-2	220	Garden City, N. Y.	Garden City	So.
54	BOYLE, RICHARD	C	20	6-1	200	Chicago, Ill.	Leo	Jr.
79	BROWN, TOM	T	19	6-4	235	Norwalk, Ohio	St. Paul	So.
64	BUONICONTI, NICHOLAS	G	19	5-11	210	Springfield, Mass.	Cathedral	So.
85	BURNELL, MAX	E	20	6-3	195	Evanston, Ill.	St. George	So.
90	CANDIDO, DON	E	18	5-11	195	St. Louis, Mo.	Bishop DuBourg	So.
73	CAROLLO, JOSEPH	T	19	6-2	230	Wyandotte, Mich.	Roosevelt	So.
2	CASTIN, JOHN	QB	20	6-0	175	Okmulgee, Okla.	Okmulgee	Jr.
77	*CIESIELSKI, RICHARD	T	22	5-11	210	South Bend, Ind.	St. Joseph	Sr.
25	CLARK, WILLIAM	HB	20	5-11	180	Youngstown, Ohio	East	Jr.
57	CLEMENTS, WILLIAM	C	18	6-4	220	Philadelphia, Pa.	LaSalle	So.
41	*COLOSIMO, JAMES	E	22	6-1	195	Eveleth, Minn.	Eveleth	Sr.
24	**CROTTY, JAMES	HB-FB	21	5-10	185	Seattle, Wash.	Int. Falls, Minn.	Sr.
33	DABIERO, ANGELO	HB	19	5-8	165	Donora, Pa.	Donora	So.
20	DE LUCA, RAYMOND	HB	20	6-0	180	Pueblo, Colo.	Pueblo Catholic	So.
32	**DOYLE, PATRICK	HB	21	6-0	180	Sioux City, Iowa	Heelan	Sr.
72	FLOR, OLIVER	T	21	6-2	200	Seattle, Wash.	Seattle Prep.	Sr.
88	FORD, WILLIAM	E	19	6-2	200	Benton H'bor, Mich.	St. John	So.
13	GARDOCKI, THOMAS	T	19	6-2	200	Wyandotte, Mich.	St. Mary (Orchard Lk.)	Jr.
49	GARGIULO, FRANK	FB	20	6-0	190	North Bergen, N. J.	W. New York, N. J.	Jr.
66	GIACINTO, MICHAEL	G	19	6-1	215	Bayside, N. Y.	St. Francis Prep.	So.
48	GRAY, GERRY	FB	18	6-2	195	Baltimore, Md.	Calvert Hall	So.
4	HAFFNER, GEORGE	QB	18	6-0	180	Chicago, Ill.	Mt. Carmel	So.
30	HEALY, PATRICK	HB	23	6-1	210	Baltimore, Md.	Loyola	Jr.
53	HECOMOVICH, THOMAS	C	19	6-3	205	Bovey, Minn.	Greenway, Coleraine	So.
83	HEENAN, PATRICK	E	22	6-2	190	Detroit, Mich.	Univ. of Detroit H. S.	Sr.
7	HENNEGHAN, WILLIAM	QB	20	6-2	190	Detroit, Mich.	De LaSalle	Jr.
70	HINDS, ROBERT	T	19	6-0	215	Cincinnati, Ohio	Xavier	So.
3	**IZO, GEORGE	QB	21	6-2	210	Barberton, Ohio	Barberton	Sr.
1	JORLING, THOMAS	QB	19	6-1	200	Cincinnati, Ohio	Xavier	So.
28	KANE, JAMES	G	20	5-6	175	Bloomington, Ill.	Holy Trinity	Jr.
68	KORECK, ROBERT	T	20	6-2	210	Philadelphia, Pa.	N. E. Catholic	Jr.
29	LIGGIO, THOMAS	HB	19	5-11	195	W. New York, N. J.	St. Joseph	So.
47	LINEHAN, EARL	T	18	6-3	220	Tulsa, Okla.	Cascia Hall	So.
51	LINEHAN, JOHN	T-C	20	6-0	205	Tulsa, Okla.	Cascia Hall	So.
74	LODISH, MICHAEL	E	21	6-0	210	Detroit, Mich.	Univ. of Detroit H. S.	Sr.
62	LOULA, JAMES	G	19	6-0	195	Rock Island, Ill.	Alleman	So.
5	LUECKE, DANIEL	QB	20	6-0	175	Los Angles, Calif.	Notre Dame (S. Oaks.)	Jr.
23	*MACK, WILLIAM	HB	22	6-0	175	Allison Pk., Pa.	Hampton Township	Jr.
44	MAGNOTTA, MIKE	G	19	5-10	210	Albion, Mich.	Albion	So.
84	MIKACICH, JAMES	E	18	6-2	205	Sacramento, Calif.	Bishop Armstrong	So.
89	MONAHAN, TOM	E	21	6-2	185	Arcola, Ill.	Arcola	Jr.
63	MUEHLBAUER, MICHAEL	G	21	5-10	200	Buffalo, N. Y.	Canisius	Sr.
45	NAAB, RICHARD	FB	18	6-0	190	Rock Island, Ill.	Alleman	So.
86	NEBEL, EDWARD	E	21	6-3	195	Mt. Clemens, Mich.	St. Mary's	Sr.
40	NICOLAZZI, ROBERT	T	21	6-2	215	Kenosha, Wis.	Mary D. Bradford	Sr.
69	NISSI, PAUL	G	20	6-0	205	Haverhill, Mass.	Haverhill	Jr.
18	O'LEARY, RICHARD	HB	20	6-0	180	Terre Haute, Ind.	Schulte	Jr.
38	PERKOWSKI, JOSEPH	FB	19	6-0	200	Wilkes Barre, Pa.	Coughlin	So.
61	PIETRZAK, ROBERT	G	20	6-3	215	Hamtramck, Mich.	Cent. Cath. (Detroit)	Jr.
75	*POTTIOS, MYRON	C	20	6-2	215	Van Voorhis, Pa.	Charleroi	Jr.
56	POWERS, JOHN	C	19	6-2	215	Harvard, Ill.	Campion (Wis.)	So.
35	RATKOWSKI, RAY	HB	20	6-1	185	Ridgewood, N. Y.	St. Francis (Brk., N. Y.)	Jr.
21	RINI, THOMAS	HB	21	5-9	185	Cleveland, Ohio	Benedictine	Sr.
59	ROTH, RICHARD	T	21	6-5	225	Toledo, Ohio	Mt. Carmel Seminary	Jr.
60	ROY, NORBERT	G	19	5-10	195	Baton Rouge, La.	Istrouma	So.
65	**SABAL, ALBIN	G-T	21	5-11	210	Chicago, Ill.	Mendel Cath.	Sr.
37	SCARPITTO, BOB	HB	20	5-11	180	Rahway, N. J.	Rahway	Jr.
55	**SCHOLTZ, BOB	C	21	6-2	235	Tulsa, Okla.	Marquette	Sr.
9	SCHULZ, CLAY	QB	19	6-1	190	Schofield, Wis.	D. C. Everest	So.
36	SEFCIK, GEORGE	HB	19	5-8	170	Cleveland, Ohio	Benedictine	So.
80	**STICKLES, MONTY	E	21	6-4	225	Poughkeepsie, N. Y.	Poughkeepsie	Sr.
81	TRAVER, LESLIE	E	19	6-2	190	Toledo, Ohio	Alliance (Ohio)	So.
52	VIOLA, GENE	C	19	6-1	215	Scranton, Pa.	Scranton Central	So.
6	**WHITE, DON	QB-FB	21	5-11	190	Haverhill, Mass.	Haverhill	Sr.
82	WILKE, HENRY	E	21	6-0	195	Hamilton, Ohio	Hamilton Catholic	Sr.
78	WILKE, ROGER	T	19	6-1	230	Hamilton, Ohio	Hamilton Catholic	So.
76	WILLIAMS, GEORGE	T	19	6-2	220	Marshfield, Mass.	Arch. Williams	So.
58	ZMARZLY, TED	G	19	5-10	215	Cleveland, Ohio	Benedictine	So.

* Denotes Monograms Won.

1959					
Coach: Joseph L. Kuharich					
Captain: Kenneth M. Adamson					
S.26	W	North Carolina (R)	28-8	H	56,746
O.3	L	Purdue	7-28	A	c50,362
O.10	W	California	28-6	A	68,500
O.17	L	Michigan State	0-19	A	73,480
O.24	L	Northwestern (R)	24-30	H	c59,078
O.31	W	Navy (0:32)	25-22	H	c58,652
N.7	L	Georgia Tech (4:27)	10-14	H	c58,575
N.14	L	Pittsburgh (R)	13-28	A	52,337
N.21	W	Iowa (3:25)	20-19	A	c58,500
N.28	W	So. California (U)	16-6	H	48,684
		(5-5-0)	171-180		584,914

AP POLL

1959
1. Syracuse
2. Mississippi
3. L.S.U.
4. Texas
5. Georgia
6. Wisconsin
7. T.C.U.
8. Washington
9. Arkansas
10. Alabama
17. NOTRE DAME

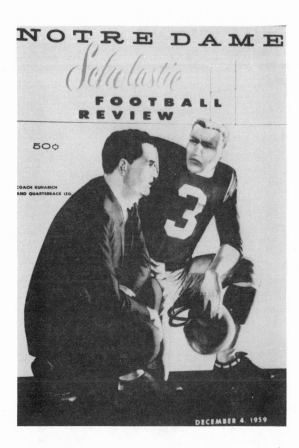

SENIORS Stickles, Flor, Scholtz, Adamson, Heenan, and Crotty line up for the last time under the scrutiny of Cardinal draft choice George Izo.

Final 1959 Season Statistics

TEAM

Notre Dame		Opponents
171	Points Scored	180
141	First Downs	137
84	by Rushing	92
53	by Passing	36
4	by Penalties	9
1352	Yards Rushing	1685
458	Times Carried	452
3.0	Yards-per-try	3.7
1431	Yards Passing	987
204	Passes Attempted	165
91	Passes Completed	65
.446	Completion Percentage	.394
13	Passes Intercepted by	19
187	Yards Int. Returned	291
2783	TOTAL OFFENSE	2672
59	Punts	62
2186	Total Yards	2139
37.0	Average	34.5
381	Yards Punts Returned	348
36	Fumbles	39
21	Ball Lost	20

PASSES CAUGHT

	Number	Yards	TD
Scarpitto	15	297	4
Heenan	12	198	1
Stickles	11	235	2
Sefcik	11	203	2
Traver	8	142	1
Crotty	8	104	0
Gray	8	56	0
Dabiero	6	64	0
Lodish	3	26	0
H. Wilke	2	27	0
Mack	2	24	0
Colosimo	2	23	0
Perkowski	2	12	0
Burnell	1	20	0

SCORING

	TD	PAT	SAF	FG	Pts.
Scarpitto	8	0	0	0	48
Stickles	2	16	0	3	37
Crotty	3	0	0	0	18
Sefcik	3	0	0	0	18
Gray	3	0	0	0	18
White	1	2	0	0	8
Ratkowski	1	1 (pass)	0	0	8
Heenan	1	0	0	0	6
Traver	1	0	0	0	6
Team	0	0	2	0	4

KICKOFFS RETURNED

	No.	Yds.	TD
Scarpitto	12	247	0
Sefcik	7	140	0
Mack	5	98	0
Dabiero	4	70	0
Ratkowski	2	43	0
Gray	2	39	0
Perkowski	2	38	0
Crotty	2	36	0
Heenan	1	26	0
Williams	1	7	0
Clark	1	5	0

RUSHING

	TC.	Yds.	Avg.
Gray	50	256	5.1
Sefcik	43	206	4.8
Scarpitto	59	199	3.8
Crotty	62	184	3.0
Perkowski	53	164	3.1
Dabiero	36	118	3.3
Ratkowski	26	108	4.2
Mack	32	86	2.7
Gargiulo	14	64	4.6
Stickles	4	27	6.9
Naab	3	26	8.7
Doyle	10	20	2.0
Schulz	1	15	15.0
Healy	1	14	14.0
Clark	7	13	1.9
Rini	1	0	0.0
Izo	6	-28	-4.6
Haffner	8	-52	-6.5
White	42	-68	-1.6

PASS INTERCEPTIONS

	No.	Yds.	TD
White	3	39	0
Sefcik	3	35	0
Scarpitto	1	48	1
Ratkowski	1	43	1
Schulz	1	13	0
Crotty	1	6	0
Perkowski	2	3	0
Hecomovitch	1	0	0

PUNTING

	No.	Yds.	Avg.
Sefcik	25	937	37.4
Scarpitto	32	1189	37.2
White	2	60	30.0

PASSING

	Att.	Comp.	Had Int.	Yds.	TD	Pct.
Izo	95	44	13	661	6	.463
White	87	39	6	653	3	.448
Haffner	22	8	0	117	1	.364

PUNTS RETURNED

	No.	Yds.	Avg.
Sefcik	10	138	13.8
Scarpitto	7	118	16.9
Ratkowski	6	52	8.7
Dabiero	4	27	6.8
Traver	1	20	20.0
Mack	3	16	5.3
White	2	8	4.0
Stickles	1	2	2.0
Clark	1	0	0.0
Haffner	1	0	0.0

DEFENSIVE STATISTICS

Opponents Fumbles Recovered

Adamson 4; Heenan and Scholtz 3; Sefcik and Traver 2; Roy, Powers, Pietrzak, Schulz, H. Wilke and Stickles 1.

Tackles

Scholtz 83; Adamson 82; Buoniconti 67; Stickles 52; Schulz 46; Flor 39; Sabal 37; Traver and Scarpitto 33; Crotty 29; Heenan and Bill 28; Pottios 24; Gray 23; Sefcik and Corollo 22; White and Muehlbauer 21; Ratkowski and Williams 18; Haffner 14; Ciesielski and Dabiero 13; Hecomovitch 12; Pietrzak and Burnell 9; Clark 6; Lodish 5; Powers and Naab 4; Roy, Doyle and Gargiulo 3; Magnotta and Colosimo 2; Koreck, Nebel, Healy, Mikacich, Augustine and Izo 1.

Passes Broken Up

Sefcik 4; Sabal and Scarpitto 3; Schulz, Ratkowski, Flor and Stickles 2; White, Mack, Buoniconti, Colosimo, Perkowski, Adamson, Traver, Corollo, Scholtz, Gray, Lodish and Heenan 1.

Blocked Kicks

Stickles, Traver and Doyle 1.

NOTRE DAME Alphabetical Roster

No.	Name	Pos.	Age	Ht.	Wt.	Hometown	High School	Cl.
59	AHERN, BILL	G	19	6-0	200	Chicago, Ill.	Loyola Academy	So.
63	AUGUSTINE, CHARLIE	G	20	6-3	205	San Rafael, Cal	Marin	Jr.
45	BARBER, DICK	HB	21	5-10	175	Logan, W. Va.	Logan	So.
71	*BILL, BOB	T	20	6-2	220	Garden City, N. Y.	Garden City	Jr.
86	BOULAC, BRIAN	E	19	6-4	195	Olympia, Wash.	Olympia	So.
64	*BUONICONTI, NICK	G	20	5-11	210	Springfield, Mass.	Cathedral	Jr.
72	BURKE, ED	T	18	6-1	225	Chicago, Ill.	Mendel	So.
85	BURNELL, MAX	E	20	6-3	195	Evanston, Ill.	St. George	Jr.
24	CAITO, LEO	HB	19	6-1	170	Cleveland, Ohio	Cathedral Latin	So.
90	CANDIDO, DON	E	20	5-11	195	Shrewsbury, Mo.	Bishop Du Bourg	Jr.
73	*CAROLLO, JOE	T	20	6-2	230	Wyandotte, Mich	Roosevelt	Jr.
2	CASTIN, JACK	QB	21	6-0	175	Okmulgee, Okla.	Okmulgee	Sr.
25	CLARK, BILL	HB	21	5-11	180	Youngstown, Ohio	East	Sr.
57	CLEMENTS, BILL	C	19	6-4	215	Philadelphia, Pa.	LaSalle	Jr.
44	DABIERO, ANGELO	HB	20	5-8	165	Donora, Pa.	Donora	Jr.
67	DEPOLA, NICK	G	19	6-2	210	Portage, Pa.	Portage	So.
88	FORD, BILL	E	20	6-2	200	Benton H'bor, Mich.	St. John's	Jr.
39	GARGIULO, FRANK	FB	21	6-0	190	North Bergen, N. J.	West New York, N. Y.	Sr.
58	GRAU, FRANCIS	G	20	6-2	210	Baltimore, Md.	Calvert Hall	Jr.
31	GRIFFITH, DAN	FB	21	5-10	185	River Forest, Ill.	Fenwick (Chi.)	Sr.
11	HAFFNER, GEORGE	QB	19	6-0	180	Chicago, Ill.	Mt. Carmel	Jr.
53	HECOMOVICH, TOM	C	20	6-3	205	Bovey, Minn.	Greenway (Coleraine)	Jr.
30	HENNEGHAN, BILL	FB	21	6-2	190	Detroit, Mich	De LaSalle	Sr.
54	HORESTER, ED	C	18	6-1	210	Chicago, Ill.	St. Rita's	So.
77	KOLASINSKI, DAN	T	19	6-2	220	Toledo, Ohio	Central Catholic	So.
91	KOLSKI, STEVE	E	19	6-3	200	Hialeah, Fla.	Archbishop Curley	So.
68	KORECK, BOB	T	21	6-2	210	Philadelphia, Pa.	N.E. Catholic	Sr.
55	KUTZAVITCH, BILL	C	18	6-2	205	Moon Run, Pa.	Montour	So.
3	LAMONICA, DARYLE	QB	19	6-2	205	Clovia, Calif.	Clovis	So.
48	LIGGIO, TOM	HB	20	5-11	195	W. New York, N. J.	St. Joseph	Jr.
32	LIND, MIKE	FB	20	6-1	195	Chicago, Ill.	Calumet	So.
51	LINEHAN, JOHN	T	21	6-0	205	Tulsa, Okla	Cascia Hall	Sr.
62	LOULA, JAMES	G	20	6-0	195	Rock Island, Ill.	Alleman	Jr.
5	LUECKE, DAN	QB	21	6-0	175	Los Angeles, Cal	Notre Dame	Sr.
70	MAGNOTTA, MIKE	G	20	5-10	205	Albion, Mich.	Albion	Jr.
41	MAXWELL, JOE	HB	19	5-11	188	Glen Side, Pa.	LaSalle	So.
84	MIKACICH, JIM	E	19	6-2	205	Sacramento, Cal.	Bishop Armstrong	Jr.
28	MINIK, FRANK	HB	19	5-7	165	Vandergrift, Pa.	Vandergrift	So.
92	MONAHAN, TOM	E	22	6-2	185	Arcola, Ill.	Arcola	Sr.
83	MURPHY, DENNIS	E	19	6-2	200	South Bend, Ind.	John Adams	So.
36	NAAB, RICHARD	FB	19	6-0	190	Rock Island, Ill.	Alleman	Jr.
69	NISSI, PAUL	G	21	6-0	205	Haverhill, Mass.	Haverhill	Sr.
21	O'HARA, CHUCK	HB	19	6-0	190	Milmont, Pa.	St. James (Chester)	So.
38	PERKOWSKI, JOE	FB	20	6-0	200	Wilkes-Barre, Pa.	Coughlin	Jr.
61	PIETRZAK, BOB	T	21	6-3	215	Hamtramck, Mich.	Detroit Cent. Cath.	Sr.
75	POTTIOS, MYRON (Capt)	G	21	6-2	215	Van Voorhis, Pa.	Charleroi	Sr.
6	RASCHER, NORB	QB	18	6-1	180	Cleveland, Ohio	Cathedral Latin	So.
35	RATKOWSKI, RAY	HB	21	6-1	185	Glendale, N. Y.	St. Francis Brooklyn)	Sr.
42	REILLY, MARSHALL	HB	20	5-11	185	Attleboro, Mass.	Attleboro	So.
60	ROY, NORB	G	20	5-10	195	Baton Rouge, La.	Istrouma	Jr.
1	RUTKOWSKI, ED	QB	19	6-1	195	Kingston, Pa.	Kingston	So.
37	SCARPITTO, BOB	HB	21	5-11	180	Rahway, N. J.	Rahway	Jr.
9	SCHULZ, CLAY	QB	20	6-1	190	Schofield, Wisc.	D. C. Everest	Jr.
22	SEFCIK, GEORGE	HB	20	5-8	170	Cleveland, Ohio	Benedictine	Jr.
89	SEILER, LEO	E	20	6-3	215	Wichita, Kans.	Kapaun	So.
87	SHERLOCK, JIM	E	19	6-0	200	Chicago, Ill.	Mt. Carmel	So.
74	SLAFKOSKY, JOHN	T	19	6-4	220	Bethlehem, Pa.	Allentown Cent. Cath.	So.
79	SNYDER, BILL	T	20	6-4	220	Hinsdale, Ill.	Hinsdale	Jr.
81	TRAVER, LES	E	20	6-2	190	Toledo, Ohio	Alliance, Ohio	Jr.
52	VIOLA, GENE	C	20	6-1	210	Scranton, Pa.	Central	Jr.
78	WILKE, ROGER	T	20	6-1	225	Hamilton, Ohio	Hamilton Catholic	Jr.
76	WILLIAMS, GEORGE	T	20	6-2	215	Marshfield, Mass.	Archbishop Williams	Jr.
66	WOOD, GREG	G	18	6-0	195	San Francisco, Cal.	St. Ignatius	So.

* Denotes Monograms Won

		1960		
		Coach: Joseph L. Kuharich		
		Captain: Myron Pottios		
S.24	W	California	21-7	H	49,286
O.1	L	Purdue	19-51	H	c59,235
O.8	L	North Carolina (R)	7-12	A	41,000
O.15	L	Michigan State	0-21	H	c59,133
O.22	L	Northwestern	6-7	A	c55,682
O.29	L	Navy (R)	7-14	N	63,000
N.5	L	Pittsburgh	13-20	H	55,696
N.12	L	Miami (Fla.) (Nt)	21-28	A	58,062
N.19	L	Iowa	0-28	A	45,000
N.26	W	So. Cal. (U) (R)	17-0	H	54,146
		(2-8-0)	111-188		540,240
N—at Philadelphia					

Drop eighth to Iowa; plug dam at S.C.

IOWA: 0-28

Iowa, already assured of a tie for the Big Ten title, lambasted Notre Dame to give Forrest Evashevsky a fitting send-off in his last game as head coach. Evashevsky, heir to the throne of Athletic Director, saw his Hawkeyes dominate every quarter against the team he most wanted to defeat in his last season.

The first half showed an ineffectual Irish offense of 21 yards, but Bob Scarpitto's booming punts kept the Hawkeyes from running rampant. Iowa's two first-half scores resulted from miscues, typical of those plaguing N.D. in previous games: the fumble and poor pass defense. On the second play of the game halfback Ed Rutkowski fumbled and alert end Bill Whisler had the ball on N.D.'s 28. After seven plays Iowa had scored. The second Iowa T.D. was credited to the combo of reserve quarterback Matt Szykowny and Bill Whisler. Whisler eluded three Irish defenders who watched the ball settle in his arms for a 28 yard score.

The Notre Dame touchdown abstinence continued in the second half while Iowa added two more scores. An unnecessary "unnecessary roughness" penalty, a 7-yard Wilburn Hollis pass, and a one-yard Hollis plunge gave the Hawks their third tally. In the fourth quarter Gene Mosley's 36-yard burst around right end set up his own two-yard T.D. plunge for the final score.

SOUTHERN CALIFORNIA: 17-0

Showing some promise for next year, Notre Dame shut out Southern California in a contest which only determined who could slip and slide farther in the mud. With intermittent downpours plaguing both teams, N.D. quarterback Daryle Lamonica literally "stuck" to a ground attack throughout the game. Lamonica, who may have insured himself a berth as next year's number one quarterback, could do nothing wrong against the Trojans as he set up all the Irish scores. On the extremely sloppy field, Lamonica rolled out for 53 yards in 10 carries, punted for a 45-yard average, and intercepted a deflected pass, returning it 18 yards.

The Irish scored all their points in the first half: a field goal by Joe Perkowski, a 9-yard touchdown slide by Bob Scarpitto, and a 1-yard lunge by Lamonica. Southern California was able to muster only seven first downs and 74 yards the entire afternoon, and their only threat came on the last play of the game. On that play, reserve quarterback Ben Charles passed to Jim Naples for what would have been a touchdown, but the halfback dropped the ball as the game ended.

The win enabled Notre Dame to match their worst season in history, 1956, when they recorded a similar 2-8 record under former coach Terry Brennan.

THE HAWKEYE LINE pinches the Irish defense to provide daylight for one of their speed merchants: Ferguson, Hollis, or Mosley.

Notre Dame 1960 Season Statistics

TEAM

Notre Dame		Opponents
111	Points Scored	188
127	First Downs	130
83	by Rushing	91
40	by Passing	33
4	by Penalties	6
1537	Yards Rushing	1608
463	Times Carried	469
3.32	Yards-per-try	3.43
900	Yards Passing	919
173	Passes Attempted	111
56	Passes Completed	53
.324	Completion Percentage	.477
8	Passes Intercepted by	21
43	Yards Int. Returned	397
2438	TOTAL OFFENSE	2527
50	Punts	57
1789	Total Yards	2100
35.8	Average	36.9
285	Yards Punts Returned	213
28	Fumbles	23
17	Ball Lost	14

SCORING

	TD	PAT	FG	TP
Scarpitto	5	0	0	30
Dabiero	3	0	0	18
Lamonica	3	0	0	18
Perkowski	0	9	1	12
Ahern	1	0	0	6
Burnell	1	0	0	6
DePola	1	0	0	6
Lind	1	0	0	6
Sherlock	1	0	0	6
Traver	0	2	0	2
Henneghan	0	1	0	1

PASSES CAUGHT

	Number	Yards	TD
Traver	14	225	0
Scarpitto	8	164	0
Burnell	6	84	1
Dabiero	5	112	1
Sefcik	5	106	0
Sherlock	5	59	1
Murphy	3	40	0
Rutkowski	2	43	0
Ratkowski	2	21	0
Lind	2	10	0
Cullen	1	22	0
Perkowski	1	10	0
Griffith	1	4	0
Gargiulo	1	1	0

PUNTING

	No.	Yards	Avg.
Lamonica	23	861	37.4
Scarpitto	15	599	40.0
Sefcik	9	239	26.6
Rutkowski	3	90	30.0

RUSHING

	TC.	Yds.	Avg.
Dabiero	80	325	4.1
Sefcik	50	248	5.0
Scarpitto	51	228	4.5
Lind	53	167	3.2
Perkowski	25	131	5.2
Ahern	24	82	3.4
Rutkowski	25	76	3.0
Lamonica	26	73	2.8
Minik	29	69	2.4
Henneghan	17	44	2.6
Liggio	10	37	3.7
Naab	12	34	2.8
Maxwell	9	30	3.3
Mack	9	29	3.2
Ratkowski	6	24	4.0
O'Hara	5	11	2.2
Griffith	3	8	2.7
Gargiulo	2	3	1.5
Caito	1	1	1.0
Rascher	7	-18	
Haffner	20	-64	

PASS INTERCEPTIONS

	No.	Yards	TD
Haffner	3	2	0
Sefcik	2	17	0
Lamonica	1	18	0
Dabiero	1	6	0
Kolski	1	0	0

PUNT RETURNS

	No.	Yards	Avg.
Dabiero	8	102	12.8
Sefcik	12	85	7.1
Minik	8	35	4.4
Scarpitto	1	16	16.0
Lamonica	1	10	10.0
DePola	1	8	8.0
Pottios	1	10	10.0
Ratkowski	1	8	8.0
Caito	1	7	7.0
Rutkowski	1	4	4.0

KICKOFF RETURNS

	No.	Yards	TD
Scarpitto	10	230	0
Sefcik	7	170	0
Dabiero	5	114	0
Minik	2	58	0
Caito	2	39	0
Rutkowski	2	37	0
Mack	1	30	0
O'Hara	1	24	0
Schulz	1	18	0
Clark	1	17	0
Haffner	1	16	0
Murphy	1	10	0
Perkowski	1	10	0

DEFENSIVE STATISTICS

Tackles

Pottios 74; Buoniconti 71; Traver 67; Roy 65; Bill 47; Linehan 41; DePola 38; Dabiero, Haffner and Schulz 37; Sefcik 35; Lamonica 33; Burke 31; Carollo 30; Murphy 26; Hoerster 25; Sherlock 23; Boulac 21; Burnell, Minik and Williams 20; Lind 17; Hecomovich 12; Castin 11; Perkowski 10; Wilke 9; Rutkowski and Scarpitto 8; Liggio 7; Grau and Powers 6; Ahern, Kolski, Pietrzak and Viola 5; O'Hara 4; Mack and Magnotta 3; Cullen, Luecke and Monahan 2; Augustine, Ford, Loula, Maxwell, Naab, Nissi, Rascher, Ratkowski and Seiler 1.

Passes Broken Up

Dabiero 6; Haffner and Sefcik 3; Lamonica, Minik, Scarpitto and Schulz 2; Boulac, Buoniconti, DePola, Gargiulo, Hoerster, Liggio, Lind, Linehan and Traver 1.

Opponents Fumbles Recovered

Traver 2; Buoniconti, Boulac, Burnell, Carollo, Haffner, Hoerster, Lind, Murphy, Schulz, Sefcik and Wilke 1.

Blocked Kicks

DePola 3; Pottios 1.

PASSES

	Att.	Comp.	Intercepted	Yards	TD	Pct.
Haffner	108	30	11	548	3	.277
Lamonica	31	15	5	242	0	.484
Rascher	30	11	3	110	0	.367
Rutkowski	3	0	1	0	0	.000
Schulz	1	0	1	0	0	.000

NOTRE DAME ALPHABETICAL ROSTER

No.	Name	Pos.	Age	Ht.	Wt.	Hometown	Class
40	*Ahern, Bill	FB	20	6-0	195	Evanston, Ill.	Jr.
59	Allen, Wayne	G	19	6-1	202	Wilmington, Del.	So.
63	Bednar, George	T	19	6-3	240	Shavertown, Pa.	So.
71	**Bill, Bob	T	21	6-2	228	Garden City, N.Y.	Sr.
61	Bitsko, Mickey	G	18	6-1	200	Van Voorhis, Pa.	So.
86	*Boulac, Brian	E	20	6-4	195	Olympia, Wash.	Jr.
2	Budka, Frank	QB	19	6-0	185	Pompano Beach, Fla.	So.
64	**Buoniconti, Nick (Co-C)	G	20	5-11	205	Springfield, Mass.	Sr.
51	*Burke, Ed	G	19	6-1	240	Chicago, Ill.	Jr.
57	Burns, Bill	C	18	6-1	200	Philadelphia, Pa.	So.
24	Caito, Leo	HB	20	6-1	175	Cleveland, Ohio	Jr.
73	**Carollo, Joe	T	21	6-2	235	Wyandotte, Mich.	Sr.
45	Costa, Paul	HB	19	6-4	230	Port Chester, N.Y.	So.
70	Cullen, Jack	T	20	6-4	220	San Francisco, Calif.	So.
44	**Dabiero, Angelo	HB	21	5-8	165	Donora, Pa.	Sr.
67	*DePola, Nick	G	20	6-2	210	Portage, Pa.	Jr.
69	DiCarlo, Mike	G	19	5-10	205	Clairton, Pa.	So.
88	Ford, Bill	E	21	6-2	200	Benton Harbor, Mich.	Sr.
93	Goberville, Tom	T-E	18	6-3	200	Chicago, Ill.	So.
58	Grau, Frank	G	20	6-2	210	Baltimore, Md.	Sr.
37	*Gray, Gerry	FB	21	6-2	195	Baltimore, Md.	Jr.
53	**Hecomovich, Tom	C	21	6-3	210	Bovey, Minn.	Sr.
54	*Hoerster, Ed	C	19	6-1	210	Chicago, Ill.	Jr.
75	Humenik, David	T	19	6-3	225	Port Vue, Pa.	So.
31	Kantor, Joseph	FB	18	6-1	190	Cleveland, Ohio	So.
89	Kelly, James	E	19	6-2	190	Clairton, Pa.	So.
50	Keneally, Patrick	C	19	6-2	215	New York, N.Y.	So.
66	Kienast, Phil	G	19	6-0	200	Oconomowoc, Wisc.	So.
77	Kolasinski, Dan	T	20	6-2	220	Toledo, Ohio	Jr.
91	Kolski, Steve	E	20	6-3	200	Hialeah, Fla.	Jr.
55	Kotzavitch, Bill	C	19	6-2	205	Moon Run, Pa.	Jr.
3	*Lamonica, Daryle	QB	20	6-2	200	Fresno, Calif.	Jr.
65	Lehmann, Bob	G	20	6-0	210	Louisville, Ky.	So.
48	*Liggio, Tom	HB	21	5-11	185	West New York, N.J.	Sr.
32	*Lind, Mike	FB	21	6-1	200	Chicago, Ill.	Jr.
62	Loula, Jim	G	21	6-0	205	Rock Island, Ill.	Sr.
23	MacDonald, Tom	HB	18	5-11	180	Downey, Calif.	So.
41	Maxwell, Joe	FB	20	5-11	185	Glenside, Pa.	Jr.
4	Meagher, Tom	QB	18	6-0	165	Louisville, Ky.	So.
68	Mikacich, Jim	G	21	6-2	205	Sacramento, Calif.	Sr.
28	*Minik, Frank	HB	20	5-7	165	Vandergrift, Pa.	Jr.
83	*Murphy, Dennis	E	20	6-2	200	South Bend, Ind.	Jr.
92	Murray, John	E	20	6-1	210	Newark, N.J.	So.
36	Naab, Dick	FB	20	6-0	190	Rock Island, Ill.	Sr.
21	O'Hara, Charlie	HB	20	6-0	190	Milmont, Pa.	Jr.
74	Olosky, Martin	T	19	6-1	220	Flint, Mich.	So.
38	**Perkowski, Joe	FB	21	6-0	200	Wilkes-Barre, Pa.	Sr.
11	Pfeiffer, Bill	QB	19	6-0	190	Chicago, Ill.	So.
43	Phillips, Dennis	HB	20	6-0	185	Pittsburgh, Pa.	So.
46	Pierson, Glen	HB	19	5-11	185	Orlando, Fla.	So.
80	Powers, John	E	20	6-2	205	Harvard, Ill.	Sr.
6	Rascher, Norb	QB	19	6-1	180	Cleveland, Ohio	Jr.
72	Reardon, Dan	T	19	6-4	225	Chicago, Ill.	So.
60	**Roy, Norb (Co-C)	G	21	5-10	215	Baton Rouge, La.	Sr.
1	*Rutkowski, Ed.	QB-HB	20	6-1	195	Kingston, Pa.	Jr.
9	**Schulz, Clay	OB	21	6-1	190	Schofield, Wisc.	Sr.
25	Secret, Bob	HB	19	6-0	180	Clarksburg, W.Va.	So.
22	**Sefcik, George	HB	21	5-8	170	Cleveland, Ohio	Sr.
87	*Sherlock, Jim	E	20	6-0	190	Chicago, Ill.	Jr.
94	Simon, John	E	18	6-3	215	St. Louis, Mo.	So.
56	Slafkosky, John	C	20	6-4	220	Bethlehem, Pa.	Jr.
33	Snowden, Jim	FB	19	6-4	235	Youngstown, Ohio	So.
79	Snyder, Bill	T	20	6-4	220	Hinsdale, Ill.	Sr.
84	Stephens, Clay	E	18	6-3	200	Burlingame, Calif.	So.
5	Szot, Denis	OB	19	6-0	185	Chicago, Ill.	So.
81	**Traver, Les	E	20	6-2	190	Toledo, Ohio	Sr.
52	Viola, Gene	C	21	6-1	220	Scranton, Pa.	Sr.
90	Vogel, Harold	E	20	6-2	190	Pittsburgh, Pa.	Jr.
78	*Wilke, Roger	T	21	6-1	230	Hamilton, Ohio	Sr.
76	**Williams, George	T	21	6-2	225	Marshfield, Mass.	Sr.
7	Zdanowicz, Wayne	QB	18	6-1	180	Jersey City, N.J.	So.

* Denotes Monograms Won

1961				
Coach: Joseph L. Kuharich				
Co-Captains: Norbert W. Roy and				
Nicholas A. Buoniconti				
S.30	W	Oklahoma	19-6	H	55,198
O.7	W	Purdue	22-20	A	c51,295
O.14	W	So. California	30-0	H	50,427
O.21	L	Michigan State	7-17	A	c76,132
O.28	L	Northwestern	10-12	H	c59,075
N.4	L	Navy	10-13	H	c59,075
N.11	W	Pittsburgh	26-20	A	50,527
N.18	W	Syracuse (0:00)	17-15	H	49,246
N.25	L	Iowa	21-42	A	c58,000
D.2	L	Duke	13-37	A	35,000
		(5-5-0)	175-182		543,975

Unhappy Ending

Durham, N. C., December 2, 1961 — The St. Valentine's Day Massacre may have been bloodier; Al Capone's gunmen used bullets. But the bodies of Bugs Moran's men could have scarcely been more riddled by Tommy Gun bullets on that sunny afternoon in Cicero than Notre Dame's defense was by Duke passes on this sunny afternoon in Durham.

Duke quarterback Walt Rappold fired 19 passes into the Irish secondary, completing 12 for 173 yards and two touchdowns. In addition, second-stringer Gil Garner threw successfully six times in nine attempts for 88 yards and two more touchdowns. The phenomenal success of the Blue Devil passing attack and the seeming inability of the Irish to stop it is largely the story of the game.

After Notre Dame won the toss and chose to receive, Reynolds kicked off to Paul Costa who returned the kick from the Notre Dame 8 to the 33. Angelo Dabiero lost two at right tackle on the first play from scrimmage, but then Mike Lind gained three up the middle and Daryle Lamonica hit Tom Goberville for 10 yards and a first down on the 44. George Sefcik gained two up the middle, and then Dabiero took a handoff from Lamonica and swung wide around left end, tight-roping 54 yards down the east sideline for the first Notre Dame touchdown. Joe Perkowski converted, and with only 2:58 elapsed in the game, Notre Dame led, 7-0. It looked very much like the Irish would crush Duke and finish the season 6-4.

Nine minutes later Duke had tied the game. Sparked by passes of 14, 6, and 22 yards by Garner, Duke moved to the Notre Dame 11. Arrington shot off his right tackle and all the way to the Irish 1, and then Garner snuck the ball across for the initial Duke score. Reynold's kick was good. Score: 7-7.

Midway through the second quarter, Notre Dame drove as far as the Duke 30 before Jack Wilson intercepted a Frank Budka pass on the nine and returned to the 32. Nine plays later, a pass interference penalty gave Duke the ball on the Notre Dame 21. On the next play Garner threw to Potts for the second Duke touchdown. Again Reynold's kick was good. Score: 14-7.

Costa returned Reynold's kick to the ND 38, and the Irish promptly got down to business. On a 15-yard burst by Lind and Budka passes of 19 yards to Goberville and 20 yards to Sefcik, the Green moved into scoring position. Mike Lind cracked off right guard one yard into the end zone for Notre Dame's final score of the season. Budka's pass for the two-point conversion was intercepted in the end zone. Score: 14-13.

But Duke was not satisfied with a one-point lead. The Blue Devils took over with only 1:10 left in the half; Rappold threw 43 yards to Widener for a first down on the Notre Dame 16, and then threw again to Widener for the tally, only 40 seconds after Duke gained possession of the ball. Halftime score: 20-13.

The third quarter brought no relief from the Duke onslaught, as the Blue Devils scored on a Reynolds field goal from the Notre Dame nine. Score: 23-13.

In the fourth quarter, Notre Dame was still unable to mount a sustained drive, but Duke continued to roll. The Blue Devils scored twice more, both times on passes. Rappold first passed 11 yards to Crisson, and then Garner hit Jay Wilkinson for 12 yards and the final Duke touchdown. Both PAT's by Reynolds were good. Final score: Duke 37, Notre Dame, 13.

Thus ended in the gloom of defeat and disappointment a season that had begun in a burst of glory.

ANGIE'S LAST

The gloom after the Duke game, though, was more than just the gloom of a so-so season; it was partly a genuine sadness, for against Duke Angelo Dabiero had made his final appearence as a Notre Dame player. And the sadness was more than the normal regret at losing a top player, because Angie himself was more than just the top Irish ground gainer in the past two seasons, the team's top defensive back, an All-American halfback, and the leading Notre Dame rusher since Don Shaefer in 1955. Angie was the classic football player: self-made by sheer work and determination, always hustling, always the leader, and pound for pound, the guttiest man on the field. . . . Notre Dame may someday have a better runner, a better blocker, or a better tackler, but there will simply never be another Angie.
— Terry Wolkerstorfer

NOTRE DAME 30 S.CAL 0

Notre Dame, Ind., Oct. 14, 1961 — On this cold and drafty October afternoon, 50,427 fans watched in awe as savage Notre Dame line play completely dominated Southern California and set 22 Irish backs loose for a net total of 322 yards rushing, as the Fighting Irish crushed the visiting Trojans, 30-0.

To say the victory was overwhelming is something of an understatement. For the first time in its 69-year football history, USC failed to gain a single yard rushing — in fact, the Trojans ended up with a four-yard deficit on the ground.

About the only thing Southern Cal could do right all afternoon was to win the toss, and this availed the visitors little as the Irish struck for two TD's in the first period and then methodically ground out the rest of the 30-point total. By the end of the game the struggle had become so one-sided that Irish coach Joe Kuharich cleared his bench, employing substitutes known only to their parents, roommates and the program printers.

The victory moved Notre Dame up to sixth place in the national polls, the highest the Irish had placed in several years, and stretched their winning streak to four games — also the best in several years. In addition, the host squad made it two years straight that USC had not scored against them, five years straight that the Trojans had not beaten Notre Dame, and twenty-one years since the visitors from the Golden State have won at Notre Dame. It was the second largest win in the 33-game series for the Irish, and the seventh time they have shut out the Trojans.

No Notre Dame player could be singled out as "the" star of the victory, unless the entire Notre Dame line be chosen for the honor. The forward wall, in addition to opening tremendous holes for the Irish backs and stifling the Trojan ground game, also proved effective on pass defense as they dropped Southern Cal quarterback Bill Nelsen for a total loss of 128 yards while he was attempting to pass.

Notre Dame gave the fans a hint of things to come the first time the ball came its way when Angelo Dabiero returned the initial Trojan punt of the afternoon for 50 yards and an apparent touchdown, only to have the score nullified by a clipping penalty. With Darlye Lamonica calling signals, the Irish then drove from their own 45 to the USC 12-yard line in eight plays. From here Lamonica circled his own right end for the first Notre Dame score of the contest — only five minutes into the game. Joe Perkowski converted, and the Irish led, 7-0.

Perkowski kicked off, and Southern Cal returned the ball to its own 28, then moved to its 44, where Ernie Jones punted on fourth down. Again the Irish were hungry for a score, and with George Sefcik, Gerry Gray and Frank Minik doing most of the ball carrying, drove down to the Trojan 17. On third and one, Lamonica passed to sophomore end Jim Kelly, who took the aerial all by himself in the end zone for the second Notre Dame score. Perkowski's placement was good and the Irish led, 14-0.

The Trojans lost end Hal Bedsole on an injury during the last series of downs in the first half, which pretty well ended their offensive performance. Nelsen was thrown for three straight losses, and USC punted. The Irish took the ball on their own 17, and, with a 43-yard dash by Angelo Dabiero providing most of the yardage, drove down to the six; then quarterback Ed Rutkowski went around left end for the tally. Perkowski's kick was wide and Notre Dame led at halftime, 20-0.

The final Notre Dame touchdown followed a fumble recovery by Joe Carollo, after he had tackled Trojan QB Bill Nelsen on the 13 while Nelsen was attempting to pass. Two plays later, a pass interference call moved the ball to the one-yard line of USC, and Daryle Lamonica plunged over for the score on the next play. Perkowski converted and the Irish led, 27-0.

In the fourth quarter, following a pass interception by Minik, the Irish moved down to the Southern Cal 32-yard line, but the Trojans, aided by a holding penalty, held fast. On fourth down, Perkowski stepped back to

In the fourth quarter, following a pass interception by Minik, the Irish moved down to the Southern Cal 32-yard line, but the Trojans, aided by a holding penalty, held fast. On fourth down, Perkowski stepped back the 39-yard line and kicked the longest field goal of his career — 49 yards — to close out the scoring as the Irish shut out USC, 30-0.
— Jerry Hea

SOUTHERN CALIFORNIA
NOTRE DAME

NOTRE DAME STADIUM
OCTOBER 14, 1961
OFFICIAL PROGRAM • FIFTY CENT

GEORGE GIPP
NOTRE DAME'S FIRST
ALL-AMERICAN
SEE PAGE 6 FOR COVER STORY

Final 1961 Season Statistics

TEAM STATISTICS

ND		Opp.
175	POINTS SCORED	182
154	FIRST DOWNS	163
39	BY PASSING	57
109	BY RUSHING	78
6	BY PENALTY	18
2245	YARDS RUSHING	1282
475	TIMES CARRIED	464
4.73	Yards-per-try	2.76
961	YARDS PASSING	1591
152	Passes Attempted	205
61	Passes Completed	107
.401	Completion Persentage	.522
17	Passes Intercepted by	20
248	Yards Int. Returned	346
3206	TOTAL OFFENSE	2873
51	PUNTS	57
1902	Total Yards	2102
37.2	Average	36.9
150	Yards Punts Returned	226
33	FUMBLES	32
20	Ball Lost	11

SCORING

Player	TD	FG	PAT	TP
Perkowski	0	5	16	31
Dabiero	4	0	0	24
Lind	4	0	0	24
Lamonica	3	0	0	18
Kelly	2	0	0	12
Naab	2	0	0	12
Sefcik	2	0	0	12
Traver	2	0	0	12
Budka	1	0	0	6
Gray	1	0	0	6
O'Hara	1	0	0	6
Rutkowski	1	0	0	6
Snowden	1	0	0	6
NOTRE DAME	24	5	16	175
OPPONENTS	23	8	20	182

PASSES CAUGHT

Player	No.	Yds.	TD
Traver	17	349	2
Dabiero	10	201	1
Kelly	9	138	2
Sefcik	5	58	0
Goberville	7	79	0
Simon	2	59	0
Lind	4	4	0
Murphy	2	19	0
Snowden	2	14	0
Perkowski	1	25	0
Powers	1	22	0
Gray	1	1	0
Minik	1	1	0
Costa	1	−9	0

RUSHING

Player	TC	Yds.	Avg.
Dabiero	92	637	6.9
Lind	87	450	5.2
Sefcik	72	335	4.7
Snowden	32	169	5.3
Gray	34	143	4.2
Lamonica	44	135	3.1
Costa	32	118	3.7
O'Hara	12	87	7.3
Rutkowski	8	41	5.1
Naab	13	37	2.9
Minik	5	39	7.8
Kantor	5	39	7.8
Phillips	5	10	2.0
Budka	31	20	
MacDonald	2	3	1.5
Perkowski	1	−8	

PUNTING

Player	No.	Yds.	Avg.
Sefcik	18	709	39.4
Lamonica	29	1113	38.4
O'Hara	2	70	35.0
Budka	1	30	30.0
TEAM	1	0	(Blk'd)

PUNT RETURNS

Player	No.	Yds.	Avg.
Dabiero	11	97	8.8
Sefcik	5	40	8.0
MacDonald	2	4	2.0
Rutkowski	1	4	4.0
Costa	1	3	3.0
Pfeiffer	1	2	2.0

KICKOFF RETURNS

Player	No.	Yds.	TD
Costa	15	359	0
Dabiero	8	203	0
Gray	4	67	0
Sefcik	3	57	0
O'Hara	1	31	0
Budka	1	10	0
Stephens	1	3	0

PASSING

Player	Att.	Comp.	Int.	Yds.	TD	Pct.
Budka	95	40	14	646	3	.421
Lamonica	52	20	4	300	2	.385
Rutkowski	5	1	2	25	0	.200

DEFENSIVE STATISTICS

TACKLES: Buoniconti 74; Bill 50; Dabiero 47; Bitsko 46; Roy 45; Sefcik and Lehmann 41; Carollo 40; Hecomovich 38; Gray and Traver 35; Lind 31; Lamonica 29; Burke 28; Kelly 26; Hoerster 24; Williams and Wilke 23; Budka 21; Murphy 20; Schulz 17; Pfeiffer and Stephens 16; Grau 15; Goberville 12; Simon 11; O'Hara 9; MacDonald 8; Rutkowski 7; Costa, Kantor and Viola 6; Minik and Olosky 5; Liggio and Powers 4; Cullen and Perkowski 3; Ahern, Boulac, and Kolski 2; Bednar, Mikacich, Murray, Naab, Snowden and Humenik 1.

PASSES INTERCEPTED

Player	No.	Yds.	TD
Dabiero	5	78	1
Sefcik	3	56	0
Lamonica	2	54	0
Budka	2	3	0
Gray	1	25	0
MacDonald	1	23	0
Hecomovich	1	4	0
Bill	1	2	0
Minik	1	2	0
Traver	1	0	0

PASSES BROKEN UP

Sefcik 9; Dabiero and Lamonica 5; Lind and Gray 4; Budka 3; Liggio and MacDonald 2; Buoniconti, Cullen, Carollo, Goberville, Kantor, O'Hara, Secret, Roy, Rutkowski and Wilke 1.

BLOCKED KICKS: Buoniconti 2.

OPPONENTS FUMBLES RECOVERED: Budka 3; Carollo 2; Wilke, Bill, Kelly, Hecomovich, Olosky and Viola 1.

NOTRE DAME ALPHABETICAL ROSTER

No.	Name	Pos.	Age	Ht.	Wt.	Hometown	Class
40	*Ahern, William	FB	21	6-0	195	Evanston, Ill.	Sr.
59	Allen, Wayne	G	20	6-1	205	Wilmington, Del.	Jr.
79	Anton, John	T	20	6-1	220	St. Louis, Mo.	Jr.
25	Antongiovanni, John	HB	19	6-0	175	Bakersfield, Cal.	So.
66	Atamian, John	G	20	6-1	205	Niagara Falls, N.Y.	So.
48	Barnard, John	HB	20	5-10	185	Kansas City, Kans.	Jr.
76	Bednar, George	T	20	6-3	234	Shavertown, Pa.	Jr.
53	Billy, Francis	C	19	6-1	215	Clairton, Pa.	So.
22	Bliey, Ronald	HB	20	6-1	190	New York, N.Y.	So.
8	Bonvechio, Alex	QB	19	5-10	185	Wainwright, Ohio	So.
86	*Boulac, Brian	E	21	6-4	205	Olympia, Wash.	Sr.
71	Brocke, James	T	18	6-2	220	Crown Point, Ind.	So.
2	*Budka, Frank	QB	20	6-0	190	Pompano Beach, Fla.	Jr.
51	**Burke, Edward	T	20	6-1	240	Chicago, Ill.	Sr.
57	Burns, William	C	19	6-1	204	Philadelphia, Pa.	Jr.
60	Carroll, James	G	19	6-1	202	Atlanta, Ga.	So.
70	Cullen, John	T	21	6-4	220	San Francisco, Cal.	Jr.
68	Dennery, Vincent	G	18	6-2	205	Philadelphia, Pa.	So.
69	DiCarlo, Michael	G	20	5-10	200	Clairton, Pa.	Jr.
20	Dupuis, Richard	HB	20	5-10	180	Windsor, Ont.	So.
78	Etten, Nicholas	T	20	6-0	220	Chicago, Ill.	Jr.
42	Farrell, Joseph	FB	20	6-0	201	Chicago, Ill.	So.
93	*Goberville, Tom	E	18	6-3	197	Chicago, Ill.	Jr.
33	**Gray, Gerard	FB	22	6-2	198	Baltimore, Md.	Sr.
58	Harding, Thomas	C	19	6-0	222	Woodstock, Ill.	So.
61	Harnisch, James	G	19	5-11	215	Poland, Ohio	So.
54	**Hoerster, Ed	C	20	6-1	216	Chicago, Ill.	Sr.
44	Hogan, Donald	HB	19	5-11	182	Chicago, Ill.	So.
7	Huarte, John	QB	18	6-0	180	Anaheim, Cal.	So.
75	Humenik, David	T	20	6-3	233	Port Vue, Pa.	Jr.
89	*Kelly, James	E	20	6-2	204	Clairton, Pa.	Jr.
52	Kostelnik, Thomas	C	19	6-2	200	Hiller, Pa.	So.
55	Kutzavitch, Bill	C	20	6-2	200	Moon Run, Pa.	Sr.
3	**Lamonica, Daryle	QB	21	6-2	202	Fresno, Cal.	Sr.
65	*Lehmann, Robert	G	21	6-0	212	Louisville, Ky.	Jr.
32	**Lind, Mike	FB	21	6-1	203	Chicago, Ill.	Sr.
23	*MacDonald, Thomas	HB	19	5-11	172	Downey, Cal.	Jr.
62	Maglicic, Kenneth	G	19	5-10	211	Cleveland, Ohio	So.
72	Mattera, Vincent	T	19	6-3	220	San Pedro, Cal.	So.
41	Maxwell, Joseph	FB	21	5-11	182	Glenside, Pa.	Sr.
63	Meyer, John	G	19	6-2	210	Chicago, Ill.	So.
28	**Minik, Frank	HB	21	5-7	161	Vandergrift, Pa.	Sr.
83	**Murphy, Dennis	E	21	6-2	203	South Bend, Ind.	Sr.
92	Murray, John	E	21	6-1	205	Newark, N. J.	Jr.
50	Nicola, Norman	C	19	6-0	235	Canton, Ohio	So.
21	O'Hara, Charles	HB	21	6-0	189	Milmont, Pa.	Sr.
74	Olosky, Martin	T	20	6-1	228	Flint, Mich.	Jr.
34	O'Rourke, James	FB	20	5-11	185	St. Louis, Mo.	Jr.
12	O'Shaughnessy, Pat	QB	19	6-2	190	Wichita, Kans.	So.
38	Paolillo, Leonard	FB	19	5-10	195	Fresno, Cal.	So.
81	Papa, Robert	E	20	6-2	202	Clifton, N. J.	So.
73	Penman, Eugene	T	19	6-2	223	Chicago, Ill.	So.
11	Pfeiffer, William	QB-HB	20	6-0	196	Chicago, Ill.	Jr.
43	Phillips, Dennis	HB	21	6-0	186	Mt. Lebanon, Pa.	Jr.
46	Pierson, Glen	HB	20	5-11	185	Orlando, Fla.	Jr.
80	Pivec, David	E	19	6-3	215	Baltimore, Md.	So.
47	Rakers, James	HB	19	6-4	196	Quincy, Ill.	So.
6	Rascher, Norbert	QB	20	6-1	187	Cleveland, Ohio	Jr.
10	Rieder, Michael	QB	20	5-11	185	Madison, Wisc.	So.
64	Ruel, John	G	18	6-1	210	Chicago, Ill.	So.
1	*Rutkowski, Edward	HB	21	6-1	202	Kingston, Pa.	Sr.
95	Schrader, Joseph	E	19	6-3	190	Lafayette, Ind.	So.
31	Selzer, Jack	HB	19	6-0	189	Fresno, Cal.	So.
87	*Sherlock, James	E	21	6-0	201	Chicago, Ill.	Sr.
94	*Simon, John	E	19	6-3	210	St. Louis, Mo.	Jr.
56	Slafkosky, John	T	21	6-4	234	Bethlehem, Pa.	Sr.
85	Snow, Jack	E	19	6-2	210	Long Beach, Cal.	So.
84	Stephens, Clay	E	19	6-3	205	Burlingame, Cal.	Jr.
5	Szot, Denis	QB	20	6-0	185	Chicago, Ill.	Jr.
79	Telfer, Robert	T	19	6-2	230	Edmore, Mich.	So.
24	Tubinis, Gerald	HB	21	6-2	200	Niagara Falls, N.Y.	So.
90	Vogel, Harold	E	21	6-2	195	Pittsourgh, Pa.	Sr.
36	Williams, Thomas	FB	19	5-10	196	Tiffin, Ohio	So.
67	Wood, Gregory	G	19	6-0	192	San Francisco, Cal.	Sr.

1962				
Coach: Joseph L. Kuharich				
Captain: Mike Lind				
S.29	W	Oklahoma	13-7	A c60,500
O.6	L	Purdue	6-24	H °c61,296
O.13	L	Wisconsin	8-17	A c61,098
O.20	L	Michigan State (R)	7-31	H c60,116
O.27	L	Northwestern	6-35	A c55,752
N.3	W	Navy (R)	20-12	N 35,000
N.10	W	Pittsburgh	43-22	H 52,215
N.17	W	North Carolina	21-7	H 35,553
N.24	W	Iowa	35-12	H 42,653
D.1	L	So. California	0-25	A 81,676
		(5-5-0)	159-192	545,859

N—at Philadelphia
°Notre Dame Stadium record

MICHIGAN STATE: 411 RUSHING YARDS

Rains, Saimes Ruin Game for Irish

Notre Dame, Ind., Oct. 20 — It appeared to many a rain spattered fan that Coach Duffy Daugherty unleashed some of the Agriculture Department's finest beef, as the mighty Spartans of Michigan State stampeded to a 31-7 rout over the Irish.

George Saimes, the man who knocked the Irish out of top contention with two touchdown runs last year, more than bettered his 1961 performance. The State captain and All-American fullback scored three touchdowns, collected 153 yards in 13 carries, and was a demon on defense. It was perhaps his finest collegiate effort.

"Let George do it" — and he did. On the fifth play of the game he dashed 54 yards for his first touchdown. Irish fans began to moan. Five plays later, another thorn in the Irish side, tiny scatback Sherman Lewis outraced the ND defenders for 72 yards and the second State touchdown. Irish hopes of an upset were nearly erased.

The early Spartan lead looked invincible, but the two teams exchanged punts and the Irish took possession inside the Spartan 50. Denis Szot was at the helm for the Irish. Szot overthrew Bliey, but connected the next time to Don Hogan for a first down on the 33. Fullback Joe Farrell hit the middle for nine; then Szot, electing to pass again, fired a strike to end Dave Pivec at the Spartan 12. Farrell carried to the eight, and twice more to the two-yard line. Then, on his fourth carry of the drive, the hard-running fullback plunged two yards to pay dirt. Ed Rutkowski added the point after and the Irish trailed 12-7 with 2:10 remaining in the first period.

The second half could be described by the word Saimes, as once again the "Golden Greek" romped for two third-quarter scores. On the Irish's second play of the half, he alertly picked off a Lamonica jump pass at the 22. Three plays gained only six yards for the Spartans and it looked like field goal time. But nothing doing. On fourth and four, the big fullback from Canton, O., took a pitchout and raced off left tackle for his second touchdown. The extra point failed again, but the Spartans, with only 3:17 gone in the third period, had jumped to an 18-7 lead.

Notre Dame's wall collapsed on the next defensive series, as the Spartans drove 57 yards for their fourth touchdown. The scoring play came when quarterback Pete Smith threw a perfect strike to end Dick Flynn. The Spartans' only noticeable weakness, extra points, was once again evident, and with 5:11 left in the third quarter, it was Michigan 24 — Notre Dame 7. Five minutes was planty of time for Saimes.

Lamonica's 59-yard punt put the Spartans on their 16, but not for long. Saimes carried twice to the 25, and Lewis followed with a 22-yard scamper to the 47. Two plays later, at the Irish 49, Big George found a hole and shot through for his third touchdown of the game. Earl Lattimer finally made good on the conversion attempt, and the Spartans increased the margin to 31-7.

Irish Coach, Joe Kuharich, disappointed with the team's third straight loss, had this to say — "They were a big, strong club with speed. They had much more depth than we did. Saimes? He's terrific. A great football player."

"Other teams might have fallen apart," said Duffy Daugherty, "but that Irish club kept scrapping." Praise comes easy to the victor though, especially to a man whose team has won its seventh straight over Notre Dame, and its tenth since 1950.

—Jack McCabe

NOTRE DAME PITTSBURGH

NOTRE DAME STADIUM • NOVEMBER 10, 19__

OFFICIAL PROGRAM • FIFTY CENTS

ND 43, PITT 22

Explosive Attack Overwhelms Pitt

Notre Dame, Ind., Nov. 10 — In this warm, sunbathed Notre Dame Stadium, a "small" homecoming crowd of 52,215 cheered as a band of Fighting Irish brutally sent the Panthers from Pittsburgh down to defeat, 43-22. The "revitalized" Notre Dame eleven hit their stride early in the game and romped to their second straight victory. Finding the field conditions considerably drier than in the previous week's encounter with Navy, the Irish unleashed a formidable offensive attack, knocking holes in Pitt's forward wall and secondary.

The victory also brought to light the passing combination of senior Daryle Lamonica to junior end Jim Kelly. Together they sparked the Irish to the victory while breaking one record and tying two. Pulling in eleven Lamonica passes for 127 yards, Kelly established a pass-receiving record, breaking the previous record of eight held by Monty Stickles. Quarterback Lamonica tossed four touchdown passes, tying Angelo Bertelli's old record, while Jim Kelly hauled in three of the four passes to equal all-pro Jim Mutscheller's twelve-year-old record. The victory was Notre Dame's second straight in the series.

Notre Dame took the opening kickoff and rolled 58 yards in 10 plays for their first score. Lamonica keyed the drive with two fourth down passes of 14 and 11 yards to Kelly. Don Hogan, a promising sophomore, carried the ball the final six yards to break the ice for the Irish. Senior Ed Rutkowski's placement split the uprights at 10:58 of the first quarter.

On Pitt's first series of downs, the stalwart Irish defense threw the Panthers for a five-yard loss, and three Notre Dame first downs later, Lamonica and Kelly were pounding at the Panthers' front door. Opportunity came with a five-yard jump pass to Kelly, and Rutkowski's two-pointer made it Notre Dame 15, Pitt 0.

The Irish defense reached for a bit of glory as they backed the Panthers into a corner and then Clay Stephens recovered a Pitt fumble to set up the third Irish touchdown. Three plays later, halfback Ron Bliey blew the

game wide open as he swept right end for seven yards and another Notre Dame touchdown.

Pitt was quick to retaliate as quarterback Jim Traficant drove the Panthers 83 yards for six points. In the remaining two quarters, the offenses pounded away, producing a seesaw battle of touchdowns.

Fighting back, the Irish moved once again with the fabulous combination of Lamonica to Kelly. Capitalizing on a blocked Pitt punt by end Tom Goberville, Lamonica rolled out and lofted a pass to Kelly in the end zone. Pitt had a few tricks of their own left. After mixing up several plays, quarterback Traficant called for the double reverse. Halfback Ed Clark responded as he rode the sideline strip 56 yards for a second Pitt tally. Pitt's All-American candidate Paul Martha picked up the two-pointer making the score Notre Dame 29, Pitt 14.

The Irish fired back with a dazzling 40-yard touchdown pass on the first play after the kickoff. This time the honors went to end Clay Stephens while Rutkowski added the extra point.

The final Irish drive of 75 yards ended as most of their touchdowns did this day — a 13-yard bomb to Jim Kelly in the end zone. It was Pitt, though, that applied the finishing touch to this sporting afternoon as quarterback Mike Mazurek took the kickoff and returned it 93 yards for the final tally of the day.

The day wasn't all Lamonica and Kelly — it was not all Notre Dame. Lamonica wouldn't have had the time to find Kelly if it hadn't have been for the superb blocking of Ed Hoerster, Bob Lehmann, Jim Carroll, and their cohorts on the offensive line. Pitt's resurgent offense might have gained more than they did had it not been for a sturdy defense which held the Panthers to half the yardage the Irish offense gained. And the powerhouse Notre Dame offense of sophomores Don Hogan, Ron Bliey, and Joe Farrell, and seniors Bill Ahern and Joe Maxwell provided the needed support. True, today there were Lamonica and Kelly; but today, there was also Notre Dame.

—Jack Gerken

Kuharich on the sidelines
in a downpour

1962 Final Statistics

TEAM STATISTICS

N.D.		OPP.
159	POINTS SCORED	192
140	FIRST DOWNS	138
1382	YARDS RUSHING	1760
449	TIMES CARRIED	435
3.08	RUSHING AVERAGE	4.05
1160	YARDS PASSING	870
195	PASSES ATTEMPTED	146
90	PASSES COMPLETED	67
.461	COMPLETION PERCENTAGE	.452
15	PASSES INTERCEPTED BY	16
166	YARDS INT. RETURNED	75
2542	TOTAL OFFENSE	2630
50	PUNTS	42
1808	TOTAL YARDS	1438
36.2	AVERAGE	33.8
11	BALLS LOST ON FUMBLES	17

DEFENSIVE STATISTICS

TACKLES:

Hoerster 73; Lehmann 61; Carroll 58; Budka 51; Gray 49; Bednar 45; Pfeiffer 39; Maglicic 35; MacDonald and Nicola 29; Goberville 25; Phillips 23; Penman 22; Kelly and Allen 21; Burns 19; Rutkowski, 17; Burke, Hogan and Olosky 15; DiCarlo, Pivec and Stephens 14; Etten and Murphy 13; Minik 12; Humenik 11; Murray and Simon 10; Ahern 9; Farrell 6; Sherlock 5; Lamonica 3; Dennery and O'Hara 1.

PASSES BROKEN UP:

Budka 8; MacDonald 5; Phillips 4; Gray and Pfeiffer 2; Burns, Goberville, Hoerster, Kelly, Lamonica and Rutkowski 1.

OPPONENTS' FUMBLES RECOVERED:

Carroll, Pfeiffer, Phillips, Pivec and Stephens 2; Gray, Hoerster, Kelly, Lehmann, Minik, Murray and Simon 1.

BLOCKED KICKS:

Goberville 2; Lehmann 1.

SCORING

Player	TD	FG	PAT	TP
Farrell	4	0	0	24
Kelly	4	0	0	24
Lamonica	4	0	0	24
Rutkowski*	1	0	17	23
Hogan**	3	0	2	20
Ahern	2	0	0	12
Minik	2	0	0	12
Bliey	1	0	0	6
Phillips	1	0	0	6
Stephens	1	0	0	6
Snow**	0	0	2	2
ND TOTALS	23	0	21	159
OPP. TOTALS	28	2	18	192

*2 on run.
**Pass for PAT.

PASSES CAUGHT

Player	No.	Yards	TD
Kelly	41	523	4
Hogan	12	146	0
Stephens	5	93	1
Minik	5	66	1
Snow	4	46	0
Murray	3	35	0
Rutkowski	3	—3	0
Phillips	2	47	1
Sherlock	2	39	0
Pivec	2	32	0
Goberville	2	29	0
Farrell	1	27	0
Simon	1	20	0
Budka	1	19	0
Bliey	1	17	0
Murphy	1	14	0
Ahern	1	9	0
Gray	1	5	0
MacDonald	1	0	0
Lind	1	—4	0

PUNTING

Player	No.	Yards	Avg.
Lamonica	49	1789	36.5
Budka	1	19	19.0

PASSING

Player	Att.	Comp.	Int.	Yards	TD	Pct.
Lamonica	128	64	7	821	6	.500
Szot	45	18	6	244	1	.400
Huarte	8	4	0	38	0	.500
Budka	9	2	3	25	0	.222
Rutkowski	2	1	0	20	0	.500
Rascher	3	1	0	12	0	.333

RUSHING

Player	TC	Yards	Avg.
Hogan	90	454	5.0
Farrell	70	278	4.0
Bliey	57	167	2.9
Lamonica	74	145	2.0
Ahern	25	97	3.9
Gray	28	94	3.4
Minik	22	61	2.8
Rutkowski	16	52	3.3
Phillips	18	38	2.1
Budka	12	21	1.8
MacDonald	10	14	1.4
Lind	8	13	1.6
Maxwell	3	9	3.0
Huarte	3	—14	--
Szot	13	—47	—

KICKOFF RETURNS

Player	No.	Yards	Avg.
Bliey	13	311	23.9
Hogan	9	206	22.9
Minik	2	61	32.0
Rutkowski	2	42	21.0
Phillips	2	39	19.5
MacDonald	2	30	15.0
Budka	1	20	—
Farrell	1	19	—
Gray	1	10	—
Burns	1	5	—
Kelly	1	3	—

PUNT RETURNS

Player	No.	Yards	Avg.
Minik	6	41	6.8
Rutkowski	2	28	14.0
Goberville	1	17	17.0
Bliey	2	10	5.0
Phillips	3	8	2.7

PASSES INTERCEPTED

Player	No.	Yards	TD
MacDonald	9	81	0
Gray	2	23	0
Murphy	1	25	0
Snow	1	23	0
Budka	1	10	0
Lamonica	1	4	0

Joe Kuharich Resigns

Hugh Devore Takes Over Irish Helm

SOUTH BEND, Ind. (P) — Joe Kuharich stepped down as head football coach at the University of Notre Dame Wednesday after four years without a winning season.

The university said the 46-year-old former Washington Redskins and Chicago Cardinals coach would take an administrative post in the National Football League.

The freshman coach, Hugh Devore, was named interim coach for the 1963 season.

The Rev. Edmund P. Joyce, executive vice president of Notre Dame, called Kuharich an able coach and said the Irish were sorry to lose him.

"We know it was a difficult decision for Mr. Kuharich to retire from the active coaching ranks," Father Joyce said.

Will Succeed Wilson

Kuharich will replace Mike Wilson as supervisor of referees and will have other administrative duties according to NFL Commissioner Pete Rozelle. Wilson is retiring on a pension at the age of 66. Kuharich will assume his new post April 15.

The South Bend native and Notre Dame alumnus left the Redskins to become Irish football boss in 1958. His teams broke even with 5-5 records in 1959, 1961 and last year, but his 2-8 slate in 1960 was the Notre Dame's worst mark in 63 years.

Devore, 52, was interim coach for Notre Dame in 1945 while Frank Leahy was in service and guided the Irish to a 7-2-1 record.

He later served as head coach at St. Bonaventure and on the staff of the professional Green Bay Packers. Devore returned as freshman coach at Notre Dame the season before Kuharich was hired.

Father Joyce said the present coaching staff would be retained.

NOTRE DAME ALPHABETICAL ROSTER

No.	Name	Pos.	Age	Ht.	Wt.	Hometown	Class
25	Andreotti, Pete	HB	19	5-9	175	Chicago, Ill.	So.
60	Anton, John	T-G	21	6-1	220	St. Louis, Mo.	Sr.
63	Arrington, Dick	T	21	5-11	227	Erie, Pa.	So.
66	Atamian, John	G	21	6-1	205	Niagra Falls, N. Y.	Jr.
48	Barnard, Jack	HB	21	5-10	185	Kansas City, Kan.	Sr.
76	*Bednar, George	G-T	21	6-3	247	Shavertown, Pa.	Sr.
59	Billy, Frank	C	20	6-1	215	Clairton, Pa.	Jr.
22	*Bliey, Ron	HB	21	6-1	190	New York City, N. Y.	Jr.
8	Bonvechio, Alex	QB	20	5-10	185	Wainwright, Ohio	Jr.
71	Brocke, Jim	T	19	6-2	220	Crown Point, Ind.	Jr.
2	**Budka, Frank	QB	21	6-0	190	Pompano Beach, Fla.	Sr.
57	*Burns, Bill	C	21	6-1	217	Philadelphia, Pa.	Sr.
1	Carey, Tony	QB	20	6-0	190	Chicago, Ill.	So.
54	*Carroll, Jim	G-C	20	6-1	225	Atlanta, Ga.	Jr.
26	Conway, Dennis	HB	20	5-9	160	Sioux City, Iowa	So.
45	*Costa, Paul	HB	21	6-4	230	Port Chester, N. Y.	Jr.
68	Dennery, Vince	G	19	6-2	215	Philadelphia, Pa.	Jr.
69	*DiCarlo, Mike	G	21	5-10	212	Clairton, Pa.	Sr.
20	Dupuis, Richard	HB	21	5-10	180	Windsor, Ont.	Jr.
32	Duranko, Pete	FB	20	6-2	228	Johnstown, Pa.	So.
78	*Etten, Nick	T	21	6-0	213	Chicago, Ill.	Sr.
42	*Farrell, Joe	HB	21	6-0	205	Chicago, Ill.	Jr.
90	Geraghty, John	E	20	6-2	190	Washington, N.Y.	Sr.
93	**Goberville, Tom	E	20	6-3	203	Chciago, Ill.	Sr.
56	Harding, Tom	C-T	20	6-0	215	Woodstock, Ill.	Jr.
44	*Hogan, Don	HB	20	5-11	190	Chicago, Ill.	Jr.
58	Hribal, Larry	G-T	19	6-2	230	Carmichaels, Pa.	So.
7	Huarte, John	QB	19	6-0	180	Anaheim, Calif.	Jr.
87	Ivan, Ken	E	18	6-1	190	Massillon, Ohio	So.
31	Kantor, Joe	FB	20	6-1	212	Cleveland, Ohio	Jr.
89	**Kelly, Jim	E	21	6-2	210	Clairton, Pa.	Sr.
67	Kolasinski, Dan	T	22	6-2	230	Toledo, Ohio	Sr.
52	Kostelnik, Tom	C	20	6-2	215	Hiller, Pa.	Jr.
65	**Lehmann, Bob (Capt.)	G	22	6-0	216	Louisville, Ky.	Sr.
37	Loboy, Alan	FB	19	6-0	195	Park Ridge, Ill.	So.
86	Long, Harry	E	18	6-0	200	LaGrange, Ill.	So.
49	Longo, Tom	HB	21	6-1	200	Lyndhurst, N.J.	So.
23	**MacDonald, Tom	HB	20	5-11	185	Downey, Calif.	Sr.
62	*Maglicic, Ken	G	20	5-10	215	Cleveland, Ohio	Jr.
53	Mattera, Vince	C	20	6-3	230	San Pedro, Calif.	Jr.
34	Mauch, Larry	HB	19	6-0	195	Belleville, Ill.	So.
3	McGinn, Dan	QB	19	5-11	180	Omaha, Nebr.	So.
51	Meeker, Bob	T	19	6-2	222	Akron, Ohio	So.
72	Meyer, John	T	20	6-2	212	Chicago, Ill.	Jr.
28	Mittelhauser, Tom	FB	20	5-11	188	Pittsburgh, Pa.	Jr.
50	*Nicola, Norm	C	20	6-0	230	Canton, Ohio	Jr.
21	O'Hara, Charlie	HB	21	6-0	190	Milmont, Pa.	Sr.
74	*Olosky, Marty	T	21	6-1	220	Flint, Mich.	Sr.
81	Papa, Bob	E	21	6-2	207	Clifton, N. J.	So.
11	*Pfeiffer, Bill	HB	21	6-0	205	Chicago, Ill.	Sr.
43	*Phillips, Denny	FB-E	22	6-0	190	Mt. Lebanon, Pa.	Sr.
80	*Pivec, Dave	E	20	6-3	220	Baltimore, Md.	Jr.
47	Rakers, Jim	FB	20	6-4	205	Quincy, Ill.	Jr.
27	Rassas, Nick	HB	19	6-0	180	Winnetka, Ill.	Jr.
70	Seymour, Herb	T	21	6-1	260	Detroit, Mich.	So.
83	Sheridan, Phil	E	19	6-4	210	Rutherford, N. J.	So.
46	**Simon, John	HB-E	20	6-3	210	St. Louis, Mo.	Sr.
64	Smith, Jim	G	19	5-10	206	Columbia, Pa.	So.
40	Snow, Jack	E-HB	20	6-2	215	Long Beach, Calif.	Jr.
73	Snowden, Jim	E-T	21	6-4	235	Youngstown, Ohio	Jr.
84	**Stephens, Clay	E	20	6-3	215	Burlingame, Calif.	Sr.
55	Sullivan, Tom	T-G	19	6-2	230	Berkeley, Calif.	So.
5	Szot, Denis	QB	21	6-0	185	Chicago, Ill.	Jr.
82	Talaga, Tom	E	19	6-5	220	Chicago, Ill.	So.
77	Telfer, Bob	T	20	6-2	235	Edmore, Mich.	Jr.
24	Tubinis, Jerry	HB	22	6-2	200	Niagara Falls, N.Y.	Jr.
36	Vasys, Arunas	HB	19	6-2	198	Cicero, Ill.	So.
61	Wadsworth, Mike	G-T	20	6-3	242	Toronto, Ont.	So.
79	Webster, Mike	T	19	6-1	250	Vancouver, B. C.	So.
35	Wolski, Bill	HB	19	5-11	195	Muskegon, Mich.	So.
6	Zloch, Bill	QB	18	6-3	190	Ft. Lauderdale, Fla.	So.

* Denotes Monograms Won

1963

Coach: Hugh J. Devore
Captain: Joseph Robert Lehmann

S.28	L	Wisconsin (1:07)	9-14	H	56,806
O.5	L	Purdue	6-7	A	c51,723
O.12	W	So. Cal. (U) (6:28)	17-14	H	c59,135
O.19	W	U.C.L.A.	27-12	H	42,948
O.26	L	Stanford (U)	14-24	A	55,000
N.2	L	Navy	14-35	H	c59,362
N.9	L	Pittsburgh	7-27	A	41,306
N.16	L	Michigan State	7-12	A	70,128
N.23	..	Iowa*	...	A	....
N.28	L	Syracuse (3:28)	7-14	YS	56,972
		(2-7-0)	108-159		493,380

*Game cancelled because of the death of President Kennedy

Two in a row

NOTRE DAME, INDIANA, October 19—The Fighting Irish of Notre Dame, in their first meeting ever with the University of California at Los Angeles, made Coach Bill Barnes' Bruins wish they had never set foot on the damp, historic turf of Notre Dame Stadium. In this second game of a triad with West Coast opponents, the Irish completely dominated play, even more so than the 27-12 score indicated.

Touchdown drives in each quarter—engineered by senior quarterback Frank Budka—and rugged line play which held the Bruins to only 72 yards rushing, were the principal ingredients in Notre Dame's victory.

The Irish drove 72 yards in ten plays the first time they had the ball, and scored on an 11-yard screen pass from Budka to fullback Joe Kantor. Ken Ivan kicked his first of three conversions, and Notre Dame led 7-0 midway through the first quarter.

A poor UCLA punt early in the second period gave the Irish possession on the Bruins' 30-yard line. Six plays later halfback Bill Wolski took a pitchout from Budka, sprinted four yards around left end, and dove headlong into the end zone. Ivan's PAT attempt was good.

Later in the second quarter, UCLA quarterback Larry Zeno—the heir to a job once held by such greats as Paul Cameron, Bob Davenport, Ronnie Knox, and Bill Kilmer—got the Bruins moving. Though their first drive was thwarted when rover Bill Pfeiffer's jarring tackle caused a fumble on the Notre Dame two-yard line, the Uclans befuddled the Irish secondary on the next series of downs, and scored on a 12-yard tackle-eligible pass play from Zeno to Mitchell Johnson. The touchdown came with but 38 seconds left in the first half; Zeno's extra-point try was wide, and Notre Dame left the field with a 14-6 advantage.

The second half began with four penalties in the first three minutes, and action bogged down considerably.

Eventually, however, the Irish were able to mount another attack: sparked by the running of Charlie O'Hara and the clutch pass catching of Jim Kelly, Notre Dame marched the 54 yards from its own 46 to UCLA's end zone in only six plays. Kelly's nifty fake left the two Bruin safetymen as little more than spectators to his 17-yard scoring catch. Ivan's kick failed, but the Irish led 20-6 with little more than a quarter to play.

The tough defensive line—led by Bob Lehmann, Norm Nicola, Jim Carroll, and Richard Arrington—continued to suppress the UCLA ground game and harass the Bruins' passers, and UCLA was again forced to punt. Notre Dame took over at the Uclans' 45.

After two routine line plunges gained eight yards, Budka gave to O'Hara on an off-tackle slant. In a run very reminiscent of his scoring scamper in Pittsburgh two seasons ago, O'Hara broke through the line, caught the secondary bunched-up, and went outside and down the sideline for 33 yards. From the four, where O'Hara was run out of bounds, Budka capped the drive with an off-tackle dive into the end zone. Ivan's perfect kick was the twenty-seventh and last point of the afternoon for the Irish.

UCLA's second touchdown culminated an 80-yard drive which was highlighted by a 42-yard pass play from quarterback Mike Haffner to All-American end Mel Profit—who lived up to his advance billings by snaring seven passes for 104 yards. The touchdown pass, however, was a nine-yarder to Kurt Altenberg. The extra-point attempt again failed, and the Bruins finished the day with an even dozen points.

Notre Dame's complete control of the game is best indicated by the fact that Coach Hugh Devore used four full teams—44 players—against the Bruins.

—SKIP RADEY

> That Notre Dame chose not to play Iowa in football is a small but significant tribute to a man who loved sports, the late President John Fitzgerald Kennedy. May he rest in peace.

Ara Parseghian Named Notre Dame Grid Coach

SOUTH BEND, Ind. (AP)—Ara Parseghian of Northwestern University was named head football coach at Notre Dame Saturday.

The 40-year-old Parseghian replaces Hugh Devore.

Devore, "interim coach" with a 2-7 record in 1963, was elevated to the post of assistant athletic director.

Parseghian was given a four-year contract at an undisclosed sum. His reported salary at Northwestern was $18,000 yearly

"We feel very fortunate in securing the services of such an outstanding coach as Mr. Parseghian," said the Rev. Edmund P. Joyce, chairman of the Notre Dame Athletic Board.

Splendid Record

"He has had a splendid record at Miami University (Oxford, Ohio) and Northwestern University and he is one of the most respected men in the coaching profession.

"On behalf of Father Theodore Hesburgh, our university, president and the faculty board in control of athletics, I welcome him to the post of head football coach at the Universtiy of Notre Dame."

"We are delighted also to announce that Mr. Hugh Devore is appointed our new assistant athletic director," Father Joyce continued. "Coach Devore performed admirably in the assignment this year of being our interim head coach and we were most appreciative of his good efforts.

"He has won the respect and admiration of all Notre Dame men and will continue to play an extremely important role in our football program."

Athletic Director Ed (Moose) Krause said:

"I've known Ara Parseghian for many years and know he is one of the best. We are sure he will get the job done here at Notre Dame. I am also very happy at the announcement of my old teammate and classmate, Hugh Devore, as assistant athletic director. We have been working together now for many years. He is one of the finest of all Notre Dame men."

The 52-year-old Devore, father of seven, was Notre Dame co-captain in 1933. He coached at Fordham, Providence College and Holy Cross before returning to Notre Dame as end coach in 1944.

1963 FINAL STATISTICS

TEAM STATISTICS

N.D.		OPP.
108	POINTS SCORED	159
119	FIRST DOWNS	150
72	by Rushing	90
33	by Passing	48
14	by Penalties	12
1326	YARDS RUSHING	1501
409	TIMES CARRIED	405
3.24	Yards-per-try	3.71
654	YARDS PASSING	1058
125	Passes Attempted	160
54	Passes Completed	82
.432	Completion Percentage	.513
14	Passes Intercepted by	9
105	Yards Int. Returned	79
1980	TOTAL OFFENSE	2559
49	PUNTS	38
1861	Total Yards	1277
38.0	Average	33.6
127	Yards Punts Returned	231
18	FUMBLES	30
9	Ball Lost	15

SCORING

PLAYER	TD	FG	PAT	SAF	TP
Budka	4	0	0	0	24
Ivan	0	1	12	0	15
Kantor	2	0	0	0	12
Kelly	2	0	0	0	12
MacDonald	2	0	0	0	12
Wolski	2	0	0	0	12
Phillips	1	0	0	0	6
Pivec	1	0	0	0	6
Snow	1	0	0	0	6
Huarte	0	0	1	0	1
TEAM	0	0	0	1	2
ND TOTALS	15	1	13	1	108
OPP. TOTALS	23	1	18	0	159

PASS RECEIVING

PLAYER	NO.	YARDS	AVG.	TD
Kelly	18	264	14.7	2
Snow	6	82	13.7	0
Pivec	6	76	12.7	1
Farrell	3	33	11.0	0
Bliey	3	31	10.3	0
Pfeiffer	3	15	5.0	0
Wolski	3	11	3.7	0
Loboy	2	35	17.5	0
MacDonald	2	34	17.0	1
Kantor	2	24	12.0	1
O'Hara	2	18	9.0	0
Stephens	2	10	5.0	0
Simon	1	12	12.0	0
Rassas	1	9	9.0	0

PUNTING

PLAYER	NO.	YARDS	AVG.
McGinn	43	1632	38.0
Snow	6	229	38.2

RUSHING

PLAYER	TC	YARDS	AVG.
Kantor	88	330	3.8
Wolski	70	320	4.6
Bliey	30	115	3.8
Budka	47	97	2.1
O'Hara	15	94	6.3
Duranko	26	93	3.6
Costa	21	82	3.9
Farrell	33	79	3.4
Pfeiffer	20	59	3.0
Rassas	8	33	4.2
Snow	3	26	8.7
MacDonald	6	20	3.3
Phillips	8	20	2.5
Loboy	5	14	2.8
Bonvechio	11	13	1.2
Mittelhauser	1	1	1.0
Simon	1	1	1.0
Zloch	3	-3	
Szot	1	-5	
McGinn	1	-10	
Huarte	11	-53	

PASSING

Player	Att.	Comp.	Int.	Yards	TD	Pct.
Budka	41	22	3	251	4	.537
Huarte	42	20	0	243	1	.476
Szot	23	5	4	66	0	.217
Bonvechio	16	6	1	82	0	.375
McGinn	2	1	0	12	0	.500
Zloch	1	0	1	0	0	.000

PASSES INTERCEPTED

PLAYER	NO.	YARDS	TD
MacDonald	5	63	1
Longo	2	8	0
Farrell	1	14	0
Kelly	1	10	0
Pfeiffer	1	4	0
Snow	1	3	0
Pivec	1	2	0
Lehmann	1	1	0
O'Hara	1	0	0

PUNT RETURNS

PLAYER	NO.	YARDS	AVG.
MacDonald	8	56	7.0
Wolski	6	31	5.2
Bliey	1	16	16.0
Farrell	1	13	13.0
O'Hara	1	10	10.0
Pfeiffer	1	1	1.0

KICKOFF RETURNS

PLAYER	NO.	YARDS	AVG.
Wolski	16	379	23.7
MacDonald	8	146	18.3
Bliey	5	131	26.2
Duranko	1	25	25.0
Kantor	1	11	11.0
Kelly	1	9	9.0

1964 NOTRE DAME ALPHABETICAL ROSTER

No.	Name	Pos.	Age	Ht.	Wt.	Hometown	School	Cl.
77	Alexander, Harry	T	19	6-1	240	Wilmington, Del.	Salesianum	So.
25	Andreotti, Peter	HB	20	5-9	175	Chicago, Ill.	Mendel	Jr.
63	*Arrington, Richard	G	22	5-11	227	Erie, Pa.	Erie East	Jr.
66	*Atamian, John	G	21	6-1	205	Niagara Falls, N.Y.	Bishop Duffy	Sr.
90	Azzaro, Joe	HB	18	5-11	190	Pittsburgh, Pa.	Central Catholic	So.
8	*Bonvechio, Alex	QB	21	5-10	185	Wainwright, Ohio	Dennison St. Mary's	Sr.
1	Carey, Anthony	HB	21	6-0	190	Chicago, Ill.	Mt. Carmel	Jr.
60	**Carroll, James, Capt.	G-LB	21	6-1	212	Atlanta, Ga.	Marist	Sr.
26	Conjar, Lawrence	HB	18	6-0	200	Harrisburg, Pa.	Bishop McDevitt	So.
24	Conway, Dennis	HB	21	5-9	160	Sioux City, Ia.	Heelan Catholic	Jr.
84	*Costa, Paul	E	22	6-4	230	Port Chester, N.Y.	Port Chester	Sr.
68	Dennery, Vincent	G-E	21	6-2	215	Philadelphia, Pa.	LaSalle	Sr.
40	Devine, Timothy	HB	21	6-0	185	Jackson, Mich.	St. John's	Sr.
43	DiLullo, James	FB-HB	19	6-0	195	Chicago, Ill.	Fenwick	So.
20	Dupuis, Richard	HB	21	5-10	180	Windsor, Ont.	Assumption	Sr.
32	*Duranko, Peter	FB-LB	20	6-2	218	Johnstown, Pa.	Bishop McCort	Jr.
47	Eddy, Nicholas	HB	19	6-0	195	Lafayette, Calif.	Tracy	So.
42	**Farrell, Joseph	FB	21	6-0	205	Chicago, Ill.	Mendel	Sr.
80	Gmitter, Donald	E-LB	19	6-2	210	Pittsburgh, Pa.	South Hills Catholic	So.
54	Goeddeke, George	C-E	19	6-3	225	Detroit, Mich.	St. David's	So.
49	Gorman, Timothy	G	19	5-11	215	Hoboken, N.J.	St. Joseph's	So.
39	Hagerty, Robert	FB	18	6-3	230	Mingo Junction, O.	Steubenville Catholic	So.
74	Hardy, Kevin	T	19	6-5	262	Oakland, Calif.	St. Elizabeth's	So.
51	Horney, John	G	18	5-11	195	Youngstown, O.	Cardinal Mooney	So.
7	Huarte, John	QB	21	6-0	180	Anaheim, Calif.	Mater Dei	Sr.
21	Ivan, Kenneth	HB	19	6-1	190	Massillon, O.	Massillon	Jr.
65	Jeziorski, Ronald	G	19	5-10	203	South Bend, Ind.	St. Joseph's	So.
31	*Kantor, Joseph	FB	21	6-1	212	Cleveland, O.	St. Ignatius	Sr.
22	Kelly, Jim	HB	19	6-0	195	Rutherford, N.J.	St. Mary's	Jr.
52	*Kostelnik, Thomas	C-LB	21	6-2	200	Hiller, Pa.	John Brushear (Brownsville)	Sr.
57	Lium, John	C	19	6-4	235	Bronx, N.Y.	Cardinal Farley	So.
37	Loboy, Alan	FB-LB	20	6-0	195	Park Ridge, Ill.	Notre Dame (Niles)	Jr.
86	Long, Harold	E	19	6-0	200	LaGrange, Ill.	Fenwick	Jr.
9	*Longo, Thomas	HB	22	6-1	195	Lyndhurst, N.J.	Lyndhurst	Jr.
61	Lynch, James	G-LB	18	6-1	210	Lima, O.	Lima Central Catholic	So.
62	**Maglicic, Kenneth	G-LB	20	5-10	212	Cleveland, O.	St. Joseph's	Sr.
69	Marsico, Joseph	G	19	6-0	210	River Forest, Ill.	Fenwick	So.
53	Mattera, Vincent	C-E	21	6-3	230	San Pedro, Calif.	Mary Star of the Sea	Sr.
3	McGinn, Daniel	E-HB	20	5-11	180	Omaha, Neb.	Cathedral	Jr.
75	Meeker, Robert	T	20	6-2	222	Akron, O.	St. Vincent's	Jr.
38	Merkle, Robert	FB	20	6-1	197	Brandywine, Md.	St. Leo Prep (Fla.)	Jr.
72	*Meyer, John	T	22	6-2	212	Chicago, Ill.	Brother Rice	Sr.
28	Mittelhauser, Thomas	HB	21	5-11	188	Pittsburgh, Pa.	South Hills Catholic	Sr.
50	**Nicola, Norman	C	21	6-0	230	Canton, O.	Central Catholic	Sr.
2	O'Malley, Hugh	QB	18	5-10	178	South Bend, Ind.	St. Joseph's	So.
78	Page, Alan	T-E	18	6-5	230	Canton, O.	Central Catholic	So.
81	Papa, Robert	E	22	6-2	207	Clifton, N.J.	Clifton	Jr.
58	Paternostro, Victor	C	20	6-1	235	Lyndhurst, N.J.	Lyndhurst	So.
27	Rassas, Nicholas	HB	20	6-0	180	Winnetka, Ill.	Loyola Academy	Jr.
76	Regner, Thomas	T	20	6-1	245	Kenosha, Wisc.	St. Joseph's	So.
87	Rhoads, Thomas	E	19	6-2	210	Cincinnati, O.	St. Xavier	So.
11	Ryan, James	HB	20	5-10	178	Shreveport, La.	Byrd	So.
88	Sack, Allen	E	19	6-3	195	Boothwyn, Pa.	Chichester	So.
4	Sauget, Richard	LB-QB	20	6-3	205	Belleville, Ill.	Cathedral	Jr.
71	Seiler, Paul	T	18	6-4	230	Algona, Ia.	Bishop Garrigan	So.
83	Sheridan, Philip	E	20	6-4	210	Rutherford, N.J.	St. Mary's	Jr.
64	Smith, James	G	20	5-10	206	Columbia, Pa.	Columbia	Jr.
85	*Snow, Jack	E	21	6-2	215	Long Beach, Calif.	St. Anthony's	Sr.
73	**Snowden, James	T	22	6-4	235	Youngstown, O.	East Youngstown	Sr.
55	Sullivan, Thomas	G	20	6-2	230	Berkeley, Calif.	Bishop McGuiness (Okla. City)	Jr.
59	Swatland, Richard	G	18	6-2	225	Stamford, Conn.	Stamford Catholic	So.
82	Talaga, Thomas	E	20	6-5	220	Chicago, Ill.	St. Patrick's	Jr.
67	Thornton, Peter	G	21	6-2	216	Portland, Me.	Cheverus	So.
34	Tubinis, Gerald	HB	23	6-2	200	Niagara Falls, N.Y.	Niagara Falls	Sr.
36	Vasys, Arunas	G-LB	20	6-2	198	Cicero, Ill.	St. Phillip's	Jr.
70	Wadsworth, Michael	T	21	6-3	242	Toronto, Ont.	DeLaSalle	Jr.
79	*Webster, Michael	T	20	6-1	250	Vancouver, B.C.	Gladstone	So.
46	Wengierski, Timothy	HB	19	6-0	190	River Forest, Ill.	Fenwick	Jr.
35	*Wolski, William	HB	20	5-11	195	Muskegon, Mich.	Muskegon Catholic	Jr.
6	Zloch, William	QB-E	19	6-3	190	Ft. Lauderdale, Fla.	St. Thomas Academy	So.
48	Zurowski, David	HB	19	6-3	197	Oxon Hill, Md.	Gonzaga	

1964

Coach: Ara Parseghian
Captain: James S. Carroll

S.26	W	Wisconsin (R)	31-7	A	c64,398
O.3	W	Purdue	34-15	H	c59,611
O.10	W	Air Force	34-7	A	c44,384
O.17	W	U.C.L.A.	24-0	H	58,335
O.24	W	Stanford	28-6	H	56,721
O.31	W	Navy	40-0	N	66,752
N.7	W	Pittsburgh	17-15	A	56,628
N.14	W	Michigan State	34-7	H	c59,265
N.21	W	Iowa	28-0	H	c59,135
N.28	L	So. Calif. (U)(1:33)	17-20	A	83,840
		(9-1-0)	287-77		609,069

N–at Philadelphia

NAVY
NOTRE DAME
JOHN F. KENNEDY MEMORIAL STADIUM · PHILADELPHIA · OCTOBER 31, 1964

Tragedy

Los Angeles, California, November 28 — Notre Dame, hoping to crown a fantastic season with the National Championship, had its dream shattered by the Trojans of Southern California, 20-17. A shirt-sleeved crowd of 83,840 watched in awe as the No. 1-ranked Irish spurted to a 17-0 half-time lead, but could not withstand the second-half comeback of the spirited Trojans.

The Irish defense forced the first break of the game. Ken Maglicic separated USC's Rod Sherman from the ball with a jarring tackle, and Arunas Vasys recovered on the Trojan 42-yard line. Two passes moved the ball 34 yards to the Southern Cal 8-yard line. Here the attack faltered and Ken Ivan booted a field goal from the 15.

A clipping penalty forced the Trojans to punt after one set of downs, and the Irish took over on their own 41-yard line. A penalty, this one against Notre Dame, pushed them back to their 26-yard line. From there, John Huarte took to the air, hitting Jack Snow for 23 yards, Phil Sheridan for 13, and Snow again at the Trojan 35-yard line. A draw play gained 10, and then Huarte, after faking beautifully to Joe Kantor and Bill Wolski, lofted a 22-yard scoring pass to Jack Snow.

Late in the second quarter the Irish marched 72 yards in 11 plays to score their final points of the game. Huarte's quick passes to ends Snow and Sheridan, capped by Wolski's 5-yard run for the touchdown, marked Notre Dame's best offensive drive of the game.

Southern Cal opened the second half by driving 68 yards in 9 plays to make the score ND 17 — USC 7. Trojan quarterback Craig Fertig and speedster Mike Garrett, working the roll-out passes and power sweeps to perfection, narrowed the margin to 10 points when Garrett scored from the one-yard line.

Nick Eddy returned the kick-off to the 29-yard line. The Irish elected to stay on the ground, utilizing the quick bursts of Kantor and Wolski to drive down to the Southern Cal 9-yard line. A fumbled pitch-out gave the ball to the Trojans at their own 14-yard line. A pass interference penalty forced Southern Cal to punt, and once again the Irish had the ball, this time at their own 34. Huarte mixed his calls effectively, sending Wolski up the middle after a double fake, and then Eddy around end. At the 13 Joe Kantor took charge and on four carries, lead the Irish to the Trojans 6-inch line. The next play was the turning point of the game. On second down and inches, Kantor had apparently scored but Notre Dame was called for holding. A touchdown would have put the game out of reach. Instead the Irish were pushed back to the 15-yard line and were able to gain only 3 yards in their next 3 attempts.

Southern Cal took over at the 12-yard line. Craig Fertig caught the Irish by surprise with a 28-yard pass to end Fred Hill which brought the ball to the 40. Behind good protection, Fertig found his receivers Sherman and Hill for short yardage, and completed the 88-yard drive with a 23-yard scoring pass to Hill.

The Irish were forced to punt by the inspired Trojan defense. Mike Garrett returned it to the Notre Dame 40 with only two minutes left in the game. Fertig threw to Hill for 23 yards. On three plays the Trojans gained only two yards, making it fourth and 8 at the 15. But then with only 1:34 remaining, Fertig hit Rod Sherman over the middle for the winning touchdown.

Notre Dame moved to the Trojan 43 in five plays. But Nate Shaw killed any hopes of a comeback with an interception. The Trojans punted with 16 seconds remaining. On two successive down-and-out passes to Snow, the Irish moved the ball to midfield, but a last-second desperation pass was batted down.

— Mike Bradley

A Yard is a Yard is a Yard

Pittsburgh, Pa., November 7 — Heard outside Pitt stadium: "You see more people you know at a Notre Dame game than you do at a wake." Inside, this statement came near to being prophetic as an Irish wake was perilously close to reality during the second half. Fortunately, Irish skies prevailed, and Notre Dame left the Panthers in *their* wake, but barely, 17-15.

Early in the fourth quarter, the crisis of the game was passed when Fred Mazurek, in a fourth and one situation, was stopped cold on the Irish sixteen by Jim Carroll and Tom Regner. After this, the game was played at Pitt's end of the field, and their sputtering last-minute dramatics were finally snuffed out when Tom Kostelnik jumped on Mazurek's reckless lateral with only seconds remaining.

After Pitt's opening kickoff bounded over the end line, the Irish came on strong and running. Joe Farrell, Nick Eddy, and Bill Wolski took turns powering the ball to the Pitt 36. From the 34, John Huarte fired a bullet to Phil Sheridan for 11 yards, and a first down on the Panther 23. Back to the running, Farrell hit for five, Wolski drove for three, a face-mask penalty took Notre Dame to the Pitt 8, and Eddy spun himself down to the two. Two plays later, Farrell slammed into the end zone. Joe Azzaro converted, and with 9:07 left on the board, Notre Dame led 7-0.

Following the kickoff Notre Dame forced Pitt to punt and took over on their own 7. After Nick Eddy gained only two yards in two carries, John Huarte rolled back into his own end zone, and floated a pass to Eddy all alone on the Notre Dame 35. He in turn paralleled the boundary chalk, full speed ahead, for a record-breaking 91-yard touchdown pass. Azzaro made good on his kick, Notre Dame led 14-0.

Later in the quarter, Notre Dame was maneuvering in their own territory when Pete Andreotti fumbled the ball into the arms of Generalovich on the ND 31. From here, Mazurek and McKnight provided the running, and seven plays later, McKnight barrelled over the goal line from the one. He also cracked over right tackle for a two-pointer, and with 9:07 on the board, Notre Dame led 14-8.

After the kickoff, Notre Dame mounted an attack which thrived on some long gainers: a fumbling, stumbling catch by Phil Sheridan on the fifty, a 14-yard run by Farrell to the Pitt 32, and another pitch to Sheridan on the Pitt 14. The attack stalled, and with 49 seconds left in the half, Joe Azzaro kicked a 30-yard field goal which gave the Irish 17 points which they would have to make good as it breathtakingly turned out.

The third quarter was all Pittsburgh. Pitt revved their running game into high gear, and again Mazurek an McKnight were at the throttle. Methodically plodding down the field, they managed to eat up the clock and the very heart of Notre Dame's specialty, rushing defense. This time-consuming assault ran out the third quarter but on the first play of the fourth, McKnight banged the right side of the Irish line, slid off, and slipped into the end zone. Jim Jones converted, and with almost 15 minutes left to play, Notre Dame had a thin 17-15 lead.

Shortly thereafter came the moment of truth, the high water mark of Pittsburgh's desperate cause. Notre Dame held, and for the rest of the quarter, Jack Snow's punting kept Pitt within their own territory. In retrospect, the Irish probably had as many great moments as in their previous six games. Unfortunately, not enough of these great moments were spent in scoring. But then every great team needs at least one squeaker. It builds character and advances the cause of humility.

— Bill Cragg

HEISMAN TROPHY

Jefferson in 1923, 7-1-1; at Rice from 1924 to 1927, 14-16-5.

Heisman's most important accomplishments aren't given by his record; he was the innovator of many practices that are now football commonplaces. Heisman invented the "safety" position, he first thought of having the quarterback call signals to time the center snap, and he was the first to have the center hike the ball to the quarterback — originally it was rolled back!

But Heisman's most important and most relevant direct contribution to Notre Dame football was none of these. He was one of the very first, in the face of repeated rebuffs, to agitate for legislation for the forward pass. He got the idea from the instinctive reaction of a trapped fullback who, just before he was tackled, tossed the ball to one of his teammates who trotted into the end zone for the winning touchdown. In the forward pass, Heisman saw the possibility of altering the nature of football, from a brutal blood bath to a game of skill. Passing, he thought, could loosen up the game.

The fortunes of Notre Dame football have been linked with the forward pass, from the time a little end named Knute Rockne caught passes that defeated vaunted Army and gained national recognition for Notre Dame, right up to today and the latest of Notre Dame's great quarterbacks, John Huarte.

THE HIGHEST TRIBUTE that can be paid a college football player is to be awarded the Heisman Trophy. This year Notre Dame's John Huarte, was distinguished with the award. The honor places Huarte in the company of such football immortals and near-immortals as Tom Harmon (Michigan 1940), Angelo Bertelli (Notre Dame 1943), "Doc" Blanchard (Army 1945), Glenn Davis (Army 1946), Johnny Lujack (Notre Dame 1947), Doak Walker (SMU 1948), Leon Hart (Notre Dame 1949), Johnny Lattner (Notre Dame 1953), Paul Hornung (Notre Dame 1956), Joe Bellino (Navy 1960), Ernie Davis (Syracuse 1961), Roger Staubach (Navy 1963).

The Heisman Trophy was first awarded in 1935 and has been awarded each year since to the outstanding college football player as chosen by newswriters and broadcasters.

The trophy is presented each year in December at a dinner held in the Downtown Athletic Club. The Athletic Club founded the trophy thirty years ago to honor the memory of John Heisman, a football coach of the late 19th and early 20th century who became director of the Down-

town Club when he retired from coaching.

Heisman coached for thirty-seven years — from 1890 to 1927. His tenures were always interesting if not successful. His football career began at Brown where, as a 154-pounder, he played tackle in 1887 and 1889. Two pounds heavier, he played end and tackle at Pennsylvania in 1890 and 1891. Law was Heisman's choice for a career, but poor eyesight forced him to give it up. He got his law degree by having students read to him and by passing an oral exam in 1891. But actual practice was impossible.

Upon his graduation, Oberlin College offered him a job coaching. Heisman's success was hardly immediate. Oberlin didn't win a game in 1892, his first year as coach.

In 1893 he moved to Butchel College, and in 1894 he returned to Oberlin. In order, then, came coaching assignments at Auburn from 1895 to 1899, where his teams were 13-3-2; at Clemson from 1900 to 1903, 19-3-2; at Georgia Tech from 1904 to 1919, 91-30-4; at Pennsylvania from 1920 to 1922, 16-10-2; at Washington and

Huarte's story is perhaps the most remarkable of any Heisman winner's. Never had the winner been so unheralded before the season began, never had a non-monogram holder won the award. John Huarte came from nowhere, from 45 minutes' playing time, to become the winner of the nation's most coveted collegiate laurel. His accomplishment symbolized the rags-to-riches rise of the entire Notre Dame team.

In ten games Huarte and his primary receiver Jack Snow broke practically every Notre Dame passing record. Huarte attempted 205 passes, completed 114 of them for a 55.3% completion average. The passes netted 2062 yards. But these basic statistics only scratch the surface.

Without John Huarte, Notre Dame would not have had a winning season. With him, they almost became national champions. This alone warrants the accolade — Outstanding College Football Player of 1964 — and places him in the illustrious company of others who have won college football's most treasured prize: The Heisman Trophy.

—JOHN WHELAN

AP POLL

1964
1. Alabama
2. Arkansas
3. NOTRE DAME
4. Michigan
5. Texas
6. Nebraska
7. L.S.U.
8. Oregon State
9. Ohio State
10. U.S.C.

UPI POLL

1964
1. Alabama
2. Arkansas
3. NOTRE DAME
4. Michigan
5. Texas
6. Nebraska
7. L.S.U.
8. Oregon State
9. Ohio State
10. U.S.C.

By Football Writers

Parseghian Selected College Coach of Year

DES MOINES, Iowa, Dec. 19 (AP)—Ara Parseghian, who in his first season at Notre Dame guided the Irish back into the ranks of the nation's football powers, was named Coach of the Year today by the Football Writers Association of America.

The announcement, made by Bert McGrane, secretary treasurer of the football writers, said Parseghian was one of 17 coaches considered.

Parseghian, whose team lost only once this year and finished as the Nation's third ranked team, received about 60 per cent of the votes from the more than 600 writers who took part in the balloting, McGrane said.

His leading rivals, McGrane said, were Frank Broyles of Arkansas, Bump Elliott of Michigan, Bear Bryant of Alabama and Bob Devaney of Nebraska.

1964 FINAL STATISTICS

TEAM STATISTICS

N.D.		OPP.
287	POINTS SCORED	77
215	FIRST DOWNS	130
111	by Rushing	60
90	by Passing	63
14	by Penalties	7
1909	YARDS RUSHING	687
472	TIMES CARRIED	351
4.04	Yards-per-try	1.96
2105	YARDS PASSING	1376
222	Passes Attempted	230
120	Passes Completed	109
.541	Completion Percentage	.474
18	Passes Intercepted by	13
220	Yards Int. Returned	180
4014	TOTAL OFFENSE	2063
30	PUNTS	57
1097	Total Yards	2227
36.6	Average	39.1
225	Yards Punts Returned	101
16	FUMBLES	21
8	Ball Lost	14

SCORING

PLAYER	TD	FG	PAT	TP
Wolski, Bill	11	0	0	66
Snow, Jack	9	0	2-p	56
Eddy, Nick	7	0	2-p	44
Ivan, Ken	0	4	15	27
Farrell, Joe	4	0	0	24
Huarte, John	3	0	0	18
Andreotti, Pete	2	0	0	12
Azzaro, Joe	0	1	7	10
Conway, Denny	1	0	0	6
Kantor, Joe	1	0	0	6
Page, Alan	1	0	0	6
Rassas, Nick	1	0	0	6
Sheridan, Phil	1	0	0	6
ND TOTALS	41	5	26	287
OPP. TOTALS	11	0	11(2-p) (2-r)	77

PUNTING

PLAYER	NO.	YARDS	AVG.
Snow, Jack	29	1057	36.4
McGinn, Dan	1	40	40.0

RUSHING

PLAYER	TC	YARDS	AVG.
Wolski, Bill	136	657	4.8
Eddy, Nick	98	490	5.0
Farrell, Joe	93	387	4.2
Kantor, Joe	47	158	3.4
Andreotti, Pete	33	115	3.5
Conway, Denny	16	66	4.1
Rassas, Nick	3	37	12.3
Merkle, Bob	4	8	2.0
Huarte, John	37	7	
Zloch, Bill	1	1	1.0
Bonvechio, Alex	3	-8	
Carey, Tony	1	-9	

KICKOFF RETURNS

PLAYER	NO.	YARDS	AVG.
Eddy, Nick	7	148	21.1
Rassas, Nick	4	103	25.8
Wolski, Bill	2	49	24.5
Andreotti, Pete	1	12	12.0
Kantor, Joe	1	8	8.0
Meeker, Bob	1	0	

DEFENSIVE STATISTICS

TACKLES: Jim Carroll 140; Ken Maglicic 88; Tom Kostelnik 81; Tom Longo 72; Tom Regner 68; Don Gmitter 54; Nick Rassas 51; Tony Carey 46; Jim Lynch and Alan Page 41; Kevin Hardy 38; Arunas Vasys 35; Pete Andreotti and Mike Wadsworth 11; John Meyer 10; Ken Ivan and Alan Loboy 8; Paul Costa 7; John Horney 6; Vince Mattera 5; Dick Sauget 4; George Goeddeke, Harry Long 3; Bob Meeker, Norm Nicola, Phil Sheridan 2; Nick Eddy, Bob Merkle, Allen Sack, Jack Snow, Jim Snowden, Tom Talaga, Mike Webster, Bill Zloch 1.

OPPONENTS' FUMBLES RECOVERED: Don Gmitter, Ken Maglicic, Alan Page, Tom Regner 2; Tony Carey, Paul Costa, Tom Kostelnik, Tom Longo, Phil Sheridan, Arunas Vasys 1.

BLOCKED KICKS: Kevin Hardy 2.

PASSES BROKEN UP: Tony Carey and Tom Longo 10; Jim Carroll and Nick Rassas 4; Tom Kostelnik 3; Don Gmitter, Ken Ivan, Jim Lynch.

PASS RECEIVING

PLAYER	NO.	YARDS	AVG.	TD
Snow, Jack	60	1114	18.9	9
Eddy, Nick	16	352	22.0	2
Sheridan, Phil	20	320	16.0	1
Wolski, Bill	8	130	16.3	2
Farrell, Joe	6	84	14.0	1
Kantor, Joe	2	43	21.5	0
Merkle, Bob	4	32	8.0	0
Conway, Denny	1	15	15.0	0
Huarte, John	1	11	11.0	0
Rassas, Nick	2	4	2.0	1

PUNT RETURNS

PLAYER	NO.	YARDS	AVG.
Rassas, Nick	15	153	10.2
Conway, Denny	8	72	9.0

PASSES INTERCEPTED

PLAYER	NO.	YARDS	TD
Carey, Tony	8	121	0
Longo, Tom	4	27	0
Maglicic, Ken	1	25	0
Rassas, Nick	1	23	0
Kostelnik, Tom	1	11	0
Ivan, Ken	1	7	0
Carroll, Jim	1	5	0
Duranko, Pete	1	1	0

PASSING

Player	Att.	Comp.	Int.	Yards	TD	Pct.
Huarte, John	205	114	11	2062	16	.556
Bonvechio, Alex	16	5	2	32	0	.313
McGinn, Dan	1	1	0	11	0	1.000

NOTRE DAME ROSTER

No.	Name	Pos.	Wt.	Ht.	Age	Class	Home Town
77	Harry Alexander	T	240	6-1	20	Jr.	Wilmington, Delaware
25	*Peter Andreotti	HB	178	5-9	21	Sr.	Chicago, Illinois
63	**Richard Arrington	G	232	5-11	23	Sr.	Erie, Pennsylvania
28	Robert Bleier	HB	185	5-11	19	Soph	Appleton, Wisconsin
33	Mike Burgener	HB	185	5-10	19	Soph	Marion, Illinois
20	Jon Butash	HB	185	5-10	18	Soph	Akron, Ohio
1	*Anthony Carey	HB	190	6-0	22	Sr.	Chicago, Illinois
32	Lawrence Conjar	FB	205	6-0	19	Jr.	Harrisburg, Pennsylvania
24	Dennis Conway	HB	165	5-9	21	Sr.	Sioux City, Iowa
66	William Dainton	G	220	6-2	18	Soph	Gary, Indiana
64	*Peter Duranko	T	225	6-2	21	Jr.	Johnstown, Pennsylvania
47	*Nicholas Eddy	HB	195	6-0	21	Jr.	Lafayette, California
72	Louis Fournier	T	248	6-3	19	Soph	Cheboygan, Michigan
80	*Donald Gmitter	E	210	6-2	20	Jr.	Pittsburgh, Pennsylvania
54	George Goeddeke	C	225	6-3	20	Jr.	Detroit, Michigan
49	Timothy Gorman	G	205	5-11	20	Jr.	Hoboken, New Jersey
52	Chuck Grable	G-T	210	6-0	19	Soph	Oshkosh, Wisconsin
74	*Kevin Hardy	T	270	6-5	20	Jr.	Oakland, California
34	Daniel Harshman	HB	185	6-0	19	Soph	Toledo, Ohio
51	John Horney	LB	205	5-11	19	Jr.	Youngstown, Ohio
21	*Kenneth Ivan	S	185	6-1	20	Sr.	Massillon, Ohio
65	Richard Jeziorski	LB	205	5-10	20	Jr.	South Bend, Indiana
50	Gerald Kelly	C	210	6-1	19	Jr.	Los Angeles, California
2	Daniel Koenings	QB	185	6-2	19	Soph	Racine, Wisconsin
73	Rudy Konieczny	T	235	6-0	18	Soph	Fairview, Massachusetts
78	Michael Kuzmicz	T	230	6-4	18	Soph	South Bend, Indiana
86	Harold Long	E	205	6-0	21	Jr.	LaGrange, Illinois
9	**Thomas Longo	HB	195	6-1	23	Sr.	Lyndhurst, New Jersey
61	*James Lynch	LB	215	6-1	20	Jr.	Lima, Ohio
53	David Martin	E-LB	200	6-0	18	Soph	Kansas City, Kansas
31	Paul May	FB	200	5-10	19	Soph	Alexandria, Virginia
60	Michael McGill	LB-E	220	6-2	18	Soph	Hammond, Indiana
3	Daniel McGinn	HB	180	5-11	21	Sr.	Omaha, Nebraska
75	*Robert Meeker	T	235	6-2	21	Sr.	Akron, Ohio
38	Robert Merkle	FB	210	6-1	21	Sr.	Brandywine, Maryland
40	Thomas O'Leary	HB	185	5-10	19	Soph	Columbus, Ohio
81	*Alan Page	E	230	6-5	20	Jr.	Canton, Ohio
8	John Pergine	QB-LB	190	6-0	18	Soph	Norristown, Pennsylvania
27	*Nicholas Rassas	HB	185	6-0	21	Sr.	Winnetka, Illinois
76	*Thomas Regner	G	245	6-1	21	Jr.	Kenosha, Wisconsin
87	Thomas Rhoads	E	210	6-2	20	Jr.	Cincinnati, Ohio
10	James Ryan	K	185	5-10	21	Jr.	Shreveport, Louisiana
88	Allen Sack	E	200	6-3	20	Jr.	Boothwyn, Pennsylvania
4	Richard Sauget	LB	205	6-3	21	Sr.	Belleville, Illinois
7	Thomas Schoen	QB	178	5-11	19	Soph	Euclid, Ohio
71	Paul Seiler	T	235	6-4	19	Jr.	Algona, Iowa
83	*Philip Sheridan (C)	E	215	6-4	21	Sr.	Rutherford, New Jersey
85	James Smithberger	HB	185	6-1	18	Soph	Welch, West Virginia
55	Thomas Sullivan	T	230	6-2	21	Sr.	Berkeley, California
59	Richard Swatland	T-G	218	6-2	19	Jr.	Stamford, Connecticut
82	Tom Talaga	E	220	6-5	21	Sr.	Chicago, Illinois
67	Peter Thornton	G	210	6-2	22	Jr.	Portland, Maine
89	Alan VanHuffel	E-LB	215	6-2	19	Soph	South Bend, Indiana
36	*Arunas Vasys	LB	220	6-2	22	Sr.	Cicero, Illinois
70	*Michael Wadsworth	T	240	6-3	22	Sr.	Toronto, Ontario
79	*Michael Webster	T	250	6-1	21	Sr.	Vancouver, British Columbia
46	Timothy Wengierski	HB	185	6-0	20	Jr.	River Forest, Illinois
35	**William Wolski	HB	195	5-11	21	Sr.	Muskegon, Michigan
6	William Zloch	QB	190	6-3	20	Sr.	Fort Lauderdale, Florida

* Denotes Monograms Won.

Notre Dame Quarterback Huarte Bagged By Jets At Reported $200,000, Plus Fringes

1965

Coach: Ara Parseghian
Captain: Philip F. Sheridan

S.18	W	California	48-6	A	53,000
S.25	L	Purdue	21-25	A	c61,291
O.2	W	Northwestern	38-7	H	c59,273
O.9	W	Army (Nt)	17-0	N	c61,000
O.23	W	So. California (R)	28-7	H	c59,235
O.30	W	Navy	29-3	H	c59,206
N.6	W	Pittsburgh	69-13	A	c57,169
N.13	W	North Carolina	17-0	H	c59,216
N.20	L	Michigan State	3-12	H	c59,291
N.27	T	Miami (Fla.) (Nt)	0-0	A	68,077
		(7-2-1)	**270-73**		**596,758**

N—at Shea Stadium, New York

AP POLL

1965

1. Alabama
2. Michigan State
3. Arkansas
4. U.C.L.A.
5. Nebraska
6. Missouri
7. Tennessee
8. L.S.U.
9. NOTRE DAME
10. U.S.C.

UPI POLL

1965

1. Michigan State
2. Arkansas
3. Nebraska
4. Alabama
5. U.C.L.A.
6. Missouri
7. Tennessee
8. NOTRE DAME
9. U.S.C.
10. Texas Tech

Jets

New York, Jan. 9 (AP) — John Huarte, Notre Dame's star quarterback and the 1964 Heisman Trophy winner, signed to play for the New York Jets of the American Football League today, and siid he was ready to get into the high-priced quarterback derby the team will run next season.

The Jets wouldn't say how much it cost to land Huarte but guesses around town are putting the figure at $200,000, or just half of what the Jets reportedly shelled out for Joe Namath, the gimpy-kneed quarterback from Alabama.

Jets Not Saying How Much

Actually, both figures contain a lot of fringe benefits such as insurance policies and annuities, which can be listed at cash or face value, sources said.

"We've never said how much Namath got," said one Jet official, "and we aren't saying how much we paid for Huarte."

Sonny Werblin, the show business tycoon who owns the Jets, said the figure on the Huarte contract was "privileged information." He said the length of the contract was, too.

That led to speculation that the pact took all possible advantage of long-term tax write-offs.

Huarte said money wasn't everything in his choise of the Jets over the Philadelphia Eagles, who are coached by Joe Kiuharich, the man who imported the Californian to Notre Dame in the first place.

ARMY... NOTRE DAM

Pitt's football team made believers out of even the most skeptical at Pitt Stadium yesterday.

The Panthers lost convincingly to Notre Dame 69-13.

They proved that their 51-13 loss to Syracuse the week before was no fluke and they did it the hard way, giving no help to the Irish in the form of fumbles or interceptions until Notre Dame had a four-touchdown lead.

Long before the finish, the sellout crowd of 57,169 was meandering toward the exits and historians were delving into the record books, which yielded the following quaint discoveries:

1 — The only teams to score as many points against Pitt were Michigan in 1947 (69-0) and Army in 1944 (69-7).

2 — Bill Wolski's five touchdowns tied a Notre Dame record set by Red Maher in 1923 against Kalamazoo.

3 — Ken Ivan's nine extra points broke a record set by Buck Shaw against Kalamazoo.

4 — It was Notre Dame's most ferocious outburst since 1940, when the Irish beat another Pittsburgh team, Carnegie Tech, 61-0. There must be a lesson here for somebody.

It was not the worst Pitt defeat of all time because Kenny Lucas threw a touchdown pass near the end of the first half and Ed James threw another with 12 seconds to play. Another small triumph for Pitt was the fact that Lucas escaped with his life.

Wolski, his five touchdowns notwithstanding, was only the third leading rusher for Notre Dame. Both Nick Eddy and Larry Conjar outgained him, 88 yards (they finished in a tie) to 54.

Wolski's longest scoring run was seven yards. After his fourth touchdown, on which he swept Pitt's left end from the two, he joyously threw the ball into the stands.

The next time he scored, tying Maher's record against Kalamazoo, he more or less took it for granted, but maybe he was beginning to suspect that Maher had been up against a tougher defense. . . .

Conjar ran for a touchdown on the second play after the kickoff with the game less than one minute old. He burst through a hole in the middle, cut to his right, brushed off one tackler as he headed toward the corner of the field and dragged the Pitt safety man the last few yards. Eddy's lunging catch of a pass from Zloch, good for 56 yards, kept the Panthers from tightening up against the Notre Dame running game.

Before the quarter was over, Notre Dame had pounded 52 yards to make it 14-0, and 81 yards to make it 21-0, with Wolski going in from the seven and the five. . . .

The Irish would tear Pitt apart in the middle and then send Wolski outside. Often he would find the coast clear but if anybody happened to be waiting for him it didn't seem to matter. Wolski just said, "Going my way?" and gave the tacklers a lift. . . .

Notre Dame's first unit stayed in the game until the score was 35-0 and returned after Pitt's first touchdown with 32 seconds left in the half.

The score was 48-6 before Coach Ara Parseghian thought it prudent to put the second stringers back in.

Following Pitt's last touchdown, Pete Andreotti returned the kickoff to the Notre Dame 35 and with two seconds left, the Irish called time-out for one more play. They were hard guys to satisfy yesterday.

Not since the great flood of '89 has so much disaster been wrecked upon the greater Pittsburgh area. The Pittsburg Press tries to explain the great force of nature that rolled up 69 points against their Panthers.

by ROY McHUGH

THE JOHNSTOWN FLOOD OF '65

MICH. STATE WHIPS IRISH

Takes Defensive Battle At South Bend, 12-3

By W. LAWRENCE NULL
[Sun Staff Correspondent]

South Bend, Ind., Nov. 20—A fumble, a quick kick that backfired and an interception were the keys to the only scoring here today as Michigan State preserved its status as the nation's best with a 12-to-3 victory over fourth-ranked Notre Dame.

As predicted by both coaches, the game that packed 59,291 fans into Notre Dame Stadium proved to be a classic defensive struggle, but the unbeaten Spartans moved when it counted.

Rose Bowl Next

The Fighting Irish, seldom restrained by anyone since coach Ara Parseghian arrived to take charge, had a total offense of 12 yards and a net rushing mark of minus 12.

Michigan State, bound next for the Rose Bowl on January 1, discovered it didn't even need its hobbled fullback, Bob Apisa. Halfbacks Dwight Lee, a 192-pound sophomore, and Clinton Jones, a 206-pound junior, simply took over the offense and rolled up most of the Spartans' 215 yards on the ground.

The Irish, who gave up the ball three times on interceptions and once on a fumble, held a 3-0 lead for most of the first half and for half of the third quarter.

Juday Has Troubles

They got on the scoreboard at 3.23 of the first quarter when Ken Ivan booted a 32-yard field goal.

Michigan State quarterback Steve Juday, the nation's back-of-the week after last Saturday's 27-13 victory over Indiana, had his troubles, not the least of which occurred on the first series of plays.

Notre Dame won the toss and elected to kick off, but after two plays and a penalty, the Irish had the Spartans on their 24 with a first and 25. On second down, Juday, on the option, pitched back poorly to fullback Eddie Cotton who never had control of the ball but was charged with the fumble.

Tom Longo, who played a fine game for the Irish, pounced on the ball at the 19. Three running plays picked up 5 yards and Ivan came in to kick the field goal.

At that point the oddsmakers who had installed Notre Dame a one-point favorite looked good and the opinion was strengthened as the first half proceeded.

It was obvious in the third period that Daugherty decided to call the plays, but Michigan State scored its first touchdown after a Notre Dame quick kick.

On third down and 14 from the 16, the Irish kicker Dan McGinn entered the game in a tight back position, but faded back, took a pitch from Zloch and booted a low liner to the Michigan State 45 where Jess Phillips took it on the run and was finally forced out of bounds on the Irish 39.

Jones Breaks Loose

Jones broke away for 20 yards and was stopped by Longo, who managed to grab one foot as the driving halfback headed for the open. Lee and Jones got it down to the 3 and the latter bulled over the left side for the touchdown with 6.50 to play in the quarter.

Dick Kenney, who placekicks barefooted but punts with his shoe on, missed the extra point.

Statistics

	Mich. State	Notre Dame
First Downs	16	3
Rushing Yardage	215	12
Passing Yardage	71	24
Passes	6-12	2-11
Passes Intercepted By	2	2
Punts	8-42	9-37
Fumbles lost	2	1
Yards penalized	35	3
Michigan State	0 0 6	6—12
Notre Dame	3 0 0	0— 3

ND—FG. Ivan, 32.
MSU—Jones, 3, run (kick, failed).
MSU—Lee, 19, pass from Juday (pass, failed).
Attendance, 59,291.

1965 FINAL STATISTICS

TEAM STATISTICS

N.D.		OPP.
270	POINTS SCORED	73
172	FIRST DOWNS	114
128	by Rushing	54
35	by Passing	56
9	by Penalties	4
2147	YARDS RUSHING	754
566	TIMES CARRIED	389
3.79	Yards-per-try	1.94
850	YARDS PASSING	1190
118	Passes Attempted	209
53	Passes Completed	106
.449	Completion Percentage	.507
18	Passes Intercepted by	10
229	Yards Int. Returned	117
3007	TOTAL OFFENSE	1944
51	PUNTS	73
2049	Total Yards	2887
39.4	Average	39.5
468	Yards Punts Returned	196
21	FUMBLES	26
12	Ball Lost	13
329	Yards Penalized	403

SCORING

PLAYER	TD	FG-Att.	4-runs	PAT-Att.	TP
Bill Wolski	8	0			52
Ken Ivan		7-12		27-31	48
Larry Conjar	7				42
Nick Eddy	6				36
Nick Rassas	4				24
Bill Zloch	3				18
Rocky Bleier	2				12
Don Gmitter	2				12
Paul May	2				12
Denny Conway	1				6
Dan Harshman	1				6
Tom Talaga			2-pass		2
ND TOTALS	36	7-13		33	270
OPP. TOTALS	11	1		4	73

PASS RECEIVING

PLAYER	NO.	YARDS	AVG.	TD
Nick Eddy	13	233	18.0	2
Phil Sheridan	10	140	14.0	0
Don Gmitter	6	155	25.5	2
Mike Heaton	4	74	18.5	0
Larry Conjar	4	55	13.8	0
Tom Talaga	4	49	12.3	0
Rocky Bleier	3	42	14.0	0
Dan Harshman	2	39	19.5	0
Pete Andreotti	2	29	14.5	0
Paul May	2	-3	-1.3	0
Bill Zloch	1	31	31.0	0
Bill Wolski	1	8	8.0	0
Tom Schoen	1	1	1.0	0

PUNTING

PLAYER	NO.	YARDS	AVG.
Dan McGinn	51	2011	39.4

RUSHING

PLAYER	TC	YARDS	AVG.
Nick Eddy	115	582	5.1
Larry Conjar	137	535	3.9
Bill Wolski	103	452	4.4
Bill Zloch	78	162	2.1
Rocky Bleier	26	145	5.6
Paul May	30	123	4.1
Tom Schoen	35	81	2.3
Dan Harshman	19	60	3.2
Pete Andreotti	20	48	2.4
Denny Conway	1	2	2.0
Dan McGinn	1	9	

KICKOFF RETURNS

PLAYER	NO.	YARDS	AVG.
Bill Wolski	6	131	21.8
Nick Rassas	4	82	20.5
Nick Eddy	3	63	21.0
Pete Andreotti	1	39	39.0
Dan Harshman	2	27	13.5
Mike Kuzmicz	1	11	11.0
Larry Conjar	1	10	10.0
Phil Sheridan	1	0	

PUNT RETURNS

PLAYER	NO.	YARDS	AVG.	TD
Nick Rassas	24	459	19.1	3
Jim Smithberger	1	9	9.0	0

DEFENSIVE STATISTICS

TACKLES: Jim Lynch 108; Pete Duranko 95; Mike McGill 88; John Horney 77; Tom Longo 73; Dave Martin 70; Nick Rassas 53; Harry Long 38; Dick Arrington 36; Tony Carey and Tom O'Leary 34; Alan Page 30; Tom Rhoads 29; Arunas Vasys 22; Harry Alexander 16; John Pergine 15; Tom Regner 13; Jim Ryan 12; Ron Jeziorski 11; Gerald Kelly 9; Bill Wolski 7; Don Gmitter, Kevin Hardy, Allen Sack, and Jim Smithberger 6; Ken Ivan, Rudy Konieczny, and Tom Sullivan 3; Nick Eddy, Dan Harshman, Mike Heaton, Mike Kuzmicz, Bob Meeker, and Dick Swatland 2; Rocky Bleier, Larry Conjar, Tom Schoen, Tom Talaga, Alan VanHuffel, and Mike Wadsworth 1.

PASSES BROKEN UP: Mike McGill 6; Jim Lynch, Tony Carey, Nick Rassas, and Tom Rhoads 3; Tom Longo 2; Harry Long, Tom O'Leary, Alan Page, Jim Smithberger, and Alan VanHuffel 1.

OPPONENTS' FUMBLES RECOVERED: John Horney, Alan Page, and Allen Sack 2; Tony Carey, Don Gmitter, Harry Long, Tom Longo, Mike McGill, and Arunas Vasys 1.

PASSES INTERCEPTED

PLAYER	NO.	YARDS	TD
Nick Rassas	6	197	1
Tom Longo	4	7	0
Tony Carey	3	9	0
Mike McGill	2	1	0
Jim Lynch	1	8	0
Tom Rhoads	1	4	0
Dave Martin	1	3	0

PASSING

Player	Att.	Comp.	Int.	Yards	TD	Pct.
Bill Zloch	89	36	9	558	3	.405
Tom Schoen	24	13	1	229	1	.542
Dan McGinn	3	3	0	42	0	1.000
Dan Harshman	2	1	0	21	0	.500

THE FIGHTING IRISH

1966 NOTRE DAME ALPHABETICAL ROSTER

No.	Name	Pos.	Age	Ht.	Wt.	Hometown
77	*Alexander, Harry	T	21	6-1	240	Wilmington, Del.
90	Azzaro, Joe	K	20	5-11	190	Pittsburgh, Pa.
36	Bartholomew, Bill	LB	20	6-2	212	Glen Mills, Pa.
2	Belden, Bob	QB	19	6-2	205	Canton, Ohio
28	*Bleier, Bob (Rocky)	HB	20	5-11	185	Appleton, Wis.
33	Burgener, Mike	HB	20	5-10	182	Marion, Ill.
37	Collins, Leo	LB	21	5-11	200	Fargo, N. D.
32	*Conjar, Larry	FB	20	6-0	212	Harrisburg, Pa.
21	Criniti, Frank	HB	19	5-8	173	Charleston, W. Va.
64	**Duranko, Pete	T	22	6-2	235	Johnstown, Pa.
10	Earley, Mike	E	21	6-0	200	South Bend, Ind.
47	**Eddy, Nick	HB	22	6-0	195	Lafayette, Calif.
53	Fischer, Ray	G	19	6-1	220	Cleveland, Ohio
68	Fox, Roger	G	19	5-11	230	Rockford, Ill.
4	Franger, Mike	HB	19	5-11	185	Elkhart, Ind.
95	Furlong, Tom	E	20	6-2	205	Cleveland, Ohio
20	Gladieux, Bob	HB	19	5-11	185	Louisville, Ohio
80	**Gmitter, Don	E	21	6-2	210	Mt. Lebanon, Pa.
54	*Goeddeke, George	C	21	6-3	228	Detroit, Mich.
57	Gorman, Tim	G	21	5-11	220	Hoboken, N. J.
52	Grable, Chuck	LB	20	6-0	215	Oshkosh, Wis.
39	Hagerty, Bob	FB	20	6-3	230	Mingo Junction, Ohio
22	Haley, Dave	HB	19	5-11	190	Hingham, Mass.
5	Hanratty, Terry	QB	18	6-1	190	Butler, Pa.
74	*Hardy, Kevin	T	21	6-5	270	Oakland, Calif.
34	Harshman, Dan	HB	20	6-0	190	Toledo, Ohio
84	Heaton, Mike	E	19	6-2	205	Seneca, Ill.
86	Heneghan, Curt	E	18	6-3	190	Redmond, Wash.
44	Holtzapfel, Mike	FB	19	6-1	200	Ironton, Ohio
51	*Horney, John	LB	20	5-11	205	Youngstown, Ohio
65	Jeziorski, Ron	G	21	5-10	210	South Bend, Ind.
58	Kelly, Gerald	C	20	6-1	205	Los Angeles, Calif.
30	Kelly, Jim	HB	21	6-0	195	Rutherford, N. J.
66	Kiliany, Dennis	LB	19	6-1	205	Youngstown, Ohio
73	*Konieczny, Rudy	T	19	6-0	225	Fairview, Mass.
75	Kuechenberg, Bob	T	18	6-2	225	Hobart, Ind.
82	Kunz, George	E-T	19	6-5	228	Arcadia, Calif.
78	Kuzmicz, Mike	T	19	6-4	235	South Bend, Ind.
17	Landolfi, Chuck	HB	19	5-11	204	Ellwood City, Pa.
93	Lauck, Chuck	E	18	6-1	220	Indianapolis, Ind.
41	Lavin, John	LB	19	6-4	200	Spokane, Wash.
61	**Lynch, Jim (Captain)	LB	21	6-1	225	Lima, Ohio
69	Marsico, Joe	G	21	6-0	220	River Forest, Ill.
56	*Martin, Dave	LB	19	6-0	210	Roeland Park, Kan.
31	*May, Paul	FB	20	5-10	205	Alexandria, Va.
60	*McGill, Mike	LB	19	6-2	220	Hammond, Ind.
79	McKinley, Tom	T-G	19	6-1	218	Kalamazoo, Mich.
55	Monty, Tim	C	19	6-0	198	St. Albans, W. Va.
72	Norri, Eric	T	19	6-2	240	Virginia, Minn.
3	O'Brien, Coley	QB	19	5-11	173	McLean, Va.
40	*O'Leary, Tom	HB	20	5-10	185	Columbus, Ohio
81	**Page, Alan	E	21	6-5	238	Canton, Ohio
49	Paternostro, Vic	C	22	6-1	235	Lyndhurst, N. J.
50	Pergine, John	LB	19	6-0	210	Norristown, Pa.
62	*Quinn, Steve	C	20	6-1	215	Northfield, Ill.
19	Quinn, Tom	HB	19	6-1	192	Clinton, Iowa
1	Rassas, Kevin	HB	20	6-1	190	Winnetka, Ill.
76	**Regner, Tom	G	22	6-1	245	Kenosha, Wis.
12	Reynolds, Tom	LB	19	6-0	185	Ogden Dunes, Ind.
87	*Rhoads, Tom	E	21	6-2	220	Cincinnati, Ohio
11	Ryan, Jim	K	22	5-10	185	Shreveport, La.
88	Sack, Allen	E	21	6-3	205	Boothwyn, Pa.
70	Schnurr, Fred	T	20	6-3	245	Cleveland, Ohio
7	*Schoen, Tom	HB	20	5-11	178	Euclid, Ohio
71	Seiler, Paul	T	20	6-4	235	Algona, Iowa
85	Seymour, Jim	E	19	6-4	205	Berkley, Mich.
94	Skoglund, Bill	E	19	6-1	210	LaGrange Park, Ill.
18	Slettvet, Tom	FB	19	6-0	202	Sumner, Wash.
25	Smithberger, Jim	HB	19	6-1	190	Welch, W. Va.
92	Snow, Paul	E	18	6-1	180	Long Beach, Calif.
91	Stenger, Brian	E	19	6-4	210	Euclid, Ohio.
59	*Swatland, Dick	G	20	6-2	225	Stamford, Conn.
89	VanHuffel, Alan	LB	20	6-2	210	South Bend, Ind.
35	Vuillemin, Ed	LB-E	18	6-1	205	Akron, Ohio
46	Wengierski, Tim	HB	21	6-0	185	River Forest, Ill.
83	Zubek, Bob	E	19	6-2	220	Painesville, Ohio
48	Zurowski, Dave	HB	21	6-3	190	Oxon Hill, Md.

*Denotes monogram won.

front row, left to right, Don Gmitter, Paul Seiler, Tom Regner, Tom Rhoads, Nick Eddy, Captain Jim Lynch, Pete Duranko, George Goedekke, John Horney, Alan Page, Larry Conjar; second row, Bob Hagerty, Tim Gorman, Dick Swatland, Leo Collins, Jim Kelly, Joe Marsico, Angelo Schiralli, Ron Jeziorski, Harry Alexander, Hugh O'Malley, Allen Sack, Kevin Hardy, Dave Zurowski; third row, Gerald Kelly, Dave Martin, Mike Heaton, Dave Haley, Paul May, Rudy Konieczny, Tom O'Leary, Mike Kuzmicz, Steve Quinn, Bob Bleier, Tom Schoen, John Pergine, Mike McGill, Jim Ryan, Tim Wengierski; fourth row, John Lium, Alan VanHuffel, Lou Fournier, Kevin Rassas, Mike Burgener, Dan Harshman, Jim Smithberger, Chuck Grable, Dan Dickman, Joe Freebery, Mike Early, Bob Zubek, Roger Fox, Tom Quinn, Mike Bars, Bill Bartholomew, Jack Sullivan, Manager; fifth row, Al Kramer, Head Manager, Kevin Moran, Manager, Mike Holtzapfel, Chuck Landolfi, Fred Schnurr, Bill Skoglund, Chuck Lauck, Eric Norri, Tom Slettvet, Tom Reynolds, Bob Gladieux, Mike Franger, Paul Snow, Ed Vuillemin, Bob Kuechenberg, Coley O'Brien; sixth row, Pat Schrage, John Lavin, Jim Seymour, Terry Hanratty, Curt Heneghan, Jim Leahy, Frank Criniti, Tim Monty, Tom McKinley, George Kunz, Brian Stenger, Gene Paszkiet, Trainer; back row, Coaches Brian Boulac, George Sefcik, Jerry Wampfler, Tom Pagna, Head Coach Ara Parseghian, Paul Shoults, John Ray, Joe Yonto, Wally Moore.

1966

Coach: Ara Parseghian
Captain: James R. Lynch

S.24	W	Purdue	26-14	H	c59,075
O.1	W	Northwestern	35-7	A	c55,356
O.8	W	Army	35-0	H	c59,075
O.15	W	North Carolina	32-0	H	c59,075
O.22	W	Oklahoma	38-0	A	c63,439
O.29	W	Navy	31-7	N	70,101
N.5	W	Pittsburgh	40-0	H	c59,075
N.12	W	Duke	64-0	H	c59,075
N.19	T	Michigan State	10-10	A	c80,011
N.26	W	So. California	51-0	A	88,520
	(9-0-1)		362-38		652,802

N—at Philadelphia

Sophomores Lead Irish To Victory

SOUTH BEND, Ind. (AP) — Notre Dame unveiled a sensational sophomore passing combination, Terry Hanratty and Jim Seymour, who clicked for touchdown passes of 84, 39 and 7 yards, leading the Fighting Irish to a 26-14 season-opener conquest of Purdue's Boilermakers Saturday.

Seymour, 6-foot-4, 205-pounder from Berkley, Mich. speared 13 Hanratty tosses for 276 yards to completely overshadow Purdue's heralded passer, Bob Griese.

Hanratty, 6-foot-190, from Butler, Pa., completed 16 of 24 passes for 304 yards in the nationally televised game.

Purdue's secondary was demoralized by Seymour, who made one sensational catch after another. The best was his fingertip catch in full stride of Hanratty's long toss on the 84-yard scoring play which put the Irish ahead for keeps, 14-7, in the second quarter.

Avenge '65 Loss

The heroics of Seymour and Hanratty, plus halfback Nick Eddy's 96-yard touchdown run on the kickoff following Purdue's first touchdown in the opening quarter, avenged Notre Dame's 25-21 loss at Purdue last fall.

Griese completed 14 of 26 tosses in shading the Irish, was a harrassed but valiant quarterback Saturday.

Griese completed 14 of 26 tosses for 178 yards and was a dancing scrambler against the fierce Irish defense, but the Boilermakers were against much superior firepower in the amazing Hanratty-Seymour display.

HERE IS A TIME TO GAMBLE..."

by JOE FALLS

...SE ME, FATHER for I have sinned . . .

I rooted for Michigan State.

...ut now I would like to repent. The winner, and it's to say it, was Notre Dame.

...n Monday morning the vote will go out to the Associated Press in New York: 1—Notre Dame, 2—Michigan ...ate, etc., etc.

...And let's not hear any of that tripe from Birmingham ...t Alabama is the best team in the nation. Bear Bryant's ...'s snuck in the back door when the AP held that ...iculous poll last January.

...Make no mistake about it — the two best teams in the ...nd were on display here Saturday and our grudging ...miration goes to the Fighting Irish.

...They were up against everything and still managed to ...ll off a tie in the most nerve-wracking football game ...at could possibly be played. It was a classic in the ...uest sense of the word.

...The Irish lost their quarterback, Terry Hanratty, early ...the game. Their best runner, and maybe the best run...er in the country, Nick Eddy, never got onto the field.

...George Goeddeke, their first-string center, also went ...t early in the action.

And here they were, with only half a backfield, in a bull ring that rivaled anything Madrid or Mexico City could offer, with a 10-0 score against them . . . and they came back and got a 10-10 standoff and barely missed winning it with five minutes to go on Joe Azzaro's field goal try from 41 yards out.

A lesser team could have collapsed when Nick Kenney put that 47-yard field goal through the bars midway in the second half . . . because here Michigan State had all the momentum, all the drive and almost all the fans behind it.

In that moment they waited the kickoff after Kenney's field goal, my heart was pounding at the prospect of a rout, which would have made this the sweetest day of the season, and the feeling came on strong that Michigan State might even have shut out this team that was running up those ridiculous 64-0 scores against people like Duke.

From then on you had to give your admiration to these Notre Dame players. Quit? Why, they came back and played their best ball of the day through those final 40 minutes.

And as the pressure mounted, until it became almost unbearable to sit still in your seat, the Irish made all the big plays.

It was magnificent the way this little Coley O'Brien immediately rallied the Irish for their touchdown, because simply, ask yourself this question — who is Coley O'Brien?

He looks like a tumbleweed being blown across the flat prairie lands, no bigger than the quarterback at North Farmington High. And certainly, no cover boy.

The people at Time probably never heard of him.

But he fused the spark in his team and before you could utter the magic words, "We're No. 1," the Irish were on the scoreboard and back in the game.

He led them 54 yards in three quick strikes and you just can't be any more authoritative than the way he hit the streaking Bob Gladieux on the goal line for the touchdown.

Right then, I started getting scared.

You can stack up the statistics and arrange them in any order that you want but the Irish won this one and even if it might put the Spartans on top, I hope Notre Dame closes out with a victory over Southern Cal. They deserve the No. 1 ranking.

This is not an attempt to demean Michigan State to get off the hook for all the needling I've given the Irish fans in the last few weeks. But it would be less than fair to be prejudiced at a time like this. You've got to give them their due.

It was regrettable that the game ended in a chorus of boos from the highly partisan crowd as Ara Parseghian chose to settle for the tie instead of trying for a bolt of lightning in the last minute.

It would have been far better to see the Irish making an all-out effort to break the tie. But there is a time to gamble, and there isn't a time to gamble.

This wasn't the time.

It was impressive the way Michigan State kept calling time out with the seconds ticking away. But to ridicule the Irish for killing the clock. . . . Well, it's just sour grapes.

Seldom — in fact never — has a game affected me the way this one did. You can believe this or not, but I awoke with a knot in my stomach Saturday morning.

I wanted Michigan State to win so badly, it hurt. If the Spartans lost, I had my lines rehearsed. . . .

AAARGH, I would say, humble pie tastes awful . . . and don't bother writing your nasty letters, Duffy and I were taking a vacation in the upper Peninsula to see who could make the biggest splash from the middle of the Mackinac Bridge.

Well, Daugherty doesn't have to apologize for anything or explain anything. He showed more guts in this one afternoon than many coaches do in an entire career.

Fourth and one on his 30 . . . three minutes left . . . go for it and risk the chance of blowing the game and the whole season and leave yourself wide open to be second guessed the rest of your natural life?

Or punt?

Duffy didn't hesitate. He sent in a play, a keeper by Jimmie Raye, and whether it worked or not, and it did, it was the boldest move any coach could make.

And then, unwilling to settle for the tie, Daugherty kept ordering those time outs in the fading moments, hoping somehow his boys would wrest the ball loose from the Irish.

They took the coach-of-the-year honors away from Daugherty when the Spartans lost to UCLA in the Rose Bowl last January. But if there's any justice left in the land, they should give it to him this time around.

You see, Michigan State played a helluva ball game, too. The Spartans are a superb team.

Reprinted with
permission from the
Detroit Free Press

M.S.U. '66:
Ara's Locker Room Speech

IN OUR LOCKER ROOM there was a quiet, indefinable air of emptiness. Each had played his best. They were spent, they were hurt, they were proud, troubled, tearful, and angered.

No one was undressing; each slumped in his own place waiting, not really sure for what.

Ara himself needed a few moments to gather himself and then he spoke:

"Men, I'm proud of you. God knows I've never been more proud of any group of young men in my life. Get one thing straight though. We did not lose." His voice rose here. "We were number one when we came, we fell behind, had some tough things happen, but you overcame it. No one could have wanted to win this one more than I. We didn't win, but by golly we did not lose. They're crying about a tie, trying to detract from your efforts, they're trying to make it come out a win. Well, don't you believe it. Their season is over; they can't go anywhere. It is all over and we are still number one. Time will prove everything that has happened here today, and you'll see that after the rabble-rousers have their say, cooler minds who understand the true odds will know that Notre Dame is a team of champions."

His words were heard and heard well. The response was quiet, both from physical exertion and lack of any remaining emotion. We said our team prayer led by Ara, and the doors were opened for the "well-wishers" and those who didn't wish so well.

The game had claimed many victims. Eddy, of course, did not play at all, Hanratty and Goeddeke were out for the season, Bleier had traces of blood in his urine from a hard kidney blow, and Gladieux was definitely through for the year. All of this we knew while still in the locker room. Monday could possibly show more serious injuries to other players. Each was bruised; Lynch made himself play with a tremendous charley horse, Conjar's forearms were a mass of black and blue spots from fending off pass rushers, and Gmitter was going on guts with really only one good knee.

Reporters, some more understanding than others, tried to say things that they felt, and have coaches affirm or negate their words. Those that knew us merely mentioned that it had been a great game and that we had proven the fiber that we were made of by coming back from such a deficit and with so many injuries. No matter what we knew or felt, no one would make any remark that reflected poorly on our opponent. Our training prevented it. We had agreed at the team's first meeting that men who stuck knives in others were not really very big men, least of all Notre Dame's dream men. Ara had told the players his feelings about these moments. "There will be moments when you'll want to blast out at something, at someone, but remember that whatever you say, whatever you do, reflects on us, on your parents, on the team, and on Notre Dame."

Irish Crush Bowl-Bound Trojans, 51 to 0

LOS ANGELES (AP) — Awesome Notre Dame, ignited by a pair of 19-year-old sophomores, blasted Southern California 51-0 Saturday as the Irish strengthened their claim for the 1966 national collegiate football championship.

Quarterback Coley O'Brien, who took over for injured quarterback Terry Hanratty, and his 6-4 pass receiver, Jim Seymour, were the key figures as the Rose Bowl-bound Trojans, champions of the Pacific-8 Conference, were buried under the highest score ever in the 38 games between Notre Dame and Southern Cal.

A crowd of 88,520 watched Notre Dame end its season with a record of nine victories and the 10-10 tie last Saturday with Michigan State.

The Trojans head for the Rose Bowl game with Purdue with a 7-3 record.

O'Brien threw three touchdown passes in completing 21 out of 31 throws for 255 yards. Seymour caught 11 for 150 yards and two touchdowns.

Notre Dame took the opening kickoff and marched 80 yards in 17 plays to score.

Two senior backs, Larry Conjar and Nick Eddy, jolted the Trojan line from tackle to tackle and O'Brien mixed in four out of five pass completions for 34 yards as the Irish demonstrated they were here for serious business.

31-0 at Halftime

The Irish built up a 31-0 halftime lead as the O'Brien-Seymour combo starred in two second quarter touchdowns.

In the first, O'Brien traveled 64 yards through the air, hitting Seymour on four throws for 53. The final went 13 yards for the score.

With six seconds remaining in the half and after Southern California had a poor punt, O'Brien fired 39 yards on the first play to Seymour in the end zone.

Seymour leaped high to get the throw as the two top Trojan defensive men, Nate Shaw and Mike Battle, tried to knock it down.

O'Brien's third touchdown toss went 23 yards to Dan Harshman, newly converted from the defense to replace one of the Notre Dame casualties from the Michigan State game.

Conjar scored on a two-yard run and Eddy blasted nine for another tally.

Notre Dame intercepted two Trojan throws by quarterback Toby Page, returning them for touchdowns. Tom Schoen got the first, raced back 40 and went out of action the rest of the day with a hip injury.

Dave Martin stole another and returned it 33 for the final score of the day.

Six of Seven Pats

Place kicker Joe Azzaro, who converted on six of the seven Irish touchdowns, contributed a 38-yard field goal.

Previous high score in the series was Notre Dame's 48-14 victory in 1953.

Southern California reached the Notre Dame 10 in the third period, was promptly thrown back to the 28, and that was the closest they came to scoring.

Coach Ara Parseghian kept his first-line troops in the battle until midway in the fourth quarter. At that stage the second and third string players came in on offense, but it was not until later that the defensive starters were removed.

SCORING:

Notre Dame	14 17 13 7—51	
USC	0 0 0 0— 0	

ND—Conjar 2 run (Azzaro kick)
ND—Schoen 40 pass interception (Azzaro kick)
ND—FG Azzaro 38
ND—Seymour 13 pass from O'Brien (Azzaro kick)
ND—Seymour 39 pass from O'Brien (Azzaro kick)
ND—Harshman 23 pass from O'Brien (Azzaro kick)
ND—Eddy 9 run (kick failed)
ND—Martin 33 pass interception (Azzaro kick)
Attendance 88,520.

STATISTICS

	ND	SC
First downs	31	15
Rushing yardage	206	46
Passing yardage	225	142
Passes	21-31	16-38
passes intercepted by	2	2
Punts	2-39	6-39
Fumbles lost	2	2
Yards penalized	10	53

1966 FINAL STATISTICS

TEAM STATISTICS

N.D.		OPP.
362	POINTS SCORED	38
204	FIRST DOWNS	119
110	by Rushing	53
85	by Passing	60
9	by Penalties	6
2116	YARDS RUSHING	793
473	TIMES CARRIED	384
4.5	Yards-per-try	2.1
1809	YARDS PASSING	1083
232	Passes Attempted	249
120	Passes Completed	105
.517	Completion Percentage	.422
26	Passes Intercepted by	16
497	Yards Int. Returned	152
3925	TOTAL OFFENSE	1876
37	PUNTS	75
1429	Total Yards	2660
38.6	Average	35.5
269	Yards Punts Returned	76
26	FUMBLES	19
13	Ball Lost	11
484	YARDS PENALIZED	367

SCORING

PLAYER	TD	PAT	FG	TP
Eddy	10	0	0	60
Seymour	8	0	0	48
Azzaro	0	38-35	5-4	47
Conjar	7	2 run	0	44
Hanratty	5	2 run	0	32
Bleier	5	0	0	30
Gladieux	5	0	0	30
Schoen	3	0	0	18
Criniti	2	0	0	12
O'Brien	2	0	0	12
Haley	1	0	0	6
Harshman	1	0	0	6
Martin	1	0	0	6
O'Leary	1	0	0	6
Ryan	0	5-3	1-0	3
May	0	2 pass	0	2
ND TOTALS	51	43-38	6-4	362
OPP. TOTALS	5	5-5	5-1	38

INDIVIDUAL RUSHING

PLAYER	TC	YDS	AVG.	TD	LONG RUN
Eddy	78	553	7.1	8	77
Conjar	112	521	4.7	7	30
Bleier	63	282	4.5	4	22
O'Brien	40	135	3.4	2	25
Hanratty	50	124	2.5	5	52
Gladieux	27	111	4.1	3	18
Haley	19	102	5.4	1	26
May	24	65	2.7	0	10
Criniti	17	63	3.7	2	10
Dushney	9	59	6.6	0	13
Belden	17	55	3.2	0	9
Harshman	8	20	2.5	0	9
Hagerty	4	13	3.2	0	4
Quinn, T.	3	12	4.0	0	12
O'Malley	1	1	1.0	0	1
Wengierski	1	0	...	0	0

INDIVIDUAL RECEIVING

PLAYER	NO.	YDS.	AVG.	TD	LONG PASS
Seymour	48	862	18.0	8	84
Bleier	17	209	12.3	1	45
Eddy	15	123	8.2	0	16
Gladieux	12	208	17.3	2	46
Stenger	6	86	14.3	0	20
Gmitter	4	72	18.0	0	24
Conjar	4	62	15.5	0	18
Heneghan	3	46	15.3	0	18
Harshman	3	35	11.7	1	23
Rassas	2	25	12.5	0	13
Heaton	2	13	6.5	0	8
May	1	24	24.0	0	24
Haley	1	23	23.0	0	23
Snow	1	11	11.0	0	11
Quinn, T.	1	10	10.0	0	10

INDIVIDUAL PASSING

Player	Att.	Comp.	Int.	Yds.	Pct.	TD	Long Pass
Hanratty	147	78	10	1247	.531	8	84
O'Brien	82	42	6	562	.512	4	46
Belden	2	0	0	0	.000	0	
Hardy	1	0	0	0	.000	0	

PUNTING

PLAYER	NO.	YDS.	AVG.	LONG PUNT
Bleier	16	634	39.6	63
Gladieux	11	386	35.1	63
Hardy	10	409	40.9	51

KICKOFF RETURNS

PLAYER	NO.	YDS.	TD	AVG.
Eddy	4	193	2	48.3
Bleier	3	67	0	22.3
Conjar	3	39	0	13.0
Gladieux	2	48	0	24
Quinn, T.	1	38	0	38

PUNT RETURNS

PLAYER	NO.	YDS.	TD	AVG.
Schoen	29	253	1	8.7
Burgener	2	16	0	8.0
Quinn, T.	1	0	0	

SCORE BY QUARTERS

NOTRE DAME	83	116	90	73
OPPONENTS	7	10	0	21

PASSES INTERCEPTED

PLAYER	NO.	YDS.	TD
Schoen	7	118	2
Burgener	2	50	0
Pergine	5	72	0
Smithberger	4	132	0
Lynch	3	12	0
Harshman	2	25	0
O'Leary	1	35	1
Martin	1	33	1
Horney	1	20	0

DEFENSIVE STATISTICS

TACKLES: Lynch 106; Pergine 98; Hardy 79; Duranko 73; Page 63; Martin 62; Smithberger 54; Horney 51; O'Leary 46; Rhoads 41; McGill 40; Schoen 30; Lavin 21; Sack 17; Burgener 15; Harshman 14; T. Quinn 13; Van Huffel 12; Jeziorski 10; Vuillemin 9; Alexander 8; Lauck, Norri 6; Holtzapfel 4; Wisne 3; Azzaro, Eddy, G. Kelly, Seiler 2; Gladieux, Gmitter, Kuechenberg, Rassas, Regner, Ryan, Snow, Zubek 1.

PASSES BROKEN UP: Martin, O'Leary 10; Smithberger 7; Hardy, Horney, Rhoads 4; Pergine 3; Lynch 2; Burgener, Duranko, Jeziorski, McGill.

1967 NOTRE DAME ALPHABETICAL ROSTER

No.	Player	Pos.	Age	Ht.	Wt.	Hometown	High School	Cl.
90	°Azzaro, Joe	K	21	5-11	190	Pittsburgh, Pa.	Central Catholic	Sr.
2	Belden, Bob	QB	20	6-2	205	Canton, Ohio	Central Catholic	Jr.
28	°°Bleier, Bob (Captain)	HB	21	5-11	195	Appleton, Wis.	St. Xavier	Sr.
64	Brennan, Terry	OT	19	6-4	235	Chicago, Ill.	Weber	So.
33	°Burgener, Mike	DB	21	5-10	182	Marion, Ill.	Marion	Sr.
21	Criniti, Frank	HB	20	5-8	180	Charleston, West Va.	Charleston Catholic	Jr.
81	deArrieta, Jim	OE	19	6-1	190	Winnemucca, Nev.	Humboldt County	So.
10	Devine, Edgar	LB	18	6-2	195	Waldwick, N. J.	Don Bosco Prep (Ramsey)	So.
49	Donohue, Pete	HB	19	6-0	193	Cincinnati, Ohio	Mariemont (Mariemont)	So.
38	Dushney, Ron	FB	19	5-10	195	Peckville, Pa.	Blakely	Jr.
53	Fischer, Ray	G	20	6-1	230	Cleveland, Ohio	St. Ignatius	Jr.
57	Freebery, Joe	LB	20	6-0	207	Wilmington, Del.	Salesianum	Jr.
83	Furlong, Nick	OE	20	6-1	200	Pelham, N. Y.	Iona Prep (New Rochelle)	So.
88	Furlong, Tom	DE	21	6-2	205	Cleveland, Ohio	St. Ignatius	Sr.
46	Gasser, John	DB	19	6-2	185	Logan, Ohio	Logan	So.
20	°Gladieux, Bob	HB	20	5-11	185	Louisville, Ohio	Louisville	Jr.
6	Gores, Tom	QB	18	6-1	180	Bellevue, Wash.	Seattle Prep (Seattle)	So.
22	Haley, Dave	HB	20	5-11	190	Hingham, Mass.	Archbishop Williams (Braintree)	Sr.
5	° Hanratty, Terry	QB	19	6-1	200	Butler, Pa.	Butler	Jr.
74	°°Hardy, Kevin	DE	22	6-5	270	Oakland, Calif.	St. Elizabeth's	Sr.
34	°Harshman, Dan	HB	21	6-0	190	Toledo, Ohio	St. Francis DeSales	Sr.
84	Heaton, Mike	OE	20	6-2	205	Seneca, Ill.	Marquette	Sr.
86	Heneghan, Curt	DB-OE	19	6-3	190	Redmond, Wash.	Lake Washington (Kirkland)	Jr.
51	Holtzapfel, Mike	C	20	6-1	215	Ironton, Ohio	St. Joseph's	Jr.
14	Hurd, Bill	OE	20	5-11	180	Memphis, Tenn.	Manassas	Jr.
70	Jockisch, Bob	DT	21	6-3	260	Peoria, Ill.	Peoria Central	So.
71	Kelly, George	DT	19	6-3	220	Butler, Pa.	Butler	So.
76	Kennedy, Charles	OT	19	6-3	240	Claymont, Del.	Salesianum (Wilmington)	So.
48	Kiliany, Dennis	LB	20	6-1	205	Youngstown, Ohio	Ursuline	Sr.
73	°Konieczny, Rudy	OT	20	6-0	225	Chicopee, Mass.	Chicopee	Sr.
75	°Kuechenberg, Bob	OT	19	6-2	245	Hobart, Ind.	Hobart	Jr.
82	Kunz, George	OE	20	6-5	240	Arcadia, Calif.	Loyola (Los Angeles)	Jr.
78	Kuzmicz, Mike	OT	20	6-4	245	South Bend, Ind.	Central	Sr.
39	Lambert, Steve	DE	20	6-1	210	Kankakee, Ill.	Bishop McNamara	So.
17	Landolfi, Chuck	FB	20	5-11	210	Ellwood City, Pa.	Lincoln	Jr.
41	Lavin, John	LB	20	6-4	205	Spokane, Wash.	Gonzaga Prep	Jr.
93	Lauck, Chuck	DE	19	6-1	225	Indianapolis, Ind.	Sacred Heart	Jr.
87	Lawson, Tom	OE	19	6-5	230	New City, N. Y.	Clarkstown	So.
56	**Martin, Dave	LB	20	6-0	210	Roeland Park, Kan.	Bishop Miege (Shawnee Mission)	Sr.
77	McCoy, Mike	DT	18	6-5	270	Erie, Pa.	Cathedral Prep	So.
60	**McGill, Mike	LB	20	6-2	225	Hammond, Ind.	Bishop Noll	Sr.
79	*McKinley, Tom	G	20	6-1	235	Kalamazoo, Mich.	Monsignor Hackett	Jr.
30	Merlitti, Jim	LB	19	6-0	205	Akron, Ohio	St. Vincent's	So.
55	*Monty, Tim	C	20	6-0	220	St. Albans, West Va.	Charleston Catholic (Charleston)	Jr.
37	Nash, Tom	FB	19	6-1	225	Flushing, N. Y.	Holy Cross	So.
23	Ness, Rick	LB	19	6-0	215	Great Falls, Mont.	Central Catholic	So.
72	Norri, Eric	DT	20	6-2	245	Virginia, Minn.	Roosevelt	Jr.
3	*O'Brien, Coley	QB	20	5-11	180	McLean, Va.	St. John's College Prep (Wash. D.C.)	Jr.
40	**O'Leary, Tom	DB	21	5-10	185	Columbus, Ohio	St. Charles Prep	Sr.
36	Olson, Bob	LB	19	6-0	225	Superior, Wis.	Superior	So.
50	*Pergine, John	LB	20	6-0	215	Norristown, Pa.	Plymouth-Whitemarsh	Sr.
80	Poskon, Dewey	DE	19	6-4	225	Elizabeth, Pa.	Elizabeth Forward	So.
62	*Quinn, Steve	C	21	6-1	225	Northfield, Ill.	Loyola Academy (Wilmette)	Sr.
19	Quinn, Tom	DB	20	6-1	200	Clinton, Iowa	St. Mary's	Jr.
65	Racanelli, Vito	G	19	6-1	210	Chicago, Ill.	Weber	So.
89	Rassas, Kevin	DE	21	6-1	218	Winnetka, Ill.	Loyola Academy (Wilmette)	Sr.
11	Reid, Don	DB	19	6-1	185	Flint, Mich.	St. Mary's	So.
61	Reilly, Jim	G-OT	19	6-2	230	Yonkers, N. Y.	Hackley Prep (Tarrytown)	Jr.
12	Reynolds, Tom	LB	20	6-0	193	Ogden Dunes, Ind.	Portage (Portage)	So.
63	Ruzicka, Jim	G	19	6-1	235	Portland, Ore.	Jesuit High (Beaverton)	So.
43	Ryan, Kevin	HB	19	5-11	200	Columbus, Ohio	Watterson	Sr.
7	**Schoen, Tom	DB	21	5-11	178	Euclid, Ohio	St. Joseph (Cleveland)	So.
24	Schumacher, Larry	LB	19	6-0	205	East Orange, N. J.	Essex Catholic (Newark)	Jr.
85	*Seymour, Jim	OE	20	6-4	205	Berkley, Mich.	Shrine (Royal Oak)	Jr.
18	Slettvet, Tom	FB	20	6-0	202	Sumner, Wash.	Sumner	Sr.
25	*Smithberger, Jim	DB	20	6-1	190	Grundy, Va.	Welch (Welch, West Va.)	Jr.
92	Snow, Paul	OE-FL	19	6-1	180	Long Beach, Calif.	St. Anthony's	So.
26	Standring, Jay	DB	19	5-10	190	Chicago, Ill.	Leo	Jr.
91	*Stenger, Brian	DE	20	6-4	215	Euclid, Ohio	St. Joseph (Cleveland)	Sr.
59	**Swatland, Dick	G	21	6-2	235	Stamford, Conn.	Stamford Catholic	Jr.
13	Torrado, Rene	K	20	5-11	170	Bal Harbour, Fla.	Archbishop Curley (Miami)	Jr.
69	Tuck, Ed	OT	21	6-3	235	Harrison, N. J.	Harrison	Sr.
27	VanHuffel, Alan	LB	21	6-2	210	South Bend, Ind.	St. Joseph's	Jr.
35	Vuillemin, Ed	FB	19	6-1	205	Akron, Ohio	St. Vincent's	So.
54	Vuillemin, Larry	C	18	6-3	230	Akron, Ohio	St. Vincent's	Jr.
96	Winegardner, Jim	OE	20	6-4	225	Lima, Ohio	Central Catholic	Sr.
67	Wisne, Gerry	DT	21	6-4	235	Dearborn, Mich.	U. of Detroit High (Detroit)	So.
8	Wittliff, Phil	DB	19	6-2	205	Port Huron, Mich.	Port Huron Catholic	So.
32	Ziegler, Ed	FB	19	6-1	213	Woodlawn, Ky.	Newport Catholic (Newport)	So.
47	Zimmerman, Jeff	FB	19	6-1	205	Orwigsburg, Pa.	Blue Mountain	

* Denotes monogram won.

1967

Coach: Ara Parseghian
Captain: Robert P. (Rocky) Bleier

S.23	W	California	41-8	H	c59,075
S.30	L	Purdue	21-28	A	c62,316
O.7	W	Iowa	56-6	H	c59,075
O.14	L	So. California	7-24	H	c59,075
O.21	W	Illinois	47-7	A	c71,227
O.28	W	Michigan State	24-12	H	c59,075
N.4	W	Navy	43-14	H	c59,075
N.11	W	Pittsburgh	38-0	A	54,075
N.18	W	Georgia Tech	36-3	A	c60,024
N.24	W	Miami (Fla.) (Nt)	24-22	A	c77,265
		(8-2-0)	337-124		620,282

AP POLL

1967
1. U.S.C.
2. Tennessee
3. Oklahoma
4. Indiana
5. NOTRE DAME
6. Wyoming
7. Oregon State
8. Alabama
9. Purdue
10. Penn State

UPI POLL

1967
1. U.S.C.
2. Tennessee
3. Oklahoma
4. NOTRE DAME
5. Wyoming
6. Indiana
7. Alabama
8. Oregon State
9. Purdue
10. U.C.L.A.

ND's 500th Victory

Irish Romp 36-3 Over Engineers

ATLANTA, Ga. (AP) —Notre Dame hammered Georgia Tech into submission 36-3 Saturday with a three-touchdown outburst in the second quarter that continued Irish domination of the intersectional football rivalry.

Bob Gladieux and Bob Bleier each scored twice for the ninth-ranked Irish. and quarterback Terry Hanratty hit on the first seven passes he threw to boost Notre Dame's record to 7-2.

The loss was the fifth for Georgia Tech which had not lost for five times in a season since 1960.

Alert Boilermakers Defeat Irish, 28-21

LAFAYETTE, Ind. (AP) — Purdue's alert football team intercepted four passes by Notre Dame quarterback Terry Hanratty and smashed the nationally top-ranked Irish 28-21 Saturday.

The teams took turns scoring touchdowns. The lead changed hands six times — but Purdue got the last one on a 31-yard pass from sophomore Mike Phipps to Bob Baltzell.

The biggest crowd ever to see a game at Purdue's Ross-Ade Stadium, 62,316, almost tore up the stadium as the Boilermakers maintained a tradition of being bad medicine for Notre Dame.

They have licked the Irish four times in their last six meetings.

The Irish were last defeated in 1965 by Michigan State 12-3.

Burly Perry Williams, Purdue fullback, bulled his way 10 yards for a first period touchdown but the kick failed. Hanratty, who completed 28 of 51 passes, pulled Notre Dame even with a one-yard sneak and Joe Azzaro's conversion gave the Irish a 7-6 lead.

Williams carried another load of Notre Dame tacklers over the goal line from three yards out after a scoreless second quarter and Phipps hit end Jim Beirne with a two-point conversion pass that made it 14-7.

Halfback Bob Bleier, who played a magnificent ground game for the Irish, plunged for a third quarter touchdown and Azarro tied it up 14-14 going into the last period.

Phipps passed 11 yards to Leroy Keyes on the third play of the last quarter and Bob Baltzell kicked the point.

Notre Dame marched 75 yards for a tying touchdown, getting the score on Hanratty's 27-yard pitch to Paul Snow, and Azzaro kicked again.

Purdue's Jim Kirkpatrick ran the kickoff back 30 yards to his 36 and the Boilermakers charged 64 yards in five plays for the winning touchdown. A Phipps-to-Baltzell pass for 31 yards got the touchdown.

Notre Dame never quit, going to the Purdue 14 on a flurry of Hanratty passes in the closing minutes, only to lose the ball on downs.

STATISTICS

Notre Dame		7 0 7 7—21
Purdue		6 0 8 14—28

Pur—Williams 10 run (kick failed)
ND—Hanratty 1 run (Azzaro kick)
Pur—Williams 3 run (Beirne pass from Phipps)
ND—Bleier 1 run (Azzaro kick)
Pur—Keyes 11 pass from Phipps (Baltzell kick)
ND—Snow 27 pass from Hanratty (Azaro kick)
Pur—Baltzell 31 pass from Phipps (Baltzell kick)
Attendance 62,316.

Simpson TD Tidal Wave Routs Notre Dame, 24-7

STATISTICS

	USC	Notre Dame
First downs	13	17
Rushing yardage	219	93
Passing yardage	59	149
Return yardage	165	172
Passes	18-5-3	40-15-7
Punts	1	2
Fumbles lost	1	2
Yards penalized	72	15

SOUTH BEND, Ind. (AP) — O.J. "Orange Juice" Simpson was a three-touchdown tidal wave in the second half, sweeping top-ranked Southern California to a 24-7 humbling of favored Notre Dame in a wild football game Saturday.

The Trojans' fifth straight triumph impressively avenged a 51-0 massacre by Notre Dame in la t year's finale at Los Angeles.

After being throttled in the first half which produced a 7-0 Notre Dame lead, the lithe and swift Simpson, top national rusher, demorali d the Irish with touchdown runs of 35, 3, and 1 yard.

In the hard-played, but often wierd contest, in which there were a dozen turnovers on pass interceptions and fumbles, Simpson battered Notre Dame for 163 yards on 39 carries to better his season average of 150 yards per game.

Simpson was at his best in the 17-point Trojan third quarter, in which the erratic Irish collapsed badly.

Simpson's one-yard scoring smash tied the score at 7-7 when the butter-fingered Irish fumbled on the second half kickoff and the Trojans' Steve Swanson recovered on the Notre Dame 18.

Held to 41 yards on 14 first-half carries, Simpson ignited the blazing Trojan comeback by cracking 18 yards on seven carries, his last a one-yard drive for the first USC touchdown.

The real backbreaker for the Irish, whose heralded Terry Hanratty had five passes intercepted, came on a 35-yard touchdown run by Simpson, his longest scrimmage jaunt of the season, with 4:34 left in the third quarter.

USC	0 0 17 7	—24
Notre Dame	0 7 0 0	—7

ND—Hanratty 3 run (Azzaro kick)
USC—Simpson 1 rcn (Aldridge kick)
USC—Simpson 35 run (Aldridge kick)
USC—FG Aldridge 22
USC—Simpson 3 run (Aldridge kick)
Attendance 59,075

★ Johnny Lujack
★ Elmer Layden

How Johnny Lujack saved a National Title in 1946 ... Layden Rose Bowl standout against Stanford (see page 2).

Southern Cal · Notre Dame

OCTOBER 14, 1967 · NOTRE DAME STADIUM · OFFICIAL PROGRAM 50 cents

1967 FINAL STATISTICS

TEAM STATISTICS

TEAM STATISTICS	ND	OPP.
TOTAL OFFENSE	3911	2201
Total Plays	788	703
Avg. Gain per Play	5.0	3.1
Avg. Gain per Game	391	220
NET RUSHING YARDS	2170	1043
Rushing Plays	530	397
Avg. per Rush	4.1	2.6
Avg. per Game	217	104
NET PASSING YARDS	1741	1158
Passes Att.-Comp.	258-131	306-102
Completion Percentage	.508	.333
Had Intercepted	17	19
Touchdown Passes	10	4
Avg. Gain per Attempt	6.7	3.8
Avg. Gain per Completion	13.3	11.4
Avg. per Game	174	116
PASSES INTERCEPTED	19	17
Yards Returned	297	317
KICKOFF RET. YARDS	413	940
Kickoff Ret.—Avg.	21-19.7	56-16.8
PUNT RET. YARDS	520	194
Punt Rets.—Avg.	45-11.6	25-7.8
YARDS PUNTING	1586	2688
Punts—Avg.	49-32.4	79-34.0
PENALTIES—YARDS	32-299	48-386
FUMBLES—BALL LOST	29-15	23-8
FIRST DOWNS	223	126
Rushing	121	58
Passing	91	59
Penalties	11	9
TOTAL POINTS SCORED	337	124
TOUCHDOWNS	45	17
Rushing	32	12
Passing	10	4
Others	3	1
FIELD GOALS	10-8	7-3
PAT—KICK	42-39	9-7
PAT—PASS	2-1	7-2
PAT—RUSH	1-1	1-1

RUSHING

Player	TC	Yds	Avg.	TD	LG
Zimmerman	133	591	4.4	8	47
Gladieux	84	384	4.6	5	28
Bleier	77	357	4.4	5	39
Dushney	45	229	5.1	2	20
Hanratty	75	183	2.4	7	37
O'Brien	34	123	3.6	1	16
Criniti	24	90	3.8	0	16
Harshman	23	85	3.7	1	14
Haley	13	54	4.2	1	23
Ziegler	11	36	3.3	1	11
Belden	10	30	3.0	0	13
Landolfi	1	8	8.0	1	8
	530	2170	4.1	32	47

PASS RECEIVING

Player	No.	Yds	Avg.	TD	LG
Seymour	37	515	13.9	4	48
Gladieux	23	297	12.9	2	38
Bleier	16	171	10.7	2	22
Harshman	10	85	8.5	0	20
Snow	9	157	17.4	1	27
Winegardner	9	127	14.1	0	17
Kunz	7	101	14.4	0	41
Zimmerman	6	102	17.0	1	39
Criniti	3	32	10.7	0	24
Dushney	3	32	10.7	0	13
N. Furlong	2	66	33.0	0	47
Haley	2	34	17.0	0	24
Lawson	2	11	5.5	0	8
Ziegler	1	13	13.0	0	13
Hanratty	1	—2		0	
	131	1741	13.3	10	48

FUMBLES RECOVERED — O'Leary 2; Martin, McGill, Olson, Pergine, Schoen, Schumacher 1.

PASSING

Player	Att.	Comp.	Int.	Yds	TD	Pct.	LG
Hanratty	206	110	15	1439	9	.534	48
O'Brien	41	16	2	220	1	.390	47
Belden	9	5	0	82	0	.556	24
Gladieux	1	0	0	0	0	.000	
Dushney	1	0	0	0	0	.000	
	258	131	17	1741	10	.508	48

PUNT RETURNS

Player	Punts No-Yds-TD	Kickoffs No-Yds-TD	Interceptions No-Yds-TD
Schoen	42-447-1		4-108-1
T. Quinn	3- 73-1		1- 0-0
Bleier		9-201-0	
Haley		5-119-0	
Ziegler		1- 22-0	
Dushney		1- 20-0	
Gladieux		1- 19-0	
Criniti		1- 17-0	
Harshman		1- 15-0	
Kuechenberg		1- 0-0	
Poskon		1- 0-0	
Pergine			4- 19-0
Martin			3- 31-0
O'Leary			2-105-0
Smithberger			2- 29-0
McCoy			1- 3-0
Kiliany			1- 2-0
Hardy			1- 0-0
	45-520-2	21-413-0	19-297-1

PUNTING

Player	NO.	YARDS	AVG.
Bleier	23	759	33.0
Hardy	20	640	32.0
Gladieux	3	98	32.7
Torrado	3	89	27.7

SCORING

Player	TD	PAT	FG
Heaton	0	2-2	0
Azzaro	0	40-37	10-8
Zimmerman	9	0	0
Bleier	7	0	0
Gladieux	7	0	0
Hanratty	7	0	0
Seymour	4	0	0
Dushney	2	0	0
Schoen	2	0	0
O'Brien	1	1 rush	0
Haley	1	0	0
Harshman	1	0	0
Landolfi	1	0	0
T. Quinn	1	0	0
Snow	1	0	0
Ziegler	1	0	0
N. Furlong	0	2 pass	0
	45	42-39	10-8

DEFENSIVE STATISTICS

TACKLES MADE — Olson 98; McGill 93; gine 89; Martin 71; Schoen 52; Lauck 50; Nor McCoy 43; Smithberger 41; O'Leary 37; Hard Kuechenberg 32; Quinn 26; Jockisch 24; Lavi Freebery 18; Burgener, Schumacher, Stenge Reid, E. Vuillemin 7; T. Furlong, Rassas 4; ieux, Merlitti, Wisne 3; Azzaro, Haley, Henegh Brennan, Donohue, Kiliany, Reilly, Snow, Zeig

TACKLES FOR LOSS—Kuechenberg 10; McC Pergine 7; Lauck, Martin, Olson 6; Norri, O' 3; Jockisch, McCoy, Stenger, E. Vuillemin 2; bery, Smithberger 1.

PASSES BROKEN UP — Schoen 11; O'Lea Smithberger 7; Olson 5; Kuechenberg, Pe T. Quinn 4; Martin, McGill 3; Hardy, McC Norri, Reid, Stenger, E. Vuillemin 1.

Notre Dame's 500th victory... an 8-2 record ... a better season next year?

Atlanta was the site of the 500th victory in Irish football history, when the Irish easily beat a hurting Georgia Tech team, 36-3. After an early field goal, the Yellow Jackets never scored again. On the next series of downs a 38-yard pass to Bob Gladieux gave the Irish a touchdown and the lead. Once again the Irish were magnificent on defense. Defensive halfback Tom O'Leary intercepted two passes, one of them setting up a touchdown run by Bob Bleier over left tackle.

The 1967 Notre Dame team inherited and passes on more ability than most, and has thrived in a home atmosphere that prompted Sports Illustrated to devote an entire color page to an impressionistic-satirical painting of the campus sprouting with footballs. Like UCLA basketball, an unbeaten, untied year might have been the dullest thing in years. The growth and midseason development of an over-rated team—particularly the development of the ground game—made the season interesting, if at times frustrating. The 1967 team proved very human, and had much more than physical strength: it had character. It had problems. And it had pride.

NOTRE DAME ROSTER

No.	Name	Pos.	Ht.	Wt.	Age	Class	Home
22	Allan, Dennis	HB	5-11	190	19	Soph.	Ashtabula, Ohio
2	Belden, Robert	QB	6-2	205	21	Sen.	Canton, Ohio
64	Brennan, Terence	OT	6-4	230	20	Jun.	Chicago, Ill.
66	Capers, Anthony	DE-T	6-2	248	19	Soph.	Warren, Ohio
60	Cotter, Robert	OG	6-2	215	19	Soph.	Chicago, Ill.
*21	Criniti, Frank	HB	5-8	180	21	Sen.	Charleston, W. Va.
81	deArrieta, James	DHB	6-1	190	20	Jun.	Winnemucca, Nev.
10	Devine, Edgar	HB	6-2	205	19	Jun.	Waldwick, N.J.
56	DiNardo, Lawrence	OG	6-1	243	19	Soph.	Queens, N.Y.
*38	Dushney, Ronald	FB	5-10	195	21	Sen.	Peckville, Pa.
89	Eaton, George	SE	6-3	200	19	Soph.	Lancaster, Ohio
53	Fischer, Raymond	OG-T	6-1	220	21	Sen.	Cleveland, Ohio
57	Freebery, Joseph	LB	6-0	207	21	Sen.	Wilmington, Del.
*83	Furlong, Nicholas	SE	6-1	200	20	Jun.	Pelham, N.Y.
82	Gasseling, Thomas	DE	6-2	235	19	Soph.	Wapato, Wash.
46	Gasser, John	DHB	6-2	178	20	Jun.	Logan, Ohio
**20	Gladieux, Robert	HB	5-11	185	21	Sen.	Louisville, Ohio
6	Gores, Thomas	QB	6-1	180	20	Jun.	Seattle, Wash.
50	Haag, Louis	C	6-1	199	19	Soph.	King George, Va.
** 5	Hanratty, Terrence	QB	6-1	200	21	Sen.	Butler, Pa.
52	Hempel, Scott	OG	6-0	235	19	Soph.	Copley, Ohio
86	Heneghan, Curtis	DHB	6-3	190	21	Sen.	Redmond, Wash.
51	Holtzapfel, Michael	C	6-1	215	21	Sen.	Ironton, Ohio
25	Jackson, Ernest	DHB	6-0	182	19	Soph.	Bartlesville, Okla.
*70	Jockisch, Robert	DT	6-3	260	20	Jun.	Peoria, Ill.
31	Johnson, Ronald	LB	6-1	208	19	Soph.	Seattle, Wash.
42	Kelly, Timothy	LB	6-1	212	19	Soph.	Springfield, Ohio
*76	Kennedy, Charles	OT	6-3	240	20	Jun.	Claymont, Del.
34	Kondrla, Michael	LB	6-0	215	19	Soph.	Oaklyn, N.J.
62	Kos, Gary	DT	6-2	234	19	Soph.	Minneapolis, Minn.
**75	Kuechenberg, Robert	DE	6-2	245	21	Sen.	Hobart, Ind.
*78	Kunz, George	OT	6-5	240	21	Sen.	Arcadia, Cal.
39	Lambert, Stephen	FB	6-1	210	20	Jun.	Kankakee, Ill.
17	Landolfi, Charles	HB-FB	5-11	205	21	Sen.	Ellwood City, Pa.
41	Lavin, John	LB	6-4	225	21	Sen.	Spokane, Wash.
*93	Lauck, Charles	DE	6-1	225	21	Sen.	Indianapolis, Ind.
87	Lawson, Thomas	TE	6-5	230	20	Jun.	New City, N.Y.
44	Malone, Michael	DE	6-3	226	21	Sen.	Elmira, N.Y.
73	Martin, Michael	OT	6-4	260	19	Soph.	Roseburg, Ore.
*77	McCoy, Michael	DT	6-5	270	20	Jun.	Erie, Pa.
43	McHale, John	LB	5-11	205	19	Soph.	Chamblee, Ga.
**79	McKinley, Thomas	OG	6-1	235	21	Sen.	Kalamazoo, Mich.
30	Merlitti, James	LB	6-0	205	20	Jun.	Akron, Ohio
**55	Monty, Timothy	C	6-0	220	21	Sen.	St. Albans, W. Va.
74	Mudron, Patrick	DT	6-0	240	19	Soph.	Joliet, Ill.
59	Nash, Thomas	OG	6-1	225	20	Jun.	Flushing, N.Y.
88	Neidert, Robert	LB-DE	6-0	210	19	Soph.	Akron, Ohio
23	Ness, Richard	LB	6-0	215	20	Jun.	Great Falls, Mont.
*72	Norri, Eric	DT	6-2	245	21	Sen.	Virginia, Minn.
** 3	O'Brien, Coleman	DB-QB	5-11	180	21	Sen.	McLean, Va.
*36	Olson, Robert	LB	6-0	230	20	Jun.	Superior, Wis.
80	Poskon, Dewey	TE	6-4	220	20	Jun.	Elizabeth, Pa.
*19	Quinn, Thomas	DHB	6-1	200	21	Sen.	Clinton, Iowa
65	Racanelli, Vito	OG	6-1	210	20	Jun.	Chicago, Ill.
11	Reid, Donald	DHB	6-1	185	20	Jun.	Flint, Mich.
*61	Reilly, James	OG	6-2	230	20	Jun.	Yonkers, N.Y.
12	Reynolds, Thomas	LB	6-0	185	20	Jun.	Ogden Dunes, Ind.
63	Ruzicka, James	OG	6-1	235	20	Jun.	Portland, Ore.
24	Schumacher, Lawrence	LB	6-0	205	20	Jun.	East Orange, N.J.
**85	Seymour, James	SE	6-4	205	21	Sen.	Berkley, Mich.
16	Sheahan, James	DHB	5-11	188	19	Soph.	Bellevue, Wash.
*92	Snow, Paul	SE	6-1	180	21	Sen.	Long Beach, Calif.
15	Standring, John	DHB	5-10	190	20	Jun.	Chicago, Ill.
90	Stark, Craig	SE	6-5	210	19	Soph.	South Bend, Ind.
7	Theismann, Joseph	QB	6-0	170	19	Soph.	South River, N.J.
*69	Tuck, Edward	OG-T	6-3	235	21	Sen.	Harrison, N.J.
*35	Vuillemin, Edward	DE	6-2	205	20	Sen.	Akron, Ohio
14	Wack, Stephen	DHB	6-1	190	19	Soph.	Portland, Ore.
*96	Winegardner, James	TE	6-4	225	21	Sen.	Lima, Ohio
67	Wisne, Gerald	DT	6-4	230	21	Sen.	Detroit, Mich.
26	Wittliff, Phillip	DHB	6-2	205	20	Jun.	Port Huron, Mich.
32	Ziegler, Edward	HB	6-1	213	20	Jun.	Newport, Ky.
84	Zilly, John	OT	6-5	240	19	Soph.	Narragansett, R.I.
*47	Zimmerman, Geoffrey	FB	6-1	205	20	Jun.	Orwigsburg, Pa.
91	Ziznewski, Jay	DT	6-7	250	20	Jun.	Perth Amboy, N.J.
27	Zloch, Charles	DHB	5-11	180	19	Soph.	Ft. Lauderdale, Fla.

(* Letters Won)

1968
1. Ohio State
2. Penn State
3. Texas
4. So. California
5. NOTRE DAME
6. Arkansas
7. Kansas
8. Georgia
9. Missouri
10. Purdue

1968
1. Ohio State
2. Southern Cal
3. Penn State
4. Georgia
5. Texas
6. Kansas
7. Tennessee
8. NOTRE DAME
9. Arkansas
10. Oklahoma

1968

Coach: Ara Parseghian

Co-captains: George J. Kunz and Robert L. Olson

S.21	W	Oklahoma	45-21	H	c59,075
S.28	L	Purdue	22-37	H	c59,075
O.5	W	Iowa	51-28	A	58,043
O.12	W	Northwestern	27-7	H	c59,075
O.19	W	Illinois	58-8	H	c59,075
O.26	L	Michigan State	17-21	A	c77,339
N.2	W	Navy	45-14	N	63,738
N.9	W	Pittsburgh	56-7	H	c59,075
N.16	W	Georgia Tech	34-6	H	c59,075
N.30	T	So. California	21-21	A	82,659
		(7-2-1)	376-170		636,229

N—at Philadelphia

ALLOW PITT ONLY 15 RUSHING YARDS

Irish Humble Pitt, 56 to 7

SOUTH BEND, Ind. (AP) — Sophomore Joe Theismann and little Coley O'Brien, erstwhile understudy to injured Terry Hanratty, teamed for five touchdowns in a 56-7 Notre Dame football rout of pathetic Pittsburgh Saturday.

Theismann, replacing star quarterback Hanratty who suffered a severe knee injury in practice, brilliantly directed the Fighting Irish to a 43-0 lead in the first 27 minutes of play.

O'Brien, who basked in Hanratty's shadow for two previous seasons, scored three straight touchdowns as a halfback in Notre Dame's 26-point second quarter.

Two of O'Brien's three touchdowns came on passes of 15 to 31 yards from the 163-pound Theismann who scored himself on runs of 10 and 9 yards as Notre Dame stunned Pitt with 23 points in the first quarter.

Notre Dame reserves took over three minutes before half time which ended with an Irish lock up of the game at 49-0.

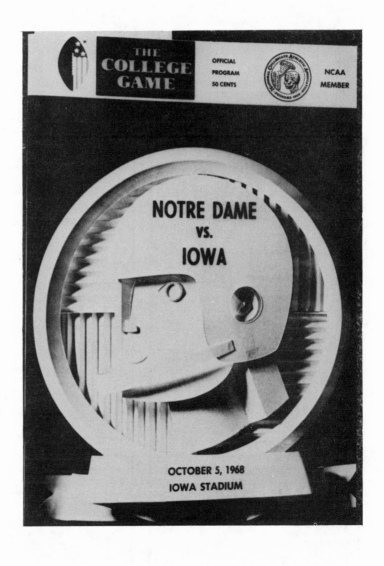

THE COLLEGE GAME
OFFICIAL PROGRAM 50 CENTS
NCAA MEMBER

NOTRE DAME vs. IOWA

OCTOBER 5, 1968
IOWA STADIUM

SCOREBOARD '68

SEASON INDIVIDUAL RECORDS

Passes Completed:
116, Terry Hanratty
*114, John Huarte, 1964

Completion Percentage:
58.8, Terry Hanratty
*56.5, Bob Williams, 1949

Kicking PAT's:
45, Scott Hempel
*40, Buck Shaw, 1921

CAREER RECORDS

Pass Attempts:
550, Terry Hanratty
*436, Ralph Guglielmi, 1951-54

Completions:
304, Terry Hanratty
*209, Ralph Gugliemmi, 1951-54

Interceptions Thrown:
34, Terry Hanratty
*30, Angelo Bertelli, 1941-43

Yards Passing:
4152, Terry Hanratty
*3117, Ralph Guglielmi, 1951-54

Total Offense Plays:
731, Terry Hanratty
*644, Ralph Guglielmi 1951-54

Total Offense Yards :
4738, Terry Hanratty
*4110, George Gipp, 1917-20

TD's Responsible For:
41, Terry Hanratty
*36, Red Salmon, 1900-03

Passes Caught:
138, Jim Seymour
*71, Joe Heap, 1951-54

Yards on Reception:
2113, Jim Seymour
*1242, Jack Snow, 1962-64

TD Catches:
16, Jim Seymour
*13, Leon Hart, 1947-49

TEAM RECORDS

SINGLE GAME
Total Plays:
104, Iowa
*101, Carnegie Tech, 1924
Yards Gained
673, Illinois
*664, Haskell Indians, 1932
First Downs:
35, Oklahoma & Iowa
*32, North Carolina, 1953
SEASON RECORDS
Most Rushes:
657
*625, 1943
Most Completions:
147
*131, 1967
Highest Completion Percentage:
.583 (147 of 252)
*.565, 1948 (61 of 108)
Total Offense Plays:
909
*788, 1967
Total Offense Yards:
5044
*4512, 1921

Highest Per Game Average:
504.4
*441.3, 1946 — 3972 in 9 games
Fewest Punts:
23
*30, 1964
First Downs:
296
*223, 1967
First Downs Rushing:
171
*156, 1943
First Downs Passing:
106
*91, 1967
First Downs Penalty:
15
*14, 1964
Fewest Punt Returns Allowed:
5
*8, 1954
GAME RECORD TIED:
18, Purdue & Michigan State
*18, Purdue (1967)

1968 RESULTS

N.D.		Opp.
45	Oklahoma	21
22	Purdue	37
51	Iowa	28
27	Northwestern	7
58	Illinois	8
17	Michigan State	21
45	Navy	14
56	Pittsburgh	7
34	Georgia Tech	6
21	Southern Cal	21

PASSING

Player	No	Comp	Int	Yds	TD	PCT	LONG
Hanratty	197	116	9	1466	10	.588	69
Theismann	49	27	5	451	2	.551	31
Belden	3	3	0	55	0	1.000	25
O'Brien	3	1	1	13	1	.333	13

RUSHING

Player	TC	YDS	AVG.	TD	LONG
Gladieux	152	713	4.7	12	57
Dushney	108	540	5.0	4	32
O'Brien	64	314	4.9	3	27
Hanratty	56	279	5.0	4	43
Zimmerman	63	267	4.2	0	33
Theismann	59	259	4.4	4	36
Landolfi	38	203	5.3	2	20
Ziegler	30	163	5.4	2	40
Criniti	33	151	4.6	3	20
Allan	33	105	3.2	3	14
Belden	18	83	4.6	0	13
Barz	1	3	3.0	0	3
Hempel	1	–12			
deArrieta	1	–13			
Seymour				1	
TOTALS	657	3059	4.6	38	57

DEFENSIVE STATISTICS

Player	TM	TL-YDS
Olson	129	8-33
Kelly	80	3-29
McCoy	72	8-34
Schumacher	51	2-12
Freebery	53	4-49
Kuechenberg	44	8-59
Lauck	45	7-59
Reid	43	1-1
Jockisch	38	3-15
Gasser	31	1-3
Zloch	27	
Lavin	17	1-1
Lambert	15	3-24
Wright	14	
Norri	18	6-42
Neidert	13	
Standring	13	
Kondria	12	
Quinn	11	
Mudron	13	1-6

RECEIVING

Player	No	Yds	Avg.	TD	Long
Seymour	53	736	13.9	4	31
Gladieux	37	442	11.9	2	69
O'Brien	16	272	17.0	4	50
Winegardner	14	179	12.8	0	22
Dushney	8	117	14.6	0	31
Allan	7	93	13.3	1	26
Eaton	5	73	14.6	0	31
Zimmerman	4	24	6.0	0	16
Landolfi	1	25	25.0	0	25
Snow	1	11	11.0	0	11
Theismann	1	13	13.0	1	13
TOTALS	147	1985	13.8	13	69

Team Statistics	N.D.	Opp.
TOTAL OFFENSE	5044	2490
Total Plays	909	629
Yards Per Play	5.5	3.9
Yards Per Game	504.4	249.0
NET YARDS RUSHING	3059	793
Rushing Plays	657	358
Yards Per Rush	4.6	2.2
Yards Per Game	305.9	79.3
NET YARDS PASSING	1985	1697
Attempts	252	286
Completions	147	137
Completion Percntage	.583	.479
Had Intercepted	15	11
Touchdown Passes	13	12
Yards Per Attempt	7.9	5.9
Yards Per Completion	13.8	12.4
Yards Per Game	198.5	169.7
INTERCEPTIONS MADE	11	15
Yards Returned	33	160
PUNT RETURN YARDS	272	52
Number of Returns	27	5
Avg. Return	10.1	10.4
TOTAL RETURN YARDS	305	212
YARDS PUNTING	820	2901
Number of Punts	23	73
Avg. Punt	35.7	39.8
KICKOFF RETURN YARDS	687	1047
Number of Returns	28	60
Avg. Return	24.5	17.5
PENALTIES AGAINST	42	45
Yards Penalized	411	422
FUMBLES — LOST	25-16	25-12

INDIVIDUAL SCORING

Player	TD	Player	TD
Gladieux	14	O'Brien	7
Seymour	5	Theismann	5
Allan	4	Dushney	4
Hanratty	4		
Criniti	3		*PAT*
Ziegler	2	Hemple	45-50
Landolfi	2	Allan (2 pt.)	1-1
Eaton	1		*FG*
Kuechenberg	1	Hemple	5-9

NOTRE DAME
Alphabetical Roster

Name	Pos.	Wt.	Ht.	Class	Home Town and High School
22 *Allan, Dennis	HB	188	5-11	Jr.	Ashtabula, O. (St. John's)
33 Barz, Bill	FB	216	6-2	Jr.	Country Club Hills, Ill. (Rich Central)
64 *Brennan, Terry	T	254	6-4	Sr.	Chicago, Ill. (Weber)
35 Cieszkowski, John	FB	218	6-2	Soph.	Detroit, Mich. (Univ. of Detroit)
81 deArrieta, Jim	E—HB	188	6-1	Sr.	Winnemucca, Nev. (Humboldt)
56 *DeNardo, Larry	G	230	6-1	Jr.	Queens, N.Y. (St. Francis)
39 Eckman, Mike	KS	190	6-0	Soph.	Lafayette (Central Catholic)
23 Ellis, Clarence	HB	176	6-0	Soph.	Grand Rapids, Mich. (Central)
2 Etter, Bill	QB	185	6-2	Soph.	Spokane, Wash. (Lewis & Clark)
83 *Furlong, Nick	E	200	6-1	Sr.	Pelham, N.Y. (Iona Prep)
82 Gasseling, Tom	T	235	6-2	Jr.	Wapato, Wash.
46 *Gasser, John	HB	186	6-2	Sr.	Logan, O.
44 Gatewood, Tom	E—HB	203	6-2	Soph.	Baltimore, Md. (City College)
91 Grenda, Ed	T	230	6-2	Soph.	Masontown, Pa. (Albert Gallatin)
12 Gulyas, Edward	HB	190	5-11	Soph.	San Carlos, Calif. (Carlmont)
68 Gustafson, Phil	G	238	6-2	Soph.	Galesburg, Ill. (Galesburg)
95 Hartzel, Nick	E	233	6-4	Jr.	White Bear Lake, Minn.
52 *Hempel, Scott	KS	235	6-0	Jr.	Copley, O.
20 Huff, Andy	HB	192	5-11	Soph.	Toledo, O. (St. Francis)
53 Humbert, Jim	G	225	6-2	Soph.	Cincinnati, O. (Roger Bacon)
72 Kadish, Mike	T	249	6-4	Soph.	Grand Rapids, Mich. (Central Catholic)
42 *Kelly, Tim	LB	212	6-1	Jr.	Springfield, O. (Catholic Central)
76 **Kennedy, Charles	T	240	6-3	Sr.	Claymont, Del. (Salesianum)
62 Kos, Gary	G	234	6-2	Jr.	Minneapolis, Minn. (DeLaSalle)
87 Lawson, Tom	E	241	6-5	Sr.	New York, New York (Clarkston)
10 Lewallen, Brian	HB	180	5-10	Sr.	South Bend (Riley)
73 Martin, Mike	T	249	6-4	Jr.	Roseburg, Ore.
75 Marx, Greg	T	240	6-5	Soph.	Redford, Mich. (Catholic Central)
86 Massey, Jim	E	205	6-4	Soph.	Farmington, Mich. (Catholic Central)
77 **McCoy, Mike	T	274	6-5	Sr.	Erie, Pa. (Cathedral Prep)
30 Merlitti, Jim	LB	205	6-0	Sr.	Akron, O. (St. Vincent's)
18 Minnix, Bob	HB	184	5-11	Soph.	Spokane, Wash. (Lewis & Clark)
74 Mudron, Pat	T	240	6-0	Jr.	Joliet, Ill. (Joliet Catholic)
59 Nash, Tom	E	235	6-1	Sr.	Flushing, N.Y. (Holy Cross)
88 Neidert, Bob	LB	216	6-0	Jr.	Akron, O. (Archbishop Hoban)
50 Novakov, Dan	C	226	6-2	Soph.	Cincinnati, O. (Moeller)
36 **Olson, Bob	LB	230	6-0	Sr.	Superior, Wis. (Superior)
54 *Oriard, Mike	C	221	6-3	Sr.	Spokane, Wash. (Gonzaga Prep)
45 Patton, Eric	LB	215	6-2	Soph.	Santa Ana, Calif. (Mater Dei)
85 Patulski, Walt	E	235	6-5	Soph.	Liverpool, N.Y. (Christian Brothers)
3 Peiffer, Mike	QB	190	6-1	Soph.	South Bend (St. Joseph's)
96 Pope, Al	T	250	6-3	Soph.	Iselin, N.Y. (J.F.X. Memorial)
80 Poskon, Dewey	E	220	6-4	Sr.	Elizabeth, Pa. (Forward)
41 Raterman, John	LB	200	6-1	Soph.	Cincinnati, O. (Elder)
11 *Reid, Don	HB	191	6-1	Sr.	Flint, Mich. (St. Mary's)
61 **Reilly, Jim	T	247	6-2	Sr.	Yonkers, N.Y. (Hackley Prep)
63 Ruzicka, Jim	T	242	6-1	Sr.	Portland, Ore. (Jesuit)
24 *Schumacher, Larry	LB	216	6-0	Sr.	East Orange, N.J. (Essex Catholic)
15 *Standring, Jay	HB	190	5-10	Sr.	Chicago, Ill. (Leo)
21 Stepaniak, Ralph	HB	195	6-2	Soph.	Alpena, Mich. (Central Catholic)
93 Swendsen, Fred	E	230	6-4	Soph.	Tacoma, Wash. (Fife)
7 *Theismann, Joe	QB	170	6-0	Jr.	South River, N.J.
38 Thomann, Rick	LB	206	6-1	Soph.	Akron, O. (Archbishop Hoban)
82 Trapp, Bill	E	197	6-3	Soph.	Chicago, Ill. (Mt. Carmel)
94 Williams, Scott	E	225	6-2	Soph.	Baltimore, Md. (Calvert Hall)
66 Witchger, Jim	LB	190	5-10	Soph.	Indianapolis (Brebeuf Prep)
40 Wright, Jim	LB	220	6-1	Jr.	Sparta, N.J.
9 Yoder, Jim	HB	178	6-0	Soph.	Alliance, O. (St. Thomas Aq.)
32 Ziegler, Ed	HB	213	6-1	Sr.	Woodlawn, Ky. (Newport Catholic)
37 Zielony, Dick	FB	204	6-0	Soph.	Vancouver, Wash. (Jesuit-Portland)
79 Zikas, Mike	T	241	6-4	Soph.	Dolton, Ill. (Thornridge)
47 **Zimmerman, Jeff	FB	208	6-1	Sr.	Orwigsburg, Pa. (Blue Mountain)
27 *Zloch, Chuck	HB	185	5-11	Jr.	Ft. Lauderdale, Fla.
49 Zuber, Tim	E—LB	216	6-2	Soph.	Garfield Heights, O.

*Indicates number of letters won.

AP POLL

1969
1. Texas
2. Penn State
3. U.S.C.
4. Ohio State
5. NOTRE DAME
6. Missouri
7. Arkansas
8. Mississippi
9. Michigan
10. L.S.U.

UPI POLL

1969
1. Texas
2. Penn State
3. Arkansas
4. U.S.C.
5. Ohio State
6. Missouri
7. L.S.U.
8. Michigan
9. NOTRE DAME
10. U.C.L.A.

Southern Cal and Notre Dame Play to Bruising 14-14 Tie

1969

Coach: Ara Parseghian
Co-captains: Robert L. Olson and Michael Oriard

S.20	W	Northwestern	35-10	H	c59,075
S.27	L	Purdue	14-28	A	c68,179
O.4	W	Michigan State	42-28	H	c59,075
O.11	W	Army	45-0	N1	c63,786
O.18	T	Southern California	14-14	H	c59,075
O.25	W	Tulane (Nt)	37-0	A	40,250
N.1	W	Navy	47-0	H	c59,075
N.8	W	Pittsburgh (R)	49-7	A	44,084
N.15	W	Georgia Tech (Nt)	38-20	A	41,104
N.22	W	Air Force	13-6	H	c59,075
		(8-1-1)	**334-113**		**552,778**

COTTON BOWL

Jan. 1	L	Texas (1:08)	17-21	N2	c73,000

N1 — at Yankee Stadium, New York
N2 — at Dallas, Texas

SOUTH BEND, Ind. (AP) — Third-ranked Southern California and favored Notre Dame played to a bristling 14-14 football tie Saturday with the Irish just missing a victory as Scott Hempel's 48-yard field goal try hit the crossbar but bounced back into the field with 2:04 left.

The 11th ranked Irish, tabbed a six-point favorite, pulled into the deadlock on a Trojan punt which was blocked by 274-pound Mike McCoy late in the fourth period and recovered on the Southern Cal 7-yard line.

In a bitter contest of big breaks, cool Jimmy Jones rifled a pair of touchdowns to rally the Trojans to a 14-7 lead after Notre Dame scored in the third period on a 74-yard march capped by Bill Barz' one-yard smash.

Jones flipped an 18-yard touchdown pass to Terry deKraai to tie it at 7-7 midway in the third period. On the first play of the fourth quarter, Trojan Tyrone Hudson intercepted a pass by Notre Dame's Joe Theismann and romped to the Irish 15. Two plays later, Jones arched a 14-yard tourhdown pass to Sam Dickerson in the corner of the end zone for a 14-7 Trojan lead.

McCoy set up the tying Irish touchdown by blocking John Young's punt on the Trojan 25 and the ball was recovered by the Irish on the Southern Cal 7-yard line.

Four plays later, Denny Allen dived over for the touchdown.

The Trojans, who also had a perfect record marred by the Irish in a 21-21 tie last year, dominated the first half completely but had a 15-yard touchdown scamper by Clarenct Davis recalled for holding in the opening quarter and saw Ron Ayala fall short on a 45-yard field goal try in the second.

The climactic moment of Notre Dame's 1969 football season came with approximately three minutes left to play in the Southern California game. Struggling to break a 14-14 tie, the Irish had third-and-four at the Trojan 30 yardline. A first down at this point may have led to six points. At least, it would have given Scott Hempel a solid shot at a game-winning field goal. Quarterback Joe Theismann (7) ordered a flat pass to fullback Bill Barz (33). Theismann rolled right, but both Barz and split end Tom Gatewood (44) were covered well. Tight end Dewey Poskon (80), however, was open over the middle; Theismann failed to spot him. Joe saw himself contained and circled to the left side. Simultaneously, Poskon cut back, hoping to throw a peel-block. Southern Cal defensive end Jim Gunn (83) had not penetrated the line of scrimmage. At the snap of the ball, Gunn saw Theismann roll to the opposite side and he drifted into the secondary. Gunn, like Poskon, reacted to Joe's scramble. Dewey met Jimmy at the 25 yardline and head linesman William Makepeace charged Poskon with clipping. Theismann hustled to the 14, but ND was penalized back to the 40.

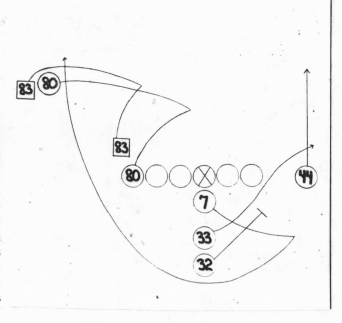

720 Yards? Yeah, Yards

Game 6

ND 47, Navy 0

THIS Naval psychology was beginning to follow a pattern.

In 1967, prior to the Irish-Middie game in ND Stadium, Navy coach Bill Elias proclaimed his signal-caller, John Cartwright, "the best college quarterback in the country."

Ara Parseghian quoted Elias at Friday's pep rally and the faithful responded with "Terry, Terry, Terry, Terry, Terry, Coley, Coley, Coley, Coley, Coley, Belden, Belden, Belden, Belden."

Sixty-minute comparisons are unfair because Hanratty played the first two quarters, O'Brien handled most of the second half and Belden quarterbacked only one series of downs.

FIRST HALF

	Att.	Comp.	Yards	Int.	TD	Tot.Off.
Hanratty	14	8	149	0	1	153
Cartwright	12	4	34	1	0	61

SECOND HALF

	Att.	Comp.	Yards	Int.	TD	Tot.Off.
Cartwright	14	6	75	0	0	108
O'Brien	3	1	47	0	0	87
Belden	0	0	0	0	0	17

GAME

	Att.	Comp.	Yards	Int.	TD	Tot.Off.
Cartwright	26	10	109	1	0	169
Irish QBs	17	9	196	0	1	257

In 1969, the new Navy coach was Rick Forzano, a more respectful fellow than Elias. His pre-game appraisal: "I've been watching the Notre Dame-Southern California film and that's the greatest collection of talent I've ever seen on a college football field. We'd have to play five to 10 times above our capabilities and Notre Dame would

have to be sub-par for us to win."

There was a brazen statesman on the '69 squad, though. He was Karl Schwelm, a tight end whose big moment had come two weeks earlier when he dropped a game-winning TD pass against Rutgers.

Perhaps to atone for that debacle, Schwelm announced that teammate Mike McNallen "is one of the five best quarterbacks in college football."

It was a prodigious statement—ranking right up there with George Wallace's "I will be your next president," Hitler's "Why can't we invade Russia?" and Sonny Liston's "I'll kill that kid Clay."

Again this year, Notre Dame divided the quarterbacking among three players. Post-game stats looked strangely familiar:

	Att.	Comp.	Yards	Int.	TD	Tot.Off.
Theismann	7	3	123	0	1	192
Etter	1	0	0	0	0	140
Gores	0	0	0	0	0	0
Irish QBs	8	3	123	0	1	332
McNallen	31	11	74	3	0	66

In other phases of the game, the contrast was about as vivid. Notre Dame stacked up 720 yards in total offense (an all-time ND record), to Navy's 93.

Navy			0	0	0	0—0
Notre Dame			7	26	14	0—47

ND—Gatewood, 35-yard pass from Theismann (Hempel kick).
ND—Allan, 1-yard run.
ND—Theismann. 46-yard run.
ND—Allan, fumble recovery in end zone.
ND—Huff, 7-yard run (Ziegler run).
ND—Etter, 15-yard run (Hempel kick).
ND—Etter, 79-yard run (Hempel kick).

FOOTBALL CLIMAX: THE COTTON BOWL

On New Year's Day, the Fighting Irish of Notre Dame ended a 45 year absence from post season play as they stormed onto the field at the Cotton Bowl in Dallas. The opposition was the best—the Texas Longhorns, who were undefeated and ranked the number one team in the country. The Irish, severely hampered by the absence of starters Jim Reilly, Terry Brennan, and Ed Ziegler, entered the game as eight point underdogs. For only the second time was a Parseghian coached Notre Dame team entering a game as an underdog.

Throughout the weeks leading up to the game there was much talk throughout the nation of a "mismatch" with the fast Longhorns running rings around the bigger slower Notre Dame defenders. This view was not shared however, by the large number of Irish supporters and Notre Dame students who came to Dallas and rampaged through the streets on New Year's Eve shouting, "The Irish are coming." Notre Dame was ready to play ball and demonstrated it to the Longhorns and a huge national television audience.

Taking the opening kickoff, the Irish marched down the field and grabbed a 3-0 lead on Scott Hempel's 26-yard field goal. Notre Dame increased its lead to 10-0 early in the second quarter as Joe Theismann, rolling left, spotted Tom Gatewood behind his defender and hit him on a 54 yard scoring play.

Texas fought back savagely as their Wishbone-T offense began to get untracked. Behind the superb ball handling of James Street and the strong running of Jim Bertelsen and Steve Worster, Texas took the ensuing kickoff and marched in for a touchdown, making the count 10-7. Texas was knocking on the door later in that quarter but were stopped as Bob Olson, playing the greatest game of his career, stopped Billy Dale of Texas at the Irish 7, inches short of a first down. The third quarter was scoreless and the score stood 10-7 as the final period began.

The last fifteen minutes of play have to be remembered as one of the most exciting quarters in Notre Dame football history.

1970 COTTON BOWL — Texas 21, Notre Dame 17

Notre Dame	3	7	0	7 — 17
Texas	0	7	0	14 — 21

Attendance: 73,000 — Weather: Fair, 48 degrees

Team	Score ND-T	Qtr.	Time Left	Play
ND	3-0	1	8:41	Hempel 26 FG
ND	10-0	2	14:40	Gatewood 54 pass from Theismann (Hempel kick)
Texas	10-7	2	11:12	Bertelsen 1 run (Feller kick)
Texas	10-14	4	10:05	Koy 3 run (Feller kick)
ND	17-14	4	6:52	Yoder 24 pass from Theismann (Hempel kick)
Texas	17-21	4	1:08	Dale 1 run (Feller kick)

Burkhart

WE ARA WITH YOU BEAT TEXAS ROYALly

OUTDOOR ADVERTISING FOUNDATION

1969 Final Statistics

TEAM STATISTICS

	ND	Opp.
Total Offense	4,489	2,187
Total Plays	868	664
Yards Per Play	5.2	3.3
Yards Per Game	448.9	218.7
Net Yards Rushing	2,905	851
Attempts	663	374
Yards Per Rush	4.4	2.3
Yards Per Game	290.5	85.1
Net Yards Passing	1,584	1,336
Attempts	205	290
Completions	113	112
Completion Percentage	.551	.368
Had Intercepted	16	21
Touchdown Passes	13	6
Yards Per Attempt	7.7	4.6
Yards Per Completion	14.0	11.9
Yards Per Game	158.4	133.6
Interceptions Made	21	16
Yards Returned	286	270
Punt Return Yards	252	171
Number of Returns	37	28
Average Return	6.8	6.1
Total Return Yards	538	441
Average Punt	34.6	36.7
Yards Punting	1,558	2,754
Number of Punts	45	75
Had Blocked	1	1
Kickoff Return Yards	427	941
Number of Returns	26	57
Average Return	16.4	16.5
Penalties Against	38	44
Yards Penalized	481	420
Fumbles (Lost)	23(13)	20(12)
Total First Downs	245	130
By Rushing	160	53
By Passing	74	66
By Penalty	11	11

TOTAL OFFENSE

	Plays	Yards	Avg.
Joe Theismann, qb	308	1,909	6.2
Denny Allan, hb	149	612	4.1
Ed Ziegler, hb	94	483	5.1
Bill Etter, qb	41	363	8.8
Bill Barz, fb	90	362	4.0
Andy Huff, hb	69	264	3.8
Mike Crotty, hb	43	183	4.3

SCORING

	TD's	Kick	Play	FG	TP
Hempel		44-41		7-5	56
Allan	9				54
Gatewood	8				48
Barz	7				42
Theismann	6		1-1		38
Huff	6				36
Ziegler	4		1-1		26
Etter	3				18
Ellis	1				6
Lewallen	1				6
Yoder	1				6
Notre Dame	46	44-41	2-1	7-5	334
Opponents	15	12-12	3-1	6-3	113

PUNTING

	No.	Yards	Avg.	Long
Jim deArrieta	36	1,245	34.5	45
Jim Yoder	8	313	39.1	49
Team	1	0	0.0	0
Notre Dame	45	1,558	34.6	49
Opponents	75	2,754	36.7	59

RUSHING

	TC	Yards	Avg.	TD	Long
Denny Allan	148	612	4.1	9	39
Ed Ziegler	94	483	5.1	2	46
Joe Theismann	116	378	3.2	6	46
Bill Barz	90	362	4.0	5	22
Bill Etter	29	310	10.7	3	79
Andy Huff	69	265	3.8	5	21
Mike Crotty	43	183	4.3	0	13
Jim Yoder	23	130	5.6	1	27
Bob Minnix	19	78	4.1	0	10
Dick Zielony	22	68	3.1	0	10
Ed Gulyas	3	20	6.7	0	14
Bill Gallagher	4	16	4.0	0	9
Tom Gatewood	1	0	0.0	0	0
Tom Gores	2	0	0.0	0	0
Notre Dame	663	2,905	4.2	31	79
Opponents	374	851	2.3	8	38

RECEIVING

	PC	Yards	Avg.	TD	Long
Tom Gatewood	47	743	15.8	8	55
Bill Barz	24	262	10.9	2	26
Denny Allan	11	199	18.1	0	56
Dewey Poskon	13	176	13.5	0	37
Ed Ziegler	7	116	16.7	2	29
Andy Huff	4	28	7.0	1	11
Jim Yoder	2	22	11.0	0	18
Bob Minnix	1	16	16.0	0	16
Nick Furlong	2	14	7.0	0	8
Mike Crotty	2	8	4.0	0	5
Notre Dame	113	1,584	14.0	13	56
Opponents	112	1,336	11.9	6	46

SCORING BY QUARTERS

Notre Dame	87	115	77	55	334
Opponents	24	30	21	38	113

RETURNS

(Number — Yards — Touchdowns)

	Interceptions	Punts	Kickoffs
Stepaniak	4- 84-0	11- 50-0	
Ellis	3- 98-1		
Gasser	3- 69-0		
Schumacher	3- 8-0		
Raterman	2- 4-0	1- 5-0	
Olson	1- 15-0		
Lewallen	1- 5-0	7- 75-1	1- 14-0
Thomann	1- 3-0		
Kadish	1- 0-0		
Kelly	1- 0-0		
McCoy	1- 0-0	1- 25-0	
Allan		1- 4-0	10-185-0
Crotty		2- 6-0	4-111-0
Gulyas		14- 87-0	1- 25-0
Huff			1- 12-0
Ziegler			3- 20-0
Barz			2- 14-0
Yoder			1- 28-0
Cieszkowski			1- 13-0
Etter			1- 5-0
Oriard			1- 0-0
Notre Dame	21-286-1	37-252-1	26-427-0
Opponents	16-270-1	28-171-0	57-941-0

PASSING

	No.	Cmp.	Int.	Yards	TD	Pct.
Theismann	192	108	16	1,531	13	.562
Etter	12	5	0	53	0	.417
Allan	1	0	0	0	0	.000
Notre Dame	205	113	16	1,584	13	.551
Opponents	290	112	21	1,336	6	.386

DEFENSIVE STATISTICS

TACKLES MADE: Olson 142; McCoy 88; Kelly 71; Kadish 68; Raterman 67; Patulski, Schumacher 54; Gasser 45; Stepaniak 37; Swendsen, Wright 32; Ellis, Neidert 31; Zikas 18; Thomann 15; Patton, Zloch 12; Merlitti 9; Lewallen 7; Eaton 6; Cloherty 5; Hempel, Reid 4; Eckman, Gasseling, McHale, Nash 3; Bossu, Witchger 1.

TACKLES FOR LOSS: Olson, McCoy 10; Kadish, Patulski 6; Schumacher 5; Swendsen, Neidert 4; Zikas, Kelly, Raterman 2; Patton, Merlitti 1.

PASSES BROKEN UP: Ellis 13; Stepaniak 10; Gasser 8; McCoy 7; Patulski 3; Kelly, Swendsen, Neidert, Merlitti 2; Olson, Kadish, Raterman, Schumacher, Wright, Zloch, Reid 1.

FUMBLES RECOVERED: Raterman 3; Patulski, Gasser 2; Olson, Schumacher, Stepaniak, Neidert, Lewallen, Allan 1.

Above: members of the football team. *First Row:* J. Wright, G. Kos, C. Zloch, J. Theismann, R. Neidert, T. Kelly, L. DiNardo, T. Eaton, W. Barz, S. Buches, S. Hempel, D. Allan. *Second row:* T. Sigrist, T. Gasseling, J. McHale, J. Witchger, C. Nightengale, J. Zilly, P. Schivarelli, R. Johnson, M. Martin, F. Bossu, J. Gardner, J. Maxim. K. Hildebrand. *Third row:* Head Manager, J. McGraw, J. Cloherty, J. Massey, W. Gallagher, J. Humbert, J. Cieszkowski, P. Mudron, N. Hartzel, R. Cotter, M. Kondrla. E. Grenda. C. Stark, J. Clements, W. Trapp. D. Denning. Assistant Manager P. McFadden. *Fourth row:* T. Gatewood. J. Dampeer. J. Cowin, J. Donahue, G. Rankin. M. Eckman. M. Peiffer, D. Novakov. J. Yoder, D. DePremio, W. Etter, T. Merritt, R. Zielony. F. Swendsen, M. Crotty, T. Menie, E. Gulyas, Assistant Manager. R. Roberts.

Fifth row: A. Huff, H. Hooten, R. Minnix, C. Ellis, G. Marx, W. Patulski, T. Phillips. J. Raterman, R. Thomann, R. Stepaniak, T. Zuber, G. Hagopian, T. McGann, D. Green. S. Smith, J. Hagger, M. Creaney, W. Holloway, E. Patton, M. Zikas, T. Robinson. *Sixth row:* R. Johnson, R. Maciag, T. Wright, H. Brück, J. Kondrk, D. Drew, R. Roemer, J. Bulger, P. Steenberge. *R. Miller, J. Roolf, J. Tereschuck, J. Mariani. M. O'Reilly, J. Borbely, T. Freistroffer, J. O'Malley, M. Webb, W. Townsend, D. O'Toole. L. Parker, D. Dewan. *Last row:* D. Gutowski, T. Garner, E. Fiber, J. Musuraca. P. McGraw, K. Schlezes. Coaching staff: G. O'Neill, W. Hickey, J. Murphy, J. Yonto. G. Kelly, P. Shoults, A. Parseghian. T. Pagna, B. Boulac, W. Moore, M. Stock, D. Murphy. L. Ballinger, G. Paszkiet.

UPI POLL

UPI POLL

1970
1. Texas
2. Ohio State
3. Nebraska
4. Tennessee
5. NOTRE DAME
6. L.S.U.
7. Michigan
8. Arizona State
9. Auburn
10. Stanford

AP POLL

1970
1. Nebraska
2. NOTRE DAME
3. Texas
4. Tennessee
5. Ohio State
6. Arizona State
7. L.S.U.
8. Stanford
9. Michigan
10. Auburn

1970

Coach: Ara Parseghian
Co-captains: Larry DiNardo and Tim Kelly

S.19	W	Northwestern	35-14	A	50,049
S.26	W	Purdue	48-0	H	c59,075
O.3	W	Michigan State	29-0	A	c76,103
O.10	W	Army	51-10	H	c59,075
O.17	W	Missouri	24-7	A	c64,200
O.31	W	Navy	56-7	N1	45,226
N.7	W	Pittsburgh	46-14	H	c59,075
N.14	W	Georgia Tech (6:28)	10-7	H	c59,075
N.21	W	Louisiana State (2:54)	3-0	H	c59,075
N.28	L	Southern Cal(R)(U)	28-38	A	64,694
	(9-1-0)		330-97		595,647

COTTON BOWL
Jan. 1 W Texas   24-11   N2 c73,000

N1 – at Philadelphia
N2 – at Dallas, Texas

NOTRE DAME

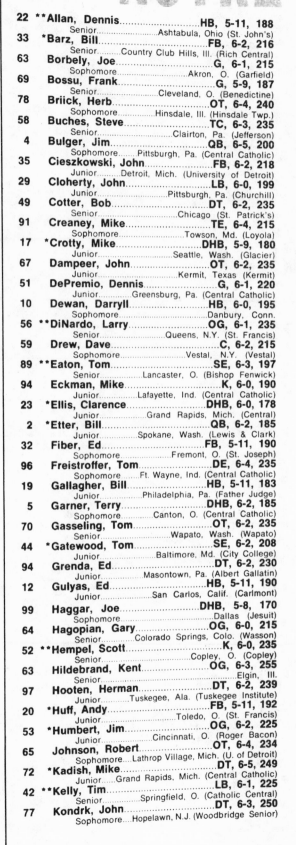

22	**Allan, Dennis**	HB, 5-11, 188	Senior..........Ashtabula, Ohio (St. John's)
33	*Barz, Bill	FB, 6-2, 216	Senior..........Country Club Hills, Ill. (Rich Central)
63	Borbely, Joe	G, 6-1, 215	Sophomore..........Akron, O. (Garfield)
69	Bossu, Frank	G, 5-9, 187	Senior..........Cleveland, O. (Benedictine)
78	Briick, Herb	OT, 6-4, 240	Sophomore..........Hinsdale, Ill. (Hinsdale Twp.)
58	Buches, Steve	TC, 6-3, 235	Senior..........Clairton, Pa. (Jefferson)
4	Bulger, Jim	QB, 6-5, 200	Sophomore..........Pittsburgh, Pa. (Central Catholic)
35	Cieszkowski, John	FB, 6-2, 218	Junior..........Detroit, Mich. (University of Detroit)
29	Cloherty, John	LB, 6-0, 199	Junior..........Pittsburgh, Pa. (Churchill)
49	Cotter, Bob	DT, 6-2, 235	Senior..........Chicago (St. Patrick's)
91	Creaney, Mike	TE, 6-4, 215	Sophomore..........Towson, Md. (Loyola)
17	*Crotty, Mike	DHB, 5-9, 180	Junior..........Seattle, Wash. (Glacier)
67	Dampeer, John	OT, 6-2, 235	Junior..........Kermit, Texas (Kermit)
51	DePremio, Dennis	G, 6-1, 220	Junior..........Greensburg, Pa. (Central Catholic)
10	Dewan, Darryll	HB, 6-0, 195	Sophomore..........Danbury, Conn.
56	**DiNardo, Larry	OG, 6-1, 235	Senior..........Queens, N.Y. (St. Francis)
59	Drew, Dave	C, 6-2, 215	Sophomore..........Vestal, N.Y. (Vestal)
89	**Eaton, Tom	SE, 6-3, 197	Senior..........Lancaster, O. (Bishop Fenwick)
94	Eckman, Mike	K, 6-0, 190	Junior..........Lafayette, Ind. (Central Catholic)
23	*Ellis, Clarence	DHB, 6-0, 178	Junior..........Grand Rapids, Mich. (Central)
2	*Etter, Bill	QB, 6-2, 185	Junior..........Spokane, Wash. (Lewis & Clark)
32	Fiber, Ed	FB, 5-11, 190	Sophomore..........Fremont, O. (St. Joseph)
96	Freistroffer, Tom	DE, 6-4, 235	Sophomore..........Ft. Wayne, Ind. (Central Catholic)
19	Gallagher, Bill	HB, 5-11, 183	Junior..........Philadelphia, Pa. (Father Judge)
5	Garner, Terry	DHB, 6-2, 185	Sophomore..........Canton, O. (Central Catholic)
70	Gasseling, Tom	OT, 6-2, 235	Senior..........Wapato, Wash. (Wapato)
44	*Gatewood, Tom	SE, 6-2, 208	Junior..........Baltimore, Md. (City College)
94	Grenda, Ed	DT, 6-2, 230	Junior..........Masontown, Pa. (Albert Gallatin)
12	Gulyas, Ed	HB, 5-11, 190	Junior..........San Carlos, Calif. (Carlmont)
99	Haggar, Joe	DHB, 5-8, 170	Sophomore..........Dallas (Jesuit)
64	Hagopian, Gary	OG, 6-0, 215	Senior..........Colorado Springs, Colo. (Wasson)
52	**Hempel, Scott	K, 6-0, 235	Senior..........Copley, O. (Copley)
63	Hildebrand, Kent	OG, 6-3, 255	Senior..........Elgin, Ill.
97	Hooten, Herman	DT, 6-2, 239	Junior..........Tuskegee, Ala. (Tuskegee Institute)
20	*Huff, Andy	FB, 5-11, 192	Junior..........Toledo, O. (St. Francis)
53	*Humbert, Jim	OG, 6-2, 225	Junior..........Cincinnati, O. (Roger Bacon)
65	Johnson, Robert	OT, 6-4, 234	Sophomore..........Lathrop Village, Mich. (U. of Detroit)
72	*Kadish, Mike	DT, 6-5, 249	Junior..........Grand Rapids, Mich. (Central Catholic)
42	**Kelly, Tim	LB, 6-1, 225	Senior..........Springfield, O. (Catholic Central)
77	Kondrk, John	DT, 6-3, 250	Sophomore..........Hopelawn, N.J. (Woodbridge Senior)

34	Kondrla, Mike	LB, 6-0, 215	Senior..........Oaklyn, N.J. (Camden Catholic)
62	*Kos, Gary	OG, 6-2, 235	Senior..........Minneapolis, Minn. (DeLaSalle)
76	Maciag, Dick	DT, 6-5, 250	Sophomore..........Buffalo, N.Y. (H.C. Technical)
73	Martin, Mike	OT, 6-4, 250	Junior..........Roseburg, Ore. (Roseburg)
75	Marx, Greg	DT, 6-5, 235	Sophomore..........Redford, Mich. (Catholic Central)
46	McGraw, Pat	LB, 6-1, 215	Sophomore..........Fort Collins, Colo. (Shattuck School)
43	McHale, John	LB, 6-1, 200	Senior..........Montreal, Quebec, Can. (Marist) (Atlanta)
14	Merritt, Tom	HB, 5-10, 190	Junior..........Tacoma, Wash. (Fife)
25	Miller, Bob	HB, 6-2, 200	Sophomore..........No. Olmsted, O. (No. Olmsted)
18	Minnix, Bob	HB, 5-11, 185	Junior..........Spokane, Wash. (Lewis & Clark)
74	Mudron, Pat	DT, 6-0, 240	Senior..........Joliet, Ill. (Joliet Catholic)
47	Musuraca, Jim	LB, 6-0, 210	Sophomore..........E. Liverpool, O. (E. Liverpool)
88	*Neidert, Bob	DE, 6-0, 220	Senior..........Akron, O. (Archbishop Hoban)
28	Nightingale, Chuck	HB, 5-10, 175	Senior..........Valparaiso, Ind.
50	*Novakov, Dan	C, 6-2, 225	Junior..........Cincinnati, O. (Moeller)
81	O'Malley, Jim	LB, 6-2, 210	Sophomore..........Youngstown, O. (Chaney High)
26	Parker, Larry	HB, 6-1, 185	Sophomore..........Cincinnati, O. (Elder)
45	Patton, Eric	LB, 6-2, 220	Junior..........Santa Ana, Calif. (Mater Dei)
85	*Patulski, Walt	DE, 6-5, 235	Junior..........Liverpool, N.Y. (Christian Brothers)
41	*Raterman, John	LB, 6-1, 200	Junior..........Cincinnati, O. (Elder)
6	Roolf, Jim	DHB, 6-0, 185	Sophomore..........Sewickley, Pa. (Quaker Valley)
68	Schivarelli, Pete	DT, 5-10, 235	Senior..........Chicago, Ill. (St. Ignatius)
16	Schlezes, Ken	DHB, 6-3, 185	Sophomore..........Rochelle, Ill. (Heelan)
3	Smith, Scott	K, 5-10, 165	Sophomore..........Dallas, Texas (Jesuit)
11	Steenberge, Pat	QB, 6-1, 175	Sophomore..........Erie, Pa. (Cathedral Prep)
21	*Stepaniak, Ralph	DHB, 6-2, 195	Junior..........Alpena, Mich. (Central Catholic)
93	*Swendsen, Fred	DE, 6-4, 235	Junior..........Tacoma, Wash. (Fife)
90	Tereschuk, John	C, 6-0, 205	Sophomore..........Long Beach, Calif. (Pius X)
7	**Theismann, Joe	QB, 6-0, 170	Senior..........South River, N.J. (South River)
38	Thomann, Rick	LB, 6-1, 205	Junior..........Akron, O. (Archbishop Hoban)
80	Townsend, Willie	SE, 6-3, 190	Sophomore..........Hamilton, O. (Garfield)
82	*Trapp, Bill	SE, 6-3, 195	Junior..........Chicago, Ill. (Mount Carmel)
61	Webb, Mike	LB, 6-2, 200	Sophomore..........New Castle, Del. (Salesianum)
66	Witchger, Jim	LB, 5-10, 190	Junior..........Indianapolis, Ind. (Brebeuf Prep)
40	*Wright, Jim	LB, 6-1, 220	Senior..........Sparta, N.J. (Sparta)
36	Wright, Tom	HB, 5-10, 190	Sophomore..........Sparta, N.J.
9	Yoder, Jim	HB, 6-0, 178	Junior..........Alliance, O. (St. Thomas Aquinas)
37	Zielony, Dick	FB, 6-0, 200	Junior..........Vancouver, Wash. (Jesuit Portland)
79	*Zikas, Mike	DT, 6-4, 240	Junior..........Dolton, Ill. (Thornridge)
84	Zilly, John	OT, 6-5, 226	Senior..........Narragansett, R.I. (Bishop Hendricken)
27	**Zloch, Chuck	DHB, 5-11, 185	Senior..........Ft. Lauderdale, Fla. (Ft. Lauderdale)
60	Zuber, Tim	OG, 6-2, 220	Junior..........Garfield Heights, O. (Garfield Hts.)

*Indicates Monograms Won.

Notre Dame lost a football game

by Terry Shields
Observer Sports Editor

Southern Cal		21	3	14	0—38
Notre Dame		7	3	7	7—28

Scoring:
ND: Theismann, 25-yard run (Hempel kick).
SC: Davis, 3-yard run (Ayala kick).
SC: Davis, 5-yard run (Ayala kick wide).
SC: Dickerson, 45-yard pass from Jones (Chandler pass).
ND: Cieszkowski, 9-yard pass from Theismann (Hempel kick).
SC: Ayala, 19-yard field goal.
SC: Adams, fumble recovery in end zone (Ayala kick).
SC: Vella, fumble recovery in end zone (Alala kick).
ND: Parker, 46-yard pass from Theismann (Hempel kick).
ND: Theismann, 1-yard run (Hempel kick).

TEAM STATISTICS		
First Downs	28	17
Yards Gained Passing	526	226
Yards Gained Rushing	31	133
Total Offensive Yardage	557	359
Passing (Att'd-Comp'd)	58-33	24-15
Interceptions by	0	4
Fumbles lost	4	0
Punting (No.-Avg.)	6-35.5	11-33
Yards Penalized	23	20

Weather: Lousy (rainy and mild).

Attendance: 64,694.

You could think up a lot of excuses why Notre Dame lost last Saturday. You could say that the pressure of the last few games finally got to the Irish and they just couldn't get "up" for this one. You could say that the absence of Larry DiNardo in the line was a psychological as well as a physical letdown to the club. Then too, you might add that it is impossible to play catch-up football in a monsoon.

Yes, each and everyone of these factors can be a sufficient alibi, but the fact of the matter is simply, Notre Dame lost a football game.

It was a typical Irish loss. They pulverized their opponents in the statistics department. It was ND with 537 yards to SC's 359. The Irish had 28 first downs to the Trojan's 17. Notre Dame ran 91 plays to Southern Cal's 76. On the huge Coliseum scoreboard, however, was the only thing that people will remember. It read 38—28. Notre Dame lost a football game.

The loss virtually eliminates any hope for the Irish to become the National Champion for which the team had worked so hard. This is the second time that Ara Parseghian has taken his team to Los Angeles with a 9—0 mark and come away with a lump on his coaching record. This was the third time that an SC team has beaten an undefeated, untied ND team in the season finale.

Many USC observers felt that their team played the kind of football that they should have been playing all season. At halftime many reporters were asking if this was the same SC team that had been pummelled the previous week by UCLA. It was.

The Trojans can point to one statistic to prove the reason for their ten point victory. The Irish handed the ball to them eight times via the fumble or interception route. SC managed to play to perfection in that department. This in itself is quite a compliment considering the abominable game conditions of the second half.

The game started as though it may be a runaway for the Irish. Joe Theismann, who was voted the outstanding offensive player of the game, hit his receivers well on an 80-yard march and then he scrambled for a 25-yard touchdown to make it 7-0 ND. This was the last time that the Irish led in the ball game.

Jimmy Jones put on quite a first quarter show once USC got the ball and by the end of the initial frame he had his mates staked to a 21-7 lead. In the first quarter Jones hit on seven of seven passes for 143 yards as he found men like Bob Chandler, Sam Dickerson, Clarence Davis and Charlie Scott continually in the clear. Davis scored the first two SC touchdowns on power sweeps after Jones passing had put the Trojans in striking range.

The third SC score was what John McKay called "the turning point." Dickerson was running a deep pattern to his favorite corner in the Coliseum end zone. Clarence Ellis was covering him as well as any receiver could be covered. Jones lofted a 45 yard bomb and both Ellis and Dickerson went for the ball. Dickerson then grabbed the ball off Ellis' shoulder pad for one of the most remarkable catches of the season.

Notre Dame came back before the half as Theismann hit John Cieszkowski with a nine yard flare. Theismann also connected with Tom Gatewood for 28 yards in this drive. Gatewood caught ten in the game giving him 77 for the season.

The Notre Dame defense took heart after this score and they never gave another legitimate touchdown to SC. Ron Ayala did hit on a 19 yard field goal following Dyer's interception of Theismann.

The third quarter is a nightmare that Irish fans won't soon forget.

On the first offensive play of the second half Darryll Dewan fumbled and SC recovered on the Notre Dame 17. Four plays later SC fumbled but the Trojans had the good fortune of being at the right place at the right time and tackle Pete Adams recovered Mike Berry's fumble for the fourth SC TD.

The darkest spot of the day was fast approaching for the Irish. Lady Luck, who had been so helpful to ND in the past few games, played the cruelest of tricks. Willie Hall threw Joe T. for an 11-yard loss on one play after the kickoff then on the following down he powdered Joe and the ball popped loose in the end zone where John Vella fell on it for SC's 38th point.

The Irish never quit even after this crushing play. Down 38-14, Theismann led his mates on what, for one brief but hopeful moment, looked like a miracle comeback.

As the all-time Irish ground gainer kept racking up the yardage and the score, it seemed that this was one of those teams that simply refused to be beaten, no matter what the odds. The Trojans burst this bubble with clutch defense.

Near the end of the third quarter Theismann found Larry Parker with a 46 yard pass. Parker broke two tackles on his way to paydirt. Larry was one of the bright spots in a gloomy afternoon.

The last ND score came early in the fourth period. Theismann went in for his second TD on a tremendous one yard squirm. He was hit at scrimmage but bounced off the tackler and wiggled into the end zone.

The remainder of the game was a ritual of frustration for the Irish. One can point to a number of plays that might be called the clincher but Willie Hall (the outstanding defensive player) made the play that killed most Irish hopes when he threw Theismann for a 15 yard loss after a Parker reception had put the Irish in a threatening position. SC fell into a prevent defense to halt the Irish and it worked as they plucked a desperation pass by Theismann for their third interception.

Theismann kept coming back after all of these crushing blows and before it was all over he had passed for an unbelievable 524 yards, only about 40 yards short of the NCAA record held by Greg Cook. Even though Theismann completed 33 of 58 passes it will be hard for Joe to remember anything but the four interceptions that the Trojans stole during the long wet afternoon.

After the game the locker rooms were a perfect contrast. John McKay said that he "knew Southern Cal was as good as Notre Dame" and that he "was proud that his men had enough pride to go out and win this satisfying victory." Still, McKay didn't feel that it made up for the disappointing season. "The Rose Bowl is always our first objective."

In the sepulchral Irish locker it was a different story. Ara was going through the post-game press ordeal with great reluctance. He stated that he "was proud of the way his team came back, but the conditions made it very difficult to play catch-up football."

Ara may have been proud of his team but there was no way of hiding his rejection as he wiped the mud from his football cleats. There was no getting away from the matter. Notre Dame lost a football game.

Irish Rope Longhorns, 24-11

Defense, Theismann Snap Texas' Streak

DALLAS (AP) — A new Notre Dame defense, nine Texas fumbles, and All-American quarterback Joe Theismann chopped off Texas' 30-game victory string in the Cotton Bowl 24-11 Friday, and probably knocked the Longhorns out of a second consecutive national title.

A glum Texas Coach Darrell Royal said:

"To quote Grantland Rice, one of your famous writers, I've learned something that victory cannot bring, to wipe the blood from my face and smile so none can see the sting."

Three Touchdowns

Theismann, Notre Dame's senior All-American, ran for two touchdowns and passed for another.

The Longhorns were tied up by a defense concocted by Notre Dame Coach Ara Parseghian. It had the Wishbone-shaped Texas backfield looking almost into a mirror of itself across the line of scrimmage.

"Basically, we tried to mirror the Wishbone with the same type of a defense," Parseghian said. "We wanted Texas to pass and Eddie Phillips did. He can throw the ball. We broke their consistency pattern."

"We learned a lot a year ago from Texas about the Wishbone and even adopted the offense so we could learn more about it.

New Alignment

"We used a new alignment—there's no way you can cover them with the typical defenses."

Royal said Notre Dame's end "was boxing us on the keep, forcing Phillips to run all the time. They were large enough physically inside that we couldn't get a crease for Worster."

Parseghian took no chances Texas would discover what the Irish planned. He even used 12 men on offense and 13 men on defense during practice sessions to confuse any would-be spies.

It was the first bowl victory for the revenge-minded Irish in 46 years and dashed the hopes of the defending national champions for a second consecutive title.

Texas fumbled the ball nine times and lost five to sixth-ranked Notre Dame, which fell 21-17 to the Longhorns last year in the Cotton Bowl when the Irish entered post-season play for the first time since 1925.

The 6-foot, 175-pound Theismann passed 26 yards to fleet Tom Gatewood for a touchdown and galloped 3 and 15 yards for two more scores as the Irish piled up a 24-11 halftime lead. The second half was a brutal defensive duel.

Texas' intricate Wishbone-T was hounded by Notre Dame's swarming defenders, although Longhorn quarterback Eddie Phillips had a great day before he was injured with 8:54 to play. All-American fullback Steve Worster fumbled four times and Notre Dame claimed three of them to blunt the Texas offense.

Phillips piled up 363 yards in total offense-164 yards on the ground and 199 yards through the air.

Theismann was at his best in the first half.

After falling behind 3-0 on Happy Feller's 23-yard field goal, Theismann rallied the Irish for touchdowns three of the next four times Notre Dame got the ball.

The senior from South River, N.J., whipped Notre Dame 80 yards in 10 plays for the first score. The payoff came on the 26-yard strike to Gatewood, who strained a hamstring muscle as he crossed the goal.

Texas' Dann Lester bobbled the ensuing kickoff and Tom Eaton claimed the ball at the Longhorns 10. Theismann sliced off right tackle from three yards away to make it 14-3.

Theismann dashed 15 yards for another touchdown around the Texas right flank early in the second quarter for a 21-3 lead.

Longhorns Dazed

The dazed Longhorns had trouble getting their famed Wishbone-T untracked because of a unique Notre Dame defensive alignment. The Irish lined up six men on the line of scrimmage but had an inverted Y with three men across from the Texas center.

Phillips abandoned the run and went to the most rusty weapon in the Longhorn arsenal-the pass. He hit tight end Deryl Comer three times in an 84-yard drive. Jim Bertlesen climaxed it with a two-yard run.

A pass from Phillips to Lester made it 24-11 at halftime.

Theismann connected on nine of 16 passes for 176 yards but gained only 22 yards running.

Notre Dame played it conservatively in the second half and let its fired-up defense take over.

Turning Point

A tremendous play on a fourth and one situation at the Notre Dame 35 helped take the steam out of a promising Longhorn drive in the third period.

Linebacker Jim Musuraca met Bertelsen head-on at the line of scrimmage to turn the ball over to the Fighting Irish, who finished the season with a 10-1 record.

Texas, the No. 1 rushing team in the nation with an average of 374 yards per game, could manage on 216 yards on the Cotton Bowl's synthetic turf. Notre Dame got only 146 yards.

Notre Dame had 213 yards passing and Texas 210.

Phillips set a Cotton Bowl record with his total yardage. Theismann set the old record last year at 279.

COTTON BOWL CLASSIC 1970 TEXAS vs. NOTRE DAME

$1 incl. tax

1971 COTTON BOWL — Notre Dame 24, Texas 11

Notre Dame		14	10	0	0 — 24
Texas		3	8	0	0 — 11

Attendance: 73,000 — Weather: Fair, 52 degrees

Team	Score T-ND	Qtr.	Time Left	Play
Texas	3-0	1	11:28	Feller 23 FG
ND	3-7	1	7:58	Gatewood 26 pass from Theismann (Hempel kick)
ND	3-14	1	5:11	Theismann 3 run (Hempel kick)
ND	3-21	2	13:28	Theismann 15 run (Hempel kick)
Texas	11-21	2	1:52	Bertelsen 2 run (Lester pass from Phillips)
ND	11-24	2	0:24	Hempel 36 FG

STATISTICS

	Notre Dame	Texas
First downs	16	20
Rushing yardage	146	216
Passing yardage	213	210
Return yardage	0	26
Passes	9-19-1	10-27-1
Punts	8-45	5-32
Fumbles lost	1	5
Yards penalized	52	33

Bag of Tricks

DALLAS, Tex. (AP) — Notre Dame Coach Ara Parseghian tossed a whole new bag of tricks at Texas in the Cotton Bowl and the Irish whipped the top-ranked Longhorns 24-11 Friday.

"Basically what we tried to do was to mirror their Wishbone," the gleeful Parseghian said, drying off from a victory splash in the shower. "We wanted to force Texas into a passing situation, to make them come out of their full-house backfield.

"After the Arkansas game— Texas' 42-7 victory over Arkansas—I became convinced that it would be impossible to stop the Wishbone with any general defense," Parseghian said. "If we had played an eight-man line today, we would have been beaten."

Parseghian said he had been "doodling with it" since the Irish's 21-17 loss to Texas in last year's Cotton Bowl. "I talked to Darrell Royal about their Wishbone during the off-season. We wanted to learn more about it."

By forcing the ground-oriented Longhorns into a passing situation, Parseghian explained, the 'Horns would be left with three backs in the backfield. Then, Notre Dame mentor "mirrored" the UT backfield with three linebackers assigned to a man.

"We wanted to force Texas to pass and this is what they did," Parseghian said. "But that (quarterback Eddie) Phillips almost ruined it for us."

The victory climaxed a 10-1 season for the Irish.

"In 21 years of coaching, I've been in some excited dressing rooms," Parseghian said. "But I've never experienced anything like this. You've gotta realize these guys just broke a 30-game winning streak. But that's what streaks are for . . . to break."

In addition to the surprise defense, Parseghian also employed a quick-kick on third down that went 74 yards and used defensive back Clarence Ellis as a receiver on offense for one play.

1970 Final Statistics

INDIVIDUAL SCORING

	TDs	Kick	Play	FG	TP
Hempel	0	36-38		4-5	48
Allan	8				48
Gatewood	7		1-1 (P)		44
Gulyas	5				30
Barz	5				30
Theismann	4		1-4 (R)		26
Cieszkowski	4				24
Dewan	3		1-1 (R)		20
Parker	3				18
Minnix	3				18
Creaney	2				12
Steenberge	1				6
Smith	0	1-1		1-4	4

INDIVIDUAL PUNTING

	No.	Yds.	Avg.	Long
Yoder	41	1589	38.7	53
Roolf	1	41	41.0	41

RUSHING

	TC	Yds.	Avg.	TDs	Long
Gulyas	118	534	4.5	3	21
Allan	111	401	3.6	7	16
Theismann	124	384	3.1	4	42
Barz	88	352	4.0	4	14
Minnix	50	230	4.6	2	33
Parker	26	201	7.7	2	63
Cieszkowski	44	187	4.3	3	35
Dewan	46	158	3.4	3	19
Steenberge	15	45	3.0	1	10
Gallagher	7	44	6.2	0	14
Trapp	2	20	10.0	0	16
Johnson	3	16	5.3	0	6
Nightingale	3	6	2.0	0	6
Garner	1	5	5.0	0	5
T. Wright	1	2	2.0	0	2
Gutowski	1	0	0.0	0	0

RETURNS
(No.—Yds.—TDs)

	Int.	Punts	Kickoffs
Stepaniak	5-39-0		
Ellis	7-25-0	5- 33-0	
Kelly	2-15-0		
Webb	1-11-0		
Wright	2- 0-0		
Crotty	1- 0-0	19-100-0	3-37-0
O'Malley	1-18-0		
Schlezes		7- 77-0	
Nightingale		2- 9-0	4-77-0
Parker		1- 3-0	4-60-0
Dewan			4-91-0
Allan			2-30-0
Minnix			2- 7-0

RECEIVING

	PC	Yds.	Avg.	TDs	Long
Gatewood	77	1123	14.6	7	39
Creaney	17	349	20.5	2	78
Parker	10	208	20.8	1	46
Gulyas	9	189	21.0	2	46
Allan	11	166	15.9	1	54
Barz	13	127	9.7	1	18
Dewan	8	87	10.9		22
Cieszkowski	7	79	11.3	1	15
Tereschuk	3	56	18.6	0	28
Minnix	1	40	40.0	1	40
Trapp	4	31	7.7	0	13
Yoder	1	15	15.0	0	15
Theismann	1	7	7.0	0	7

PASSING

	No.	Comp.	Int.	Yds.	TDs	Pct.
Theismann	268	155	14	2429	16	.574
Steenberge	14	7	1	98	0	.500
Yoder	1	0	0	0	0	.000

TEAM STATISTICS

	ND	Opp.
Total Offense	5105	2178
Total Plays	927	716
Yards Per Play	5.5	3.0
Yards Per Game	510.5	217.8
Net Yards Rushing	2578	950
Attempts	641	375
Yards Per Rush	4.0	2.5
Yards Per Game	278.8	95.0
Net Yards Passing	2527	1228
Attempts	283	281
Completions	162	106
Completion Pct.	.573	.377
Had Intercepted	15	20
Touchdown Passes	16	4
Yards Per Attempt	8.9	4.4
Yards Per Completion	15.6	11.6
Yards Per Game	252.7	122.8
Punt Return Yards	222	304
No. of Returns	33	22
Avg. Per Return	6.7	13.8

Punts	7-	85
Yards Punting	1630	3033
Avg. Per Punt	38.8	35.7
Had Blocked	0	1
Penalties	43	33
Yards Penalized	397	363
Fumbles (Lost)	25(20)	18(8)
Total First Downs	264	125
Rushing	146	53
Passing	105	62
Penalty	13	10

INDIVIDUAL TOTAL OFFENSE LEADERS

	Games	Plays	Yards	Avg.
Theismann	10	391	2801	7.2
Gulyas	10	118	534	4.5
Barz	10	88	352	4.0
Allan	8	11	401	3.6

TEAM SCORING

	ND	Opp.
Total Points	330	97
Avg. Per Game	33.0	9.7
No. of TD's	45	13
By Rushing	29	8
By Passing	16	4
By Return	0	1
Field Goals (Att-Made)	9-5	7-2
Safeties	1	0

Won 9, Lost 1, Tied 0

N.D. 48, Northwestern	14	(50,409)
N.D. 35, Purdue	0	(59,075) C
N.D. 29, Michigan State	0	(76,103) C
N.D. 51, Army	10	(59,075) C
N.D. 24, Missouri	7	(64,200) C
N.D. 56, Navy	7	(45,226)
N.D. 46, Pitt	14	(59,075) C
N.D. 10, Georgia Tech	7	(59,075) C
N.D. 3, Louisiana State	0	(59,075) C
N.D. 28, Southern California	38	(64,694)

Notre Dame 1971 Varsity Roster

NO.	NAME	POS.	HT.	WT.	CLASS	HOMETOWN
52	Alvarado, Joe	C	6-1	218	So.	East Chicago, Ind.
62	Bolger, Tom	OG	6-2	232	So.	Cincinnati, O.
63	Borbely, Joe	OG	6-1	215	Jr.	Akron, O.
70	Brenneman, Mark	OT	6-4	230	So.	York, Pa.
78	Briick, Herb	OT	6-4	240	Jr.	Hinsdale, Ill.
8	Brown, Cliff	QB	6-0	185	So.	Middleton, Pa.
4	Bulger, Jim	QB	6-5	200	Jr.	Pittsburgh, Pa.
88	Casper, Dave	TE	6-3	228	So.	Chilton, Wis.
35	Cieszkowski, John*	FB	6-2	218	Jr.	Detroit, Mich.
48	Clemente, Brian	LB	6-2	215	So.	Loudonville, N.Y.
91	Creaney, Mike*	TE	6-4	215	Jr.	Towson, Md.
17	Crotty, Mike**	DHB	5-9	180	Sr.	Seattle, Wash.
67	Dampeer, John*	OT	6-4	240	Jr.	Kermit, Texas
51	DePrimio, Dennis*	OG	6-1	220	Sr.	Greensburg, Pa.
43	Devine, Tom	LB	6-3	210	So.	Jackson, Mich.
10	Dewan, Darryll,*	HB	6-0	195	Jr.	Danbury, Conn.
28	Diminick, Gary	HB	5-9	170	So.	Mount Carmel, Pa.
9	Doherty, Brian	QB	6-2	180	So.	Portland, Ore.
59	Drew, Dave	C	6-2	215	Jr.	Vestal, N.Y.
94	Eckman, Mike	K	6-0	190	Sr.	Lafayette, Ind.
23	Ellis, Clarence**	DHB	6-0	178	Sr.	Grand Rapids, Mich.
89	Frazier, Algery	SE	6-5	195	So.	Calvert, Texas
96	Freistroffer, Tom	DE	6-4	235	Jr.	Fort Wayne, Ind.
19	Gallagher, Bill	HB	5-11	183	Sr.	Philadelphia, Pa.
5	Garner, Terry	DHB	6-2	185	Jr.	Canton, Ohio
44	Gatewood, Tom**	SE	6-2	208	Sr.	Baltimore, Md.
12	Gulyas, Ed*	HB	5-11	190	Sr.	San Carlos, Calif.
64	Hagopian, Gary	OG	6-0	215	Sr.	Colorado Springs, Colo.
95	Hayduk, George	DE	6-3	225	So.	Factoryville, Pa.
99	Hein, Jeff	DE	6-1	210	So.	Cincinnati, O.
22	Hill, Greg	HB	6-1	180	So.	Pilot Mountain, N.C.
97	Hooten, Herman	DT	6-2	239	Sr.	Tuskegee, Ala.
20	Huff, Andy*	FB	5-11	192	Jr.	Toledo, O.
53	Humbert, Jim**	OG	6-2	225	Jr.	Cincinnati, O.
72	Kadish, Mike**	DT	6-5	260	Sr.	Grand Rapids, Mich.
77	Kondrk, John*	OT	6-5	260	Jr.	Hopelawn, N.J.
76	Maciag, Dick	DT	6-5	250	Jr.	Buffalo, N.Y.
30	Mariani, John	LB	5-11	195	Jr.	Philadelphia, Pa.
75	Marx, Greg*	DT	6-5	235	Jr.	Redford, Mich.
86	Massey, Jim	DE	6-4	205	Sr.	Farmington, Mich.
74	McBride, Mike	OT	6-5	230	So.	Michigan City, Ind.
46	McGraw, Pat	LB	6-1	215	Jr.	Fort Collins, Colo.
1	Menie, Tom	DHB	6-1	190	Sr.	Ebensburg, Pa.
18	Minnix, Bob*	HB	5-11	185	Sr.	Spokane, Wash.
66	Morrin, Dan	DT	6-4	230	So.	Croydon, Pa.
47	Musuraca, Jim	LB	6-0	210	Jr.	East Liverpool, O.
49	Naughton, Mike	DHB	6-3	180	So.	Bloomfield Hills, Mich.
50	Novakov, Dan**	C	6-2	225	Sr.	Cincinnati, O.
81	O'Malley, Jim	LB	6-2	210	Jr.	Youngstown, O.
39	O'Toole, Dan	DHB	6-1	180	Jr.	Oklahoma City, Okla.
26	Parker, Larry*	HB	6-1	185	Jr.	Cincinnati, O.
34	Parker, Mike	DHB	5-10	175	So.	Cincinnati, O.
45	Patton, Eric*	LB	6-2	235	So.	Santa Ana, Calif.
85	Patulski, Walt**	DE	6-6	260	Sr.	Liverpool, N.Y.
87	Peiffer, Mike	SE	6-1	190	Sr.	South Bend, Ind.
56	Pomarico, Frank	OG	6-1	238	So.	Howard Beach, N.Y.
40	Potempa, Gary	FB	6-0	227	So.	Niles, Ill.
57	Rankin, George	OT	6-2	235	Sr.	Jeannette, Pa.
41	Raterman, John*	LB	6-1	200	Sr.	Cincinnati, O.
83	Robinson, Tyrone	DE	6-2	220	Jr.	Philadelphia, Pa.
6	Roolf, Jim	DHB-P	6-0	185	Jr.	Sewickley, Pa.
7	Rudnick, Tim	S	5-10	170	So.	Chicago, Ill.
16	Schlezes, Ken	DHB	6-3	185	Jr.	Rochelle, Ill.
3	Smith, Scott	K	5-10	165	Jr.	Dallas, Texas
11	Steenberge, Pat	QB	6-1	175	Jr.	Erie, Pa.
21	Stepaniek, Ralph**	DHB	6-2	195	Sr.	Alpena, Mich.
42	Sullivan, Tim	LB	6-3	217	So.	Des Moines, Ia.
93	Swendsen, Fred**	DE	6-4	235	Sr.	Tacoma, Wash.
65	Szatko, Greg	TE	6-4	220	So.	Western Springs, Ill.
90	Tereschuk, John*	TE-C	6-0	200	Jr.	Long Beach, Calif.
38	Thomann, Rick*	LB	6-1	225	Sr.	Akron, O.
98	Thomas, Robert	K	5-10	175	So.	Rochester, N.Y.
27	Townsend, Mike	DHB	6-3	178	So.	Hamilton, O.
80	Townsend, Willie	SE	6-3	190	Jr.	Hamilton, O.
82	Trapp, Bill*	SE	6-3	195	Sr.	Chicago, Ill.
31	Washington, Bob	SE	6-0	175	So.	Steubenville, O.
61	Webb, Mike	LB	6-2	220	Jr.	New Castle, Del.
79	Zikas, Mike**	DT	6-4	240	Sr.	Dolton, Ill.
60	Zuber, Tim	OG	6-2	220	Sr.	Garfield Heights, O.

1971

Coach: Ara Parseghian
Co-Captains: Walter Patulski and Thomas Gatewood

S.18	W	Northwestern	50-7	H	c59,075
S.25	W	Purdue (2:58) (R)	8-7	A	c69,765
O.2	W	Michigan State	14-2	H	c59,075
O.9	W	Miami (Fla.) (Nt)	17-0	A	66,039
O.16	W	North Carolina	16-0	H	c59,075
O.23	L	So. California (U)	14-28	H	c59,075
O.30	W	Navy	21-0	H	c59,075
N.6	W	Pittsburgh	56-7	A	55,528
N.13	W	Tulane	21-7	H	c59,075
N.20	L	Louisiana State (Nt)	8-28	A	c66,936
	(8-2-0)		225-86		612,718

7 INTERCEPTIONS

Northwestern	7	0	0	0 —	7
Notre Dame	7	23	6	14 —	50

Scoring:
ND: Gulyas, 3-yard run (Brown kick).
NU: Cooks, 7-yard pass from Daigneau (Planisek kick).
ND: Minnix, 4-yard run (Brown kick).
ND: Gatewood, 8-yard pass from Steenberge (Brown kick).
ND: Thomas, 36-yard field goal.
ND: Cieszkowski, 4-yard run (Kick failed).
ND: Stepaniak, 40-yard interception return (Kick failed)
ND: Crotty, 65-yard interception return (Thomas kick).
ND: Hill, 4-yard run (Thomas kick).

TEAM STATISTICS	ND	NU
Total First Downs	21	16
Yards Gained Rushing	242	37
Yards Gained Passing	114	215
Total Offensive Yardage	356	252
Passing (Att'd–Com'd)	27–9	44–19
Interceptions by	7	2
Fumbles lost	2	2
Punting (No.–Ave.)	5–42.5	7–36.4
Total Yards Penalized	41	50
Weather: Cloudy and warm.		Attendance: 59,075

PITT·NOTRE DAME

November 6, 1971
Pitt Stadium
Official Program $1.00

1971 final statistics

SCORING BY QUARTERS

Notre Dame	52	60	48	55 —	225
Opponents	30	42	7	7 —	86

TEAM STATISTICS

	ND	Opp.
Total Offense	3,329	1,969
Totals Plays	819	598
Yards Per Play	4.0	3.2
Yards Per Game	332.9	196.9
Net Yards Rushing	2,321	864
Attempts	613	383
Yards Per Rush	3.7	2.2
Yards Per Game	232.1	86.4
Net Yards Passing	1,008	1,105
Attempts	206	215
Completions	87	89
Completion Percentage	.422	.414
Had Intercepted	12	13
Touchdown Passes	5	8
Yards Per Attempt	4.9	5.1
Yards Per Completion	11.5	12.4
Yards Per Game	100.8	110.5
Interceptions Made	13	12
Yards Returned	203	129
Punt Return Yards	316	97
Number of Returns	36	24
Average Return	8.7	4.0
Kickoff Return Yards	417	813
Number of Returns	19	37
Average Return	21.9	21.9
Total Return Yards	936	1,039
Average Punt	38.9	37.4
Yards Punting	2,259	3,034
Had Blocked	0	2
Penalties Against	44	42
Yards Penalized	442	395
Fumbles (Lost)	20(14)	22(15)
Total First Downs	206	110
By Rushing	154	48
By Passing	47	50
By Penalty	5	12

INDIVIDUAL TOTAL OFFENSE

	Plays	Yards	Avg.
Cliff Brown	196	922	4.7
Bob Minnix	78	337	4.3
John Cieszkowski	69	316	4.6
Larry Parker	80	299	3.7

RESULTS

Won 8, Lost 2, Tied 0

	Opp.	Attendance
Northwestern (H)	7	59,075 (C)
Purdue (A)	7	69,765 (C)
Michigan State (H)	2	59,075 (C)
Miami (Fla.) (A)	0	66,039
North Carolina (H)	0	59,075 (C)
Southern Cal (H)	28	59,075 (C)
Navy (H)	0	59,075 (C)
Pittsburgh (A)	7	55,528 (C)
Tulane (H)	7	59,075 (C)
Louisiana State (A)	28	66,936 (C)

TEAM SCORING

	ND	Opp.
Total Points	225	86
Average	22.5	8.6
Touchdowns	29	12
By Rushing	22	3
By Passing	5	8
By Return	2	1
By Recovery	1	0
Field Goals (Made-Att.)	5-9	0-3
Safeties	0	1
PAT — Kick	24-27	12-12
PAT — Run	1-1	0-0
PAT — Pass	2-2	0-0

INDIVIDUAL SCORING

P.A.T.

	TD'S	Kick	R P A	FG	TP
Thomas	5	21-22		5-9	36
Minnix	5		2-0		34
Gulyas	5				30
Gatewood	4				24
Brown	2	3-5			15
Huff	2				12
Cieszkowski	2				12
Dewan	2				12
Parker	2				12
Creaney	1		0-1		8
Crotty	1				6
Stepaniak	1				6
Swendsen	1				6
W. Townsend	1				6
Notre Dame	29	24-27	2-1	5-9	225
Opponents	12	12-12		0-3	84

PUNTING

	No.	Yards	Avg.	Long
Doherty	58	2,259	38.9	61
Notre Dame	58	2,259	38.9	61
Opponents	81	3,034	37.4	63

PASSING

	No.	Comp.	Int.	Yards	TD's
Brown	111	56	9	669	4
Steenberge	47	13	1	168	1
Etter	26	15	1	140	0
Bulger	11	3	1	31	0
Gallagher	1	0	0	0	0
Gulyas	1	0	0	0	0
Parker	1	0	0	0	0
Notre Dame	206	87	12	1,008	5
Opponents	215	89	13	1,105	8

RUSHING

	TC	Yards	Avg.	TD	Long
Minnix	78	337	4.3	5	16
Parker	80	299	3.7	2	20
Cieszkowski	69	316	4.6	2	17
Huff	68	295	4.3	2	21
Brown	77	253	3.2	2	47
Gallagher	49	180	3.6	0	15
Gulyas	56	220	4.4	5	19
Dewan	35	119	3.4	2	9
Etter	35	114	3.3	0	19
Hill	16	84	5.2	1	20
Diminick	17	61	3.4	0	16
Steenberge	23	5	0.2	0	7
Rudnick	1	2	2.0	0	2
Bulger	4	-1	0.2	0	10
Gatewood	2	-7	-3.5	0	3
Townsend	3	32	10.6	1	34
Notre Dame	613	2,321	3.7	22	47
Opponents	383	964	2.2	3	29

PASS RECEIVING

	PC	Yards	Avg.	TD	Long
Gatewood	33	417	12.6	4	39
Townsend	8	95	11.8	0	23
Creaney	11	151	13.7	1	42
Minnix	5	29	5.8	0	13
Huff	4	39	9.7	0	11
Gallagher	4	69	17.2	0	32
Dewan	4	42	10.5	0	13
Parker	10	109	10.9	0	35
Diminick	2	14	7.0	0	9
Trapp	1	8	8.0	0	8
Gulyas	3	16	5.3	0	16
Hill	1	7	7.0	0	7
Casper	1	12	12.0	0	12
Notre Dame	87	1,008	11.5	5	42
Opponents	89	1,105	12.4	8	42

RETURNS

(Number - Yards - TD's)

	Intercep.	Punts	Kickoffs
Schlezes	4- 63-0		
Crotty	2- 66-1	33-297-0	
Ellis	3- 34-0		
Stepaniak	3- 40-1		
Garner	1- 0-0		
Hill		2- 7-0	7-147-0
Diminick			7-199-0
Gallagher			3- 53-0
Rudnick			2- 18-0
Patulski		1- 12-0	
Notre Dame	13-203-2	36-316-0	19-417-0
Opponents	12-129-0	24- 97-0	37-813-0

DEFENSIVE STATISTICS

	TM	TL-Yards	PBU	FR
Kadish	97	8-40	6	
Marx	85	12-44	8	
Patulski	74	17-129	6	1
Patton	79	2-9	3	
O'Malley	72			
Musuraca	66	1-4	6	5
Crotty	65	1-1	9	
Thomann	48	2-12	2	
Swendsen	40	11-76	3	2
Stepaniak	39	1-3	4	
Schlezes	30	1-4	6	
Ellis	35		8	
Raterman	15		1	
Zikas	21	2-23		
Webb	8			
Garner	7			
Townsend M.	5			
Freistroffer	5			
Sullivan	4			
Hooten	4			
Potempa	4			
McGraw	3			
Hayduk	3			
Devine	2		1	
Rudnick	1			
Cloherty	1			
Tereschuk	1			
Townsend				1
Notre Dame		59-349	54	13
Opponents		48-68	39	11

Key: TM—Tackles Made; TL-Yards—Tackles made from minus yardage to opponent; PBU—Passes Broken Up; FR—Fumbles Recovered.

ABOVE, Members of the Football Team. FIRST ROW: B. Etter, T. Wright, A. Huff, J. Rooff, M. Creaney, J. Cieszkowski, J. Dampeer, G. Marx, K. Schlezes, J. Haggar, D. Drew, D. Dewan, T. Freistroffer, J. O'Malley. SECOND ROW: H. Briick, E. Fiber, D. Gutowski, T. Garner, J. Mariani, T. Robinson, W. Townsend, J. Kondrk, W. Holloway, J. Borbely, D. Maciag, F. Pumarico, D. Morrin, J. Bulger, P. Steenberge, D. O'Toole, B. Johnson, S. Smith. THIRD ROW: E. Scales, T. Rudnick, M. McBride, B. Washington, M. Townsend, C. Brown, G. Hill, P. Hartman, G. Diminick, G. Lane, M. Naughton, M. Zloch, B. Doherty, B. Thomas, P. Sawicz, L. Susko, G. Szatko. FOURTH ROW: R. Barnett, A. Stroughter, F. Bossu, D. Casper, J. Hein, G. Hayduk, J. Alvarado, P. McPartland, T. Devine, T. Sullivan, T. Creevey, D. Lozzi, M. Wasilevich, T. Bolger, G. Potempa, S. Sylvester, C. Kelly, J. O'Donnell, J. Gambone. FIFTH ROW: K. Nosbusch, D. Schwarber, P. Demmerle, E. Penick, W. Bullock, A. Samuel, R. Goodman, J. Audino, J. Riepenhoff, B. McGreevey, F. Allocco, T. Clements, D. Mahalic, S. Quehl, B. Sweeney, T. Miller, M. Fanning, T. Fine, G. DiNardo, T. Laney, J. Chauncey, S. Smith. SIXTH ROW: I. Brown, T. Maschmeier, A. Best, B. Zanot, B. Messaros, J. Pszeracki, T. Loplenski, J. Stock, P. Linehan, G. Collins, S. Neece, E. Bauer, B. Arment, A. Rohan, T. Bake, C. Balliet, P. Sarb, A. Wujciak, B. Walsh, K. Doherty, J. Achterhoff, F. Rutkowski, J. Novakov, B. Michuta. SEVENTH ROW: P. Pohlen, K. Andler, K. Horton, J. Galanis, T. Brantley, R. Payne, R. Korman, N. Federenko, S. Niehaus, R. Weber, S. Lopardo, R. Slager, T. Parise. EIGHTH ROW: L. Ferrallo, M. Busick, G. Biache, B. Hickey, J. Yonto, G. Kelly, P. Shoults, Head Coach A. Parseghian, T. Pagna, W. Moore, B. Boulac, M. Stock, L. DiNardo, G. Pazkiet, M. Dwyer.

1972

Coach: Ara Parseghian
Co-Captains: John Dampeer and Greg Marx

S.23	W	Northwestern	37-0	A	c55,155
S.30	W	Purdue	35-14	H	c59,075
O.7	W	Michigan State	16-0	A	c77,828
O.14	W	Pittsburgh	42-16	H	c59,075
O.21	L	Missouri (U) (R)	26-30	H	c59,075
O.28	W	TCU	21-0	H	c59,075
N.4	W	Navy	42-23	N1	43,089
N.11	W	Air Force	21-7	A	c48,671
N.18	W	Miami (Fla.)	20-17	H	c59,075
D.2	L	Southern Cal	23-45	A	75,243
		(8-2-0)	283-152		595,361

ORANGE BOWL
J.1   L   Nebraska (Nt)   6-40   N2 c80,010
N1—at Philadelphia; N2—at Miami

1972 Alphabetical Roster

No.	Name	Pos.	Ht.	Wt.	Class	Hometown
52	ALVARADO, JOE	C	6-1	224	Jr.	E. Chicago, Mich.
14	BARNETT, REGGIE	DHB	5-11	180	So.	Flint, Mich.
62	BOLGER, TOM	OG	6-2	225	Jr.	Cincinnati, Ohio
63	BORBELY, JOE	OG	6-1	232	Sr.	Akron, Ohio
78	BRIICK, HERB	OT	6-4	230	Sr.	Hinsdale, Ill.
8	BROWN, CLIFF	QB	6-0	196	Jr.	Middletown, Pa.
68	CASPER, DAVE	OT-TE	6-3	240	Jr.	Chilton, Wisc.
35	CIESZKOWSKI, JOHN	FB	6-2	220	Sr.	Detroit, Mich.
2	CLEMENTS, TOM	QB	6-0	180	So.	McKees Rocks, Pa.
50	COLLINS, GREG	LB	6-3	216	So.	Troy, Mich.
91	CREANEY, MIKE	TE	6-4	232	Sr.	Towson, Md.
67	DAMPEER, JOHN	OT	6-4	237	Sr.	Kermit, Texas
10	DEWAN, DARRYLL	HB	6-0	204	Sr.	Danbury, Conn.
28	DIMINICK, GARY	HB	5-9	168	Jr.	Mt. Carmel, Mich.
72	DINARDO, GERRY	OG	6-1	240	So.	Howard Beach, N.Y.
9	DOHERTY, BRIAN	QB-B	6-2	188	Jr.	Portland, Ore.
59	DREW, DAVE	C	6-2	220	Sr.	Vestal, N.Y.
19	ETTER, BILL	QB	6-2	185	Sr.	Spokane, Eash.
88	FANNING, MIKE	DE	6-6	260	So.	Tulsa, Okla.
32	FIBER, ED	LB	5-11	185	Sr.	Fremont, Ohio
96	FREISTROFFER, TOM	DE	6-4	234	Sr.	Fort Wayne, Inc.
5	GARNER, TERRY	S	6-1	185	Sr.	Canton, Ohio
25	GUTOWSKI, DENNIS	DB	5-10	181	Sr.	Hobart, Ind.
33	HAGGAR, JOE	DHB	5-11	172	Sr.	Dallas, Taxas
53	HARTMAN, PETE	C	6-1	233	Jr.	San Francisco, Calif.
95	HAYDUK, GEORGE	DE	6-3	240	Jr.	Factoryville, Pa.
99	HEIN, JEFF	DE	6-1	224	Jr.	Cincinnati, Ohio
22	HILL, GREG	HB	6-1	185	Jr.	Pilot Mountain, N.C.
20	HUFF, ANDY	FB	5-11	210	Sr.	Toledo, Ohio
77	KONDRK, JOHN	OG	6-5	257	Sr.	Hopelawn, N.J.
69	LOZZI, DENNIS	T	6-3	253	Jr.	Whitman, Mich.
76	MACIAG, DICK	DT	6-5	277	Sr.	Buffalo, N.Y.
45	MAHALIC, DREW	LB	6-4	213	So.	Birmingham, Mich.
31	MARIANI, JOHN	LB	5-11	195	Sr.	Chester Heights, Pa.
75	MARX, GREG	DT	6-5	260	Sr.	Redford, Mich.
74	McBRIDE, MIKE	OT	6-5	256	Jr.	Michigan City, Ind.
46	McGRAW, PAT	LB	6-1	221	Sr.	Ft Collins, Colo.
66	MORRIN, DAN	OG	6-4	230	Jr.	Croydan, Pa.
47	MUSURACA, JIM	LB	6-0	214	Sr.	East Liverpool, Ohio
49	NAUGHTON, MIKE	DHB	6-3	186	Jr.	Bloomfield Hills, Ohio
60	NOSBUSCH, KEVIN	DT	6-4	267	So.	Milwaukee, Wisc.
81	O'MALLY, JIM	LB	6-2	221	Sr.	Youngstown, Ohio
44	PENICK, ERIC	HB	6-1	195	So.	Clevland, Ohio
56	POMARICO, FRANK	OG	6-1	238	Jr.	Howard Beach, N.Y.
40	POTEMPA, GARY	LB	6-0	225	Jr.	Niles, Ill.
90	QUEHL, STEVE	TE	6-4	220	So.	Cincinnati, Ohio
83	ROBINSON, TYRONE	DE	6-2	226	Sr.	Philadelphia, Pa.
6	ROOLF, JIM	SE	6-0	185	Sr.	Sewickly, Pa.
7	RUDNICK, TIM	DHB	5-10	185	Jr.	Chicago, Ill.
24	SAMUEL, AL	SE	6-1	178	So.	Newport News, Va.
16	SCHLEZES, KEN	DHB	6-3	192	Sr.	Rochelle, Ill.
3	SMITH, SCOTT	K	5-10	153	Sr.	Dallas, Texas
55	SMITH, SHERMAN	LB	6-2	208	So.	Chillicothe, Mo.
42	SULLIVAN, TIM	LB	6-3	219	Jr.	DesMoines, Iowa
71	SYLVESTER, STEVE	OT	6-4	248	So.	Milford, Ohio
65	SZATKO, GREG	DT	6-4	251	Jr.	Western Springs, Ill.
98	THOMAS, ROBERT	K	5-10	178	Jr.	Rochester, N.Y.
27	TOWNSEND, MIKE	DHB	6-3	183	Jr.	Hamilton Ohio
80	TOWNSEND, WILLIE	SE	6-3	196	Jr.	Hamilton, Ohio
34	ZANOT, ROBERT	DB	6-0	183	Fr.	Riverton Ill.

THE COLLEGE GAME
January 1, 1973

39th
ANNUAL
CLASSIC
UNIVERSITY OF
NOTRE DAME
vs.
UNIVERSITY OF
NEBRASKA

'Huskers Rout Irish

1973 ORANGE BOWL — Nebraska 40, Notre Dame 6

Nebraska	7	13	20	0 — 40
Notre Dame	0	0	0	6 — 6

Attendance: 80,010 — Weather: Fair, 74 degrees

Team	Score N-ND	Qtr.	Time Left	Play
Neb	7-0	1	11:19	Rodgers 8 run (Sanger kick)
Neb	14-0	2	14:21	Dixon 1 run (Sanger kick)
Neb	20-0	2	12:20	Anderson 52 pass from Rodgers (Sanger kick failed)
Neb	26-0	3	11:17	Rodgers 4 run (Humm pass failed)
Neb	33-0	3	7:33	Rodgers 5 run (Sanger kick)
Neb	40-0	3	6:00	Rodgers 50 pass from Humm (Sanger kick)
ND	40-6	4	13:51	Demmerle 5 pass from Clements (Clements pass failed)

SCORING

Notre Dame		0 0 0 6— 6
Nebraska		7 13 20 0—40

Neb—Rodgers 8 run (Sanger kick)
Neb—Dixon 1 run (Sanger kick)
Neb—Anderson 52 pass from Rodgers (kick failed)
Neb—Rodgers 4 run (pass failed)
Neb—Rodgers 5 run (Sanger kick)
Neb—Rodgers 50 pass from Humm (Sanger kick)
ND—Demmerle 5 pass from Clements (Sanger kick)
ND—Demmerle 5 pass from Clements (pass failed)
A—80,010

STATISTICS

	Notre Dame	Nebraska
First downs	13	30
Rushes yards	44-124	64-300
Passing yards	103	260
Return yards	18	3
Passes	9-23-3	19-26-1
Punts	6-37	4-38
Fumbles-lost	3-0	1-1
Penalties-yards	1-15	5-68

INDIVIDUAL LEADERS

RUSHING—Nebraska, Rodgers 15-81, Dixon 9-69, Goeller 11-43. Notre Dame, Penick 8-48, Huff 11-22.

RECEIVING—Nebraska, Rodgers 3-71, Revelle 3-62, List 3-25. Notre Dame, Dewan 3-46, Creaney 2-28.

PASSING—Nebraska, Humm 13-19-0, 185 yards. Notre Dame, Clements 9-22-3, 103.

MIAMI (AP) — Johnny Rodgers, flashing the brilliant moves that earned him the Heisman Trophy, scored four touchdowns and passed for another as ninth-ranked Nebraska smashed Notre Dame 40-6 Monday night in the Orange Bowl, New Year's Day's third and final postseason football game.

Rodgers scored on runs of eight, four, and five yards, hugged the sideline on a 50-yard touchdown pass play from Dave Humm and hurled a 52-yard scoring pass to Frosty Anderson as the two-time national champion Cornhuskers rolled to their third consecutive Orange Bowl conquest.

The Big Eight power, finishing a 9-2-1 campaign, sent Coach Bob Devaney into retirement with the worst defeat of a Notre Dame team since Ara Parseghian began coaching the Fighting Irish nine years ago.

Devaney announced before the season began that this would be his last, turning full-time to his duties as Nebraska's athletic director.

Rodgers' four touchdowns cracked the Orange Bowl scoring mark of 19 points set by Alabama's Bobby Luna in 1953 against Syracuse.

The Cornhuskers bolted to a 20-0 halftime lead and added three more touchdowns—all by Rodgers—in the third period.

The Nebraska All-American did not handle the ball again after turning in the play of the night with a 50-yard pass reception with six minutes left in the third period.

Rodgers stepped back one yard, caught Humm's pass on the right sideline and then did his thing, hugging the chalk to the 25 where he cut inside, then faked the final defender off his feet at the Irish 10.

Notre Dame, which had not been shut out in 72 games, kept the streak alive with a 77-yard touchdown drive that ended on Tom Clement's five-yard scoring pass to Pete Demmerle with 13:51 left in the game.

Nebraska's other score came early in the second period on a one-yard plunge by Gary Dixon, who had sparked the 80-yard drive with a 37-yard scamper to the Notre Dame 27.

Notre Dame, ranked 12th nationally, closed the year with an 8-3 record—first time the Irish have lost three in the Parseghian era.

The Cornhuskers, who lost their chance for a third straight national crown with regular season losses to UCLA and Oklahoma and a tie with Iowa State, set the tempo of this 39th Orange classic on the first possession of the game.

notre dame football statistics/ten games

SCORING BY QUARTERS

Notre Dame	75	89	55	64 —	283
Opponents	29	14	41	68 —	152

TEAM STATISTICS

	ND	OPP
Total Offense	4238	2571
Total Plays	766	682
Yards Per Play	5.5	3.8
Yards Per Game	424	257
Net Yards Rushing	3043	1427
Attempts	594	481
Yards Per Rush	5.1	3.0
Yards Per Game	304	143
Net Yards Passing	1195	1144
Attempts	172	201
Completions	85	86
Completion Percentage	.494	.428
Had Intercepted	13	23
Touchdown Passes	8	4
Yards Per Attempt	6.9	5.7
Yards Per Completion	14.0	13.3
Yards Per Game	120	114
Interceptions Made	23	13
Yards Returned	222	158
Punt Return Yards	235	86
Number of Returns	23	19
Average Return	10.2	4.5
Kickoff Return Yards	488	863
Number of Returns	30	38
Average Return	16.2	22.7
Total Return Yards	774	809
Average Punt	38.4	37.1
Number of Punts	43	70
Yards Punting	1650	2595
Had Blocked	0	0
Penalties Against	46	55
Yards Penalized	526	514
Fumbles (lost)	35(22)	26(11)
Total First Downs	218	148
by rushing	154	80
by passing	53	61
by penalty	11	7

INDIVIDUAL TOTAL OFFENSE LEADERS

	G	PLAYS	YARDS	AVG.
Tom Clements	10	248	1534	6.2
Eric Penick	9	115	735	6.4
Andy Huff	10	118	607	5.1

RESULTS . . . . Won 8, Lost 2, Tied 0

ND		OPP	Attendance	
37	Northwestern (a)	0	55,155	(c)
35	Purdue	14	59,075	(c)
16	Michigan State (a)	0	77,828	(c)
42	Pittsburgh	16	59,075	(c)
26	Missouri	30	59,075	(c)
21	Texas Christian	0	59,075	(c)
42	Navy (a)	23	43,089	
21	Air Force (a)	7	48,671	(c)
20	Miami	17	59,075	(c)
23	Southern Cal (a)	45	75,243	

January 1   Orange Bowl

TEAM SCORING

	ND	OPP
Total Points	283	152
Average	28.3	15.2
Touchdowns	38	20
by rushing	28	14
by passing	8	4
by return	2	2
by recovery	0	0
Field Goals (Made-Att)	7-11	4-10
Safeties	0	0
PAT — Kick	34-34	10-13
PAT — Run	0-2	1-2
PAT — Pass	0-2	4-5

INDIVIDUAL SCORING

	G	TD	Kick	R-PA	FG	TP
Huff	10	10				60
Thomas	10		34-34		7-11	55
Penick	9	5				30
Clements	10	4				24
Diminick	10	4				24
W. Townsend	8	4				24
Cieszkowski	8	3				18
Best	4	2				12
Creaney	10	2				12
Dewan	8	1				6
Mahalic	10	1				6
Roolf	5	1				6
Samuel	9	1				6
Notre Dame	10	38	34-34	0-4	7-11	283
Opponents	10	20	10-13	5-7	4-10	152

INDIVIDUAL PUNTING

	G	NO.	YDS.	AVG	LONG
Doherty	10	43	1650	38.4	52
Notre Dame	10	43	1650	38.4	52
Opponents	10	70	2595	37.1	77

RUSHING

	G	TC	Yds	Avg	TD	Long
Penick	9	124	727	5.9	5	38
Huff	10	115	567	4.9	10	21
Diminick	10	71	377	5.3	2	42
Clements	10	86	341	4.0	4	26
Dewan	8	62	319	5.1	1	30
Cieszkowski	8	54	212	3.9	3	16
Best	4	17	158	9.3	2	57
Bullock	9	27	123	4.5	0	14
Kornman	4	10	79	7.9	0	29
Roolf	5	2	49	24.5	0	37
W. Townsend	9	2	43	21.5	0	31
Samuel	9	14	41	2.9	1	19
Demmerle	5	1	23	23.0	0	23
Washington	4	1	8	8.0	0	8
Goodman	4	4	-3	-0.7	0	4
Etter	1	1	-9	-9.0	0	-9
Brown	10	3	-12	-4.0	0	6
Notre Dame	10	594	3043	5.1	23	57
Opponents	10	481	1427	3.0	14	52

PASSING

	G	NO.	Comp.	Pct.	INT.	YDS	TD
Clements	10	162	83	.512	12	1163	8
Brown	10	7	2	.286	0	32	0
Dewan	8	1	0	.000	0	0	0
Etter	1	1	0	.000	0	0	0
Samuel	9	1	0	.000	1	0	0
Notre Dame	10	172	85	.495	13	1195	8
Opponents	10	201	86	.428	23	1144	4

PASS RECEIVING

	G	PC	Yds	Avg	TD	Long
W. Townsend	9	25	369	14.8	4	62
Creaney	10	17	321	18.9	2	41
Diminick	10	14	143	10.2	1	36
Huff	10	9	102	11.3	0	17
Roolf	5	6	108	18.0	1	36
Cieszkowski	8	4	40	10.0	0	13
Dewan	8	4	53	13.3	0	23
Bullock	9	2	32	16.0	0	18
Penick	9	2	9	4.5	0	5
Washington	4	1	12	12.0	0	12
Casper	10	1	6	6.0	0	6
Notre Dame	10	85	1195	14.0	8	62
Opponents	10	86	1144	13.3	4	38

RETURNS

	Interceptions	Punts	Kickoffs
M. Townsend	10-39-0		
Mahalic	2-59-1		
Musuraca	2-28-0		
Barnett	2-16-0		
O'Malley	1-12-0		
Rudnick	3-18-0	13-106-0	
Schlezes	2-16-0	9-122-0	
Zanot	1-34-0	1-7-0	2-4-0
Diminick			15-331-1
Dewan			5-77-0
Huff			2-40-0
Penick			2-20-0
Cieszkowski			1-7-0
Goodman			1-7-0
W. Townsend			1-2-0
Bolger			1-0-0
Notre Dame	23-222-1	23-235-0	30-488-1
Opponents	13-158-0	19-86-0	38-863-2

DEFENSIVE STATISTICS

	TM	TL-YDS	PBU	FR
O'Malley	122	3-31	1	1
Marx	96	6-36	1	
Musuraca	85	3-16	1	1
Mahalic	77	4-15	1	
Schlezes	49	4-18	3	
Sullivan	49	4-22		1
Niehaus	47	2-14		
Maciag	39	3-21	1	
Nosbusch	39	3-9		
Hayduk	37	5-23		2
M. Townsend	34		4	
Freistroffer	29	2-2		2
Barnett	24		4	1
Rudnick	21	2-13	2	
Collins	18			
Fanning	13	2-10		
Smith	12			
Potempa	9	1-28		1
Zanot	6			
Alvarado	5			
Hein	5			
McGraw	5			
Naughton	4		1	
Garner	3			
Stock	3			1
Casper	2			
Creaney	2			
Diminick	2			
Mariani	2			
O'Donnell	2			
Roolf	2			
Brown	1			1
Cieszkowski	1			
Dampeer	1			
DiNardo	1			
Huff	1			
Lopienski	1			
O'Toole	1			
Team	9			
Notre Dame		44-258	19	11
Opponents		39-175	25	22

KEY: TM — Tackles Made; TL-YDS —• Tackles made for minus yardage to the opponent; PBU — Passes Broken Up; FR — Fumble Recoveries.

1973 NOTRE DAME FOOTBALL ROSTER

No.	NAME	Pos	Ht	Wt	Class	HOMETOWN
79	Achterhoff, Jay	DT	6-4	249	Soph	Muskegon, Mich.
12	Allocco, Frank	QB	6-1	178	Jr	New Providence, N.J.
52	Alvarado, Joe	C	6-1	232	Sr	East Chicago, Ind.
17	Bake, Tom	HB	5-10	180	Jr	Middletown, Ohio
63	Balliet, Calvin	OG	6-4	220	Soph	Moorestown, N.J.
14	Barnett, Reggie	DHB	5-11	182	Jr	Flint, Mich.
23	Best, Art	HB	6-1	200	Soph	Gahanna, Ohio
62	Bolger, Tom	OG	6-2	229	Sr	Cincinnati, Ohio
20	Bradley, Luther	DHB	6-2	194	Fr	Muncie, Ind.
4	Brantley, Tony	P	6-0	200	Soph	Oklahoma City, Okla.
59	Brenneman, Mark	C	6-4	230	Sr	York, Pa.
8	Brown, Cliff	QB	6-0	193	Sr	Middletown, Pa.
46	Brown, Ivan	DE	6-3	220	Soph	LeRoy, Ill.
89	Browner, Ross	DE	6-3	218	Fr	Warren, Ohio
30	Bullock, Wayne	FB	6-1	210	Jr	Newport News, Va.
86	Casper, Dave	TE	6-3	240	Sr	Chilton, Wisc.
2	Clements, Tom	QB	6-0	185	Jr	McKees Rocks, Pa.
50	Collins, Greg	LB	6-3	220	Jr	Troy, Mich.
41	Creevey, Tom	DE	6-3	210	Sr	Mishawaka, Ind.
85	Demmerle, Pete	SE	6-1	190	Jr	New Canaan, Conn.
28	Diminick, Gary	HB	5-9	166	Sr	Mt. Carmel, Pa.
72	Dinardo, Gerry	OG	6-1	242	Jr	Howard Beach, N.Y.
9	Doherty, Brian	P	6-2	186	Sr	Portland, Ore.
32	Doherty, Kevin	SE	6-0	174	Soph	Portland, Ore.
88	Fanning, Mike	DT	6-6	254	Jr	Tulsa, Okla.
76	Fedorenko, Nick	DT	6-5	255	Soph	Chicago, Ill.
93	Fine, Tom	TE	6-5	234	Jr	Apple Valley, Calif.
94	Fry, Willie	DE	6-3	220	Fr	Memphis, Tenn.
96	Galanis, John	DE	6-4	223	Soph	Ipswich, Mass.
21	Goodman, Ron	HB	5-11	192	Jr	Mt. Sinai, N.Y.
43	Harchar, John	LB	6-3	219	Fr	Clairton, Pa.
95	Hayduk, George	DE	6-3	240	Sr	Factoryville, Pa.
99	Hein, Jeff	FB	6-1	235	Sr	Cincinnati, Ohio
25	Hunter, Al	HB	5-11	189	Fr	Greenville, N.C.
15	Kornman, Russ	FB	6-0	200	Soph	Wauwatosa, Wisc.
51	Lane, Gary	LB	6-0	221	Sr	Kalamazoo, Mich.
58	Laney, Tom	OT	6-2	242	Jr	Sprague, Wash.
26	Lopienski, Tom	DHB	6-1	182	Soph	Akron, Ohio
78	Lozzi, Dennis	OT	6-3	245	Sr	Whitman, Mass.
45	Mahalic, Drew	LB	6-4	224	Jr	Birmingham, Mich.
31	Maschmeier, Tom	DHB	5-11	185	Soph	Cincinnati, Ohio
74	McBride, Mike	OT	6-5	234	Sr	Michigan City, Ind.
37	Miller, Tim	LB	6-2	215	Jr	Pittsburgh, Pa.
92	Miskowitz, Lew	LB	5-11	234	Sr	Rock Island, Ill.
57	Moore, Elton	OG	6-1	230	Fr	Portland, Ore.
66	Morrin, Dan	OG	6-3	235	Sr	Croydan, Pa.
49	Naughton, Mike	DHB	6-3	185	Sr	Bloomfield Hills, Mich.
64	Neece, Steve	OT	6-3	253	Jr	Janesville, Wisc.
70	Niehaus, Steve	DT	6-5	265	Soph	Cincinnati, Ohio
60	Nosbusch, Kevin	DT	6-4	259	Jr	Milwaukee, Wisc.
38	Novakov, Tony	LB	5-11	195	Soph	Cincinnati, Ohio
33	Parker, Mike	DHB	5-11	175	Jr	Cincinnati, Ohio
16	Payne, Randy	DHB	5-9	175	Soph	Palmer Park, Md.
44	Penick, Eric	HB	6-1	213	Jr	Cleveland, Ohio
40	Potempa, Gary	LB	6-0	227	Sr	Niles, Ill.
47	Pszeracki, Joe	LB	5-11	214	Soph	Ambridge, Pa.
77	Quehl, Steve	OT	6-4	238	Jr	Cincinnati, Ohio
65	Rohan, Andy	C	6-1	234	Jr	Cincinnati, Ohio
7	Rudnick, Tim	DHB	5-10	187	Sr	Chicago, Ill.
24	Samuel, Al	HB	6-1	178	Jr	Newport News, Va.
29	Sarb, Pat	DHB	6-0	181	Soph	Dearborn, Mich.
69	Sawicz, Paul	OG	6-4	238	Sr	Lackawanna, N.Y.
97	Simon, Tim	SE	5-10	165	Fr	Pontiac, Mich.
11	Slager, Rick	QB	5-11	192	Soph	Columbus, Ohio
55	Smith, Sherm	LB	6-2	210	Jr	Chillicothe, Mo.
48	Stock, Jim	DE	6-3	210	Soph	Barberton, Ohio
42	Sullivan, Tim	LB	6-3	227	Sr	Des Moines, Iowa
73	Susko, Larry	DT	6-1	262	Sr	Sharpsville, Pa.
71	Sylvester, Steve	OT	6-4	236	Jr	Milford, Ohio
98	Thomas, Bob	K	5-10	171	Sr	Rochester, N.Y.
27	Townsend, Mike	DHB	6-3	178	Sr	Hamilton, Ohio
80	Townsend, Willie	SE	6-3	196	Sr	Hamilton, Ohio
82	Washington, Bob	SE	6-0	173	Sr	Steubenville, Ohio
67	Wasilevich, Max	OG	6-3	224	Sr	Dearborn Heights, Mich.
61	Webb, Mike	LB	6-2	228	Sr	New Castle, Del.
91	Weber, Robin	TE	6-5	236	Soph	Dallas, Tex.
35	Weiler, Jim	FB	6-0	215	Fr	Cleveland Heights, Ohio
81	Wujciak, Al	DT	6-2	230	Soph	Newark, N.J.
39	Zappala, Tony	DHB	6-0	205	Fr	Elmwood Park, N.J.
34	Zanot, Bob	DHB	6-0	177	Soph	Riverton, Ill.

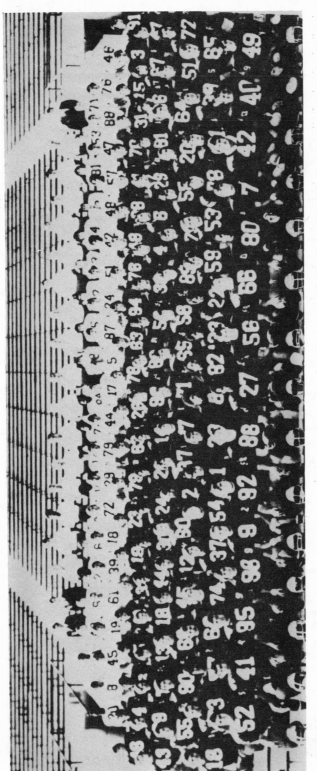

ABOVE *Members of the Football Team.* FIRST ROW: J. Alvarado, T. Creevey, G. Havduk, B. Thomas, B. Doherty, L. Miskowitz, D. Casper, M. Townsend, F. Pomanco, D. Morra, W. Townsend, T. Rudnick, T. Sullivan, G. Potempa, M. Naughton. SECOND ROW: J. Gambone, L. Susko, M. Wasilevich, T. Bolger, M. McBride, J. Zloch, G. Lane, K. Kinealy, G. Dimnick, C. Brown, B. Washington, M. Parker, G. Hill, M. Brennaman, P. Hartmann, D. Lozzi, M. Webb, E. Scales, G. Szatko. THIRD ROW: S. Smith, S. Quehl, B. Sweeney, D. Manalio, F. Allocco, K. Nosbusch, T. Clements, T. Miller, T. Bake, S. Sylvester, A. Rohan, T. Laney, P. Demmerle, B. Arment, S. Bossu, J. Audino, S. Neece, J. O'Donnell, G. DiNardo. FOURTH ROW: M. McGuire, J. Hein, P. Sawitz, J. Chauncey, B. McGreevy, E. Penick, W. Bullock, A. Samuel, R. Goodman, R. Barnett, T. Fine, M. Fanning, G. Collins, T. Parise, T. Brantley, K. Horton, P. Sarb, A. Wujciak, J. Galanis, P. Pohlen, J. Pszeracki. FIFTH ROW: B. Brown, B. Zanot, R. Payne, B. Walls, F. Trosko, P. Linehan, K. Doher-

ty, A. Best, J. Achterhoff, B. Messaros, T. Lopienski, F. Rutkowski, C. Balliet, K. Andler, N. Fedorenko, J. Stock, T. Novakov, R. Slager, S. Niehaus, T. Maschmeier, R. Kornman, F. McDonald, R. Weber. SIXTH ROW: L. Bradley, K. Moriarty, T. Eastmann, M. Ostrander, E. Sharkey, T. Zappala, J. Rufo, D. Pattyn, R. Bonder, T. Gullickson, E. Gieckler, J. Soutner, S. Bobowski, M. Kafka, M. Banks, S. Humbert, M. Russell, J. Likovich, E. Moore, J. Lloyd, D. Buth, D. Rodenkirk, D. Malinak. SEVENTH ROW: R. Browner, J. Harchar, T. Katenkamp, D. Knott, M. Ewald, A. Hunter, R. Henry, T. Unis, G. Smith, W. Fry, B. Sahm, J. Weiler, R. Allocco, T. Leary, J. Dubenetzky, T. Simon, D. Kelleher, V. Klees, D. Buck. EIGHTH ROW: J. Sweeney, K. Flanagan, G. O'Neill, M. Creaney, G. Blanche, J. Murphy, J. Yonto, G. Kelley, P. Shoults. Head Coach Ara Parseghian, T. Pagna, W. Moore, B. Boulac, M. Stock, D. Murphy, B. Hickey, L. Dinardo, G. Paszkiet, G. Bockrath.

1973

Coach: Ara Parseghian
Tri-Captains: Dave Casper, Frank Pomarico (Off.)
and Mike Townsend (Def.)

S.22	W	Northwestern	44-0	H	c59,075
S.29	W	Purdue	20-7	A	c69,391
O.6	W	Michigan State	14-10	H	c59,075
O.13	W	Rice (Nt)	28-0	A	50,321
O.20	W	Army	62-3	A	c42,503
O.27	W	Southern Cal (R)	23-14	H	c59,075
N.3	W	Navy	44-7	H	c59,075
N.10	W	Pittsburgh (S)	31-10	A	c56,593
N.22TH	W	Air Force	48-15	H	57,236
D.1	W	Miami (Fla.) (Nt)	44-0	A	42,968

(10-0-0) 358-66 555,312

SUGAR BOWL

D.31	W	Alabama	24-23	N1	c85,161

(4:26) (Nt)

N1—at New Orleans

AP POLL

1973
1. NOTRE DAME
2. Ohio State
3. Oklahoma
4. Alabama
5. Penn State
6. Michigan
7. Nebraska
8. Southern Cal
9. Arizona State
9. Houston

UPI POLL

1973
1. Alabama
2. Oklahoma
3. Ohio State
4. NOTRE DAME
5. Penn State
6. Michigan
7. Southern Cal
8. Texas
9. UCLA
10. Arizona State

Eyeing Perfect Season
Irish Rip Air Force, 48-15

SOUTH BEND, Ind. (AP — Notre Dame made Air Force its Thanksgiving Day feast as the fifth-ranked Irish remained on the hunt for a national championship and their first perfect season since 1949.

The Irish devoured the visiting Falcons 48-15 Thursday before a national television audience and their first below-capacity home crowd since 1964.

Notre Dame, heading for a New Year's Eve showdown with No. 2 Alabama in the Sugar Bowl, stomped to a 28-0 lead with the aid of three Air Force fumbles in the first period. They were in charge the rest of the way.

"We got a lot of early breaks and capitalized on them, getting the ball into the end zone very quickly," Irish Coach Ara Parseghian said. "When we get a 28-0 nothing, we get a tendency to lose our concentration. But that's a very human tendency."

Asked if this was his best team, Parseghian said, "This team has as fine a team leadership and team unity as any I have had. They have a willing-ness to sacrifice to achieve the team's goal."

That goal—though unspoken by Parseghian after the game—is the national championship and the perfect season that likely will be needed to get there.

In a fitting tribute, the late Frank Leahy was honored in a halftime salute. Leahy was the Irish coach when they rolled to a 10-0 record and the national crown in 1949.

Parseghian's best of his first nine seasons at Notre Dame was 1966 when only a 10-10 tie with Michigan State blemished the Irish record in another national championship year.

The victory over Air Force moved Parseghian closer to Leahy's Irish coaching record of 87-11-9.

SCORING

Air Force	0	6	3	6—15
Notre Dame	28	6	0	14—48

ND—Casper 14 pass from Clements (Thomas kick)
ND—Penick 6 run (Thomas kick)
ND—Bullock 8 run (Thomas kick)
ND—Penick 4 run (Thomas kick)
AF—Bready 21 pass from Haynie (kick failed)
ND—FG Thomas 36
ND—FG Thomas 32
AF—FG Lawson 51
ND—Dennerie 22 pass from Brown (Thomas kick)
ND—Samuel 5 run (Thomas kick)
AF—Reiner 18 run (kick failed)
A—57,236

rsity of Miami

ty of Notre Dame

*Special
Hall
of
Fame
Issue*

THE
COLLEGE
GAME

Price
tax included
50c

Bowl - December 1, 1973

10-0-0 SEASON

By virtue of victory over Miami and the fortunate 10-10 Michigan-Ohio State tie, the Irish found themselves in third place with two first-place votes in the AP poll. The *Football News* named Ara Coach of the Year and Mike Townsend, Dave Casper and Greg Collins received individual honors from the press associations. Though the honors were beginning to flow in, the team didn't relax; for the most important game of the entire season was still ahead of them.

"How does it feel?" asked Brian Doherty after the Miami victory. "It feels like the end of four long waiting years. It feels like the top of the world. And only one thing could possibly beat this — 11-0."

1974 SUGAR BOWL — Notre Dame 24, Alabama 23

Notre Dame	6	8	7	3 — 24
Alabama	0	10	7	6 — 23

Attendance: 85,161 — Weather: Fair, 55 degrees

Team	Score ND-A	Qtr.	Time Left	Play
ND	6-0	1	3:19	Bullock 6 run (kick failed, bad center snap)
Ala	6-7	2	7:30	Billingsley 6 run (Davis kick)
ND	14-7	2	7:17	Hunter 93 kickoff return (Demmerle pass from Clements)
Ala	14-10	2	0:39	Davis 39 FG
Ala	14-17	3	11:02	Jackson 5 run (Davis kick)
ND	21-17	3	2:30	Penick 12 run (Thomas kick)
Ala	21-23	4	9:33	Todd 25 pass from Stock (Davis kick failed)
ND	24-23	4	4:26	Thomas 19 FG

Sugar Bowl Battle

Official Sugar Bowl Souvenir Brochure $1.00
Complete Schedule of Events for Football, Basketball, Tennis, and Regatta

Fighting Irish of Notre Dame vs. Crimson Tide of Alabama

Sugar Bowl, Alabama

The Alabama-Notre Dame game would have been one of the biggest games of the season if it had been for nothing. But considering it matched two undefeated, top-ranked teams vying for the Sugar Bowl and the national championship, you have what some called the game of the century.

The winner of this game would be the national champion, and each school knew exactly what that meant. Alabama had three national championships to its credit, the last coming in '65, while the Irish had earned five, their last coming in '66.

Though the teams were quite similar in some aspects, their offensive techniques differed. Alabama, running out of the Wishbone offense, often had to rely on its bench to wear down opponents; consequently, they won many games in the late stages. Notre Dame, on the other hand, used its powerful first team to destroy its opponents very quickly in the contest. Against their one common opponent (Miami), both teams played predictably. The Tide seemed uncertain until a number of turnovers helped them increase the score while the Irish dominated the game from the very beginning.

Alabama had gone to more bowls than any other college in the country, but they went into the Sugar Bowl with a four-game Bowl losing streak, and Coach Bear Bryant was anticipating a change. Notre Dame had also lost its last bowl game to national champs Nebraska in the Orange Bowl. Overall, Notre Dame had a 2-2 Bowl record compared to the Alabama mark of 12-11-3. Under Coach Bryant, Alabama had attended 15 straight post-season bowls, making them the "bowlingest" college team in the country.

The Sugar Bowl clash of the two teams was their first meeting, though they do have regular season games scheduled for 1976 at South Bend and some time in the 80's for the return engagement. The Irish, in fact, have faced Southeastern Conference competition just twice before, that being against Louisiana State. Notre Dame won the first encounter in South Bend, 3-0, and the Tigers got even the following year in Baton Rouge, 28-8.

Statistically speaking, both Alabama and Notre Dame ranked high in regular season performance. The Irish ranked fifth in total offense, but the Tide ranked second with slightly over 18 yards more per game. The same held true for rushing offense, where Alabama racked up 16 yards per game more than the Irish. In scoring, Alabama ranked third with 41.3 points per game, while the Irish claimed eighth spot with 35.8 points per game. The Irish shone in defensive statistics, where they allowed only 201.2 yards per game, good enough for second place; while Alabama maintained eleventh place with 244.8 yards per game. In rushing defense, the Irish placed third with 82.4 yards per game, while the Tide didn't place at all. The Irish remained consistently high in scoring defense with a third-place mark of 6.6 points per game, while the Tide allowed a fifth-place total of 8.1 points per game. Finally, 'Bama was averaging a sixth-place 42.8 yards per punt, while ND's Bob Thomas ranked eighth with 42.4 yards per punt.

Most prognosticators, professional and otherwise, believed that the Alabama offense would be too much for the Notre Dame defense. Critics pointed to a weak secondary and claimed Bear would riddle the field with long-gain passes. Again, most of the Irish defensive work had come against straight-ahead, methodical offenses, they claimed, while Alabama used an explosive, lightning-quick wishbone offense to offset their opponents.

To a certain extent, they were right, but only as correct as any seer can be; for the Notre Dame defense learned with each play, gradually holding the Alabama offense to limited yardage.

The first-quarter statistics made believers out of all the skeptics. The Irish defense could do no wrong as they shut out the mighty wishbone—zero yardage with zero first downs. From the 20, Clements handed off twice to Bullock, who broke for 7 and 15 yards. Penick crossed over left tackle for 6, followed by Bullock again for 10. Here, the Irish drive began to falter, as Best and Bullock could only make three yards, and Clements could only add two, forcing Doherty to punt to the Alabama 16.

The defense forced a loss of two and a quick return of the punt to the ND 40. Two series later, the Irish finally mounted a drive, beginning at the ND 36. Clements' first pass to Demmerle netted 19 yards, followed by another for 26 and a third for 14 yards. Clements to Demmerle had just moved 59 yards in less than one minute. Bullock broke over from the one, putting the Irish on the scoreboard first, though a missed PAT kept the score at 6-0.

Excellent field position greatly helped the Irish; but the inability of the Tide to move was a little more difficult to explain. Ara credited it to the defense, though it appeared as if Alabama was scouting the Irish defense up close, looking for cracks and weaknesses.

They seemed to have found some. They were able immediately to put together an impressive drive that ended on the ten with a very fortunate fumble, recovered by Jim Stock. Initial sweeps of 16, 15 and 10 yards accompanied more conservative gains as the Tide rolled closer to the ND goal line. A bad Rutledge pitch went down as a fumble, though, and the Irish took over on their own 36.

On the second play from scrimmage, a Clements-Bullock connection missed its mark, and Alabama recovered on their own 48. It took Rutledge only seven plays to score, passing for 15 yards, handing off four times for 24 and keeping once for 12. The PAT was good, making the score 7-6.

But what should have been a change in momentum was rendered meaningless on the next play as Al Hunter returned the kickoff 93 yards for the second Notre Dame touchdown of the evening. The run set a new record for kickoff returns, originally held by Monk Simons, who was serving as a Sugar Bowl official. Clements passed to Demmerle for the two-point conversion, and the Irish had the lead at 14-7.

Alabama mounted one more serious attack before the half, settling for a field goal when the Irish defense stopped them at the ND 22.

The Irish found themselves within field goal range also, as Diminick's return of 25 yards gave the Irish good field position. Clements bootlegged twice for 27 yards, but Thomas missed the 48-yard attempt, falling short as the half ended.

I get a Kick out of Life

Notre Dame kicker Bob Thomas had been experiencing a frustrating season until the Irish beat Southern Cal when his three field goals proved the difference in the 23-14 game.

And some of Thomas' biggest frustrations were with his coach, Ara Parseghian.

"It all started the week of the Northwestern game," Thomas remembers. "I made up a cheer (a Notre Dame football custom) and I was supposed to pat Coach Parseghian on the back at the end. Instead I got carried away and slapped him on the face.

"That's the first time since sophomore year I've checked the bulletin board to see if I was dressing for the game," he laughs.

Thomas hasn't tried to make any alibis for his kicking this season either. After connecting on two field goal attempts at Purdue he missed eight more before his three-for-three day against the Trojans.

"I had some tough tries during that streak. Against Michigan State I tried kicks of 42, 49 and 55 yards into the wind. And I just plain missed some chip shots. But calling it a slump doesn't justify it."

"I said a prayer at the beginning of the season and told God that I didn't want any recognition all season if I could just have it for the Southern Cal game," Thomas relates. "After breaking my PAT streak at Army and missing two field goals, one of which I thought was good, I walked back to my sixth-floor room. I opened the curtains and looked toward heaven and said, 'I know I told you I didn't want any big games until USC, but this is getting ridiculous.'"

Thomas was granted his request but not before he took some more ribbing from his coach.

"One day at practice Coach drop-kicked a field goal 32-yards," says Thomas. "He turned to me and asked if I had seen that. I nodded and he quickly reminded me that I had missed a few from just that far.

"But then he told me not to worry about it because I was going to beat USC with my field goals. Can you imagine how great that made me feel?"

Thomas' performance against the Trojans marked the fourth time in his Notre Dame career that he connected on three field goals. That ties him with Gus Dorais for the single-game record. It also earned him the offensive player of the game award from Chevrolet and the Notre Dame Quarterback Club.

But his most important, and certainly most remembered, field goal of the season was the 19-yard completion against Alabama in the closing minutes of the Sugar Bowl. Thomas had already tried a 48-yard boot that fell short just as the first half ended. This left the score 14-10, Notre Dame, but the extra points might have meant a bit more breathing room.

With 9:33 left in the final quarter, Bryant showed a little of his razzle-dazzle, sending in Todd to replace Rutledge at quarterback. Todd handed off to Mike Stock, who turned and whipped a pass right back to the reserve who raced all alone for the tally.

With the score 23-21, Davis missed the PAT, leaving the Irish with a possible field goal victory. Twelve plays later, Thomas had his golden opportunity — of the game, of the season, and, certainly, of his career. From 19 yards out, the senior split the uprights with a chip shot to send the Irish ahead for good, 24-23.

"I thought about it during the whole drive," Thomas later explained. "I wouldn't have minded if we scored a touchdown, but I wasn't on the sidelines saying 'please score and take a burden off my head.'

"Normally I don't chip the ball, but I decided to this time, and I decided not to follow through as much to make sure I got it over their rush. I knew it would probably go a little to the right or left, but at 19 yards I knew it couldn't drift far enough to miss. I knew I could put points on the board."

Thomas finished the season with a bevy of records to his credit. He has the best career percentage for extra points, .970 (98 out of 101) and the best percentage for one season, 1.000 (34 out of 34, 1972); the most field goals in a game, 3 (four times), most in a season, 9 (1973), most in a career, 21 of 38; most kicking points in a game, 13 (vs. Northwestern, 1972), most in a season, 70 (1973, to lead the team) and is second in career, 161 (Scott Hempel, 164); most field goal attempts in a season, 18 (1973) and most in a career, 38; he connected on 62 straight extra points, missing this year in the Army game, for a mark that was second best in NCAA history.

Bob Thomas' 19-yard field goal that won the Sugar Bowl and the National Championship.

NOTRE DAME FOOTBALL STATISTICS
(TEN GAMES)

SCORING BY QUARTERS

Notre Dame	78	120	79	81 —	358
Opponents	10	16	13	27 —	66

TEAM STATISTICS

	ND	OPP
Total Offense	4614	2012
Total Plays	815	615
Yards Per Play	5.7	3.3
Yards Per Game	461	201
Net Yards Rushing	3502	824
Attempts	673	390
Yards Per Rush	5.2	2.1
Yards Per Game	350	82.4
Net Yards Passing	1112	1188
Attempts	142	225
Completions	75	88
Completion Percentage	.528	.391
Had Intercepted	7	20
Touchdown Passes	11	4
Yards Per Completion	14.8	13.5
Yards Per Attempt	7.8	5.3
Yards Per Game	111	119
Interceptions Made	20	7
Yards Returned	178	55
Punt Return Yards	269	60
Number of Returns	29	10
Average Return	9.4	6.0
Kickoff Return Yards	454	851
Number of Returns	19	46
Average Return	23.9	18.5
Total Return Yards	901	966
Average Punt	42.4	38.1
Number of Punts	41	78
Yards Punting	1738	2972
Had Blocked	0	1
Penalties Against	54	28
Yards Penalized	567	259
Fumbles (lost)	38 (23)	34 (19)
Total First Downs	244	119
by rushing	181	54
by passing	57	51
by penalty	6	14

INDIVIDUAL TOTAL OFFENSE LEADERS

	G	Plays	Yards	Avg.
Clements	10	149	1242	8.3
Bullock	10	162	752	4.6
Best	10	118	700	5.9

RESULTS — Won 11, Lost 0, Tied 0

ND		OPP	Attendance
44	Northwestern	0	59,075 (c)
20	Purdue (a)	7	69,391 (c)
14	Michigan State	10	59,075 (c)
28	Rice (a)	0	50,000
62	Army (a)	3	42,503 (c)
23	Southern Cal	14	59,075 (c)
44	Navy	7	59,075 (c)
31	Pittsburgh (a)	10	56,593 (c)
48	Air Force	15	57,236
44	Miami (a)	0	42,968
24	Alabama	23	85,161 (c)

TEAM SCORING

	ND	OPP
Total Points	358	66
Average	35.8	6.6
Touchdowns	47	8
by rushing	35	3
by passing	11	4
by return	1	1
by recovery	0	0
Field Goals (Made-Att.)	9-18	4-9
Safeties	2	0
PAT — Kick	43	6
PAT — Run	1	0
PAT — Pass	0	0

INDIVIDUAL SCORING

	G	TD	Kick	R	FG	TP
Thomas	10		43-45		9-18	70
Bullock	10	11				66
Penick	10	7				42
Demmerle	10	5				30
Clements	10	4				26
Casper	10	4				24
Best	10	3				18
Hunter	10	3				18
Samuel	8	2				12
Brown	7	2				12
Diminick	10	1				6
Allocco	5	1				6
Goodman	9	1				6
W. Townsend	7	1				6
Parise	5	1				6
Simon	7	1				6
Stock	10		Safety—1			2
Browner	10		Safety—1			2
Notre Dame	10	47	43-46 2 1		9-18	358
Opponents	10	8	6-8 0 0		4-9	66

INDIVIDUAL PUNTING

	G	No.	Yds.	Avg.	Long
B. Doherty	10	39	1664	42.7	66
Brantley	1	2	74	37.0	38
Notre Dame	10	41	1738	42.4	66
Opponents	10	78	2972	38.1	64

PASSING

	G	No.	Comp.	Pct.	Int.	Yds.	TD
Clements	10	113	60	.531	6	882	8
Brown	7	28	14	.500	1	228	3
Allocco	5	1	1	1.000	0	2	0
Notre Dame	10	142	75	.528	7	1112	11
Opponents	10	225	88	.391	20	1188	4

RUSHING

	G	TC	Yds.	Avg.	TD	Long
Bullock	10	162	752	4.6	10	32
Best	10	118	700	5.9	3	69
Penick	10	102	586	5.7	7	85
Clements	10	89	360	4.0	4	30
Samuel	8	33	221	6.7	2	42
Parise	5	31	164	5.3	1	29
Hunter	10	32	150	4.7	3	22
Brown	8	22	134	6.1	2	38
Diminick	9	19	121	6.4	1	44
Kornman	5	21	94	4.5	0	19
Allocco	5	16	86	5.4	1	17
Goodman	9	21	86	4.1	1	10
Simon	7	2	24	12.0	0	33
Gambone	1	1	8	8.0	0	8
Knott	1	1	7	7.0	0	7
Weiler	1	1	4	4.0	0	4
W. Townsend	1	1	4	4.0	0	4
Hill	1	1	1	1.0	0	1
Notre Dame	10	673	3502	5.2	35	85
Opponents	10	390	824	2.1	3	65

PASS RECEIVING

	G	PC	Yds.	Avg.	TD	Long
Demmerle	10	26	404	15.5	5	30
Casper	10	19	317	16.7	4	35
Goodman	9	4	84	21.0	0	28
Bullock	10	8	83	10.4	1	25
W. Townsend	7	4	68	17.0	1	28
Best	10	4	48	12.0	0	17
Kornman	5	1	35	35.0	0	35
Diminick	9	2	21	10.5	0	14
Penick	10	2	16	8.0	0	10
Weber	9	1	11	11.0	0	11
Samuel	8	1	11	11.0	0	11
Hunter	10	2	12	6.0	0	7
Weiler	1	1	2	2.0	0	2
Notre Dame	10	75	1112	14.8	11	35
Opponents	10	88	1188	13.8	4	53

RETURNS

	Interceptions	Punts	Kickoffs
Zanot	2-20	20-149	
Goodman			5-113
Fine			1-7
M. Townsend	3-47		
Rudnick	3-49	5-34	
Bradley	6-37		
Diminick			8-181
Simon		4-86	
Barnett	1-0		
Bullock			2-39
Hunter			3-114
Collins	3-25		
Parker	1-0		
Mahalic	1-0		
Notre Dame	20-178	29-269	19-454
Opponents	7-55	11-60	46-851

DEFENSIVE STATISTICS

	TM	TL-Yds.	PBU	FR	BK
Collins	133	11-58	1	2	0
Potempa	75	7-41	0	1	0
Browner	68	15-104	1	2	1
Fanning	61	12-76	0	1	0
Mahalic	59	1-1	2	1	0
S. Smith	44	4-14	1	1	0
Rudnick	43	1-17	10	0	0
Stock	41	11-66	0	4	0
Niehaus	35	3-12	0	0	0
Barnett	29	1-2	6	2	0
Bradley	27	1-2	11	1	0
M. Townsend	23	0-0	6	3	0
Nosbusch	21	4-34	0	0	0
Hayduk	14	2-2	0	0	0
Fry	12	2-16	1	0	0
Parker	10	0-0	0	0	0
Lopienski	9	0-0	1	2	0
Achterhoff	8	3-24	0	0	0
Creevey	7	2-17	0	0	0
Novakov	7	1-1	0	1	0
Naughton	5	1-2	0	0	0
Sullivan	3	0-0	0	0	0
Parise	2	0-0	0	0	0
Zanot	6	0-0	0	1	0
Goodman	2	0-0	0	0	0
Thomas	1	0-0	0	0	0
Best	1	0-0	0	1	0
Webb	6	1-1	1	0	0
Sarb	3	0-0	0	0	0
G. Smith	1	0-0	0	0	0
Casper	1	0-0	0	0	0
Brown	1	0-0	0	0	0
Scales	1	0-0	0	0	0
Sylvester	1	0-0	0	1	0
Team	1	0-0	0	0	0
Notre Dame	769	83-468	43	24	1
Opponents	963	37-170	25	22	0

NOTRE DAME

No.	Name	Pos/Ht/Wt	Class/Hometown
79	Achterhoff, Jay	DT, 6-4, 251	Junior, Muskegon, Mich.
12	Allocco, Frank	QB, 6-1, 178	Senior, New Providence, N.J.
37	Allocco, Rich	HB, 6-2, 200	Sophomore, New Providence, N.J.
56	Andler, Ken	C, 6-5, 178	Junior, Cleveland, Ohio
73	Arment, Bill	DT, 6-4, 234	Senior, Muncie, Ind.
28	Bake, Tom	HB, 5-10, 188	Senior, Middletown, Ohio
63	Balliet, Cal	OG, 6-3, 234	Junior, Moorestown, N.J.
14	Barnett, Reggie	DHB, 5-11, 175	Senior, Flint, Mich.
68	Bauer, Ed	OT, 6-3, 234	Senior, Cincinnati, Ohio
43	Becker, Doug	OLB, 6-0, 210	Freshman, Hamilton, Ohio
23	Best, Art	HB, 6-1, 196	Junior, Gahanna, Ohio
34	Bonder, Frank	FB, 6-1, 207	Sophomore, Niles, Ohio
56	Bossu, Steve	C, 5-11, 202	Junior, Maple Heights, Ohio
4	Brantley, Tony	P, 6-0, 195	Junior, Oklahoma City, Okla.
59	Brenneman, Mark	C, 6-3, 233	Senior, York, Pa.
30	Bullock, Wayne	FB, 6-1, 223	Senior, Newport News, Va.
18	Burgmeier, Ted	FS, 6-0, 182	Freshman, East Dubuque, Ill.
83	Buth, Doug	TE, 6-5, 230	Sophomore, Green Bay, Wisc.
61	Carney, Mike	MLB, 6-2, 220	Freshman, LaMirada, Calif.
13	Chauncey, Jim	FS, 6-0, 184	Senior, Wheat Ridge, Colo.
2	Clements, Tom	QB, 6-0, 188	Senior, McKees Rocks, Pa.
50	Collins, Greg	OLB, 6-3, 230	Senior, Troy, Mich.
33	Cullins, Ron	DHB, 6-1, 183	Freshman, Warren, Ohio
85	Demmerle, Pete	SE, 6-1, 190	Senior, New Canaan, Conn.
72	DiNardo, Gerry	OG, 6-1, 248	Senior, Howard Beach, N.Y.
32	Doherty, Kevin	SE, 6-0, 181	Junior, Portland, Ore.
41	Dubenetzky, John	SS, 6-3, 215	Sophomore, Hobart, Ind.
42	Eastman, Tom	MLB, 6-0, 230	Sophomore, Elkhart, Ind.
40	Eurick, Terry	HB, 5-11, 193	Freshman, Saginaw, Mich.
88	Fanning, Mike	DT, 6-6, 253	Senior, Tulsa, Okla.
93	Fine, Tom	TE, 6-5, 225	Senior, Apple Valley, Calif.
75	Frericks, Tom	DT, 6-5, 230	Sophomore, Circleville, Ohio
96	Galanis, John	DT, 6-4, 244	Junior, Ipswich, Mass.
49	Gleckler, Ed	OLB, 6-2, 235	Sophomore, Bay Shore, N.Y.
21	Goodman, Ron	HB, 5-11, 195	Senior, Mt. Sinai, N.Y.
73	Gullickson, Tom	OT, 6-2, 235	Sophomore, Joliet, Ill.
10	Harrison, Randy	FS, 6-2, 192	Freshman, Hammond, Ind.
95	Hughes, Ernie	DE, 6-2, 220	Freshman, Boise, Id.
51	Johnson, Pete	OLB, 6-3, 215	Freshman, Fond du Lac, Wisc.
7	Kasparek, Ed	SS, 6-1, 185	Freshman, Livonia, Mich.
97	Kelleher, Dan	SE, 5-11, 184	Sophomore, Ellensburg, Wash.
19	Kelly, Chuck	FB, 5-11, 190	Senior, St. Paul, Minn.
52	Klees, Vince	C, 6-4, 222	Sophomore, Costa Mesa, Calif.
15	Kornman, Russ	FB, 6-0, 195	Junior, Wauwatosa, Wisc.
58	Laney, Tom	OT, 6-2, 235	Senior, Sprague, Wash.
53	Likovich, John	DE, 6-2, 207	Sophomore, Phoenix, Ariz.
46	Lloyd, Jack	OLB, 6-2, 210	Sophomore, Rolling Meadows, Ill.
26	Lopienski, Tom	DHB, 6-0, 180	Junior, Akron, Ohio
81	MacAfee, Ken	TE, 6-5, 235	Freshman, Brockton, Mass.
45	Mahalic, Drew	OLB, 6-3, 220	Senior, Farmington, Mich.
82	Malinak, Don	DE, 6-2, 208	Sophomore, Flemington, Pa.
31	Maschmeier, Tom	DHB, 5-11, 182	Junior, Cincinnati, Ohio
22	McLane, Mark	HB, 6-1, 204	Sophomore, Wilmington, Del.
99	McLaughlin, Pat	K, 6-2, 217	Junior, Santa Barbara, Calif.
57	Moore, Elton	OG, 6-1, 231	Sophomore, Portland, Ore.
1	Moriarty, Kerry	QB, 5-9, 163	Sophomore, Santa Barbara, Calif.
64	Neece, Steve	OT, 6-3, 264	Senior, Janesville, Wisc.
70	Niehaus, Steve	DE, 6-5, 266	Junior, Cincinnati, Ohio
60	Nosbusch, Kevin	DT, 6-4, 265	Senior, Milwaukee, Wisc.
38	Novakov, Tony	OLB, 5-11, 205	Junior, Cincinnati, Ohio
61	O'Donnell, John	OG, 6-1, 216	Senior, Woodside, N.Y.
6	Ostrander, Mike	DHB, 5-9, 177	Sophomore, Galesburg, Ill.
36	Parise, Tom	FB, 6-0, 215	Junior, Longmont, Colo.
5	Parseghian, Mike	HB, 5-8, 174	Sophomore, South Bend, Ind.
16	Payne, Randy	DHB, 5-9, 180	Junior, Palmer Park, Md.
44	Penick, Eric	HB, 6-1, 200	Senior, Cleveland, Ohio
55	Ploszek, Mike	C, 6-3, 220	Sophomore, Bedford Park, Ill.
67	Pohlen, Pat	OT, 6-4, 241	Junior, Downey, Calif.
47	Pszeracki, Joe	MLB, 5-11, 213	Junior, Ambridge, Pa.
3	Reeve, Dave	K, 6-2, 195	Freshman, Bloomington, Ind.
87	Rodenkirk, Don	DT, 6-4, 258	Sophomore, Milwaukee, Wisc.
65	Rohan, Andy	C, 6-1, 230	Senior, Cincinnati, Ohio
9	Rufo, John	HB, 5-11, 191	Sophomore, Lansdowne, Pa.
54	Russell, Marv	MLB, 6-0, 220	Sophomore, Ford City, Pa.
78	Rutkowski, Frank	DT, 6-4, 226	Junior, Middletown, Del.
24	Samuel, Al	HB, 6-1, 181	Senior, Newport News, Va.
29	Sarb, Pat	DHB, 6-0, 184	Junior, Dearborn, Mich.
11	Slager, Rick	QB, 5-11, 186	Junior, Columbus, Ohio
8	Soutner, John	FS, 6-2, 183	Sophomore, Steelton, Pa.
48	Stock, Jim	DE, 6-3, 214	Junior, Barberton, Ohio
69	Sweeney, Bob	OT, 6-5, 245	Senior, Salem, Mass.
71	Sylvester, Steve	OT, 6-4, 245	Senior, Cincinnati, Ohio
91	Weber, Robin	TE, 6-5, 235	Junior, Dallas, Texas
35	Weiler, Jim	FB-HB, 6-2, 212	Sophomore, Cleveland Hgts., Ohio
74	Weston, Jeff	DT, 6-5, 240	Freshman, Rochester, N.Y.
77	Woebkenberg, Harry	OT, 6-3, 252	Freshman, Cincinnati, Ohio
66	Wujciak, Al	OG, 6-2, 230	Junior, Newark, N.J.
39	Zappala, Tony	DE, 6-0, 205	Sophomore, Elmwood Park, N.J.

1974

Coach: Ara Parseghian
Co-Captains: Tom Clements and Greg Collins

S.9	W	Georgia Tech	31-7	A	45,228
S.21	W	Northwestern	49-3	A	c55,000
S.28	L	Purdue (U) (R)	20-31	H	c59,075
O.5	W	Michigan State	19-14	H	c77,431
O.12	W	Rice (3:08)	10-3	A	c59,075
O.19	W	Army (S)	48-0	H	c59,075
O.26	W	Miami (Fla.)	38-7	H	c59,075
N.2	W	Navy	14-6	N1	48,634
N.16	W	Pitt (R) (2.49)	14-10	H	c59,075
N.23	W	Air Force (R)	38-0	H	c59,075
N.30	L	Southern Cal	24-55	A	83,522

(9-2-0) 305-136 664,265

ORANGE BOWL

J.1	W	Alabama (U)	13-11	N2	71,801

N1—at Philadelphia; N2—at Miami

ND = 36 FIRST DOWNS

NOTRE DAME 48, ARMY 0

STATISTICS

	Army	ND
First downs	6	36
Rushes yards	49-81	83-525
Passing yards	8	68
Return yards	0	13
Passes	1-14-0	5-07-1
Punts	10-28.7	1-36
Fumbles lost	4-2	5-4
Penalties yards	3-36	7-95

Army	0 0 00	— 0
Notre Dame	7 13 21 7	— 48

ND—Bullock 6 run Reeve kick)
ND—Bullock 9 run (Reeve kick)
ND—Clements 7 run (Kick failed)
ND—Kornman 4 run (Reeve kick)
ND—Samuel 35 run (Reeve kick)
ND—Kornman 7 run (Reeve kick)
ND—Bake 6 run (Reeve kick)
A—59,075

NOTRE DAME PITTSBURGH

NOV 18 1974

ARA PARSEGHIAN RESIGNS

In eleven years beneath the Golden Dome, Ara Parseghian's Fighting Irish had marched to victory 94 times, suffered only 17 losses, and tied 4—with one more chapter remaining to be written New Year's Day in the Orange Bowl. Two of Parseghian's squads captured national championships—one in 1966 and the other in 1973—and both were undefeated.

Through the years, Ara and Notre Dame should have mutually fond memories of one another. They will recall that initial 1964 season when a young coach guided his first Notre Dame team to a 9-1 miracle, a Heisman Trophy for quarterback John Huarte and coach of the year honors for himself. They will reminisce about the late autumn of 1966, when Terry Hanratty, Jim Seymour, Coley O'Brien and the Irish ended their season with a 51-0 victory over the Trojans of Southern California. It was Ara's one hundredth coaching victory, and secured his first national championship. And they will ever remember that night in New Orleans when Ara made the choice already lauded as the gutsiest play ever conceived by a college coach—the Tom Clements to Robin Weber pass that turned a dangerous third and eight situation into the climactic play of the most exciting college football game ever—Notre Dame's 24-23 thriller over Alabama Crimson Tide in the 1973 Sugar Bowl classic.

Anecdotes about Ara are many and oft-repeated, as befits a man who represented his university with great dignity and a great sense of humor. The controversy will always rage about whether it is more difficult to spell Parseghian or Presbyterian . . . Students will debate whether he really could stop the rain. And the alumni will chuckle about May 1974 when the Alumni Association named the Miami of Ohio graduate the first honorary Notre Dame Alumnus. It seems Ara considered it a great honor but wondered "why it took most people four years and him ten."

And they will always be proud of the fact that Ara Parseghian chose to devote eleven years of his life to "Our Lady's tough guys," and their university.

ORANGE BOWL '75: ALABAMA

1975 ORANGE BOWL — Notre Dame 13, Alabama 11				
Notre Dame 7	6	0	0 — 13	
Alabama 0	3	0	8 — 11	

Attendance: 71,801 — Weather: Fair, 70 degrees

Team	Score ND-A	Qtr.	Time Left	Play
ND	7-0	1	6:41	Bullock 4 run (Reeve kick)
ND	13-0	2	8:29	McLane 9 run (Reeve kick failed)
Ala	13-3	2	1:45	Ridgeway 21 FG
Ala	13-11	4	3:13	Schamun 48 pass from Todd (Pugh pass from Todd)

The skies were clear over Miami on New Year's Night, although if rumors printed in the *San Francisco Chronicle* were to be believed things had been stormy in the Notre Dame football program for most of the season. But if disharmony existed, it was not in evidence in this year's Orange Bowl. A team effort knocked Alabama out of the national championship by a 13-11 score and sent Ara Parseghian out of the college ranks a winner.

Ron Goodman started the game with Notre Dame's longest kickoff return of the season, advancing 30 yards to the 38. But Wayne Bullock missed a first down by a yard after three consecutive cracks at the line and Tony Brantley shanked a 20-yard punt out of bounds.

As was to be the case most of the evening, the Irish defense shackled the 'Bama attack. Eric Penick picked up a first down on Notre Dame's second possession of the game with an eight-yard burst around left end, but the attack stalled and once again the Irish punted. This time Brantley's punt was in play and the Tide's Willie Shelby fumbled it. Al Samuel came up with the recovery at the Alabama 16.

Three plays later the Irish were faced with a fourth-and-one at the seven. Bullock came up with a big play, powering over the left side for three yards and the first down. On the next play he slid over the other side for the evening's first score. Dave Reeve's extra point gave the Irish a 7-0 lead with less than seven minutes gone. The remainder of the quarter was scoreless as both teams played outstanding defense to go with their own jittery offenses. The Irish took over on their own 23 with fifty seconds left and controlled the ball for 6:31, running off 17 plays on a 77-yard touchdown march. The Irish attempted only one pass on the drive, a nine-yard completion from Clements to Mark McLane. The remainder of the drive was on the ground with McLane and Samuel picking up good yardage on sweeps while Bullock worked the middle. The drive appeared to stall at the 'Bama 28 when a fourth and four confronted Notre Dame. Alabama's Ricky Davis went all out to block the attempted field goal but in the process jumped offside giving the Irish new life. Mark McLane then finished off the resurrection, taking a pitchout 12 yards around the left end. Two plays later he twisted reminiscent of Chubby Checker nine yards for the score off left tackle. Reeve's conversion barely missed to the left and the Irish lead stood at 13-0.

Bullock lost a fumble on Notre Dame's next possession putting the Irish defense on the spot with the Tide just 40 yards from the end zone. 'Bama quarterback Richard Todd hit receivers twice on third down to move the Tide to a first and goal at the eight-yard line. But the Irish defense dug in and Alabama had to settle for Ridgeway's 21-yard field goal. The Irish ran all but eight seconds of the half to take a 13-3 lead into the locker room as a horde of bands, floats, clowns, singers, balloons and stiltwalkers took over the field.

To the casual observer, the scoreless third quarter of the Orange Bowl may have appeared very dull. But to a team that had been outscored 35-0 in their last third period, as the Irish had against Southern Cal, it was welcome fifteen minutes of peace indeed. The Irish frontal defense keyed by Steve Niehaus and Tom Eastman stifled the fabled Alabama rushing attack. Alabama attempted to pass, but their inexperience in aerial football was evident. Unable to take consistent advantage of openings in the Irish secondary, the Tide managed just three first downs in the quarter, all by passing; Notre Dame's offense was also stagnant, converting zero of four as the Irish failed to add to their lead.

Notre Dame took over on their own eight to start the final period and spurred by necessity, the offense surged into life. Samuel picked up twenty yards on a pair of sweeps to spring Notre Dame from the hole and then McLane and Bullock took over. Faced with fourth-and-one at the Alabama 42, the Irish went for it with Bullock. And as usual, Wayne picked up the key yard. Out of gas, the train left the game at this point and his absence was felt when Woodrow Lowe and Mike Turpin stopped another fourth down try on the next series.

Inspired by the defensive play, the Tide put together its first sustained offense of the evening, racking up four first downs in as many plays, three on passes by Todd. The whirlwind attack carried to the Irish 12 but there it abruptly ended when Todd delivered an interception to John Dubenetzky, who returned the ball 16 yards out of danger to the 26.

Four plays later Brantley punted and the Crimson Tide took over on their own 47 with 4:29 left. Todd hit two of his first three passes but only for five yards. On 4th and 5 Steve Schamun ran a simple down-and-out. Randy Payne gambled for an interception and missed, allowing Schamun to catch the pass unimpeded and sprint down the sideline for a 48-yard touchdown. The Tide got the two-point conversion when Willie Pugh made a fantastic diving catch in the end zone. Trailing 13-11, Alabama needed only a field goal to win the na-

tional championship and gain revenge for last year's one point Sugar Bowl loss.

Bullock picked up one first down but Frank Allocco (replacing the injured Clements) was sacked trying to pass and Brantley punted to 'Bama with just under two minutes remaining.

On his first play from the 'Bama 38, Todd picked on the now over-cautious Payne for a 16-yard gain to Schamun. He then came back with an 8-yard completion to Randy Billingsley that put the ball on the Irish 38. On the next play Todd proved him a prophet, throwing an interception which Reggie Barnett claimed. Barnett weaver back and forth across the field with the ball before crashing, like Alabama's title hopes, among the wreckage of the Tide bench.

One minute and eight seconds later, the Era of Ara was over as players and fans carried the victorious coach off the field for the last time with the familiar navy blue jacket on. After the game the now gray-haired cocah preferred to emphasize the team aspect. "I didn't overburden the team with this being my last game. The kids won the game. They played with as much pain and injury as I've ever seen." Kevin Nosbusch, Greg Collins, Mark Brenneman and Wayne Bullock were among those who played with injuries that might well have sidelined them. It was fitting that there were no great individual stars in the game for quite properly the win was Parseghian's.

Alabama	0	3	0	8 — 11
Notre Dame	7	6	0	0 — 13

Scoring:
ND: Bullock, 4-yard run (Reeve kick).
ND: McLane, 9-yard run (Kick no good).
ALA: Ridgeway, 21-yard field goal.
ALA: Todd to Schamun, 48 yards (Two-point attempt good).

NOTRE DAME FOOTBALL STATISTICS
(ELEVEN GAMES)

SCORING BY QUARTERS

Notre Dame	73	101	66	65 —	305
Opponent	37	16	55	28 —	136

TEAM STATISTICS

	ND	OPP
Total Offense	4779	2147
Total Plays	919	693
Yards Per Play	5.2	3.1
Yards Per Game	434.5	195.2
Net Yards Rushing	3119	1131
Attempts	684	488
Yards Per Rush	4.6	2.3
Yards Per Game	283.5	102.8
Net Yards Passing	1660	1016
Attempts	235	205
Completions	132	82
Completion Percentage	.562	.400
Had Intercepted	12	8
Touchdown Passes	9	7
Yards Per Completion	12.6	12.4
Yards Per Attempt	7.1	5.0
Yards Per Game	150.9	92.4
Interceptions Made	8	12
Yards Returned	119	191
Punt Return Yards	173	252
Number of Returns	28	21
Average Return	6.2	12.0
Kickoff Return Yards	408	918
Number of Returns	25	44
Average Return	16.3	20.9
Total Return Yards	292	443
Average Punt	38.8	39.5
Number of Punts	49	82
Yards Punting	1903	3238
Had Blocked	1	0
Penalties Against	58	45
Yards Penalized	577	382
Fumbles (Lost)	24(18)	23(15)
Total First Downs	273	133
by rushing	175	76
by passing	87	50
by penalty	11	7

INDIVIDUAL TOTAL OFFENSE LEADERS

	G	Plays	Yards	Avg.
Clements	11	310	1918	6.2
Bullock	10	203	855	4.2
Samuel	11	96	525	5.5

RESULTS ... Won 9, Lost 2, Tied 0

ND		OPP	Attendance
31	at Georgia Tech	7	45,228
49	at Northwestern	3	55,000(c)
20	PURDUE	31	59,075(c)
19	at Michigan St.	14	77,431(c)
10	RICE	3	59,075(c)
48	ARMY	0	59,075(c)
38	MIAMI	7	59,075(c)
14	at Navy	6	48,634
14	PITTSBURGH	10	59,075(c)
38	AIR FORCE	0	59,075(c)
24	at Southern Cal	55	83,552
Jan. 1—Alabama (Orange Bowl)			

INDIVIDUAL PUNTING

	G	No.	Yds.	Avg.	Long
Brantley	11	48	1903	39.6	69
Team (Blocked)		1	0	0.0	0
Notre Dame	11	49	1903	38.8	69
Opponents	11	82	3238	39.5	65

PASS RECEIVING

	G	PC	Yds.	Avg.	TD	Long
Demmerle	10	43	667	15.5	6	47
Weber	8	13	206	15.8	1	28
Samuel	11	14	134	9.6	0	17
Goodman	11	14	149	10.6	0	21
Bullock	10	11	103	9.4	0	17
MacAfee	10	14	146	10.4	1	24
Doherty	5	4	59	14.8	1	25
Kornman	7	6	57	9.5	0	17
Best	7	3	54	18.0	0	27
McLane	8	5	56	11.2	0	16
Weiler	11	3	21	7.0	0	10
Eurick	7	1	6	6.0	0	6
Penick	4	1	2	2.0	0	2
Notre Dame	11	132	1660	12.6	9	47
Opponents	11	82	1016	12.4	7	29

TEAM SCORING

	ND	OPP
Total Points	305	136
Average	27.7	12.4
Touchdowns	41	17
by rushing	30	7
by passing	9	7
by return	2	3
by recovery	0	0
Field Goals (Made-Att.)	7-10	6-14
Safeties	0	0
PAT — Kick	38-40	14-15
PAT — Run	0-0	1-2
PAT — Pass	0-0	0-0

PASSING

	G	No.	Comp.	Pct.	Int.	Yds.	TD
Clements	11	215	122	.567	11	1549	8
Allocco	11	10	7	.700	1	72	1
Slager	4	8	3	.375	0	39	0
Goodman	11	1	0	.000	0	0	0
Samuel	11	1	0	.000	0	0	0
Notre Dame	11	235	132	.562	12	1660	9
Opponents	11	205	82	.400	8	1016	7

RUSHING

	G	TC	Yds.	Avg.	TD	Long
Bullock	10	203	855	4.2	12	16
Samuel	11	95	525	5.5	2	35
Clements	11	95	369	3.9	4	35
Best	7	51	241	4.7	0	29
McLane	8	42	207	4.9	2	16
Parise	9	40	207	5.2	1	62
Goodman	11	25	144	5.8	1	62
Weiler	11	30	133	4.4	0	15
Eurick	7	19	131	6.9	1	28
Kornman	7	25	99	4.0	4	13
Slager	4	12	82	6.8	0	17
Allocco	11	17	36	2.1	2	12
Parseghian	3	7	32	4.6	0	12
Bake	2	5	23	4.6	1	9
Penick	4	12	14	1.2	0	9
Doherty	5	2	9	4.5	0	7
Rufo	2	2	8	4.0	0	4
Kelly	1	1	3	3.0	0	3
Moriarty	1	1	1	1.0	0	1
Notre Dame	11	684	3119	4.6	30	62
Opponents	11	488	1131	2.3	7	52

RETURNS

	Interceptions	Punts	Kickoffs
Bullock			1- 7
Goodman		15-80	5- 81
Samuel			8-150
Barnett	1-0		
Harrison	2-84-2	6-42	
Payne	2-19		
Burgmeier		6-46	3- 52
Dubenetzky	2-16		
Best			1- 15
Chauncey		1-5	
Mahalic	1-0 -		
McLane			6- 95
Weiler			1- 8
Notre Dame	8-119-2	28-173	25-408-0
Opponents	12-191-2	21-252	44-918-1

INDIVIDUAL SCORING

	G	TD	Kick	R-PA	FG	TP
Bullock	10	12				72
Reeve	11	0	38-40	*7-10		59
Demmerle	10	6				36
Kornman	7	4				24
Clements	11	4				24
Samuel	11	2				12
Harrison	11	2				12
Allocco	11	2				12
McLane	8	2				12
Goodman	11	1				6
Weber	8	1				6
Eurick	7	1				6
Bake	2	1				6
MacAfee	10	1				6
Parise	9	1				6
Doherty	5	1				6
Notre Dame	11	41	38-40	0-0	7-10	305
Opponents	11	17	14-15	1-0	6-14	136

*22 yards vs. Georgia Tech
38 and 32 yards vs. Michigan State
45 yards vs. Rice
28 yards vs. Miami
33 yards vs. Air Force
20 yards vs. Southern Cal

DEFENSIVE STATISTICS

	*TM	TL-Yds.	PBU	FR	BK
Collins	144	6-22	0	1	0
Mahalic	117	6-27	4	1	0
Niehaus	95	13-82	2	1	0
Fanning	85	12-52	1	1	0
Nosbusch	76	9-40	0	1	1
Stock	76	19-120	2	3	0
Harrison	57	1-3	7	1	0
Dubenetzky	56	6-12	4	1	0
Russell	52	1-2	1	0	0
Eastman	43	2-12	0	0	0
Payne	40	3-12	6	1	0
Barnett	37	3-10	9	0	0
Weston	3i	2-22	0	0	0
Novakov	19	0-0	1	0	0
Lopienski	18	0-0	2	0	0
Becker	12	1-19	0	2	0
Johnson	11	1-12	1	0	0
Zappala	7	2-12	0	0	0
Burgmeier	6	0-0	0	0	0
Wujciak	5	0-0	0	0	0
S. Smith	4	1-2	0	0	0
Hughes	4	0-0	0	0	0
Achterhoff	4	1-3	1	0	0
Pszeracki	3	0-0	0	0	0
Banks	3	0-0	1	1	0
Carney	3	0-0	0	0	0
Reeve	2	0-0	0	0	0
Cullins	2	0-0	0	0	0
Galanis	2	1-13	0	0	0
Demmerle	1	0-0	0	0	0
Bullock	1	0-0	0	0	0
Brenneman	1	0-0	0	0	0
Best	1	0-0	0	0	0
Rohan	1	0-0	0	0	0
Chauncey	1	0-0	0	0	0
Arment	0	0-0	1	0	0
Parise	1	0-0	0	0	0
DiNardo	1	0-0	0	0	0
Sylvester	1	0-0	0	0	0
Eurick	1	0-0	0	0	0
Laney	1	0-0	0	0	0
Notre Dame	1025	90-477	43	14	1
Opponents	1108	45-132	24	18	1

*TM — Includes solos and assists

DAN DEVINE
HEAD FOOTBALL COACH

		1975			
		Coach: Dan Devine			
		Co-Captains: Ed Bauer and Jim Stock			
S.15	W	Boston College	17-3	N	c61,501
S.20	W	Purdue	17-0	A	c69,795
S.27	W	Northwestern	31-7	H	c59,075
O.4	L	Michigan State (3:50)	3-10	H	c59,075
O.11	W	No. Carolina (1:03)	21-14	A	c49,500
O.18	W	Air Force (3:23)	31-30	A	43,204
O.25	L	Southern Cal	17-24	H	c59,075
N.1	W	Navy (R)	31-10	H	c59,075
N.8	W	Georgia Tech	24-3	H	c59,075
N.15	L	Pittsburgh (U)	20-34	A	c56,480
N.22	W	Miami (Fla.) (Nt)	32-9	A	24,944
		(8-3-0)	244-144		600,799
N—at Foxboro					

UPI POLL

1975
1. Oklahoma
2. Arizona State
3. Alabama
4. Ohio State
5. UCLA
6. Arkansas
7. Texas
8. Michigan
9. Nebraska
10. Penn State
17. NOTRE DAME (tie)

Dan Devine knows what it's like to follow legends. He did it at Missouri with Don Faurot, Green Bay with Vince Lombardi and now Notre Dame with Ara Parseghian. This last act may have been the toughest because he inherited just six starters from 1974—and only one on offense. But he was able to mold a youthful unit that finished 8-3 against the toughest schedule in years. Along the way his squad came up with two of the greatest comeback wins in Notre Dame history (North Carolina and Air Force) and wound up 17th in the final UPI poll.

When Ara Parseghian resigned his post as head football coach, Notre Dame athletic officials sought a man with a winning tradition equal to the school's outstanding football heritage. Dan Devine, former coach and general manager of the tradition-rich Green Bay Packers, certainly has those qualifications.

Devine, Notre Dame's 23rd coach in 87 seasons, has a collegiate record of 128-43—compiled at Arizona State, Missouri and Notre Dame—which ranks him among the 30 winningest major college coaches of all time.

An intense, thoroughgoing fundamentalist, Devine launched an imposing success pattern in his very first coaching assignment, at little East Jordan (Michigan) High School, where his 1948 team went undefeated.

He continued it during 16 years as a collegiate head coach, a span in which he compiled the nation's third highest winning percentage, and enhanced his stature upon entering the pro ranks in 1971.

In only his second season he led the Packers to a 10-4 record and the National Football Conference's Central Division championship in 1972, Green Bay's first division title since 1967.

That accomplishment brought him NFC "Coach of the Year" recognition from the Pro Football Writers' Association of America and United Press International, as well as a salute from Pro Football News as its "Man of the Year." He is the third winningest coach in Packer history with a 25-27-4 record.

The 51-year-old Wisconsin native may have been best depicted by Andy Russell, one of the many collegiate stars he developed, who now is the all-pro defensive captain of the Pittsburgh Steelers. Of him he said, "He looks like a college professor, but there's steel inside that mild-mannered exterior."

NOTRE DAME

79	Achterhoff, Jay	DT, 6-4, 248
	Senior	Muskegon, Mich.
12	Allocco, Frank	QB, 6-1, 176
	Senior	New Providence, N.J.
56	Andler, Ken	C, 6-6, 238
	Senior	Cleveland, Ohio
63	Balliet, Cal	OG, 6-4, 225
	Senior	Moorestown, N.J.
17	Banks, Mike	SS, 6-2, 194
	Junior	Youngstown, Ohio
68	Bauer, Ed (Capt.)	OT, 6-3, 248
	Senior	Cincinnati, Ohio
43	Becker, Doug	OLB, 6-0, 220
	Sophomore	Hamilton, Ohio
44	Bonder, Frank	FB, 6-1, 199
	Junior	Niles, Ohio
20	Bradley, Luther	CB, 6-2, 198
	Sophomore	Muncie, Ind.
4	Brantley, Tony	P, 6-0, 200
	Senior	Oklahoma City, Okla.
46	Brown, Ivan	DE, 6-3, 221
	Senior	LeRoy, Ill.
33	Browner, Jim	FB, 6-3, 207
	Freshman	Warren, Ohio
89	Browner, Ross	DE, 6-3, 235
	Sophomore	Warren, Ohio
61	Buck, Dave	OT, 6-5, 234
	Junior	Austin, Tex.
18	Burgmeier, Ted	SE-CB, 5-11, 179
	Sophomore	E. Dubuque, Ill.
83	Buth, Doug	TE, 6-5, 228
	Junior	Green Bay, Wis.
73	Calhoun, Mike	DT, 6-5, 241
	Freshman	Youngstown, Ohio
64	Carney, Mike	OG, 6-2, 215
	Sophomore	LaMirada, Calif.
61	Case, Jay	DE, 6-3, 225
	Freshman	Cincinnati, Ohio
29	Christensen, Ross	FS, 6-1, 190
	Sophomore	Racine, Wis.
84	Crews, Ron	DE, 6-4, 223
	Freshman	Columbia, Mo.
23	Cullins, Ron	CB, 6-0, 190
	Sophomore	Warren, Ohio
24	DeCicco, Nick	OLB, 5-10, 188
	Sophomore	South Bend, Ind.
72	Dike, Ken	DT, 6-2, 235
	Sophomore	Crown Point, Ind.
32	Doherty, Kevin	SE, 6-0, 178
	Senior	Portland, Ore.
87	Driscoll, John	TE, 6-1, 219
	Sophomore	Cincinnati, Ohio
41	Dubenetzky, John	SS, 6-5, 213
	Junior	Hobart, Ind.
42	Eastman, Tom	MLB, 6-1, 229
	Junior	Elkhart, Ind.
40	Eurick, Terry	HB, 5-10, 190
	Sophomore	Saginaw, Mich.
76	Fedorenko, Nick	DT, 6-5, 257
	Senior	Chicago, Ill.
8	Forystek, Gary	QB, 6-2, 202
	Sophomore	Livonia, Mich.
94	Fry, Willie	DE, 6-3, 226
	Sophomore	Memphis, Tenn.
96	Galanis, John	DE, 6-4, 245
	Senior	Ipswich, Mass.
55	Golic, Bob	MLB, 6-3, 240
	Freshman	Cleveland, Ohio
69	Gullickson, Tom	DT, 6-2, 243
	Junior	Joliet, Ill.
82	Haines, Kris	SE, 6-0, 174
	Freshman	Sidney, Ohio
50	Harchar, John	OLB, 6-3, 220
	Junior	Jefferson Boro, Pa.
37	Harris, Kenny	SE, 6-1, 190
	Sophomore	Gary, Ind.
10	Harrison, Randy	FS, 6-1, 206
	Sophomore	Hammond, Ind.
30	Heavens, Jerome	FB, 6-0, 203
	Freshman	E. St. Louis, Ill.
58	Heimkrieter, Steve	OLB, 6-2, 216
	Freshman	Cincinnati, Ohio
86	Heitzman, Tim	TE, 6-1, 186
	Freshman	Cincinnati, Ohio
62	Huffman, Dave	OT, 6-5, 228
	Freshman	Dallas, Tex.
65	Hughes, Ernie	OG, 6-3, 237
	Sophomore	Boise, Ida.
25	Hunter, Al	HB, 5-11, 191
	Sophomore	Greenville, N.C.
51	Johnson, Pete	OLB-TE, 6-4, 221
	Sophomore	Fond du Lac, Wis.
85	Kafka, Mike	TE-OG, 6-3, 224
	Junior	Antigo, Wis.

80	Kelleher, Dan	SE, 5-11, 183
	Junior	Ellensburg, Wash.
52	Klees, Vince	C, 6-4, 236
	Junior	Costa Mesa, Calif.
21	Knott, Dan	HB, 6-1, 197
	Sophomore	Chowchilla, Calif.
53	Likovich, John	OLB, 6-2, 211
	Junior	Phoenix, Ariz.
26	Lopienski, Tom	CB, 6-1, 176
	Senior	Akron, Ohio
81	MacAfee, Ken	TE, 6-4, 251
	Sophomore	Brockton, Mass.
91	Malinak, Don	DE, 6-4, 204
	Junior	Flemington, Pa.
31	Maschmeier, Tom	CB, 5-11, 180
	Senior	Cincinnati, Ohio
71	McDaniels, Steve	OT, 6-6, 264
	Sophomore	Seattle, Wash.
22	McLane, Mark	HB, 6-1, 204
	Junior	Wilmington, Del.
99	McLaughlin, Pat	K, 6-0, 225
	Senior	Santa Barbara, Calif.
60	Meyer, Howard	OG, 6-3, 219
	Freshman	San Jose, Calif.
3	Montana, Joe	QB, 6-2, 184
	Sophomore	Monongahela, Pa.
57	Moore, Elton	OG, 6-1, 230
	Junior	Portland, Ore.
70	Niehaus, Steve	DT, 6-5, 270
	Senior	Cincinnati, Ohio
38	Novakov, Tony	OLB, 5-11, 200
	Senior	Cincinnati, Ohio
14	Orsini, Steve	FB, 5-10, 199
	Sophomore	Hummelstown, Pa.
36	Parise, Tom	FB, 6-0, 211
	Senior	Longmont, Colo.
88	Pattillo, Reynold	OG, 6-1, 227
	Sophomore	Los Angeles, Calif.
16	Payne, Randy	CB, 5-9, 170
	Senior	Palmer Park, Md.
67	Pohlen, Pat	OT, 6-4, 242
	Senior	Downey, Calif.
47	Pszeracki, Joe	MLB, 5-11, 212
	Senior	Ambridge, Pa.
77	Quehl, Steve	C, 6-4, 241
	Senior	Cincinnati, Ohio
13	Reeve, Dave	K, 6-3, 198
	Sophomore	Bloomington, Ind.
7	Restic, Joe	P-QB, 6-2, 175
	Freshman	Milford, Mass.
93	Rodenkirk, Don	DT, 6-4, 248
	Junior	Milwaukee, Wis.
45	Ruettiger, Dan	DE, 5-8, 185
	Senior	Joliet, Ill.
9	Rufo, John	HB, 5-11, 194
	Junior	Lansdowne, Pa.
54	Russell, Marv	MLB, 6-0, 225
	Junior	Ford City, Pa.
86	Rutkowski, Frank	DT, 6-4, 220
	Senior	Middletown, Del.
28	Sarb, Pat	CB, 6-0, 176
	Senior	Dearborn, Mich.
19	Schmitz, Steve	HB, 5-11, 185
	Sophomore	Lakewood, Ohio
59	Sharkey, Ed	C, 6-3, 242
	Junior	Renton, Wash.
27	Simon, Tim	FS, 5-10, 170
	Senior	Pontiac, Mich.
11	Slager, Rick	QB, 5-11, 188
	Senior	Columbus, Ohio
90	Smith, Gene	OLB, 6-2, 215
	Junior	Cleveland, Ohio
23	Soutner, John	SS, 6-2, 189
	Junior	Steelton, Pa.
48	Stock, Jim (Capt.)	OLB, 6-3, 215
	Senior	Barberton, Ohio
50	Tull, Bob	OT, 6-3, 234
	Sophomore	South Bend, Ind.
59	Vinson, Dave	MLB, 6-2, 224
	Sophomore	Liberty, Tex.
85	Walls, Bob	SE, 5-11, 166
	Senior	Cohasset, Mass.
35	Weiler, Jim	HB, 6-2, 200
	Junior	Cleveland Hgts., Ohio
74	Weston, Jeff	DT, 6-3, 255
	Sophomore	Rochester, N.Y.
78	Woebkenberg, Harry	OT, 6-2, 260
	Sophomore	Cincinnati, Ohio
66	Wujciak, Al	OG, 6-2, 232
	Senior	Newark, N.J.
34	Zanot, Bob	CB, 6-0, 182
	Senior	Riverton, Ill.
39	Zappala, Tony	DE, 6-0, 209
	Junior	Elmwood Park, N.J.

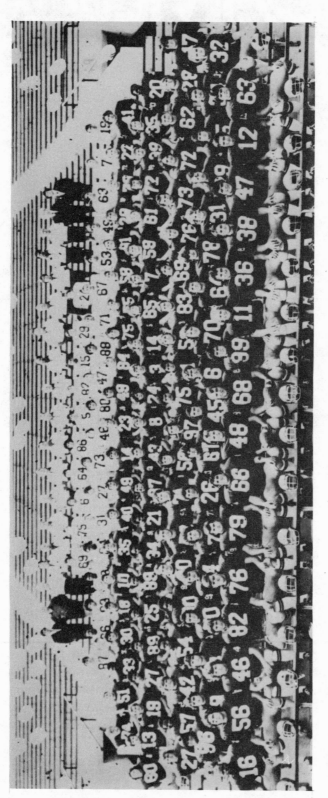

THE 1975-76 NOTRE DAME FOOTBALL TEAM: **Back Row:** D. Hadley, J. Whitmer, G. O'Neill, D. Novakov, R. Stevenson, E. Chlebek, P. Shoults, M. Johnson, G. Kelly, Dan Devine, (head coach), J. Yonto, J. Roland, B. Boulac, H. Kuhlmann, S. Bossu, G. Blache, G. Paszkiet, M. Navarre, D. Dempsvey. **Second Row:** M. Calhoun, J. Case, J. Pasazola, D. Huffman, A. Alvarado, R. Lisch, K. Haines, V. Rachal, S. Dover, P. Pallas. **Third Row:** D. Grindinger, J. Heavens, C. McPherson, J. Browner, R. Crews, P. Johnson, T. Domin, J. Hager, S. Heimkrieter, T. Heitzman, D. Hughes, K. Hart, B. Golic, T. Horansky, L. Graziani, H. Meyer, J. Hautman, J. Restic, T. Flynn. **Fourth Row:** J. Weston, P. Johnson, R. Cullins, A. Bucci, T. Burgmeier, R. Harrison, J. Weiler, T. Eurick, S. Bobowski, T. Unis, J. Soutner, E. Gleckler, D. Malinak, T. Frericks, T. Murphy, B. Tull, K. MacAfee, K. Uniacke, H. Woebkenberg, M. McLane, J. Dubenetzky. **Fifth Row:** J. Driscoll, D.

Reeve, S. Schmitz, K. Harris, R. Pattillo, A. Hunter, R. Browner, W. Fry, D. Knott, R. Allocco, D. Becker, G. Forstek, N. DeCicco, J. Montana, S. Orsini, E. Hughes, M. Falash, D. Vinson, D. Buck, K. Dike, T. Zappala, T. Leary, L. Bradley. **Sixth Row:** T. Simon, E. Moore, T. Eastman, M. Russell, G. Smith, D. Kelleher, V. Klees, S. McDaniels, A. McMurry, B. Adams, B. Duncan, K. Moriarty, J. Likovich, D. Buth, T. Gullickson, M. Ewald, D. Rodenkirk, E. Sharkey, M. Kafka, R. Christenson, M. Banks. **Seventh Row:** J. Galanis, J. Rufo, T. Brantley, J. Harchar, F. Bonder, S. Quehl, T. Lopienski, P. Pohlen, D. Ruettiger, F. McDonald, S. Niehaus, M. Carney, F. Rutkowski, T. Maschmeier, P. Sarb, R. Kornman, B. Zanot, K. Doherty. **Bottom Row:** R. Payne, K. Andler, I. Brown, B. Walls, N. Fedorenko, J. Achterhoff, A. Wujiak, J. Stock, E. Bauer, P. McLaughlin, R. Slager, T. Parise, T. Novakov, J. Pszeracki, F. Allocco, C. Balliet.

EDWARD W. KRAUSE
Athletic Director

Michigan State Upsets Irish, 10-3;
Long Run Sets Up Spartan Victory

By The Associated Press

SOUTH BEND, Ind., Oct. 4 —Tyrone Wilson's 76-yard burst set up Levi Jackson's 4-yard touchdown run with 3 minutes 50 seconds left, as Michigan State upset eighth-ranked Notre Dame, 10-3, today.

The quick, two-play scoring strike came 23 seconds after Dave Reeve's 35-yard field goal had tied the score for the Irish.

It was Notre Dame's first defeat in four games under Coach Dan Devine and the first time in 49 games the Irish had failed to score a touchdown.

Michigan State, a one-touchdown underdog, won its third in a row after dropping its opener.

Notre Dame did everything but score in the first half. The error-plagued Irish wasted four opportunities, lost two fumbles early in the third quarter and the momentum slowly swung to State.

Hans Nielsen, a native of Denmark, gave State a 3-0 lead with a 37-yard field goal 12 seconds before the end of the third period. It came after the Spartans had **driven from the Notre Dame 49 to the 21 following a punt.**

Jackson contributed a key 14-yard run around left end, and later cracked the left side for 6 and a crucial first down at the 22.

With five minutes left in the game, Notre Dame, which started from its 45, had a first down at State's 5. Three plays lost 13 yards against the swarming State defense and the Irish were forced to settle for Reeve's field goal.

Wilson returned the ensuing kickoff 13 yards to his 20. On the first play, he bolted through the right side and raced to the Notre Dame 4, where Luther Bradley hauled him down.

Jackson then took a pitchout to the right and dived into the end zone just inside the flag.

Notre Dame lost three of six fumbles and suffered two interceptions. The final blow came when Kim Rowekamp intercepted Rick Slager's pass at the State 32 with 1:36 remaining after the Irish had moved from their 18 to the Spartans' 45.

Despite good field position on five of their six possessions in the first half, the Irish were frustrated on a fourth-down gamble that failed at the State 22, an end-zone interception, a missed field goal attempt and a fumble at the Spartan 23.

While Notre Dame was threatening continuously, Michigan State mounted only one serious drive in the first half, going from their 23 to the Irish 20. But a 38-yard field-goal effort was wide with 53 seconds left.

Wilson's stunning 76-yard run allowed the Spartans, who failed to complete any of their four passes, to outrush Notre Dame, 241 yards to 195.

	Michigan State	Notre Dame
Michigan State	0 0 3 7—10	
Notre Dame	0 0 0 3— 3	

M.S.U.—FG, Nielsen, 37.
N.D.—FG, Reeve, 35.
M.S.U.—Jackson, 4, run (Nielsen, kick).
A—59,075.
Attendance—59,075.

STATISTICS OF THE GAME

	Mich. St.	N.D.
First downs	11	17
Rushing yardage	54-241	53-105
Passing yardage	0	123
Passes	0-4	9-18
Interceptions by	2	1
Punts	6-37	4-36
Fumbles lost	2	3
Yards penalized	0	10

Notre Dame 17, Purdue 0

WEST LAFAYETTE. Ind., Sept. 20 (AP)—Notre Dame's Luther Bradley, returning after a year's suspension, intercepted two passes today and returned one 99 yards for a touchdown as the Irish swamped Purdue, 17-0, in a nonconference football contest.

The ninth-ranked Irish, was held to Dave Reeve's 29-yard field goal through the first three quarters before breaking it open when Bradley ended the Boilermakers best scoring threat of the game.

Notre Dame	3 0 0 14—17
Purdue	0 0 0 0— 0

FG, Reeve, 29.
Bradley, 99, return of interception (Reeve, kick).
Hunter, 1, run (Reeve, kick).
Attendance—69,795.

STATISTICS OF THE GAME

	Notre Dame	Purdue
First downs	19	11
Rushing yardage	58-238	35-66
Passing yardage	53	134
Passes	4-12	13-24
Interceptions by	3	1
Punts	5-39	7-38
Fumbles lost	1	0
Yards penalized	54	37

Notre Dame, 31-30

AIR FORCE ACADEMY.
Colo. (AP) — Halfback Al
Hunter ran 43 yards to set up
Notre Dame's winning
touchdown Saturday as the 15-
ranked Irish survived a
determined challenge by
inspired Air Force in a 31-30
college football victory.

Hunter's run, to the Air
Force 2-yard line with just
over four minutes to go, came
after a 28-yard Air Force punt
that gave Notre Dame the ball
at the Falcon 45.

Devine Supported
By Irish Players

MIAMI, Nov. 21 (AP)—Notre Dame's 48-man travel-
ing football squad gave a vote of confidence tonight to
Coach Dan Devine on the eve of its game with the
University of Miami in the Orange Bowl.

Roger Valdiserri, sports information director for the
Irish, said Ed Bauer, a co-captain, handed him a slip of
paper during a practice session and told him, "I would
like you to handle this. Nobody knows anything about
this except the players."

Valdiserri said he showed the note to Devine, who
was visibly moved.

The note said:

"With an effort to clarify certain issues raised recently by elements of the media, the following members of
the Notre Dame football team wish to convey their un-
qualified support for Dan Devine and his entire staff
and the operation of the 1975 football season."

It was signed by the entire traveling squad.

Devine had admitted concern during the week about
reports of team dissension after last Saturday's 34-20
loss to Pittsburgh, in which the Panthers' Tony Dorsett
gained 303 yards. The defeat made Notre Dame's won-
lost record, 7-3.

Statistics of the Game

	notre Dame	Miami
First downs	16	14
Rushes-yards	49-191	50-78
Passing yards	104	174
Return yards	34	108
Passes	10-23-2	7-21-0
Punts	9-41	4-41
Fumbles lost	0-0	4-3
Penalties-yards	3-35	1-31

Notre Dame	3	16	0	13—32
Miami	3	0	6	0— 9

ND—FG Reeve 26
Mia—FG Dennis 29
ND—Heavens 2 run (Reeve kick)
ND—Safety Archer tackled end zone
ND—MacAfee 3 pass from Stager
(Reeve kick)
Mia—Cain 38 pass from Baker (run
failed)
ND—Hunter 4 run (kick failed)
ND—MacAfee 10 pass from Restic
(Reeve kick)
A—24,944

Notre Dame Vanquishes
Fumbling Miami by 32-9

1975 NOTRE DAME FOOTBALL STATISTICS
(ELEVEN GAMES)

SCORING BY QUARTERS

Notre Dame	43	60	31	110	— 244
Opponent	27	33	57	27	— 144

TEAM STATISTICS

	ND	OPP
Total Offense	3586	2971
Total Plays	780	729
Yards Per Play	4.6	4.1
Yards Per Game	326.0	270.1
Net Yards Rushing	2400	1889
Attempts	569	543
Yards Per Rush	4.2	3.5
Yards Per Game	218.2	171.7
Net Yards Passing	1186	1082
Completion Percentage	.455	.440
Attempts	211	186
Completions	96	82
Had Intercepted	12	13
Touchdown Passes	7	6
Yards Per Completion	12.4	13.2
Yards Per Attempt	5.6	5.8
Yards Per Game	107.8	98.4
Interceptions Made	13	12
Yards Returned	297	106
Punt Return Yards	196	242
Number of Returns	31	33
Average Return	6.3	7.3
Kickoff Return Yards	772	508
Number of Returns	29	34
Average Return	26.6	14.9
Total Return Yards	493	367
Average Punt	41.3	38.7
Number of Punts	64	78
Yards Punting	2640	3020
Had Blocked	1	3
Penalties Against	43	39
Yards Penalized	408	378
Fumbles (Lost)	28 (18)	31 (16)
Yards Returned	0	19
Total First Downs	182	162
by rushing	118	107
by passing	57	46
by penalty	7	9

INDIVIDUAL TOTAL OFFENSE LEADERS

	G	Plays	Yards	Avg.
Heavens	10	129	756	5.9
Slager	10	190	713	3.8
Hunter	10	117	558	4.8

RESULTS . . . Won 8, Lost 3, Tied 0

ND		OPP	Attendance
17	at Boston College	3	61,501 (c)
17	at Purdue	0	69,795 (c)
31	NORTHWESTERN	7	59,075 (c)
3	MICHIGAN STATE	10	59,075 (c)
21	at North Carolina	14	49,500 (c)
31	at Air Force	30	43,204
17	SOUTHERN CAL	24	59,075 (c)
31	NAVY	10	59,075 (c)
24	GEORGIA TECH	3	59,075 (c)
20	at Pittsburgh	34	56,480 (c)
32	at Miami (Fla.)	9	24,944

PUNTING

	G	No.	Yds.	Avg.	Long
Restic	6	40	1739	43.5	61
Brantley	5	23	901	39.2	52
Team	1	1	0	0.0	0
Notre Dame	11	64	2640	41.3	61
Opponents	11	78	3020	38.7	57

TEAM SCORING

	ND	OPP
Total Points	244	144
Average	22.2	13.1
Touchdowns	30	16
by rushing	19	10
by passing	7	6
by return	4	0
by recovery	0	0
Field Goals (Made-Att.)	11-18	11-21
Safeties	1	0
PAT—Kick	25-27	15-15
PAT—Run	0	0-1
PAT—Pass	2-3	0

PASS RECEIVING

	G	PC	Yds.	Avg.	TD	Long
MacAfee	11	26	333	12.8	5	29
McLane	11	21	277	13.2	1	66
Burgmeier	9	10	185	18.5	1	80
Kelleher	11	12	171	14.3	0	39
Hunter	10	10	87	8.7	0	28
Heavens	11	8	64	8.0	0	20
Eurick	10	3	30	10.0	0	17
J. Browner	9	2	16	8.0	0	12
Huffman	6	1	16	16.0	0	16
Schmitz	2	1	9	9.0	0	9
Weiler	11	2	-2	-1.0	0	15
Notre Dame	11	96	1186	12.4	7	80
Opponents	11	82	1082	13.2	6	62

PASSING

	G	No.	Comp.	Pct.	Int.	Yds.	TD
Slager	10	139	66	.475	3	686	2
Montana	7	66	28	.424	8	507	4
Restic	6	1	1	1.000	0	10	1
Allocco	6	2	0	.000	1	0	0
Forystek	1	1	0	.000	0	0	0
Brantley	5	1	1	1.000	0	-17	0
Burgmeier	9	1	0	.000	0	0	0
Notre Dame	11	211	96	.455	12	1186	7
Opponents	11	186	82	.440	13	1082	6

RUSHING

	G	TC	Yds.	Avg.	TD	Long
Heavens	11	129	756	5.9	5	73
Hunter	10	117	558	4.8	8	52
J. Browner	9	104	394	3.9	2	18
McLane	11	54	228	4.2	0	41
Eurick	10	36	154	4.3	0	15
Orsini	10	28	95	3.4	0	9
Burgmeier	9	1	50	50.0	0	50
Weiler	11	9	46	5.1	0	15
Knott	8	9	46	5.1	1	10
Haines	8	1	28	28.0	0	28
Slager	10	51	27	0.5	1	10
Schmitz	2	1	9	9.0	0	9
Allocco	6	3	8	2.7	0	4
Kornman	1	1	6	6.0	0	6
Montana	7	25	-5	-0.2	2	9
Notre Dame	11	569	2400	4.2	19	73
Opponents	11	543	1889	3.5	10	76

RETURNS

	Interceptions	Punts	Kickoffs
Harrison	1- 7-0	2- 11-0	
Burgmeier		9- 52-0	
Bradley	4-135-1	1- 18-0	
Lopienski	4- 79-0	1- 19-1	
MacAfee			1- 0-0
Simon	1- 0-0	15- 61-0	
Eurick			13-347-0
Haines		1- 3-0	
Christensen		1- 5-0	
Hunter			5-141-0
Knott			10-284-0
Dubenetzky	1- 0-0		
R. Browner		1- 27-1	
Eastman	1- 23-0		
Weston	1- 53-1		
Notre Dame	13-297-2	31-196-2	29-772-0
Opponents	12-106-0	33-242-0	34-508-0

SCORING

	G	TD	PAT	S	R-PA	FG	TP
Reeve	10	0	24-26			11-16*	57
Hunter	10	8					48
Heavens	11	5					30
MacAfee	11	5					30
Montana	7	2					12
J. Browner	9	2					12
R. Browner	10	1		1			8
Bradley	11	1					6
McLane	11	1					6
Burgmeier	9	1					6
Lopienski	11	1					6
Weston	11	1					6
Knott	8	1					6
Slager	10	1					6
Buth	7	0			0-1		2
Haines	8	0			0-1		2
McLaughlin	7	0	1-1			0-2	1
Notre Dame	11	30	25-27	1	0-2	11-18	244
Opponents	11	16	15-15	0	0-0	11-21	144

*30 yards vs. Boston College
29 yards vs. Purdue
44 yards vs. Northwestern
35 yards vs. Michigan State
31 yards vs. Air Force
27 yards vs. Southern Cal
35 yards vs. Navy
29 yards vs. Georgia Tech
48 and 47 yards vs. Pittsburgh
26 yards vs. Miami

DEFENSIVE STATISTICS

	*TM	TL-Yds.	PBU	FR	BK
Niehaus	113	7-20	0	0	0
Weston	101	9-61	0	1	0
Stock	84	2-12	1	0	0
Golic	82	2-13	0	0	0
Fry	78	14-100	0	2	1
Becker	72	4-8	1	3	0
R. Browner	71	16-78	2	4	1
Banks	61	3-8	3	0	1
Bradley	56	2-5	2	0	0
Harrison	54	1-2	2	0	0
Johnson	49	0-0	0	0	0
Lopienski	49	3-15	2	0	3
Dubenetzky	48	0-0	1	1	0
Achterhoff	27	2-9	0	1	0
Eastman	26	1-3	0	0	0
Likovich	23	0-0	2	0	0
Heimkrieter	22	0-0	0	1	0
Simon	20	0-0	0	0	0
Zappala	16	1-10	0	1	0
Orsini	10	0-0	0	1	0
Galanis	7	2-25	0	0	0
Cullins	6	0-0	0	0	0
Meyer	5	0-0	0	0	0
Maschmeier	5	0-0	1	0	0
McLane	4	0-0	0	0	0
Burgmeier	4	1-3	0	0	0
Christensen	4	0-0	0	0	0
Hughes	4	0-0	0	1	0
Knott	3	0-0	0	0	0
Weiler	3	0-0	0	0	0
Carney	2	0-0	0	0	0
J. Browner	2	0-0	0	0	0
Russell	1	1-1	0	0	0
Heavens	1	0-0	0	0	0
Ruettiger	1	1-5	0	0	0
Fedorenko	1	0-0	0	0	0
Notre Dame	1115	72-378	17	16	6
Opponents	1046	41-178	23	18	2

*Includes solos and assists

1976 NOTRE DAME VARSITY ROSTER
ALPHABETICAL

NO.	PLAYER	POS.	HT.	WT.	CL.
12	Allocco, Rich	HB	6-2	196	Sr.
15	Alvarado, Art	CB	6-2	202	So.
17	*Banks, Mike	SS	6-2	199	Sr.
43	**Becker, Doug	LB	6-0	231	Jr.
	Bobowski, Stan	CB	6-0	185	Sr.
47	Bonder, Frank	FB	6-1	194	Sr.
20	**Bradley, Luther	CB	6-2	202	Jr.
33	*Browner, Jim	SS-FB	6-3	214	So.
89	**Browner, Ross	DE	6-3	248	Jr.
72	Buck, Dave	OT	6-5	216	Sr.
18	**Burgmeier, Ted	CB-WR	5-11	189	Jr.
83	*Buth, Doug	TE	6-5	228	Sr.
77	Calhoun, Mike	DT	6-5	235	So.
64	*Carney, Mike	OG	6-2	226	Jr.
75	Case, Jay	DT	6-3	239	So.
28	Christensen, Ross	SS	6-1	195	Jr.
95	Crews, Ron	DE	6-4	222	So.
49	DeCicco, Nick	LB	5-10	196	Jr.
79	Dike, Ken	DT	6-2	227	Jr.
26	Domin, Tom	HB	6-3	205	So.
23	Dover, Steve	HB	6-1	190	So.
61	Driscoll, John	OG	6-1	219	Jr.
84	Driscoll, Leo	WR	5-11	165	Jr.
41	**Dubenetzky, John	LB-SS	6-5	213	Sr.
	Duncan, Bob	OG	5-11	230	Jr.
42	**Eastman, Tom	MLB	6-1	236	Sr.
40	**Eurick, Terry	HB	5-10	190	Jr.
76	Ewald, Mark	OT	6-4	236	Sr.
	Falash, Mike	QB	6-1	197	Jr.
23	Flynn, Tom	CB	6-0	170	So.
8	Forystek, Gary	QB	6-2	202	Jr.
	Frericks, Tom	OT	6-5	223	Sr.
94	**Fry, Willie	DE	6-3	236	Jr.
46	Gleckler, Ed	LB	6-2	228	Sr.
55	*Golic, Bob	MLB	6-3	250	So.
67	Graziani, Larry	OG	6-2	220	So.
96	Grindinger, Dennis	TE	6-6	223	So.
69	Gullickson, Tom	OT	6-2	245	Sr.
76	Hager, John	DT	6-6	254	So.
82	*Haines, Kris	WR	6-0	173	So.
87	Harris, Kenny	WR	6-1	195	So.
10	**Harrison, Randy	FS	6-1	212	Jr.
98	Hart, Kevin	TE	6-4	225	So.
63	Hautman, Jim	C	6-3	237	So.
30	*Heavens, Jerome	FB	6-0	209	So.
58	*Heimkreiter, Steve	LB	6-2	237	So.
66	Horansky, Ted	OT	6-3	240	So.
56	*Huffman, Dave	C	6-5	228	So.
38	Hughes, Dick	LB	6-2	215	So.
65	*Hughes, Ernie	OG	6-3	248	Jr.
25	**Hunter, Al	HB	5-11	190	Jr.
51	**Johnson, Pete	LB	6-4	220	Jr.
29	Johnson, Phil	CB	6-0	185	So.
70	Kafka, Mike	OG	6-3	228	Sr.
80	*Kelleher, Dan	WR	5-11	183	Sr.
52	**Klees, Vince	C	6-4	223	Sr.
21	*Knott, Dan	HB	6-1	200	Jr.
34	Leary, Terry	LB	6-2	189	Sr.
53	*Likovich, John	LB	6-2	211	Sr.
6	Lisch, Russ	QB	6-4	203	So.
81	**MacAfee, Ken	TE	6-4	251	Jr.
91	Malinak, Don	DE	6-4	198	Sr.
71	*McDaniels, Steve	OT	6-6	279	Jr.
22	**McLane, Mark	HB	6-1	204	Sr.
93	McPherson, Charles	TE	6-4	240	So.
60	*Meyer, Howard	OG	6-3	233	So.
3	*Montana, Joe	QB	6-2	184	Jr.
57	***Moore, Elton	OT	6-1	239	Sr.
1	Moriarty, Kerry	WR	5-9	164	Sr.
	Mullins, Brian	C	6-1	200	So.
	Murphy, Terry	OG	6-1	215	Jr.
14	*Orsini, Steve	FB	5-10	199	Jr.
45	Pallas, Pete	FB	6-2	210	So.
68	Pattillo, Rey	OT	6-1	227	Jr.
31	Rachal, Vince	CB	6-2	190	So.
13	**Reeve, Dave	K	6-3	198	Jr.
7	*Restic, Joe	P-FS	6-2	182	So.
73	Rodenkirk, Don	DT	6-4	242	Sr.
26	Rufo, John	HB	5-11	181	Sr.
54	*Russell, Marvin	MLB	6-0	225	Sr.
19	Schmitz, Steve	HB	5-11	185	Jr.
67	Sharkey, Ed	OG	6-3	235	Sr.
27	*Simon, Tim	FS	5-10	187	Jr.
11	*Slager, Rick	QB	5-11	190	Sr.
90	Smith, Gene	LB	6-2	229	Sr.
16	Soutner, John	SS	6-2	197	Sr.
79	Tull, Bob	OT	6-3	234	Jr.
34	Uniacke, Kevin	HB	6-2	203	Sr.
36	Unis, Tom	CB	5-10	177	Sr.
59	Vinson, Dave	OG	6-2	246	Jr.
35	**Weiler, Jim	TE-HB	6-2	216	Sr.
74	**Weston, Jeff	DT	6-3	267	Jr.
78	*Woebkenberg, Harry	OT	6-2	269	Jr.
39	**Zappala, Tony	DE	6-0	209	Sr.

Pitt Overpowers Notre Dame, 31-10

By The Associated Press

SOUTH BEND, Ind., Sept. 11—Pittsburgh turned a pair of interceptions into quick touchdowns in the second period today and the Panthers rolled to a 31-10 victory. Tony Dorsett again tormented the Irish by rushing for 181 yards. It was the first opening-game loss in 13 years for Notre Dame.

Robert Haygood, the Pitt quarterback, scored twice on 1-yard dives in 2 minutes 11 seconds early in the second quarter. The touchdowns came after interceptions of Rick Slager's passes by LeRoy Felder and Jeff Delaney in Irish territory.

Meanwhile, a swarming Pitt defense led by Randy Holloway a tackle, stiffened after Notre Dame stormed 86 yards on 11 plays for a touchdown after receiving the opening kickoff.

Slager, who completed all three passes on the drive for 52 yards, threw 25 yards to Ken MacAfee, a right end, giving Notre Dame a 7-0 lead after less than five minutes of play.

However, Dorsett, who stunned Notre Dame with a record 209 yards a a freshman in 1973 and eclipsed that with 303 a year ago, quickly swung the momentum to Pitt.

On the Panthers' first play from scrimmage, he burst through the right side on a 61-yard gallop to the Irish 23. Five pays later, he tied the score, 7-7, with a 5-yard dash around right end.

In four games against Notre Dame, Dorsett has rushed for a record 754 yards on 96 carries. He rushed 22 times today.

Notre Dame 23, Purdue 0

SOUTH BEND, Ind., Sept. 18 (AP)—Al Hunter ran for one touchdown and passed for another today as Notre Dame ground out a 23-0 victory over Purdue. Hunter, named the game's outstanding offensive player, picked up 96 yards on 23 carries and threw a 33-yard scoring pass to Mark McLane. Jerome Heavens added 73 yards on 21 carries.

Notre Dame, which led by 3-0 on a 39-yard field goal by Dave Reeve, went ahead by 10-0 at the half after Hunter's pass to McLane. The Irish got a 1-yard touchdown plunge by Rick Slager, the quarterback, midway into the third quarter. Hunter's 2-yard scoring run early in the final period completed the scoring.

Slager, who was booed last week when he completed only 6 of 22 passes and had two intercepted in Notre Dame's loss to Pittsburgh, completed three passes for 29 yards today as the Irish relied almost totally on the running of Hunter and Heavens.

All three touchdowns were set up by Purdue mistakes—a bobbled fake punt, an offside penalty that nullified the Boilermakers' block of an Irish field-goal attempt and an interception.

Notre Dame 23, Purdue 0

```
Purdue          0  0  0  0— 0
Notre Dame      3  7  7  6—23
ND—FG Reeve 39
ND—McLane 33 pass from Hunter (Reeve
kick)
ND—Slager 1 run (Reeve kick)
ND—Hunter 2 run (kick failed)
A—59,075
```

Notre Dame 41, Oregon 0

SOUTH BEND, Ind., Oct. 16 (AP) — Al Hunter rushed for three touchdowns, and Notre Dame's defense recorded its third shutout of the season, as the Irish swamped Oregon, 41-0, in a college football game today.

Notre Dame, whose won-lost record is now 4-1, has yielded just two field goals since its season-opening 31-10 loss to Pittsburgh. Oregon dropped to 3-3 and suffered its second shutout this year.

The Irish dominated from the start, fashioning touchdown drives on four of their first five possessions and keeping the Ducks from a first down until 3 minutes 26 seconds was left in the first half. Notre Dame led by 27-0 at intermission.

Rick Slager, Notre Dame quarterback, plunged over from the 1-yard line with 4:54 left in the opening period, after a 33-yard completion of a double reverse, and the rout was on.

Notre Dame 41, Oregon 0

```
Oregon          0  0  0  0— 0
Notre Dame     14 13  7  7—41
ND—Slager 1 run (Reeve kick)
ND—McLane 11 pass from Slager
(Reeve kick)
ND—Hunter 9 run (kick failed)
ND—Hunter 6 run (Reeve kick)
ND—Hunter 31 run (Reeve kick)
ND—Ferguson 2 run (Reeve kick)
A—59,075
```

	Oregon	Notre Dame
First downs	11	28
Rushes-yards	26-0	61-305
Passing yards	145	213
eturn yards	5	85
Passes	14-32-3	16-26-1
Punts	10-32	3-35
Fumbles-lost	3-1	0-0
Penalties-yards	2-20	7-95

SEPT. 25

Notre Dame 48, Northwestern 0

```
Notre Dame      0 14 21 13—48
Northwestern    0  0  0  0— 0
ND—Hunter 16 run (kick failed)
ND—W. Browner 8 pass from Salger
(Kelleher pass from W. Browner)
ND—Domin 70 pass from Slager (Reeve
kick)
Notre D—Hunter 37 run (Reed kick)
ND—MacAfee 7 pass from Slager
ND—Lisch 4 run (Reeve kick)
ND—Leopold 57 pass interception (pass
failed)
A—44,936
```

Notre Dame 13, S. Carolina 6

COLUMBIA, S.C., Oct. 23 (AP)—Willard Browner, a freshman, scored on a 9-yard pass in the first quarter and his brother, Jim, mde a key interception in the closing minutes to lead Notre Dame to 13-6 victory over South Carolina today.

It was the Irish's fifth victory in a row, against one defeat. The Gamecocks fell to 5-3. Notre Dame's Al Hunter put on a brilliant show as he rushed for 181 yards.

Ten first-quarter points wwere all Notre Dame needed, but ts defense had to come up with several big plays to stop the Gamecacks in the second half. President Ford attended the game.

Notre Dame 13, S. Carolina 6

```
Notre Dame ............... 10  3  0  0—13
South Carolina ........... 0  3  0  3— 6
ND—W. Brower 9 pass from Rick Slager
(Reeve kick).
ND—FG Reeve 37.
ND—FG Reeve 30.
SC—Parrish 49.
SC—FG Parrish 35.
A—56,721.
```

	Notre Dame	So. Carolina
First downs	16	19
Rushes-yards	54-224	52-149
Passings yards	111	90
Return yards	14	13
Passes	7-17-2	7-21-1
Punts	6-44	9-37
Fumbles-lost	0-0	3-1
Penalties-yards	5-55	3-35

Notre Dame 24, Michigan State 6

EAST LANSING, Mich., Oct. 2 (AP) Rick Slager passed for two touchdowns as Notre Dame defeated Michigan State, 24-6.

Notre Dame shredded the Spartan defense in the first quarter, with Dave Reeve hitting a field goal and Al Hunter diving for a touchdown, to give the Irish a 10-0 lead after their first two possessions.

Slager connected with Terry Eurick early in the second quarter for a 20-yard touchdown play to cap an 80-yard drive. The final Irish touchdown came when Slager hit Ken MacAfee for a 1-yard scoring toss with less than a minute to play.

The Spartan's defense gave up 10 first downs and 181 yards in the first half, and their attack stayed bottled up in its end of the fild, getting only 60 yards.

This was the third straight game the Irish defense held the opponent without a touchdown.

Hans Nielsen tried for five field goals in the second half for Michigan State, in addition to one in the first half, ranging up to 55 yards. Nielsen hit on kicks of 48 and 29 yards to tie Michigan State's career record of 19 field goals, by Dick Kenney.

Notre Dame 24, Michigan St. 6

```
Notre Dame     10  7  0  7—24
Mich State      0  0  6  0— 6
ND—FG Reeve 47
ND—Hunter 1 run (Reeves kick)
NC—Eurick 20 pass from Slager
(Reeves kick)
MSU—FG Nielsen 48
MSU—FG Nielsen 29
ND—MacAfee 1 pass from Slager
(Reeves kick)
A—77,081
```

	Notre Dame	Mich State
First downs	16	10
Rushes-yards	56-181	31-25
Passing yards	111	149
Return yards	61	94
Passes	9-19-1	11-34-2
Punts	7-46	7-45
Fumbles-lost	2-2	0-0
Penalties-yards	5-53	3-15
West Virginia-Richmond Stax		

Irish Rally From 14-3 Deficit

CLEVELAND, Oct. 30 (AP)—Rick Slager's passing and a pair of field goals by Dave Reeve led Notre Dame to a 27-21 victory over Navy today in the 50th renewal of their rivalry. Notre Dame won its sixth straight game, overcoming a 14-3 deficit with 21 points in the second period and holding off an aroused Midshipman offense in the second half.

Reeve, who opened the scoring with a 47-yard field goal in the first quarter, added a 24-yarder with 11:49 left in the game, giving the Irish a 27-14 lead.

Bob Leszczynski, whose pinpoint passing kept Navy in the game, directed a long drive late in the fourth period that moved the team from its 20 to Notre Dame's 16. There, a fourth-down pass was tipped away by Dave Waymer, a defensive back, at the goal line with 4:30 remaining.

The Irish, who broke a school record by holding Navy without a touchdown in the first quarter—their 21st straight quarter without yielding a touchdown—checked Navy's last offensive thrust with an interception in the end zone by Luther Bradley as time ran out.

Slager accounted for two touchdowns and set up Reeve's second field goal with his passing. He hit Dave Kelleher for 58 yards on Notre Dame's first touchdown, threw 28 yards to Al Hunter for another score and hit Kelleher with a 45-yard scoring pass.

Notre Dame 27, Navy 21

```
Notre Dame      0 21  0  3—27
Navy            3 14  0  7—21
ND—FG Reeve 47
Nav—King 17 pass from Leszczynski
(Tata kick)
Nav—Klawinski 1 run (Tata kick)
ND—Kelleher 58 pass from Slager
(Reeve kick)
ND—Hunter 1 run (Reeve kick)
ND—Hunter 28 pass from Slager
(Reeve kick)
Nav—Thompson 1 run (Tata kick)
ND—FG Reeve 24
A—61,172.
```

	Notre Dame	Navy
First downs	16	19
Rushes-yards	49-139	44- 55
Passing yards	243	294
Return yards	93	130
Passes	13-27-2	21-45-1
Punts	6-45	9-35
Fumbles-lost	4-3	6-2
Penalties-yards	5-72	5-70

Georgia Tech Rallies, Upsets Notre Dame

ATLANTA, Nov. 6 (AP)—David Sims scored two touchdowns in the second half and gave Georgia Tech a 23-14 college upset over Notre Dame today.

Sims, Tech's career rushing leader, ran for 122 yards in sparking the Yellow Jacket's rushing offense to 368 yards. Tech did not throw a pass.

Tech trailed, 14-10, at the half. Then Sims scored in the third quarter on a 10-yard run and assured the Yellow Jackets of victory with a 16-yard scoring run with 3 minutes 58 seconds to play.

Notre Dame, which now has a 6-2 won-lost record, got two first-half touchdown runs from Al Hunter. The Irish loss followed six consecutive victories.

A homecoming crowd of 50,079 saw the Tech defense limit Notre Dame to only four first downs in the second half.

The Yellow Jackets took the lead for good on Sims' 10-yard run with 2:59 left in the third period. A sophomore, Bo Thomas, led the 80-yard scoring drive with a 45-yard burst, and Sims ran for 20 yards two plays before the touchdown.

Tech surprised the Irish by taking a 3-0 lead on Danny Smith's 31-yard field goal at 3:59 of the second period. The score was set up by Sims' 31-yard run and another of 15 yards by Eddie Lee Ivery.

Notre Dame then exploded for both touchdowns, marching 67 yards in eight plays with Hunter going the last 2. Rick Slager passed to Ken MacAfee three times for 48 yards in the drive.

On the next series, Georgia Tech's punter, Harper Brown, bobbled the snap and the Irish took over on the Yellow Jacket's 35. Six plays later, Hunter scored from the 3 for a 14-3 lead 1:58 before the half.

Tech's Gary Lanier scored with only 23 seconds left on an 8-yard run, capping an 84-yard, five-play drive.

Georgia Tech 23, Notre Dame 14

```
Notre Dame        0 14 0  0—14
Georgia Tech      0 10 6  7—23
  Tech—FG Smith 31
  ND—Hunter 2 run (Reeve kick)
  ND—Hunter 3 run (Reeve kick)
  Tech—Lanier 8 run (Smith kick)
  Tech—Sims 10 run (kick failed)
  Tech—Sims 16 run (Smith kick)
  A—50,079
```

	Notre Dame	Ga. Tech
First Downs	14	18
Rushes-yards	42-107	50-368
Passing yards	71	0
Return yards	3	57
Passes	8-19-1	0-0-0
Punts	6-46	4-41
Fumbles-lost	1-0	0-0
Penalties-yards	4-49	3-32

Nov. 13

Notre Dame Trips Bama

SOUTH BEND, Ind. (AP) — Notre Dame continued its mastery over Alabama Saturday as Rick Slager passed for 208 yards in the first half, including a 56-yard touchdown bomb to Dan Kelleher, and led the Irish to a 21-18 victory in the first regular-season meeting between two of college football's greatest names.

Notre Dame built a 21-7 halftime lead but survived a series of second-half scares and didn't nail down the victory until Jim Browner intercepted Jeff Rutledge's pass in the end zone with 4:17 left and halfback Pete Cavan wide open and waving for the ball across the field. Rutledge, however, never saw him.

The triumph gave 18th-ranked Notre Dame a 7-2 record and kept its hopes alive for a major bowl bid. Alabama, which was ranked 10th, had a five-game winning streak snapped and dropped to 7-3 over-all, the most losses for the Crimson Tide since 1970.

Slager picked Alabama's secondary apart in the first half, completing 12 of 19 passes. His long heave to Kelleher on the first play of the second period started the scoring and the Irish added touchdowns the next two times they had the ball on Al Hunter's two-yard run and a 17-yard dash by freshman Vagas Ferguson.

The only two previous meetings between the traditional gridiron powers came in post-season action. Notre Dame nipped Alabama 24-23 in a Sugar Bowl showdown for the 1973 national championship and edged the Tide 13-11 the following season in the Orange Bowl.

Strong running by Hunter and Ferguson complimented Slager's precision passing as Notre Dame's Wing-T misdirection offense gobbled up 365 yards in the first half alone. Ferguson, in his first starting assignment, gained 76 yards on 12 carries in the first two periods and Hunter added 71 on 11 rushes. For the game, they had 113 and 90, respectively.

On three consecutive first half possessions, Notre Dame reeled off scoring drives of 80, 60 and 72 yards. The last one, capped by Ferguson's nifty 17-yard run on which he cut sharply around defensive back Phil Allman at the five, came just after Jack O'Rear scored Alabama's first touchdown on a one-yard run.

The score by Ferguson made it 21-7 and equalled the most points yielded by one of Bear Bryant's teams since Notre Dame's dramatic Sugar Bowl triumph three years ago.

Slager's aerial dynamics came against an Alabama pass defense which ranked fifth in the nation, allowing an average of 83.2 yards in nine previous games.

```
Alabama ............... 0  7  3.  8—18
Notre Dame ........... 0 21  0   0—21
  ND—Kelleher 56 pass from Slager (Reeve kick).
  ND—Hunter 2 run (Reeve kick).
  Ala—O'Rear 1 run (Berrey kick).
  ND—Ferguson 17 run (Reeve kick).
  Ala—FG Berrey 38.
  Ala—Newsome 30 pass from Rutledge (Newsome run).
  A—59,075.
```

	Ala.	N. D.
First downs	20	22
Rushes yards	42-170	57-249
Passing yards	231	235
Return yards	31	5
Passes	14-25-2	15-25-1
Punts	1-28	5-37
Fumbles-lost	0-0	2-2
Penalties-yards	1-5	4-20

Nov. 20

Irish Beat Miami, Take Bowl Bid

Notre Dame 40, Miami [Fla.] 27

```
Miami          0  0 14 13—27
Notre Dame    17  6  7 10—40
  ND—FG Reeve 31
  ND—Kelleher 4 pass from Browner (Reeve kick)
  ND—Kelleher 42 pass from Lisch (Reeve kick)
  ND—Lisch 7 run (Kick failed)
  ND—Lisch 1 run (Reeve kick)
  Mia—Morgan 93 kickoff return (Dennis kick)
  Mia—Claude 1 pass from Baker (Dennis kick).
  Mia—Bennett 3 pass from Baker (Pass failed)
  ND—FG Reeve 42
  Mia—Tokarski 9 pass from Mason (Dennis kick)
  A—59,075.
```

	Miami	Notre Dame
Rushes-yards	36-6	61-162
Passing-yards	246	105
Return yards	16	45
Passes	20-45-3	6-16-1
First Downs	20	16
Punts	8-33	7-40
Fumbles-lost	5-4	2-2
Penalties-yards	7-86	8-86

Nov. 27

Evans Paces 17-14 Win

USC Conquers Irish

LOS ANGELES (AP) — Trojans' quarterback Vince Evans and his understudy, Rob Hertel, each threw touchdown passes and Glen Walker tacked on a 46-yard field goal Saturday as third-ranked Southern California downed error-prone Notre Dame 17-13.

Notre Dame, down 14-0, scored twice in the final quarter, but their final touchdown came with just four seconds remaining and Southern Cal recovered an onside kick attempt.

Hertel, coming off the bench late in the first half, staked the Trojans to a 7-0 lead when he marched them 68 yards, capping the drive with a six-yard scoring toss to Shelton Diggs.

Evans came back to stun Notre Dame with a quick touchdown in the opening moments of the second half as he connected with Randy Simmrin for a 63-yard scoring pass on the fourth play of the third quarter.

After the Irish, ranked 13th, had closed the gap to seven on a 17-yard touchdown pass from Rusty Lisch to Vegas Ferguson early in the final quarter, Walker booted his field goal to give the Trojans a 10-point pad.

Lisch brought the Irish to within four points when, following a pass interference call against USC that moved the ball to the Trojans one, he broke over for a touchdown. But the two-point conversion attempt failed and USC got the ensuing onside kick to nail down the triumph.

A victory in the regular season finale for the Trojans gave them a 10-1 record. Their next date is with second-ranked Michigan in the Rose Bowl.

Notre Dame, which squandered numerous scoring opportunities against USC, finishes regular season play with an 8-3 mark and will meet Penn State in the Gator Bowl Dec. 27.

Notre Dame held Trojans tailback Ricky Bell to 75 yards on 21 carries while Irish halfback Al Hunter became the first Notre Dame back to go over 1,000 yards in a season as he gained 115 yards on 21 carries.

Simmrin, playing one of the finest games of his Trojan career, caught six passes for 121 yards, including the scoring bomb from Evans.

Evans, a senior who has blossomed into one of the top quarterbacks on the West Coast, completed six of his 14 throws for 106 yards, while his junior backup, Hertel, hit six of nine for 61 yards in the two series he played.

The Trojans' first two fullbacks were ailing, and Bell was used at that position frequently against the Irish, with freshman Charles White moving into Bell's tailback spot.

Dec. 9

Notre Dame's Browner wins Outland

Oklahoma City (AP) — Ross Browner of the University of Notre Dame won the prestigious Outland Award as the outstanding collegiate lineman in the nation yesterday when the Football Writers Association of America announced its 1976 All-Star team.

Browner, the 31st recipient of the award that began in 1946, is a 6-foot-3, 248-pound junior from Warren, Ohio. He has started for the Fighting Irish since his freshman year.

Browner topped the writers' list of 25 All-Star picks, announced here by Volney Meece, sports writer for the Oklahoma City *Times* and secretary-treasurer of the 905-member association.

As a sophomore, Browner was expected to be the bulwark of the Notre Dame defense as the Irish went into the 1975 season as defending national champions under new coach Dan Devine.

Devine had replaced Ara Parsehgian, who had guided the Irish to that national title, highlighted by a 24-to-23 victory over the University of Alabama in the Sugar Bowl, a

victory that vaulted Notre Dame into the national championship.

However, Browner, along with five other players, including defensive end Willie Fry, running backs Al Hunter and Don Knott and defensive backs Luther Bradley and Roy Henry, were suspended for a full academic year for allegedly breaking dormitory rules.

Browner returned this season and will cap his campaign when he leads the Irish (8-3) against Penn State University in the Gator Bowl December 27 in Jacksonville, Fla.

In addition to 11 offensive and 11 defensive players, the association cited punter and placekicker Tony Franklin of Texas A. & M. University, punter-place-kicker Russell Erxleben of the University of Texas and kick returner Jim Smith of the University of Michigan.

The only repeaters from the 1975 writers' squad were running backs Ricky Bell of the University of Southern California and Tony Dorsett of the University of Pittsburgh. The third running back is Terry Miller of Oklahoma

State University.

The quarterback is Gifford Nielsen, a Brigham Young University junior who rewrote the Western Athletic Conferencee passing records while leading the Cougars to a league co-championship, a 9-2 record and a date in the Tangerine Bowl opposite Oklahoma State.

In South Bend, Ind., where Browner received word of his honor, he said "It's a great feeling. I was really shocked and overwhelmed when I got the word."

The lineman returned to his dormitory after running a few errands when his younger brother, Jim, a defensive back on the team, gave him the good news.

"He came in the room with Willie [a third brother on the team] and I said 'Ross, you got the Outland,'" Jim said.

"The Outland," Ross said. "Oh, wow. It's really the Outland."

Browner said the award surprised him because he figured the board would choose a senior.

DEC. 27
GATOR BOWL

Notre Dame Staves Off Penn State

Notre Dame	7	13	0	0—20	
Penn State	3	0	0	6— 9	

PS—FG Capozzoli 26
ND—Hunter 1 run (Reeve kick)
ND—F GReeve 23
ND—Hunter 1 run (Reeve kick)
ND—FG Reeve 23
PS—M. Suhey 8 pass from Fusina (run failed)
A—67,827.

	Notre Dame	Penn St.
First downs	17	16
Rushes-yards	48-132	39-147
Passing yards	141	118
Return yards	34	21
Passes	10-20-0	14-33-2
Punts	5-33	5-29
Fumbles-lost	2-0	4-1
Penalties-yards	5-62	6-55

INDIVIDUAL LEADERS
RUSHING—Notre Dame, Hunter 26-102, Ferguson 10-22. penn State, Torrey 12-63, M.Suhey 9-40, Geise 12-36.
RECEIVING—Notre Dame, MacAfee 5-78, Kelleher 3-46. Penn State, Cefalo 5-60, M. Suhey 2-17.
PASSING—Notre Dame, Slager 10-19-0, 141 yards. penn State, Fusina 14-33-2, 118.

JACKSONVILLE, Fla. (AP) — Al Hunter, the only runner in Notre Dame history to gain 1,000 yards in one season, scored a pair of one-yard touchdowns in the first half and led the Fighting Irish to a 20-9 victory over penalty-plagued Penn State in the Gator Bowl Monday night.

Hunter, who gained 1,058 yards during the regular season, scored in each of the first two periods. Dave Reeve kicked a pair of 23-yard field goals, one on the final play of the half, as 15th-ranked Notre Dame piled up a 20-3 halftime lead.

The Irish finished the campaign with a 9-3 record. Penn State, which was tied for 20th in the ratings, wound up 7-5, the most losses since a 5-5 mark in Joe Paterno's first year as head coach a decade ago.

Penn state took a 3-0 lead on Tony Capozzoli's 26-yard field goal midway through the opening period. Then Notre Dame's defense, seventh-best in the nation against the run, took over and stifled the Nittany Lions.

Led by linebackers Bob Golic, Doug Becker and Steve Heimkreiter and strong safety Jim Browner, the Irish clamped down on Penn State's offense. They never let the Lions beyond their own 32 in the first half after their initial possession.

And despite good yardage in the second half, Penn State was unable to score a touchdown until Bruce Clark blocked a punt deep in Notre Dame territory with 9:14 left in the game. Chuck Fusina passed eight yards to Matt Suhey for the score.

A 65-yard kickoff return by Terry Eurick got Notre Dame started following Penn state's field goal and Hunter put the Irish in front to stay 10 plays later with a burst through the left side. The Lions helped out with a key offsides penalty, one of several costly infractions.

They also were socked with a 15-yard personal foul penalty that moved the football to their 13-yard line four plays before Hunter's second touchdown made it 17-3 with 2:20 peft in the second quarter.

And 17 seconds before the half, they were charged with punt interference, giving Notre Dame the ball at the Penn State 32. Rick Slager quickly passed 26 yards to Dan Kelleher and two plays later Reeve booted his second field goal as the gun sounded.

A Gator Bowl crowd of 67,827, almost 3,000 short of capacity, sat in breezy weather. Temperatures were in the 40s as Notre Dame and Penn State, two of the top names in college football history, met for the first time in 48 years in the nationally televised contest.

On its first possession, Penn State drove from its own 35 to the Notre Dame 10 and Capozzoli gave the Lions a 3-0 edge. But they never got their offense untracked again until the Irish had built a commanding half-time lead.

The 20-3 margin could have been wider, but Notre Dame managed only three points despite twice having a first down at the Penn State nine-yard line. That field goal gave the Irish a 10-3 lead and came after Browner recovered a fumble by Mike Guman at the Penn state 23.

Notre Dame then wrapped it up late in the half with a 51-yard march which included passes of 12 and 13 yards from Slager to tight end Ken MacAfee and a 12-yard toss to Hunter.

Although the Irish were set back 15 yards by a holding penalty, a personal foul against Penn State put the ball on the 13. Hunter, who gained 10 yards on 26 carries, burst through left guard for 11 yard and then plowed the other way for his second touchdown.

Penn State moved the ball well on its first two possessions of the second half, but each time Notre Dame's defense stiffened when it had to. The first drive reached the Irish 32 before ends Willie Fry and Outland Trophy winner Ross Browner made key tackles, forcing the desperate Lions to try a fourth-down pass with 14 yards to go.

FINAL 1976 NOTRE DAME FOOTBALL STATISTICS
(11 Games)

ND		OPP	ATTN.
10	PITTSBURGH	31	59,075 (c)
23	PURDUE	0	59,075 (c)
48	at Northwestern	0	44,936
24	at Michigan State	6	77,081 (c)
41	OREGON	0	59,075 (c)
13	at South Carolina	6	56,721 (c)
27	at Navy (Cleveland)	21	61,172
14	at Georgia Tech	23	50,079
21	ALABAMA	18	59,075 (c)
40	MIAMI	27	59,075 (c)
13	at Southern Cal	17	76,561

SCORING BY QUARTERS

Notre Dame	64	109	49	52	274
Opponent	7	55	36	51	149

RESULTS — WON 8, LOST 3, TIED 0

TEAM STATISTICS	ND	OPP
Total Offense	4001	3011
Total Plays	847	776
Yards Per Play	4.7	3.9
Yards Per Game	363.7	273.7
Net Yards Rushing	2280	1324
Attempts	609	483
Yards Per Rush	3.7	2.7
Yards Per Game	207.3	120.4
Net Yards Passing	1721	1687
Comp. Percentage	.466	.419
Attempts	238	291
Completions	111	122
Had Intercepted	17	16
Touchdown Passes	15	7
Yards Per Comp.	15.5	13.8
Yards Per Attempt	7.2	5.8
Yards Per Game	156.5	153.4
Interceptions Made	16	17
Yards Returned	233	217

NOTRE DAME FOOTBALL STATISTICS

RUSHING	G	TC	YDS	AVG	TD	LONG
Hunter	11	233	1058	4.5	12	64
Ferguson	8	81	350	4.3	2	24
Eurick	10	46	230	5.0	0	59
Heavens	3	54	204	3.8	0	12
W. Browner	10	41	170	4.1	0	15
Orsini	11	33	159	4.8	0	26
Lisch	6	37	77	2.1	4	21
McLane	7	18	56	3.1	0	13
Knott	2	5	25	5.0	0	13
Domin	11	5	18	3.6	0	24
Waymer	10	2	17	8.5	0	14
Forystek	3	5	—6	—1.2	0	6
Slager	10	49	—78	—1.6	2	13
ND	11	609	2280	3.7	20	64
OPP	11	483	1324	2.7	10	61

PASS RECEIVING	G	PC	YDS	AVG	TD	LG
Kelleher	11	24	522	21.8	4	58
MacAfee	11	34	483	14.2	3	26
Hunter	11	15	189	12.6	1	28
Domin	11	5	124	24.8	1	70
McLane	7	9	110	12.2	2	33
Eurick	10	5	65	13.0	1	38
Haines	11	3	64	21.3	0	35
W. Browner	10	5	53	10.6	2	15
Orsini	11	4	47	11.8	0	14
Ferguson	8	3	27	9.0	1	17
Heavens	3	2	22	11.0	0	12
S. Hart	3	1	9	9.0	0	9
Schmitz	11	1	6	6.0	0	6
ND	11	111	1721	15.2	15	70
OPP	11	122	1687	13.8	7	63

PUNTING	G	NO	YDS	AVG	LONG
Restic	11	63	2627	41.7	63
ND	11	63	2627	41.7	63
OPP	11	90	3283	36.5	62

PASSING	G	NO	COMP	PCT	INT	YDS	TD
Slager	10	172	86	.500	12	1281	11
Lisch	6	41	16	.390	2	267	2
Forystek	3	17	5	.294	2	99	0
Hunter	11	1	1	1.000	0	33	1
Waymer	10	1	1	1.000	0	33	0
Restic	11	2	1	.500	0	4	0
W. Browner	10	4	1	.250	1	4	1
ND	11	238	111	.466	17	1721	15
OPP	11	291	122	.419	16	1687	7

SCORING	G	TD	PAT	R-PA	FG	TP
Hunter	11	13	0-0	0-0	0-0	78
Reeve	11	0	29-33	0-0	*9-18	56
Kelleher	11	4	0-0	0-1	0-0	26
Lisch	6	4	0-0	0-0	0-0	24
MacAfee	11	3	0-0	0-0	0-0	18
Ferguson	8	3	0-0	0-0	0-0	18
Slager	10	2	0-0	0-0	0-0	12
McLane	7	2	0-0	0-0	-00	12
W. Browner	10	2	0-0	0-0	0-0	12
Domin	11	1	0-0	0-0	0-0	6
Leopold	10	1	0-0	0-0	0-0	6
Eurick	10	1	0-0	0-0	0-0	6
ND	11	36	29-33	0-1	9-18	274
OPP	11	18	15-16	1-0	8-15	149

*53 yards vs. Pittsburgh
 39 yards vs. Purdue
 47 yards vs. Michigan State
 37 & 30 yards vs. So. Carolina
 47 & 24 yards vs. Navy
 31 & 42 yards vs. Miami

RETURNS	INTER- CEPTIONS	PUNTS	KICKOFFS
Hunter		4- 1-0	12-241-0
Eurick			10-181-0
Harrison		2- 17-0	
Burgmeier	2- 42-0	20-138-0	
Schmitz		18-168-0	1- 28-0
Leopold	1- 57-1		
Waymer	1- 24-0		
Restic	4- 92-0		
Becker	1- 0-0		
Banks	1- 0-0		
Christensen	1- 16-0		
MacAfee			3- 34-0
J. Browner	2- 0-0		
Bradley	2- 0-0		
Weiler			3- 27-0
Orsini			3- 30-0
Golic	1- 2-0		
ND	16-233-1	44-324-0	32-541-0
OPP	17-217-0	30-163-0	42-704-1

AP POLL

1. Pittsburgh
2. Southern Calif.
3. Michigan
4. Houston
5. Oklahoma
6. Ohio State
7. Texas A & M
8. Maryland
9. Nebraska
10. Georgia
11. Alabama
12. Notre Dame

UPI POLL

1. Pittsburgh
2. Southern Calif.
3. Michigan
4. Houston
5. Ohio State
6. Oklahoma
7. Nebraska
8. Texas A & M
9. Alabama
10. Georgia
11. Maryland
12. Notre Dame

HEAD FOOTBALL COACHES

YEAR	COACH	WON	LOST	TIED	
1887-88-89·92-93	No head coaches	7	4	1	.636
1894	J. L. Morison	3	1	1	.750
1895	H. G. Hadden	3	1	0	.750
1896-98	Frank E. Hering	12	6	1	.667
1899	James McWeeney	6	3	1	.667
1900-01	Patrick O'Dea	14	4	2	.778
1902-03	James Faragher	14	2	2	.875
1904	Louis Salmon	5	3	0	.625
1905	Henry J. McGlew	5	4	0	.556
1906-07	Thomas Barry	12	1	1	.923
1908	Victor M. Place	8	1	0	.889
1909-10	Frank C. Longman	11	1	2	.917
1911-12	L. H. Marks	13	0	2	1.000
1913-17	Jesse C. Harper	34	5	1	.872
1918-30	Knute Rockne	105	12	5	.897
1931-33	Heartley (Hunk) Anderson	16	9	2	.640
1934-40	Elmer Layden	47	13	3	.783
1941-43, 46-53	Frank Leahy	87	11	9	.888
1944	Edward McKeever	8	2	0	.800
1945; 1963	Hugh Devore	9	9	1	.500
1954-58	Terry Brennan	32	18	0	.640
1959-62	Joseph Kuharich	17	23	0	.425
1964-74	Ara Parseghian	95	17	4	.848
1975-76	Dan Devine	17	6	0	.739
		580	156	38	.788

FUTURE

1977

September 10 — Pittsburgh
September 17 — Mississippi
September 24 — Purdue
October   1 — MICHIGAN STATE
October 15 — Army
October 22 — SOUTHERN CAL
October 29 — NAVY
November 5 — GEORGIA TECH
November 12 — Clemson
November 19 — AIR FORCE
December 2 — Miami

1978

September 9 — MISSOURI
September 23 — MICHIGAN
September 30 — PURDUE
October   7 — Michigan State
October 14 — PITTSBURGH
October 21 — Air Force
October 28 — MIAMI
November 4 — Navy
November 11 — TENNESSEE
November 18 — Georgia Tech
November 25 — Southern Cal

1979

September 15 — Michigan
September 22 — Purdue
September 29 — MICHIGAN STATE
October   6 — GEORGIA TECH
October 13 — Air Force
October 20 — SOUTHERN CAL
October 27 — SOUTH CAROLINA
November 3 — NAVY
November 10 — Tennessee
November 17 — CLEMSON
November 24 — Miami

1980

September 20 — MICHIGAN
September 27 — PURDUE
October   4 — Michigan State
October 11 — MIAMI
October 18 — ARMY
October 25 — Arizona
November 1 — Navy
November 8 — Georgia Tech
November 15 — Alabama
November 22 — AIR FORCE
November 29 — Southern Cal

Home games in capital letters.

Notre Dame Stadium, used exclusively for football, measures a half-mile around and 45 feet high. It seats 59,075 fans. There are more than 2,000,000 bricks in the edifice which, if laid end to end, would reach from Notre Dame to the Cleveland waterfront 300 miles away. If the 400 tons (approximately 20 carloads) of steel used in its construction were converted into nails, almost 6,500,000 could be made.

The 15,000 cubic yards of concrete, if made into a tower 10 feet square, would reach a height four times that of the Hancock Building in Chicago. If a table were made of the 100,000 feet of California Redwood used originally for seats, it could seat 20,000 persons at one time.

The original sod of Cartier Field, where Notre Dame did not lose a home game in 23 years, was moved into the Stadium. Southern Methodist played the first game on the field in 1930, losing 20-14.

Stadium personnel for each game totals nearly 800 persons. The parking lots immediately adjacent to the arena easily accommodate more than 15,000 cars.

The press box, glass-enclosed on the west side of the structure, rises 60 feet above the ground. This facility, considered one of the best in the nation, can accommodate 375 writers, announcers and cameramen.

The Stadium is open for public inspection during the summer months from 8 to 5 p.m.